AF814405

Recommended by **Teachers**
Trusted by **Toppers**

All in one®

INFORMATICS PRACTICES

WITH PYTHON PANDAS

Class 12

EVERYTHING YOU NEED TO SCORE

- Simplified Theory
- Topic & Chapter Exercises
- Solved NCERT Exercise
- All Types of Exam Pattern Questions
- CBQs; MCQs, A-R, Case Based
- Board Questions Upto 2025
- Sample Question Papers

CBSE Exams 2026

Recommended by **Teachers**
Trusted by **Toppers**

All in One

INFORMATICS PRACTICES
WITH PYTHON PANDAS
Class 12

EVERYTHING YOU NEED TO SCORE

- Simplified Theory
- Topic & Chapter Exercises
- Solved NCERT Exercise
- All Types of Exam Pattern Questions
- CBQs; MCQs, A-R, Case Based
- Board Questions Upto 2025
- Sample Question Papers

CBSE Exams 2026

Author
Lalita Kaler

arihant
SUCCESS AND NOTHING LESS

arihant
SUCCESS AND NOTHING LESS

ARIHANT PRAKASHAN
(School Division Series)

卐 ADMINISTRATIVE & PRODUCTION OFFICES

Regd. Office
'Ramchhaya' 4577/15, Agarwal Road, Darya Ganj, New Delhi -110002
Tele: 011- 47630600, 43518550; Fax: 011- 23280316

卐 *Head Office*
Kalindi, TP Nagar, Meerut (UP) - 250002, Tel: 0121-7156203, 7156204

卐 SALES & SUPPORT OFFICES
Agra, Ahmedabad, Bengaluru, Bareilly, Chennai, Delhi, Guwahati, Hyderabad, Jaipur, Jhansi, Kolkata, Lucknow, Nagpur & Pune.

PO No : TXT-XX-XXXXXXX-X-XX

Published By Arihant Publications (India) Ltd.

For further information about the books published by Arihant, log on to www.arihantbooks.com or e-mail at info@arihantbooks.com

Follow us on

卐 PRICE ₹ 300.00

PRODUCTION TEAM

Publishing Managers
Mahendra Singh Rawat & Keshav Mohan

Cover Designer
Rakesh Rawat

Inner Designer
Ankit Tyagi

Project Head
Shruti Aggarwal

Page Layouting
Ravinder Kumar

Index *cum* Study Planner

One Book- Endless Features
to Help you Succeed

01
CHAPTER

Python Pandas is a Python package providing fast, flexible and expressive data structures designed for high level data manipulation.

▼ **YOUR STUDY GOALS**
1.1 Introduction to various Python Libraries
1.2 Data Structure
1.3 Pandas Series

▼ **YOUR PRACTICE GOAL**
Objective Type Questions
(101 Qs ; MCQs, Fill Ups, True/False, A-R)
Subjective Type Questions

Data Handling using Pandas-I

Python PANDAS (PANel DAta) was developed by Wes Mckinney in 2008 and is used for data analysis in Python. Data analysis requires lots of processing, such as restructuring, cleaning, merging etc., using different tools available such as NumPy, Scipy, Cython and Pandas.

Using Pandas, we can accomplish five typical steps in the processing and analysis of data, such as load, prepare, manipulate, model and analyse.

In this Chapter

At the start of each chapter, all the chapter topics have been listed , so that students may know what they are going to study.

1.1 Introduction to various Python Libraries

A Python library is a collection of built-in modules. It contains bundles of code that can be used repeatedly in different programs. It makes Python Programming simpler and convenient for the programmer. As we don't need to write the same code again and again for different programs.

Python libraries play a very vital role in fields of Machine Learning, Data Science, Data Visualization, etc. Let's learn about the three important libraries that allow us to manipulate transform and visualize data easily and efficiently.

* *Jupyter Notebook is an open source web application, which discussed in Class XI.*

TEACHER TIP
Explicit call to a mathematical operation is preferred when series may have missing values and we want to replace it by a specific value to have a concrete output in place of NaN.

Simplified Theory

Each chapter contains the necessary study material well supported by Definitions, Facts, Figures, Flow Charts, etc.

Teacher Tips

Important Points related to given concept to bring students focus on important points.

Quick Test 1

1. Python pandas was develop by **CBSE SQP 2021-22 Term I**
   (a) Guido van Rossum (b) Travis Oliphant
   (c) Wes Mckinney (d) Brendan Eich
2. Give the full form of 'Pandas'.
3. What does the term 'library' signify in Python? Mention one use for each of the following libraries:
   • Pandas • Matplotlib **CBSE SQP 2024-25**
4. While importing Pandas, is it mandatory to always use pd as an alias name? What would happen if we give any other name? **NCERT**

Quick Tests

To make students understand the chapter in a smooth part-by-part manner, Quick Tests have been given in each chapter. These Exercises help students to assess the understanding of related concepts at regular interval.

One Book- Endless Features

to Help you Succeed

NCERT Questions

To make students completely understand NCERT books, answers of selected NCERT questions have been given in each chapter.

NCERT Folder

Activity Based Questions

1. Create a series having names of any five famous monuments of India and assign their States as index values.

Ans.
```
import pandas as pd
monuments = pd.Series(
    ["Taj Mahal", "Qutub Minar", "Gateway
     of India", "Charminar", "Hawa Mahal"],
    index=["Uttar Pradesh", "Delhi",
           "Maharashtra", "Telangana",
                          "Rajasthan"]
)
# Creating the Series
print(monuments)
```

2. Consider the given below code:
```
import pandas as pd
import numpy as np
s2 = pd.Series([12, np.nan, 10])
print(s2)
```
Find output of the above code and write a Python statement to count and display only non null values in the above series.

```
d 4
e 5
dtype: int64
seriesB = pd.Series([10,20,-10,-50,100],
index = ['z', 'y', 'a', 'c', 'e'])
seriesB
z 10
y 20
a -10
c -50
e 100
dtype: int64
```

Table 1 Subtraction Without Replacing Missing Values

INDEX	VALUE FROM SERIES A	VALUE FROM SERIES B	SERIESA - SERIESB
a	1	-10	11.0
b	2		NaN
c	3	-50	53.0
d	4		NaN
e	5	100	-95.0
y		20	NaN
z		10	NaN

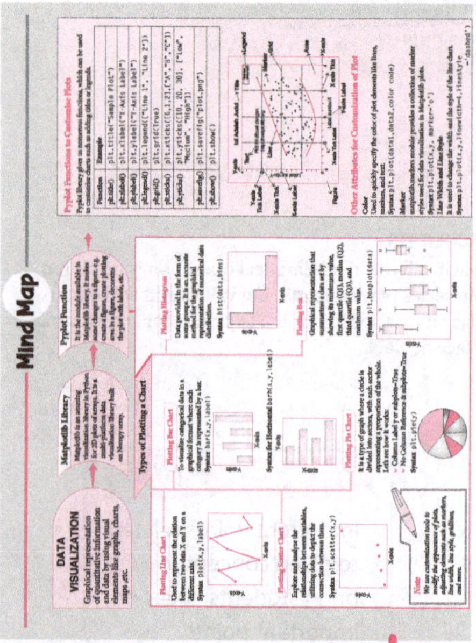

Sample Question Papers

To make students practice of examination in real sense, there are 3 Sample Question Papers at the end. All these Sample Questions Papers are exactly prepared on the latest syllabus & pattern of examination.

Mind Map

A quick revision visual tool for the complete chapter.

SAMPLE QUESTION PAPER 1

A Highly Simulated Sample Question Paper for CBSE Class XII Examination

INFORMATICS PRACTICES

Time : 3 Hours Max. Marks : 70

General Instructions

1. Please check this question paper contains 37 questions.
2. All questions are compulsory. However, internal choices have been provided in some questions. Attempt only one of the choices in such questions.
3. The paper is divided into 5 Sections- A, B, C, D and E.
4. Section A consists of 21 questions (1 to 21). Each question carries 1 Mark.
5. Section B consists of 7 questions (22 to 28). Each question carries 2 Marks.
6. Section C consists of 4 questions (29 to 32). Each question carries 3 Marks.
7. Section D consists of 2 case study type questions (33 to 34). Each question carries 4 Marks.
8. Section E consists of 3 questions (35 to 37). Each question carries 5 Marks.
9. All programming questions are to be answered using Python Language only.
10. In case of MCQ, text of the correct answer should also be written.

SECTION A

[21 × 1 = 21]

1. State whether the following statement is True and False:
A pandas Series cannot have string values as indices.

2. The MySQL function returns the specified number of characters from a particular position of a given string.
(a) MID () (b) SUBSTRING ()
(c) SUBSTR () (d) All of these

3. Which type of network is formed, when you connect two mobiles using bluetooth to transfer a picture file?
(a) LAN (b) MAN (c) PAN (d) WAN

4. Consider a table DOCTOR(ID, DocName, Department, DOJ,Gender, Salary) . Which of the following query will display the names and salaries of doctors in descending order of salaries.
(a) `SELECT DocName, Salary FROM DOCTOR ORDER BY Salary DESC;`
(b) `SELECT DocName, Salary FROM DOCTOR WHERE ORDER BY Salary ASC;`
(c) `SELECT DocName, Salary FROM DOCTOR ORDER BY Salary ASC;`
(d) `SELECT DocName, Salary FROM DOCTOR WHERE ORDER BY Salary DESC;`

5. .... is a cyber crime in which a target or targets are contacted by E-mail, telephone or text message by someone posing as a legitimate institution to lure individuals into providing sensitive data such as personally identifiable information, banking and credit card details and passwords.
(a) Plagiarism (b) Phishing (c) Cyber stalking (d) Hacking

6. What is a correct syntax to return the values of first row of a Pandas DataFrame? Assuming the name of the DataFrame is dfRent.
(a) `dfRent[0]` (b) `dfRent.loc[1]`
(c) `dfRent.loc[0]` (d) `dfRent.iloc[0]`

7. Out of the following, which function cannot be used for customization of charts in Python?
(a) xlabel() (b) color() (c) title() (d) xticks()

8. State whether the following statement is True and False:
The SQL DISTINCT keyword is used to return only duplicate rows from a query result.

9. Which of the following statements will read a csv file "Emp.csv" from "c:\\Data" folder.
(a) pd.readcsv('C:\\Data\\Emp.csv')
(b) pd.read ('C:\\Data\\Emp.csv')
(c) pd.read_csv('C:\\Emp.csv')
(d) pd.read_csv('C:\\Data\\Emp.csv')

10. Which of the following is/are the benefit(s) of e-Waste management?
(a) Saving the environment (b) Creating jobs
(c) Recovery of precious metals (d) All of these

Latest Course *Structure*

PREREQUISITE

In Formatics Practices Class XI

LEARNING OUTCOMES

At the end of this course, students will be able to:

- Create Series, Data frames and apply various operations.
- Visualize data using relevant graphs.
- Design SQL queries using aggregate functions.
- Import/Export data between SQL database and Pandas.
- Learn terminology related to networking and internet.
- Identify internet security issues and configure browser settings.
- Understand the impact of technology on society including gender and disability issues.

DISTRIBUTION OF MARKS AND PERIODS:

Unit No.	Unit Name	Marks
1	Data Handling using Pandas and Data Visualization	25
2	Database Query using SQL	25
3	Introduction to Computer Networks	10
4	Societal Impacts	10
	Project	-
	Practical	30
	TOTAL	**100**

UNIT WISE SYLLABUS

UNIT 1

Data Handling using Pandas -I

Introduction to Python libraries- Pandas, Matplotlib.

Data structures in Pandas - Series and Data Frames.

Series: Creation of Series from – ndarray, dictionary, scalar value; mathematical operations; Head and Tail functions; Selection, Indexing and Slicing.

Data Frames: creation - from dictionary of Series, list of dictionaries, Text/CSV files; display; iteration; Operations on rows and columns: add, select, delete, rename; Head and Tail functions; Indexing using Labels, Boolean Indexing;

Importing/Exporting Data between CSV files and Data Frames.

Data Visulization

Purpose of plotting; drawing and saving following types of plots using Matplotlib – line plot, bar graph, histogram Customizing plots: adding label, title, and legend in plots.

UNIT 2 Database Query using SQL

Revision of database concepts and SQL commands covered in Class XI

Math functions: POWER (), ROUND (), MOD ().

Text functions: UCASE ()/UPPER (), LCASE ()/LOWER (), MID ()/SUBSTRING ()/SUBSTR (), LENGTH (), LEFT (), RIGHT (), INSTR (), LTRIM (), RTRIM (), TRIM ().

Date Functions: NOW (), DATE (), MONTH (), MONTHNAME (), YEAR (), DAY (), DAYNAME ().

Aggregate Functions: MAX (), MIN (), AVG (), SUM (), COUNT (); using COUNT (*).

Querying and manipulating data using Group by, Having, Order by. Working with two tables using equi-join

UNIT 3 Introduction to Computer Networks

Introduction to networks, Types of network: PAN, LAN, MAN, WAN.

Network Devices: modem, hub, switch, repeater, router, gateway

Network Topologies: Star, Bus, Tree, Mesh.

Introduction to Internet, URL, WWW, and its applications- Web, email, Chat, VoIP.

Website: Introduction, difference between a website and webpage, static vs dynamic web page, web server and hosting of a website.

Web Browsers: Introduction, commonly used browsers, browser settings, add-ons and plug-ins, cookies.

UNIT 4 Societal Impacts

Digital footprint, net and communication etiquettes, data protection, intellectual property rights (IPR), plagiarism, licensing and copyright, free and open source software (FOSS), cybercrime and cyber laws, hacking, phishing, cyber bullying, overview of Indian IT Act.

E-waste: hazards and management.

Awareness about health concerns related to the usage of technology.

PROJECT WORK

The aim of the class project is to create tangible and useful IT application. The learner may identify a real-world problem by exploring the environment. e.g. Students can visit shops/business places, communities or other organizations in their localities and enquire about functioning of the organization, and how data are generated, stored, and managed.

The learner can take data stored in csv or database file and analyze using Python libraries and generate appropriate charts to visualize.

Learners can use Python libraries of their choice to develop software for their school or any other social good.

Learners should be sensitized to avoid plagiarism and violation of copyright issues while working on projects. Teachers should take necessary measures for this. Any resources (data, image etc.) used in the project must be suitably referenced.

The project can be done individually or in groups of 2 to 3 students. The project should be started by students at least 6 months before the submission deadline.

PRACTICAL MARKS DISTRIBUTION

Unit No.	Unit Name	Marks
1	Programs using Pandas and Matplotlib	8
2	SQL Queries	7
3	Practical file (minimum of 15 programs based on Pandas, 4 based on Matplotlib and 15 SQL queries must be included)	5
4	Project Work (using concepts learned in class XI and XII)	5
5	Viva-Voce	5
	TOTAL	**30**

SUGGESTED PRACTICALS LIST

1. Data Handling

1. Create a panda's series from a dictionary of values and a ndarray
2. Given a Series, print all the elements that are above the 75th percentile.
3. Create a Data Frame quarterly sales where each row contains the item category, item name, and expenditure. Group the rows by the category and print the total expenditure per category.
4. Create a data frame for examination result and display row labels, column labels data types of each column and the dimensions
5. Filter out rows based on different criteria such as duplicate rows.
6. Importing and exporting data between pandas and CSV file

2. Visualization

1. Given the school result data, analyses the performance of the students on different parameters, e.g subject wise or class wise.
2. For the Data frames created above, analyze, and plot appropriate charts with title and legend.
3. Take data of your interest from an open source (e.g. data.gov.in), aggregate and summarize it. Then plot it using different plotting functions of the Matplotlib library.

3. Data Management

1. Create a student table with the student id, name, and marks as attributes where the student id is the primary key.
2. Insert the details of a new student in the above table.
3. Delete the details of a student in the above table.
4. Use the select command to get the details of the students with marks more than 80.
5. Find the min, max, sum, and average of the marks in a student marks table.
6. Find the total number of customers from each country in the table (customer ID, customer Name, country) using group by.
7. Write a SQL query to order the (student ID, marks) table in descending order of the marks.

01 CHAPTER

Python Pandas is a Python package providing fast, flexible and expressive data structures designed for high level data manipulation.

Data Handling using Pandas-I

▼ **YOUR STUDY GOALS**

▼ **YOUR PRACTICE GOAL**

- Objective Type Questions (101 Qs ; MCQs, True or False, Fill in the Blanks, Assertion and Reason)
- Subjective Type Questions (62 Qs ; VSA, SA, LA)
- Case Study Based Questions (Objective Case Studies-7)

Python **PANDAS (PANel DAta)** was developed by **Wes Mckinney** in **2008** and is used for data analysis in Python. Data analysis requires lots of processing, such as restructuring, cleaning, merging etc., using different tools available such as NumPy, Scipy, Cython and Pandas.

Using Pandas, we can accomplish five typical steps in the processing and analysis of data, such as load, prepare, manipulate, model and analyse.

This chapter will introduce **Python's Pandas library**, its data structures **Series** and **DataFrame** and some useful functions with these data structures.

In this chapter, we will use Jupyter Notebook for programming.*

1.1 Introduction to various Python Libraries

A Python library is a collection of built-in modules. It contains bundles of code that can be used repeatedly in different programs. It makes Python Programming simpler and convenient for the programmer. As we don't need to write the same code again and again for different programs.

Python libraries play a very vital role in fields of Machine Learning, Data Science, Data Visualization, etc. Let's learn about the three important libraries that allow us to manipulate transform and visualize data easily and efficiently.

* *Jupyter Notebook is an open source web application, which discussed in Class XI.*

1. **Pandas (Panel data)** It is a popular Python library used to analyze and manipulate large datasets. It provides easy-to-use data structures like DataFrames and Series, which make it simple to import, clean, and explore data. With Pandas, you can perform various data analysis tasks, from basic calculations to complex statistical modeling.
2. **Matplotlib (MATLAB, plot, and library)** It is a versatile library for creating a wide range of visualizations, including line plots, bar charts, histograms, and scatter plots. By combining it with Pandas, you quickly generate insightful visualizations to understand your data better. Matplotlib allows you to customize your plots to suit your specific needs, making it a powerful tool for data exploration and presentation.
3. **NumPy (Numerical Python)** It is an open source Python library that provides support for large, multi-dimensional arrays and matrices.

   It also have a collection of high-level mathematical functions to operate on arrays.

Features of Python Pandas

- **Data Handling** Pandas provides efficient ways to manage and explore data using structures like Series and DataFrames, allowing for effective data representation and manipulation.
- **Input/Output Tools** It offers a wide range of built-in tools for reading and writing data easily.
- **Visualization** Pandas enables data visualization, allowing users to plot and view various types of graphs.
- **Grouping** With the help of this feature of Pandas you can split data into categories of your choice, according to the criteria you set. The GROUP BY function helps split data into categories, apply functions, and combine results.
- **Merging and Joining of Datasets** Pandas efficiently merges and joins datasets, crucial for comprehensive data analysis.
- **Optimized Performance** With core code in C or Cython, Pandas delivers fast and responsive performance.

To Work with Pandas

The first step in working with Pandas is to ensure whether it is installed in the system or not. If not, then we need to install it on our system using the **pip** command.

Installing Pandas

Follow these steps to install Pandas:

Step 1 Type **cmd** in the search box and open it.

Step 2 Locate the folder using the cd command where the python-pip file has been installed.

Step 3 After locating it, type the command:

```
pip install pandas
```

Importing Pandas

To work with Pandas in Python, you need to import Pandas library. By the following command either on shell prompt or script file, you can import pandas

```
import pandas as pd
```

Note *Here, pd is referred to as an alias for the pandas. While importing pandas, it is not mandatory to use pd as an alias for pandas. You can use any valid identifier as an alias when importing a library in Python.*

1.2 Data Structure

It is a specialised format for organising, processing, retrieving and storing data. Any data structure is designed to arrange data to suit a specific purpose so that it can be accessed and worked with in appropriate ways.

Pandas provide three data structures for processing the data as : Series , DataFrame and Panels. In this chapter , we will study about **Series** and **DataFrames.**

A **Series** is a one-dimensional array-like object that holds an array of data and associated labels, which are called **indices.**

A **DataFrame** is a two-dimensional labelled data structure with columns and rows. Pandas store such tabular data using a DataFrame.

Quick Test 1

1. Python pandas was develop by **CBSE SQP 2021-22 Term I**
   (a) Guido van Rossum (b) Travis Oliphant
   (c) Wes Mckinney (d) Brendan Eich
2. Give the full form of 'Pandas'.
3. What does the term 'library' signify in Python? Mention one use for each of the following libraries:
   • Pandas • Matplotlib **CBSE SQP 2024-25**
4. While importing Pandas, is it mandatory to always use pd as an alias name? What would happen if we give any other name? **NCERT**

1.3 Pandas Series

A Pandas Series is a one-dimensional labelled array capable of holding sequence of values of any type (integer, string, float, list,Python objects, etc.). The axis labels are collectively called **indexes.**

We can easily convert the list and dictionary into series using series() method. Example of series containing name of students given below:

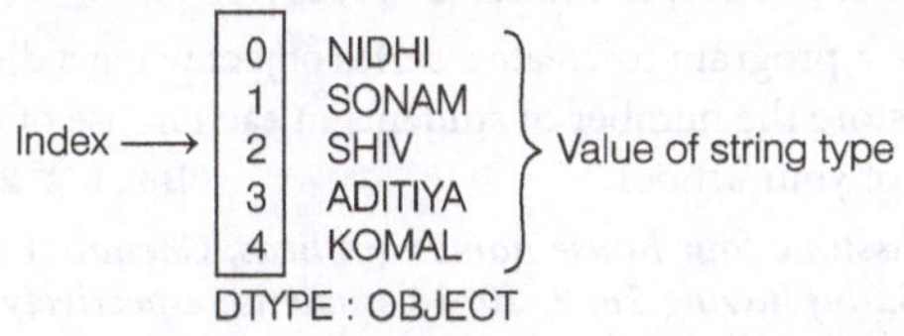

Syntax `pandas.Series(data, index, dtype, copy)`

where,

- **data** It can be any list, dictionary, or scalar value.
- **index** The value of the index should be unique and hashable.
- **dtype** It refers to the data type of series.
- **copy** It is used for copying the data.

Creating a Series

In Pandas, series can be created in two ways as :

1. Create an Empty Series

We can easily create an empty series in Pandas which means it will not have any value.

Syntax

```
Series_Object = pandas.Series()
```

Mistake Alert!

S is always in Uppercase

Example 1

```
import pandas as pd    # import pandas with alias pd
x = pd.Series()        # creating a series
print(x)               # Display the series
```

Output

Series([], dtype: float64)

Note By default, the data type of Series is float 64.

2. Creating a Series using Inputs

We can create series by using various inputs as

Creating a Series from Lists

- To create a series from list, we have to first create a list after that we can create a series from list.

Example 2

```
import pandas as pd
list = ['A', 'r', 'i', 'h', 'a','n','t']  # a simple list
ser = pd.Series(list)            # create series from a list
print(ser)
```

Output

```
0  A
1  r
2  i
3  h
4  a
5  n
6  t
dtype: object
```

In the above example, the output is shown in two columns - the index is on the left and the data value is on the right. If we did not pass any index value, it took by default indexes ranging from 0 to len(data)-1 i.e., 0 to 6.

- If we pass an index values, then the customised index value will be shown in the output as shown in given below example.

Example 3

```
ser = pd.Series(list,index= ['a','b','c','d','e',
                                           'f','g'])
                                 # create series from a list
print(ser)
```

Output

```
a  A
b  r
c  i
d  h
e  a
f  n
g  t
dtype: object
```

Creating a Series from Dictionary

When we create a series from dictionary and dictionary object is being passed as an input. If index is not specified, then the dictionary keys are taken in a sorted order to construct the index.

If index is passed, then corresponding values to a particular label in the index will be extracted from the dictionary.

Example 4

```
import pandas as pd
dict = {'Books': 10,'Pen': 20,'Notebooks': 30}
                                  # a simple dictionary
```

```
ser = pd.Series(dict)        # create series from dictionary
print(ser)
```

Output

Books 10
Pen 20
Notebooks 30
dtype: int64

Creating a Series from Scalar Value

To create a series from scalar value, an index must be provided.

The scalar value will be repeated to match the length of the index.

Example 5

```
import pandas as pd
ser = pd.Series(10, index=[0, 1, 2, 3, 4, 5])
                # giving a scalar value with index
print(ser)
```

Output

0 10
1 10
2 10
3 10
4 10
5 10
dtype: int64

Note If data is a scalar value, then the index argument to Series() function must be provided.

Creating a Series from Array

To create a series from array, we have to import a numpy module and have to use array() function.

Example 6

```
import pandas as pd
import numpy as np              # import numpy with alias np
data = np.array(['P','y','t','h','o','n']) # simple array
ser = pd.Series(data)
print(ser)
```

Output

0 P
1 y
2 t
3 h
4 o
5 n
dtype: object

Note If index is passed then the length index should be equal to the length of arrays. If no index is passed, then index will be range(n), where n is the array length.

Quick Test 2

1. Insert the correct Pandas method to create a Series.
   pd.______(mylist)
2. How do you create a simple pandas Series from a list, my_list = [10, 20, 30]?
3. What is the default index used when creating a Series from a list or array in pandas?
4. How can you assign custom indices ['a', 'b', 'c'] to a pandas Series created from the list [5, 10, 15]?
5. Write a program to create a series object using a dictionary that store the number of students in each house of class 12D of your school. **CBSE SQP 2022-23**

Note Assume four house names are Beas, Chenab, Ravi and Satluj having 18, 2, 20, 18 students respectively and pandas library has been imported as pd.

1.4 Attributes of Pandas Series

Lists some attributes of Pandas series using seriesCapCntry as an example in given below table:

Example 7

```
import pandas as pd
seriesCapCntry = pd.Series(['NewDelhi', 'WashingtonDC',
        'London', 'Paris'], index=['India', 'USA', 'UK',
                                               'France'])
print(seriesCapCntry)
```

Output

India NewDelhi
USA WashingtonDC
UK London
France Paris
dtype : object

Table 1 : Attributes of Series

Attribute	Description	Example

name	Assigns a name to the Series.	`seriesCapCntry.name = 'Capitals'`
		`print(seriesCapCntry)`
		Output
		India NewDelhi
		USA WashingtonDC
		UK London
		France Paris
		Name : Capitals, dtype: object

values	Prints a list of the values in the Series.	`print(seriesCapCntry.values)` **Output** ['NewDelhi' 'WashingtonDC' 'London' 'Paris']

Attribute	Description	Example

index.name	Assigns a name to the index of the Series.	`seriesCapCntry.index.name = 'Countries'`
		`print(seriesCapCntry)`
		Output
		Countries
		India NewDelhi
		USA WashingtonDC
		UK London
		France Paris
		Name : Capitals, dtype : object

size	Returns the number of values in the Series object.	`print(seriesCapCntry.size)` **Output** 4

empty	Prints True if the Series is empty, and False otherwise.	`print(seriesCapCntry.empty)`
		Output
		`False`
		`seriesEmpt = pd.Series()`
		`print(seriesEmpt.empty)`
		Output
		True

1.5 Selection in Series

Series provides index labels loc, iloc, and [] to access rows and columns.

1. Selection Using loc Index Label

loc is used to access a group of rows and columns by labels or a boolean array. It includes the last index in the specified range.

Syntax

```
series_name.loc[StartRange: StopRange]
```

Example 8

```
import pandas as pd
import numpy as np
arr = np.array([10, 15, 18, 22, 55, 77])
s = pd.Series(arr)
print(s)
print(s.loc[:2])
        # Selects values from index 0 to 2
print(s.loc[3:4])
        # Selects value at index 3 to 4
print(s.loc[2:3])
        # Selects value at index 2 to 3
```

Output

```
0   10
1   15
2   18
3   22
4   55
5   77
dtype: int64
0   10
1   15
2   18
dtype: int64
3   22
4   55
dtype: int64
2   18
3   22
dtype: int64
```

where, s.loc[:2] → Selects values from index 0 to 2.
s.loc[3:4] → Selects values from index 3 to 4.
s.loc[2:3] → Selects values from index 2 to 3.

2. Selection Using iloc Index Label

iloc is used for integer-location based indexing. It excludes the last index in the specified range (like standard Python slicing).

Syntax

```
series_name.iloc[StartRange : StopRange]
```

Example 9

```
import pandas as pd
import numpy as np
arr = np.array([10, 15, 18, 22, 55, 77])
s = pd.Series(arr)
print(s)
print(s.iloc[:2])
        # Selects values from index 0 to 1
print(s.iloc[3:4])
        # Selects values at index 3
print(s.iloc[2:3])
        # Selects values at index 2
```

Output

```
0   10
1   15
2   18
3   22
4   55
5   77
dtype: int64
```

```
0   10
1   15
dtype: int64
3   22
dtype: int64
2   18
dtype: int64
```

where, s.iloc[:2] → Selects values from index 0 to 1.
s.iloc[3:4] → Selects values from index 3.
s.iloc[2:3] → Selects values from index 2.

1.6 Accessing Elements from Series (Indexing and Slicing)

Accessing elements from a Pandas Series can be done using **indexing** and **slicing**.

Indexing allows you to retrieve individual elements by their label or position, while slicing enables you to extract a subset of the Series using a range of index labels or positions.

Elements of a series can be accessed in two ways:

Accessing Element from Series with Position

In order to access the series element refers to the index number. Use the **index operator** [ ] to access an element in a series. The index must be an integer.

In order to access multiple elements from a series, we use **Slice operation**.

Slice operation is performed on Series with the use of the colon(:).

Different forms of slice operations as:

[:Index]	To print elements from beginning to a range
[:-Index]	To print elements from end
[Index:]	To print elements from specific Index till the end
[Start Index: End Index]	To print elements within a range
[:]	To print whole Series
[::-1]	To print the whole Series in reverse order

Example 10

```
import pandas as pd
data = pd.Series([10, 20, 30, 40, 50, 60, 70, 80, 90, 100])
        # Creating a pandas Series
print("Original Series:")
        # Original Series
print(data)
print("\nElements from the beginning to index 5
(excluding index 5):")
        # To print elements from the beginning
                                    to a range-use [:Index]
print(data[:5])
print("\nElements from the beginning to index -3
                                    (excluding last 3 elements):")
        # To print elements from the end-use [:-Index]
print(data[:-3])
print("\nElements from index 4 to the end:")
        # To print elements from a specific index
                                    till the end-use [Index:]
print(data[4:])
print("\nElements from index 2 to index 7 (excluding
                                    index 7):")
        # To print elements within a range-use
                                    [Start Index:End Index]
print(data[2:7])
print("\nPrint the whole Series using slicing:")
        # To print the whole Series with the use of slicing
                                    operation-use [:]
print(data[:])
print("\nPrint the whole Series in reverse order:")
        # To print the whole Series in reverse
                                    order-use [::-1]
print(data[::-1])
```

Output

```
Original Series:
0   10
1   20
2   30
3   40
4   50
5   60
6   70
7   80
8   90
9   100
dtype: int64
Elements from the beginning to index 5 (excluding
index 5):
0   10
1   20
2   30
3   40
```

4 50
dtype: int64

Elements from the beginning to index -3 (excluding last 3 elements):

0 10
1 20
2 30
3 40
4 50
5 60
6 70
dtype: int64

Elements from index 4 to the end:

4 50
5 60
6 70
7 80
8 90
9 100
dtype: int64

Elements from index 2 to index 7 (excluding index 7):

2 30
3 40
4 50
5 60
6 70
dtype: int64

Print the whole Series using slicing:

0 10
1 20
2 30
3 40
4 50
5 60
6 70
7 80
8 90
9 100
dtype: int64

Print the whole Series in reverse order:

9 100
8 90
7 80
6 70
5 60
4 50
3 40
2 30
1 20
0 10
dtype: int64

Access an Element in Pandas Using Label (index)

In order to access an element from series, we have to set values by **index label**. A Series is like a fixed-size dictionary in that you can get and set values by index label. Here, we will access an element in Pandas using label.

Accessing a Single Element Using Index Label

In this example, a Pandas Series 'ser' is created from a NumPy array 'data' with custom indices provided. The element at index 17 is accessed and printed using `print(ser[17])`.

Example 11

```
import pandas as pd
import numpy as np
data = np.array(['P','y','t','h','o','n',' ',
        'P','r','o','g','r','a','m','m','i','n','g'])
        # creating simple array
ser = pd.Series(data, index=[10, 11, 12, 13, 14, 15, 16,
        17, 18, 19, 20, 21, 22, 23, 24, 25, 26, 27])
        # accessing a element using index element
print("The element at 17th index is ",ser[17])
```

Output

The element at 17th index is P

Accessing a Multiple Element Using Index Label

In above example, a Pandas Series 'ser' is created from a NumPy array 'data' with custom indices provided. Multiple elements at indices 17, 18, 19, 20, 21, 22 and 23 are accessed and printed using print(ser[[17,18,19,20,21,22,23]]).

Example 12

```
import pandas as pd
import numpy as np
data = np.array(['P','y','t','h','o','n','
        ','P','r','o','g','r','a','m','m','i','n','g'])
```

```
ser = pd.Series(data, index=[10, 11, 12, 13, 14, 15, 16,
                17, 18, 19, 20, 21, 22, 23, 24, 25, 26, 27])
print(ser[[17,18,19,20,21,22,23]])
```

Output

17 P
18 r
19 o
20 g
21 r
22 a
23 m
dtype: object

Access Multiple Elements by Providing Label of Index

In this example, a Pandas Series 'ser' is created using NumPy's arange() function with values from 3 to 8 and custom indices.

Elements at indices 'a', 'd' are accessed and printed using print(ser[['a', 'd']]).

Example 13

```
import pandas as pd
import numpy as np
ser = pd.Series(np.arange(3, 9), index=['a', 'b', 'c',
                                        'd', 'e', 'f'])
print(ser[['a', 'd']])
```

Output

a 3
d 6
dtype: int64

Note To create multiple values for Series arange() function is used.

1.7 Methods of Series

In this section, we are going to discuss some of the methods which are available in the Pandas Series.

Consider the given below example:

Example 14

```
import pandas as pd
ser = pd.Series([2,3.5,4,5.5,6,6.5,7,7.5,8,'Hi', 14])
print(ser)
```

Output

0 2
1 3.5
2 4
3 5.5
4 6
5 6.5
6 7
7 7.5
8 8
9 Hi
10 14
dtype: object

Table 2 : Methods of Series

Methods	Explanation	Example

head()
<pandas object>.head([n])
	• Method is used to return a specified number of rows from the beginning of a Series.
	• If the value of n is not passed, then by default n takes 5 and first five values are displayed.
		`print(ser.head(2))`
		Output
		0 2
		1 3.5
		dtype: object
		`print(ser.head())`
		Output
		0 2
		1 3.5
		2 4
		3 5.5
		4 6
		dtype: object

tail()
<pandas object>.tail([n])
	• Method is used to return a specified number of rows from the end of a Series.
	• If the value of n is not passed, then by default n takes 5 and last five values are displayed.
		`print(ser.tail(3))`
		Output
		8 8
		9 Hi
		10 14
		dtype: object
		`print(ser.tail())`
		Output
		6 7
		7 7.5
		8 8
		9 Hi
		10 14
		dtype: object

count()	Returns number of non-NaN values in the Series.	`print("count:",ser.count())` **Output** count: 11

1.8 Mathematical Operation on Series

We can perform the mathematical operations (like : addition, subtraction, multiplication, division, etc) on series objects but only on the matching indexes.

If data items of two indexes are not compatible, then it will produce the result as NaN (Not a Number).

Consider the following example, for understanding the mathematical operation:

Example 15

```
import pandas as pd
data1 = [1, 2, 3, 4, 5]
series1 = pd.Series(data1,index=['a','b','c','d','e'])
print(series1)
print ("--------------------")
data2 = [10, - 20, 30, - 40, 50]
series2 = pd.Series(data2,index=['p','a','r','b','e'])
print(series2)
```

Output

```
a  1
b  2
c  3
d  4
e  5
dtype: int64
--------------------
p      10
a     -20
r      30
b     -40
e      50
dtype: int64
```

(i) Addition of two Series

This operation can be done by two ways:

1. print(series1 + series2)

In first method , two series are simply added together as shown in the given below example

Example 16

```
series1 = pd.Series(data1,index=['a','b','c','d','e'])
series2 = pd.Series(data2,index=['p','a','r','b','e'])
print(series1 + series2)
```

Output

```
a   -19.0
b   -38.0
c    NaN
d    NaN
e    55.0
p    NaN
r    NaN
dtype: float64
```

2. add() Method

In second method, we use add() method and a parameter fill_value to replace missing value with a specified value. This method is applied when we do not want to have NaN values in output. Consider the following example

Example 17

```
print(series1.add(series2,fill_value = 0))
```

Output

```
a   -19.0
b   -38.0
c     3.0
d     4.0
e    55.0
p    10.0
r    30.0
dtype: float64
```

(ii) Subtraction of two Series

It can also done by two ways, shown in the following examples:

1. print(series1 - series2)

Example 18

```
series1 = pd.Series(data1,index=['a','b','c','d','e'])
series2 = pd.Series(data2,index=['p','a','r','b','e'])
print(series1 - series2)
```

Output

```
a    21.0
b    42.0
c    NaN
d    NaN
e   -45.0
p    NaN
r    NaN
dtype: float64
```

2. sub() Method

The missing value is replace by 100 before subtracting the series2 from series1 using explicit subtraction method sub().

Example 19

```
print(series1.sub(series2,fill_value = 100))
```

Output

```
a    21.0
b    42.0
c   -97.0
d   -96.0
e   -45.0
p    90.0
r    70.0
dtype: float64
```

(iii) Multiplication of two Series

This is also done by two ways, as shown in the given below examples:

1. print(series1 * series2)

Example 20

```
series1 = pd.Series(data1,index=['a','b','c','d','e'])
series2 = pd.Series(data2,index=['p','a','r','b','e'])
print(series1 * series2)
```

Output

```
a   -20.0
b   -80.0
c     NaN
d     NaN
e   250.0
p     NaN
r     NaN
dtype: float64
```

2. mul() Method

Let us now replace the missing value with 0 before multiplication of series2 with series1 using explicit multiplication method mul().

Example 21

```
print(series1.mul(series2, fill_value = 0))
```

Output

```
a   -20.0
b   -80.0
c     0.0
d     0.0
e   250.0
p     0.0
r     0.0
dtype: float64
```

(iv) Division of two Series

This also can be done in two different ways, as shown in the following examples

1. print(series1/series2)

Example 22

```
series1 = pd.Series(data1,index=['a','b','c','d','e'])
series2 = pd.Series(data2,index=['p','a','r','b','e'])
print(series1/series2)
```

Output

```
a   -0.05
b   -0.05
c     NaN
d     NaN
e    0.10
p     NaN
r     NaN
dtype: float64
```

2. div() Method

Let us now replace the missing value with 0 before dividing series1 by series2 using explicit division method div().

Example 23

```
print(series1.div(series2, fill_value=0))
```

Output

```
a   -0.05
b   -0.05
c     inf
d     inf
e    0.10
p    0.00
r    0.00
dtype: float64
```

TEACHER TIP

Explicit call to a mathematical operation is preferred when series may have missing values and we want to replace it by a specific value to have a concrete output in place of NaN.

Quick Test 3

1. How to check if a Series is empty or not?
2. Find the output of the following Python code: **CBSE 2024**
```
import pandas as pd
com = pd. Series ([45, 12, 15, 200], index
=['mouse', 'printer', 'webcam', 'keyboard'])
print (com [1 : 3])
```
3. Write a Python Program to create a Pandas Series as shown below using a dictionary. **CBSE SQP 2024-25**

Note that the left column indicates the indices and the right column displays the data

Russia	Moscow
Hungary	Budapest
Switzerland	Bern

1.9 DataFrame

DataFrame is two dimensional data structure with labelled axes, i.e. rows and columns. Pandas DataFrame consists of three principal components, i.e. data, rows and columns.

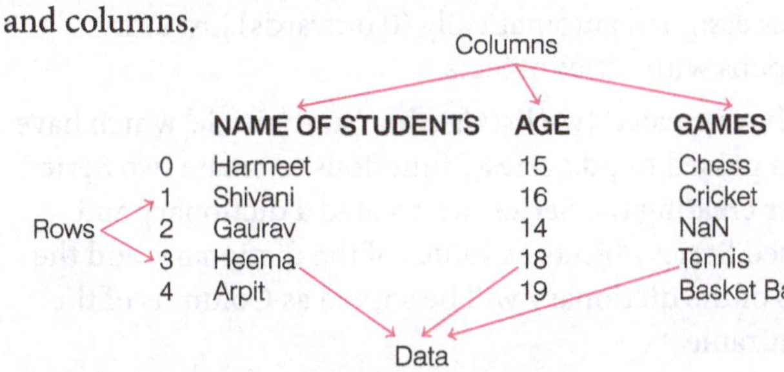

There are following characteristics of DataFrame

(i) There are two indexes in DataFrame named row index (axis = 0) and column index (axis = 1).

(ii) It looks like spreadsheet which contains row index and column index combination, where row index is known as index and column index is known as column name.

(iii) Indexes can be contain numbers, or letters or strings.

(iv) Columns of DataFrame can be heterogeneous.

Syntax

```
DataFrame_Object = pandas.DataFrame (data,
                          index, columns, dtype, copy)
```

Here,

- **data** Different form like ndarray, series, list etc.
- **index** For row label, if no index is passed in DataFrame then default np.arange(n) is used.
- **columns** For column label
- **dtype** Datatype of each column
- **copy** Used for copying data

Creating a DataFrame

To create a DataFrame, we use many ways such as:

(i) Create an Empty DataFrame

The below example shows how to create an empty DataFrame in Pandas:

Example 24

```
import pandas as pd        # importing the pandas library
df = pd.DataFrame()
print(df)
```

Mistake Alert!

Both D and F are always in capital letters.

Output

Empty DataFrame

Columns: []

Index: []

(ii) Create DataFrame from NumPy ndarrays

Creating a DataFrame from NumPy ndarrays using pandas.

Consider the following example in which we create a simple DataFrame without any column labels:

Example 25

```
import pandas as pd
import numpy as np
array_1 = np.array([1, 2, 3, 4, 5])
                    # Creating a NumPy ndarray
df1 = pd.DataFrame(array_1)
                    # Creating a DataFrame from the ndarray
print(df1)
```

Output

```
   0
0  1
1  2
2  3
3  4
4  5
```

***Note** The DataFrame df1 has a single column (with a default label 0), and the rows are indexed from 0 to 4.*

We can also create a DataFrame using more than one ndarrays, as shown in the following example:

Example 26

```
import pandas as pd
import numpy as np
array_1 = np.array([1, 2, 3, 4])
array_2 = np.array([10, 20, 30])
array_3 = np.array([100, 200, 300, 400, 500])
df2 = pd.DataFrame([array_1,array_2,array_3], columns
                   =['A','B','C','D','E'])
        # Creating a DataFrame from the three arrays
print(df2)
```

Output

	A	B	C	D	E
0	1	2	3	4.0	NaN
1	10	20	30	NaN	NaN
2	100	200	300	400.0	500.0

If we pass a dictionary to pd.DataFrame where each key corresponds to a column name, and each value is one of the arrays.

Example 27

```
array_1 = np.array([1, 2, 3, 4, 5])
array_2 = np.array([10, 20, 30, 40, 50])
```

```
array_3 = np.array([100, 200, 300, 400, 500])
df_multiple = pd.DataFrame({
    'Column1': array_1,
    'Column2': array_2,
    'Column3': array_3
})
print(df_multiple)
```

Note *All array (array_1, array_2, array_3) must be of same length, if the length of arrays do not match, then Python show ValueError.*

Output

	Column1	Column2	Column3
0	1	10	100
1	2	20	200
2	3	30	300
3	4	40	400
4	5	50	500

indexes are automatically generated

(iii) Create a DataFrame from Series

Series can only contain a single list with an index, whereas DataFrame can be made of more than one series or we can say that a DataFrame is a collection of series that can be used to analyze the data.

Example 28

```
import pandas as pd
author = ['Jitender', 'Purnima', 'Arpit', 'Jyoti']
article = [210, 211, 114, 178]
# Creating two lists
auth_series = pd.Series(author, index=['a', 'b', 'c', 'd'])
article_series = pd.Series(article, index=['a', 'b',
                                           'c', 'd'])
# Creating two Series by passing lists and specifying index
frame = {'Author': auth_series, 'Article':
article_series}
# Creating a dictionary by passing Series objects as values
result = pd.DataFrame(frame)
# Creating DataFrame by passing Dictionary
print(result)
```

Output

	Author	Article
a	Jitender	210
b	Purnima	211
c	Arpit	114
d	Jyoti	178

As you can see that the created DataFrame object has its index assigned automatically (0 onwards) just as it happens with series objects.

We have created two lists 'author' and 'article' which have been passed to pd.Series() functions to create two Series. After creating the Series, we created a dictionary and passed Series objects as values of the dictionary, and the keys of the dictionary will be served as Columns of the Dataframe.

You should provide matching indices when creating the Series or pass the custom index when creating the Series itself. As shown in below line of above example

```
auth_series = pd.Series(author, index=['a', 'b', 'c', 'd'])
article_series = pd.Series(article, index=['a', 'b',
                                           'c', 'd'])
```

Output

	Author	Article
a	Jitender	210
b	Purnima	211
c	Arpit	114
d	Jyoti	178

(iv) Create a DataFrame from Dictionary of Series

To create a DataFrame from a dictionary of Series in pandas, each key in the dictionary represents a column in the DataFrame, and the corresponding value is a pandas Series. The index of each Series represents the row labels for that column.

Example 29

```
import pandas as pd
info = {'one' : pd.Series([1, 2, 3, 4, 5, 6], index=['a',
  'b', 'c', 'd', 'e', 'f']), 'two' : pd.Series([1, 2, 3, 4,
    5, 6, 7, 8], index=['a', 'b', 'c', 'd', 'e', 'f', 'g',
                        'h'])}
d1 = pd.DataFrame(info)
print (d1)
```

Output

	one	two
a	1.0	1
b	2.0	2
c	3.0	3
d	4.0	4
e	5.0	5
f	6.0	6
g	NaN	7
h	NaN	8

(v) Create DataFrame from Dictionary of Lists

Using the pandas library, you can create a DataFrame from a dictionary of lists.

Each key in the dictionary represents a column in the DataFrame, and each list associated with a key represents the data for that column.

Let's create a DataFrame using a dictionary of lists that includes information about different states, their geographical area (GArea), and the area covered by Very Dense Forest (VDF).

Example 30

```
data = {
  "State": ["Maharashtra", "Madhya Pradesh",
            "Chhattisgarh", "Odisha", "Arunachal Pradesh"],
  "GArea": [307713, 308350, 135192, 155707, 83743],
                    # Geographical Area in square kilometers
  "VDF": [15600, 10800, 13800, 7016, 20088]
                 # Very Dense Forest area in square kilometers
}
df = pd.DataFrame(data)
print(df)
```

Output

	State	GArea	VDF
0	Maharashtra	307713	15600
1	Madhya Pradesh	308350	10800
2	Chhattisgarh	135192	13800
3	Odisha	155707	7016
4	Arunachal Pradesh	83743	20088

We can change the sequence of columns in a DataFrame. This can be done by assigning a particular sequence of the dictionary keys as columns parameters as shown below

```
df = pd.DataFrame(data, columns=['State','VDF','GArea'])
print(df)
```

Output

VDF is now displayed as the middle column

	State	VDF	GArea
0	Maharashtra	15600	307713
1	Madhya Pradesh	10800	308350
2	Chhattisgarh	13800	135192
3	Odisha	7016	155707
4	Arunachal Pradesh	20088	83743

(vi) Create DataFrame from List of Dictionaries

To create a DataFrame from a list of dictionaries in Python using pandas, you can follow the example below.

Example 31

```
students_data = [
    {"Name": "Shivam", "Age": 18, "Marks": 85},
    {"Name": "Ravi", "Marks": 90},
    {"Name": "Nayra", "Age": 18, "Marks": 88},
]
# List of dictionaries
students_df = pd.DataFrame(students_data)
# Creating a DataFrame from the list of dictionaries
print(students_df)
```

Output

	Name	Age	Marks
0	Shivam	18.0	85
1	Ravi	NaN	90
2	Nayra	18.0	88

Note *If the corresponding value for a column is missing, then NaN is inserted by default.*

Each dictionary in the list represents one student. The keys in the dictionary ("Name", "Age", "Marks") become the column names in the DataFrame, and the values become the corresponding data in each row. Number of columns in a DataFrame is equal to the maximum number of keys in any dictionary of the list.

Quick Test 4

1. Sneha is writing a Python program to create a DataFrame using a list of dictionaries. However, her code contains some mistakes. Identify the errors, rewrite the correct code, and underline the corrections made.

```
import Pandas as pd
D1 = {'Name': 'Rakshit', 'Age': 25}
D2 = {'Name': 'Paul', 'Age': 30}
D3 = {'Name': 'Ayesha", 'Age': 28}
data = [D1,D2,D3)
df = pd.Dataframe(data)
print(df)
```

CBSE SQP 2024-25

2. Write a Python program to create the following DataFrame using a list of dictionaries. **CBSE SQP 2024-25**

	Product	Price
0	Laptop	60000
1	Desktop	45000
2	Monitor	15000
3	Tablet	30000

3. Write a Python code to create a DataFrame with appropriate column headings from the list given below: **CBSE SQP 2022-23**

[[101,'Gurman',98],[102,'Rajveer',95],[103,'Samar',96],[104,'Yuvraj',88]]

4. Kabir, a data analyst, has stored the voter's name and age in a dictionary. Now, Kabir wants to create a list of dictionaries to store data of multiple voters. He also wants to create a DataFrame from the same list of dictionaries having appropriate row labels as shown below: **CBSE 2024**

	Voter_Name	Voter_Age
Ar1001	Arjun	35
Ba3002	Bala	23
Go4002	Govind	25
Dh4007	Dhruv	19
Na6005	Navya	18

Help Kabir in writing a Python program to complete the task.

1.10 Operations on Rows and Columns on DataFrame

We can perform basic operations on rows/columns like selecting, deleting, adding, and renaming. In this section we will discuss some basic operations:

(i) Add/Modify a New Column to a DataFrame

To add a new column to a DataFrame in pandas, you can use the assignment operator (=) to create or modify columns.

Example 32

```
import pandas as pd
data = {'Name': ['Arjun', 'Gaurav', 'Jatin'], 'Age':
                                          [25, 30, 35]}
ResultDF = pd.DataFrame(data)
print(ResultDF)
```

Output

	Name	Age
0	Arjun	25
1	Gaurav	30
2	Jatin	35

To add a new column, you simply assign a value or a sequence of values to a new column name, as shown below

```
ResultDF['City'] = ['New York', 'Los Angeles', 'Chicago']
```

Output

	Name	Age	City
0	Arjun	25	New York
1	Gaurav	30	Los Angeles
2	Jatin	35	Chicago

If the column already exists in the DataFrame, then the assignment statement will update the values of the already existing column as shown below

```
ResultDF['Age'] = [24,26,28]
ResultDF['Country'] = 'USA'
```

Output

	Name	Age	City	Country
0	Arjun	24	New York	USA
1	Gaurav	26	Los Angeles	USA
2	Jatin	28	Chicago	USA

(ii) Add/Modify a New Row to a DataFrame

The loc() method allows you to add/modify a new row by specifying the index label for the new row. This is particularly useful if you want to add a row with a specific index or if you're working with a DataFrame where indices are not simple integers.

We can consider the above DataFrame 'ResultDF' and add a new row of data{'Name': 'Ronit', 'Age': 35}

Example 33

```
ResultDF.loc[len(ResultDF)] = {'Name': 'Ronit', 'Age':
35}
```

Output

	Name	Age	City	Country
0	Arjun	24	New York	USA
1	Gaurav	26	Los Angeles	USA
2	Jatin	28	Chicago	USA
3	Ronit	35	NaN	NaN

We can add a row with index value, but we have give all values of all columns otherwise it shows ValueError.

```
ResultDF.loc[3] = ['Ronit', 35, 'Phoenix' 'USA']
print(ResultDF)
```

(iii) Deleting Rows or Columns from a DataFrame

To delete rows or columns from the ResultDF DataFrame using the drop() method.

drop() function is used to delete rows or columns using an index label or column name.

Syntax

```
DataFrame.drop(labels=None, axis=0,
index=None, columns=None, level=None,
inplace=False, errors='raise')
```

where,

- **labels** String or list of strings referring row or column name.
- **axis** int or string value, 0 'index' for Rows and 1 'columns' for Columns.

- **index or columns** Single label or list. index or columns are an alternative to axis and cannot be used together.
- **level** Used to specify level in case data frame is having multiple level index.
- **inplace** Makes changes in original Data Frame if True.
- **errors** Ignores error if any value from the list doesn't exists and drops rest of the values when errors = 'ignore'.

Return type Dataframe with dropped values

Consider the following example:

	Name	Age	City	Country
0	Arjun	24	New York	USA
1	Gaurav	26	Los Angeles	USA
2	Jatin	28	Chicago	USA
3	Ronit	35	Phoenix	USA

(a) To delete a row, you would set the axis parameter to 0. For example, if you want to delete the 2nd row:

```
ResultDF = ResultDF.drop(2, axis=0)
```

Output

	Name	Age	City	Country
0	Arjun	24	New York	USA
1	Gaurav	26	Los Angeles	USA
3	Ronit	35	Phoenix	USA

(b) To delete a column, set the axis parameter to 1. For example, if you want to delete the "Country" column:

```
ResultDF = ResultDF.drop('Country', axis=1)
```

Output

	Name	Age	City
0	Arjun	24	New York
1	Gaurav	26	Los Angeles
3	Ronit	35	Phoenix

TEACHER TIP

Python del keyword can also be used to directly flush the column from the data frame. The del keyword is usually used to delete or flush out objects in Python. del is also an option, you can delete a column by del df['column name'].

(iv) Rename Row Labels of a DataFrame

To rename the row labels of a DataFrame using the DataFrame.rename() method.

rename() function is used to rename any index, column or row. This method is useful when we need to rename some selected columns because we need to specify information only for the columns which are to be renamed.

Syntax

```
DataFrame.rename(mapper=None, index=None,
columns=None, axis=None, copy=True,
inplace=False, level=None)
```

where,

- **mapper, index and columns** Dictionary value, key refers to the old name and value refers to new name. Only one of these parameters can be used at once.
- **axis** int or string value, 0/'row' for Rows and 1/'columns' for Columns.
- **copy** Copies underlying data if True.
- **inplace** Makes changes in original Data Frame if True.
- **level** Used to specify level in case data frame is having multiple level index.
- **Return Type** Data frame with new names.

The example below demonstrates how to rename the row indices 0, 1 and 3 to Row1, Row2 and Row3, respectively:

```
ResultDF = ResultDF.rename({0: 'Row1', 1: 'Row2', 3:
'Row3'}, axis='index')
```

\# Renaming the row labels

```
print(ResultDF)
```

Output

	Name	Age	City
Row1	Arjun	24	New York
Row2	Gaurav	26	Los Angeles
Row3	Ronit	35	Phoenix

The axis='index' parameter specifies that you want to rename the row labels.

If you omit a label in the dictionary, that label will remain unchanged in the DataFrame as shown below

```
ResultDF = ResultDF.rename({0: 'Row1', 1: 'Row2'},
axis='index')
```

\# Renaming only some of the row labels

```
print(ResultDF)
```

Output

	Name	Age	City
Row1	Arjun	24	New York
Row2	Gaurav	26	Los Angeles
Row3	Ronit	35	Phoenix

(v) Renaming Column Labels of a DataFrame

When using rename() in pandas to change column labels, any non-existent column labels specified will be ignored, and no error will be raised. Existing columns will be renamed as specified, while unmatched columns remain unchanged as shown below

```
ResultDF = ResultDF.rename({'Name': 'Full Name'},
axis='columns')
print(ResultDF)
```

Output

	Full Name	Age
Row1	Arjun	24
Row2	Gaurav	26
Row3	Ronit	35

Note *The column Age remains unchanged since we did not pass any new label.*

1.11 Accessing DataFrame Element Through Indexing

When working with DataFrames in pandas, indexing is a key concept for accessing and manipulating the data. There are two main types of indexing:

(i) Label Based Indexing

Label-based indexing is used to access DataFrame elements by specifying the row and/or column labels. This can be done using .loc[], which allows you to select rows and columns by their labels.

Example 34

```
ResultSheet={'Arnab': pd.Series([90, 91, 97,97],
         index=['Maths','Science','English','Hindi']),
'Ramit': pd.Series([92, 81, 96,89],
         index=['Maths','Science','English','Hindi']),
'Samridhi': pd.Series([89, 91, 88,78],
         index=['Maths','Science','English','Hindi']),
'Riya': pd.Series([81, 71, 67,60],
         index=['Maths','Science','English','Hindi']),
'Mallika': pd.Series([94, 95, 99,45],
         index=['Maths','Science','English','Hindi'])}
ResultDF = pd.DataFrame(ResultSheet)
print(ResultDF)
```

Output

	Arnab	Ramit	Samridhi	Riya	Mallika
Maths	90	92	89	81	94
Science	91	81	91	71	95
English	97	96	88	67	99
Hindi	97	89	78	60	45

(a) When a single row label is passed, it returns the row as a Series.

```
print(ResultDF.loc['Science'])
```

Output

Arnab	91
Ramit	81
Samridhi	91
Riya	71
Mallika	95

Name: Science, dtype: int64

(b) When a single column label is passed, it returns the column as a Series.

```
print(ResultDF.loc[:,'Arnab'])
```

Output

Maths	90
Science	91
English	97
Hindi	97

Name: Arnab, dtype: int64

Note *If you want to read more than one row from a DataFrame, a list of row labels is used as shown below*

```
print(ResultDF.loc[['Science','Hindi']])
```

Here, [[]] returns a DataFrame.

(ii) Boolean Indexing

In boolean indexing, we will select subsets of data based on the actual values of the data in the DataFrame and not on their row/column labels or integer locations. In boolean indexing, we use a boolean vector to filter the data.

We want to filter the DataFrame to only include rows where Arnab's score is greater than 95.The condition ResultDF['Arnab'] > 95 returns a boolean Series:

Maths	False
Science	False
English	True
Hindi	True

Name: Arnab, dtype: bool

Here, False indicated by 0 and True indicated by 1.

We can use the conditions on column names to filter data values. The following statement displays True or False depending on whether the data value satisfies the given condition or not.

```
print(ResultDF.loc['Science'] > 90)
```

Output

Arnab	True
Ramit	False
Samridhi	True
Riya	False
Mallika	True

Name: Science, dtype: bool

Accessing DataFrames Elements through Slicing

When accessing elements of a DataFrame in Pandas, slicing is a powerful technique that allows you to select subsets of rows and columns.

Consider the following DataFrame:

	Name	Age	City
0	Riya	25	New Delhi
1	Arnab	30	Mumbai
2	Rahul	35	Pune
3	Mallika	40	Indore
4	Harry	22	Goa

(i) Row Slicing

To select specific rows, use slicing with : inside iloc[] or loc[]:

Example 35

```
import pandas as pd
# Create the DataFrame
data = {'Name': ['Riya', 'Arnab', 'Rahul', 'Mallika',
                                              'Harry'],
     'Age': [25, 30, 35, 40, 22],
     'City': ['New Delhi', 'Mumbai', 'Pune', 'Indore',
                                              'Goa']}

df = pd.DataFrame(data)
sliced_rows = df.iloc[0:3]
print(sliced_rows)
```

Output

	Name	Age	City
0	Riya	25	New Delhi
1	Arnab	30	Mumbai
2	Rahul	35	Pune

(ii) Column Slicing

To select specific columns, you can pass a list of column names to the DataFrame:

```
sliced_columns = df[['Name', 'City']]
# Slicing specific columns
print(sliced_columns)
```

Output

	Name	City
0	Riya	New Delhi
1	Arnab	Mumbai
2	Rahul	Pune
3	Mallika	Indore
4	Harry	Goa

(iii) Slicing with loc[]

The loc[] method is label-based and can be used with labels for rows and columns:

```
sliced_loc = df.loc[1:3, 'Name':'Age'] # Slicing with loc
print(sliced_loc)
```

Output

	Name	Age
1	Arnab	30
2	Rahul	35
3	Mallika	40

The result shows only the selected rows and columns.

Note *loc() and iloc() are one of those methods. These are used in slicing data from the Pandas DataFrame. They help in the convenient selection of data from the DataFrame in Python. They are used in filtering the data according to some conditions.*

1.12 Attributes of DataFrame

Attributes are the properties of a DataFrame that can be used to fetch data or any information related to a particular DataFrame.

Syntax

```
DataFrame_name.attribute_name
```

Example 36

```
ForestArea = {
'Assam': pd.Series([78438, 2797, 10192, 15116],
        index=['GeoArea', 'VeryDense', 'ModeratelyDense',
                                          'OpenForest']),
'Kerala': pd.Series([38852, 1663, 9407, 9251],
        index=['GeoArea', 'VeryDense', 'ModeratelyDense',
                                          'OpenForest']),
'Delhi': pd.Series([1483, 6.72, 56.24, 129.45],
        index=['GeoArea', 'VeryDense', 'ModeratelyDense',
                                          'OpenForest'])
}
# Create DataFrame
ForestAreaDF = pd.DataFrame(ForestArea)
# Display DataFrame
print(ForestAreaDF)
```

Output

	Assam	Kerala	Delhi
GeoArea	78438	38852	1483.00
VeryDense	2797	1663	6.72
ModeratelyDense	10192	9407	56.24
OpenForest	15116	9251	129.45

Table 3 : Attributes of Pandas DataFrame

Attribute	Description	Example
DataFrame.index	Displays row labels (index).	`print( ForestAreaDF.index )` **Output** index(['GeoArea', 'VeryDense', 'ModeratelyDense', 'OpenForest'], dtype='object')
DataFrame.T	Transposes the DataFrame (row indices and column labels switch positions).	`print(ForestAreaDF.T)` **Output** GeoArea VeryDense ModeratelyDense OpenForest Assam 78438.0 2797.00 10192.00 15116.00 Kerala 38852.0 1663.00 9407.00 9251.00 Delhi 1483.0 6.72 56.24 129.45

DataFrame.empty	Returns True if the DataFrame is empty, otherwise returns False.	`print (ForestAreaDF.empty)`
		Output False
		`df = pd.DataFrame()`
		`print(df.empty)`
		Output True

DataFrame.columns	Displays column labels.	`print(ForestAreaDF.columns )` **Output** Index(['Assam', 'Kerala', 'Delhi'], dtype='object')
DataFrame.dtypes	Displays the data type of each column.	`print( ForestAreaDF.dtypes)` **Output** Assam int64 Kerala int64 Delhi float64 dtype: object
DataFrame.values	Displays a NumPy array of all values without axes labels.	`print (ForestAreaDF.values )` **Output** array([[7.8438e+04, 3.8852e+04, 1.4830e+03], [2.7970e+03, 1.6630e+03, 6.7200e+00], [1.0192e+04, 9.4070e+03, 5.6240e+01], [1.5116e+04, 9.2510e+03, 1.2945e+02]])
DataFrame.shape	Displays a tuple representing the dimensionality of the DataFrame.	`print( ForestAreaDF.shape )` **Output** (4, 3)
DataFrame.size	Displays the total number of elements (values) in the DataFrame.	`print( ForestAreaDF.size )` **Output** 12

Table 4 : Some Methods of DataFrame

DataFrame.head(n)	To display the first n rows in the DataFrame Default value of n = 5.	`print(ForestAreaDF.head(2))` **Output** Assam Kerala Delhi GeoArea 78438 38852 1483.00 VeryDense 2797 1663 6.72
DataFrame.tail(n)	To display the last n rows in the DataFrame Default value of n = 5.	`print(ForestAreaDF.tail(2))` **Output** Assam Kerala Delhi ModeratelyDense 10192 9407 56.24 OpenForest 15116 9251 129.45

Iteration

Iteration is a general term for taking each item of something, one after another. We have to iterate a DataFrame like iterate over dictionary because DataFrame includes rows and columns.

In DataFrame, we can iterate an element in two ways as follows

Iterating Over Rows

Use methods like .iterrows() or .itertuples() to access each row one by one.

Example 37

We use .iterrows() to loop through each row as a (index, Series) pair.

```
import pandas as pd
df = pd.DataFrame({'Name': ['Amit', 'Sara'], 'Marks':
                                                [85, 90]})
for index, row in df.iterrows():
    print(row['Name'], row['Marks'])
```

Output

Amit 85

Sara 90

Iterating Over Columns

We can loop through each column name using for col in df: or df.items().

Example 38

```
for col in df:
    print(col)
    print(df[col].values)
```

Output

Name

['Amit' 'Sara']

Marks

[85 90]

1.13 Importing and Exporting Data between CSV Files and DataFrames

A Comma-Separated Value (CSV) file is a text file where values are separated by comma. Each line represents a record (row). Each row consists of one or more fields (columns). They can be easily handled through a spreadsheet application. In Pandas, we need to deal with huge datasets, which is usually available in CSV file format. Various advantages of CSV files are

- CSV format is universal and supported by any spreadsheet package and database.
- CSV files are simple to understand and debug with a basic text editor.
- CSV files are quick to create and load into memory before analysis.

Loading Data from CSV to DataFrames

There are two library functions in Python which are used to load data from CSV files into DataFrame.

These functions are

- read_csv()
- to_csv()

To load data, first prepare the CSV file in Excel as well as notebook. CSV file can also be created using MS-Excel file by same as command.

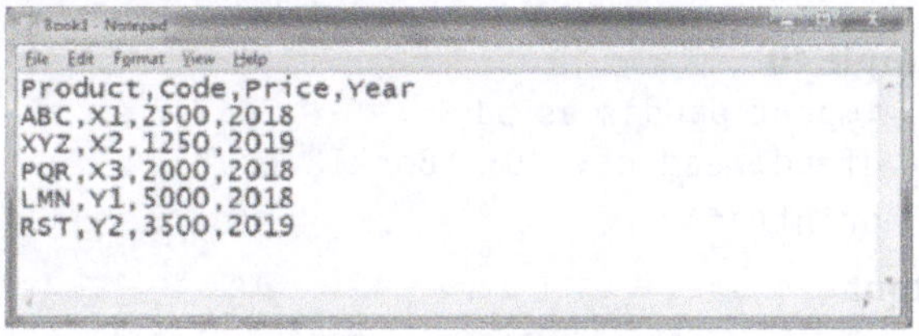

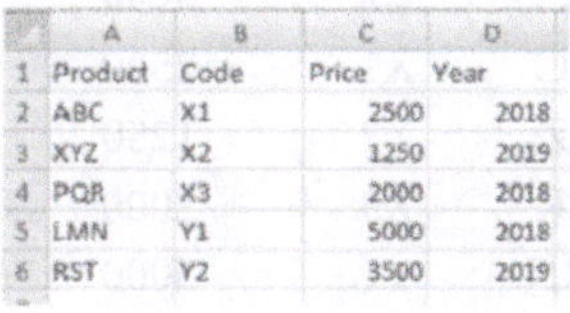

To work in Pandas, first import the library by following command

```
import pandas as pd
```

Reading from a CSV File to DataFrame

Using the **read_csv** function from the pandas package, you can import tabular data from CSV files into Pandas dataframe by specifying a parameter value for the file name.

To import the CSV file named Book.csv which is stored in folder D, follow the given code

Example 39

```
import pandas as pd
df = pd.read_csv("D:\\Book.csv")
print(df)
```

Output

	Product	Code	Price	Year
0	ABC	X1	2500	2018
1	XYZ	X2	1250	2019
2	PQR	X3	2000	2018
3	LMN	Y1	5000	2018
4	RST	Y2	3500	2019

Reading CSV File and Specifying Own Column Names

Suppose you have data without header row, as shown below

	A	B	C	D
1	AAA	Z1	3000	2018
2	ABC	X1	2500	2018
3	XYZ	X2	1250	2019
4	PQR	X3	2000	2018
5	LMN	Y1	5000	2018
6	RST	Y2	3500	2019

When you want to display this data, which is stored in folder D.

Example 40

```
import pandas as pd
df=pd.read_csv("D:\\Book12.csv")
print(df)
```

Output

	AAA	Z1	3000	2018
0	ABC	X1	2500	2018
1	XYZ	X2	1250	2019
2	PQR	X3	2000	2018
3	LMN	Y1	5000	2018
4	RST	Y2	3500	2019

In above example, first row acts as header row. But this is not right way what we wanted.

In such type of situation, we can mention the header row in read_csv() function by following syntax

```
DataFrame = pandas.read_csv (filepath,
names = "sequence containing column names")
```

Example 41

```
import pandas as pd
df=pd.read_csv("D:\\Book12.csv",names=["Pr
oduct","Code","Price","Year"])
print(df)
```

Output

	Product	Code	Price	Year
0	AAA	Z1	3000	2018
1	ABC	X1	2500	2018
2	XYZ	X2	1250	2019
3	PQR	X3	2000	2018
4	LMN	Y1	5000	2018
5	RST	Y2	3500	2019

If you want to overwrite the default header names, you can pass the header = None keyword argument.

Syntax

```
DataFrame = pandas.read_csv (filepath,
header = None)
```

Example 42

```
import pandas as pd
df=pd.read_csv("D:\\Book12.csv", header =
None)
print(df)
```

Output

	0	1	2	3
0	AAA	Z1	3000	2018
1	ABC	X1	2500	2018
2	XYZ	X2	1250	2019
3	PQR	X3	2000	2018
4	LMN	Y1	5000	2018
5	RST	Y2	3500	2019

skiprows argument with int value is used to skip those rows from top while reading CSV file and initializing a data frame.

Syntax

```
DataFrame = pandas.read_csv(filepath,
skiprows = n)
```

Example 43

```
import pandas as pd
df=pd.read_csv("D:\\Book.csv", skiprows =
[2,4])
print(df)
```

Output

	Product	Code	Price	Year
0	ABC	X1	2500	2018
1	XYZ	X2	1250	2019
2	LMN	Y1	5000	2018

Reading Specified Number of Rows from the CSV File

If you want to read a specified number of rows, instead of all the rows in a dataset, use nrows attribute. This is especially useful when reading a large file from a Pandas DataFrame.

Syntax

```
DataFrame = pandas. read_csv (filepath,
nrows = n)
```

Example 44

```
import pandas as pd
df=pd.read_csv("D:\\Book.csv",nrows=2)
print(df)
```

Output

	Product	Code	Price	Year
0	ABC	X1	2500	2018
1	XYZ	X2	1250	2019

Storing DataFrame Data to CSV File

Pandas DataFrame to_csv() function converts DataFrame into CSV data file.

We can pass a file object to write the CSV data into a file, otherwise the CSV data is returned in the string format.

Syntax `DataFrame.to_csv (filepath)`

or `DataFrame.to_csv (filepath, sep = separator_character)`

Example 45

```
import pandas as pd
data = {
'Name': ['Rahul', 'Shrey', 'Rishi',
                    'Muskan'],
'Salary': [18000, 20000, 21000, 17500],
'Dept': ['Analyst','DBA','Programmer',
                    'Tester']
}
df1 = pd.DataFrame(data)
print(df1)
```

Output

	Name	Salary	Dept
0	Rahul	18000	Analyst
1	Shrey	20000	DBA
2	Rishi	21000	Programmer
3	Muskan	17500	Tester

We have a DataFrame df1 and want to display its CSV file then following statement is used.

To display CSV file, give the path where you want to save that file

```
>>> df1.to_csv("D:\\neetu1\\AIO 12th IP
with Pandas\\Extra\\new.csv")
```

It will display the following CSV file with default separator character comma because we did not mention any separator in above code.

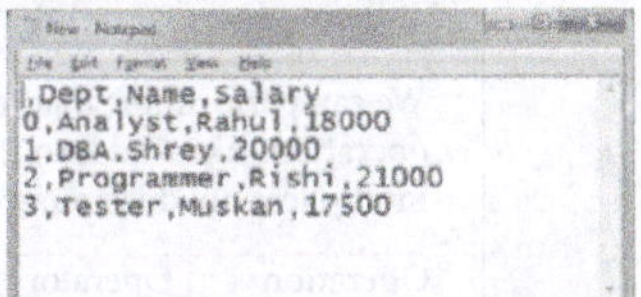

If you want to specify separator character in CSV file, mention this with sep attribute as

```
>>> df1.to_csv ("D:\\neetu1\\AIO 12th IP
with Pandas\\ Extra\\new1.csv", sep = "#")
```

Handling NaN Values with to_csv()

In dataframe, some values are missing. For these missing values, we assign NaN with following code.

Syntax

```
DataFrame.loc [index, columnname] = np.NaN
```

Example 46

```
import numpy as np
df1.loc [2, 'Name'] = np.NaN
df1.loc [3, 'Salary'] = np.NaN
print (df1)
```

Output

	Dept	Name	Salary
0	Analyst	Rahul	18000.0
1	DBA	Shrey	20000.0
2	Programmer	NaN	21000.0
3	Tester	Muskan	NaN

If you want to display above dataframe as CSV file named "hello" with separator #, type following statement

```
>>> df1.to_csv ("D:\\neetu1\\AIO 12th IP
with Pandas\\Extra\\hello.csv", sep = "#")
```

Quick Test 5

1. Can you write a program to count the number of rows and columns in a DataFrame?
2. What happens if we pass a row label that does not exist in the rename() function?
3. What would happen if the label or row index passed is not present in the DataFrame?
4. How can you check whether a given DataFrame has any missing value or not?
5. What are the other parameters that can be used with read_csv() function? You may explore from https://pandas.pydata.org.
6. Besides comma, what are the other allowed characters that can be used as a separator while creating a CSV file from a DataFrame?

Mind Map

PYTHON LIBRARIES

A Python library is a collection of built-in modules that perform specific tasks.

NumPy (Numerical Python)

It is an open source Python library that provides support for multi-dimensional arrays and matrices.
Syntax `import numpy as np`

Matplotlib
(MATLAB, plot, and library)

It is an amazing visualization library in Python which is used for 2D plots of array.
Syntax `import matplotlib.pyplot`

Pandas (Panel data)

It is a free open source Python library that helps with data analysis and manipulation.
Syntax `import'pandas as pd`

Series

Index→		
0	NIDHI	Value of string type
1	SONAM	
2	SHIV	
3	ADITIYA	
4	KOMAL	

DTYPE : OBJECT

* A Pandas Series is a one-dimensional labelled array capable of holding sequence of values of any type (integer, string, float, list, Python objects, etc.). The axis labels are collectively called indexes.

* The data in series is mutable i.e. it can be changed but the size of series is immutable i.e. size of the series cannot be changed.
Syntax `pandas.Series(data, index, dtype, copy)`

Creating a Series

Empty Series
Syntax `Series_Object=pandas.Series()`

Using Inputs

From Lists
```
e.g. list=['A','B','C']
     ser=pd.Series()
```
From Dictionary
```
e.g. dict={'Books' : 10, 'Pen' : 20}
     ser=pd.Series(dict)
```
From Scalar Value
```
e.g. ser=pd.Series(10,index=[0,1,3,4])
```
From Array
```
e.g. data=np.array(['A', 'B', 'C'])
     ser=pd.Series(data)
```

Attributes of Series

name Assigns a name to the Series.
Syntax `Series_name.name ='Any_Name'`

values Prints a list of the values in the Series.
Syntax `Series_name.values`

index.name Assigns a name to the index of the Series.
Syntax `Series_name.index.name="Any_name"`

size Returns the number of values in the Series object.
Syntax `Series_name.size`

empty Prints True if the Series is empty, and False otherwise.
Syntax `Series_name.empty`

Accessing Elements from Series

Accessing elements from a Pandas Series can be done using indexing and slicing.

Indexing
Allows to retrieve individual elements by their label or position,

4 **Positional indexes** are used to extract a data element present at a particular index location from a series.

4 **Label indexes** are used to extract a data element present at a particular index label from a series.

slicing
Enables to extract a subset of the Series using a range of index labels or positions. Slice operation is performed on Series with the use of the colon(:). Different forms of slice operations as:

[:Index]	To print elements from beginning to a range
[:-Index]	To print elements from end
[Index:]	To print elements from specific Index till the end
[Start Index: End Index]	To print elements within a range
[:]	To print whole Series
[::-1]	To print the whole Series in reverse order

Methods of Series

head Used to return a specified number of rows from the beginning of a Series.
Syntax `<pandas object>.head(n)`

Note If the value of n is not passed, then by default n takes 5 and first five values are displayed.

tail() Used to return a specified number of rows from the end of a Series.
Syntax `<pandas object>.tail(n)`

Note If the value of n is not passed, then by default n takes 5 and last five values are displayed.

count() Returns number of non-NaN values in the Series.
Syntax `count()`

Mathematical Operation on Series

We can perform the mathematical operations like – addition, subtraction, multiplication, division, etc. on series.

Operation	Operator	Function
Addition	+	add()
Subtraction	–	sub()/subtract()
Multiplication	×	mul()/multiply()
Division	/	div()/divide()

Note All these operations are done by index matching and missing values are filled in with NaN by default.

DataFrame

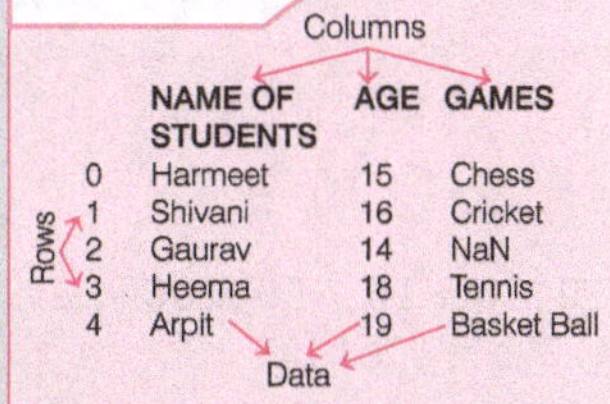

DataFrame is two dimensional data structure with labelled axes, i.e. rows and columns. Pandas DataFrame consists of three principal components, i.e. data, rows and columns.

Data and size both are mutable in DataFrame.

Syntax

```
DataFrame_Object = pandas.DataFrame
                    (data, index, columns,
                              dtype, copy)
```

Importing and Exporting Data between CSV Files and DataFrames

Comma-Separated Value (CSV) file is a text file where values are separated by comma.

Reading from a CSV File to DataFrame

read_csv import tabular data from CSV files into Pandas dataframe by specifying a parameter value for the file name.

Storing DataFrame Data to CSV File

to_csv() converts DataFrame into CSV data.

Operations on Rows/Columns on DataFrame

Add/Modify a New Column

Syntax `DataFrame_object[column]=new_data`

Add/Modify a New Row

Syntax
```
DataFrame_object.loc[row_number,:]
                              =new_data
```

Deleting Rows or Columns

Syntax for rows
```
DataFrame_object.drop(rows_indexes, axis=0)
```
Syntax for columns
```
DataFrame_object.drop(['columns'], axis=1)
```

Rename Row and Column Labels

Syntax
```
df_rename(index={<dic_names>},
   columns={<dic_names}, inplace=false)
```

Selecting/Accessing DataFrame Element

Indexing

- **Label-based indexing** is used to access DataFrame elements by specifying the row and/or column labels. This can be done using .loc[], which allows you to select rows and columns by their labels.
- In **boolean indexing,** we will select subsets of data based on the actual values of the data in the DataFrame and not on their row/column labels or integer locations. In boolean indexing, we use a boolean vector to filter the data.

Slicing

- **Row Slicing** To select specific rows, use slicing with : inside iloc[] or loc[].
- **Column Slicing** To select specific columns, you can pass a list of column names to the DataFrame.
- **Slicing with loc[]** The loc[] method is label-based and can be used with labels for rows and columns.

Note *loc() and iloc() are one of those methods. These are used in slicing data from the Pandas DataFrame. They help in the convenient selection of data from the DataFrame in Python. They are used in filtering the data according to some conditions.*

Creating a DataFrame

Empty DataFrame

Syntax `df = pd.DataFrame()`

NumPy ndarrays

Syntax
```
array_1=np.array([1,2,3,4,5])
df1=pd.DataFrame(array_1)
```

Series

Syntax
```
ser=pd.Series(data, index = [])
df=pd.DataFrame(ser)
```

Dictionary of Series

Syntax
```
info = {'one' : pd.Series
([1,2,3,4,5,6],index=['a','b',
'c','d','e','f'])}
df = pd.DataFrame(info)
```

Dictionary of Lists

Syntax
```
data = {"State":["Maharashtra",
"Madhya Pradesh","Chhattisgarh",
"Odisha"],"GArea":[307713,308350,
135192, 155707]}
df = pd.DataFrame(data)
```

List of Dictionaries

Syntax
```
data = [
{"Name": "Shivam", "Age": 18,"Marks":85},
{"Name": "Nayra", "Age":18,"Marks":88}]
df = pd.DataFrame(data)
```

Note *If the corresponding value for a column is missing, then NaN is inserted by default.*

Attributes of DataFrame

Used to fetch data or any information related to a particular DataFrame.

Attribute	Description	Syntax
DataFrame.index	Displays row labels (index).	`DataFrame_name.index`
DataFrame.T	Transposes the DataFrame (row indices and column labels switch positions).	`DataFrame_name.T`
DataFrame.empty	Returns True if the DataFrame is empty, otherwise returns False.	`DataFrame_name.empty`
DataFrame.columns	Displays column labels.	`DataFrame_name.columns`
DataFrame.dtypes	Displays the data type of each column.	`DataFrame_name.dtypes`
DataFrame.values	Displays a NumPy array of all values without axes labels.	`DataFrame_name.values`
DataFrame.shape	Displays a tuple representing the dimensionality of the DataFrame.	`DataFrame_name.shape`
DataFrame.size	Displays the total number of elements (values) in the DataFrame.	`DataFrame_name.size`

Methods of DataFrame

DataFrame.head(n)	To display the first n rows in the DataFrame	`DataFrame_name.head(n)`
DataFrame.tail(n)	To display the last n rows in the DataFrame	`DataFrame_name.tail(n)`

NCERT Folder

Activity Based Questions

1. Create a series having names of any five famous monuments of India and assign their States as index values.

Ans.
```
import pandas as pd
monuments = pd.Series(
    ["Taj Mahal", "Qutub Minar", "Gateway
      of India", "Charminar", "Hawa Mahal"],
    index=["Uttar Pradesh", "Delhi",
                "Maharashtra", "Telangana",
                                  "Rajasthan"]
)
# Creating the Series
print(monuments)
```

2. Consider the given below code:

```
import pandas as pd
import numpy as np
s2 = pd.Series([12, np.nan, 10])
print(s2)
```

Find output of the above code and write a Python statement to count and display only non null values in the above series.

Ans. Output

```
0   12.0
1   NaN
2   10.0
dtype: float64
print(s2.count())
```

This will output the count of non-null values, which is 2 in this case.

3. Draw two tables for subtraction similar to tables 2.2 and 2.3 of NCERT Book showing the changes in the series elements and corresponding output without replacing the missing values, and after replacing the missing values with 1000.

Ans. To create tables showing the subtraction of two Series, we will follow the same format as the addition tables, one without replacing the missing values and the other by replacing the missing values with 1000.

```
seriesA = pd.Series([1,2,3,4,5], index =
['a', 'b', 'c', 'd', 'e'])
seriesA
a 1
b 2
c 3
d 4
e 5
dtype: int64
seriesB = pd.Series([10,20,-10,-50,100],
index = ['z', 'y', 'a', 'c', 'e'])
seriesB
z 10
y 20
a -10
c -50
e 100
dtype: int64
```

Table 1 Subtraction Without Replacing Missing Values

INDEX	VALUE FROM SERIES A	VALUE FROM SERIES B	SERIESA - SERIESB
a	1	-10	11.0
b	2		NaN
c	3	-50	53.0
d	4		NaN
e	5	100	-95.0
y		20	NaN
z		10	NaN

Table 2 Subtraction Using sub() Method with Missing Values Replaced by 1000

INDEX	VALUE FROM SERIES A	VALUE FROM SERIES B	SERIESA - SERIESB
a	1	-10	11.0
b	2	1000	-998.0
c	3	-50	53.0
d	4	1000	-996.0
e	5	100	-95.0
y	1000	20	980.0
z	1000	10	990.0

4. Draw two tables for multiplication similar to Tables 2.2 and 2.3 of NCERT Book showing the changes in the series elements and corresponding output without replacing the missing values, and after replacing the missing values with 0.

Ans. To create two tables similar to the ones for addition but for multiplication, we'll demonstrate how to multiply two series, one without replacing missing values (NaN) and one using the multiply() method with fill_value=0 to replace missing values with 0.

Table 1 Multiplication Without Replacing Missing Values

INDEX	VALUE FROM SERIESA	VALUE FROM SERIESB	SERIESA × SERIESB
a	1	-10	-10.0
b	2	–	NaN
c	3	-50	-150.0
d	4	–	NaN
e	5	100	500.0
y	–	20	NaN
z	–	10	NaN

Table 2 Multiplication After Replacing Missing Values with 0

INDEX	VALUE FROM SERIESA	VALUE FROM SERIESB	SERIESA × SERIESB
a	1	-10	-10.0
b	2	0	0.0
c	3	-50	-150.0
d	4	0	0.0
e	5	100	500.0
y	0	20	0.0
z	0	10	0.0

5. Draw two tables for division similar to tables 2.2 and 2.3 of NCERT Book showing the changes in the series elements and corresponding output without replacing the missing values, and after replacing the missing values with 0.

Ans. To illustrate the division of two series similar to the addition example provided, we'll create two tables for both cases: one without replacing missing values and one where missing values are replaced with 0.

Table 1 Division Without Replacing Missing Values

INDEX	VALUE FROM SERIESA	VALUE FROM SERIESB	SERIESA / SERIESB
a	1	-10	-0.10
b	2	–	NaN
c	3	-50	-0.06
d	4	–	NaN
e	5	100	0.05
y	–	20	NaN
z	–	10	NaN

Table 2 Division After Replacing Missing Values with 0

INDEX	VALUE FROM SERIESA	VALUE FROM SERIESB	SERIESA / SERIESB
a	1	-10	-0.1
b	2	0	Inf
c	3	-50	-0.06
d	4	0	Inf
e	5	100	0.05
y	0	20	0.00
z	0	10	0.00

6. Use the type function to check the datatypes of ResultSheet and ResultDF. Are they the same?

```
# Define ResultSheet and ResultDF
ResultSheet = {
'Arnab': pd.Series([90, 91, 97], index=['Maths',
'Science', 'Hindi']),
'Ramit': pd.Series([92, 81, 96], index=['Maths',
'Science', 'Hindi']),
'Samridhi': pd.Series([89, 91, 88],
index=['Maths', 'Science', 'Hindi']),
'Riya': pd.Series([81, 71, 67], index=['Maths',
'Science', 'Hindi']),
'Mallika': pd.Series([94, 95, 99],
index=['Maths', 'Science','Hindi'])
}
ResultDF = pd.DataFrame(ResultSheet)
# Check the types
type_result_sheet = type(ResultSheet)
type_result_df = type(ResultDF)
print("Type of ResultSheet:", type_result_sheet)
print("Type of ResultDF:", type_result_df)
```

Ans. Type of ResultSheet will be
<class 'dict'>, as ResultSheet is a dictionary.

Type of ResultDF will be
<class 'pandas.core.frame.DataFrame'>, as ResultDF is a pandas DataFrame.

So, the types are not the same. ResultSheet is a dictionary where each key corresponds to a pd.Series, while ResultDF is a DataFrame created from this dictionary.

7. (a) Using the above DataFrame ResultSheet, write the statement to access Marks of Arnab in Maths.

(b) Create a DataFrame having 5 rows and write the statement to get the first 4 rows of it.

Ans. (a)

```
marks_arnab_maths =
ResultDF.loc['Maths', 'Arnab']
print(marks_arnab_maths)
```

(b)

```
import pandas as pd
# Create a DataFrame with 5 rows
data = {
'Column1': [1, 2, 3, 4, 5],
'Column2': ['A', 'B', 'C', 'D', 'E']
}
df = pd.DataFrame(data)
# Get the first 4 rows
first_4_rows = df.head(4)
print(first_4_rows)
```

Exercise Questions

1. What is a DataFrame and how is it different from a 2-D array?

Ans. A DataFrame is a 2-D labelled data structure in pandas, similar to a table with rows and columns. Unlike a 2-D array, a DataFrame has labelled rows and columns, allowing for more flexible data manipulation and indexing.

2. How are DataFrames related to Series?

Ans. A DataFrame is essentially a collection of Series objects, each representing a column in the DataFrame.

3. What do you understand by the size of (i) a Series, (ii) a DataFrame?

Ans. Size of Series and DataFrame:

- **Series** Size refers to the number of elements in the Series.
- **DataFrame** Size refers to the total number of elements (rows × columns) in the DataFrame.

4. Create the following Series and do the specified operations:

(a) EngAlph, having 26 elements with the alphabets as values and default index values.

(b) Vowels, having 5 elements with index labels 'a', 'e', 'i', 'o' and 'u' and all the five values set to zero. Check if it is an empty series.

(c) Friends, from a dictionary having roll numbers of five of your friends as data and their first name as keys.

(d) MTseries, an empty Series. Check if it is an empty series.

(e) MonthDays, from a numpy array having the number of days in the 12 months of a year. The labels should be the month numbers from 1 to 12.

Ans. (a)
```
import pandas as pd
EngAlph = pd.Series([chr(i) for i in range(65,
91)])
```
(b)
```
Vowels = pd.Series(0, index=['a', 'e', 'i',
'o', 'u'])
is_empty = Vowels.empty  # Check if empty
```
(c)
```
friends_dict = {'Alice': 101, 'Bob': 102,
'Charlie': 103, 'David': 104, 'Eve': 105}
Friends = pd.Series(friends_dict)
```
(d)
```
MTseries = pd.Series([])
is_empty = MTseries.empty  # Check if empty
```
(e)
```
import numpy as np
days_in_months = np.array([31, 28, 31, 30, 31,
30, 31, 31, 30, 31, 30, 31])
MonthDays = pd.Series(days_in_months,
index=range(1, 13))
```

5. Using the Series created in Question 4, write commands for the following:

(a) Set all the values of Vowels to 10 and display the Series.

(b) Divide all values of Vowels by 2 and display the Series.

(c) Create another series Vowels1 having 5 elements with index labels 'a', 'e', 'i', 'o' and 'u' having values [2,5,6,3,8] respectively.

(d) Add Vowels and Vowels1 and assign the result to Vowels3.

(e) Subtract, Multiply and Divide Vowels by Vowels1.

(f) Alter the labels of Vowels1 to ['A', 'E', 'I', 'O', 'U'].

Ans. (a)
```
Vowels[:] = 10
print(Vowels)
```
(b)
```
Vowels = Vowels / 2
print(Vowels)
```
(c)
```
Vowels1 = pd.Series([2, 5, 6, 3, 8],
index=['a', 'e', 'i', 'o', 'u'])
print(Vowels1)
```
(d)
```
Vowels3 = Vowels + Vowels1
print(Vowels3)
```
(e)
```
Vowels_sub = Vowels - Vowels1
Vowels_mul = Vowels * Vowels1
Vowels_div = Vowels / Vowels1
print(Vowels_sub)
print(Vowels_mul)
print(Vowels_div)
```
(f)
```
Vowels1.index = ['A', 'E', 'I', 'O', 'U']
print(Vowels1)
```

6. Using the Series created in Question 4, write commands for the following:

(a) Find the dimensions, size and values of the Series EngAlph, Vowels, Friends, MTseries, MonthDays.

(b) Rename the Series MTseries as SeriesEmpty.

(c) Name the index of the Series MonthDays as monthno and that of Series Friends as Fname.

(d) Display the 3rd and 2nd value of the Series Friends, in that order.

(e) Display the alphabets 'e' to 'p' from the Series EngAlph.

(f) Display the first 10 values in the Series EngAlph.

(g) Display the last 10 values in the Series EngAlph.

(h) Display the MTseries.

Ans. (a)
```
# EngAlph
engalph_shape = EngAlph.shape
engalph_size = EngAlph.size
```

```
engalph_values = EngAlph.values
# Vowels
vowels_shape = Vowels.shape
vowels_size = Vowels.size
vowels_values = Vowels.values
# Friends
friends_shape = Friends.shape
friends_size = Friends.size
friends_values = Friends.values
# MTseries
mtseries_shape = MTseries.shape
mtseries_size = MTseries.size
mtseries_values = MTseries.values
# MonthDays
monthdays_shape = MonthDays.shape
monthdays_size = MonthDays.size
monthdays_values = MonthDays.values
```

(b) `SeriesEmpty = MTseries.rename("SeriesEmpty")`

(c) `MonthDays.index.name = 'monthno'`
`Friends.index.name = 'Fname'`

(d) `Friends.iloc[[2, 1]]`

(e) `EngAlph[4:16]`

(f) `EngAlph.head(10)`

(g) `EngAlph.tail(10)`

(h) `print("MTseries :", MTseries)`

7. Using the Series created in Question 4, write commands for the following:

(a) Display the names of the months 3 through 7 from the Series MonthDays.

(b) Display the Series MonthDays in reverse order.

Ans. (a) `print(MonthDays[3:8])`

(b) `print(MonthDays[::-1])`

8. Create the following DataFrame Sales containing year wise sales figures for five sales persons in INR. Use the years as column labels, and sales person names as row labels.

	2014	2015	2016	2017
Madhu	100.5	12000	20000	50000
Kusum	150.8	18000	50000	60000
Kinshuk	200.9	22000	70000	70000
Ankit	30000	30000	100000	80000
Shruti	40000	45000	125000	90000

Ans.

```
import pandas as pd
data = {
'2014': [100.5, 150.8, 200.9, 30000, 40000],
'2015': [12000, 18000, 22000, 30000, 45000],
'2016': [20000, 50000, 70000, 100000, 125000],
'2017': [50000, 60000, 70000, 80000, 90000]
}
sales_persons = ['Madhu', 'Kusum',
'Kinshuk', 'Ankit', 'Shruti']
Sales = pd.DataFrame(data,
index=sales_persons)
print(Sales)
```

9. Use the DataFrame created in Question 8 above to do the following:

(a) Display the row labels of Sales.

(b) Display the column labels of Sales.

(c) Display the data types of each column of Sales.

(d) Display the dimensions, shape, size and values of Sales.

(e) Display the last two rows of Sales.

(f) Display the first two columns of Sales.

(g) Create a dictionary using the following data. Use this dictionary to create a DataFrame Sales2.

	2018
Madhu	160000
Kusum	110000
Kinshuk	500000
Ankit	340000
Shruti	900000

(h) Check if Sales2 is empty or it contains data.

Ans. (a) `print(Sales.index)`

(b) `print(Sales.columns)`

(c) `print(Sales.dtypes)`

(d)
```
print("Dimensions:", Sales.ndim)
print("Shape:", Sales.shape)
print("Size:", Sales.size)
print("Values:\n", Sales.values)
```

(e) `print(Sales.tail(2))`

(f) `print(Sales.iloc[:, :2])`

(g)
```
import pandas as pd
# Data for the DataFrame
data = {
   '2014': [100.5, 150.8, 200.9, 30000, 40000],
   '2015': [12000, 18000, 22000, 30000, 45000],
   '2016': [20000, 50000, 70000, 100000, 125000],
   '2017': [50000, 60000, 70000, 80000, 90000]
}
# Creating the DataFrame
sales2 = pd.DataFrame(data, index=['Madhu',
'Kusum', 'Kinshuk', 'Ankit', 'Shruti'])
print(sales2)
```

(h)
```
# Check if Sales2 is empty
is_empty = sales2.empty
print(sales2)
print(f"Sales2 is empty: {is_empty}")
```

10. Use the DataFrame created in Question 8 above to do the following:

(a) Append the DataFrame Sales2 to the DataFrame Sales.

(b) Change the DataFrame Sales such that it becomes its transpose.

(c) Display the sales made by all sales persons in the year 2017.

(d) Display the sales made by Madhu and Ankit in the year 2017 and 2018.

(e) Display the sales made by Shruti 2016.

(f) Add data to Sales for salesman Sumeet where the sales made are [196.2, 37800, 52000, 78438, 38852] in the years [2014, 2015, 2016, 2017, 2018] respectively.

(g) Delete the data for the year 2014 from the DataFrame Sales.

(h) Delete the data for sales man Kinshuk from the DataFrame Sales.

(i) Change the name of the salesperson Ankit to Vivaan and Madhu to Shailesh.

(j) Update the sale made by Shailesh in 2018 to 100000.

(k) Write the values of DataFrame Sales to a Comma Seperated file SalesFigures.csv on the disk. Do not write the row labels and column labels.

(l) Read the data in the file SalesFigures.csv into a DataFrame SalesRetrieved and Display it. Now Update the row labels and column labels of SalesRetrieved to be the same as that of Sales.

Ans. (a)
```
Sales = Sales.append(Sales2)
print(Sales)
```
(b) `Sales_transposed = Sales.T`

(c) `sales_2017 = Sales['2017']`

(d)
```
print(Sales.loc[['Madhu', 'Ankit'], ['2017',
'2018']])
```
(e) `sales_shruti_2016 = Sales.loc['Shruti', '2016']`

(f)
```
Sales.loc['Sumeet'] = [196.2, 37800, 52000,
78438, 38852]
```
(g) `Sales = Sales.drop(columns='2014')`

(h) `Sales = Sales.drop('Kinshuk', axis=0)`

(i)
```
Sales = Sales.rename(index={'Ankit': 'Vivaan',
'Madhu': 'Shailesh'})
```
(j) `Sales.loc['Shailesh', '2018'] = 100000`

(k)
```
Sales.to_csv('SalesFigures.csv', header=False,
index=False)
```
(l)
```
SalesRetrieved =
pd.read_csv('SalesFigures.csv', header=None)
SalesRetrieved.columns = Sales.columns
SalesRetrieved.index = Sales.index
print(SalesRetrieved)
```

EXAM PATTERN QUESTIONS

Objective Type Questions

Multiple Choice Questions

1. The name "Pandas" is derived from the term **CBSE SQP 2021-22 Term-I**

(a) Panel Data (b) Panel Series
(c) Python Document (d) Panel Data Frame

2. Which of the following import statement is not correct? **CBSE SQP 2021-22 Term-I**

(a) import pandas as class12
(b) import pandas as 1pd
(c) import pandas as pd1
(d) import pandas as pd

3. Which of the following statement will import pandas library? **CBSE SQP 2022-23**

(a) Import pandas as pd
(b) import Pandas as py
(c) import pandas as pd
(d) import panda as pd

4. Which is incorrect statement for the Python package Numpy ? **CBSE 2021-22 Term-I**

(a) It is a general-purpose array-processing package.
(b) Numpy arrays are faster and more compact.
(c) It is multi-dimensional arrays.
(d) It is proprietary software.

5. The command to install the pandas is: CBSE SQP 2021-22 Term I

(a) install pip pandas
(b) install pandas
(c) pip pandas
(d) pip install pandas

6. Which Python library is not used for data science? CBSE 2021-22 Term I

(a) Panda
(b) Numpy
(c) Matplotlib
(d) Tkinter

7. Pandas Series is: CBSE SQP 2021-22 Term I

(a) 2 Dimensional
(b) 3 Dimensional
(c) 1 Dimensional
(d) Multidimensional

8. A social science teacher wants to use a pandas series to teach about Indian historical monuments and its states. The series should have the monument names as values and state names as indexes which are stored in the given lists, as shown in the code. Choose the statement which will create the series: CBSE SQP 2021-22 Term I

```
import pandas as pd
Monument=['Qutub Minar','Gateway of
India','Red Fort','Taj
Mahal']
State=['Delhi','Maharashtra','Delhi','Utta
r Pradesh']
```

(a) `S=df.Series(Monument,index=State)`
(b) `S=pd.Series(State,Monument)`
(c) `S=pd.Series(Monument,index=State)`
(d) `S=pd.series(Monument,index=State)`

9. What is the syntax for creating a series

(a) `<series name>=pandas.Series(<list name>,...)`
(b) `<series name>=pandas.Series(<dictionary name>,...)`
(c) `<series name>=pandas.Series(<array name>,...)`
(d) All of the above

10. Which of the following is used to create an empty series object

(a) pd.Series(empty)
(b) pd.Series(np.NaN)
(c) pd.Series( )
(d) All of the above

11. Minimum number of argument we require to pass in pandas series ?

(a) 1.0
(b) 2.1
(c) 3.2
(d) 4.3

12. Which of the following is used to get the number of elements in a Series object

(a) index
(b) size
(c) itemsize
(d) ndim

13. Which of the following is used to get the number of dimensions of a Series object

(a) index
(b) size
(c) itemsize
(d) ndim

14. Which of the following is used to check whether a Series object has NaN values

(a) nbytes
(b) hasnans
(c) dtype
(d) ndim

15. While creating a Series using a dictionary, the keys of the dictionary become: CBSE SQP 2024-25

(a) Values of the Series
(b) Indices of the Series
(c) Data type of the Series
(d) Name of the Series

16. Assuming the given series, named stud, which command will be used to print 5 as output? CBSE SQP 2021-22 Term I

```
Amit      90
Ramesh   100
Mahesh    50
John      67
Abdul     89
Name: Student, dtype: int64
```

(a) stud.index
(b) stud.length
(c) stud.values
(d) stud.size

17. Which of the following statement is wrong? CBSE 2021-22 Term-I

(a) Cannot change the index of the Series.
(b) We can easily convert the list, tuple and dictionary into a Series.
(c) A Series represents a single column in memory.
(d) We can create empty Series.

18. Which attribute is used with Series to count the total number of NaN values? CBSE 2021-22 Term I

(a) size
(b) len
(c) count
(d) count total

19. Given the following code snippet:

```
import pandas as pd
s = pd.Series([1, 2, 3, 4, 5], index=['a',
'b', 'c', 'd', 'e'])
```

What will be the output of s['d':'e']?

(a)
```
d  4
e  5
dtype: int64
```

(b)
```
a  1
b  2
c  3
d  4
e  5
dtype: int64
```

(c)
```
d  4
dtype: int64
```

(d)
```
e  5
dtype: int64
```

20. What will be the output of the following code? CBSE 2023

```
import pandas as pd
myser = pd.Series([0,0,0])
print (myser)
```

(a) 0 0
0 0
0 0

(b) 0 1
0 1
0 2

(c) 0 0
1 0
2 0

(d) 0 0
1 1
2 2

21. What will be the output of the following Python code? CBSE 2024

```
import pandas as pd
dd = {'One':1, 'Two': 2, 'Three': 3,
'Seven': 7}
rr = pd. Series (dd)
rr ['Four'] = 4
print(rr)
```

(a) One 1
Two 2
Three 3
Seven 7
dtype: int64

(b) One 1
Two 2
Three 3
Four 4
Seven 7
dtype: int64

(c) Four 4
One 1
Two 2
Three 3
Seven 7
dtype: int64

(d) One 1
Two 2
Three 3
Seven 7
Four 4
dtype: int64

22. Given the following code snippet:

```
import pandas as pd
data = [10, 20, 30, 40, 50]
s = pd.Series(data)
```

What will be the output of s[2]?

(a) 10 (b) 20
(c) 30 (d) 40

23. What is the use of head( ) function with a Series

(a) Display the last five elements of a Series
(b) Displays the first five elements of a Series
(c) Removes the first five elements of a Series
(d) Removes the last five elements of a Series

24. Which of the following command will not show first five rows from the Pandas series named S1? CBSE 2024

(a) S1 [0 : 5]
(b) S1. head ( )
(c) S1. head (5)
(d) S1. head [0 : 5]

25. To display last five rows of a series object 'S', you may write: CBSE SQP 2022-23

(a) S.Head() (b) S.tail(5)
(c) S.Head(5) (d) S.tail()

26. What will be the output of the given code?

```
import pandas as pd
s = pd.Series([1,2,3,4,5],
index=['akram','brijesh','charu','deepika','era'
])
print(s['charu'])
```

CBSE SQP 2021-22 Term-I

(a) 1 (b) 2
(c) 3 (d) 4

27. Consider the following series named animal: CBSE SQP 2021-22 Term I

L Lion
B Bear
E Elephant
T Tiger
W Wolf
dtype: object

Write the output of the command:
`print(animal[::-3])`

(a) L Lion
T Tiger
dtype: object

(b) B Bear
E Elephant
dtype: object

(c) W Wolf
B Bear
dtype: object

(d) W Wolf
T Tiger
dtype: object

28. What type of error is returned by the following statement?

```
import pandas as pa
pa.Series ( [1,2,3,4], index = ['a', 'b',
'c' ] )
```

CBSE 2021-22 Term-I

(a) Value Error (b) Syntax Error
(c) Name Error (d) Logical Error

29. Consider the following Series in Python

```
data = pd.Series([5, 2, 3,7], index=['a', 'b',
'c', 'd'])
```

Which statement will display all odd values? CBSE 2021-22 Term-I

(a) `print(data%2==0)`
(b) `print(data(data%2!=0))`
(c) `print(data mod 2!=0)`
(d) `print(data[data%2!=0])`

30. What will be the output of the following code?

```
import pandas as pd
import numpy
```

```
s=pd.Series(data=[31, 54, 34, 89, 12, 23],
                                dtype=numpy.int)
print(s>50)
```
CBSE 2021-22 Term-I

(a)	(b)	(c)	(d)
0 False	1 54	0 31	1 True
1 True	3 89	1 54	3 True
2 False	dtype: int64	2 34	dtype: bool
3 True		3 89	
4 False		4 12	
5 False		5 23	
dtype: bool		dtype: int64	

31. Consider the following code: **CBSE 2021-22 Term I**

```
import numpy as np
import pandas as pd
L = np.array([10,20])
x = pd.Series(________) #statement 1
print(x)
```

Output of the above code is:

0 1000
1 8000
dtype: int64

What is the correct statement for the above output in the following statement 1?

(a) d = L*3
(b) data = L**3
(c) L*3
(d) [10,20] **3

32. Consider a following DataFrame **CBSE 2021-22 Term I**

```
import pandas as pd
s=pd.Series(data=[31, 54, 34, 89, 12, 23])
df=pd.DataFrame(s)
```

Which statement will be used to get the output as 2?

(a) print(df.index)
(b) print(df.shape())
(c) print(df.ndim)
(d) print(df.values)

33. Write the output of the given code.

```
import pandas as pd
S1=pd.Series([5,6,7,8,10],index=['v','w','x',
                                     'y','z'])
l=[2,6,1,4,6]
S2=pd.Series(l,index=['z','y','a','w','v'])
print(S1-S2)
```
CBSE SQP 2021-22 Term-I

(a)		(b)		(c)		(d)	
a	0	a	NaN	v	– 1.0	a	NaN
v	–1.0	v	– 1.0	w	2.0	v	– 1.0
w	2.0	w	2.0	y	2.0	w	2.0
x	NaN	x	NaN	z	8.0	x	3.0
y	2.0	y	2.0	dtype: float64		y	2.0
z	8.0	z	8.0			z	8.0
dtype: float64		dtype: float64				dtype: float64	

34. DataFrames can be created from **CBSE 2021-22 Term-I**

(a) lists
(b) dictionaries
(c) series
(d) All of these

35. Which of the following is a two-dimensional labelled data structure of Python? **CBSE 2023**

(a) Relation
(b) DataFrame
(c) Series
(d) Square

36. Name a data structure where two-dimensional labelled array that is ordered collection of columns is used to store heterogeneous data types.

(a) Series
(b) NumPy Array
(c) DataFrame
(d) Panel

37. In a dataframe, what does axis=0 represents?

(a) Columns
(b) Rows
(c) Rows and Columns both
(d) None of these

38. All pandas data structures are ___________ mutable but not always __________ mutable.

(a) size, value
(b) semantic, size
(c) value, size
(d) none of the mentioned

39. Which among the following options can be used to create a DataFrame in Pandas?

(a) A scalar value
(b) An ndarray
(c) A python dict
(d) All of these

40. Which function is used to rename the existing column or index?

(a) ren( )
(b) rename( )
(c) changename( )
(d) namechange( )

41. Which of the following Python statements can be used to select a column column_name from a DataFrame df? **CBSE SQP 2024-25**

(a) df.getcolumn('column_name')
(b) df['column_name']
(c) df.select('column_name')
(d) df(column_name)

42. Which of the following can be used to specify the data while creating a DataFrame? **CBSE SQP 2022-23**

(a) Series
(b) List of Dictionaries
(c) Structured ndarray
(d) All of these

43. Pandas data frame cannot be created using: CBSE SQP 2021-22 Term -I

(a) Dictionary of tuples (b) Series
(c) Dictionary of List (d) List of Dictionaries

44. Which of the following statement is wrong in context of DataFrame? CBSE 2021-22 Term I

(a) Two-dimensional size is mutable.
(b) Can perform Arithmetic operations on rows and columns.
(c) Homogeneous tabular data structure.
(d) Create DataFrame from numpy ndarray.

45. When we create a DataFrame from a list of Dictionaries the columns labels are formed by the CBSE 2021-22 Term-I

(a) union of the keys of the dictionaries
(b) intersection of the keys of the dictionaries
(c) union of the values of the dictionaries
(d) intersection of the values of the dictionaries

46. While accessing the column from the dataframe, we can specify the column name. In case column does not exist, which type of error it will raise? CBSE SQP 2021-22 Term-I

(a) Key Error (b) Syntax Error
(c) Name Error (d) Runtime Error

47. Method or function to add a new row in a dataframe is CBSE SQP 2021-22 Term-I

(a) .loc() (b) .iloc()
(c) join() (d) add()

48. What is a correct syntax to return the values of first row of a Pandas DataFrame? Assuming the name of the DataFrame is dfRent. CBSE SQP 2021-22 Term-I

(a) `dfRent[0]`
(b) `dfRent.loc[1]`
(c) `dfRent.loc[0]`
(d) `dfRent.iloc[1]`

49. Function to display the first n rows in the DataFrame is CBSE SQP 2021-22 Term-I

(a) tail (n) (b) head (n)
(c) top (n) (d) first (n)

50. Consider the following dataframe df1:

	EName	Sal	Bonus
0	Kavita	50000	3000
1	Sudha	60000	4000
2	Garima	55000	5000

Write the output of the given command:
`df1.loc[:0,'Sal']` CBSE SQP 2021-22 Term-I

(a) 0 Kavita 50000 3000 (b) 50000
(c) 3000 (d) 55000

51. Difference between loc() and iloc().: SQP 2021-22 Term I

(a) Both are Label indexed based functions.
(b) Both are Integer position-based functions.
(c) loc() is label based function and iloc() integer position based function.
(d) loc() is integer position based function and iloc() index position based function.

52. Which method is used to Delete row(s) from DataFrame ? CBSE 2021-22 Term I

(a) .drop() method
(b) .del() method
(c) .remove() method
(d) .delete() method

53. Identify the correct option to select first four rows and second to fourth columns from a DataFrame 'Data'. CBSE 2021-22 Term-I

(a) `display(Data.iloc[1 : 4, 2 : 4])`
(b) `display(Data.iloc[1 : 5, 2 : 5])`
(c) `print(Data.iloc[0 : 4, 1 : 4])`
(d) `print(Data.iloc[1 : 4, 2 : 4])`

54. Consider the following statements CBSE 2021-22 Term I

Statement A .loc() is a label based data selecting method to select a specific row(s) or column(s), which we want to select.

Statement B .iloc() cannot be used with default indices, if customised indices are provided.

(a) Statement A is true but statement B is false.
(b) Statement A is false but statement B is true.
(c) Statement A and statement B both are false.
(d) Statement A and statement B both are true.

55. Mr. Raman created a DataFrame from a Numpy array

```
arr = np. array ([[2, 4, 8], [3, 9, 27], [4, 16, 64 ]] )
df=pd. DataFrame(arr,index=['one', 'two', 'three'], ________ )
print(df)
```

Help him to add a customised column labels to the above DataFrame. CBSE 2021-22 Term-I

(a) columns='no', 'sq', 'cube'
(b) column=['no', 'sq', 'cube']
(c) columns=['no', 'sq', 'cube']
(d) columns=[['no', 'sq', 'cube']]

56. What will be the output of the following program?

```
import pandas as pd
dic={'Name': ['Sapna', 'Anmol', 'Rishul',
'Sameep'], 'Agg' : [56, 67 , 75 , 76], ' Age'
:[16, 18,  16, 19]}
df=pd.DataFrame(dic,columns=['Name', 'Age'])
print(df)
```

CBSE 2021-22 Term I

(a)

	Name	Agg	Age
101	Sapna	56	16
102	Anmol	67	18
103	Rishul	75	16
104	Sameep	76	19

(b)

	Name	Agg	Age
0	Sapna	56	16
1	Anmol	67	18
2	Rishul	75	16
3	Sameep	76	19

(c)

	Name
0	Sapna
1	Anmol
2	Rishul
3	Sameep

(d)

	Name	Age
0	Sapna	16
1	Anmol	18
2	Rishul	16
3	Sameep	19

57. Sudhanshu has written the following code to create a DataFrame with boolean index

```
import numpy as np
import pandas as pd
df=pd.DataFrame(data=[[5,6,7]], index=[true,
false, true])
print (df)
```

While executing the code, she is getting an error, help her to rectify the code. **CBSE 2021-22 Term I**

(a) `df=pd.DataFrame([True,False,True], data=[5, 6, 7])`

(b) `df=pd.DataFrame (data=[5, 6, 7],index = [True, False, True])`

(c) `df=pd.DataFrame ([true, false, true] data =[5, 6, 7])`

(d) `df=pd.DataFrame(index=[true, false, true], data=[[5, 6, 7]])`

58. What will be the output of the following code snippet?

```
import pandas as pd
data = {'A': [1, 2, 3], 'B': [4, 5, 6]}
df = pd.DataFrame(data)
print(df.loc[1, 'B'])
```

(a) 4 (b) 5

(c) 6 (d) Error

59. Fill in the Blank

Boolean indexing in Pandas DataFrame can be used for ________. **CBSE SQP 2024-25**

(a) Creating a new DataFrame

(b) Sorting data based on index labels

(c) Joining data using labels

(d) Filtering data based on condition

60. Given the following code snippet, what will be the output of df.head(2)?

```
import pandas as pd
data = {
    'Name': ['John', 'Anna', 'Peter', 'Linda'],
    'Age': [23, 21, 24, 22],
    'City': ['New York', 'Paris', 'Berlin',
                                       'London']
}
df = pd.DataFrame(data)
print(df.head(2))
```

(a)

	Name	Age	City
0	John	23	New York
1	Anna	21	Paris

(b)

	Name	Age	City
0	John	23	Paris
1	Anna	21	New York

(c)

	Name	Age	City
0	Peter	24	Berlin
1	Linda	22	London

(d)

	Name	Age	City
0	Anna	21	Paris
1	John	23	New York

61. Abhay is a student of class 'XII' and he is aware of some concepts of Python. He has created the DataFrame but he is getting errors after executing the code. Help him by identifying the correct statement that will create the DataFrame. **CBSE 2021-22 Term I**

```
import pandas as pd
stuname=[ 'Muskan', 'Radhika', 'Gopar',
'Pihu']
term1 =[70, 63, 74, 90]
term2 =[67, 70, 86, 95]
```

(a) `df=pd. DataFrame({"Name":stuname, "marks1":term 1,"marks2":term 2})`

(b) `df=pd.DataFrame ([stuname. term1, term2], columns=['stuName',"marks1", marks2"])`

(c) `df=pd.DataFrame({stuname, term1, term2})`

(d) `df=pD.dataframe({stuname, term1, term2})`

62. In a Pandas DataFrame, if the tail() function is used without specifying the optional argument indicating the number of rows to display, what is the default

number of rows displayed, considering the DataFrame has 10 entries? CBSE SQP 2024-25

(a) 0 (b) 1
(c) 4 (d) 5

63. Which of the following is not an attribute of Pandas dataframe? CBSE SQP 2021-22 Term-I

(a) length (b) T
(c) size (d) shape

64. Which command will be used to delete 3 and 5 rows of the dataframe. Assuming the dataframe name as DF. CBSE SQP 2021-22 Term-I

(a) `DF.drop([2,4],axis=0)`
(b) `DF.drop([2,4],axis=1)`
(c) `DF.drop([3,5],axis=1)`
(d) `DF.drop([3,5])`

65. Read the statements given below. Identify the right option from the following for attribute and method/function.

Statement A Attribute always ends without parenthesis.
Statement B Function/Method cannot work without arguments. CBSE SQP 2021-22 Term-I

(a) Both statements are correct.
(b) Both statements are incorrect.
(c) Statement A is correct, but Statement B is incorrect.
(d) Statement A is incorrect, but Statement B is correct.

66. Ritika is a new learner for the python pandas, and she is aware of some concepts of python. She has created some lists, but is unable to create the data frame from the same. Help her by identifying the statement which will create the data frame. CBSE SQP 2021-22 Term I

```
import pandas as pd
Name=['Manpreet','Kavil','Manu','Ria']
Phy=[70,60,76,89]
Chem=[30,70,50,65]
```

(a) `df=pd.DataFrame({"Name":Name,"Phy":Phy,"Chem":Chem})`
(b) `d=("Name":Name,"Phy":Phy,"Chem":Chem)`
`df=pd.DataFrame(d)`
(c) `df=pd.DataFrame([Name,Phy,Chem],columns=['Name',"Phy","Chem","Total"])`
(d) `df=pd.DataFrame({Name:"Name", Phy:"Phy",Chem: "Chem"})`

67. Which of the following would give the same output as DF/DF1, where DF and DF1 are DataFrames? CBSE 2021-22 Term-I

(a) DF.div(DF1)
(b) DF1.div(DF)
(c) Divide(DF, DF1)
(d) Div(DF, DF1)

68. Sandhya wants to display the last four rows of the dataframe df and she has written the following command:

```
df. tail( )
```

But the first 5 rows are being displayed. To rectify this problem, which of the following statement should be written? CBSE 2021-22 Term I

(a) df.head( ) (b) df.last(4) (c) df.tail(4) (d) df.rows(4)

69. Which object do you get after reading a CSV file using pandas.read.csv()?

(a) DataFrame (b) ND array
(c) Char Vector (d) None

70. Which of the following Python statements is used to import data from a CSV file into a Pandas DataFrame (Note: pd is an alias for pandas)? CBSE SQP 2024-25

(a) pd.open_csv('filename.csv')
(b) pd.read_csv('filename.csv')
(c) pd.load_csv('filename.csv')
(d) pd.import_csv('filename.csv')

71. Which of the following is not true with respect to CSV files? CBSE 2024

(a) Values are separated by commas.
(b) to_csv ( ) can be used to save a dataframe to a CSV file.
(c) CSV file is created using a word processor.
(d) CSV file is a type of text file.

72. Which function will be used to read data from a CSV file into Pandas dataframe? CBSE SQP 2021-22 Term-I

(a) readcsv() (b) to_csv()
(c) read_csv() (d) csv_read()

73. The data of any CSV file can be shown in which of the following software? CBSE 2021-22 Term-I

(a) MS Word (b) Notepad
(c) Spreadsheet (d) All of these

74. Now-a-days, for developing machine learning projects programmers rely on CSV files rather than databases. Why? CBSE 2021-22 Term I

(a) CSV can be used with proprietary softwares only
(b) CSV files can be downloaded from open source websites free of cost
(c) CSV files need not be imported while creating the projects
(d) CSV is a simple and well formatted mode for data Storage

Fill in the Blanks

75. Series is ______ dimensional array with homogeneous data.

76. Size of series is ______ .

77. The operation is performed only on the ______ indexes.

78. _______ can be done either in ascending or descending order.

79. _________ slice operation is used to print whole series.

80. DataFrame has _____ value means its value can be change easily.

81. iloc stands for _______ .

82. ______ files are simple to understand and debug with a basic text editor.

State whether True or False

83. "In a Python program, if a break statement is given in a nested loop, it terminates the execution of all loops in one go." **CBSE SQP 2023-24**

84. List and tuple can be easily converted into Series by Series( ) method.

85. The data value of series object can be modified using value assignment.

86. To short the series values using values, use sort_values( ) function.

87. Slicing can be used to extract a specific portion from a Pandas Series. **CBSE SQP 2024-25**

88. In DataFrame, name( ) function is used to rename any index, column or row.

89. An exception may be raised even if the program is syntactically correct. **CBSE SQP 2023-24**

90. CSV file can be viewed as word file.

91. CSV files are quick to create and load into memory before analysis.

Assertion and Reason Based Questions

Assertion and Reason Based Questions. Mark the correct choice as

(a) Both Assertion (A) and Reason (R) are true and Reason (R) is the correct explanation for A

(b) Both Assertion (A) and Reason (R) are true and Reason (R) is not the correct explanation for A

(c) Assertion (A) is True but Reason (R) is False

(d) Assertion (A) is false but Reason (R) is True

92. **Assertion (A)** A Series is a one dimensional array and a DataFrame is a two-dimensional array containing sequence of values of any data type. (int, float, list, string, etc.) **CBSE 2024**

Reason (R) Both Series and DataFrames have by default numeric indexes starting from zero.

93. **Assertion(A)** Python Standard Library consists of various modules. **CBSE SQP 2023-24**

Reason (R) A function in a module is used to simplify the code and avoids repetition.

94. **Assertion (A)** To create a series from array, we have to import the NumPy module and then use array() method.

Reason (R) NumPy is an open-source numerical Python library. NumPy contains a multidimensional array and matrix data structures.

95. **Assertion (A)** A dict can be passed as an input to the series.

Reason (R) If index is passed, then corresponding values to a particular label in the index will be extracted from the dictionary.

96. **Assertion (A)** The output of addition of two series will be NaN, if one of the elements or both the elements have no value(s). **CBSE 2023**

Reason (R) While performing mathematical operations on a series by default all missing values are filled in with 0.

97. **Assertion (A)** DataFrame is two dimensional labelled array. It's columns types can be heterogeneous i.e., of varying objects.

Reason (R) We need a DataFrame with a boolean index to use the boolean indexing.

98. **Assertion (A)** We can add a new column in an existing DataFrame. **CBSE SQP 2024-25**

Reason (R) DataFrames are size mutable.

99. **Assertion (A)** DataFrame has both a row and column index. **CBSE SQP 2022-23**

Reason (R) A DataFrame is a two-dimensional labelled data structure like a table of MySQL.

100. **Assertion (A)** List of dictionary can be passed to form a DataFrame.

Reason (R) Keys of dictionary area taken as row names by default.

101. **Assertion (A)** CSV files are available to open in any spreadsheet program, including Google sheets, Open Office, and Microsoft Excel.

Reason (R) Using a spreadsheet program can serve a user's needs better since it has cells where data is sorted in rows and columns.

Answers

1. (a) Panel Data
2. (b) import pandas as 1pd
3. (d) import panda as pd
4. (d) It is proprietary software.
5. (d) pip install pandas
6. (d) Tkinter
7. (c) 1 Dimensional
8. (c) `S=pd.Series(Monument,index=State)`
9. (d) All of the above
10. (c) pd.Series( )
11. (a) 1.0
12. (b) size
13. (d) ndim
14. (b) hasnans
15. (b) Indices of the Series
16. (d) stud.size
17. (a) Cannot change the index of the Series.
18. (c) count
19. (a)
```
d    4
e    5
dtype: int64
```
20. (c)
```
   0
1  0
2  0
```
21. (d)
```
One      1
Two      2
Three    3
Seven    7
Four     4
dtype: int64
```
22. (c) 30
23. (b) Displays the first five elements of a Series
24. (d) S1. head [0 : 5]
25. (b) S.tail(5)
26. (c) 3
27. (c)
```
W    Wolf
B    Bear
dtype: object
```
28. (a) Value Error
29. (c) `print(data mod 2!=0)`
30. (a)
```
0    False
1    True
2    False
3    True
4    False
5    False
dtype: bool
```
31. (b) data = L**3
32. (c) print(df.ndim)
33. (b)
```
a    NaN
v    – 1.0
w    2.0
x    NaN
y    2.0
z    8.0
dtype: float64
```
34. (d) All of these
35. (b) DataFrame
36. (c) DataFrame
37. (b) Rows
38. (c) value, size
39. (d) All of these
40. (b) rename( )
41. (b) df['column_name']
42. (d) All of these
43. (a) Dictionary of tuples
44. (c) Homogeneous tabular data structure.
45. (a) union of the keys of the dictionaries
46. (a) Key Error
47. (a) .loc()
48. (c) `dfRent.loc[0]`
49. (b) head (n)
50. (b) 50000
51. (c) loc() is label based function and iloc() integer position based function.
52. (a) .drop() method
53. (a) `display(Data.iloc[1 : 4, 2 : 4])`
54. (a) Statement A is true but statement B is false.
55. (c) columns=['no', 'sq', 'cube']
56. (d)

	Name	Age
0	Sapna	16
1	Anmol	18
2	Rishul	16
3	Sameep	19

57. (b) `df=pd.DataFrame (data=[5, 6, 7],index = [True, False, True])`
58. (b) 5
59. (d) Filtering data based on condition
60. (a)
```
  Name  Age      City
0 John   23  New York
1 Anna   21     Paris
```
61. (b) `df=pd.DataFrame ([stuname. term1, term2], columns=[‘stuName’,“marks1”, marks2”])`
62. (d) 5
63. (a) length
64. (a) `DF.drop([2,4],axis=0)`
65. (c) Statement A is correct, but Statement B is incorrect.
66. (a) `df=pd.DataFrame({"Name":Name, "Phy": Phy,"Chem":Chem})`
67. (a) DF.div(DF1)
68. (c) df.tail(4)
69. (a) DataFrame
70. (b) pd.read_csv('filename.csv')
71. (c) CSV file is created using a word processor.

72. (c) read_csv()
73. (d) All of these
74. (d) CSV is a simple and well formatted mode for data
75. one
76. immutable
77. matching
78. Sorting
79. [:]
80. mutable
81. integer location
82. CSV
83. False
84. True
85. True
86. True
87. True
88. False
89. True
90. False
91. True
92. (b) Both Assertion (A) and Reason (R) are true and Reason (R) is not the correct explanation for A
93. (a) Both Assertion (A) and Reason (R) are true and Reason (R) is the correct explanation for A
94. (a) Both Assertion (A) and Reason (R) are true and Reason (R) is the correct explanation for A
95. (a) Both Assertion (A) and Reason (R) are true and Reason (R) is the correct explanation for A
96. (c) Assertion (A) is True but Reason (R) is False
97. (c) Assertion (A) is True but Reason (R) is False
98. (a) Both Assertion (A) and Reason (R) are true and Reason (R) is the correct explanation for A
99. (a) Both Assertion (A) and Reason (R) are true and Reason (R) is the correct explanation for A
100. (c) Assertion (A) is True but Reason (R) is False
101. (a) Both Assertion (A) and Reason (R) are true and Reason (R) is the correct explanation for A

Subjective Type Questions

Very Short Answer Types Questions

1. Name some common data structures of Python's pandas library?

Ans. DataFrame, Series.

2. Which platform is required to work on DataFrame?

Ans. Any platform that supports Python, such as Jupyter Notebook, PyCharm, or Google Colab.

3. Mention four features of Pandas.

Ans. Four features of Pandas:

- Handles missing data efficiently.
- Provides tools for reshaping and pivoting data.
- Supports merging and joining of datasets.
- Offers powerful group-by functionality for data aggregation.

4. What is a Series in Python Pandas? Also, give a suitable example to support your answer. **CBSE SQP 2024-25**

Ans. A Series in Pandas is a one-dimensional labeled array that can hold data of any type (integers, strings, floats, etc.). It is similar to a column in a spreadsheet or a single-column DataFrame.

Example:

```
import pandas as pd
data = pd.Series([10, 20, 30, 40])
print(data)
```

5. What will the output produced by following code?

```
stationary = ['pencils', 'notebooks',
'scales', 'erasers']
S=pd.Series([20,30,52,10],index=stationary)
S2=pd.Series([17,13,32,21],index=stationary)
print(S+S2)
S=S+S2
print(S+S2)
```

Ans.

```
pencils      37
notebooks    43
scales       84
erasers      31
dtype: int64
pencils      54
notebooks    56
scales      116
erasers      52
dtype: int64
```

6. Find the error in following code fragment:

```
S2=pd.Series([101,102,102,104])
S2.index=[0,1,2,3,4,5]
S2[5]=220
print(S2)
```

Ans. The error is in setting the index length longer than the Series.

7. Complete the given Python code to get the required output (ignore the dtype attribute) as **CBSE SQP 2024-25**

Output

Tamil Nadu	**Chennai**
Uttar Pradesh	**Lucknow**
Manipur	**Imphal**

Code

```
import ________ as pd
data = ['Chennai','________','Imphal']
indx = ['Tamil Nadu','Uttar
Pradesh','Manipur']
```

```
s = pd.Series(________, indx)
print(________)
```

Ans.
```
import pandas as pd
data = ['Chennai','Lucknow','Imphal']
indx = ['Tamil Nadu','Uttar
Pradesh','Manipur']
s = pd.Series(data, indx)
print(s)
```

8. Write a Python program to create a series object, country using a list that stores the capital of each country. **CBSE 2023**

Note Assume four countries to be used as index of the series object are India, UK, Denmark, and Thailand having their capitals as New Delhi, London, Copenhagen, and Bangkok respectively.

Ans.
```
import pandas as pd
data=["New Delhi", "London",
"Copenhagen", "Bangkok"]
ind = ["India", "UK", "Denmark",
"Thailand"]
country = pd.Series(data, ind)
print(country)
```

9. The Python code written below has syntactical errors. Rewrite the correct code and underline the correction(s) made. **CBSE 2024**

```
import Pandas as pd
stud = ['Name': 'Ramya', 'Class': 11, 'House':
'Red']
s = p.Series(s)
print(s)
```

Ans. Correct code :
```
import pandas as pd
stud={'Name':'Ramya','Class':11,'House':'Red'}
s=pd.Series(stud)
print(s)
```

10. What will be the output for the below program?
```
import pandas as pd
import numpy as np
s = pd.Series(5, index=[10, 11, 12, 13])
print(s)
```

Ans.
```
10  5
11  5
12  5
13  5
dtype: int64
```

11. How does dataframe assign row index to its rows in two dimensional dictionaries?

Ans. The keys of the outer dictionary become the column names, and the keys of the inner dictionaries become the row indices.

12. Hitesh wants to display the last four rows of the dataframe df and has written the following code :
```
df.tail( )
```
But last 5 rows are being displayed. Identify the error and rewrite the correct code so that last 4 rows get displayed.

Ans. df.tail(4)

13. Consider the following code and predict the output
```
import pandas as pd
s1 = pd.Series(range (1,9,2),index =
list("abcd"))
print(s1[::2])
```

Ans.
```
a  1
c  5
dtype: int64
```

14. Consider the following Python code and write the output for statement:
```
values = ['India','Canada']
code = ['IND','CAN']
df = pd.DataFrame(values,index=code,
columns =['Country'])
print(df)
```

Ans.
```
     Country
IND  India
CAN  Canada
```

15. Carefully observe the following code **CBSE 2023**
```
import pandas as pd
dic={'pid':[101,102,103,104,105],
'pname':['Shyam ','Roushan','Archit',
              'Medha','Lalit'],
'sports':['Cricket','Tennis',
          'Football','Cricket','Cricket'],
'points':[45000,20000,15000,53000, 60000]}
player=pd.DataFrame(dic)
print(player)
```

Write Python statements for the following

(i) In the DataFrame player created above, set the row labels as 'Player1', 'Player2', 'Player3', 'Player4', 'Player5'.

(ii) Rename the column 'points' to 'netpoint' in the DataFrame player.

Ans. (i)
```
player =pd.DataFrame(dic,index =
['Player1','Player2','Player3',
'Player4','Player5'])
```

(ii)
```
new_df=player.rename({'points':
'netpoint'},axis=1)
print (new_df)
```

16. Carefully observe the following code:

```
import pandas as pd
Year1 = {'Q1': 5000, 'Q2': 8000, 'Q3':
12000, 'Q4': 18000}
Year2 = {'A': 13000, 'B': 14000, 'C': 12000}
totSales = {1: Year1, 2: Year2}
df = pd.DataFrame(totSales)
print(df)
```

Answer the following:

(i) List the index of the DataFrame df

(ii) List the column names of DataFrame df. **CBSE 2023, SQP 2022-23**

Ans. (i) Index(['Q1', 'Q2', 'Q3', 'Q4', 'A', 'B', 'C'], dtype='object')

(ii) Index([1, 2], dtype='object')

17. Consider the following Python code: **CBSE 2024**

```
import pandas as pd
S1 = pd. Series (['Rubina', 'Jaya', 'Vaibhav'],
index = [10, 16, 18])
S2 = pd. Series ( ______, index = [10, 16, 18])
S3 = pd. Series ([56, 67, 86], ______)
xiia = {'Name': ______, 'Subject': S2, 'Marks': S3}
df = pd. DataFrame (______)
print (df)
```

Complete the above Python code to display the following output

	Name	Subject	Marks
10	Rubina	IP	56
16	Jaya	HSc	67
18	Vaibhav	IP	86

Ans. Complete code:

```
import pandas as pd
S1=pd.Series(['Rubina','Jaya','Vaibhav'],index=[1
0,16,18])
S2=pd.Series(['IP','HSc','IP'], index = [10, 16, 18])
S3= pd.Series([56,67,86],index=[10,16,18])
xiia={'Name':S1,'Subject':S2,'Marks':S3}
df=pd.DataFrame(xiia)
print(df)
```

Short Answer Type I Questions

18. What is data structure?

Ans. Refer to text on page no. 2 (Data Structure).

19. How to create a Series from Scalar value?

Ans. Refer to text on page no. 4 (Creating a Series from Scalar value).

20. How to create a Series from lists?

Ans. Refer to text on page no. 3 (Creating a Series from lists).

21. What will be the output of the given code?

```
import pandas as pd
s=pd.Series([3,6,9,12,14],index=['a','b','
c','d','e'])
print(s['a']+s['c'])
```

Ans. 12

22. Write the output of the following code.

```
import pandas as pd
import numpy as up
in = [1, 2, 3, 4, 5]
data1 = ['a', 'b', 'c', 'd', 'e']
a=pd. Series (data = in, index=data1,
dtype = np.float64)
print(a)
```

Ans. Output

```
a    1.0
b    2.0
c    3.0
d    4.0
e    5.0
dtype : float64
```

23. Write the output of the following code, considering the Series sr as given below

0 Computer
1 Maths
2 Science
3 English
4 Hindi
5 Social Science

(i) print (sr [3 : 5])

(ii) print (sr.index)

(iii) print (sr. values)

(iv) print (sr [0:2])

Ans. (i)
```
3    English
4    Hindi
dtype:object
```

(ii) RangeIndex (start=0, stop=6, step=1)

(iii) ['Computer', 'Maths', 'Science', 'English', 'Hindi', 'Social Science']

(iv)
```
0    Computer
1    Maths
dtype:object
```

24. Write the code to produce following Series and also display this Series in descending order of its index.

d 225
b 720
a 840
c 650
e 950

Ans.
```
import pandas as pd
x=pd. Series (data=[225, 720, 840, 650, 950],
```

```
    index = ['d', 'b', 'a', 'c', 'e'])
print(x)
print("Descending Order")
print(x.sort_index(ascending=False))
```

25. Write the output of following code.

```
import pandas as pd
import numpy as np
data = np.array (['Computer', 'SST',
      'Science', 'English', 'Math', 'Hindi'])
a=pd.Series(data)
hd=a.head(4)
print("First output")
print(hd)
tl=a.tail(3)
print("Second output")
print(tl)
```

Ans. First output

0	Computer
1	SST
2	Science
3	English

dtype:object

Second output

3	English
4	Math
5	Hindi

dtype:object

26. Consider the series object sr1 that stores the salary of teacher, as shown below. Here Teacher's name represents by their initial names.

R 15000
K 12000
N 20000
L 22000

Write the code to modify the salary of K as 18000 and for N and L as 25000. Print the changed Series.

Ans.

```
import pandas as pd
sr1[1]=18000
sr1[2:]=25000
print(sr1)
```

Output

R	15000
K	18000
N	25000
L	25000

27. Write the output of the given program:

```
import pandas as pd
S1=pd.Series([5,6,7,8,10],
index=['v','w',' x','y','z'])
l=[2,6,1,4,6]
S2=pd.Series(l,index=['z','y','a','w','v'])
print(S1-S2)
```

Ans. x NaN
a NaN
v -1.0
w 2.0
y 2.0
z 8.0
dtype: float64

28. Consider the following Series

Series A		Series B	
0	5	0	3
1	6	1	4
2	7	2	5
3	2	3	12
4	10	4	2
		5	15

Write the output of the following statements.

(i) print(A–B) **(ii) print(A*B)**

Ans.

(i)

0	+2.0
1	2.0
2	2.0
3	–10.0
4	8.0
5	NaN

dtype: float 64

(ii)

0	15.0
1	24.0
2	35.0
3	24.0
4	20.0
5	NaN

dtype: float 64

29. Define DataFrame in Pandas.

Ans. DataFrame is two dimensional data structure with heterogeneous data, usually represented in the tabular format. The data is represented in rows and columns. Each column represents an attribute and each row represents a person.

30. What will be the output of following code and Answer the following:

(i) List the index of the DataFrame df

(ii) List the column names of DataFrame df.

```
import pandas as pd
Year1={'Q1':5000,'Q2':8000,'Q3':12000,'Q4':
18000}
Year2={'A' :13000,'B':14000,'C':12000}
totSales={1:Year1,2:Year2}
df=pd.DataFrame(totSales)
print(df)
```

Ans. Output

	1	2
Q1	5000.0	NaN

```
Q2    8000.0      NaN
Q3   12000.0      NaN
Q4   18000.0      NaN
A        NaN  13000.0
B        NaN  14000.0
C        NaN  12000.0
```

(i) The index of the DataFrame df is:
Index(['Q1', 'Q2', 'Q3', 'Q4', 'A', 'B', 'C'], dtype='object')

(ii) The column names of the DataFrame df are:
Int64Index([1, 2], dtype='int64')

31. Write a Python code to create a DataFrame with appropriate headings from the list given below:
['S101', 'Amy', 70], ['S102', 'Bandhi', 69], ['S104', 'Cathy', 75], ['S105', 'Gundaho', 82]

Ans.
```
import pandas as pd
data=[['S101', 'Amy', 70],
      ['S102', 'Bandhi', 69],
      ['S104', 'Cathy', 75],
      ['S105', 'Gundaho', 82]]
df=pd.DataFrame (data, columns=['ID',
                          'Name', 'Marks'])
print(df)
```

32. Write the code to create the following DataFrame

	Name	Marks	Subject
a	Abhi	75	Maths
b	Chirag	82	Science
c	Tushar	69	English
d	Mahi	70	Science
e	Vanshika	92	Computer

Ans.
```
import pandas as pd
data = {'Name' : ['Abhi', 'Chirag', 'Tushar',
  'Mahi', 'Vanshika'],
  'Marks' : [75, 82, 69, 70, 92],
  'Subject' : ['Maths', 'Science',
  'English', 'Science', 'Computer']}
df=pd.DataFrame (data, index = ['a', 'b',
                          'c', 'd', 'e'])
print(df)
```

33. Write a small Python code to create a DataFrame with headings (a and b) from the list given below:
[[10, 20], [30, 40], [50, 60], [70, 80]]

Ans.
```
import pandas as pd
df=pd.DataFrame ([[10, 20], [30, 40]],
      columns = ['a', 'b'])
df2=pd.DataFrame ([[50, 60], [70, 80]],
      columns = ['a', 'b'])
df = df.append (df2)
```

34. Write a program to change the order of a DataFrame columns.

e.g. Original DataFrame

	Col1	Col2	Col3
0	10	40	70
1	40	50	80
2	30	60	90
3	40	70	0
4	50	80	10

After altering col1 and col3

	Col3	Col2	Col1
0	70	40	10
1	80	50	40
2	90	60	30
3	0	70	40
4	10	80	50

Ans.
```
import pandas as pd
d = {'col1': [10,40 , 30, 40, 50], 'col2': [40, 50,
60, 70, 80], 'col3': [70, 80, 90, 0, 10]}
df = pd.DataFrame(data=d)
print("Original DataFrame")
print(df)
print('After altering col1 and col3')
df = df[['col3', 'col2', 'col1']]
print(df)
```

35. Given a DataFrame df as shown below:

	A	B	C
0	21	12	69
1	45	45	84
2	23	86	70
3	17	33	78

What will be the result of the following code statements?

(i) df['D']=np.NaN (ii) df['D'] = [23, 41, 32]
(iii) df['D'] = [23, 41, 32, 9]

Ans. (i)

	A	B	C	D
0	21	12	69	NaN
1	45	45	84	NaN
2	23	86	70	NaN
3	17	33	78	NaN

(ii) ValueError : Length of values does not match with the length of index.

(iii)

	A	B	C	D
0	21	12	69	23
1	45	45	84	41
2	23	86	70	32
3	17	33	78	9

36. Give an example to create a DataFrame from the list of dictionary. Also, display its output.

Ans.
```
import pandas as pd
A = {'One' : 23, 'Two' : 44, 'Three' : 54,
                              'Four' : 77}
```

```
B = {'One' : 44, 'Two' : 75, 'Three' : 89,
                              'Four' : 29}
C = {'One' : 29, 'Two' : 52, 'Three' : 63,
                              'Four' : 38}
D = {'One' : 12, 'Two' : 42, 'Three' : 7,
                              'Four' : 16}
data = [A, B, C, D]
df=pd.DataFrame(data)
print(df)
```

Output

	One	Two	Three	Four
0	23	44	54	77
1	44	75	89	29
2	29	52	63	38
3	12	42	7	16

37. Define the following terms

(i) .loc[] **(ii) .iloc[]**

Ans. (i) .loc[]: A pandas function used to access rows and columns of a DataFrame by label or a boolean array.
Syntax: Series.loc

(iii) .iloc[]: A pandas function used to access rows and columns of a DataFrame by index position (integer-based indexing).
Syntax: Series.iloc

38. Consider a DataFrame of Sales data of four months stored with name sales_df.

	April	May	June	July
Delhi	75	90	54	67
Mumbai	78	65	87	84
Kolkata	84	79	92	79
Chennai	65	78	94	90

(i) Write a Python code to find total sales of July month.

(ii) Write a Python code to add the sales of August month with [70, 94,80,93] data.

Ans. (i) `print(sales_df.sum().loc['July'])`

(ii) `sales_df.insert(4,column="August", value=[70,94,80,93])`

39. Consider the following DataFrame dfn that contain vegetables.

	Color	Quantity	Price
Capsicum	Red	12	60
Capsicum	Green	22	100
Chilli	Red	50	40
Chilli	Green	65	55
Lime	Green	20	35

Write the code statement to the following:

(i) Find all rows with the label "Chilli". Extract all columns.

(ii) List 2nd, 3rd and 4th rows.

(iii) List only the columns Quantity and Price using loc.

Ans. (i) dfn. loc ['Chilli', :]

(ii) dfn. iloc [0 : 3, :]

(iii) dfn. loc [:, ['Quantity', 'Price']]

40. Consider the given DataFrame 'password': **CBSE 2024**

	CodeName	Category	Frequency
0	aaaaaa	alpha	6.91
1	dragon	animal	18.52
2	baseball	sport	1.29
3	football	sport	11.11
4	monkey	animal	3.72
5	qwerty	alpha	1.85
6	abcde	alpha	3.19

Write suitable Python statements for the following:

(i) To add a new row with following values:
CodeName – 'abc123'
Category – alphanumeric
Frequency – 12.8

(ii) To delete the row with the row label 2.

(iii) To delete the column having column label as Frequency.

Ans. (i) password.loc[7]=['abc123','alphanumeric',12.8]

(ii) password =password.drop(2)

(iii) password.pop('Frequency')

41. Kavyanjali, a chemical analyst, needs to arrange data of few elements in the form of two series containing symbols and their atomic numbers respectively. Thereafter, the data of these two series has to be arranged and displayed in the for of DataFrame as shown below: **CBSE 2023**

	Symbol	Atomic Number
Hydrogen	H	1
Helium	He	2
Lithium	Li	3
Beryllium	Be	4

Help her in writing suitable Python code to complete the task.

Ans.
```
import pandas as pd
index = ["Hydrogen", "Helium", "Lithium",
"Beryllium"]
sym = ["H", "He", "Li", "Be"]
atom = [1, 2, 3, 4]
Symbol=pd.Series (sym, index)
Atomic_Number = pd.Series (atom, index)
```

```
df = pd.DataFrame
({"Symbol":Symbol,"Atomic Number":
Atomic_Number})
print(df)
```

42. **Consider the given DataFrame 'health'.** **CBSE 2023**

	Diseasename	Agent
0	Common cold	Virus
1	Chickenpox	Virus
2	Cholera	Bacteria
3	Tuberculosis	Bacteria

Write suitable Python statements for the following:

(i) **Remove the row containing details of disease named Tuberculosis.**

(ii) **Add a new disease named 'Malaria' caused by 'Protozoa'.**

(iii) **Display the last 2 rows.**

Ans. (i) `df = df.drop(3)`

(ii) `df.loc[4, :] = ["Malaria", "Protozoa"]`

(iii) `t = df.tail(2)`

43. **What do you mean by CSV file?**

Ans. A Comma Separated Values (CSV) file is a plain text file that contains a list of data. These files are often used for exchanging data between different applications. For example, databases and contact managers often support CSV files.

These files may sometimes be called Character Separated Values or Comma Delimited Files. They mostly use the comma character to separate data, but sometimes use other characters like semicolons.

44. **Consider the following CSV file Student.csv, write the program to read data from this file and create a DataFrame from it.**

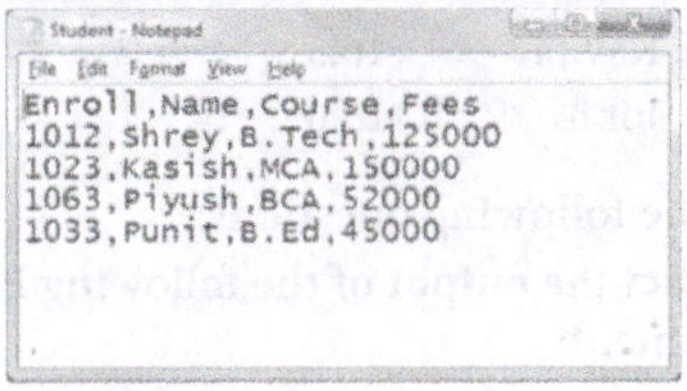

```
Enroll,Name,Course,Fees
1012,Shrey,B.Tech,125000
1023,Kasish,MCA,150000
1063,Piyush,BCA,52000
1033,Punit,B.Ed,45000
```

Ans.
```
import pandas as pd
df1=pd.read_csv("D:\\neetu1\\AIO 12th IP
with Pandas\\Chapter-4\\Student.csv")
print(df1)
```

Output

	Enroll	Name	Course	Fees
0	1012	Shrey	B.Tech	125000
1	1023	Kasish	MCA	150000
2	1063	Piyush	BCA	52000
3	1033	Punit	B.Ed	45000

45. **Consider the following code and identify the command.**

(i) **pd.read_csv("Hello.csv",sep="#")**

(ii) **pd.read_csv("Hello.csv",nrows=5)**

Ans. (i) This code is reading a file "Hello.csv" which contains separator character as '#'.

(ii) This code is reading a file "Hello.csv" which will read the first 5 rows from given file.

46. **Write a program that read CSV file named Student.csv and convert it into DataFrame with new column's header. Also, find the minimum fees from given data.**

Ans.
```
import pandas as pd
df1=pd.read_csv("D:\\neetu1\\AIO 12th IP
with Pandas\\Chapter-4\\Student.csv",
names=['RollNo','SName','Learning',
                   'Fees'],skiprows=1)
print(df1)
print("Minimum fees from given
                   data:",df1.Fees.min())
```

Output

	RollNo	SName	Learning	Fees
0	1012	Shrey	B.Tech	125000
1	1023	Kasish	MCA	150000
2	1063	Piyush	BCA	52000
3	1033	Punit	B.Ed	45000

47. **Consider the following DataFrame df**

	Dept	Employee	Salary
0	Analyst	Rahul	28000
1	DBA	Shreya	35000
2	Programmer	Kiyaan	42000
3	Tester	Rishi	30000
4	DBA	Nishi	32000

Write the program to export DataFrame to a CSV file.

Ans.
```
import pandas as pd
df.to_csv("D:\\neetu1\\AIO 12th IP with
Pandas\\Chapter-4\\Employee.csv")
print("Export successfully")
```

Output

Export successfully

CSV file Employee.csv

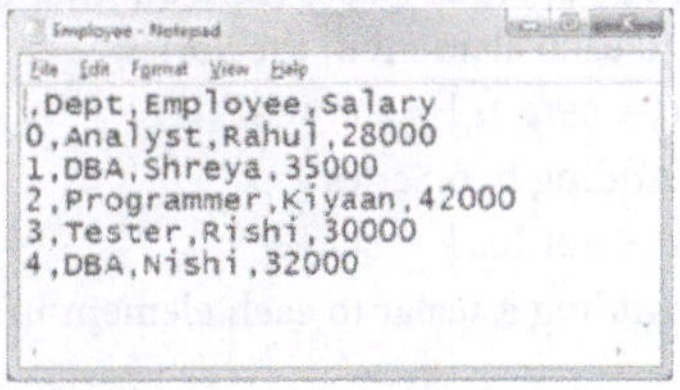

```
,Dept,Employee,Salary
0,Analyst,Rahul,28000
1,DBA,Shreya,35000
2,Programmer,Kiyaan,42000
3,Tester,Rishi,30000
4,DBA,Nishi,32000
```

48. **Find output of following code**

```
import pandas as pd
Year1={'Q1':[5000,10],'Q2':[8000,20],'Q3':
[12000,30],'Q4':[18000,40]}
totSales={1:Year1}
df=pd.DataFrame(totSales)
print(df)
```

Ans.

	1
Q1	[5000, 10]
Q2	[8000, 20]
Q3	[12000, 30]

49. **Consider the given DataFrame 'Stock':** **CBSE SQP 2022-23**

	Name	Price
0	Nancy Drew	150
1	Hardy boys	180
2	Diary of a wimpy kid	225
3	Harry Potter	500

Write suitable Python statements for the following:

(i) **Add a column called Special_Price with the following data:**
[135,150,200,440].

(ii) **Add a new book named 'The Secret' having price 800.**

(iii) **Remove the column Special_Price.**

Ans. (i)
```
Stock['Special_Price'] = [135, 150, 200,
440]
```

(ii)
```
new_book = pd.DataFrame({'Name': ['The
Secret'], 'Price': [800],
'Special_Price': [None]}) Stock =
pd.concat([Stock, new_book],
ignore_index=True)
```

(iii)
```
Stock = Stock.drop(columns
=['Special_Price'])
```

Short Answer Type II Questions

50. **Give any three mathematical operations that can be performed on series with syntax.**

Ans. In pandas, you can perform various mathematical operations directly on Series objects. Three common operations along with their syntax are:

1. **Addition (+)** Adds values from another Series or a scalar to each element in the Series.
```
result = series1 + series2
    # Adding two Series
result = series1 + scalar
    # Adding a scalar to each element in Series
```

2. **Subtraction (-)** Subtracts values from another Series or a scalar from each element in the Series.
```
result = series1 - series2
    # Subtracting one Series from another
result = series1 - scalar
    # Subtracting a scalar from each element in Series
```

3. **Multiplication (*)** Multiplies each element in the Series by values from another Series or a scalar.
```
result = series1 * series2
    # Multiplying two Series
result = series1 * scalar
    # Multiplying each element in Series by a scalar
```

51. **Write code for selecting a column from the DataFrame.**

Ans.
```
import pandas as pd
d = {'One': pd.Series([1, 2, 3],
index=['a', 'b', 'c']),
    'Two': pd.Series([1, 2, 3, 4],
index=['a', 'b', 'c', 'd'])}
df = pd.DataFrame(d)
print(df['One'])
```

Output

a 1.0
b 2.0
c 3.0
d NaN
Name: One, dtype: float64

52. **Ms. Ritika conducted an online assessment and stored the details in a DataFrame result as given below:** **CBSE 2024**

	Name	Score	Attempts	Qualify
a	Atulya	12.5	1	yes
b	Disha	9.0	3	no
c	Kavita	16.5	2	yes
d	John	15.0	1	no

Answer the following questions:

(i) **Predict the output of the following Python statement:**
```
print(result.loc [: ,'Attempts'] > 1)
```

(ii) **Write the Python statement to display the last three records.**

(iii) **Write Python statement to display records of 'a' and 'd' row labels.**

***Or* (Option for Part (iii) only)**

(iii) **Write suitable Python statement to retrieve the data stored in the file, 'registration. csv' into a DataFrame, 'regis'.**

Ans. (i)

	Name	Score	Attempts	Qualify
b	Disha	9.0	3	no
c	Kavita	16.5	2	yes

(ii) result.tail(3)

(iii) result.loc[['a':'d'],[:]]

Or

(iii) regis=p.read_csv("registration.csv")

53. Consider the following DataFrame 'mdf'. **CBSE 2023**

	Rollno	Name	English	Hindi	Maths
0	1	Aditya	23	20	28
1	2	Balwant	18	1	25
2	3	Chirag	27	23	30
3	4	Deepak	11	3	7
4	5	Eva	17	21	24

(a) Write Python statements for the DataFrame 'mdf'

(i) To display the records of the students having roll numbers 2 and 3.

(ii) To increase the marks of subject Math by 4, for all students.

(b) Write Python statement to display the Rollno and Name of all students who secured less than 10 marks in Maths.

***Or* (Option for Part (b) only)**

Write Python statement to display the total marks i.e., sum of marks secured in English, Hindi and Maths for all students.

Ans. (a) (i)
```
print(mdf.loc[mdf['Rollno'].isin
([2, 3])])
```
(ii)
```
mdf['Maths']=mdf['Maths'] +4
print(mdf)
```
(b)
```
print (mdf.loc [mdf['Maths']<10,
['Rollno', 'Name']])
```
Or
```
mdf['Maths'] + mdf['English'] + mdf
['Hindi']
```

54. Mr. Som, a data analyst has designed the DataFrame df that contains data about Computer Olympiad with 'CO1', 'CO2', 'CO3', 'CO4', 'CO5' as indexes shown below. Answer the following questions: **CBSE SQP 2022-23**

	School	Tot_students	Topper	First_Runnerup
CO1	PPS	40	32	8
CO2	JPS	30	18	12
CO3	GPS	20	18	2
CO4	MPS	18	10	8
CO5	BPS	28	20	8

A. Predict the output of the following python statement:

(i) df.shape

(ii) df[2:4]

B. Write Python statement to display the data of Topper column of indexes CO2 to CO4.

Or

Write a Python statement to computer and display the difference of data of the Tot_students column and First_Runnerup column of the above given DataFrame.

Ans. A.(i) (5, 4)

(ii)

	School	Tot_students	Topper	First_Runnerup
CO3	GPS	20	18	2
CO4	MPS	18	10	8

B.
```
print (df.loc['CO2':'CO4', 'Topper'])
```
Or
```
print(df.Tot_students-df.First_Runnerup)
```

Long Answer Type Questions

55. Write the difference between Pandas Series and NumPy Arrays

Ans. The comparison between Pandas Series and NumPy Arrays:

Pandas Series	NumPy Arrays
In a Series, you can define your own labeled index to access elements, which can be numbers, strings, or a combination.	NumPy arrays are accessed by their integer position, using numbers only.
The elements can be indexed in descending order or any other custom order based on the labels.	NumPy arrays are indexed starting from zero, and the index is fixed in a sequential order.
If two Series are not aligned, NaN (Not a Number) or missing values are automatically generated.	NumPy arrays do not handle misalignment of data. If the arrays do not match, alignment fails.
Pandas Series can hold a variety of data types including strings, integers, and floats, and can handle missing data.	NumPy arrays require elements to be of a single data type, such as integers or floats.
Series can be more flexible for handling data with labels, making it suitable for data analysis tasks.	NumPy arrays are more efficient for numerical computations but lack built-in label handling.
Series require more memory due to the extra overhead of maintaining labels along with the data.	NumPy arrays are more memory-efficient because they store elements without extra metadata.

Pandas Series	NumPy Arrays
Pandas Series support operations like addition, subtraction, multiplication, and division that align by index labels.	NumPy arrays support element-wise operations, but indexing is strictly positional (no label handling).
Series offer built-in functions for handling missing data, such as .fillna(), .dropna().	NumPy arrays do not have built-in methods to handle missing values or gaps in data.

56. Consider the following DataFrame 'Employees' containing information about employees in a company:

Employee_ID	Name	Age	Department	Salary
101	Ravi Kumar	30	HR	50000
102	Sita Patel	28	Marketing	55000
103	Ajay Singh	35	IT	60000
104	Neha Agarwal	25	Finance	45000
105	Rahul Mehta	40	HR	65000

Write Python code for the following:

(i) Add a column Experience to the DataFrame with the following data: [5, 6, 8, 3, 10].

(ii) Add a new employee to the DataFrame with the name 'Priya Sharma', age 32, department 'IT', and salary 70000.

(iii) Remove the 'Salary' column from the DataFrame.

(iv) Filter the DataFrame to show employees who belong to the 'HR' department and have a salary greater than 55000.

Ans.

```
import pandas as pd
# Creating the DataFrame
data = {'Employee_ID': [101, 102, 103,
                        104, 105],
'Name': ['Ravi Kumar', 'Sita Patel',
      'Ajay Singh', 'Neha Agarwal', 'Rahul
                           Mehta'],
'Age': [30, 28, 35, 25, 40],
'Department': ['HR', 'Marketing', 'IT',
            'Finance', 'HR'],
'Salary': [50000, 55000, 60000, 45000,
                        65000]}
employees = pd.DataFrame(data)
(i) employees['Experience'] = [5, 6, 8, 3, 10]
(ii) employees.loc[len(employees)] = [106, 'Priya
     Sharma', 32, 'IT', 70000, 6]
(iii) employees = employees.drop(columns=['Salary'])
(iv) hr_above_55000 =
     employees[(employees['Department'] == 'HR') &
     (employees['Salary'] > 55000)]
```

57. Consider the given DataFrame 'temp':

	city	Maxtemp	Mintemp	Rainfall
0	Delhi	40	32	24.1
1	Bengaluru	31	25	36.2
2	Chennai	35	27	40.8
3	Mumbai	29	21	35.2

Write suitable Python statements for the following:

(i) Add a column called area with the following data: [135455,153330,225000,442540].

(ii) Add a new city named 'calcutta having maxtemp 20,mintemp 12 and rainfall

(iii) Remove the column rainfall.

(iv) Remove first and third rows from DataFrame

Ans. (i) temp['area ']=[135,150,200,440]

(ii) temp.loc[4]=['calcutta',20,12,10.2,252522]

(iii) temp.drop(['rainfall'],axis=1,inplace=True)

(iv) temp.drop([0,2],axis=0,inplace=True)

58. Write the code in Pandas to create the following DataFrames

df1

	Mark1	Mark2
0	30	20
1	40	45
2	15	30
3	40	70

df2

	Mark1	Mark2
0	10	15
1	20	25
2	20	30
3	50	30

Write the commands to do the following operations on the dataframes given above:

(i) To display both the dataframes.

(ii) To add dataframes df1 and df2.

(iii) To subtract df2 from df1.

(iv) To rename column Mark1 as Marks1 in both the dataframes df1 and df2.

(v) To change index label of df1 from 0 to zero and 1 to one.

Ans.

```
import numpy as np
import pandas as pd
df1 = pd.DataFrame({'Mark1':[30,40,15,40],
   'Mark2':[20,45,30,70]})
df2 = pd.DataFrame({'Mark1':[10,20,20,50],
   'Mark2':[15,25,30,30]})
```

(i) print(df1)

print(df2)

(ii) print(df1.add(df2))

(iii) print(df1.subtract(df2))

(iv) df1.rename (columns = {'Mark1' : 'Marks1'}, inplace = True)

(v) df1.rename (index = {0 : 'zero', 1 : 'one'}, inplace = True)

59. Write a Pandas program to sort the DataFrame first by Name in descending order, then by 'Score' in ascending order.

Sample DataFrame :

```
exam_data={'Name':['Abhi','Chirag','Tarun',
'Anjali','Mahi','Tushar','Shubham','Harsh',
'Vanshika','Kartik'],
'Score':[12.5,9,16.5,np.NaN,9,20,14.5,
np.NaN,8,19],
'Attempts':[1,3,2,3,2,3,1,1,2,1],
'Qualify':['Yes','No','Yes' 'No','No','Yes',
'Yes','No','No','Yes']}
labels=['a','b','c','d','e','f','g','h',
'i','j']
```

Ans.

```
import pandas as pd
import numpy as np
exam_data = {'Name': ['Abhi', 'Chirag',
    'Tarun', 'Anjali', 'Mahi', 'Tushar',
    'Shubham', 'Harsh', 'Vanshika',
    'Kartik'],
  'Score': [12.5, 9, 16.5, np.NaN, 9, 20,
    14.5, np.NaN, 8, 19],
  'Attempts': [1, 3, 2, 3, 2, 3, 1, 1, 2, 1],
  'Qualify': ['Yes', 'No', 'Yes', 'No', 'No'
    'Yes', 'Yes', 'No', 'No', 'Yes']}
labels = ['a', 'b', 'c', 'd', 'e', 'f', 'g',
    'h', 'i', 'j']
df = pd.DataFrame(exam_data , index=labels)
print("Orginal rows:")
print(df)
result=df.sort_values(by=['Name', 'Score'],
    ascending=[False, True])
print("Sort the DataFrame first by 'Name'
    in descending order, then by 'Score'
    in ascending order:")
print(result)
```

60. Write the code in Pandas to create the following DataFrame

	Name	Designation	Salary
1	Abhi	DBA	35000
2	Vanshika	Pragrammer	40000
3	Riya	Tester	32000
4	Chirag	Content Writer	25000
5	Tushar	Business Analyst	30000
6	Khushal	Sales Executive	37000
7	Mahi	Web Designer	42000

Write the commands to do the following operations on the DataFrame given above:

(i) To select the column Designation.

(ii) To change index label from 1 to E101, 2 to E102, ... and so on.

Ans.

```
import pandas as pd
import numpy as np
array = np.array([['Abhi','DBA',35000],
        ['Vanshika','Programmer',40000],
        ['Riya','Tester',32000],
        ['Chirag','Content Writer',25000],
        ['Tushar','Business Analyst',30000],
        ['Khushal','Sales Executive',37000],
        ['Mahi','Web Designer',42000]])
index_values = [1,2,3,4,5,6,7]
column_values =['Name','Designation',
                              'Salary']
df = pd.DataFrame(data = array,
        index = index_values,
        columns = column_values)
print(df)
```

(i) df['Designation']

(ii) df.rename (index={1 : 'E101', 2 : 'E102', 3 : 'E103', 4 : 'E104', 5 : 'E105', 6 : 'E106', 7 : 'E107'}, inplace = True)

61. Write a code to create the following DataFrame

	RNo	Name	Marks
SecA	21	Abhi	69.5
SecB	45	Anjali	84.5
SecC	23	Tushar	70.0
SecD	17	Mahi	78.0

Write the commands to do the following operations on the DataFrame given above:

(i) To add new section SecE with the values [08, 'Kushal', 80.0].

(ii) To modify the marks of SecC to 68.5.

Ans.

```
import pandas as pd
data = {'RNo':[21,45,23,17],
  'Name': ['Abhi','Anjali','Tushar','Mahi'],
  'Marks':[69.5,84.5,70.0,78.0]}
df = pd.DataFrame(data,index=['SecA',
  'SecB','SecC','SecD'])
print(df)
```

(i) df.loc['SecE',:]=[08,'Kushal',80.0]
print(df)

(ii) df.Marks['SecC']=68.5
print(df)

62. Consider the DataFrame df shown below. CBSE SQP 2024-25

	MovieID	Title	Year	Rating
0	1	LAGAAN	2001	8.4
1	2	TAARE ZAMEEN PAR	2007	8.5
2	3	3 IDIOTS	2009	8.4
3	4	DANGAL	2016	8.4
4	5	ANDHADHUN	2018	8.3

Write Python statements for the DataFrame df to:

I. Print the first two rows of the DataFrame df.

II. Display titles of all the movies.

III. Remove the column rating.

IV. Display the data of the 'Title' column from indexes 2 to 4 (both included).

V. Rename the column name 'Title' to 'Name'.

Ans. I. `print(df.head(2))`

II. `print(df['Title'])`

III. `df = df.drop(columns=['Rating'])`

IV. `print(df.loc[2:4, 'Title'])`

V. `df = df.rename(columns={'Title': 'Name'})`

Case Study Based Questions

Case Study 1

Mr. Sharma is working with an IT company, and he has provided some data. On which hewants to do some operations, but he is facing some problem, help him: CBSE SQP 2021-22 Term 1

```
import pandas as pd
ResultSheet={
'Naveen': pd.Series([90, 91, 97],
        index=['Maths','Science','Hindi']),
'Rehana': pd.Series([92, 81, 96],
        index=['Maths','Science','Hindi']),
'John': pd.Series([89, 91, 88],
        index=['Maths','Science','Hindi']),
'Roja': pd.Series([81, 71, 67],
        index=['Maths','Science','Hindi']),
'Mannat': pd.Series([94, 95, 99],
        index=['Maths','Science','Hindi'])}
DF = pd.DataFrame(ResultSheet)
print(DF)
```

Output of the above code:

	Naveen	Rehana	John	Roja	Mannat
Maths	90	92	89	81	94
Science	91	81	91	71	95
Hindi	97	96	88	67	99

Based on the given information, answer the questions (i)-(vi).

(i) He wants to add a new column with name of student 'Prem' in above DataFrame

Choose the right command to do so:

(a) DF['Prem']=[89,78,76]
(b) df['Prem']=[89,78,76]
(c) DF['Prem']=[89,78,76,67]
(d) DF['Name']=[89,78,76]

(ii) He wants to set all the values to zero in data frame, choose the right command to do so:

(a) DF=0 (b) DF[]=0
(c) DF[:]=0 (d) DF[:]==0

(iii) He wants to delete the row of science marks:

(a) DF.drop('Science', axis=1)
(b) DF.drop('Science', axis=0)
(c) DF.drop('Science', axis=-1)
(d) DF.drop('Science', axis==0)

(iv) The following code is to create another data frame, which he wants to add to the existing Data frame. Choose the right command to do so:

```
Sheet1={'Aaradhya': pd.Series([90, 91,
97], index=['Maths','Science','Hindi'])}
S1=pd.DataFrame(Sheet1)
```

(a) DF.append(S1,axis=0) (b) DF.append(S1)
(c) DF.insert(S1) (d) DF.join(S1)

(v) What will be the output of the given command?

```
DF.index=['A','B','C']
```

(a)

	Naveen	Rehana	John	Roja	Mannat
Maths	90	92	89	81	94
Science	91	81	91	71	95
Hindi	97	96	88	67	99

(b)

	Naveen	Rehana	John	Roja	Mannat
A	90	92	89	81	94
B	91	81	91	71	95
C	97	96	88	67	99

(c)

	A	B	C	Roja	Mannat
Maths	90	92	89	81	94
Science	91	81	91	71	95
Hindi	97	96	88	67	99

(d) Error, Index already exists and cannot be overwritten.

(vi) What will be the output of the given command?

	Naveen	Rehana	John	Roja	Mannat
Maths	90	92	89	81	94
Science	91	81	91	71	95
Hindi	97	96	88	67	99

```
print(DF.size)
```

(a) 15 (b) 18 (c) 21 (d) 23

Ans. (i) (a) DF['Prem']=[89,78,76]

(ii) (c) DF[:]=0

(iii) (b) DF.drop('Science', axis=0)

(iv) (b) DF.append(S1)

(v) (b)

	Naveen	Rehana	John	Roja	Mannat
A	90	92	89	81	94
B	91	81	91	71	95
C	97	96	88	67	99

(vi) (a) 15

Case Study 2

Mr. Ankit is working in an organisation as data analyst. He uses Python Pandas and Matplotlib for the same. He got a dataset of the passengers for the year 2010 to 2012 for January, March and December. His manager wants certain information from him, but he is facing some problems. Help him by answering few questions given below:

	Year	Month	Passengers
0	2010	Jan	25
1	2010	Mar	50
2	2012	Jan	35
3	2010	Dec	55
4	2012	Dec	65

Code to create the above data frame:

```
import pandas as ________        #Statement 1
data={"Year":[2010,2010,2012,2010,2012],"Month":
["Jan","Mar","Jan","Dec","Dec"],
"Passengers":[25,50,35,55,65]}
df=pd.________(data)             #Statement 2
print(df)
```

CBSE Question Bank

(i) Choose the right code from the following for Statement 1.

(a) pd (b) df
(c) data (d) p

(ii) Choose the right code from the following for the Statement 2.

(a) Dataframe (b) DataFrame
(c) Series (d) Dictionary

(iii) Choose the correct statement/method for the required output:
(5,3)

(a) df.index (b) df.shape()
(c) df.shape (d) df.size

(iv) He wants to print the details of "January" month along with the number of passengers, identify the correct statement.

	Month	Passengers
0	Jan	25
2	Jan	35

(a) `df.loc[['Month','Passengers']][df['Month']=='Jan']`

(b) `df[['Month','Passengers']][df['Month']=='Jan']`

(c) `df.iloc[['Month','Passengers']][df['Month']=='Jan']`

(d) `df(['Month','Passengers'])[df['Month']=='Jan']`

(v) Mr. Ankit wants to change the index of the DataFrame and the output for the same is given below. Identify the correct statement to change the index.

	Year	Month	Passengers
Air India	2010	Jan	25
Indigo	2010	Mar	50
Spicejet	2012	Jan	35
Jet	2010	Dec	55
Emirates	2012	Dec	65

(a) df.index[]=["Air India","Indigo,"Spicejet","Jet","Emirates"]

(b) df.index["Air India","Indigo","Spicejet","Jet","Emirates"]

(c) df.index=["Air India","Indigo","Spicejet","Jet","Emirates"]

(d) df.index()=["Air India","Indigo","Spicejet","Jet","Emirates"]

Ans. (i) (a) While creating the dataframe the object used is pd, so pandas is to be imported as pd.

(ii) (b) The DataFrame() function creates a dataframe in Python Pandas.

(iii) (c) The shape attribute displays the number of rows and columns in a dataframe.
(iv) (b) Since only data of "Jan" is to be displayed the 'Month'=='Jan' condition is applied , along with the columns to be displayed as the 1st parameter.
(v) (c) To change the indexes of a dataframe, the new list of indexes can be specified as a list with the index property.

Case Study 3

Pushp, a student of Class XII, has been assigned a code to create a pandas Series 'S1', as shown below.

```
a       100
b       200
c       300
d       400
e       500
dtype:  int64
```

With reference to the above information, answer given questions: **[CBSE Question Bank]**

(i) Choose the command that will give the following output.

```
b       200
c       300
dtype:  int64
```

(a) print(S1[:3]) (b) print(S1[0:3])
(c) print(S1[1:3]) (d) print(S1[2:4])

(ii) Help him to identify the correct statement that can be used to extract the value with the index 'c'.

(a) print(S1[c]) (b) print(S1(c))
(c) print('S1' ['c']) (d) print(S1 ['c'])

(iii) Which of the following command will give the following output?

```
b       200
d       400
dtype:  int64
```

(a) print(S1.iloc[1:4]) (b) print(S1.iloc[2:4])
(c) print(S1.iloc(1:4)) (d) print(S1.iloc[1:4:2])

(iv) Which of the following command will display the series by adding 10 in each value?

(a) print(S1 [+10])
(b) print(S1+10)
(c) print(S1)+10
(d) print(S1)+print(10)

(v) Pushp wants to delete the value against index 'd'. Help him to choose the suitable option to do so.

(a) S1=S1.drop(d) (b) S1=S1.drop('d')
(c) S1=drop('d') (d) S1=S1.drop['d']

Ans. (i) (c) S1[1:3] returns index, values from index 1 to (3–1) , that is 1 to 2.
(ii) (b) print (S1(c))
(iii) (d) Here, 1 is the start index, 3(4–1) is the end index and progression is by 2 giving 200 and 400.
(iv) (b) If an integer is added to a series ,it is added to all the values , if they are numbers.
(v) (b) The drop() function removes an element from a series . It is called with the series name and parameter as the index.
(vi) (b) To get value at index 'c', the index is to be subscripted with series name.

Case Study 4

Zeenat has created the following data frame dataframe1 to keep track of data Rollno, Name, Marks1 and Marks2 for various students of her class where row indexes are taken as the default values:

Rollno	Name	Marks1	Marks2
1	Swapnil Sharma	30	50
2	Raj Batra	75	45
3	Bhoomi Singh	82	95
4	Jay Gupta	90	95

CBSE Question Bank

(i) Which among the following option will give 90, 95 as output?

(a) `print(max(dataframe1['Marks1', 'Marks2'])`
(b) `print((dataframe1.Marks1.max(), (dataframe1.Marks2.max()))`
(c) print(max(dataframe1['Marks1'])
(d) print(max(dataframe1['Marks2'])

(ii) She needs to know the marks scored by Rollno 2. Help her to identify the correct set of statement(s) from the given options.

(a) print(dataframe1[dataframe1['Rollno']= =2])
(b) print(dataframe1['Rollno']= =2)
(c) print(dataframe1[dataframe1. Rollno = =2])
(d) print(dataframe1[dataframe1 ['Rollno']])

(iii) Which of the following statement(s) will delete the 3rd column?

A. del dataframe1['Marks1']
B. dataframe1.pop('Marks1')
C. drop dataframe1['Marks1']
D. pop dataframe1['Marks1']

Choose the correct option.

(a) Both A and B (b) Only B
(c) A, B and C (d) A, B and D

(iv) Which of the following command will display the total number of elements in the dataframe?
(a) print(dataframe1.shape)
(b) print(dataframe1.num)
(c) print(dataframe1.size)
(d) print(dataframe1.elements)

(v) Now she wants to add a new column "Marks3" with relevant data. Help her to choose the command to perform this task.
(a) dataframe1.column=[45,52,90,95]
(b) dataframe1 ['Marks3']= [45,52,90,95]
(c) dataframe1.loc['Marks3']= [45,52,90,95]
(d) Both (b) and (c)

Ans. (i) (b) The max() function calculates the maximum value of a numeric column of a dataframe. Hence, Mark1., max() ,Marks2.max() displays 90,95.
(ii) (c) Dataframes can be indexed with a condition to extract rows matching the condition , here Rollno==2 condition has been extracted.
(iii) (a) Both del and pop() can be used to remove columns from a dataframe permanently. Using del the column name has to be written in indexed form.
(iv) (c) The size property of a dataframe returns the total number of elements in it.
(v) (b) To add a column to a dataframe the column name can be indexed to the dataframe and the values can be assigned as a list.

Case Study 5

Naman has created the following dataframe "Climate" to record the data about climatic conditions of four years.

Year	MaxTemp	MinTemp	Rainfall
2017	32	20	123
2018	33	22	140
2019	35	21	135
2020	34	23	160

CBSE Question Bank

(i) Which of the following code snippets will return the MaxTemp and Rainfall for year 2018 and 2019?
(a) Climate[['MaxTemp','Rainfall']][1:3]
(b) Climate['MaxTemp', 'Rainfall'][1:3]
(c) Climate.iloc[1:3]
(d) Climate.iloc[1:3,1:2]

(ii) Display the temperature difference between MaxTemp and MinTemp for all the rows in the dataframe Climate.
(a) Climate=Climate["MaxTemp"]–Climate["MinTe mp"]
(b) print(Climate["maxt"]–Climate["mint"])
(c) print(Climate["MaxTemp"]–Climate["MinTemp "])
(d) print(Climate.Climate["MaxTemp"]–Climate[" MinTemp"])

(iii) To display two rows from the top in the dataframe, which of the following statement is correct?
(a) print (Climate.head()=2)
(b) print (Climate.head(n==2))
(c) print (Climate.head(range(2)))
(d) print (Climate.head(2))

(iv) Which of the following statement(s) will give the exact number of values in each column of the dataframe?
A. print(Climate.count())
B. print(Climate.count(0))
C. print(Climate.count)
D. print(Climate.count(axis='index'))
Choose the correct option.
(a) Both A and B
(b) Only B
(c) A, B and C
(d) A, B and D

(v) To display two rows from the bottom in the dataframe, which of the following statement is correct:
(a) print (Climate.tail()=2)
(b) print (Climate.tail(n==2))
(c) print(Climate.tail(range(2)))
(d) print (Climate.tail(2))

Ans. (i) (a) This option selects the MaxTemp and Rainfall columns first, and then uses slicing [1:3] to get rows for the years 2018 and 2019.
(ii) (c) The dataframe numeric columns can be subtracted from each other by indexing them to the dataframe names.
(iii) (d) The head() function can be used to display the first n rows from a dataframe.Here Climate.head(2) will return the first two rows.
(iv) (d) The call to count() , count(0) and count(axis='index') all return the exact number of values in each column . The count() is an aggregate function that counts the number of records..
(v) (d) The tail() function displays the last n values from a dataframe. Hence, Climate.tail(2) will return the last two rows.

Case Study 6

HR department of ABC Tech has created following dataframe to store data about salaries and bonus paid to their employees:

```
import pandas as pd
import numpy as np
d1={'EName':[ 'Kavita', 'Sudha',
'Garima']'],'Sal':[50000,60000,55000],
                    'Bonus':[3000,4000,5000]}
Df1=pd.DataFrame(d1)
```

Choose the Python statement using suitable functions for the following tasks. CBSE Question Bank

(i) Display the columns Sal and Bonus.
(a) Df1 [:Sal :Bonus]
(b) Df1.loc(['Sal','Bonus'])
(c) Df1.iloc(['Sal','Bonus'])
(d) Df1[['Sal','Bonus']]

(ii) Display the details of employee Kavita.
(a) Df1[df1.EName='Kavita']
(b) Df1.loc[df1.EName=='Kavita']
(c) Df1.iloc[df1.EName=='Kavita']
(d) Df1[EName='Kavita']

(iii) Display the details of the last employee.
(a) Df1.tail(1) (b) Df1.tail (–1)
(c) Df1.head(n=1) (d) Df1.head()

(iv) Add a new column named 'Email' with the value "abc@gmail.com".
(a) Df1['Email']= 'abc@gmail.com'
(b) Df1[Email]='abc@gmail.com'
(c) Df1.loc['Email']='abc@gmail.com'
(d) Df1('Email')='abc@gmail.com'

(v) Write a Python statement to print the details of employees having Sal more than 50000.
(a) Df1.Sal>=50000
(b) Df1[Df1.Sal>=50000]
(c) Df1[Df1.'Sal'>=50000]
(d) Df1.iloc[Df1.Sal>=50000]

Ans. (i) (d) This syntax correctly selects the columns sal and bonus.

(ii) (b) The loc() function can have the condition for display the data from a dataframe indexed .
Here the EName=='Kavita' condition has been indexed to the dataframe df1 to get details of Kavita.

(iii) (a) The tail() function displays the last n rows from a dataframe. So tail(1) will display the last record.

(iv) (a) To add a new column to a dataframe the dataframe can be indexed with the column name and the value set can be assigned as a list of items to it or as a single value that will be used for all the rows.

(v) (b) To extract values from a dataframe that match a certain condition , the dataframe name can be indexed with the condition, as done here Df1[Df1.Sal>=50000].

Case Study 7

A data analyst is working with the Pandas library in Python to analyze sales data. The data is stored in a CSV file, and he imports it into a Pandas DataFrame. He performs various operations such as selecting specific columns, renaming them, and applying mathematical functions on the numerical data. The dataset contains information about sales, product categories, and revenue.

Answer the following Questions:

(i) Which Python library is primarily used for handling structured data like tables?
(a) NumPy (b) Matplotlib
(c) Pandas (d) Scikit-learn

(ii) How can the analyst read a CSV file into a Pandas DataFrame?
(a) pd.load_csv('data.csv')
(b) pd.read_csv('data.csv')
(c) pd.import_csv('data.csv')
(d) pd.open_csv('data.csv')

(iii) If the analyst wants to view the first five rows of the DataFrame, which function should he use?
(a) df.head(5) (b) df.tail(5)
(c) df.first(5) (d) df.show(5)

(iv) To rename a column from "Revenue" to "Sales Revenue", which command should be used?
(a) df.rename(columns={'Revenue': 'Sales Revenue'})
(b) df.rename('Revenue', 'Sales Revenue')
(c) df.modify(columns={'Revenue': 'Sales Revenue'})
(d) df.change_name('Revenue', 'Sales Revenue')

(v) Which function allows the selection of specific rows based on a condition, such as selecting all rows where sales exceed 10,000?
(a) df.loc[df['Sales'] > 10000]
(b) df.select(df['Sales'] > 10000)
(c) df.filter(Sales > 10000)
(d) df.pick(df['Sales'] > 10000)

Ans. (i) (c) Pandas
(ii) (b) pd.read_csv('data.csv')
(iii) (a) df.head(5)
(iv) (a) df.rename(columns={'Revenue': 'Sales Revenue'})
(v) (a) df.loc[df['Sales'] > 10000]

SELF ASSESSMENT TEST

Multiple Choice Questions

1 For fast data processing, how many different tools are available?
(a) NumPy (b) Scipy (c) Cython (d) All of these

2 Identify the parameter(s) of Series()
(a) data (b) index (c) dtype (d) All of these

3 Which function is used to convert DataFrame into CSV file?
(a) read_csv() (b) to_csv() (c) Either (a) or (b) (d) None of these

4 To access a row, use .... after comma(,).
(a) semicolon(;) (b) hash(#) (c) colon(:) (d) dot(.)

Fill in the Blanks

5 Pandas provide various methods to have purely label based ....

6 Pandas dataframe consists of .... principle components.

7 .... is used to the whole series in reverse order.

8 Pandas is the most important library coming to ....

State whether True or False

9 loc attribute can add/modify a row in DataFrame.

10 In head( ) function, the default value of n is 4.

Assertion and Reason Based Questions

Assertion and Reason Based Questions. Mark the correct choice as

(a) Both Assertion (A) and Reason (R) are true and Reason (R) is the correct explanation for A
(b) Both Assertion (A) and Reason (R) are true and Reason (R) is not the correct explanation for A
(c) Assertion (A) is True but Reason (R) is False
(d) Assertion (A) is false but Reason (R) is True

11 **Assertion** The drop() method in pandas can be used to remove rows or columns from a DataFrame.
Reason The drop() method requires the axis parameter to specify whether rows or columns are to be dropped, where axis=0 indicates rows and axis=1 indicates columns.

12 **Assertion** The .loc[] function in pandas is used for label-based indexing to access data.
Reason The .loc[] function allows the selection of rows and columns by their labels and can also handle conditional filtering based on row values.

Very Short Answer Type Questions

13 What is the use of nrows attribute?

14 Which attribute is used for specifying axis?

Short Answer Type Questions

15 How to work with Pandas?

16 How to specify data type along with data and index?

17 How to access multiple columns from DataFrame?

Long Answer Type Questions

18 Write a code to create the following DataFrame:

	RNo	Name	Designation
Class 10	21	Abhay	Monitor
Class 11	42	Shrey	Head
Class 12	16	Kirti	Head

Write the commands to do the following operations on the DataFrame given above:

(i) To add new Class 9 with the values [15, 'Shivi', 'Monitor'].

(ii) To select the column Name.

19 Write the program for adding new column to an existing dataframe.

Case Study Based Question

20 Consider the following DataFrame emp and answer any four question from (i)-(iii):

Empno	Name	Dept	Salary	Experience (in years)
1	Ram singh	IT	15000	2.5
2	Shyam singh	HR	18000	3
3	Nidhi gupta	IT	9000	2
4	Puja sharma	EXE	24000	8
5	Pohan malik	HR	20000	6

(i) Write down the command that will give the following output.

```
Empno        5
Name         Shayam singh
Dept         HR
Salary       24000
Experience   8
dtype: object
```

(ii) The CEO needs to know the salary of the employee with empno 4. Help him to identify the correct set of statement/s.

(iii) Which command will display the column labels of the DataFrame?

Answers

1. (d)	2. (d)	3. (b)	4. (c)	5. indexing/selection/access
6. two	7. Series.iloc[:: –1]	8. data analysis	9. True	
10. False	11. (a)	12. (a)		

02 CHAPTER

Data visualization helps people to understand the significance of data by summarizing and presenting a huge amount of data in a simple and easy format.

▼ **YOUR STUDY GOALS**

2.1 Using Pyplot of Matplotlib Library
2.2 Other Attributes for Customization of Plot
2.3 Using plot() with Pandas
2.4 Plots/Charts Types

▼ **YOUR PRACTICE GOAL**

- Objective Type Questions (54 Qs ; MCQs, True or False, Fill in the Blanks, Assertion and Reason)
- Subjective Type Questions (39 Qs ; VSA, SA, LA)
- Case Study Based Questions (Subjective Case Studies-3)

Data Visualization

Data visualization is a graphical representation of quantitative information and data by using visual elements like **graphs, charts, maps** ,etc.

We can see visualizations in the form of line charts to display changes over time, bar and column charts are useful for observing relationships and making comparisons, etc.

2.1 Using Pyplot of Matplotlib Library

Matplotlib is a powerful plotting library in Python used for creating static, animated, and interactive visualizations.

Matplotlib's primary purpose is to provide users with the tools and functionality to represent data graphically, making it easier to analyze and understand. It was originally developed by **John D. Hunter** in **2003** and is now maintained by a large community of developers.

- To install Matplotlib, you can use the following command in the command prompt:

```
pip install matplotlib
```

- To plot using Matplotlib, you need to import its Pyplot module:

```
import matplotlib.pyplot as plt
```

  In this case, plt is an alias for matplotlib.pyplot. You can use any other alias if you prefer.

Pyplot is a collection of command style functions that make matplotlib work like **MATLAB.** It is the module available in matplotlib library. It makes some change to a figure : e.g. Create a figure, create a plotting area in a figure, decorates the plot with labels, etc.

Key characteristics of Matplotlib include

- **Versatility** It can create a wide range of static, animated, and interactive plots.
- **Customizability** Almost every element of a plot (like sizes, colors, and fonts) can be customized.
- **Extensibility** It can be used with a variety of GUI modules to create graphical applications.
- **Integration** Easily integrates with other libraries like NumPy and Pandas for efficient data manipulation.
- **Output Formats** Supports many output formats, including PNG, PDF, SVG, EPS, and interactive backends.

Components of a Chart

When working with data visualisation in Python, you'll want to have control over all aspects of your figure. In this section, you'll learn about the main components that make up a figure in Matplotlib.

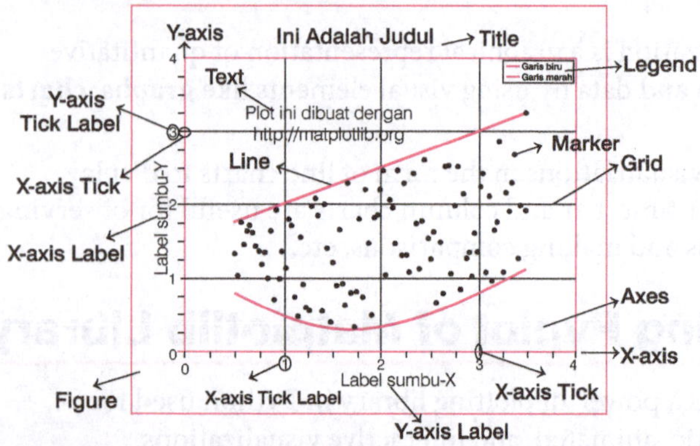

The components of a graph are as follows:

1. **Figure** This is the entire space where the graph and its components are drawn. It is the container for the plot, including all axes, labels, titles, and data.
2. **Axis** The axes provide a reference for the graph's data. The x-axis runs horizontally and typically represents the independent variable, while the y-axis runs vertically and represents the dependent variable. The axis establishes the coordinate system for the data points.
3. **Title** The title is a concise description of what the graph represents. It gives context and names the graph, helping viewers understand its purpose.
4. **X-axis Label** The X-axis label describes the variable on the X-axis. It often includes the units of measurement for clarity (e.g., "Time (seconds)", "Temperature (°C)").
5. **Y-axis Label** Similar to the x-axis label, the y-axis label describes the variable on the y-axis, along with its units (e.g., "Speed (km/h)", "Height (meters)").
6. **Legend** The legend explains the meaning of the different data representations (such as different lines, colors, or markers) in the graph. It helps viewers identify and differentiate between multiple datasets or variables.
7. **Ticks and Tick Labels** Ticks are small marks along the axis that represent specific values. Tick labels are the numeric or categorical values placed next to the ticks, showing the exact value represented by each tick on the axis. They guide users in understanding the scale of the graph.
8. **Line Plots** These are the actual plotted data points connected by lines. Line plots are useful for showing trends over time or relationships between variables.
9. **Markers** Markers are visual symbols (such as dots, squares, or triangles) placed at specific data points on the graph. These help highlight the exact locations of data points on a line plot or scatter plot.
10. **Spines** Spines are the lines that form the border around the graph, outlining the area of the plot. They typically define the boundary of the graph, with the x-axis and y-axis spines intersecting at the origin (0,0).

Pyplot Functions

List of common Pyplot functions used to create various types of charts in Matplotlib:

Table 1 : List of Pyplot functions to plot different charts

Chart Type	Pyplot Function	Example
Line Plot	plt.plot()	plt.plot(x, y)
Bar Chart	plt.bar()	plt.bar(x, height)
Horizontal Bar Chart	plt.barh()	plt.barh(y, width)
Histogram	plt.hist()	plt.hist(data, bins)
Scatter Plot	plt.scatter()	plt.scatter(x, y)
Pie Chart	plt.pie()	plt.pie(sizes, labels=labels)
Box Plot	plt.boxplot()	plt.boxplot(data)
Area Plot	plt.fill_between()	plt.fill_between(x, y1, y2)

Customisation of Plots

Pyplot library gives us numerous functions, which can be used to customise charts such as adding titles or legends. Some of the customisation options are listed below:

Table 2 : List of Pyplot functions to customise plots

Function	Description	Example
plt.title()	Adds a title to the plot.	plt.title("Sample Plot")
plt.xlabel()	Sets the label for the x-axis.	plt.xlabel("X-Axis Label")
plt.ylabel()	Sets the label for the y-axis.	plt.ylabel("Y-Axis Label")
plt.legend()	Adds a legend to the plot.	plt.legend(["Line 1", "Line 2"])
plt.grid()	Adds a grid to the plot.	plt.grid(True)
plt.xticks()	Customizes the tick marks on the x-axis.	plt.xticks([0, 1, 2], ["A", "B", "C"])
plt.yticks()	Customizes the tick marks on the y-axis.	plt.yticks([10, 20, 30], ["Low", "Medium", "High"])
plt.savefig()	Saves the current figure to a file.	plt.savefig("plot.png")
plt.show()	Display all figures	plt.show()

Example 1. Plotting a line chart of date *versus* temperature by adding Label on X and Y axis, and adding a Title and Grids to the chart.

Solution.

```
import matplotlib.pyplot as plt
date = ["25/12", "26/12", "27/12"]
temp = [8.5, 10.5, 6.8]                  # Create the plot
plt.plot(date, temp)
plt.xlabel("Date")                       # Label for x-axis
plt.ylabel("Temperature")                # Label for y-axis
plt.title("Date wise Temperature")       # Title of the chart
plt.grid(True)                           # Add grid to the plot
plt.yticks(temp) # Set y-axis ticks to match temperature values
plt.show()                               # Display the plot
```

Output

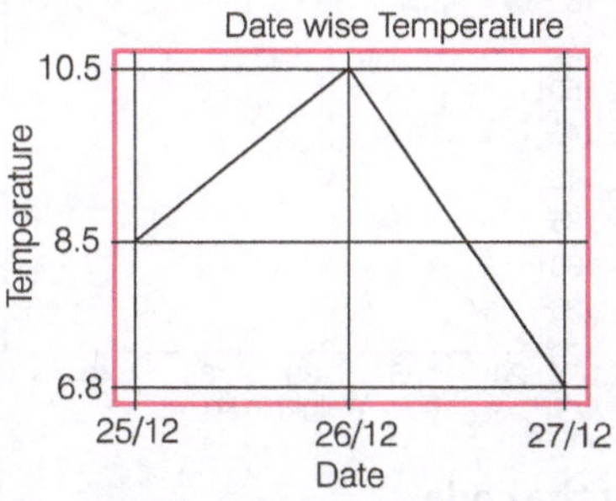

Note *We can click on the save button on the output window and save the plot as an image. A figure can also be saved by using the savefig() function. The name of the figure is passed to the function as a parameter.*

For example `plt.savefig('temperature_plot.png')`

2.2 Other Attributes for Customization of Plot

Color

In Matplotlib, color abbreviations are used to quickly specify the color of plot elements like lines, markers, and text. These abbreviations are single-character strings that represent common colors.

Syntax `plt.plot(data1,data2,color code)`

Table 3 : Color abbreviation for plotting

Abbreviation	Color
'b'	Blue
'g'	Green
'r'	Red
'c'	Cyan
'm'	Magenta
'y'	Yellow
'k'	Black
'w'	White

Marker

The matplotlib.markers module provides a collection of marker styles used for data visualization in Matplotlib plots. These markers represent individual data points, enhancing clarity and distinction within graphs and charts.

Syntax `marker = marker_type,`
`marker_size = in_points,markeredgecolor=validcolor`

Table 4 : Some of the matplotlib markers

Marker	Description	Marker	Description
"."	point	"p"	pentagon
","	pixel	"P"	plus (filled)
"o"	circle	"*"	star
"v"	triangle_down	"h"	hexagon1
"^"	triangle_up	"H"	hexagon2
"<"	triangle_left	"+"	plus
">"	triangle_right	"x"	x
"1"	tri_down	"X"	x (filled)
"2"	tri_up	"D"	diamond
"3"	tri_left	"d"	thin_diamond
"4"	tri_right	"|"	vline
"8"	octagon	"_"	hline
"s"	square		

Line Width and Line Style

The linewidth and linestyle property can be used to change the width and the style of the line chart. Linewidth is specified in pixels. The default line width is 1 pixel showing a thin line. Thus, a number greater than 1 will output a thicker line depending on the value provided.

We can also set the line style of a line chart using the linestyle parameter. It can take a string such as "solid(-)", "dotted (:) ", "dashed(--)" or "dashdot (-.)".

e.g.
```
plt.plot(x,a,linewidth=2)
plt.plot(x,b,linewidth=4,linestyle= 'dashed')
```

2.3 Using plot( ) with Pandas

You can call the plot() method on a Series or DataFrame object like this:

```
import pandas as pd
s = pd.Series([1, 3, 2, 4])        # Example with a Series
s.plot()
df = pd.DataFrame({                # Example with a DataFrame
  'A': [1, 2, 3, 4],
  'B': [4, 3, 2, 1]
})
df.plot()
```

Plot Types with kind Argument

The kind argument in the .plot() method allows you to specify the type of plot you want to generate.

Common plot types include:

- **line** for line plots (default)
- **bar** for vertical bar plots
- **barh** for horizontal bar plots
- **hist** for histograms
- **box** for box plots
- **pie** for pie charts
- **scatter** for scatter plots (requires x and y arguments)
- **area** for area plots

The plot() method accepts numerous arguments to customize the appearance of the plots, such as color, label, grid, title, legend, and more.

Example 2. Consider the average heights and weights of persons aged 8 to 16 stored in the following two lists:

height = [121.9, 124.5, 129.5, 134.6, 139.7, 147.3, 152.4, 157.5, 162.6]

weight = [19.7, 21.3, 23.5, 25.9, 28.5, 32.1, 35.7, 39.6, 43.2]

Let us plot a line chart where:

(i) x axis will represent weight
(ii) y axis will represent height
(iii) x axis label should be "Weight in kg"
(iv) y axis label should be "Height in cm"
(v) colour of the line should be green
(vi) use * as marker
(vii) Marker size as 10
(viii) The title of the chart should be "Average weight with respect to average height".
(ix) Line style should be dashed
(x) Linewidth should be 2.

Solution.

```
import matplotlib.pyplot as plt
import pandas as pd
height = [121.9,124.5,129.5,134.6,139.7,147.3,152.4,
          157.5, 162.6]                          # List of height
weight = [19.7, 21.3, 23.5, 25.9,28.5, 32.1, 35.7,39.6, 43.2]
                                                 # List of weight
df = pd.DataFrame({"height": height, "weight": weight})
                                                 # Create DataFrame
plt.xlabel('Weight in kg')                       # Set xlabel for the plot
plt.ylabel('Height in cm')                       # Set ylabel for the plot
plt.title('Average weight with respect to average height')
                                                 # Set chart title
plt.plot(df['weight'],df['height'],
marker='*', markersize=10, color='green',
linewidth=2, linestyle='--')
                         # Plot using marker '*' and line color as green
plt.show()
```

Output

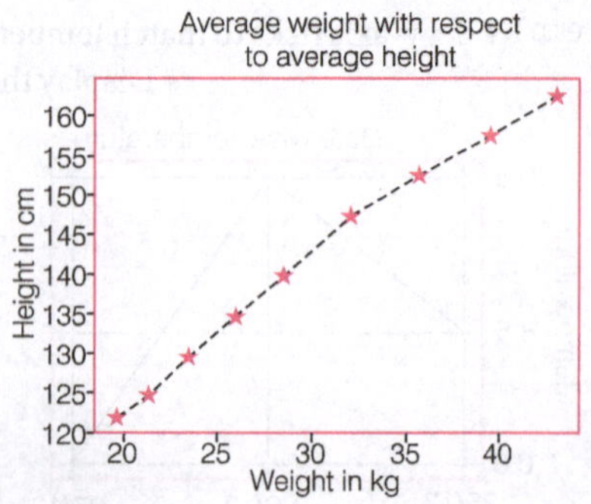

Key points of the code

- **x-axis** (Weight in kg) Represents the weight from the list.
- **y-axis** (Height in cm) Represents the height from the list.

- **Line Style** Dashed line ('--').
- **Line Color** Green ('green').
- **Marker** Asterisk ('*') with size 10.
- **Chart Title** "Average weight with respect to average height".

Note *Continuous data are measured while discrete data are obtained by counting. Height, weight are examples of continuous data. It can be in decimals. Total number of students in a class is discrete. It can never be in decimals.*

Quick Test 1

1. Write a command to install matplotlib.
2. What is matplotlib used for?
3. What is the pyplot module in matplotlib?
4. How can you display a plot in matplotlib?
5. How do you add a title to a plot in matplotlib?
6. How can you plot a line graph in matplotlib?
7. How can you change the size of a plot in matplotlib?

2.4 Plots/Charts Types

Types of plots we are going to study in this chapter are:

- Line Chart
- Bar Chart
- Histogram
- Scatter Chart
- Pie Chart
- Quartiles and Box plot

Plotting and Customization a Line Chart

Line charts are used to represent the relation between two data X and Y on a different axis. It is used to show continuous dataset. A line plot is used to visualise growth or decline in data over a time interval.

Example 3. Plot and customize the temperature variation over a week.

Solution. **Plotting a line chart**

```
import pandas as pd
import matplotlib.pyplot as plt
# Data
data = {
    'Days': ['Monday', 'Tuesday',
        'Wednesday', 'Thursday', 'Friday',
                    'Saturday', 'Sunday'],
    'Temperature': [22, 24, 19, 23, 25, 20,
                                         21]
}
df = pd.DataFrame(data)
plt.plot(df['Days'], df['Temperature'])
plt.show()
```

Output

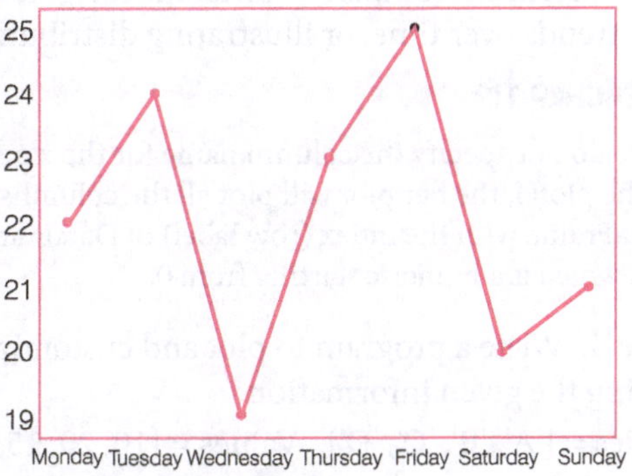

Customization a line chart

```
import pandas as pd
import matplotlib.pyplot as plt
data = {
    'Days': ['Monday', 'Tuesday', 'Wednesday',
            'Thursday', 'Friday', 'Saturday', 'Sunday'],
    'Temperature': [22, 24, 19, 23, 25, 20, 21]
}
df = pd.DataFrame(data)                    # Creating DataFrame
    plt.plot(df['Days'], df['Temperature'],
    color='red', linestyle='--', marker='o')
                    # Plotting the line chart using the DataFrame
    plt.title('Temperature Variation Over a Week')
    plt.xlabel('Days')
    plt.ylabel('Temperature (°C)')  # Customizing the chart
    plt.grid(True)
    plt.show()                              # Display the chart
```

Mistake Alert! If we have a Series or DataFrame type object (let's say 's' or 'df') we can call the plot method by writing: s.plot() or df.plot()

Output

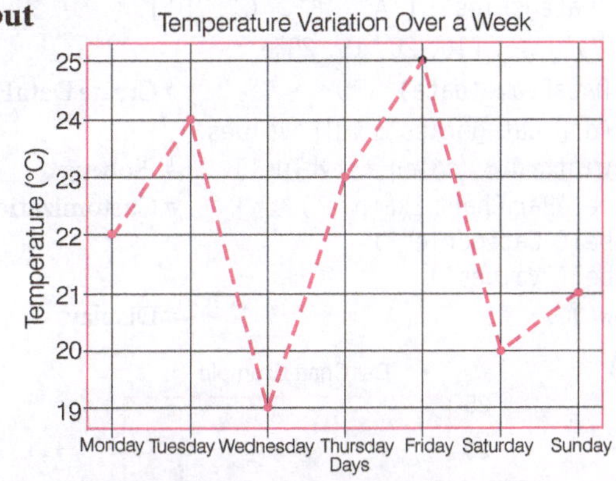

Plotting and Customization a Bar Chart

Plotting a bar chart is a common way to visualize categorical data in a graphical format where each category is represented by a bar. The length or height of the bar is proportional to the values it represents. Bar charts are useful for comparing different categories, showing trends over time, or illustrating distributions.

TEACHER TIP

If we do not specify the column name for the x parameter in the plot(), the bar plot will plot all the columns of the DataFrame with the index (row label) of DataFrame at x axis which is a numeric starting from 0.

Example 4. Write a program to plot and customize a bar chart using the given information.

Categories = ['A', 'B', 'C', 'D'], Values = [10, 20, 15, 25]

***Solution.* Plotting a bar chart**

```
import pandas as pd
import matplotlib.pyplot as plt
data = {'Categories': ['A', 'B', 'C', 'D'],
  'Values': [10, 20, 15, 25]}
df = pd.DataFrame(data)          # Create DataFrame
plt.bar(df['Categories'], df['Values'])
plt.show()
```

Output

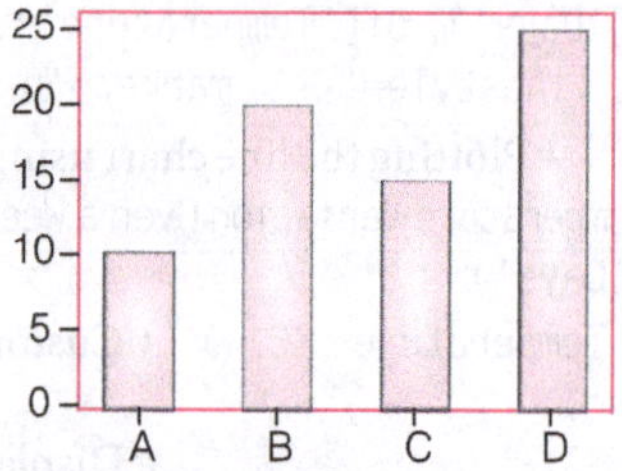

Customization a bar chart

```
import pandas as pd
import matplotlib.pyplot as plt
data = {'Categories': ['A', 'B', 'C', 'D'],
  'Values': [10, 20, 15, 25]}
df = pd.DataFrame(data)                      # Create DataFrame
plt.bar(df['Categories'], df['Values'],
     width=0.5, color='skyblue')             # Plotting
plt.title('Bar Chart Example')               # Customization
plt.xlabel('Categories')
plt.ylabel('Values')
plt.show()                                   # Display
```

Output

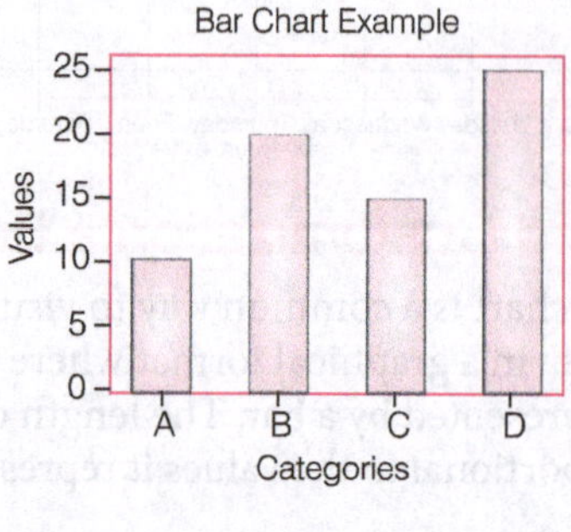

Additional Customizations

Horizontal Bar Chart Use plt.barh() for horizontal bars.

```
plt.barh(df['Categories'], df['Values'],
         height=0.5, color='skyblue')
```

Output

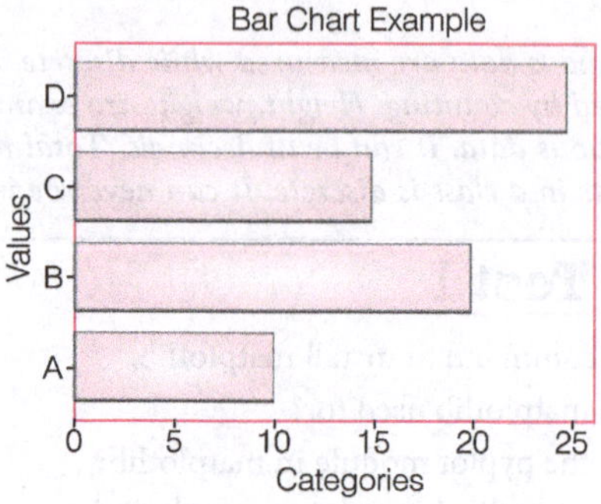

Plotting Histogram

A Histogram represents data provided in the form of some groups. It is an accurate method for the graphical representation of numerical data distribution.

It is a type of bar plot where the X-axis represents the bin ranges while the Y-axis gives information about frequency.

The df.plot(kind='hist') function in pandas can be used to create them. The bins parameter allows for flexibility in defining the bin edges or the number of bins. It is also possible to set value for the bins parameter:

Example 5. Write a program to plot a histogram using the given information.

Name = ['Arnav', 'Sheela', 'Azhar', 'Bincy', 'Yash', 'Nazar']

Height = [60, 61, 63, 65, 61, 60]

Weight = [47, 89, 52, 58, 50, 47]

Solution.

```
import pandas as pd
```

Mistake Alert ! import pandas before using DataFrame

```
import matplotlib.pyplot as plt
data = {'Name': ['Arnav', 'Sheela', 'Azhar',
  'Bincy', 'Yash', 'Nazar'], 'Height': [60, 61, 63, 65, 61,
           60], 'Weight': [47, 89, 52, 58, 50, 47]}
                # Automatic binning
df = pd.DataFrame(data)
df.plot(kind='hist', alpha=0.5)   # alpha for
transparency
plt.show()
                # Setting number of bins
df.plot(kind='hist', bins=20, alpha=0.5)
plt.show()
                # Custom bin edges
```

```
df.plot(kind='hist', bins=[47, 50, 55, 60, 65,70],
alpha=0.5)
plt.show()          # Using a range for bins
df.plot(kind='hist', bins=range(45, 75, 5), alpha=0.5)
plt.show()
```

Output

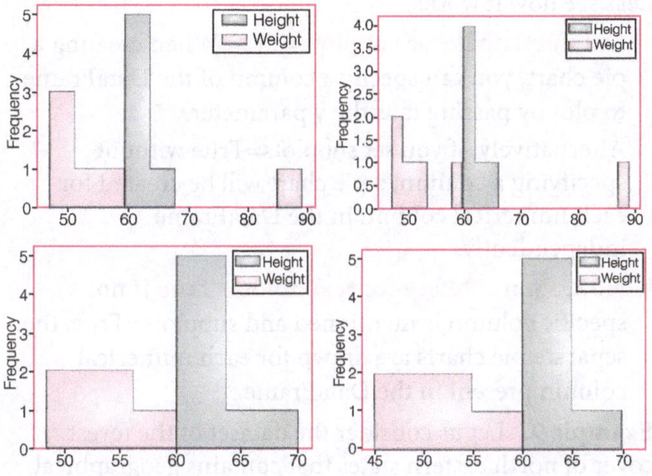

Customising Histogram

Taking the same data as above, now let see how the histogram can be customised. Let us change the edgecolor, which is the border of each hist, to green.

Also, let us change the line style to ":" and line width to 2. Let us try another property called **fill**, which takes boolean values.

The default True means each hist will be filled with color and False means each hist will be empty. Another property called **hatch** can be used to fill to each hist with pattern ('-', '+', 'x', '\\', '*', 'o', 'O', '.').

Example 6. Write a program to customize histogram using the given information.

Name = ['Arnav', 'Sheela', 'Azhar', 'Bincy', 'Yash', 'Nazar'],

Height = [60, 61, 63, 65, 61, 60]

Weight = [47, 89, 52, 58, 50, 47]

Solution.

```
import pandas as pd
import matplotlib.pyplot as plt
data = {'Name': ['Arnav', 'Sheela', 'Azhar',
 'Bincy', 'Yash', 'Nazar'], 'Height': [60, 61, 63, 65, 61,
                    60], 'Weight': [47, 89, 52, 58, 50, 47]}
df = pd.DataFrame(data)    # Create DataFrame
df['Height'].plot(kind='hist', edgecolor='Green',
      linewidth=2, linestyle=':', fill=False, hatch='o')
                          # Plot histograms for Height and Weight
plt.title('Height Distribution')
plt.xlabel('Height')
plt.show()
```

Output

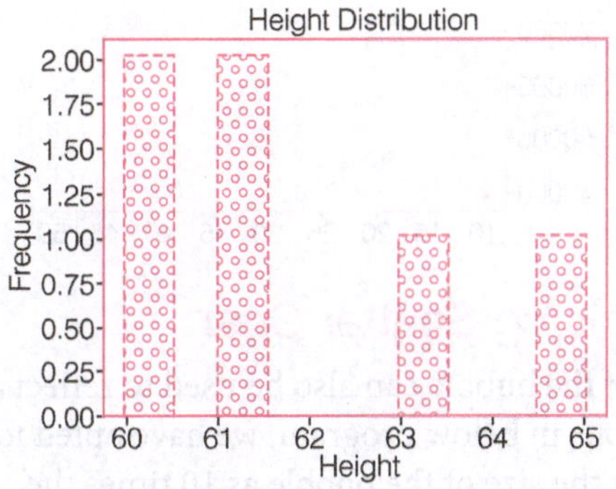


```
df['Weight'].plot(kind='hist',
            edgecolor='Green', linewidth=2,
    linestyle=':', fill=False, hatch='o')
plt.title('Weight Distribution')
plt.xlabel('Weight')
plt.show()
```

Output

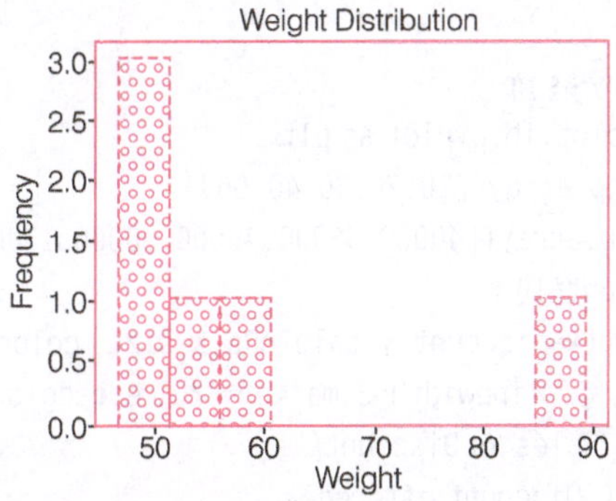

Plotting Scatter Chart

The matplotlib.pyplot.scatter() plots serve as a visual tool to explore and analyze the relationships between variables, utilizing dots to depict the connection between them.

Example 7. Prayatna sells designer bags and wallets. During the sales season, he gave discounts ranging from 10% to 50% over a period of 5 weeks. He recorded his sales for each type of discount in an array. Draw a scatter plot to show a relationship between the discount offered and sales made.

Solution.

```
import numpy as np
import matplotlib.pyplot as plt
discount= np.array([10,20,30,40,50])
saleInRs=np.array([40000,45000,48000,50000,100000])
plt.scatter(x=discount,y=saleInRs)
plt.show()
```

Output

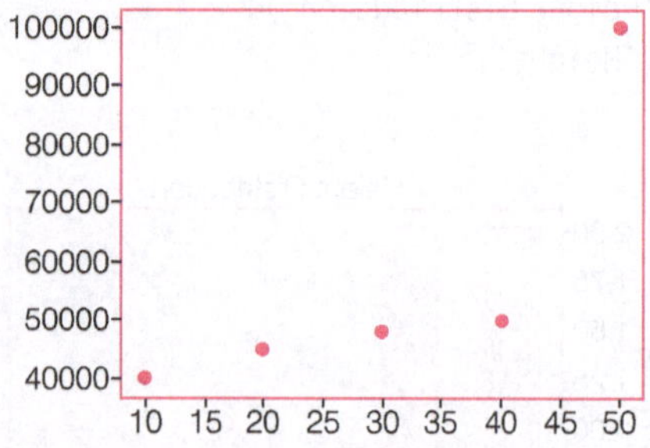

Customising Scatter Chart

The size of the bubble can also be used to reflect a value. For example, in below program, we have opted for displaying the size of the bubble as 10 times the discount.

The colour and markers can also be changed in the above plot by adding the following statements:

Example 8. Write the program to demonstrate customization in a scatter chart using a NumPy array.

Solution.

```
import numpy as np
import matplotlib.pyplot as plt
discount= np.array([10,20,30,40,50])
saleInRs=np.array([40000,45000,48000,50000,100000])
size=discount*10
plt.scatter(x=discount,y=saleInRs,s=size, color='red',
            linewidth=3,marker='*', edgecolor='blue')
plt.title('Sales Vs Discount')
plt.xlabel('Discount offered')
plt.ylabel('Sales in Rs')
plt.show()
```

Output

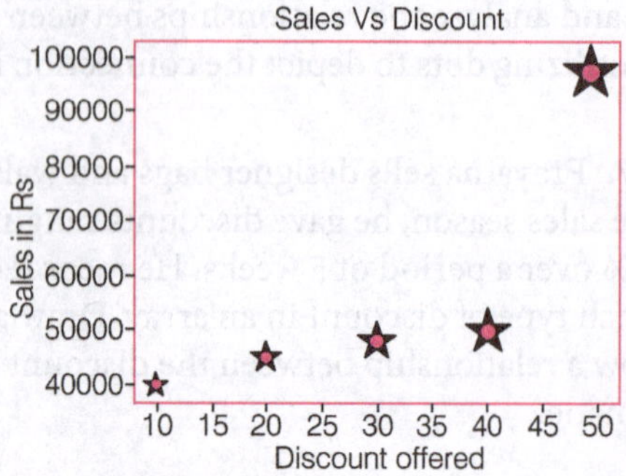

Plotting Pie Chart

A pie chart is a type of graph where a circle is divided into sectors, with each sector representing a proportion of the whole.

The size of each sector is proportional to the numerical data it represents, making pie charts ideal for showing the relative sizes of parts to a whole.

In Python's pandas library, you can create a pie chart using the df.plot(kind='pie') function.

Let's see how it works:

- **Column Label y or subplots=True** When creating a pie chart, you can specify a column of the DataFrame to plot by passing it as the y parameter.
  Alternatively, if you set subplots=True without specifying a column, a pie chart will be created for each numerical column in the DataFrame independently.
- **No Column Reference & subplots=True** If no specific column is mentioned and subplots=True, then separate pie charts are drawn for each numerical column present in the DataFrame.

Example 9. Let us consider the dataset of the forest cover of north eastern states that contains geographical area and corresponding forest cover in sq km along with the names of the corresponding states.

State	GeoArea	ForestCover
Arunachal Pradesh	83743	67353
Assam	78438	27692
Manipur	22327	17280
Meghalaya	22429	17321
Mizoram	21081	19240
Nagaland	16579	13464
Tripura	10486	8073

Solution. **Plotting a pie chart**

```
import pandas as pd
import matplotlib.pyplot as plt # Data for the DataFrame
data =
{
 'GeoArea': [83743, 78438, 22327, 22429, 21081, 16579,
     10486], 'ForestCover': [67353, 27692, 17280, 17321,
                                  19240, 13464, 8073]
}
df = pd.DataFrame(data, index=['Arunachal Pradesh',
           'Assam', 'Manipur', 'Meghalaya', 'Mizoram',
                              'Nagaland', 'Tripura'])
   # Creating DataFrame with state names as index
df.plot(kind='pie', y='ForestCover')
plt.show()
```

Output

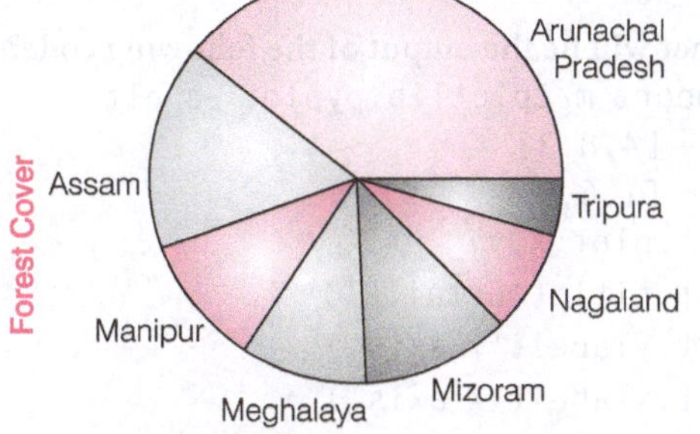

Customization a pie chart

```
import pandas as pd
import matplotlib.pyplot as plt  # Data for the DataFrame
data = {
    'GeoArea': [83743, 78438, 22327, 22429, 21081,
      16579, 10486], 'ForestCover': [67353, 27692, 17280,
                              17321, 19240, 13464, 8073]
}
df = pd.DataFrame(data, index=['Arunachal Pradesh',
                'Assam', 'Manipur', 'Meghalaya', 'Mizoram',
                                 'Nagaland', 'Tripura'])
                 # Creating DataFrame with state names as index
exp = [0.1, 0, 0, 0, 0.2, 0, 0]    # Explode and color settings
colors = ['r', 'g', 'm', 'c', 'brown', 'pink', 'purple']
df.plot(kind='pie', y='ForestCover',
           title='Forest Cover of North Eastern States',
           legend=False, explode=exp, autopct="%.2f%%",
                                         colors=colors)
                             # Plotting the pie chart
plt.show()                   # Display the plot
```

Output

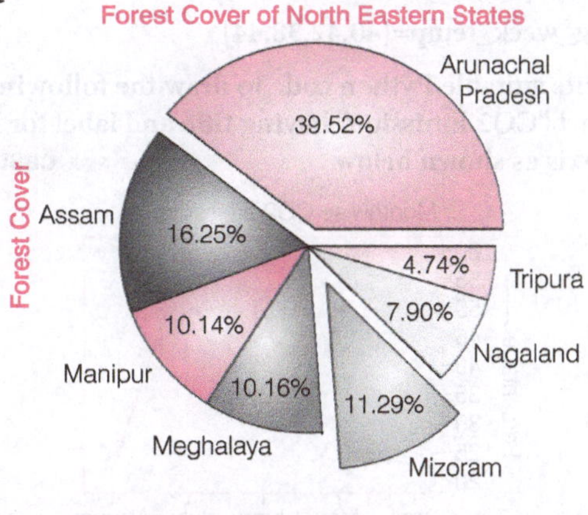

Plotting Quartiles and Box plots

Quartiles are statistical measures that divide a data set into four equal parts, each containing an equal number of observations.

To calculate quartiles, you first need to determine the median of the data set. Quartiles are useful in various contexts, such as educational achievement data, sales figures, and survey results.

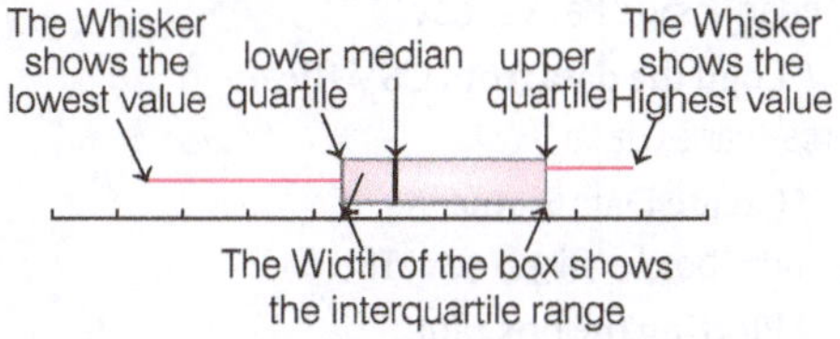

For example, quartiles can help identify the top 25% of students based on their exam scores.

A Box Plot (or Box-and-Whisker Plot) is a graphical representation that summarizes a data set by showing its minimum value, first quartile (Q1), median (Q2), third quartile (Q3), and maximum value.

The plot consists of a rectangular box, which represents the interquartile range (IQR) from Q1 to Q3. Whiskers extend from the box to the minimum and maximum values within a specified range.

Box plots also highlight outliers, which are values that lie significantly outside the range of the rest of the data.

Example 10. In order to assess the performance of students of a class in the annual examination, the class teacher stored marks of the students in all the 5 subjects in a CSV "Marks.csv" file as shown in Table. Plot the data using boxplot and perform a comparative analysis of performance in each subject.

Name	English	Maths	Hindi	Science	Social Studies
Rishika Batra	95	95	90	94	95
Waseem Ali	95	76	79	77	89
Kulpreet Singh	78	81	75	76	88
Annie Mathews	88	63	67	77	80
Shiksha	95	55	51	59	80
Naveen Gupta	82	55	63	56	74
Taleem Ahmed	73	49	54	60	77
Pragati Nigam	80	50	51	54	76
Usman Abbas	92	43	51	48	69
Gurpreet Kaur	60	43	55	52	71
Sameer Murthy	60	43	55	52	71
Angelina	78	33	39	48	68
Angad Bedi	62	43	51	48	54

Solutions. **Plotting the box plot**

```
import numpy as np
import pandas as pd
import matplotlib.pyplot as plt
data = pd.read_csv('Marks.csv')
            # Load the data from CSV file
df = pd.DataFrame(data)
            # Create DataFrame
df.plot(kind='box', figsize=(10, 6))
            # Plotting the box plot
plt.show()
```

Output

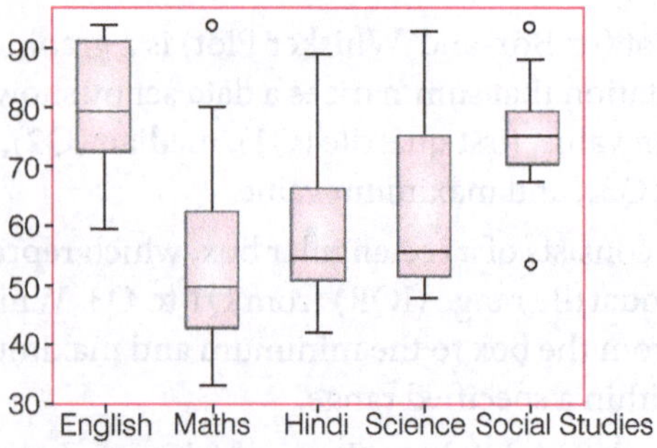

Customization the box plot

```
import numpy as np
import pandas as pd
import matplotlib.pyplot as plt
data = pd.read_csv('Marks.csv')
            # Load the data from CSV file
df = pd.DataFrame(data)
            # Create DataFrame
plt.figure(figsize=(10, 6))
df.plot(kind='box', figsize=(10, 6))
            # Plotting the box plot
plt.title('Performance Analysis') # Set title
plt.xlabel('Subjects')            # Set xlabel
plt.ylabel('Marks')               # Set ylabel
plt.show()                        # Show the plot
```

Output

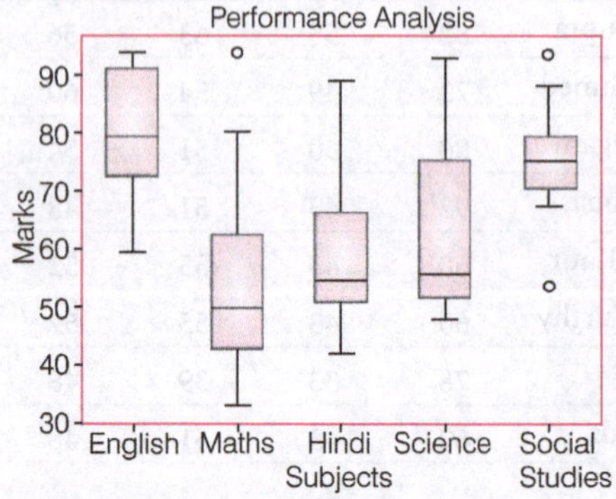

Quick Test 2

1. **What will be the output of the following code?**

```
import matplotlib.pyplot as plt
x = [4,8,3]
y = [1,6,9]
plt.plot(x,y)
plt.title('Details')
plt.ylabel('Y axis')
plt.xlabel('X axis')
plt.show()
```

2. **Write Python code to draw the following bar graph representing the total sales in each quarter. Add the Title , Label for X-axis and Y-axis. Use the following data for plotting the graph**
   Sales =[450,300,500,650]
   qtr=["QTR1", QTR2", "QTR3", "QTR4"]

3. **Write Python code to draw a pie chart representing the nutrition values given in the lists nutrition, Nvalues, and colval.**

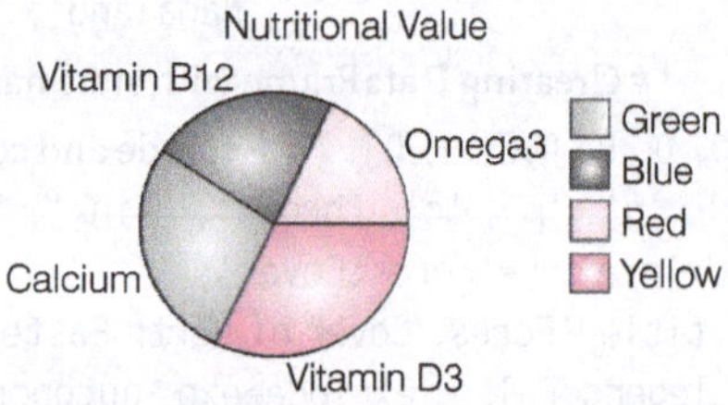

4. **Write a Python program to plot a line chart based on the given data to depict the changing weekly average temperature in Delhi for four weeks.** **CBSE SQP 2023-24**
   Week=[1,2,3,4]
   Avg_week_temp=[40,42,38,44]

5. **Write suitable Python code to draw the following line chart "CO2 Emission" having title and label for X and Y axis as shown below.** **CBSE 2024**

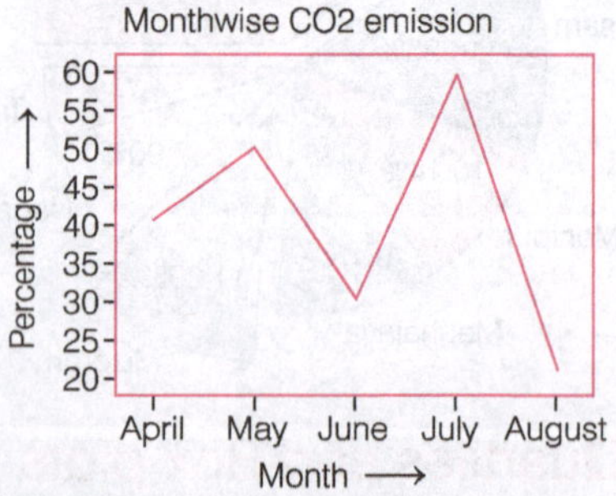

Also give suitable Python statement to save this chart with the name, emission.png.

Mind Map

DATA VISUALIZATION

Graphical representation of quantitative information and data by using visual elements like graphs, charts, maps ,etc.

Matplotlib Library

Matplotlib is an amazing visualization library in Python for 2D plots of arrays. It is a multi-platform data visualization library built on Numpy array.

Pyplot Function

It is the module available in Matplotlib library. It makes some changes to a figure. e.g. create a figure, create plotting area in a figure, decorates the plot with labels, etc.

Types of Plotting a Chart

Plotting Line Chart

Used to represent the relation between two data X and Y on a different axis.

Syntax `plot(x,y,label)`

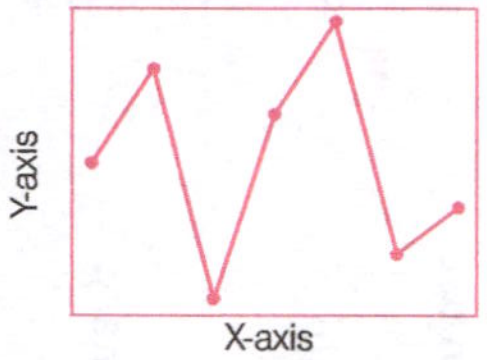

Plotting Scatter Chart

Explore and analyze the relationships between variables, utilizing dots to depict the connection between them.

Syntax `plt.scatter(x,y)`

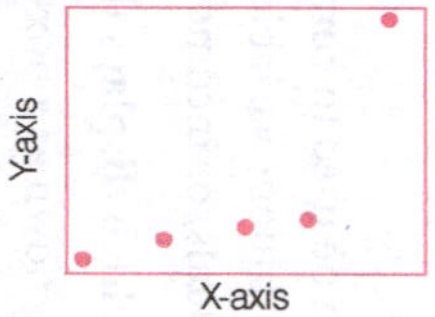

Plotting Bar Chart

To visualize categorical data in a graphical format where each category is represented by a bar.

Syntax `bar(x,y,label)`

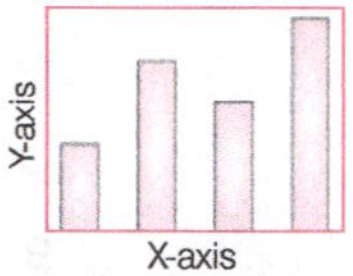

Syntax for Horizontal `barh(x,y,label)`

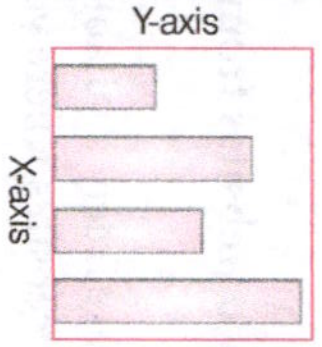

Plotting Pie Chart

It is a type of graph where a circle is divided into sectors, with each sector representing a proportion of the whole. Let's see how it works:

- Column Label y or subplots=True
- No Column Reference & subplots=True

Syntax `plt.pie(y)`

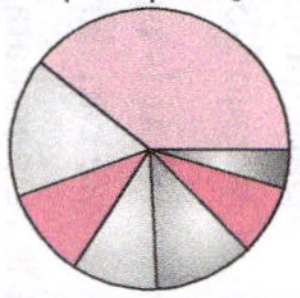

Plotting Histogram

Data provided in the form of some groups. It is an accurate method for the graphical representation of numerical data distribution.

Syntax `hist(data,bins)`

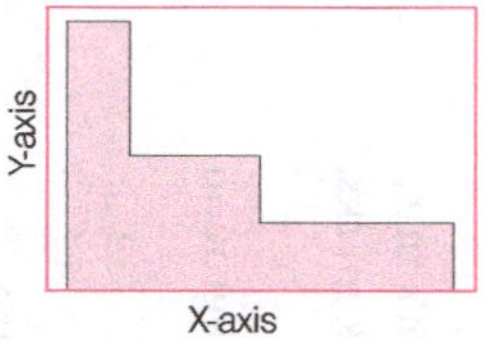

Plotting Box

Graphical representation that summarizes a data set by showing its minimum value, first quartile (Q1), median (Q2), third quartile (Q3), and maximum value.

Syntax `plt.boxplot(data)`

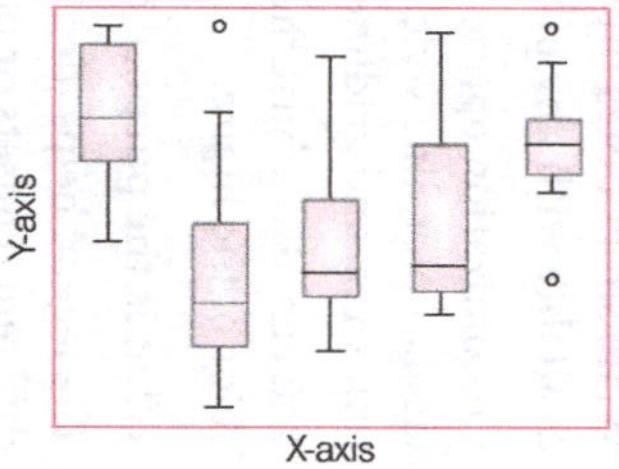

> ***Note***
> *We use customization tools to modify the appearance of plots, adjusting elements such as markers, line width, line style, gridlines, and more.*

Pyplot Functions to Customise Plots

Pyplot library gives us numerous functions, which can be used to customise charts such as adding titles or legends.

Function	Example
plt.title()	`plt.title("Sample Plot")`
plt.xlabel()	`plt.xlabel("X-Axis Label")`
plt.ylabel()	`plt.ylabel("Y-Axis Label")`
plt.legend()	`plt.legend(["Line 1", "Line 2"])`
plt.grid()	`plt.grid(True)`
plt.xticks()	`plt.xticks([0,1,2],["A","B","C"])`
plt.yticks()	`plt.yticks([10, 20, 30], ["Low", "Medium", "High"])`
plt.savefig()	`plt.savefig("plot.png")`
plt.show()	`plt.show()`

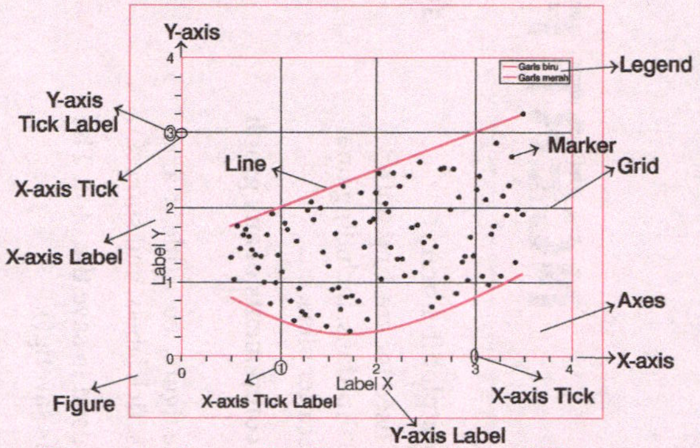

Other Attributes for Customization of Plot

Color

Used to quickly specify the color of plot elements like lines, markers, and text.

Syntax `plt.plot(data1,data2,color code)`

Marker

matplotlib.markers module provides a collection of marker styles used for data visualization in Matplotlib plots.

Syntax `plt.plot(x,y, marker='o')`

Line Width and Line Style

It is used to change the width and the style of the line chart.

Syntax `plt.plot(x,y,linewidth=4,linestyle='dashed')`

NCERT Folder

1. What is the purpose of the Matplotlib library?

Ans. Matplotlib is a Python library used for creating static, animated, and interactive visualizations, including line plots, bar charts, histograms, scatter plots, etc.

2. What are some of the major components of any graph or plot?

Ans. Major components include the figure, axes, title, x-axis label, y-axis label, legend, ticks, tick labels, and spines.

3. Name the function which is used to save the plot. The function used to save a plot is savefig().

Ans. plt.savefig('plot.png')

4. Write short notes on different customisation options available with any plot.

Ans. Customization options include changing the plot's title, labels, color, line styles, markers, axes limits, tick marks, font sizes, and gridlines.

You can also adjust the size, resolution, and background color of the figure.

5. What is the purpose of a legend?

Ans. The legend helps identify and distinguish between different datasets or plot elements by providing a description of what each line, color, or marker represents.

6. Define Pandas visualization.

Ans. Pandas visualization is a feature within the pandas library that allows easy plotting of data directly from a DataFrame using built-in plotting functions that utilize Matplotlib.

7. What is open data? Name any two websites from which we can download open data.

Ans. Open data refers to datasets that are freely available for public use and distribution. Two websites where you can download open data are:

1. Kaggle
2. Government Open Data Portal (data.gov)

8. Give an example of data comparison where we can use the scatter plot.

Ans. A scatter plot can be used to compare the relationship between two continuous variables, such as height vs. weight of individuals, or income vs. education level.

9. Name the plot which displays the statistical summary.

Ans. A box plot (also known as a box-and-whisker plot) displays the statistical summary of data, showing the median, quartiles, and outliers.

10. Plot the following data using a line plot:

Day	1	2	3	4	5	6	7
Tickets Sold	2000	2800	3000	2500	2300	2500	1000

- **Before displaying the plot display "Monday, Tuesday, Wednesday, Thursday, Friday, Saturday, Sunday" in place of Day 1, 2, 3, 4, 5, 6, 7**
- **Change the color of the line to 'Magenta'.**

Ans.

```
import matplotlib.pyplot as plt
days = ['Monday', 'Tuesday', 'Wednesday',
'Thursday', 'Friday', 'Saturday', 'Sunday']
tickets_sold = [2000, 2800, 3000, 2500,
                                2300, 2500, 1000]
  # Plotting the data
plt.figure(figsize=(10, 6))
plt.plot(days, tickets_sold,
                color='magenta', marker='o')
  # Setting the title and labels
plt.title('Tickets Sold Over a Week')
plt.xlabel('Day of the Week')
plt.ylabel('Tickets Sold')
  # Display the plot
plt.grid(True)
plt.show()
```

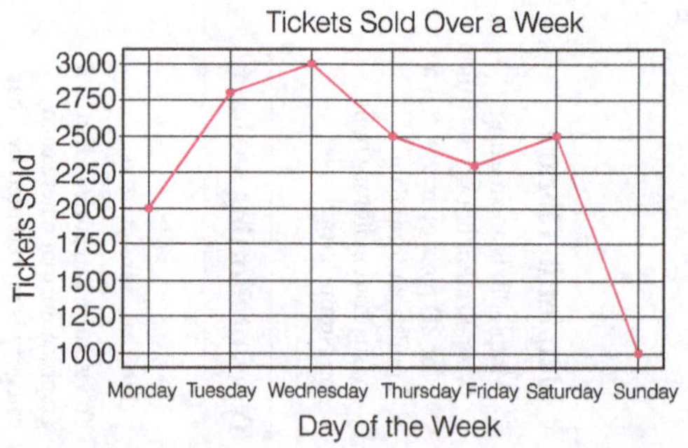

11. Collect data about colleges in Delhi University or any other university of your choice and number of courses they run for Science, Commerce and Humanities, store it in a CSV file and present it using a bar plot.

Ans. Data about colleges and the number of courses they offer in Science, Commerce, and Humanities:

College	Science Courses	Commerce Courses	Humanities Courses
Deen Dayal Upadhyaya College	15	10	12
Maitreyi College	20	12	15
Shri Venkateshwara College	18	8	14

```
import pandas as pd
import matplotlib.pyplot as plt
 # Load the CSV file into a DataFrame
df = pd.read_csv('college_courses.csv')
# Set the index to the College column for easy plotting
df.set_index('College', inplace=True)
# Plot the data
df.plot(kind='bar', figsize=(10, 6))
plt.title('Number of Courses Offered by
                                Colleges')
plt.xlabel('Colleges')
plt.ylabel('Number of Courses')
plt.xticks(rotation=45)
plt.legend(title='Course Type')
plt.tight_layout()
# Show the plot
plt.show()
```

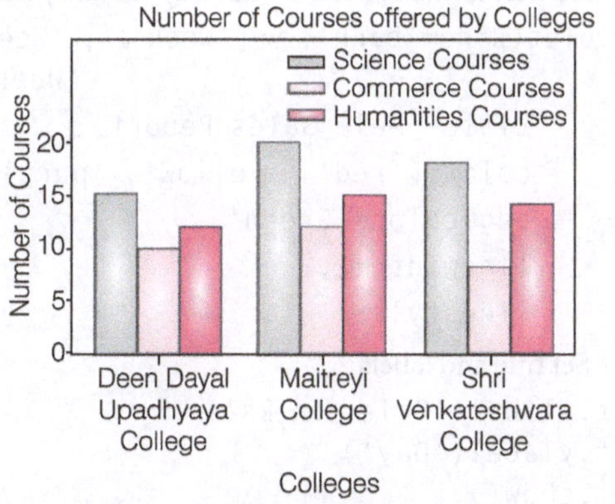

12. Collect and store data related to the screen time of students in your class separately for boys and girls and present it using a boxplot.

Ans. Data for screen time (in hours) for boys and girls:

Student	Gender	Screen Time (hours)
1	Boys	2.5
2	Boys	3.0
3	Boys	2.8
4	Boys	4.1
5	Boys	3.7
6	Girls	1.8
7	Girls	2.2
8	Girls	2.5
9	Girls	3.0
10	Girls	2.7

```
import matplotlib.pyplot as plt
 # Example data
screen_time =
{
    'Boys': [2.5, 3.0, 2.8, 4.1, 3.7],
    'Girls': [1.8, 2.2, 2.5, 3.0, 2.7]
}
  # Create a boxplot
plt.figure(figsize=(8, 6))
plt.boxplot(screen_time.values(),
labels=screen_time.keys())
plt.title('Screen Time Distribution by
                                    Gender')
plt.xlabel('Gender')
plt.ylabel('Screen Time (hours)')
plt.grid(True)
plt.show()
```

Output

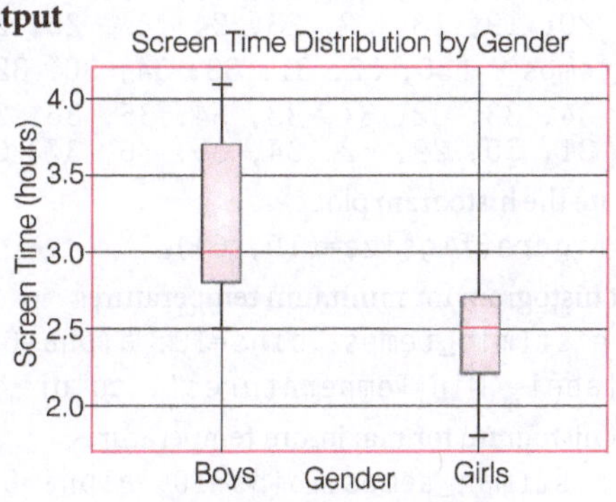

13. Explain the findings of the boxplot of Figure below by filling the following blanks:

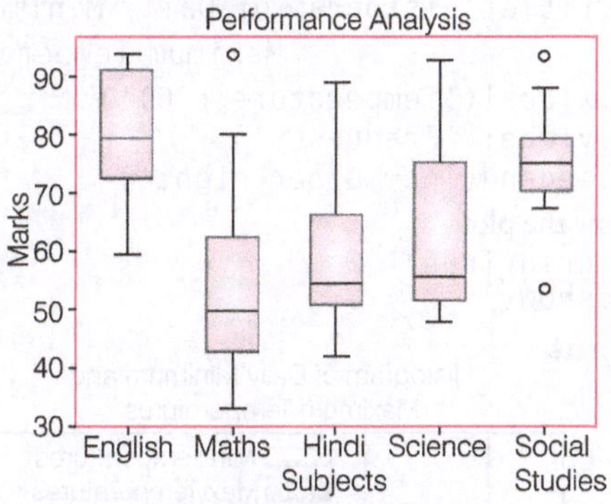

(a) **The median for the five subjects is ______, ______, ______, ______, ______**

(b) **The highest value for the five subjects is ______, ______, ______, ______, ______**

(c) **The lowest value for the five subjects is ______, ______, ______, ______, ______**

(d) ______ **subject has two outliers with the value ______ and ______**

(e) ______**subject shows minimum variation.**

Ans. (a) The median for the five subjects is 80, 50, 55, 56, 76.

(b) The highest value for the five subjects is 95, 95, 90, 94, 95.

(c) The lowest value for the five subjects is 60, 33, 39, 48, 54.

(d) Social Studies subject has two outliers with the value 95 and 54.

(e) Social Studies subject shows minimum variation.

14. Collect the minimum and maximum temperature of your city for a month and present it using a histogram plot.

Ans.
```
import matplotlib.pyplot as plt
# Sample data: replace these with your actual temperature data
min_temps = [20, 22, 19, 21, 23, 20, 22, 24,
 25, 23, 21, 20, 22, 24, 26, 25, 24, 23, 22,
 21, 20, 19, 18, 22, 23, 24, 25, 26, 27, 28]
max_temps = [30, 32, 31, 33, 34, 30, 32, 33,
 35, 34, 33, 32, 31, 33, 34, 35, 36, 34, 33,
 32, 31, 30, 29, 32, 34, 35, 36, 37, 38, 39]
# Create the histogram plot
plt.figure(figsize=(10, 6))
# Plot histogram for minimum temperatures
plt.hist(min_temps, bins=10, alpha=0.5,
   label='Min Temperatures', color='blue')
# Plot histogram for maximum temperatures
plt.hist(max_temps, bins=10, alpha=0.5,
    label='Max Temperatures', color='red')
# Add titles and labels
plt.title('Histogram of Daily Minimum and
                    Maximum Temperatures')
plt.xlabel('Temperature (°C)')
plt.ylabel('Frequency')
plt.legend(loc='upper right')
# Show the plot
plt.grid(True)
plt.show()
```

Output

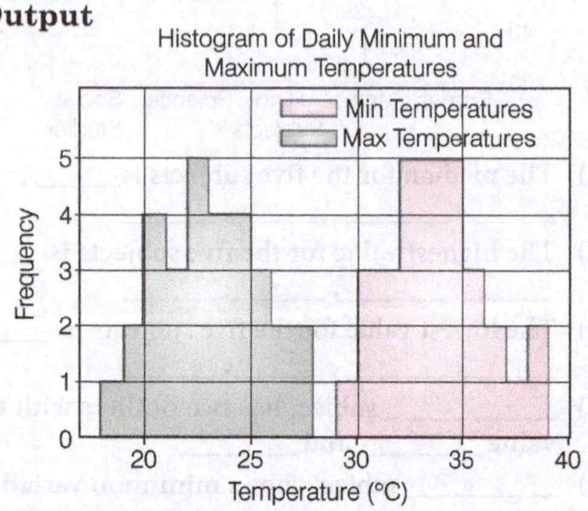

15. How can we make the bar chart of given table horizontal?

Week 1	Week 2	Week 3	Day
5000	4000	4000	Monday
5900	3000	5800	Tuesday
6500	5000	3500	Wednesday
3500	5500	2500	Thursday
4000	3000	3000	Friday
5300	4300	5300	Saturday
7900	5900	6000	Sunday

Ans.
```
import pandas as pd
import matplotlib.pyplot as plt
# Load the data from the CSV file
df = pd.read_csv('MelaSales.csv')
# Plot a horizontal bar chart with 'Day' as  the y axis
df.plot(kind='barh', y=['Week 1', 'Week 2',
                                  'Week 3'],
    title='Mela Sales Report',
    color=['red', 'yellow', 'purple'],
    edgecolor='Green',
    linewidth=2,
    linestyle='--')
# Set title and labels
plt.xlabel('Sales in Rs')
plt.ylabel('Day')
plt.show()
```

Output

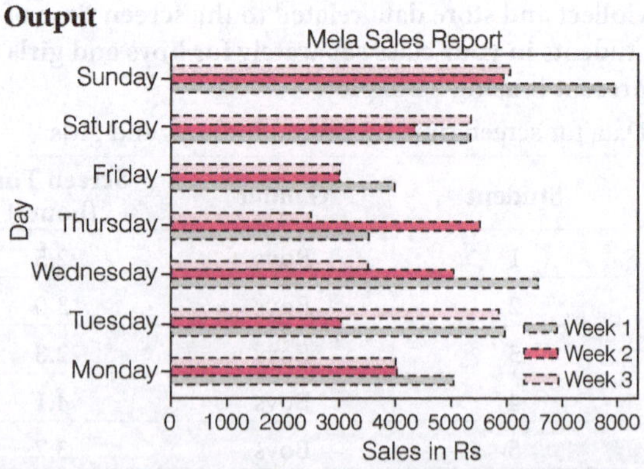

16. What would happen if we use df.plot(kind='scatter') instead of plt.scatter()?

Ans. df.plot(kind='scatter') provides a more integrated way of plotting directly from DataFrame columns without explicitly passing the data to plt.scatter().

plt.scatter() offers more fine-grained control over the appearance of the scatter plot, like setting linewidth, edgecolor, etc., which might not be as straightforward with df.plot(kind='scatter').

17. What effect did 'legend= False' in Program have on the output?

```
import pandas as pd
import matplotlib.pyplot as plt
  # Create DataFrame
df = pd.DataFrame({
    'GeoArea': [83743, 78438, 22327, 22429,
                        21081, 16579, 10486],
    'ForestCover': [67353, 27692, 17280,
                    17321, 19240, 13464, 8073]
}, index=['Arunachal Pradesh', 'Assam',
          'Manipur', 'Meghalaya', 'Mizoram',
                       'Nagaland', 'Tripura'])
  # Plot pie chart
df['ForestCover'].plot(kind='pie',
        title='Forest Cover of North Eastern
  States', legend=False, autopct='%1.1f%%')
plt.ylabel('')
        # Hides the y-label to make the pie chart cleaner
plt.show()              # Display the plot
```

Ans. In Program, setting legend=False in the df.plot method removes the legend from the pie chart, which means the pie chart will display without the label indicating which color corresponds to which state.

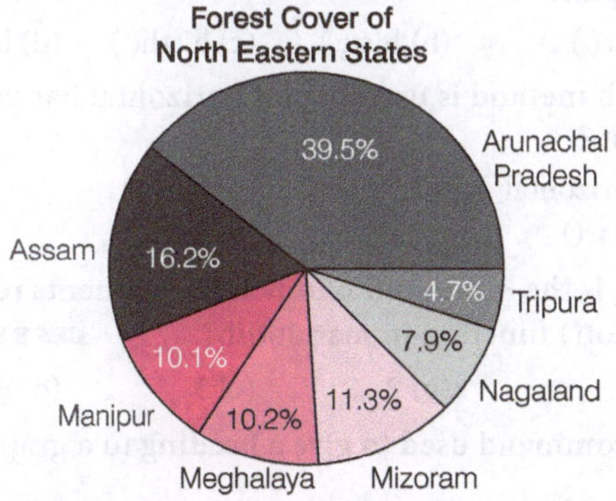

18. Create the MelaSale. csv using Python Pandas containing data as shown in Table.

Week 1	Week 2	Week 3
5000	4000	4000
5900	3000	5800
6500	5000	3500
3500	5500	2500
4000	3000	3000
5300	4300	5300
7900	5900	6000

Ans. To create the MelaSale.csv file with the given data using Python and pandas, follow these steps:

1. **Import pandas** Make sure you have pandas installed. If not, install it using pip install pandas.
2. **Create a DataFrame** Define the data and structure it in a pandas DataFrame.
3. **Save to CSV** Write the DataFrame to a CSV file.

```
import pandas as pd
  # Define the data
data = {
    'Week 1': [5000, 5900, 6500, 3500, 4000,
                                 5300, 7900],
    'Week 2': [4000, 3000, 5000, 5500, 3000,
                                 4300, 5900],
    'Week 3': [4000, 5800, 3500, 2500, 3000,
                                 5300, 6000]
}
  # Create a DataFrame
df = pd.DataFrame(data)
  # Save the DataFrame to a CSV file
df.to_csv('MelaSale.csv', index=False)
print("MelaSale.csv has been created.")
```

19. What value does each bubble on the plot at Figure below represent?

Ans. In the scatter plot you've created, each point (or bubble) represents a pair of values from the discount and saleInRs arrays. Specifically:

- **discount values** represent the x-axis and show the discount offered.
- **saleInRs values** represent the y-axis and show the sales amount in rupees corresponding to each discount.

So, each bubble on the plot corresponds to a specific discount and its associated sales amount.

For example, a bubble at (10, 40000) means that a 10% discount corresponds to sales of ₹ 40,000.

20. Plot a pie to display the radius of the planets and also give an appropriate title to the plot.

Ans.
```
import pandas as pd
import matplotlib.pyplot as plt
# Creating DataFrame
df = pd.DataFrame({'mass': [0.330, 4.87,
5.97], 'radius': [2439.7, 6051.8, 6378.1]},
index=['Mercury', 'Venus', 'Earth'])
# Plotting pie chart for the radius
df['radius'].plot(kind='pie',
        title='Radius of Planets',
        autopct='%1.1f%%')
# Displaying the plot
plt.show()
```

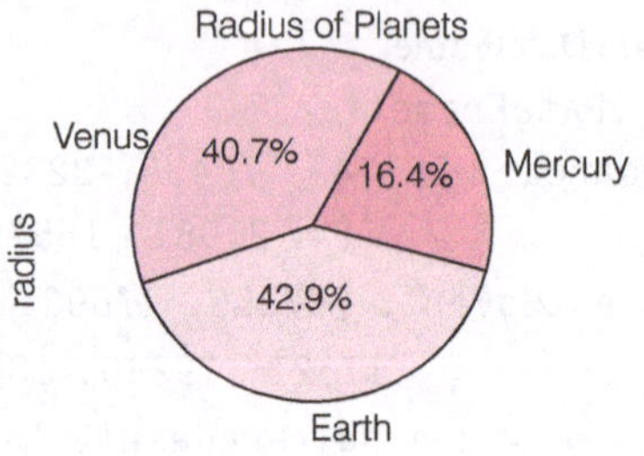

EXAM PATTERN QUESTIONS

Objective Type Questions

Multiple Choice Questions

1. What is not true about Data Visualisation? CBSE 2021-22 Term-I

(a) Graphical representation of information and data.
(b) Helps users in analysing a large amount of data in a simpler way.
(c) Data Visualisation makes complex data more accessible, understandable and usable.
(d) No library needs to be imported to create charts in Python language.

2. To install matplotlib, the following function will be typed in your command prompt. What does -U represent?

```
Python -m pip install -U pip
```

(a) Downloading pip to the latest version
(b) Upgrading pip to the latest version
(c) Removing pip
(d) Upgrading matplotlib to the latest version

3. Which library is imported to draw charts in Python? CBSE 2021-22 Term-I

(a) csv (b) matplotlib
(c) numpy (d) pandas

4. Which of the following command is used to import matplotlib for coding? CBSE 2021-22 Term-I

(a) import matplotlib.pyplot as plt
(b) import plt.matplotlib as plt
(c) import py.matplotlib as plt
(d) import pyplot.matplotlib as plt

5. Which method is used to plot histogram in pyplot?

(a) his() (b) hist() (c) Hist() (d) histogram()

6. Which of the following is not a valid plotting function of pyplot?

(a) bar( ) (b) hist( ) (c) histh( ) (d) barh( )

7. Which method is used to plot horizontal bar graph in pyplot ?

(a) horizontal_bar() (b) barh()
(c) hbar() (d) bar()

8. What is the minimum number of arguments required for plot() function in matplotlib? CBSE SQP Term-I

(a) 1 (b) 2 (c) 3 (d) 4

9. The command used to give a heading to a graph is ________

(a) plt.show() (b) plt.plot()
(c) plt.xlabel() (d) plt.title()

10. Which method will be add inside the file to display plot?

(a) show() (b) display() (c) execute() (d) plot()

11. Out of the following, which function cannot be used for customization of charts in Python? CBSE SQP Term-I

(a) xlabel() (b) color() (c) title() (d) xticks()

12. .... is the function to save the graph. CBSE SQP 2021-22 Term-I

(a) savefig() (b) savefigure()
(c) savegraph() (d) savechart()

13. In Python which function of matplotlib library is used to save a plot? **CBSE 2025**

(a) save () (b) saveplot() (c) export() (d) savefig()

14. By default, the plot() function of Matplotlib draws a ______ plot. **CBSE SQP 2024-25**

(a) histogram (b) column (c)bar (d)line

15. Using Python Matplotlib __________ can be used to display information as a series of data points.

(a) line chart (b) bar graph
(c) histogram (d) None of these

16. Which Matplotlib plot is best suited to represent changes in data over time? **CBSE SQP 2024-25**

(a) Bar plot (b) Histogram
(c) Line plot (d) Histogram & Bar plot

17. To compare data values of commission earned by salesmen over a year, which of the following type of graph should preferably be used? **CBSE 2023**

(a) Line (b) Area
(c) Bar (d) Scatter

18. Which type of chart shows the relationship between a numerical variable and a categorical variable?

(a) Line (b) Bar
(c) Pie (d) X-Y plot

19. To change the width of bars in a bar chart, which of the following arguments with a float value is used? **CBSE 2021-22 Term-I**

(a) hwidth (b) width
(c) breath (d) barwidth

20. Consider the following statements with reference to Line charts. **CBSE 2021-22 Term-I**

Statement A Line graphs is a tool for comparison and is created by plotting a series of several points and connecting them with a straight line.

Statement B You should never use line chart, when the chart is in a continuous data set.

(a) Statement A is correct.
(b) Statement B is correct.
(c) Statement A is correct but statement B is incorrect.
(d) Statement A is incorrect but statement B iscorrect.

21. Read the statements given below and identify the right option to draw a histogram. **CBSE SQP 2021-22 Term-I**

Statement A To make a histogram with matplotlib, we can use the plt.hist() function.

Statement B The bins parameter is compulsory to create histogram.

(a) Statement A is correct.
(b) Statement B is correct.
(c) Statement A is correct, but Statement B is incorrect.
(d) Statement A is incorrect, but Statement B is correct.

22. Ms. Kalpana is working with an IT company and she wants to create charts from the data provided to her. She generates the following graph. Which statement is used to mark the line as given in the above graph? **CBSE 2021-22 Term-I**

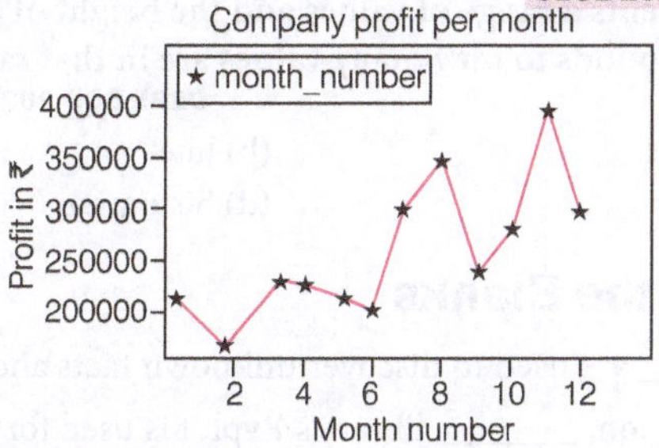

(a) plt. plot(x,y, marker=#, markersize= 10, color=red, linestyle=dashdot)
(b) plt.plot(x,y,marker=star, markersize = 10, color=red)
(c) plt.plot(x,y,marker = @, markersize=10, color=red, linestyle = dashdot)
(d) plt.plot(x,y,marker=*, markersize = 10, color = red)

23. Mohit is trying to create a histogram of "STEP" type with 10 bins. Help him to identify the correct statement from the following statements **Competency Based Que.**

(a) plt.hist(x,bins=10, histype="barstacked")
(b) plt.hist(x,bins=11)
(c) plt.hist(x, bins=10, histype="step")
(d) plt.hist(x, bins=10, histytpe="Dashed")

24. Point out the correct combination with regards to kind keyword for graph plotting.

(a) hist for histogram (b) box for boxplot
(c) area for area plot (d) All of these

25. Observe the following figure. Identify the code for obtaining this as output. **CBSE SQP 2021-22 Term-I**

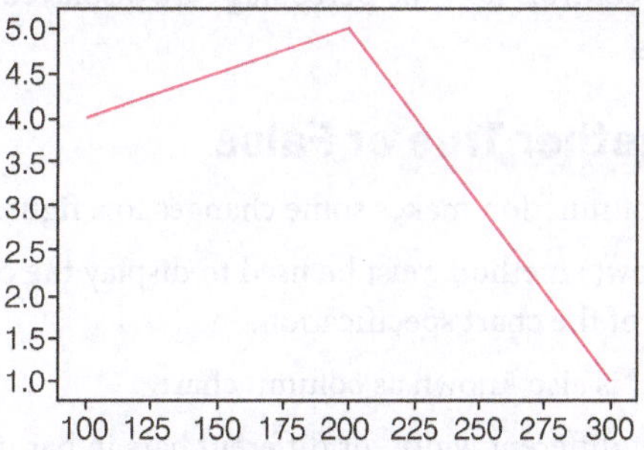

(a)
```
import matplotlib.pyplot as plt
plt.plot([1,2],[4,5])
plt.show()
```
(b)
```
import matplotlib.pyplot as plt
plt.plot([1,2,3],[4,5,1])
plt.show()
```
(c)
```
import matplotlib.pyplot as plt
plt.plot([2,3],[5,1])
plt.show()
```

(d)
```
import matplotlib.pyplot as plt
plt.plot([1,3],[4,1])
plt.show()
```

26. **Which graph should be used where each column represents a range of values and the height of a column corresponds to how many values are in that range?** CBSE SQP 2021-22 Term-I

(a) plot (b) line
(c) bar (d) histogram

Fill in the Blanks

27. ______ are used to discover unknown facts and trends.

28. In Python, ______ library's Pyplot is used for data visualization.

29. The ______ library provides the interface and functionality for plotting the graphs.

30. The pyplot module provides the ______ function which is frequently use to plot graph.

31. A ______ chart displays information as a markers connected by a straight lines.

32. Pyplot's ______ function is used to create a vertical bar charts.

33. The bars in bar chart can be plotted ______ or ______.

34. A/An ______ is an accurate graphical representation of the distribution of numerical data.

35. Histograms are type of chart for numeric data that group the data into ______.

36. ______ attribute in legend() can be a string specifying the legend location.

37. ______ controls how the percentage are displayed on the wedges.

State whether True or False

38. Each pyplot function makes some changes to a figure.

39. The plt.show() method must be used to display the chart in the end of the chart specification.

40. A bar chart is also known as column chart.

41. You can set different width for different bars in bar chart.

42. To create a horizontal bar chart, bar() function is used.

43. A bar chart can only display one series of data.

44. grid( ) method of axes class adds a legend to the plot figure.

45. A frequency polygon is a graphical form of representation of data.

Assertion and Reason Based Questions

Assertion and Reason based questions. Mark the correct choice as:

(a) Both A and R are true and R is the correct explanation for A
(b) Both A and R are true and R is not the correct explanation for A
(c) A is True but R is False
(d) A is false but R is True

46. Assertion (A) Data visualization refers to the graphical representation of information and data using visual elements like charts, graphs and maps etc.

Reason (R) To install matplotlib library we can use the command pip install matplotlib.

46. Assertion (A) Matplotlib library was introduced by John Hunter in the year 2003.

Reason (R) Matplotlib.submodule is a collection of functions that make Matplotlib work like MATLAB.

48. Assertion (A) We import matplotlib to create charts in Python.

Reason (R) In matplotlib there is pyplot which is used to create 2d charts.

49. Assertion (A) Line graph is a tool for comparison and is created by plotting a series of several points and connecting them with a straight line.

Reason (R) You should never use a line chart when the chart is in a continuous data set. CBSE 2021-22 Term I

50. Assertion (A) Bar charts can be two dimensional and 3 dimensional.

Reason (R) Bar charts are used to show individual figures at a specific time or to compare different items.

51. Assertion (A) To plot a bar graph in Matplotlib, the plt.plot() function should be used.

Reason (R) The plt.bar() function is specifically designed for creating bar graphs.

52. Assertion (A) The plt.hist() function in Matplotlib is used to create a histogram.

Reason (R) The plt.hist() function requires a sequence of data values and a number of bins to divide the data into.

53. Assertion (A) Matplotlib.pyplot.hist() function is used to compute and create histogram of x.

Reason (R) X.axis is about frequency where Y-axis is about bin ranges.

54. Assertion (A) Histograms are used to describe distributions.

Reason (R) To specify the intervals in X-axis, the property used is "interval".

Answers

1. (d) No library needs to be imported to create charts in Python language.
2. (b) Upgrading pip to the latest version
3. (b) matplotlib
4. (a) import matplotlib.pyplot as plt
5. (b) hist() 6. (c) histh() 7. (b) barh()
8. (a) 1 9. (d) plt.title() 10. (a) show()
11. (b) color() 12. (a) savefig() 13. (d) savefig()
14. (d)line 15. (a) line chart 16. (c) Line plot
17. (c) Bar 18. (b) Bar 19. (b) width
20. (c) Statement A is correct but statement B is incorrect.
21. (c) Statement A is correct, but Statement B is incorrect.
22. (d)plt.plot(x,y,marker=*, markersize = 10, color = red)
23. (c) plt.hist(x, bins=10, histype="step")
24. (d) All of these
25. (b)

```
import matplotlib.pyplot as plt
plt.plot([1,2,3],[4,5,1])
plt.show()
```

26. (d) histogram 27. Data visualizations
28. matplotlib 29. matplotlib 30. plot()
31. line 32. bar()
33. vertically, horizontally
34. histogram 35. bins 36. loc
37. autopct 38. True 39. True
40. True 41. True 42. False
43. False 44. False 45. True
46. (b) Both A and R are true and R is not the correct explanation for A
47. (b) Both A and R are true and R is not the correct explanation for A
48. (a) Both A and R are true and R is the correct explanation for A
49. (c) A is True but R is False
50. (b) Both A and R are true and R is not the correct explanation for A
51. (d) A is false but R is True
52. (a) Both A and R are true and R is the correct explanation for A
53. (c) A is True but R is False
54. (b) Both A and R are true and R is not the correct explanation for A

Subjective Type Questions

Very Short Answer Type Questions

1. Which statement is used to import library?

Ans. import matplotlib.pyplot as plt

2. What is marker?

Ans. The data points being plotted on a graph/chart are called markers.

3. Write the symbol for following markers:

(i) tri_right marker

(ii) vline marker

Ans. (i) '4' (ii) '|'

4. Write the syntax for grid.

Ans. <matplotlib.pyplot>.grid (b = None, which major, axis both)

5. Which function is used to set the y-limits of the current axis?

Ans. ylim()

6. What is the purpose of the plt.xlabel() and plt.ylabel() functions in Matplotlib?

Ans. The plt.xlabel() and plt.ylabel() functions are used to set the labels of the x-axis and y-axis, respectively, in a Matplotlib plot. They take a string argument that specifies the label text for each axis.

7. How can you add a title to a Matplotlib plot, and which function is used to set it?

Ans. You can add a title to a Matplotlib plot using the plt.title() function. This function takes a string as an argument, which specifies the title of the plot.

8. What are ticks?

Ans. Ticks are the markers denoting data points on axes.

9. Give the syntax to save the figure.

Ans. <matplotlib.pyplot>.savefig (filename and path)

10. How can you change the line style and color in a Matplotlib plot? Provide an example of how to plot a dashed red line.

Ans. Line style and color in Matplotlib can be changed using the linestyle and color parameters in the plot() function. For example, to plot a dashed red line, you can use:

```
plt.plot(x, y, linestyle='--', color='red')
```

11. What do you mean by line chart?

Ans. Line chart can be 2 or 3-dimensional. Line charts are used to compare trends over time.

12. What is the use of multiple bar plot?

Ans. Multiple bar plots are used when comparison among the data sets is to be done when one variable is changing.

13. What is the utility of pie chart?

Ans. Pie chart illustrates the proportion of each category within a whole, making it useful for showing percentage distributions.

14. What is Scatter chart? How is it different from line chart?

Ans. Displays points representing values for two different variables. Each point's position is determined by its x and y values. A scatter chart shows individual data points without connecting them, while a line chart connects data points with lines, showing trends over time.

15. What is the default value of loc in legend?

Ans. Default value of loc is best (upper left)

Short Answer Type I Questions

16. What is Python's support for Data Visualisation?

Ans. Python offers extensive support for data visualization through various libraries like Matplotlib, Seaborn, Plotly, and others. These libraries provide tools to create a wide range of charts and plots, making it easier to understand and analyze data.

17. Which library is used for plotting in python language ?

Ans. The most commonly used library for plotting in Python is Matplotlib, which provides tools for creating a wide variety of static, animated, and interactive visualizations. Another popular option is Seaborn, built on Matplotlib, offering enhanced features for statistical plots and attractive designs.

18. What is subplots() function?

Ans. Matplotlib's pyplot API has a convenience function called subplots() which acts as a utility wrapper and helps in creating common layouts of subplots, including the enclosing figure object, in single call.

Syntax `plt.subplots (nrows, ncols)`

18. Mr. Sanjay wants to plot a bar graph for the given set of values of subjects on x-axis and number of students who opted for that subject on y-axis. Competency Based Que.

Complete the code to perform the following operations:

(i) To plot the bar graph in statement 1

(ii) To display the graph in statement 2

```
import matplotlib.pyplot as plt
x = ['Hindi', 'English', 'Science','SST']
y = [10, 20, 30, 40]
...........          #statement 1
............          # statement 2
```

CBSE SQP 2020

Ans. (i) plt.bar (x, y)

(ii) plt.show()

20. Compare bar() and barh() functions.

Ans. Both bar() and barh() are used to plot bar charts. barh() just plots horizontal bar charts.

e.g. **bar('cities','popul')** #cities in the horizontal axis and bars grows upwards

barh('cities','popul') #cities in vertical axis and bars grow toward the right.

21. What do you understand by x limit and ylimit ? How are these linked to data being plotted?

Ans. xlimit and ylimit are used to set limit on the x & y axis range on which the data being plotted is shown. xlim() & ylim() functions are used for this.e.g. plt.xlim(-2.0,4.0)

The data on the chart will now be plotted only for the range from -2 to 4.

22. Name the function you will use to create a (i) Line chart (ii) Bar chart (iii) Scatter chart

Ans. The functions to create specific charts using Matplotlib are:

1. **Line chart** plt.plot() 2. **Bar chart** plt.bar()
3. **Scatter chart** plt.scatter()

23. Mr. Harry wants to draw a line chart using a list of elements named LIST. Complete the code to perform the following operations:

(i) To plot a line chart using the given LIST.

(ii) To give a y-axis label to the line chart named Sample Number.

```
import matplotlib.pyplot as PLINE
LIST= [10, 20, 30, 40, 50, 60]
........     # statement 1
........     # statement 2
PLINE.show()
```

CBSE SQP 2020

Ans. (i) PLINE.plot(LIST)

(ii) PLINE.ylabel('Sample Number')

24. Following code is plotting the desired graph but legends are not showing despite giving the legend() of PyPlot. What could be the reason? Suggest a solution for the problem.

```
plt.plot(x,y)
plt.plot(x,z)
plt.legend(loc ="upper left")
```

Ans. The legend might not be showing because no labels were provided for the plotted lines. You need to include label arguments in the plot functions to identify each line. The correct code:

```
plt.plot(x, y, label='Line 1')
plt.plot(x, z, label='Line 2')
plt.legend(loc='upper left')
```

Short Answer Type II Questions

25. When should you use (i) a line chart (ii) a bar chart (iii)a pie chart?

Ans. (i) line chart : Line charts should be used when we need to connect all the data points and see patterns.

(ii) bar chart: Bar charts should be used when we need to visualize categorical data. It helps to see trends.

(iii) Pie chart: A pie chart shows how some total amount is divided among distinct categories as a circle (the namesake pie) divided into radial slices. Each category is associated with a single slice whose size corresponds with the category's proportion of the total.

26. Write the code to display the following graph.

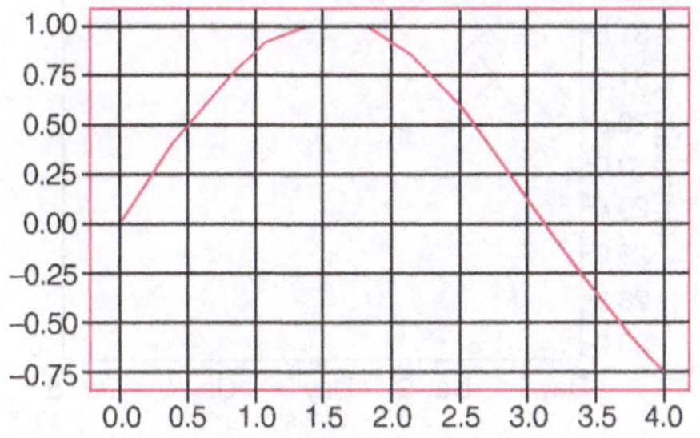

Ans.

```
import matplotlib.pyplot as plt
plt.style.use('seaborn-whitegrid')  # style name
import numpy as np
x = np.linspace(0, 4, 12)
y = np.sin(x)
plt.plot(x, y, 'c')  # the plot line style
plt.grid()
plt.show()         # Added this line to display the plot
```

27. Write the code for the following graph which display the different style multiline in same plot.

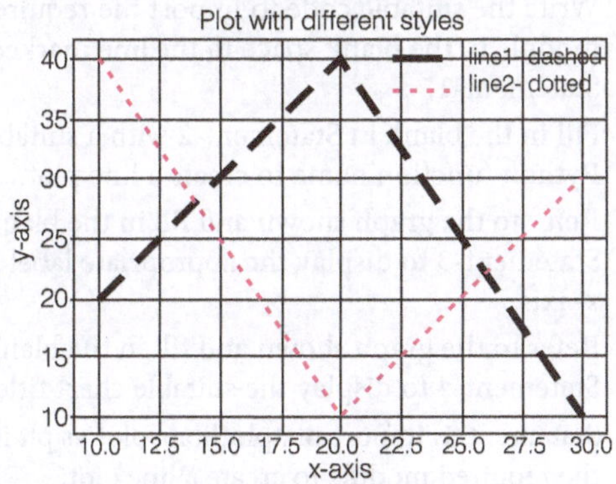

Ans.

```
import matplotlib.pyplot as plt
x1 = [10, 20, 30]
y1 = [20, 40, 10]
x2 = [10, 20, 30]
y2 = [40, 10, 30]
plt.xlabel('x - axis')
plt.ylabel('y - axis')
plt.plot(x1, y1, color='black', linewidth=5,
         label='line1-dashed', linestyle='dashed')
plt.plot(x2, y2, color='magenta', linewidth=3,
         label='line2-dotted', linestyle='dotted')
plt.title('Plot with different styles')
plt.legend()
plt.grid()
plt.show()
```

28. Write a Python program to plot the below given line chart with suitable label in the x-axis, y-axis and a title. Also give suitable python statement to save this chart.

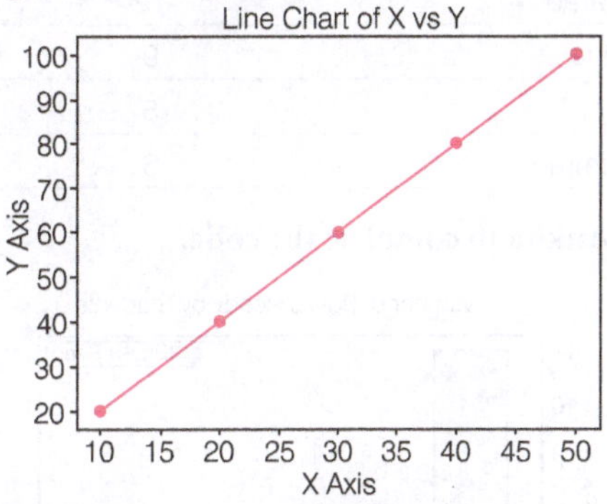

Ans.

```
import matplotlib.pyplot as plt
x_axis = [10, 20, 30, 40, 50]
y_axis = [20, 40, 60, 80, 100]
      # Plotting the line chart
plt.plot(x_axis, y_axis, marker='o')
      # Adding labels and title
plt.xlabel('X Axis')
plt.ylabel('Y Axis')
plt.title('Line Chart of X vs Y')
      # Save the chart as an image file
plt.savefig('line_chart.png')
      # Display the chart
plt.show()
```

29. Write a code to plot a bar chart to depict the pass percentage of students in CBSE exams for the years 2015 to 2018 as shown below.

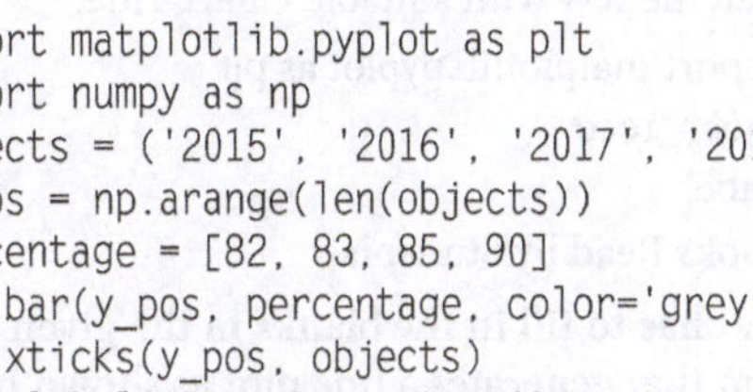

Ans.

```
import matplotlib.pyplot as plt
import numpy as np
objects = ('2015', '2016', '2017', '2018')
y_pos = np.arange(len(objects))
percentage = [82, 83, 85, 90]
plt.bar(y_pos, percentage, color='grey')
plt.xticks(y_pos, objects)
plt.ylabel('Pass Percentage')
plt.xlabel('Years')
plt.show()
```

30. **During a practical exam, a student Ankita has to fill in the blanks in a Python program that generates a bar chart. This bar chart represents the number of books read by four students in one month.** **CBSE SQP 2024-25, Competency Based Que.**

Student Name	Books Read
Karan	12
Lina	9
Raj	5
Simran	3

Help Ankita to complete the code.

```
import _____ as plt #Statement-1
students = ['Karan', 'Lina', 'Raj', 'Simran']
books_read = [12, 9, 5, 3]
plt.bar( students, _____, label='Books Read')
#Statement-2
plt.xlabel('Student Name')
plt._____('Books Read') #Statement-3
plt.legend()
plt.title('_____') #Statement-4
plt.show()
```

I. Write the suitable code for the import statement in the blank space in the line marked as Statement-1.

II. Refer to the graph shown above and fill in the blank in Statement-2 with suitable Python code.

III. Fill in the blank in Statement-3 with the name of the function to set the label on the y-axis.

IV. Refer the graph shown above and fill the blank in Statement-4 with suitable Chart Title.

Ans. I. import matplotlib.pyplot as plt

II. books_read

III. ylabel

IV. Books Read by Students

31. **Gurkirat has to fill in the blanks in the given Python program that generates a line plot as shown below. The given line plot represents the temperature (in degree Celcius) over five days as given in the table**

Days	Temperature
Day 1	30
Day 2	32
Day 3	31
Day 4	29
Day 5	28

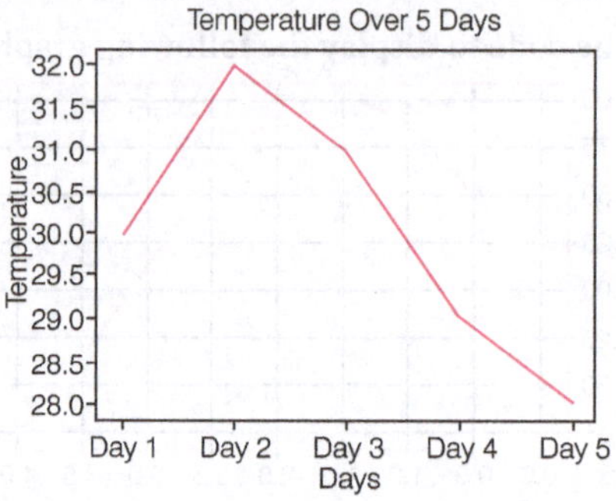


```
import_____ as plt # Statement-1
days = ['Day 1', 'Day 2', 'Day 3', 'Day 4', 'Day 5']
temp = [30, 32, 31, 29, 28]
plt. ____ (days, temp) # Statement-2
plt.xlabel ('____') # Statement-3
plt.ylabel ('Temperature')
plt.title ('____') # Statement-4
plt.show()
```

Write the missing statements according to the given specifications:

(i) Write the suitable code to import the required module in the blank space in the line marked as Statement-1.

(ii) Fill in the blank in Statement-2 with a suitable Python function name to create a line plot.

(ii) Refer to the graph shown and fill in the blank in Statement-3 to display the appropriate label for x-axis.

(iv) Refer to the graph shown and fill in the blank in Statement-4 to display the suitable chart title.

Ans. (i) Statement-1: import matplotlib.pyplot as plt imports the required module to create a line plot.

(ii) Statement-2: plt.plot(days, temp) is used to generate a line plot.

(iii) Statement-3: plt.xlabel('Days') labels the x-axis as "Days" based on the given graph.

(iv) Statement-4: plt.title('Temperature Over Five Days') gives an appropriate title to the chart.

32. **Consider the following graph. Write the Python code to plot it. Also add the Title, label for X and Y-axes. Use the following data for plotting the graph.** **CBSE 2023**

```
smarks=[10,40,30,60,55]
```

```
sname=["Sahil", "Deepak", "Anil", "Ravi","Riti"]
```

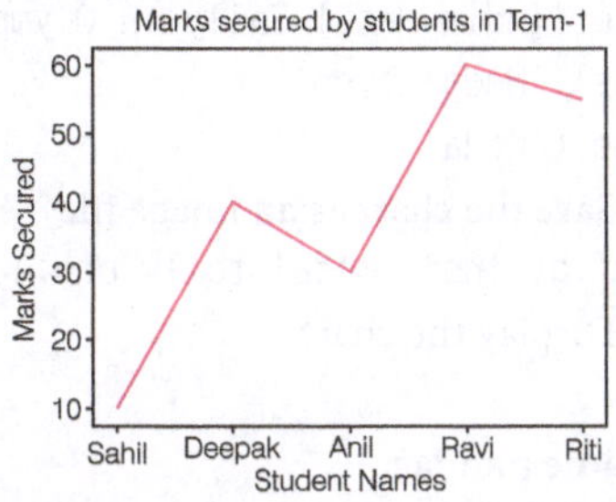

Ans.
```
import matplotlib.pyplot as plt
    # Data
smarks = [10, 40, 30, 60, 55]
sname = ["Sahil", "Deepak","Anil", "Ravi", "Riti"]
    # Plotting the plot chart
plt.plot(sname, smarks)
    # Adding title and labels
plt.title('Marks secured by students in Term-1')
plt.xlabel('Student Names')
plt.ylabel('Marks Secured')
    # Display the plot
plt.show()
```

33. Write a Python program to plot a line chart based on the given data to depict the changing weekly average temperature in Delhi for four weeks. **CBSE SQP 2022-23**

```
Week=[1,2,3,4]
Avg_week_temp=[40,42,38,44]
```

Ans.
```
import pandas as pd
import matplotlib.pyplot as plt
    # Data
data = {'Week': [1, 2, 3, 4],
 'Average Temperature (°C)': [40, 42, 41, 43]}
    # Create DataFrame
df = pd.DataFrame(data)
    # Create a line plot
plt.figure(figsize=(8, 5))
plt.plot(df['Week'], df['Average Temperature
(°C)'], marker='o', linestyle='-', color='b')
    # Add titles and labels
plt.title('Weekly Average Temperature in Delhi')
plt.xlabel('Week')
plt.ylabel('Average Temperature (°C)')
    # Display grid lines for better readability
plt.grid(True)
    # Show the plot
plt.show()
```

Long Answer Type Questions

34. A bar graph is used to show individual figures at a specific time or to compare different items. Similarly, a bar graph which is showing the marks of different subjects. You have to write the code that will represent the given graph.

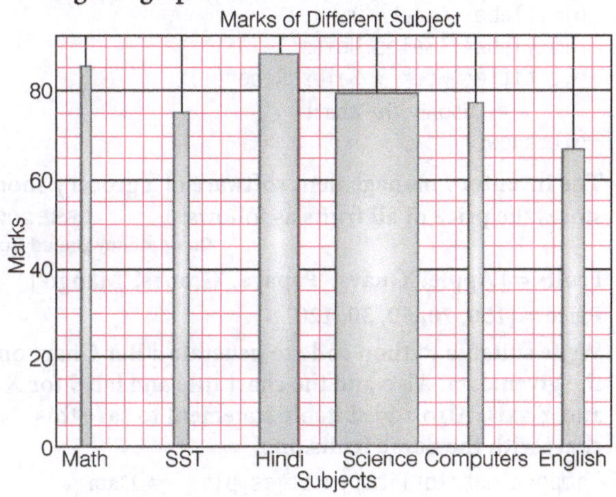

Ans.
```
import matplotlib.pyplot as plt
    # Data
x = ['Math', 'SST', 'Hindi', 'Science',
'Computers', 'English']
marks = [85, 75, 88, 80, 77, 67]
    # Position of bars
x_pos = [i for i, _ in enumerate(x)]
    # Plotting the bar chart
plt.xlabel('Subjects')
plt.ylabel('Marks')
plt.title('Marks of Different Subjects')
plt.xticks(x_pos, x)
    # Bar chart
width = [0.1, 0.2, 0.5, 1.1, 0.2, 0.3]
plt.bar(x_pos, marks, width=[w * 0.8 for w in
width], align='center')
    # Grid settings
plt.minorticks_on()
plt.grid(which='major', linestyle='-',
linewidth=0.5, color='black')
plt.grid(which='minor', linestyle=':',
linewidth=0.5, color='magenta')
    # Show plot
plt.show()
```

35. You are given the following data for a month's sales of a product:

Week 1: 150 units

Week 2: 200 units

Week 3: 180 units

Week 4: 220 units

Write a Python program using Matplotlib to create a bar chart that shows the sales units for each week.

Ans.
```
import matplotlib.pyplot as plt
weeks = ['Week 1', 'Week 2', 'Week 3', 'Week 4']
sales = [150, 200, 180, 220]
    # Creating the bar chart
```

```
plt.bar(weeks, sales)
        # Adding labels and title
plt.xlabel('Weeks')
plt.ylabel('Sales Units')
plt.title('Weekly Sales Report')
        # Display the chart
plt.show()
```

36. The inventory management software of a grocery shop stores the price of all fruits as follows: CBSE 2024 Competency Based Que.

Fruits = ['Apple', 'Guava', 'Papaya', 'Grapes', 'Mango']
Price = [150, 70, 50, 30, 120]
Write suitable Python code to generate a Bar Chart on the given data. Also add the chart title and label for X and Y axis. Also add suitable statement to save this chart with the name fruits.png.

Ans.

```
import matplotlib.pyplot as plt    # Data
fruits = ['Apple', 'Guava', 'Papaya', 'Grapes',
                                        'Mango']
price = [150, 70, 50, 30, 120]
        # Create a bar chart
plt.bar(fruits, price, color='skyblue')
plt.title('Fruit Prices')    # Add title and labels
plt.xlabel('Fruits')
plt.ylabel('Price (in INR)')
plt.savefig('fruits.png')
                # Save the chart as 'fruits.png'
plt.show()        # Display the chart
```

37. Write Python code to plot a bar chart for India's medal tally as shown below: SQP 2023-24

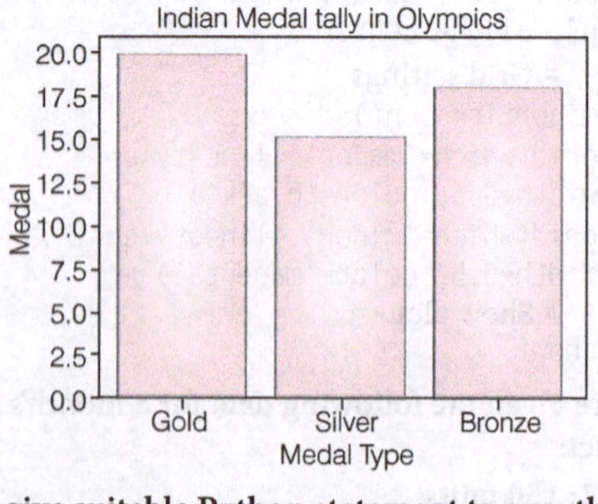

Also give suitable Python statement to save this chart.

Ans.

```
import matplotlib.pyplot as plt
        # Data for the bar chart
medal_types = ['Gold', 'Silver', 'Bronze']
medal_counts = [ 20.0, 15.5,18.0 ]
        # Medal counts for each type
        # Create the bar chart
plt.figure(figsize=(8, 6))
plt.bar(medal_types, medal_counts)
        # Add title and labels
plt.title('India Metal Tally in Olympics')
plt.xlabel('Medal Type')
plt.ylabel('Medal')
        # Save the chart as an image file
plt.savefig('india_medal_tally.png')
        # Display the chart
plt.show()
```

38. A Data Frame pandas:

	1990	2000	2010
1.	54	345	895
2.	64	485	562
3.	79	690	1100
4.	96	770	890

Write Code to Create:-

(a) A scatter chart from 1990 and 2010 of data framepd.

(b) A line chart from the 1990 and 2000 of data framepd.

(c) A bar chart to plotting the three columns of data framepd.

Ans. (a)

```
import matplotlib.pyplot as pl
import pandas as pd
data = {'1990':[54,64,79,96],
        '2000':[345,485,690,770],'2010':
                        [895,562,1100,890]}
d = pd.DataFrame(data,columns=
                {'1990','2000','2010'})
pl.scatter(d['1990'],d['2010'])
pl.show()
```

(b)

```
import matplotlib.pyplot as  pl
import pandas as pd
data = {'1990':[54,64,79,96],
        '2000':[345,485,690,770],'2010':
                        [895,562,1100,890]}
d = pd.DataFrame(data,columns=
                {'1990','2000','2010'})
pl.plot(d['1990'],d['2000'])
pl.show()
```

(c)

```
import matplotlib.pyplot as pl
import pandas as pd
data = {'1990':[54,64,79,96],
        '2000':[345,485,690,770],'2010':
                        [895,562,1100,890]}
d = pd.DataFrame(data,columns=
                {'1990','2000','2010'})
pl.bar(d['1990'],d['2000'],d['2010'])
pl.show()
```

39. **Write the code for the following bar graph.**

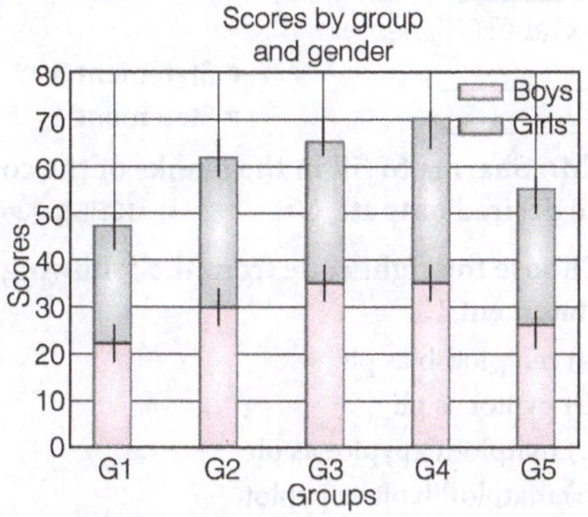

Ans.

```
import numpy as np
import matplotlib.pyplot as plt
N = 5
boys = (22, 30, 35, 35, 26)
girls = (25, 32, 30, 35, 29)
boyStd = (4, 3, 4, 1, 5)
girlStd = (3, 5, 2, 3, 3)
ind = np.arange(N)
width = 0.35
p1 = plt.bar(ind, boys, width, yerr=boyStd,
color='blue')
p2 = plt.bar(ind, girls, width, bottom=boys,
yerr=girlStd, color='green')
plt.ylabel('Scores')
plt.xlabel('Groups')
plt.title('Scores by group\n and gender')
plt.xticks(ind, ('G1', 'G2', 'G3', 'G4', 'G5'))
plt.yticks(np.arange(0, 81, 10))
plt.legend((p1[0], p2[0]), ('Boys', 'Girls'))
plt.show()
```

Case Study Based Questions

Case Study 1

Consider the following program and answer the any four questions from (i) to (v):

```
import ________ as plt                        # line 1
plt.bar([2, 3, 4, 8, 1], [2, 4, 7, 3, 5], label=
________)                                     # line 2
plt.legend()
plt.xlabel(________)                          # line 3
plt.ylabel('Height')
plt.________('Vertical Bar Chart')
plt.show()
```

(i) Which module will be imported in Line 1 for given program?

(a) matplot (b) matplotlib.pyplot

(c) plotlib (d) None of these

(ii) Name the label that can be used to represent the bar chart in Line 2.

(a) Data (b) Data value

(c) Depend on user (d) All of these

(iii) Which message is best suited for xlabel?

(a) X values (b) Y values

(c) legend (d) vertical

(iv) Which function is used to show the title of bar chart?

(a) tit ( ) (b) title

(c) title ( ) (d) All of these

(v) Choose the statement to display the bar chart.

(a) plt.print()

(b) plt.show()

(c) plt.display()

(d) plot.show()

Ans. (i) (b) matplotlib.pyplot

(ii) (d) All of these

(iii) (a) X values

(iv) (c) title ( )

(v) (b) plt.show()

Case Study 2

Consider the following program and answer any four questions from (i) to (v):

```
from matplotlib import ______ as plt       # Line 1
import numpy as np                          # Line 2
fig, ax = plt.________ (1, 1)               # Line 3
a = np.array([26, 59, 44, 39, 76, 16, 23,
              11, 18, 78])                  # Line 4
ax.hist(a, bins=[0, 10, 20, 30, 40])        # Line 5
ax.__________ ('Histogram')                 # Line 6
ax.set_xticks([0, 10, 20, 30, 40])          # Line 7
ax.set_xlabel('Percentage')                 # Line 8
ax.________ ('Students')                    # Line 9
plt.______                                  # Line 10
```

(i) Choose the correct option to import for given program.

(a) matplotlib (b) matplot
(c) pyplot (d) plot

(ii) Fill the blank in Line 3.

(a) subplots (b) subplot
(c) plot (d) subplt

(iii) Which statement is used to set title in Line 6?

(a) title (b) set_title
(c) set (d) tit

(iv) How to set the Y-axis label?

(a) label( ) (b) set_y
(c) set_ylab( ) (d) set_ylabel

(v) Fill the blank in Line 10 to show the histogram.

(a) plt.show() (b) plot_show()
(c) show() (d) plt.show

Ans. (i) (c) pyplot
(ii) (a) subplots
(iii) (b) set_title
(iv) (d) set_ylabel
(v) (c) show()

Case Study 3

Mr. Sharma is working in a game development industry and he was comparing the given chart on the basis of the rating of the various games available on the play store. He is trying to write a code to plot the graph.

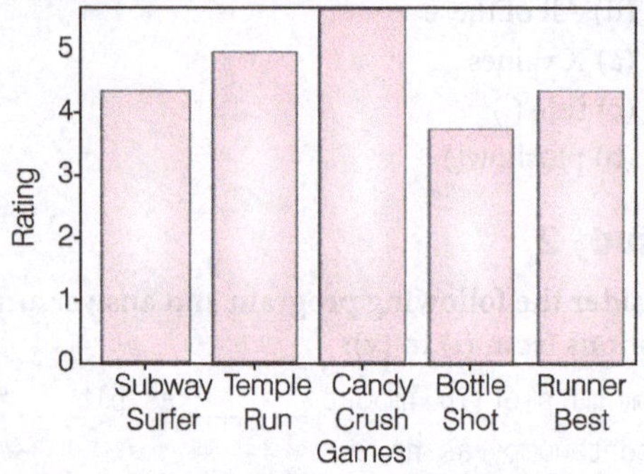


```
import _______                          # Statement 1
Games = ['Subway Surfer', 'Temple Run', 'Candy
Crush', 'Bottle Shot', 'Runner Best']
Rating = [4.2, 4.8, 5.0, 3.8, 4.1]
plt._______(Games, Rating)  # Statement 2
plt.xlabel('Games')
plt._______                 # Statement 3
plt._______                 # Statement 4
```

Help Mr. Sharma to fill in the blanks of the code and get the desired output. **[CBSE Question Bank]**

(i) Choose the right code from the following for Statement 1.

(a) matplotlib as plt
(b) pyplot as plt
(c) matplotlib.pyplot as plt
(d) matplotlib.plt as pyplot

(ii) Identify the name of the function that should be used in Statement 2 to plot the above graph.

(a) line() (b) bar()
(c) hist() (d) barh()

(iii) Choose the correct option for the Statement 3.

(a) title(Rating) (b) ytitle(Rating)
(c) ylabel(Rating) (d) yaxis(Rating)

(iv) Choose the right function/method from the following for the Statement 4.

(a) display() (b) print()
(c) bar() (d) show()

(v) In case Mr. Sharma wants to change the above plot to the any other shape, which statement should he change?

(a) Statement 1 (b) Statement 2
(c) Statement 3 (d) Statement 4

Ans. (i) (c) The pyplot module in matplotlib carries the functions related to charts. Hence, it has to be imported.

(ii) (b) The chart is a bar chart ,hence the bar () function is to be used to plot the chart.

(iii) (c) As seen from the plot the y-axis has a label "Rating". In charts the y-axis label is given using the ylabel() function.

(iv) (d) A chart needs to be shown using the show() function after plotting it.

(v) (b) Since Statement 2 is plotting the chart , it has to be changed to change the type of chart.

SELF ASSESSMENT TEST

Multiple Choice Questions

1 Matplotlib was introduced by John Hunter in year
(a) 2003 (b) 2004
(c) 2005 (d) 2006

2 You can use .... method to create a plot of points on the graphs.
(a) show() (b) plot()
(c) bar() (d) pie()

3 Which marker is used Tri-up marker?
(a) . (b) ,
(c) ^ (d) <

Fill in the Blanks

4 The required positional arguments supplied to .... are two lists or arrays.

5 The .... can be plotted vertically or horizontally.

6 The data for the .... is in the form of list of lists or list of arrays or tuple of arrays.

State whether True or False

7 matplotlib. pyplot. hist ( ) function is used to compute and create histogram of *x*.

8 Ticks are the markers denoting data points on axes.

9 title() function is used to add the title to a chart.

10 Matplot library's Pyplot is used for data visualisation.

Assertion and Reason Based Questions

Assertion and Reason based questions. Mark the correct choice as:

(a) Both A and R are true and R is the correct explanation for A
(b) Both A and R are true and R is not the correct explanation for A
(c) A is True but R is False
(d) A is False but R is True

11 **Assertion (A)** A line plot is a graph that shows bends or relationship between variables, typically by connecting data points with a line.

Reason (R) The legend is displayed by default associating the colours with the plotted data.

12 **Assertion (A)** A legend is an area describing the elements of the graph.

Reason (R) In the matplotlib library, there's a function called leg() which is used to Place a legend on the axes.

Very Short Answer Type Questions

13 Write the symbol for following markers:
(i) Tri_left marker
(ii) Hline marker

14 Which function is used to set the x-limits of the current axis?

15 Give the code for the following location strings:
(i) upper left
(ii) upper center

Short Answer Type Questions

16 Differentiate between histogram chart and bar graph.

17 Write the code for the following graph:

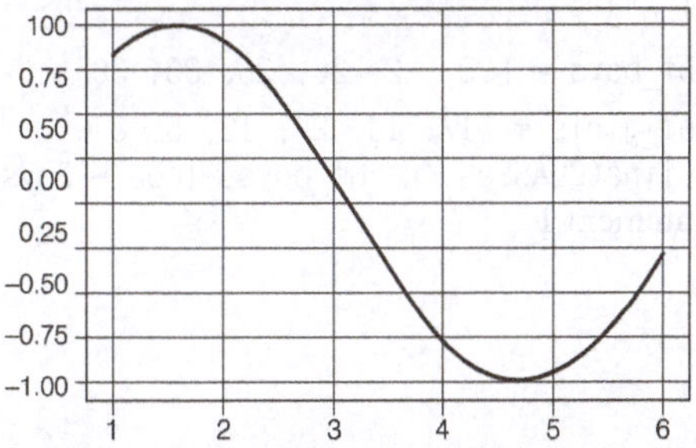

18 Write a code to plot a bar chart to depict the pass percentage of students in ISC exams for the months January to April as show below:

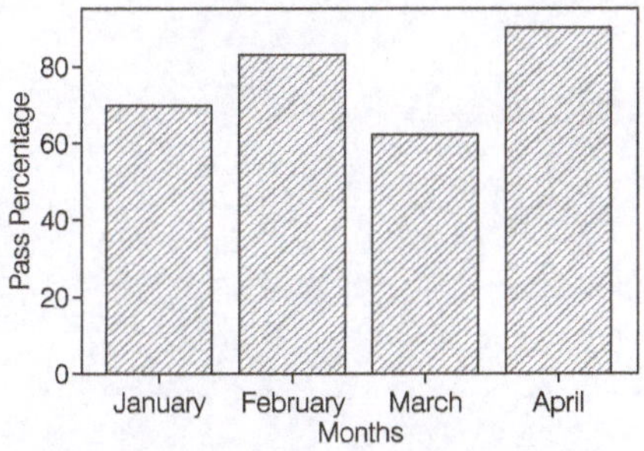

Long Answer Type Questions

19 How to set the ticks for axes? Explain.

20 Define the adding legends with labels in detail.

21 Define the following terms:
(i) xlabel()

(ii) subplots()
(iii) legend()

Case Study Based Questions

22. Mrs. Ankita is a coordinator in the senior section school. She represented data on number of students who passed the exam on line chart as follows:

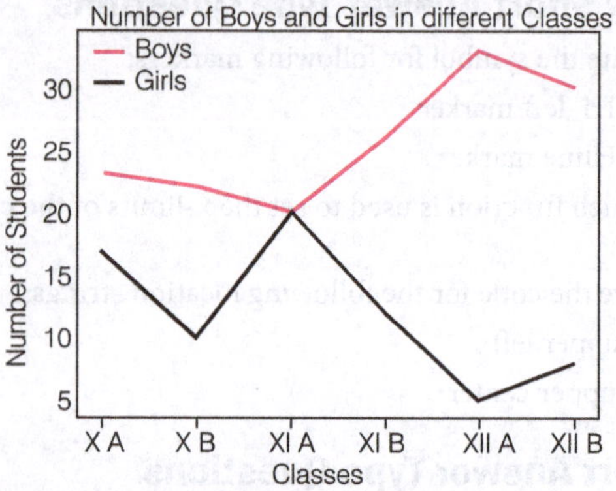


```
import matplotlib.pyplot as plt
CLASSes = ["X A", "X B", "XI A", "XI B", "XII A",
"XII B"]
no_of_boys = [23, 22, 20, 26, 33, 30]
no_of_girls = [17, 10, 20, 12, 5, 8]
plt.line(CLASSes, no_of_boys, label='Boys')
# Statement 1
plt.line(CLASSes, no_of_girls, label='Girls')
# Statement 2
plt.ylabel("Classes")
# Statement 3
plt.xlabel("Number of Students")
# Statement 4
plt.title("Number of Boys and Girls in Different
Classes")
plt.legend()
plt.show()
```

(i) What will be the correct code for Statement 1 and Statement 2?

(ii) What is the correct function name for Statement 3 and Statement 4?

(iii) Write a method and parameter required to display legends?

(iv) Name the parameter and values used to apply the marker as given in the output.

(v) Name the parameter and values used to apply linestyle as given in the output.

Answers

1. (a)	2. (b)	3. (c)	4. plt.plot()
5. bar graph		6. Scatter plot	7. True
8. False	9. True	10. True	11. (c) 12. (c)

03

CHAPTER

RDBMS store data in the form of related tables. RDBMS are powerful because they require few assumptions about how data is related or how it will be extracted from the database.

Revision Tour of RDBMS

▼ **YOUR STUDY GOALS**

▼ **YOUR PRACTICE GOAL**

- Objective Type Questions (59 Qs ; MCQs, True or False, Fill in the Blanks, Assertion and Reason)
- Subjective Type Questions (56 Qs ; VSA, SA, LA)
- Case Study Based Questions (Objective Case Study-1, Subjective Case Study-1)

In Class XI, we understood database concepts and learned how to create databases using MySQL. We also learned how to manipulate and retrieve data from a database using SQL queries.

In this chapter, we will revise all those topics related to MySQL databases and practice some questions.

3.1 Database Concepts

A database is an organised collection of data that can be easily accessed, managed, updated and operations such as adding, updating and deleting can be performed on it.

The contents of a database are obtained by combining the data from all different sources in an organisation.

A database has the following properties

- It is a collection of data elements representing real-world information.
- It is logical, coherent and internally consistent.

e.g. consider the names, telephone numbers and addresses of the relatives. You may have recorded this data in an indexed address book or you may have stored it on a hard drive, using application software such as Microsoft Access or Excel. This collection of related data with an implicit meaning is known as a DATABASE.

Database Management System (DBMS)

A Database Management System is a software system that enables users to define, create, and maintain the database and provides controlled access for it.The primary goal of a DBMS is to provide a way to store and retrieve database information that is both convenient and efficient. Using DBMS, data in a database can be added, deleted, changed, sorted or searched.

Application program accesses the data stored in the database by sending request to the DBMS.

e.g. MySQL, INGRES, MS-ACCESS etc.

The purpose of a Database Management System is to bridge the gap between information and data. The data stored in memory or on disk must be converted to usable information.

The basic processes that are supported by a DBMS are

- Specification of data types, structures and constraints to be considered in an application.
- Storing the data itself into persistent storage.
- Manipulation of the database.
- Querying the database to retrieve desired information.
- Updating the content of the database.

Advantages of DBMS

- Reduced data redundancy
- Elimination of inconsistency
- Data sharing
- Data integrity
- Data security
- Backup and recovery

Limitations of DBMS

- High cost
- Database failure
- Data quality
- Confidentiality, privacy and security

3.2 Relational Data Model

In a relational data model, data is stored in different tables related to each other. These tables are called **relations**. These tables communicate and show information which facilitates data search ability, organisation and reporting.

Various terms related to relational model are as follows

Relation

A relation is a table with columns and rows, which represent the data items and relationships among them.

Relations have three important properties as

(i) **Name** The first property of a relation is its name, which is represented by the title or the entity identifier.

(ii) **Cardinality** The second property of a relation is its cardinality, which refers to the number of tuples (rows) in a relation.

(iii) **Degree** The third property of a relation is its degree, which refers to the number of attributes (columns) in a table.

Domain

A domain is a collection of all possible values from which the values for a given column or an attribute is drawn. A domain is said to be atomic if elements are considered to be indivisible units.

Tuples

The rows in a relation are also known as tuples. Each row or tuple has a set of permitted values for each attribute.

Attributes

The heading columns of a table are known as attributes. Each attribute of a table has a distinct name.

Relational Database Management System (RDBMS)

- A Relational Database Management System is a Database Management System (DBMS) that uses relational data model. It is developed by Dr. E.F. Codd, of IBM's San Jose Research Laboratory.
- RDBMS store data in the form of related tables. RDBMS are powerful because they require few assumptions about how data is related or how it will be extracted from the database.
- An important feature of relational system is that a single database can be spread across several tables. Today, popular commercial for large databases include Oracle, Microsoft SQL Server, Sybase, etc.

Keys

Key is defined as the column or set of columns in a table that is used to identify either row of data in a table or establish relationship with another table.

If a table has Id, Name and Address as the column names then each one is known as the key for that table. The keys are also used to uniquely identify each record in the database table.

A key is also used to arrange the records either in ascending or descending order. It also controls and maintains the integrity of information store in the database.

e.g. CourseId column of Student table work as a foreign key for Student table, as well as a primary key for Course table (referenced table).

Candidate Keys | Alternate Keys | Foreign Key | Primary Key

StudentId	FirstName	LastName	CourseId
L0002345	Jim	Black	C002
L0001254	James	Harradine	A004
L0002349	Amanda	Holland	C002
L0001198	Simon	McCloud	S042
L0023487	Peter	Murray	P301
L0018453	Anne	Norris	S042

Primary Key

Student table

CourseId	CourseName
A004	Accounts
C002	Computing
P301	History
S042	Short Course

Course table

There are various types of keys, which are as follows:

Primary Key

The primary key of a relational table uniquely identifies each record in the table. In some tables, combination of more than one attributes is declared as primary key.

In that case, primary key is also known as composite key and the value of primary key must be unique and it cannot accept NULL value. Every relation does have a primary key.

e.g. In the given table Student, column StudentId works as a primary key because it contains Id's, which are unique for each student.

> **Mistake Alert!**
>
> Sometimes Students forgot that primary key do not accept NULL value.

Candidate Key

The set of all attributes which can uniquely identify each tuple of a relation are known as candidate keys. Each table may have one or more candidate keys and one of them will become the primary key.

e.g. In the given table Student, column StudentId and the combination of column FirstName and LastName work as the candidate keys for the given table.

A candidate key must possess the following properties

- For each row, the value of the key must be uniquely identify that row.
- No attribute in the key can be discarded without destroying the property of unique identification.

Alternate Key

From the set of candidate keys after selecting one of the key as primary key, all other remaining keys are known as alternate keys. These keys are also unique but they allow nulls.

e.g. In the given table Student from the candidate keys (StudentId, FirstName and LastName), StudentId chosen as a primary key then the FirstName and LastName column work as alternate keys.

Foreign Key

A foreign key is a non-key attribute whose value is derived from the primary key of another table. The relationship between two tables is established with the help of foreign key.

A table may have multiple foreign keys and each foreign key can have different referenced table. Foreign keys play an essential role in database design, when tables are broken apart then foreign keys make it possible for them to be reconstructed.

Quick Test 1

1. Define RDBMS. Name any two RDBMS software. **NCERT**
2. Define the term domain with respect to RDBMS. Give one example to support your answer.
3. Define the term primary key in a database. Explain how it is different from a candidate key. **CBSE SQP 2024-25**
4. Give one difference between alternate key and candidate key.
5. In a table in MYSQL database, an attribute A of datatype varchar (20) has the value "Keshav". The attribute B of datatype char (20) has value "Meenakshi". How many characters are occupied by attribute A and attribute B? **CBSE SQP 2023-24**
   (a) 20, 6 (b) 6, 20 (c) 9, 6 (d) 6, 9
6. In MYSQL database, if a table, Alpha has degree 5 and cardinality 3, and another table, Beta has degree 3 and cardinality 5, what will be the degree and cardinality of the Cartesian product of Alpha and Beta? **CBSE SQP 2023-24**
   (a) 5, 3 (b) 8, 15 (c) 3, 5 (d) 15, 8

3.3 MySQL

MySQL is an open source Relational Database Management System (RDBMS) based on SQL (Structured Query Language).

In MySQL database, information is stored in tables and runs virtually on all platforms including Linux, Unix and Windows.

MySQL provides many features such as storing, maintaining and controlling data in a secured environment.

It is a fast, reliable, scalable substitute to many of the commercial RDBMSs available today. MySQL works with many languages like PHP, Perl, C, C++, Java, etc.

Components of MySQL

A database is a structured collection of amount of information. To add, access and process data stored in a computer database, you need a database management system such as MySQL server.

MySQL can be used for variety of applications but it is mostly used for the web applications on the Internet.

MySQL database system consists of the following three components

Server (MySQL Server)

MySQL server is an engine which provides access to databases, responsible for creating, managing database, executing and returning queries and maintaining security together with additional tools to manage multiple MySQL servers.

Client

A client is a program that connects to the database server and issues queries in a pre-specified format. In MySQL, you can enter command-line queries to manage user permissions and utilities to import and export MySQL database.

Client Library

A client library is an Application Programming Interface (API) where a client can write their own programs using a programming language like C, C++, Java, etc.

Basic Elements of MySQL

MySQL, the implementation of SQL has certain elements that play an important role in querying from a database. These certain elements are very helpful for the user even if he/she wants to write the most elementary SQL queries. These basic elements are

(i) Literals

A literal is a constant value written into a query. A literal does not change its value during the execution of a query.

Literals can be divided into multiple groups depending upon the type of data it is representing. These are Numeric literal, Character literal, Boolean literal and String literal.

(ii) NULLs or Null Values

If a column in a table has no value, then the column is said to be a null. NULL values are treated differently from other values.

NULL can appear in columns of any data type provided they are not restricted by NOT NULL or PRIMARY KEY integrity constraints. It is used as a placeholder for unknown or inapplicable values, but NULL and 0 are not equivalent.

(iii) Comments

It is the text that is not executed and is used only for documentation purpose. Comments within SQL statement do not affect the statement execution. Comments can be written in MySQL in following three ways

(a) Double hyphen "_ _" precedes a comment within a single line.

(b) Comment beginning with a "#" symbol. This is a single line comment.

(c) Comment enclosed in /*……………..*/. This is multiline comment.

Data Types

A data type is a data storage format that can contain a specific type or range of values. The fields within a database often require a specific type of data to be input.

e.g. a school's record for a table Student may use a character data type for the students first name and last name. The student's date of admission and date of birth would be stored in a date format, while his or her marks in each subject may be stored as a numeric.

Some mainly used data types in DBMS are as follows

(i) Numeric data type
(ii) Text/string data type
(iii) Date and time data type

(i) Numeric Data Type

It allows the database server to store numbers such as integers and real numbers in a column.
e.g. age of the students, numbers obtained in subjects, etc.

Types	Length in Bytes	Minimum Value (Signed)	Maximum Value (Signed)	Minimum Value (Unsigned)	Maximum Value (Unsigned)
TINYINT	1	-128	127	0	255
SMALLINT	2	-32768	32767	0	65535
MEDIUMINT	3	-8388608	8388607	0	16777215
INT	4	-2147483648	2147483647	0	4294967295
BIGINT	8	-9223372036854775808	9223372036854775807	0	18446744073709551615

FLOAT (N, D) A small number with floating decimal point. It cannot be unsigned. Its size is 4 bytes. Here, N represents the total number of digits (including decimals) and D represents the number of decimals.

DOUBLE (N, D) A large number with floating decimal point. It cannot be unsigned. Its size is 8 bytes.

DECIMAL (N, D) It cannot be unsigned. The maximum number of digits may be specified in the N parameter. The maximum number of digits to the right of the decimal point is specified in the D parameter.

(ii) String/Text Data Type

It allows the database server to store string values such as Name of the Students, Address, etc.

Types	Description	Display Format	Range in Characters
CHAR	Contains non-binary strings. Length is fixed as you declare while creating a table. When stored, they are right-padded with spaces to the specified length.	Trailing spaces are removed	The length can be any value from 0 to 255.
VARCHAR	Contains non-binary strings. Columns are variable length strings.	As stored	A value from 0 to 255 before MySQL 5.0.3.
BLOB or TEXT	BLOB are "Binary Large Objects" and are used to store large amount of binary data.	As stored	0 to 65535 characters.

(iii) Date and Time Data Type

It allows the database server to store a date using the fields YEAR, MONTH and DAY in the format YYYY-MM-DD.

e.g. Date of admission, Date of birth, etc.

Types	Description	Display Format	Range
DATETIME	Use when you need values containing both date and time information.	YYYY-MM-DD HH:MM:SS	'1000-01-01 00:00:00' to '9999-12-31 23:59:59'.
DATE	Use when you need only date information.	YYYY-MM-DD	'1000-01-01' to '9999-12-31'.
TIMESTAMP	Values are converted from the current time zone to UTC (Co-ordinated Universal Time) while storing and converted back from UTC to the current time zone when retrieved.	YYYY-MM-DD HH:MM:SS	'1970-01-01 00:00:01' UTC to '2038-01-19 03:14:07' UTC.

3.4 Structured Query Language (SQL)

Structured Query Language is a computer language, aimed to store, manipulate and query data stored in a relational database. The first incarnation of SQL appeared in 1974, when a group in IBM developed the first prototype of a relational database. The first commercial relational database was released by Relational Software (later becoming Oracle).

SQL Commands

In order to access data from MySQL database, all applications, programmers and users must use SQL. SQL commands are the instructions used to communicate with the database to perform specific task.

SQL commands can be used not only for searching the database but also to perform various other functions like create tables, add data to tables, modify data, drop the table, set permissions for users and many more.

SQL commands can be classified into following categories

(i) **Data Definition Language (DDL)** It is used to define the structure of your tables and other objects in the database. In DBMS, it is used to specify a database schema as a set of definitions. These commands are CREATE, ALTER, DROP, RENAME, TRUNCATE and COMMENT.

(ii) **Data Manipulation Language (DML)** DML provides various commands used to access and manipulate data in existing database. The manipulation involves inserting data into database tables, retrieving existing data, deleting data from existing tables and modifying existing data. These commands are SELECT, INSERT, UPDATE and DELETE.

(iii) **Transaction Control Language (TCL)** TCL is playing an important role in SQL. TCL commands are used to manage transactions in database. These commands are COMMIT, ROLLBACK and SAVEPOINT.

(iv) **Data Control Language (DCL)** DCL commands are used to assign security levels in database which involve multiple user setups. These commands are GRANT and REVOKE.

MySQL Basic Commands

MySQL database is a way of organising a group of tables and table stores the data in the form of rows and columns. To create a bunch of different tables that share a common theme, you would group them into one database to make the management process easier. So, for manipulating data, we need to know about MySQL commands, which are described below:

Commands	Description	Syntax	Example
Create database	Creating database is an easier task. You need to just type the name of the database in a CREATE DATABASE command.	`CREATE DATABASE databasename;`	`mysql>CREATE DATABASE BOOK;`
Access database	Creating database is not enough for use. Before working with tables, first you have to use the database.	`USE databasename;`	`mysql>USE BOOK;`
Show database	To check the database names on the server you need to use the SHOW command. This will provide you the information about databases.	`SHOW DATABASES;`	`mysql>SHOW DATABASES;`
Drop database	Database can be removed or deleted using DROP command. But before deleting a database make sure that you do not need the data stored in different tables of a database because when you delete a database, all its tables also get removed alongwith it.	`DROP DATABASE databasename;`	`mysql>DROP DATABASE BOOK;`
Create table	Database is a collection of tables. The main purpose for creating tables is to store information in an orderly fashion. Each database table consists of columns and rows-just like a graphical table. The columns specify what data is going to be stored, while the rows contain the actual data. Tables are created using CREATE TABLE command.	`CREATE TABLE table_name ( column_name1 data_type(size), column_name2 data_type(size) ... );`	`mysql>CREATE TABLE STUDENT(Roll_No INTEGER, Name CHAR(10), Subject CHAR(20));`

Commands	Description	Syntax	Example
Insert into table	Inserting is a process of adding information into a table. When a table is created, it does not contain any data. Data is inserted in one row at a time.	`INSERT INTO <table_name>(col_1, col_2, col_3,... col_n) VALUES(value_1, value_2,... value_n);`	`mysql>INSERT INTO STUDENT(Roll_No, Name, Subject) VALUES(101, 'Anuj', 'Maths');`

Display table	DESCRIPTION or DESC command is used to verify the structure of a table that you have created. This command displays the column names, available data items with their data types.	`DESCRIBE <table_name>;`
		or
		`DESC <table_name>;`
			`mysql>DESC STUDENT;`

Making Simple Queries in MySQL

A modern database is an efficient way to organise and gain access to large amount of data. A relational database (e.g. MySQL) is able to create relationship between database elements, to show your desired results in desired format from the database. This thing can be achieved by making queries in database.

Some queries of MySQL are as follows

SELECT Statement

The most commonly used SQL command is SELECT statement. The SELECT statement is used to query or retrieve data from a table in the database. A query may retrieve information from specified columns or from all of the columns in the table.

Syntax `SELECT column_list FROM table_name;`

Selecting Specific Columns

To select any specific column or information from the table, we use the following command

Syntax `SELECT<column_name1>,[<column_name2>,.........., <column_nameN>] FROM <table_name>;`

Example 1 To display the column Emp_Code and Emp_Salary from table COMPANY

Table : COMPANY

Emp_Code	Emp_Name	Emp_Salary	Emp_Dep	Joining_Date
101	Ravi	28000	D02	2010-10-10
102	Neeru	70000	D03	2013-06-04
103	Swarg	60000	D05	2011-03-02
104	Puneet	15000	D07	2009-05-01
105	Sneha	12000	D08	2008-04-03

```
mysql>SELECT Emp_Code, Emp_Salary FROM COMPANY;
```

Output

Emp_Code	Emp_Salary
101	28000
102	70000
103	60000
104	15000
105	12000

Selecting All Columns

To select all columns of a table or entire table, we can use an asterisk (*) symbol in place of column_name list.

Syntax `SELECT * FROM <table_name>;`

Example 2 To display all the columns of table COMPANY.

```
mysql>SELECT * FROM COMPANY;
```

Output

Emp_Code	Emp_Name	Emp_Salary	Emp_Dep	Joining_Date
101	Ravi	28000	D02	2010-10-10
102	Neeru	70000	D03	2013-06-04
103	Swarg	60000	D05	2011-03-02
104	Puneet	15000	D07	2009-05-01
105	Sneha	12000	D08	2008-04-03

Column Alias

Column alias is used to temporarily rename a table's column for the purpose of a particular query. This renaming is a temporary change and the actual column name does not change in the database.

Syntax `SELECT <column_name> AS <Alias_name>`
`FROM <table_name>;`

Example 3 To display the column Joining_Date from table COMPANY, here the column_name is rename by JDate.

```
mysql>SELECT Joining_Date AS JDate FROM COMPANY;
```

Output

JDate
2010-10-10
2013-06-04
2011-03-02
2009-05-01
2008-04-03

Eliminating Redundant Data

When you are working with the SELECT statement, you will get duplicate rows when viewing your query results. To remove this redundancy, the SQL DISTINCT keyword is used.

Syntax `SELECT DISTINCT <column_name>`
`FROM <table_name>;`

Example 4 To display the distinct Roll_No from table SCHOOL.

Table: SCHOOL

Roll_No	Book	Price
1FF	Maths	250
3SS	English	300
2MM	Science	250
1FF	G.Studies	350
3SS	Maths	270

```
mysql>SELECT DISTINCT Roll_No FROM SCHOOL;
```

Output

Roll_No
1FF
3SS
2MM

WHERE Clause

The WHERE clause is used when you want to retrieve specific information from a table excluding other irrelevent data.

WHERE clause can be used alongwith SELECT, DELETE and UPDATE statements.

The WHERE command (clause) with SELECT command (clause) can retrieve records from a table with some given conditions.

As the select query executes, SQL processes one row at a time. Each time the conditional statement is met (returns true), a row is returned as a result.

Syntax `SELECT <column_name>`
`FROM <table_name> WHERE<condition>;`

Example 5 To display the Emp_Name, Emp_Salary from table COMPANY whose Emp_Dep is 'D05'.

```
mysql>SELECT Emp_Name, Emp_Salary
FROM COMPANY WHERE Emp_Dep = 'D05';
```

Output

Emp_Name	Emp_Salary
Swarg	60000

SQL Operators

The SQL reserved words and characters are called operators which are used with a WHERE clause in a SQL query.

Some operators are described below

Arithmetic Operators

These operators are used to perform mathematical calculations, such as

Operators	Description
+ (Addition)	Add two arguments together.
– (Subtraction)	Subtract the second argument from the first argument.
* (Multiplication)	Multiplies the two arguments.
/ (Division)	Divide the first argument by the second argument.
% (Modulo)	Divide the first argument from the second argument and provides the remainder of that operation.

Syntax

```
SELECT <expression1> <arithmetic operator>
<expression2>
FROM <table_name>
WHERE <condition>;
```

Example 6 To display Emp_Name, Emp_Dep and 20% of Emp_Salary from table COMPANY for each employee for social fund.

```
mysql> SELECT Emp_Name, Emp_Dep, Emp_Salary*0.20
FROM COMPANY;
```

Output

Emp_Name	Emp_Dep	Emp_Salary*0.20
Ravi	D02	5600
Neeru	D03	14000
Swarg	D05	12000
Puneet	D07	3000
Sneha	D08	2400

Comparison Operators

These operators are used to test or compare the value of two operands, i.e. between two variables or between a variable and a constant.

If the condition is false, then the result is zero (0) and if the condition is true, then the result is non-zero. These operators are also called **relational operators.**

Some of the comparison/relational operators used in MySQL are as follows:

Operators	Description
=	Equal to
>	Greater than
<	Less than
>=	Greater than or equal to
<=	Less than or equal to
<> or !=	Not equal to
!<	Not less than
!>	Not greater than

Syntax

```
SELECT <column_name>|*|expression
FROM <table_name> WHERE <condition>
<comparison operator> <expression>;
```

Example 7 To display Emp_Name and Emp_Salary from table COMPANY for those employees whose salary is greater than or equal to 25000.

```
mysql> SELECT Emp_Name,Emp_Salary
FROM COMPANY
WHERE Emp_Salary>= 25000;
```

Output

Emp_Name	Emp_Salary
Ravi	28000
Neeru	70000
Swarg	60000

Logical Operators

The logical operators compare two conditions at a time to determine whether a row can be selected for the output or not. Logical operators are also called **boolean operators**, because these operators return a boolean data type value as TRUE or FALSE.

When retrieving data using a SELECT statement, you can use these operators in the WHERE clause, which allow you to combine more than one conditions.

Some of the boolean/logical operators used in MySQL are as follows

Operators	Description
AND	Logical AND compares two expressions and return True, when both expressions are true otherwise False.
OR	Logical OR compares two expressions and return True, when atleast one of the expressions is true otherwise False.
NOT	NOT takes a single expression as an argument and changes its value from False to True or from True to False. You can use an exclamation point (!) in place of NOT operator.

Syntax

```
SELECT <column_name>|*|<expression>
FROM <table_name>
WHERE <expressions> <boolean operator>
<expression>;
```

Example 8 To display Emp_Code and Emp_Name for those employees whose Emp_Dep is D05 and Emp_Salary is greater than 22000.

```
mysql> SELECT Emp_Code,Emp_Name
FROM COMPANY WHERE(Emp_Dep='D05'AND
                    Emp_Salary >22000);
```

Output

Emp_Code	Emp_Name
103	Swarg

BETWEEN Operator

The BETWEEN operator is used in a WHERE clause to check that, the field values are within a specified inclusive range.

Values can be numbers, text or dates. The range consists of a beginning expression, followed by an AND keyword and an end expression.

The operator returns 1 if the search value is present within the range otherwise returns 0. BETWEEN clause is sensitive in order and the first value in the clause must be first in alphabetic or numeric order.

Syntax

```
SELECT <column_name>|*| <expression>
FROM <table_name>
WHERE <column_name> BETWEEN <value1>
                              AND <value2>;
```

Example 9 To display Emp_Code, Emp_Name and Emp_Salary for those employees whose Emp_Salary lies between 23000 to 28000.

```
mysql> SELECT Emp_Code,Emp_Name, Emp_Salary
FROM COMPANY
WHERE (Emp_Salary BETWEEN 23000 AND 28000);
```

Output

Emp_Code	Emp_Name	Emp_Salary
101	Ravi	28000

IN Operator

This operator checks a value within a set of values separated by commas and retrieve the rows from the table, which are matching. The IN operator returns 1 when the search value is present within the set, otherwise returns 0. The IN operator allows you to specify multiple values in a WHERE clause.

Syntax

```
SELECT <column_name>|*|<expression>
FROM <table_name>
WHERE <column_name>IN<(value1,
                        value2,… valuen)>;
```

Example 10 To display Emp_Code, Emp_Name and Emp_Salary of the employees whose Emp_Code is 101,104,105.

```
mysql> SELECT Emp_Code, Emp_Name,
Emp_Salary FROM COMPANY
WHERE Emp_Code IN (101,104,105);
```

Output

Emp_Code	Emp_Name	Emp_Salary
101	Ravi	28000
104	Puneet	15000
105	Sneha	12000

LIKE Operator

This operator is used to search a specified pattern in a column. It is useful when you want to search rows to match a specific pattern, or when you do not know the entire value.

The SQL LIKE clause is used to compare a value to similar values using wildcard operators.

We describe patterns by using two special wildcard operators, given below

- **The Per cent Sign** (%) It is used to match any substring.
- **The Underscore** (_) It is used to match any character.

The symbols can also be used in combinations.

Syntax

```
SELECT <column_name> |*| <expression>
<column_name> FROM <table_name>
WHERE <column_name> LIKE <pattern>;
```

Example 11 To display Emp_Name, Emp_Salary whose name is start from 'S'.

```
mysql> SELECT Emp_Name, Emp_Salary FROM COMPANY
WHERE Emp_Name LIKE 'S%';
```

Output

Emp_Name	Emp_Salary
Swarg	60000
Sneha	12000

There are various commands and their descriptions are given below

Commands	Description
WHERE SALARY LIKE '100%'	Find any values that start with 100.
WHERE SALARY LIKE '%100%'	Find any values that have 100 in any position.
WHERE SALARY LIKE '_00%'	Find any values that have 00 in the second and third positions.
WHERE SALARY LIKE '1_%_%'	Find any values that start with 1 and are atleast 2 characters in length.
WHERE SALARY LIKE '%2'	Find any values that end with 2.
WHERE SALARY LIKE '_2%3'	Find any values that have a 2 in the second position and end with a 3.
WHERE SALARY LIKE '2__3'	Find any values in a four-digit number that start with 2 and end with 3.

Quick Test 2

1. The purpose of WHERE clause in a SQL statement is to: **CBSE SQP 2024-25**
   (a) Create a table
   (b) Filter rows based on a specific condition
   (c) Specify the columns to be displayed
   (d) Sort the result based on a column
2. Which of the following clause cannot work with SELECT statement in MySQL? **CBSE 2024**
   (a) FROM (b) INSERT INTO
   (c) WHERE (d) GROUP BY
3. Name the server used in DBMS.
4. How many types of literals are there in SQL?
5. Give two DCL commands.
6. Write the syntax to insert a row in a table.
7. Define the relational operator in one line.

3.5 Creating a Table

Database is a collection of tables. The main purpose for creating tables is to store information in an orderly fashion. Each database table consists of columns and rows-just like a graphical table. The columns specify what data is going to be stored, while the rows contain the actual data. MySQL Command Line Client allows you to create a table using the CREATE TABLE statement. This method requires specifying the table name, column names, and data types.

Syntax

```
CREATE TABLE table_name (
    column1_name datatype constraints,
    column2_name datatype constraints,
    ...
    columnN_name datatype constraints
);
```

Where,

- **column_name** This is the name of each column in the table.
- **datatype** This is the data type of the column (e.g., INT, VARCHAR, DATE, etc.).
- **constraints** These are optional and define rules for the data in the column, such as NOT NULL, UNIQUE, PRIMARY KEY, FOREIGN KEY, etc.

e.g.
```
mysql > CREATE TABLE STUDENT
  (
  Student_Code INTEGER,
  Student_Name CHAR(20),
  Sex CHAR(1),
  Grade CHAR(2),
  Total_Marks DECIMAL
  );
```

Output

Query OK, 0 rows affected

<0.06 sec>

Rules for Creating Tables

- The table and column names must start with a letter and can be followed by letters, numbers, or underscores.
- Table or column names not to exceed a total of 30 characters in length and not use any SQL reserved keywords as names for tables or column names (such as 'select', 'create', 'insert', etc).
- It is important to make sure that you are using an open parenthesis before the beginning of a table definition and a closing parenthesis after the end of the last column definition.
- Separate each column definition with a comma (,).
- All SQL statements should end with a semicolon (;).

Data Integrity through Constraints

Constraints are the rules enforced on data columns on table. These are used to limit the type of data that can go into a table. This ensures the accuracy and reliability of the data in the database.

Basically, constraints maintain the data integrity. So, these are also known as data integrity constraints. If there is any violation between the constraint and the data action, the action is aborted by the constraint.

There are two types of constraints as follows

- **Column Constraints** It applies only to individual column.
- **Table Constraints** It applies to groups of one or more columns.

Constraints can be specified when the table is created by the following syntax

Syntax

```
CREATE TABLE table_name
(
column_name1 data_type(size)
constraint_name,
column_name2 data_type(size)
constraint_name,
------
);
```

Database Integrity Constraints

Some of the database integrity constraints are as follows

(i) **Unique Constraints** It ensures that no two rows have the same value in the specified columns but null values are allowed.

e.g.
```
CREATE TABLE Employee (Emp_Code
INTEGER UNIQUE, Emp_Name CHAR (20));
```

(ii) **Default Constraints** If a user does not enter a value for the column, the defined default value by this constraint is inserted in the field automatically.

e.g.
```
CREATE TABLE Employee (Emp_Code
INTEGER, Emp_Name CHAR(20), Salary
INTEGER DEFAULT 10000);
```

(iii) **Primary Key Constraints** It is similar to unique constraints except that this constraint can be applied to only one column and it does not allow null values.

e.g.
```
CREATE TABLE Employee (Emp_Code
INTEGER PRIMARY KEY, Emp_Name CHAR(20));
```

(iv) **Foreign Key Constraints** It is a constraint that ensures that columns in one table match the primary key column of same or another table.

e.g.
```
CREATE TABLE Items (Order_No INTEGER
PRIMARY KEY, Item_No INTEGER
REFERENCES Items (Order_No));
```

(v) **Check Constraints** It is used to limit the value range that can be placed in a column.

e.g.
```
CREATE TABLE Employee (Emp_Code
INTEGER PRIMARY KEY, Salary DECIMAL
CHECK (Salary>5000));
```

When a check constraint involves more than one column from the same table, it is specified after all columns have between defined.

e.g.
```
CREATE TABLE Items (I_Code INTEGER, Rol
INTEGER, Quantity INTEGER CHECK
(Rol<Quantity));
```

(vi) **Not Null Constraints** This constraint ensures that all rows in the table contain a definite value for the column which is specified as not null, which means a null value is not allowed.

e.g.
```
CREATE TABLE Employee (Emp_Code
INTEGER NOT NULL, Emp_Name CHAR(20));
```

Displaying the Table Structure

DESCRIBE or DESC command is used to verify the structure of a table that you have created.

This command display the column names, available data items with their data types.

Syntax
```
DESCRIBE <table_name>;
```
Or
```
DESC <table_name>;
```

e.g.
```
mysql>DESC STUDENT;
```

Output

Field	Type	Null	Key	Default	Extra
Student_Code	Int	NO	PRI		
Student_Name	Char(20)	YES			
Sex	Char(1)	YES			
Grade	Char(2)	YES			
Total_Marks	Decimal	YES			

Changing Data with DML Commands

DML (Data Manipulation Language) is a category of SQL used to access and manipulate data in existing database. In DML, INSERT command is used to insert the data into a table.

Inserting Data

Inserting is a process of adding information into a table. When a table is created, it does not contain any data. Data is inserted in one row at a time.

Inserting a New Row-INSERT INTO Command

The INSERT command is used to add a single record or multiple records into a table.

Syntax

```
INSERT INTO <table_name>(col_1, col_2,
col_3,.., col_n) VALUES(value_1,
value_2,... value_n);
```

Where,

- **table_name** defines the name of a table, where data will be inserted.
- **col_1, col_2, col_3,..., col_n** are the columns of the current table.
- **value_1, value_2,..., value_n** are the data values against each column.

Consider the following table STUDENT

Roll_No	Name	Subject
101	Rahul	Art
102	Vikas	Science
103	Puneet	Science
104	Sachin	Art
105	Uday	Commerce

Example 12 To add a new row into the STUDENT table use the INSERT INTO command as follow

```
mysql>INSERT INTO STUDENT(Roll_No, Name,
Subject) VALUES(106, 'Ajay', 'Science');
```

Output

Roll_No	Name	Subject
101	Rahul	Art
102	Vikas	Science
103	Puneet	Science
104	Sachin	Art
105	Uday	Commerce
106	Ajay	Science

Inserting Null Values

When you execute the INSERT statement, the database server inserts a NULL value into any column for which you did not provide any value, as well as for all columns that have no default values.

e.g.
```
mysql>INSERT INTO STUDENT(Roll_No, Name)
VALUES(107, 'Viku');
```

The above command inserts only **Roll_No** and **Name** of the table **STUDENT** but the remaining column **Subject** (as same in previous table) becomes NULL.

You can also specify the NULL keyword in the VALUES clause to indicate that a column should be assigned a NULL value.

e.g.
```
mysql>INSERT INTO STUDENT(Roll_No, Name,
Subject) VALUES(107, 'Viku', NULL);
```

Now, the table STUDENT will look like as follows

Roll_No	Name	Subject
101	Rahul	Art
102	Vikas	Science
103	Puneet	Science
104	Sachin	Art
105	Uday	Commerce
106	Ajay	Science
107	Viku	NULL

Inserting Numeric and Character Values

We insert both numeric and character type values in a table. In MySQL, we give the char values in quotes (' ') and numerical values without quotes.

e.g.
```
mysql> INSERT INTO STUDENT1(Roll_No, Name,
Total, Percentage) VALUES (129,'Vinay',
1560, 70.5);
```

The above command inserts both character and numeric values.

Here,	**Roll_No**	Integer value
	Name	Character value
	Total	Double int value
	Percentage	Float value

Output

```
Query OK, 1 row affected <0.03 sec>
```

The column in which a value is not inserted in the above command contains NULL value.

Inserting Date Values

A simple date value in MySQL exists in 'YYYY-MM-DD' format.

Here, first four digits YYYY depicting Year, next two digits MM depicting Month and last two digits DD depicting Date.

e.g.
```
mysql> INSERT INTO STUDENT1(Roll_ No, Name,
Total, DOB) VALUES(129, 'Vinay', 1560,
'1984-12-29');
```

Output

```
Query OK, 1 row affected <0.03 sec>
```

Manipulating Data of a Table/Relation

UPDATE Command

The UPDATE command is used to update a single record or multiple records in a table. The UPDATE command is used to modify the existing rows in a table. To update multiple fields, each field assignment is separated with a comma(,) symbol.

The WHERE clause in the UPDATE syntax specifies which record or records should be updated. If you omit the WHERE clause, all records will be updated.

Syntax

```
UPDATE<table_name > SET <column1>
= <value1>, [<column2> = <value2> ,.....]
WHERE <condition>;
```

Let us consider the following table COMPANY.

EMP_CODE	EMP_NAME	EMP_ADDRESS	EMP_SALARY	EMP_DEPT_NO	DOJ
100	Rahul Sharma	C-21, Arya Nagar	25600	D05	2012-02-06
101	Vikas Mittal	A/44, Mayur Vihar	26000	D03	2002-12-04
102	Puneet Jain	50-MIG, Rohini	21000	D05	2004-08-06
103	Sachin Vats	A-21, Ankur Vihar	23500	D02	2007-09-06
104	Uday Singh	D-34, Indraprasth	26000	D03	2001-07-06
105	Ravi Shukla	45/A, Vivek Nagar	23500	D01	2012-05-06
106	Vinay Rana	120, DDA Colony	24000	D03	2001-02-06

Example 13 To update the EMP_SALARY from the given table COMPANY.

```
mysql>UPDATE COMPANY SET EMP_SALARY=28000
      WHERE EMP_CODE=100;
```

To view the output of the above query, use SELECT command.

```
mysql>SELECT * FROM COMPANY;
```

Output

EMP_CODE	EMP_NAME	EMP_ADDRESS	EMP_SALARY	EMP_DEPT_NO	DOJ
100	Rahul Sharma	C-21, Arya Nagar	28000	D05	2012-02-06
101	Vikas Mittal	A/44, Mayur Vihar	26000	D03	2002-12-04
102	Puneet Jain	50-MIG, Rohini	21000	D05	2004-08-06
103	Sachin Vats	A-21, Ankur Vihar	23500	D02	2007-09-06
104	Uday Singh	D-34, Indraprasth	26000	D03	2001-07-06
105	Ravi Shukla	45/A, Vivek Nagar	23500	D01	2012-05-06
106	Vinay Rana	120, DDA Colony	24000	D03	2001-02-06

Using Expressions in UPDATE

Expressions are also used in the SET clause of the UPDATE command to manipulate the values.

Example 14 If you want to increase the salary of each employee by 1000. Then, you could use the following query

```
mysql>UPDATE COMPANY SET EMP_SALARY=EMP_SALARY+1000;
```

To view the output of the above query, use SELECT command.

```
mysql>SELECT * FROM COMPANY;
```

Output

EMP_CODE	EMP_NAME	EMP_ADDRESS	EMP_SALARY	EMP_DEPT_NO	DOJ
100	Rahul Sharma	C-21, Arya Nagar	29000	D05	2012-02-06
101	Vikas Mittal	A/44, Mayur Vihar	27000	D03	2002-12-04
102	Puneet Jain	50-MIG, Rohini	22000	D05	2004-08-06
103	Sachin Vats	A-21, Ankur Vihar	24500	D02	2007-09-06
104	Uday Singh	D-34, Indraprasth	27000	D03	2001-07-06
105	Ravi Shukla	45/A, Vivek Nagar	24500	D01	2012-05-06
106	Vinay Rana	120, DDA Colony	25000	D03	2001-02-06

Example 15 You can use the WHERE command to update the salary of some employees' as follows

```
mysql>UPDATE COMPANY
      SET EMP_SALARY = EMP_SALARY + 1000
      WHERE EMP_DEPT_NO = 'D05';
```

To view the output of the above query, use SELECT command.

```
mysql>SELECT * FROM COMPANY;
```

Output

EMP_CODE	EMP_NAME	EMP_ADDRESS	EMP_SALARY	EMP_DEPT_NO	DOJ
100	Rahul Sharma	C-21, Arya Nagar	30000	D05	2012-02-06
101	Vikas Mittal	A/44, Mayur Vihar	27000	D03	2002-12-04
102	Puneet Jain	50-MIG, Rohini	23000	D05	2004-08-06
103	Sachin Vats	A-21, Ankur Vihar	24500	D02	2007-09-06
104	Uday Singh	D-34, Indraprasth	27000	D03	2001-07-06
105	Ravi Shukla	45/A, Vivek Nagar	24500	D01	2012-05-06
106	Vinay Rana	120, DDA Colony	25000	D03	2001-02-06

Updating to NULL Values

You can use UPDATE command to enter the NULL values just as other values.

Example 16 The address of the employee Ravi Shukla is changed. But for the time being, the new address is not known, thus NULL value is to be inserted for the address of Ravi Shukla.

```
mysql>UPDATE COMPANY SET EMP_ADDRESS = NULL
      WHERE EMP_NAME = 'Ravi Shukla';
```

To view the ouput of the above query, use SELECT command.

```
mysql>SELECT * FROM COMPANY;
```

Output

EMP_CODE	EMP_NAME	EMP_ADDRESS	EMP_SALARY	EMP_DEPT_NO	DOJ
100	Rahul Sharma	C-21, Arya Nagar	30000	D05	2012-02-06
101	Vikas Mittal	A/44, Mayur Vihar	27000	D03	2002-12-04
102	Puneet Jain	50-MIG, Rohini	23000	D05	2004-08-06
103	Sachin Vats	A-21, Ankur Vihar	24500	D02	2007-09-06
104	Uday Singh	D-34, Indraprasth	27000	D03	2001-07-06
105	Ravi Shukla	NULL	24500	D01	2012-05-06
106	Vinay Rana	120, DDA Colony	25000	D03	2001-02-06

DELETE Command

To discard unwanted data from a database, the DELETE command is used. The DELETE command is used with a WHERE clause. If you don't use a WHERE clause, all rows in the table will be deleted.

Syntax DELETE FROM <table name> WHERE <condition>;

Example 17 Query to delete the record of employee Puneet Jain from the table COMPANY.

```
mysql> DELETE FROM COMPANY WHERE EMP_NAME ='Puneet Jain';
```

To view the output of the above query, use SELECT command.

```
mysql>SELECT * FROM COMPANY;
```

Output

EMP_CODE	EMP_NAME	EMP_ADDRESS	EMP_SALARY	EMP_DEPT_NO	DOJ
100	Rahul Sharma	C-21, Arya Nagar	30000	D05	2012-02-06
101	Vikas Mittal	A/44, Mayur Vihar	27000	D03	2002-12-04
103	Sachin Vats	A-21, Ankur Vihar	24500	D02	2007-09-06
104	Uday Singh	D-34, Indraprasth	27000	D03	2001-07-06
105	Ravi Shukla	NULL	24500	D01	2012-05-06
106	Vinay Rana	120, DDA Colony	25000	D03	2001-02-06

Delete All Rows

To delete all rows in a table without deleting the table structure, the following command is used

Syntax DELETE FROM <table name>;

or DELETE * FROM <table name>;

It is very easy to drop an existing MySQL table, but you need to be very careful while deleting any existing table because lost data will not be recovered after deleting a table.

Restructuring a Table (ALTER TABLE Command)

One can change the structure of a table after creating it, by using ALTER command. To restructure a table either by adding new rows or deleting existing rows, the ALTER command is used. It is also used to modify the structure of a table by modifying the definition of its columns.

Adding a Column in a Table

Syntax ALTER TABLE <table_name> ADD <column_name> datatype <value>;

Example 18 Query to add a column named "EXPERIENCE" of data type INT of size 3 to the table COMPANY used in above section.

```
mysql>ALTER TABLE COMPANY ADD EXPERIENCE INT(3);
```

To view the output of the above query, use SELECT command.

```
mysql>SELECT * FROM COMPANY;
```

Output

EMP_CODE	EMP_NAME	EMP_ADDRESS	EMP_SALARY	EMP_DEPT_NO	DOJ	EXPERIENCE
100	Rahul Sharma	C-21, Arya Nagar	30000	D05	2012-02-06	NULL
101	Vikas Mittal	A/44, Mayur Vihar	27000	D03	2002-12-04	NULL
103	Sachin Vats	A-21, Ankur Vihar	24500	D02	2007-09-06	NULL
104	Uday Singh	D-34, Indraprasth	27000	D03	2001-07-06	NULL
105	Ravi Shukla	NULL	24500	D01	2012-05-06	NULL
106	Vinay Rana	120, DDA Colony	25000	D03	2001-02-06	NULL

Deleting a Column from a Table

Syntax ALTER TABLE<table_name> DROP COLUMN<column_name>;

or ALTER TABLE<table_name> DROP <column_name>;

Example 19 Query to drop a column named "EXPERIENCE" from the table COMPANY.

```
mysql>ALTER TABLE COMPANY DROP COLUMN EXPERIENCE;
```

To view the output of the above query, use SELECT command.

```
mysql>SELECT * FROM COMPANY;
```

Output

EMP_CODE	EMP_NAME	EMP_ADDRESS	EMP_SALARY	EMP_DEPT_NO	DOJ
100	Rahul Sharma	C-21, Arya Nagar	30000	D05	2012-02-06
101	Vikas Mittal	A/44, Mayur Vihar	27000	D03	2002-12-04
103	Sachin Vats	A-21, Ankur Vihar	24500	D02	2007-09-06
104	Uday Singh	D-34, Indraprasth	27000	D03	2001-07-06
105	Ravi Shukla	NULL	24500	D01	2012-05-06
106	Vinay Rana	120, DDA Colony	25000	D03	2001-02-06

Changing the Data Type of a Column in a Table

Syntax ALTER TABLE <table_name> MODIFY COLUMN <column_name> datatype<value>;

or ALTER TABLE <table_name> MODIFY <column_name> datatype<value>;

Example 20 Query to change the data type of a column DOJ to datatype VARCHAR (15) from the table COMPANY used in above section.

```
mysql>ALTER TABLE COMPANY MODIFY COLUMN DOJ
VARCHAR (15);
```

Output

```
+-------------------------------------------+
| Query OK, 6 rows  affected (0.17 sec)     |
| Records : 6 Duplicates : 0 Warnings : 0   |
+-------------------------------------------+
```

DROP TABLE Command

SQL DROP TABLE statement is used to remove table in a database. When you use the DROP TABLE statement to remove a table, the database deletes all objects.

Syntax `DROP TABLE table_name;`

Here, `table_name` is the name of table to be deleted.

Quick Test 3

1. Identify the SQL command used to delete a relation (table) from a relational database. **CBSE SQP 2024-25**
   (a) DROP TABLE
   (b) REMOVE TABLE
   (c) DELETE TABLE
   (d) ERASE TABLE
2. Which MySQL command helps to add a primary key constraint to any table that has already been created? **CBSE 2024**
   (a) UPDATE (b) INSERT INTO
   (c) ALTER TABLE (d) ORDER BY
3. Write any two differences between UPDATE and ALTER TABLE commands of MySQL. **CBSE 2024**
4. How to update the null value?
5. Which command is used to remove a table in a database?

Mind Map

Terminologies

Relation
A relation is a table with columns and rows, which represent the data items and relationships among them.
- **Name** It is represented by the title or the entity identifier.
- **Cardinality** It refers to the number of tuples (rows) in a relation.
- **Degree** It refers to the number of attributes (columns) in each tuple.

Domain
A domain is a collection of all possible values from which the values for a given column or an attribute is drawn.

Tuples
The rows in a relation are also known as tuples. Each row or tuple has a set of permitted values for each attribute.

Attributes
The heading columns of a table are known as attributes. Each attribute of a table has a distinct name.

Keys
Used to uniquely identify and record or row of data from the table.
- **Primary Key** is a column or set of columns in a table that uniquely identifies each row in the table.
- Minimal set of attributes that can uniquely identify a tuple is known as a **candidate key**.
- An **alternate key** is any candidate key in a table that is not chosen as the primary key.
- A **foreign key** is an attribute in one table that refers to the primary key in another table.

Components
- **Server (MySQL Server)** Manages the data
- **Client** It connects to the database server and queries in a pre-specified format.
- **Client Library** It is an Application Programming Interface where a client can write their own programs using a programming language

Elements
- **Literals** A constant value written into a query.
- **NULLs or Null Values** If a column in a table has no value, then the column is said to be a null.
- **Comments** These statements do not affect the statement execution.

Data Types
- **Numeric Data Type** Store numbers such as integers and real numbers in a column.
  Types – INT, FLOAT, DOUBLE, DECIMAL
- **String/Text Data Type** Store string values such as Name of the Students, Address, etc.
  Types –CHAR, VARCHAR, TEXT
- **Date and Time Data Type** Store a date using the fields YEAR, MONTH and DAY in the format YYYY-MM-DD.
  Types – DATETIME, DATE, TIMESTAMP

RELATIONAL DATA MODEL
It represents how data is stored in Relational Databases.

MySQL
It is an open source Relational Database Management System (RDBMS) based on SQL (Structured Query Language).

RDBMS (Relational Database Management System) Stores data in tables and uses a relational model to organize data.

SQL (Structured Query Language)
Programming language for storing and processing information in a relational database.

DBMS
A Database Management System is a collection of programs that enables users to create, maintain and use a database.

DATABASE
Collection of related data that has been recorded, organized and made available for searching is called a Database.

DATA
Data is a collection of raw facts which have not been processed to reveal useful information.

DATABASE CONCEPTS

SQL Commands
- **Data Definition Language (DDL)** Define the structure of your tables and other objects in the database. **Commands** CREATE, ALTER, DROP, RENAME, TRUNCATE, COMMENT.
- **Data Manipulation Language (DML)** Access and manipulate data in existing database. **Commands** SELECT, INSERT, UPDATE, DELETE.
- **Transaction Control Language (TCL)** Manage transactions in database. **Commands** COMMIT, ROLLBACK and SAVEPOINT.
- **Data Control Language (DCL)** Assign security levels in database. **Commands** GRANT and REVOKE.

SQL Operators
- **Arithmetic Operators**
  +, –, *, /, %
- **Comparison Operators**
  = , > , < , >=, <=, <> or != , !< , !>
- **Logical Operators**
  AND, OR, NOT
- **BETWEEN Operator**
  Used to check range
- **IN Operator**
  Check a value within a set of values.
- **LIKE Operator** Used to search a specific pattern in a column.

Constraints
- **Unique Constraints** No two rows have the same value in the specified columns
- **Default Constraints** Default value is inserted in the field automatically.
- **Primary Key Constraints** Unique identification of each rows and do not allow NULL value.
- **Foreign Key Constraints** It ensures that values in one table match values in another table.
- **Check Constraints** Used to limit the value range that can be placed in a column.
- **Not Null Constraints** Enforces a column to NOT accept NULL values.

EXAM PATTERN QUESTIONS

Objective Type Questions

Multiple Choice Questions

1. Which of the following is the organised collection of large amount of interrelated data stored in a meaningful way used for manipulation and updating?

(a) Database (b) File
(c) Folder (d) Data Source

2. The database stores information in

(a) blocks (b) tracks and sectors
(c) rows and columns (d) None of these

3. What is the overall term for creating, editing, formatting, storing, retrieving a text document?

(a) Word processing
(b) Spreadsheet
(c) Web design
(d) Database management system

4. DBMS helps to achieve

(a) data independence
(b) centralised control of data
(c) selection of data
(d) Both (a) and (b)

5. Which out of the following is not a DBMS software?

(a) MySQL (b) Oracle
(c) MS-Access (d) Database 2000

6. An advantage of the database management approach is

(a) data is dependent on programs
(b) data redundancy increases
(c) backup and recovery
(d) All of the above

7. Which of the following is the drawback of DBMS?

(a) Improvement in data
(b) Backup and recovery
(c) Complexity
(d) Maintenance of data integrity

8. In which of the following, databases are used?

(a) Banking (b) Finance
(c) Sales (d) All of these

9. In a relational database, a data structure that organises the information about a single topic into rows and columns is

(a) block (b) table (c) record (d) tuple

10. The cardinality property of a relation refers to the

(a) number of database (b) number of columns
(c) number of rows (d) number of tables

11. A set of possible data values is called

(a) attribute (b) degree (c) tuple (d) domain

12. Rows of a relation are called

(a) relation (b) tuples
(c) data structure (d) entity

13. In files, there is a key associated with each record which is used to differentiate among different records. For every file, there is atleast one set of keys that is unique. Such key is called

(a) Unique key (b) Prime attribute
(c) Index key (d) Primary key

14. Key to represent relationship between tables is called

(a) primary key (b) secondary key
(c) foreign key (d) composite key

15. Which of the following constraint ensures that columns in one table match the primary key column of same or another table?

(a) Default (b) Primary key
(c) Foreign key (d) Check

16. Which of the following statements is FALSE about keys in a relational database? **CBSE SQP 2023-24**

(a) Any candidate key is eligible to become a primary key.
(b) A primary key uniquely identifies the tuples in a relation.
(c) A candidate key that is not a primary key is a foreign key.
(d) A foreign key is an attribute whose value is derived from the primary key of another relation.

17. Which of the following is an open source RDBMS based on SQL?

(a) MSQL (b) MySQL
(c) Both (a) and (b) (d) None of these

18. In which format, a simple date value in MySQL exists?

(a) MM-YYYY-DD (b) YYYY-MM-DD
(c) DD-MM-YYYY (d) None of these

19. It is a program that connects to the database server and issues queries in a pre-specified format.

(a) Server (b) Client library
(c) Client (d) None of these

20. Which of the following is a constant value written into a query?

(a) Literals (b) Comments
(c) Commands (d) Null values

21. In which of the following syntax, you have to use the database?

(a) `CREATE database_name;`
(b) `USE database_name;`
(c) `SHOW database_name;`
(d) None of the above

22. Which SQL statement is used to query or retrieve data from a table in the database?

(a) SELECT (b) ALTER
(c) CREATE (d) UPDATE

23. This operator is used to search a specified pattern in a column.

(a) IN (b) BETWEEN
(c) WHERE (d) LIKE

24. .... are the rules enforced on data columns on table.

(a) Accuracy (b) Constraints
(c) Syntax (d) None of these

25. Which DML command is used to add a single or multiple records into a table?

(a) INSERT (b) SELECT
(c) MERGE (d) UPDATE

26. Which of the following keywords is used to remove the redundancy from the database?

(a) Different (b) Unique
(c) Distinct (d) None of these

27. Which of the following command is used to discard unwanted data from a database?

(a) DROP (b) WHERE
(c) DELETE (d) ALTER

28. Which of the following commands is not a data manipulation command?

(a) SELECT (b) INSERT
(c) UPDATE (d) ALTER

Fill in the Blanks

29. Oracle is a/an ....

30. The number of attributes in a relation is called ....

31. The .... is defined as the attribute or a combination of attributes that is used to identify records of the database table.

32. The purpose of the primary key in a database is to ....

33. Each table may have one or more .... and one of them will become the ....

34. A .... is a data storage format that, can contain a specific range of values.

35. The range of char data type can be ....

36. A/An .... is an application programming interface where a client can write their own programs using a programming language.

37. A/An .... is a language that enables users to access and manipulate data in a database.

38. TCL commands are used to manage .... in a database.

39. To check the database names on the server, you need to use the .... command.

40. ...... command is used to retrieve data from a database.

41. .... is used to temporarily rename a table's column for the purpose of a particular query.

42. Logical operators are also called ....

43. Tables are created using .... command.

44. .... statement is used to add one or more records to a database.

45. .... applies to group of one or more columns.

46. .... command is used to verify the structure of a table that you have created.

47. The WHERE clause in the .... syntax specifies which record or records should be updated.

State Whether True or False

48. Data is logical, coherent and internally consistent.

49. RDBMS store data in the form of related tables.

50. Cardinality refers to the number of columns.

51. Comments can be written in MySQL in two ways.

52. Comparison operators are also known as logical operators.

Assertion and Reason Based Questions

Assertion (A) and Reason (R) based questions. Mark the correct choice as

(a) Both (A) and (R) are true and (R) is the correct explanation for (A).
(b) Both (A) and (R) are true and (R) is not the correct explanation for (A).
(c) (A) is true and (R) is false.
(d) (A) is false but (R) is true.

53. **Assertion (A)** A Database Management System (DBMS) allows users to define, create, and maintain a database efficiently.

Reason (R) The primary goal of a DBMS is to provide controlled access to database information, making data operations convenient and efficient.

54. **Assertion (A)** In a relational data model, tables are known as relations and can store data in rows and columns.

Reason (R) The cardinality of a relation refers to the number of attributes in each tuple.

55. **Assertion (A)** The cardinality of a relation refers to the number of attributes (columns) in a relation.

Reason (R) The degree of a relation refers to the number of tuples (columns) in a relation.

56. **Assertion (A)** A primary key in a relational table can accept NULL values.

Reason (R) The primary key must uniquely identify each record in the table.

57. **Assertion (A)** The NOT NULL constraint ensures that every row in a table has a defined value for a specified column.

Reason (R) If a column is defined as NOT NULL, it can still accept NULL values if not specified otherwise.

58. **Assertion (A)** The DESCRIBE command is used to insert data into a table in SQL.

Reason (R) The INSERT command is used to add records to a table.

59. **Assertion (A)** In SQL, INSERT INTO is a Data Definition Language (DDL) Command.

Reason (R) DDL commands are used to create, modify, or remove database structures, such as tables.

CBSE SQP 2024-25

Answers

1. (a) Database
2. (c) rows and columns
3. (d) Database management system
4. (d) Both (a) and (b)
5. (d) Database 2000
6. (c) backup and recovery
7. (c) Complexity
8. (d) All of these
9. (b) table
10. (c) number of rows
11. (d) domain
12. (b) tuples
13. (d) Primary key
14. (c) foreign key
15. (c) Foreign key
16. (c) A candidate key that is not a primary key is a foreign key.
17. (b) MySQL
18. (b) YYYY-MM-DD
19. (c) Client
20. (a) Literals
21. (b) `USE database_name;`
22. (a) SELECT
23. (d) LIKE
24. (b) Constraints
25. (a) INSERT
26. (c) Distinct
27. (c) DELETE
28. (d) ALTER
29. Relational database management system
30. degree
31. key
32. Uniquely identify a record.
33. Candidate keys, primary key
34. data type
35. 0 to 255
36. Client library
37. Data Manipulation Language (DML)
38. transaction
39. SHOW
40. SELECT
41. COLUMN ALIAS
42. boolean operators
43. CREATE TABLE
44. INSERT
45. GROUP BY
46. DESC
47. UPDATE
48. True
49. True
50. False
51. False
52. False
53. (a) Both (A) and (R) are true and (R) is the correct explanation for (A).
54. (c) (A) is true and (R) is false.
55. (d) (A) is false but (R) is true.
56. (d) (A) is false but (R) is true.
57. (c) (A) is true and (R) is false.
58. (d) (A) is false but (R) is true.
59. (d) (A) is false but (R) is true.

Subjective Type Questions

Very Short Answer Type Questions

1. What is a database?

Ans. A database is a collection of data that is organised so that its contents can be easily accessed, managed and updated.

2. Write two examples of DBMS software.

Ans. Two examples of DBMS software are

(i) MySQL (ii) Oracle

3. What is a Database Management System (DBMS)? Mention any two examples of DBMS. CBSE 2025

Ans. Database Management System (DBMS) is software that enables users to create, manage, and manipulate databases efficiently. It provides tools to store, retrieve, and manage data in a structured way, ensuring data integrity and security.

Examples of DBMS:

1. Oracle Database
2. MySQL

4. Who developed RDBMS?

Ans. The RDBMS (Relational Database Management System) was developed by Dr. E.F. Codd.

5. On which language, MySQL does work?

Ans. MySQL works with many languages like PHP, Perl, C, C++, Java, etc.

6. Expand the following abbreviations.

(i) RDBMS (ii) SQL

Ans. (i) **RDBMS** Relational Database Management System

(ii) **SQL** Structured Query Language

7. If R1 is a relation with 8 rows and 5 columns, then what will be the cardinality of R1?

Ans. The cardinality of R1 will be 8.

8. Write one difference between degree and cardinality.

Ans. Degree refers to the number of columns while cardinality refers to the number of rows in a relation.

9. List different types of keys used in a table in DBMS.

Ans. There are various types of keys used in a table in DBMS, such as

(i) Primary key (ii) Candidate key

(iii) Alternate key (iv) Foreign key

10. Can a table have multiple foreign keys?

Ans. Yes, a table may have multiple foreign keys and each foreign key can have different referenced table.

11. Mention two characteristics of SQL.

Ans. (i) SQL is very simple and easy to learn.

(ii) SQL allows the user to create, update, delete and retrieve data from a database.

12. What are clients in a database system?

Ans. Clients are the programs that connect to the database server and issue queries in a pre-specified format.

13. Name any two DDL commands.

Ans. Two DDL commands are

(i) Create

(ii) Alter

14. Mention the names of the three Transaction Control Language (TCL) commands.

Ans. The three transaction control language commands are

(i) Commit

(ii) Rollback

(iii) Save point

15. Write MySQL command which is used to open an already existing database 'LIBRARY'.

Ans. `USE LIBRARY;`

16. Seema had previously created a table named 'PRODUCT' in a database using MySQL. Later on she forgot the table structure. Suggest her the suitable MySQL command through which she can check the structure of the already created table.

Ans. `DESC PRODUCT;`

Or `DESCRIBE PRODUCT;`

17. How do you select all the rows from a table named 'SCHOOL', where the value of the column 'SNAME' starts with 'P'?

Ans. `SELECT*FROM SCHOOL WHERE SNAME LIKE 'P%';`

18. Which operator can replace the OR condition in the WHERE clause for the following query?

```
SELECT EMP_NO, ENAME FROM EMPLOYEE
WHERE EMP_NO = 101 OR EMP_NO = 121;
```

Ans. In this query, IN operator can replace the OR condition in the WHERE clause.

19. When using the LIKE clause, which wildcard symbol represents any sequence of none, one or more characters?

Ans. The % wildcard symbol is used in LIKE clause to represent any sequence of none, one or more characters.

20. How can you create table using CREATE command?

Ans.
```
CREATE TABLE table_name
(
column_name1 data_type (size),
column_name2 data_type (size),
:
);
```

21. Rewrite the following SQL statement after correcting error(s). Underline the corrections made.
```
INSERT IN STUDENT (RNO, MARKS)
VALUE (5, 78.5);
```

Ans. Correct statement is
```
INSERT INTO STUDENT (RNO, MARKS) VALUES
(5, 78.5);
```

22. Write the UPDATE statement in MySQL to increase commission by 100.00 in 'Commission' column in the 'EMP' table.

Ans. The SQL statement to UPDATE the commission is :
```
UPDATE EMP SET Commission = Commission +
100;
```

23. Mr. William wants to remove all the rows from table INVENTORY to release the storage space, but he does not want to remove the structure of the table. What MySQL statement will he use?

Ans. The command to delete all rows from the INVENTORY table without deleting the structure of the table will be as follows:
```
DELETE FROM INVENTORY;
```

24. Ms. Shalini has just created a table named "Employee" containing columns Ename, Department and Salary. After creating the table, she realized that she has forgotten to add a primary key column in the table. Help her in writing an SQL command to add a primary key column EmpId of integer type to the table Employee. **CBSE SQP 2023-24**

Thereafter, write the command to insert the following record in the table:

EmpId- 999

Ename- Shweta

Department: Production

Salary: 26900

Or

Zack is working in a database named SPORT, in which he has created a table named "Sports" containing columns SportId, SportName, no_of_players, and category.

After creating the table, he realized that the attribute, category has to be deleted from the table and a new attribute TypeSport of data type string has to be added. This attribute TypeSport cannot be left blank. Help Zack write the commands to complete both the tasks.

Ans. The SQL command to add a primary key column EmpId of integer type to the table Employee is
```
ALTER TABLE Employee ADD EmpId INT PRIMARY KEY;
```
The command to insert the record in the table is
```
INSERT INTO Employee (EmpId, Ename,
Department, Salary)
VALUES (999, 'Shweta', 'Production', 26900);
```

Or

SQL command to delete the attribute category from the table Sports:
```
ALTER TABLE Sports DROP category;
```
SQL command to add the attribute TypeSport to the table Sports:
```
ALTER TABLE Sports
ADD TypeSport char(10) NOT NULL;
```

Short Answer Type I Questions

25. Differentiate between an attribute and a tuple with an example.

Ans. The columns of a table are referred to as attributes. It is also known as field which is reserved for a specific piece of data.

The rows of a table are referred to as tuples.

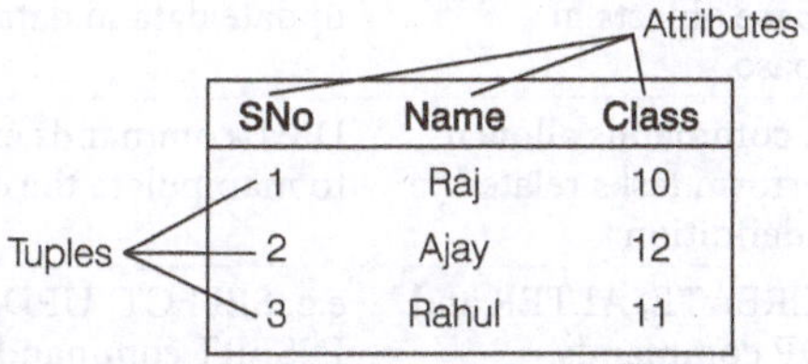

26. Give any two characteristics of primary key.

Ans. Two characteristics of primary key are

(i) All the values in the primary key field are unique.

(ii) Does not allow NULL values.

27. What is the difference between alternate key and candidate key?

Ans. The set of all attributes which can uniquely identify each tuple of relationship are known as candidate keys whereas the set of candidate keys, after selecting one of the keys as primary key, all other remaining keys are known as alternate keys.

28. Explain the following terms:

(i) Relation

(ii) Primary key

(iii) Alternate key

Ans. (i) **Relation** All data items and relationships among them are represented in a two dimensional table known as a relation.

(ii) **Primary key** The key that uniquely identifies each record in a table is known as a primary key.

(iii) **Alternate key** From the set of candidate keys after selecting one of the keys as primary key, all other remaining keys are known as alternate keys.

29. What do you mean by data type?

Ans. Refer to text on page no. 86 (Datatype).

30. MySQL is the world's most popular open source database software. Justify this statement.

Ans. MySQL is the world's most popular open source database software because it supports the basic principles of database and data manipulation used to retrieve, insert and update stored data. It is available to user free or at minimum cost and allows user to use and change the software according to their needs.

31. Differentiate between DDL and DML commands.

Ans. Differences between DDL and DML commands are as follows

DDL	DML
DDL is the abbreviation of Data Definition Language.	DML is the abbreviation of Data Manipulation Language.
It is used to create and modify the structure of database objects in database.	It is used to retrieve, store, modify, delete, insert and update data in database.
DDL commands allow us to perform tasks related to data definition.	DML commands are used to manipulate the data.
e.g. CREATE, ALTER and DROP commands.	e.g. SELECT, UPDATE and INSERT commands.

32. Which commands are used to control user's privileges and how?

Ans. There are two commands that are used to control a user's privileges

(i) GRANT (ii) REVOKE

The GRANT command is used to give an existing user privileges, and REVOKE is used to remove privileges of a user does not exist, GRANT will create a new user at the same time and give them all privileges.

33. Mrs. Kumar is using table STUDENTS with the following columns:

RNO, ADMNO, NAME, AGGREGATE

She wants to display all information of students in descending order of name within ascending order of aggregate. She wrote the following SQL query but she did not get the desired output.

```
SELECT * FROM STUDENTS
ORDER BY NAME, AGGREGATE DESC;
```

Rewrite the above query to get the desired output.

Ans.

```
SELECT * FROM STUDENTS
ORDER BY AGGREGATE, NAME DESC;
```

34. Mr. Ram is using a table with following columns Name, Class, StreamID, StreamName. He needs to display name of students who have not been assigned any stream or have been assigned StreamName that ends with "Computers". He wrote the following command, which did not give the desired result:

```
SELECT Name, Class FROM STUDENTS
WHERE StreamName = NULL OR StreamName=
                                   "%Computers";
```

Help Mr. Ram to run the query by removing the errors and write correct query.

Ans.

```
SELECT Name, Class FROM STUDENTS
WHERE StreamName IS NULL
OR StreamName LIKE "%Computers";
```

35. The Mname column of a table Members is given below

Mname
Akash
Hirav
Vinayak
Sheetal
Rajeev

Based on the given information, find the output of the following queries

(i) `SELECT Mname FROM Members WHERE Mname LIKE "%v";`

(ii) `SELECT Mname FROM Members WHERE Mname LIKE "%e%";`

Ans. (i) Hirav
Rajeev

(ii) Sheetal
Rajeev

36. Write an SQL command to create the table BANK whose structure is given below

FieldName	Data_type	Size	Constraint
ID_Number	integer	10	Primary key
Name	varchar	20	
B_Date	date		
Address	varchar	50	

Ans. The SQL command to create a table as per given structure is as follows

```
mysql > CREATE TABLE BANK (ID_Number integer
(10) PRIMARY KEY, Name varchar (20), B_Date
date, Address varchar (50));
```

37. Write SQL command to create the table VEHICLES with given constraints and also add some information in it.

ColumnName	Data_type (size)	Constraints
Reg_No	char (15)	Primary key
Reg_Date	date	
Owner_Name	varchar (20)	
Address	varchar (40)	

Ans. To create a table using the CREATE TABLE command is

```
mysql > CREATE TABLE VEHICLES (Reg_No char
(15) PRIMARY KEY, Reg_Date date, Owner_Name
varchar (20), Address varchar (40));
```

To add information using the INSERT command is

```
mysql > INSERT INTO VEHICLES (Reg_No,
Reg_Date, Owner_Name, Address) VALUES (100,
12-12-13, 'VIKAS', 'MEERUT');
```

38. I. Write an SQL statement to create a table named STUDENTS, with the following specifications:

Column Name	Data Type	Key
StudentID	Numeric	Primary Key
FirstName	Varchar(20)	
LastName	Varchar(10)	
DateOfBirth	Date	
Percentage	Float(10,2)	

II. Write SQL query to insert the following data in the Students Table

1, Supriya, Singh, 2010-08-18, 75.5

CBSE SQP 2024-25

Ans. I.

```
CREATE TABLE STUDENTS (
StudentID NUMERIC PRIMARY KEY,
FirstName VARCHAR(20),
LastName VARCHAR(10),
DateOfBirth DATE,
Percentage FLOAT(10,2)
);
```

II.

```
INSERT INTO STUDENTS (StudentID, FirstName,
LastName, DateOfBirth, Percentage)
VALUES (1, 'Supriya', 'Singh', '2010-08-18', 75.5);
```

39. (i) Write the SQL statement to create a table, Customer with the following specifications

Table : Customer

Column Name	Data Type	Key
CID	Int	Primary Key
FName	Varchar (20)	
LName	Varchar (20)	
Age	Int	

(ii) Write the SQL query to display all records in descending order of LName from the Table Customer.

CBSE 2025

Ans. (i) SQL statement to create the Customer table:

```
CREATE TABLE Customer (
    CID INT PRIMARY KEY,
    FName VARCHAR(20),
    LName VARCHAR(20),
    Age INT
);
```

(ii) SQL query to display all records in descending order of LName:

```
SELECT * FROM Customer ORDER BY LName DESC;
```

40. What is the difference between "%" and "_" wild card characters with reference to LIKE clause of MySQL?

Ans. Differences between '%' and '_' given below:

'%' Operator	'_' Operator
It represents any number of character.	It represents a single character.
Syntax `SELECT FROM table_name WHERE column LIKE 'XX%';`	**Syntax** `SELECT FROM table_name WHERE column LIKE 'XX_';`

41. Insert any two rows into a table COLLEGE, whose structure is given below:

Roll_No	Name	Class	Branch

Ans. (i)

```
mysql > INSERT INTO COLLEGE (Roll_No,
Name, Class, Branch) VALUES
(2, 'VIKAS', 12, 'SCIENCE');
```

(ii)

```
mysql > INSERT INTO COLLEGE (Roll_No,
Name, Class, Branch) VALUES
(3, 'RAJ', 10, 'SCIENCE');
```

42. In a database SAM with the following information with reference to SAMS table, which column should be set as the primary key? Which column is the foreign key? Give reasons.

Table : SAMS

ICode	IName	Price	Color	VCode
S001	Refrigerator	20000	Blue	P01
S002	Mobile Phone	45000	Black	P02
S003	LCD	60000	Silver	P03
S004	Washing Machine	12500	Smoke	P01
S005	Air Conditioner	16000	White	P03

Table : VENDOR

VCode	VName
P01	Satish
P02	Manoj
P03	Subodh
P04	Jacob

Ans. In the SAMS table, ICode column should be set as primary key because it can uniquely identify each item. VCode should be set as foreign key because it is referring to the VCode column of VENDOR table.

43. Observe the given statements carefully:

(i) `SELECT * FROM CLUB WHERE Salary BETWEEN 30000 AND 40000;`

(ii) `SELECT * FROM CLUB WHERE Salary IN (30000, 40000);`

(iii) `SELECT * FROM CLUB WHERE Salary > = 30000 AND Salary < = 40000;`

Make pairs of the equivalent SQL statements given above (which give the same output) and place each pair in a group.

Ans. We can categorise the equivalent SQL statements in two groups.

Group A In (i) and (iii) query are equivalent. Both are used to calculate the salary between 30000 to 40000.

Group B In (ii) query IN operator is used to compare the values.

44. What do you mean by UPDATE command?

Ans. Refer to text on page no. 95 (UPDATE Command).

Short Answer Type II Questions

45. Differentiate between DBMS and RDBMS.

Ans. Differences between DBMS and RDBMS are as follows

DBMS	RDBMS
In DBMS, relationship between two tables or files are maintained programmatically.	In RDBMS, relationship between two tables or files can be specified at the time of table creation.
DBMS doesn't support client server architecture.	Most of the RDBMS support client server architecture.
DBMS does not support distributed databases.	Most of the RDBMS support distributed databases.
In DBMS, there is no security of data.	In RDBMS, there are multiple levels of security such as command level, object-level.
Each table is given an extension in DBMS.	Many tables are grouped in one database in RDBMS.

46. Explain the Text data types in brief.

Ans. Refer to text on page no. 87 (String/Text DataType).

47. Explain the various components of a MySQL database system.

Ans. Refer to text on page no. 86 (Components of MySQL).

Long Answer Type Questions

48. Explain the database and DBMS in detail.

Ans. **Database** It is a shared collection of logically related data and designed to meet the information needs of an organisation. A database is a computer based record keeping system whose over all purpose is to record and maintain information.

The database holds not only the organization's operational data but also a description of this data. For this reason, a database is also defined as a self-describing collection of integrated records. The description of the data is known as the dictionary or metadata (data about data).

DBMS A Database Management System (DBMS) is a collection of programs that enables users to store, modify and extract information from a database as per the requirements.

It acts as an interface between the application programs and the operating system to access or manipulate the database. A database management system is a piece of software that provides services for accessing a database, while maintaining the required features of the data. Commercially available database management system in the market are dbase, FoxPro, Oracle, MySQL, DB2, etc.

49. Write down some differences between primary key and candidate key.

Ans. Differences between primary key and candidate key are as follows

Primary Key	Candidate Key
▪ A primary key is a column or a combination of columns that uniquely identify a record.	▪ A candidate key can be any column or a combination of columns that can identify as unique key in database.
▪ A table cannot have more than one primary key.	▪ A table can have multiple candidate keys.
▪ Only one candidate key can be primary key.	▪ Each candidate key can identify as primary key.

Primary Key	Candidate Key
▪ Primary key column value cannot be null.	▪ Candidate key column can have null value.
▪ It is most important part of any relation or table.	▪ It signifies as which key can be used as primary key.

50. What do you understand by DDL? Explain the various functions performed by DDL.

Ans. A database scheme is specified by a set of definitions which are expressed by a special language called Data Definition Language (DDL). Data Definition Language statements are used to build and modify the structure of tables and other objects in the database.

Functions performed by DDL are:

(i) It identifies the types of data division such as data item, segment, record and database file.
(ii) It gives a unique name to each data_item_type, record type, database and other data subdivision.
(iii) It specifies the proper data types.
(iv) It specifies how the record types are related to make structures.
(v) It defines the type of encoding the program uses in the data items.
(vi) It defines the length of the data items.
(vii) It defines the range of values that a data_item can assume.
(viii) It specifies means of checking for errors in the data.
(ix) It specifies privacy locks for preventing unauthorized reading or modification of the data.
(x) It should not specify addressing, indexing or searching techniques or the placement of data on the storage units.

51. Define the following terms:

(i) INSERT Command
(ii) SELECT Command
(iii) DELETE Command
(iv) DCL Command
(v) WHERE Clause

Ans. (i) **INSERT Command** It is used to add a single record or multiple records into a table.

Syntax

```
INSERT INTO <table_name>
(cal1, cal2 …) VALUES (val1, val2);
```

(ii) **SELECT Command** It is used to query or retrieve data from a table in the database.

Syntax

```
SELECT column_list FROM table_name;
```

(iii) **DELETE Command** To discard unwanted data from a database, the DELETE command is used.

Syntax

```
DELETE FROM <table_name>
WHERE <condition>;
```

(iv) **DCL Command** These commands are used to assign security levels in database which involve multiple user setups. They are used to grant defined role and access privileges to the users.

(v) **WHERE Clause** It is used when you want to retrieve specific information from a table excluding other irrelevent data.

52. Write SQL queries for the questions from (i) to (v) on the basis of table Class.

No	Name	Stipend	Subject	AvgMark	Grade
01	Vikas	1200	Medical	67	B
02	Boby	1400	Humanities	78.4	B
03	Tarun	1000	Medical	64.8	C
04	Varun	1600	Non-medical	84	A
05	Atul	1800	Non-medical	92	A

(i) Select all the non-medical stream students from the table Class.
(ii) Arrange the records of Class name wise.
(iii) List the records whose grade is B or C.
(iv) Insert the new row with the following data. (06, 'Jack', 2800, 'Humanities', 98, 'A')
(v) Identify the attribute suitable for primary key.

Ans. (i) `SELECT * FROM Class WHERE Subject= 'Non-medical';`

(ii) `SELECT * FROM Class ORDER BY Name;`

(iii) `SELECT * FROM Class WHERE Grade IN ('B','C');`

(iv) `INSERT INTO Class VALUES (06, 'Jack', 2800, 'Humanities' 98, 'A');`

(v) No attribute suitable for primary key.

53. Write SQL commands for the questions from (i) to (v) on the basis of table SHOP.

S_NO	P_Name	S_Name	Qty	Cost	City
S1	Biscuit	Priyagold	120	12.00	Delhi
S2	Bread	Britannia	200	25.00	Mumbai
S3	Chocolate	Cadbury	350	40.00	Mumbai
S4	Sauce	Kissan	400	45.00	Chennai

(i) Display all products whose quantity in between 100 and 400.
(ii) Display data for all products sorted by their quantity.
(iii) To list S_Name, P_Name, Cost for all the products whose quantity is less than 300.
(iv) Give S_Name for products whose name starts with 'B'.

(v) To display the name of product whose cost is less than 40.

Ans. (i) SELECT * FROM SHOP WHERE Qty BETWEEN 100 and 400;
(ii) SELECT * FROM SHOP ORDER BY Qty;
(iii) SELECT S_Name, P_Name, Cost FROM SHOP WHERE Qty <300;
(iv) SELECT S_Name FROM SHOP WHERE P_Name LIKE 'B%';
(v) SELECT P_Name FROM SHOP WHERE Cost<40;

54. Write the SQL commands for the questions from (i) to (v) on the basis of table Employee.

Emp_no	E_name	Profile	Manager	Hire_date	Salary	Commission	Dept_no
8369	SMITH	CLERK	8902	1990-12-18	8000	NULL	20
8499	ANYA	SALESMAN	8698	1991-02-20	16000	300.00	30
8521	SETH	SALESMAN	8698	1991-02-22	12500	500.00	30
8566	MAHADEVAN	MANAGER	8839	1991-04-02	29850	NULL	20
8654	MOMIN	SALESMAN	8698	1991-09-28	12500	1400.00	30
8698	BINA	MANAGER	8839	1991-05-01	28500	NULL	30
8882	SHIVANSH	MANAGER	8839	1991-06-09	24500	NULL	10
8888	SCOTT	ANALYST	8566	1992-12-09	30000	NULL	20
8839	AMIR	PRESIDENT	NULL	1991-11-18	50000	NULL	10
8844	KULDEEP	SALESMAN	8698	1991-09-08	15000	0.00	30

(i) Display employee name and salary of those employees whose salary is greater than or equal to 22000.
(ii) Display employee name and salary of those employees who have their salary in range of 2000 to 4000.
(iii) Display the name, profile and salary of employee(s) who doesn't hold any profile.
(iv) Display the name of employee whose name contains "A" as fourth alphabet.
(v) Display the detail of employee whose name is AMIR.

Ans. (i) SELECT E_name, Salary FROM Employee WHERE Salary> = 22000;
(ii) SELECT E_name, Salary FROM Employee WHERE Salary BETWEEN 2000 and 4000;
(iii) SELECT E_name, Profile, Salary FROM Employee WHERE Profile IS NULL;
(iv) SELECT E_name FROM Employee WHERE E_name LIKE '_ _ _ A%';
(v) SELECT * FROM Employee WHERE E_name ="AMIR";

55. Write SQL commands for the questions from (i) to (v) on the basis of table MASTER.

SNo	Name	Age	Department	Salary
1	Shyam	21	Computer	12000
2	Shiv	25	Maths	15000
3	Rakesh	31	Hindi	14000
4	Sharmila	32	History	20000
5	Dushyant	25	Software	30000

(i) Write a command to update the salary of the employee to 40000, whose SNo is 3.
(ii) Write a query to add a column Date_of_ Joining to the table MASTER.
(iii) Select Age and Department of those employees whose salary is greater than 12000.
(iv) List all data of table MASTER.
(v) Write a query to display Name whose Salary is more than 15000 and Department is Computer.

Ans. (i) UPDATE MASTER SET Salary= 40000 WHERE SNo =3;
(ii) ALTER TABLE MASTER ADD Date_of_Joining Date;
(iii) SELECT Age, Department FROM MASTER WHERE Salary>12000;
(iv) SELECT * FROM MASTER;
(v) SELECT Name FROM MASTER WHERE Department = "Computer" AND Salary > 15000;

56. Excellent Consultancy Pvt. Ltd. maintains two tables for all its employees. **CBSE 2024**

Table : Employee

Employee_Id	First_Name	Last_Name	Salary	Joining_Date	Department
E101	Monika	Das	100000	2019-01-20	Finance
E102	Mehek	Verma	600000	2019-01-15	IT
E103	Manan	Pant	890000	2019-02-05	Banking
E104	Shivam	Agarwal	200000	2019-02-25	Insurance
E105	Alisha	Singh	220000	2019-02-28	Finance
E106	Poonam	Sharma	400000	2019-05-10	IT
E107	Anshuman	Mishra	123000	2019-06-20	Banking

Table : Reward

Employee_Id	Date_Reward	Amount
E101	2019-05-11	1000
E102	2019-02-15	5000
E103	2019-04-22	2000
E106	2019-06-20	8000

Write suitable SQL queries to perform the following task :

(i) Change the Department of Shivam to IT in the table Employee.

(ii) Remove the record of Alisha from the table Employee.

(iii) Add a new column Experience of integer type in the table Employee.

(iv) Display the first name, last name and amount of reward for all employees from the tables Employee and Reward.

(v) Display first name and salary of all the employees whose amount is less than 2000 from the tables Employee and Reward.

Ans. (i) `Update Employee set Department = "IT" where First_Name="Shivam";`

(ii) `Delete from Employee where First_Name ="Alisha";`

(iii) `Alter table Employee ADD Experience integer;`

(iv) `Select A.First_Name, A. Last_Name, B.Amount from Employee A, Reward B where A.Employee_Id= B. Employee_Id;`

(v) `Select A.First_Name, A.Salary from Employee A, Reward B where A.Employee_Id= B. Employee_Id and B.Amount<2000;`

Case Study Based Questions

Case Study 1

Consider the following table Doctor and answer the following questions from (i) to (iv):

ID	DocName	Department	DOJ	Gender	Salary
1	Amit Kumar	Orthopaedics	1993-02-12	M	35000
2	Anita Hans	Paediatrics	1998-10-16	F	30000
3	Sunita Maini	Gynaecology	1991-08-23	F	40000
4	Joe Thomas	Surgery	1994-10-20	M	55000
5	Gurpreet Kaur	Paediatrics	1999-11-24	F	52000
6	Anandini Burman	Oncology	1994-03-16	F	31000
7	Siddharth Dang	Surgery	1995-09-08	M	47000
8	Rama Mukherjee	Oncology	2000-06-27	F	54500

(i) **Correct query to display the names and dates of joining of doctors of oncology department.**
(a) SELECT * FROM Doctor WHERE Department = "Oncology";
(b) SELECT DocName, DOJ FROM Doctor WHERE Department = "Oncology";
(c) SELECT DocName, DOJ FROM Doctor WHERE Department LIKE Oncology;
(d) None of the above

(ii) **Find the correct output.**
SELECT Department FROM Doctor WHERE Salary > = 55000;

(a)

Department
Oncology

(b)

Department
Surgery

(c)

Department
Paediatrics

(d)

Department
Gynaecology

(iii) **Which column is used for primary key?**
(a) DOJ (b) Gender (c) Salary (d) ID

(iv) **Choose the correct output.**
SELECT SUM (Salary) FROM Doctor WHERE Department = "Surgery";

(a)

SUM (Salary)
102000

(b)

SUM (Salary)
10200

(c)

SUM (Salary)
202000

(d)

SUM (Salary)
20200

Ans. (i) (b) SELECT DocName, DOJ FROM Doctor WHERE Department = "Oncology";

(ii) (b)

Department
Surgery

(iii) (d) ID

(iv) (a)

SUM (Salary)
102000

Case Study 2

Consider the table SHOP and answer any four questions from (i) to (v):

Code	Name	Type	Cost	Margin	Qty
1001	Samsung	A1	50000	2.00	1000
1002	Galaxy	A2	40000	2.00	200
1003	MotoG	A1	30000	NULL	500
1004	Nokia	A3	20000	4.00	1500
1005	Samsung	A1	50000	NULL	1200
1006	MotoG	A2	35000	3.00	300

(i) **What will be the output of the following query?**
SELECT Name, Cost FROM SHOP WHERE Margin = NULL;

(ii) **Write the query that will give the output as**

Code	Name	Margin
1004	Nokia	4.00
1005	Samsung	NULL

(iii) **Shrey has given the following query to set the margin NULL for type A3.**
ALTER SHOP SET Margin = NULL WHERE Type = A3;
But he is not getting the desired result. Help him by writing the correct statement.

(iv) **The primary key for SHOP table will be ....**

(v) **To add a new row in table SHOP, the correct query is ......, where row data [1007, Nokia, A2, 22000, 2.00, 250]**

Ans. (i)

Name	Cost
MotoG	30000
Samsung	50000

(ii) SELECT Code, Name, Margin FROM SHOP WHERE Qty > 1000;
(iii) UPDATE SHOP SET Margin = NULL WHERE Type = A3;
(iv) Code
(v) INSERT INTO SHOP (Code, Name, Type, Cost, Margin, Qty) VALUES (1007, 'Nokia', 'A2', 22000, 2.00, 250);

SELF ASSESSMENT TEST

Multiple Choice Questions

1. Facilities offered by database are
   (a) the ability to store a large amount of data in a structured format, easy update, sort query and production of reports.
   (b) easy edition, spell check, perform calculations, library of mathematical functions and replication.
   (c) the ability to rotate images, copy and paste, fill scale.
   (d) None of the above
2. Which of the following commands are used to manage transactions in database?
   (a) DDL (b) DML
   (c) TCL (d) DCL
3. Which of the following operators compare two conditions at a time to determine whether a row can be selected for the output?
   (a) Comparison operators
   (b) Logical operators
   (c) Arithmetic operators
   (d) Between operator
4. DBMS is a program that controls the creation, maintenance and use of database. Here DBMS referred to
   (a) Digital Base Management System
   (b) Data Build Management System
   (c) Database Management System
   (d) Database Management Service
5. Which of the following constraints applies only to individual column?
   (a) Column constraint
   (b) Table constraint
   (c) Both (a) and (b)
   (d) None of the above

Fill in the blanks

6. A foreign key is a reference of the ……… key in another table.
7. ……… precedes a comment within a single line.
8. ……… is used to match any character.
9. All SQL statements should end with a ……… .
10. Three popular DBMS software are ……… , ……… & ……… .

State whether True or False

11. Every relation does have a primary key.
12. NULL values are treated differently from other values.
13. COMMIT, ROLLBACK, etc. are examples of TCL.
14. To remove redundancy, the NULL keyword is used.

Assertion and Reason Based Questions

Assertion (A) and Reason (R) based questions. Mark the correct choice as

(a) Both (A) and (R) are true and (R) is the correct explanation for (A).
(b) Both (A) and (R) are true and (R) is not the correct explanation for (A).
(c) (A) is true and (R) is false.
(d) (A) is false but (R) is true.

15. **Assertion (A)** RDBMS stands for Relational Database Management System.
    Reason (R) RDBMS does not allow relating or associating two tables in a database.
16. **Assertion (A)** A database is the largest component for holding and storing data and may contain several tables.
    Reason (R) Each table comprises multiple rows and records.
17. **Assertion (A)** A foreign key is an attribute whose value is derived from the primary key of another relation.
    Reason (R) A foreign key is used to represent the relationship between tables or relations.

Very Short Answer Type Questions

18. Who developed the SQL?
19. What are the limitations of DBMS software?
20. Define the syntax to verify the structure of table.
21. How will you calculate the degree of a relation?

Short Answer Type Questions

22. Write a short note on domain.
23. State some key features of MySQL.
24. What is the use of DML command?

25. What do you mean by relational data model? Explain the various terms related to relational database.

26. State the relationship and difference between a primary and foreign key.

Long Answer Type Questions

27. Name two categories into which SQL commands may be categorised. Also, give one example of SQL commands in each categories.

28. List the data types used in DBMS/RDBMS.

Case Study Based Questions

29. Consider the table STUDENT with the following detail

STU_ID	NAME	STREAM	MARKS	CLASS
1	Aditya	Science	87.5	12A
2	Vikram	Commerce	88.7	12B
3	Astha	Humanities	76.8	12C
4	Varsha	Science	79.5	12A
5	Kanishka	Science	77.9	12A
6	Anand	Commerce	86.7	12B

Now answer the question given below

(i) Delete records that belongs to Humanities stream.

(ii) A tuple in RDBMS is referred to as ..... of a table.

(iii) What is the degree and cardinality of STUDENT table.

(iv) The primary key for STUDENT table ....

Answers

1. (a) 2. (c) 3. (b) 4. (c) 5. (a)
6. primary key 7. --
8. _(Underscore) 9. semicolon
10. Oracle, MySQL & Microsoft SQL Server
11. True 12. True 13. True 14. False 15. (c)
16. (a) 17. (a)

04

CHAPTER

SQL querying is the process of retrieving specific data from a database using SQL (Structured Query Language) commands. It involves writing queries to select, filter, and manipulate data stored in tables.

Database Query Using SQL

YOUR STUDY GOALS

- 4.1 Types of SQL Functions
- 4.2 Single-Row Functions
- 4.3 Aggregate Functions
- 4.4 Join on Two Tables

YOUR PRACTICE GOAL

- Objective Type Questions (62 Qs ; MCQs, True or False, Fill in the Blanks, Assertion and Reason)
- Subjective Type Questions (95 Qs ; VSA, SA, LA)
- Case Based Questions (Objective Case Studies-3)

MySQL function performs a pre-defined task and returns a single value such as a numerical, string or date/time value.

Functions operate on zero, one, two or more values provided to them, these values are called **parameters** or **arguments**. While using functions, arguments or parameters are often supplied that provide these functions with the information they needs to perform the task.

These arguments are usually in the form of column names, literal values or other expressions.

MySQL supports number of built-in functions that are already implemented in MySQL. These functions allow to perform different types of operations on the data such as find the ASCII value of the string stored in column or convert all characters of a string to uppercase and so on.

Example 1 To use any function, we need to specify the column to which the function should be applied.

```
SELECT function (column_name)
FROM table_name;
```

To specify multiple columns, you can write a query like either of these.

```
SELECT *, function (column_name)
FROM table_name;
```

Or

```
SELECT column_name1, function (column_name2),
column_name3 FROM table_name;
```

4.1 Types of SQL Functions

SQL provides two types of functions

(i) Single-row Functions

This type of function work with a single-row at a time. It returns a result for each row of the table, on which the query is performed. This is also known as **Scalar functions.**

Examples Single-row functions include CHAR(), CONCAT(), INSTR() etc.

(ii) Multiple-row Functions

Multiple row functions are also called as **Aggregate functions**. This type of functions work with data of multiple-rows at a time and return a single output value. This is also known as Group functions.

We often use aggregate functions with **GROUP BY** and **HAVING** clauses of the SELECT Statement.

TEACHER TIP

Except for count(*), aggregate functions totally ignore NULL values and considers all values present in a column.

Examples of multiple-row functions include SUM(), AVG(), COUNT(), etc.

4.2 Single-Row Functions

(a) String/Text Functions

The string/text functions of SQL are used to extract, change, format or alter character strings. They accept a character string as an input and provides character string or numeric values as an output.

Some string/text functions are explained with example as follows:

Function	Description	Syntax	Example
UCASE() / UPPER()	Converts a string to uppercase.	UCASE(string) / UPPER(string)	SELECT UPPER('hello'); **Output** HELLO
LCASE() / LOWER()	Converts a string to lowercase.	LCASE(string) / LOWER(string)	SELECT LOWER('HELLO'); **Output** hello
MID() / SUBSTRING() / SUBSTR()	Extracts a substring from a string.	MID(string, start, length) / SUBSTRING(string, start, length) / SUBSTR(string, start, length)	SELECT SUBSTRING('Hello World', 1, 5); **Output** Hello
LENGTH()	Returns the length of a string.	LENGTH(string)	SELECT LENGTH('Hello'); **Output** 5
LEFT()	Returns the leftmost characters from a string.	LEFT(string, length)	SELECT LEFT('Hello', 2); **Output** He
RIGHT()	Returns the rightmost characters from a string.	RIGHT(string, length)	SELECT RIGHT('Hello', 3); **Output** llo
INSTR()	Returns the position of the first occurrence of a substring within a string.	INSTR(string, substring)	SELECT INSTR('Hello World', 'o'); **Output** 5
LTRIM()	Removes leading spaces from a string.	LTRIM(string)	SELECT LTRIM(' Hello'); **Output** Hello
RTRIM()	Removes trailing spaces from a string.	RTRIM(string)	SELECT RTRIM('Hello '); **Output** Hello
TRIM()	Removes both leading and trailing spaces from a string.	TRIM(string)	SELECT TRIM(' Hello '); **Output** Hello

(b) Mathematical Functions

MySQL provides a number of functions used for performing mathematical calculations on database. These mathematical functions accept numeric values and after performing the required operation, return numeric values. Some mathematical functions are explained with examples as follows

Function	Description	Syntax	Example
POWER()	Returns the value of a number raised to the power of another number.	POWER(base, exponent)	`SELECT POWER(2, 3);` **Output 8**
ROUND()	Rounds a number to a specified number of decimal places.	ROUND(number, decimals)	`SELECT ROUND(123.4567, 2);` **Output 123.46**
MOD()	Returns the remainder of a division operation.	MOD(dividend, divisor)	`SELECT MOD(10, 3);` **Output 1**

TEACHER TIP

Students should remember that first argument is base value and second argument as exponent value in power function and in Mod function, first argument represents dividend and second argument represents divider.

There are some additional mathematical functions given below:

Function	Description	Syntax	Example
ABS()	Returns the absolute value of a number.	ABS(number)	`SELECT ABS(-5);` **Output 5**
SQRT()	Returns the square root of a number.	SQRT(number)	`SELECT SQRT(16);` **Output 4**
CEIL()	Rounds a number up to the nearest integer.	CEIL(number)	`SELECT CEIL(5.3);` **Output 6**
FLOOR()	Rounds a number down to the nearest integer.	FLOOR(number)	`SELECT FLOOR(5.9);` **Output 5**

(c) Date/Time Functions

MySQL stores date in date/time format, representing the century, month, year, day and hours. The date and time functions are used to perform operations on the date/time data stored in the database. The default date format is YYYY-MM-DD in MySQL.
Some date/time functions are explained with examples as follows

Function	Description	Syntax	Example
NOW()	Returns the current date and time.	NOW()	`SELECT NOW();` **Output 2024-10-07 12:00:00**
DATE()	Extracts the date part from a date or datetime expression.	DATE(date_expression)	`SELECT DATE(NOW());` **Output 2024-10-07**
MONTH()	Returns the month from a date (1-12).	MONTH(date_expression)	`SELECT MONTH('2024-10-07');` **Output 10**
MONTHNAME()	Returns the name of the month for a date.	MONTHNAME(date_expression)	`SELECT MONTHNAME('2024-10-07');` **Output October**
YEAR()	Returns the year from a date.	YEAR(date_expression)	`SELECT YEAR('2024-10-07');` **Output 2024**
DAY()	Returns the day of the month (1-31) from a date.	DAY(date_expression)	`SELECT DAY('2024-10-07');` **Output 7**
DAYNAME()	Returns the name of the day for a date.	DAYNAME(date_expression)	`SELECT DAYNAME('2024-10-07');` Output Monday

Quick Test 1

1. Predict the output of the following queries: **CBSE SQP 2021-2022 Term-II**
   (i) Select power(5,3); (ii) Select mod(5,3);
2. Briefly explain the purpose of the following SQL functions: **CBSE SQP 2021-2022 Term-II**
   (i) power() (ii) mod()
3. Help Reshma in predicting the output of the following queries: **CBSE SQP 2021-2022 Term-II**
   (i) select round(8.72,3); (ii) select round(9.8);
4. Write suitable SQL query for the following: **CBSE SQP 2022-2023**
   (i) Display 7 characters extracted from 7th left character onwards from the string 'INDIA SHINING'.
   (ii) Display the position of occurrence of string 'COME' in the string 'WELCOME WORLD'.
   (iii) Round off the value 23.78 to one decimal place.
   (iv) Display the remainder of 100 divided by 9.
   (v) Remove all the expected leading and trailing spaces from a column userid of the table 'USERS'.
5. What will be the output of the following SQL queries? **CBSE 2024**
   (i) SELECT RIGHT ("CHANDRAYAN", 4); (ii) SELECT ROUND (76345.456,2);

4.3 Aggregate Functions

Aggregate functions are also known as **group functions**, they return a result only in single row based on group of rows, rather than on single row. It always used with SELECT command and in ORDER BY and HAVING clauses. They are commonly used with the GROUP BY clause in a SELECT statement. Some of the aggregate functions are MIN, MAX, SUM, AVG, COUNT. The SQL aggregate functions return a single value, calculated from values in a column.

Function	Description	Syntax	Example
MAX()	Returns the maximum value from a set of values.	MAX(column_name)	`SELECT MAX(salary) FROM employees;`
MIN()	Returns the minimum value from a set of values.	MIN(column_name)	`SELECT MIN(age) FROM employees;`
AVG()	Returns the average value of a numeric column.	AVG(column_name)	`SELECT AVG(salary) FROM employees;`
SUM()	Returns the total sum of a numeric column.	SUM(column_name)	`SELECT SUM(salary) FROM employees;`
COUNT()	Returns the number of rows that match a specified criteria.	COUNT(column_name) or COUNT(*)	`SELECT COUNT(*) FROM employees;`

COUNT( ) Function

This function returns the total number of values or rows of the specified field or column. COUNT (*) is a special function, as it returns the count of all rows in a specified table. It includes all the null and duplicate values.

Syntax `SELECT COUNT(*) FROM table_name;`

Consider the following table PAYMENTS:

Empid	Emp_Name	Salary	Department
1	Ridhi	20000	D1
2	Rohit	25000	D2
3	Rakesh	20000	D2
4	Roshan	44000	D1
5	Rohini	15000	D3
6	Radha	14000	D1

Example 2 To count the total number of employees from table PAYMENTS.

```
SELECT COUNT(*) "Employees" FROM PAYMENTS;
```

Above query produces the following output

Employees
6

DISTINCT Keyword with COUNT() Function

The DISTINCT keyword helps us in removing the duplicates from the result. When it is used with aggregate function COUNT, it returns the number of distinct rows in a specified table.

Syntax
```
SELECT COUNT(DISTINCT column_name)
FROM table_name;
```

Example 3 To count total number of rows in Department column from PAYMENTS table.

```
SELECT COUNT(Department) "Deptid"
FROM PAYMENTS;
```

Above query produces the following output

Deptid
6

Example 4 To count distinct values of column Department from PAYMENTS table.

```
SELECT COUNT(DISTINCT Department) "Deptid"
FROM PAYMENTS;
```

Above query produces the following output

Deptid
3

ORDER BY Clause

The ORDER BY clause is used to sort the result set along a specified column. The ORDER BY clause sorts the records in ascending order by default. If you want to sort the records in descending order, you can use the DESC keyword.

Syntax
```
SELECT column_name(s)
FROM table_name
ORDER BY column_name(s)ASC/DESC;
```

Example 5 If we have the following table PERSONS

P_ID	LastName	FirstName	Address	City
1	Hansen	Ola	Timoteivn 10	Sandnes
2	Svendson	Tove	Borgvn 23	Sandnes
3	Pettersen	Kari	Storgt 20	Stavanger

Now, we want to select all the persons from the table PERSONS. However, we want to sort the persons by their last name in ascending order. We will use the following statement

```
SELECT * FROM PERSONS
ORDER BY LastName ASC;
```

The result set will look like this

P_ID	LastName	FirstName	Address	City
1	Hansen	Ola	Timoteivn 10	Sandnes
3	Pettersen	Kari	Storgt 20	Stavanger
2	Svendson	Tove	Borgvn 23	Sandnes

GROUP BY Clause

The GROUP BY clause can be used with SELECT statement, if we want to select multiple records and group of results by one or more columns.

Note *AS keyword is optional and is used to assign a temporary name to the column or table.*

Example 6 To display sum of salary from table PAYMENTS using SUM() function on Salary column group by Department column.

```
SELECT Empid, SUM(Salary) AS "TotalSalary"
FROM PAYMENTS GROUP BY Department;
```

Above query produces the following output

Empid	TotalSalary
1	78000
2	45000
5	15000

Example 7 To return the name of the department and number of employees (in the associated department) who makes over 25000 from table PAYMENTS.

```
SELECT Department, COUNT(*)
AS "NumberofEmployees"
FROM PAYMENTS
WHERE Salary>25000 GROUP BY Department;
```

Above query produces the following output

Department	NumberofEmployees
D1	1

Example 8 To provide the result as the name of each department and the minimum salary in the department from table PAYMENTS.

```
SELECT Department, MIN(Salary)
AS "LowestSalary"
FROM PAYMENTS GROUP BY Department;
```

Above query produces the following output

Department	LowestSalary
D1	14000
D2	20000
D3	15000

Example 9 To return the name of department and the maximum salary in the department from table PAYMENTS.

```
SELECT Department, MAX(Salary)
AS "HighestSalary"
FROM PAYMENTS
GROUP BY Department;
```

Above query produces the following output

Department	HighestSalary
D1	44000
D2	25000
D3	15000

HAVING Clause

The HAVING clause can be used only with the SELECT statement.

HAVING is applied to summarised rows (summarised with GROUP BY).

In which the completed data is firstly fetched and then separated according to condition.

The HAVING clause was added to MySQL because the WHERE keyword could not be used with aggregate functions. Consider the following table ORDER:

Table: ORDER

O_ID	OrderDate	OrderPrice	Customer
1	2015/01/23	1000	Rubeen
2	2014/11/15	1600	Sheena
3	2014/11/12	700	Jensen
4	2013/10/22	500	Rubeen
5	2013/10/16	2000	Jensen
6	2012/09/30	300	Sheena

Example 10 To display customer name and sum of order price if any of the customers have a total order of less than 2000 from table ORDER.

```
SELECT Customer, SUM(OrderPrice) FROM
ORDER GROUP BY Customer
HAVING SUM(OrderPrice)<2000;
```

Above query produces the following output

Customer	SUM(OrderPrice)
Rubeen	1500
Sheena	1900

4.4 JOIN on Two Tables

The JOIN operation combines rows from two tables based on specified conditions. This is different from a cartesian product, which generates all possible combinations of rows. Using the JOIN clause in SQL, we specify conditions on the related attributes of the two tables within the FROM clause. Typically, such an attribute is a primary key in one table and a foreign key in the other.

EQUI JOIN in SQL

An EQUI JOIN is a specific type of INNER JOIN that retrieves rows from two or more tables where the values in the related columns are equal. It's used to combine rows based on matching values in common columns.

Key Characteristics

- **Equality Condition**: It uses the equality operator (=) to compare values between columns.
- **Inner Join Behavior** It only returns rows where there's a match in both tables.
- **No Nulls/Unmatched Data** Rows with null values or unmatched data in the joined columns are excluded.

Syntax

There are two common ways to write an EQUI JOIN:

1. Using WHERE clause

```
SELECT * FROM TableName1, TableName2 WHERE
TableName1.ColumnName = TableName2
.ColumnName;
```

2. Using JOIN and ON clause

```
SELECT * FROM TableName1 JOIN TableName2 ON
TableName1.ColumnName = TableName2
.ColumnName;
```

where, JOIN keyword specifies the join operation, ON keyword defines the equality condition.

Example 11 Consider two tables:

Table state

State_ID	State_Name
1	Uttar Pradesh
2	Uttarakhand
3	Madhya Pradesh

Table city

City_ID	City_Name
1	Lucknow
1	Gorakhpur
1	Noida
2	Dehradun
2	Rishikesh
3	Gwalior

From all possible combinations of tuples of relations state and city display only those rows such that the attribute name in both have the same value.

```
SELECT * FROM state JOIN city ON
state.State_ID = city.City_ID;
```

Above query produces the following output.

Output

State_ID	State_Name	City_ID	City_Name
1	Uttar Pradesh	1	Lucknow
1	Uttar Pradesh	1	Gorakhpur
1	Uttar Pradesh	1	Noida
2	Uttarakhand	2	Dehradun
2	Uttarakhand	2	Rishikesh
3	Madhya Pradesh	3	Gwalior

This result shows the cities matched with their corresponding states based on the State_ID and City_ID columns.

Quick Test 2

1. Aryan, a database administrator, has grouped records of a table with the help of group by clause.
   He needs to further filter groups of records generated through group by clause.
   Suggest suitable clause for it and properly explain its usage with the help of an example. **CBSE SQP 2021-2022 Term-II**
2. Based on table STUDENT given here, write suitable SQL queries for the following: **CBSE SQP 2022-2023**

Roll No	Name	Class	Gender	City	Marks
1	Abhishek	XI	M	Agra	430
2	Prateek	XII	M	Mumbai	440
3	Sneha	XI	F	Agra	470
4	Nancy	XII	F	Mumbai	492
5	Himnashu	XII	M	Delhi	360
6	Anchal	XI	F	Dubai	256
7	Mehar	X	F	Moscow	324
8	Nishant	X	M	Moscow	429

   (i) Display gender wise highest marks.
   (ii) Display city wise lowest marks.
   (iii) Display total number of male and female students.
3. Differentiate between COUNT( ) and COUNT(*) functions in MySQL. Give suitable examples to support your answer. **CBSE 2023**
4. Write the SQL queries which will perform the following operations. **CBSE 2023**
   (i) To display the year from your Date of Admission which is '2023-05-15'.
   (ii) To convert your email id 'ABC@XYZ.com' to lowercase.
   (iii) To remove leading spaces from a string 'my country'.
   (iv) To display current date.
   (v) To display the value of 10^6

Mind Map

Types of SQL Functions

MySQL function performs a pre-defined task and returns a single value such as a numerical, string or date/time value.

Single-row Functions

This type of function work with a single-row at a time. It returns a result for each row of the table, on which the query is performed. This is also known as Scalar functions.

Types of Single-row Functions

String/Text Functions

The string/text functions of SQL are used to extract, change, format or alter character strings. They accept a character string as an input and provides character string or numeric values as an output.

Function	Syntax
UCASE() / UPPER()	`UCASE(string) / UPPER(string)`
LCASE() / LOWER()	`LCASE(string) / LOWER(string)`
MID()/SUBSTRING() /SUBSTR()	`MID(string, start, length) / SUBSTRING(string, start, length) / SUBSTR(string, start, length)`
LENGTH()	`LENGTH(string)`
LEFT()	`LEFT(string, length)`
RIGHT()	`RIGHT(string, length)`
INSTR()	`INSTR(string, substring)`
LTRIM()	`LTRIM(string)`
RTRIM()	`RTRIM(string)`
TRIM()	`TRIM(string)`

Mathematical Functions

MySQL provides a number of functions used for performing mathematical calculations on database. It accepts numeric values and after performing the required operation, return numeric values.

Function	Syntax
POWER()	`POWER(base,exponent)`
ROUND()	`ROUND(number,decimals)`
MOD()	`MOD(dividend,divisor)`

Note Some additional mathematical functions are ABS(), SQRT(), CEIL(), FLOOR().

Date/Time Functions

MySQL stores date in date/time format, representing the century, month, year, day and hours. The date and time functions are used to perform operations on the date/time data stored in the database.

Function	Syntax
NOW()	`NOW()`
DATE()	`DATE(date_expression)`
MONTH()	`MONTH(date_expression)`
MONTHNAME()	`MONTHNAME(date_expression)`
YEAR()	`YEAR(date_expression)`
DAY()	`DAY(date_expression)`
DAYNAME()	`DAYNAME(date_expression)`

Multiple-row Functions

It is also known as **Aggregate functions** and **Group functions**. This functions work with data of multiple-rows at a time and return a single output value.

Types of Multiple-row Functions

MAX() Returns the maximum value from a set of values.

Syntax `MAX(column_name)`

MIN() Returns the minimum value from a set of values.

Syntax `MAX(column_name)`

AVG() Returns the average value of a numeric column.

Syntax `AVG(column_name)`

SUM() Returns the total sum of a numeric column.

Syntax `SUM(column_name)`

COUNT() Returns the number of rows that match a specified criteria.

Syntax `COUNT(column_name)` *Or* `COUNT(*)`

Or

The COUNT DISTINCT function returns the number of unique values in the column or expression.

Syntax
```
SELECT COUNT(DISTINCT column_name)FROM
                              table_name;
```

CLAUSE

- The **ORDER BY clause** sorts the records in ascending order by default. If you want to sort the records in descending order, you can use the DESC keyword.

  Syntax
  ```
  SELECT column_name(s)FROM table_name ORDER BY column_name
                                                (s)ASC/DESC;
  ```
- The **GROUP BY clause** can be used with SELECT statement, if we want to select multiple records and group of results by one or more columns.

  Syntax
  ```
  SELECT Empid, SUM(Salary) AS "TotalSalary" FROM PAYMENTS
                                      GROUP BY Department;
  ```
- The **HAVING clause** can be used only with the SELECT statement. HAVING is applied to summarised rows (summarised with GROUP BY).

  Syntax
  ```
  SELECT Customer, SUM(OrderPrice) FROM ORDER GROUP BY Customer
  HAVING SUM(OrderPrice)<2000;
  ```
- **JOIN clause** is used to combine rows from two or more tables based on a related column between them.

NCERT Folder

1. Answer the following questions:

(a) What is the purpose of the following clauses in a select statement?

(i) ORDER BY (ii) HAVING

(b) Site any two differences between Single_row functions and Aggregate functions.

(c) What do you understand by Cartesian Product?

(d) Write the name of the functions to perform the following operations:

(i) To display the day like "Monday", "Tuesday", from the date when India got independence.

(ii) To display the specified number of characters from a particular position of the given string.

(iii) To display the name of the month in which you were born.

(iv) To display your name in capital letters.

Ans. (a) Purpose of the clauses in a SELECT statement:

(i) **ORDER BY** The ORDER BY clause is used to sort the result set of a query in either ascending (ASC) or descending (DESC) order based on one or more columns. By default, it sorts the data in ascending order.

e.g.
```
SELECT * FROM Employees ORDER BY
Salary DESC;
```

This query sorts the employees' data by salary in descending order.

(ii) **HAVING** The HAVING clause is used to filter the results after the GROUP BY operation, applying conditions to groups of rows, unlike the WHERE clause which filters rows before the grouping. It is typically used with aggregate functions like SUM(), COUNT(), etc.

e.g.
```
SELECT Department, COUNT(*)
                    AS EmployeeCount
FROM Employees
GROUP BY Department
HAVING COUNT(*) > 10;
```

(b) Differences between Single Row Functions and Aggregate Functions

Single Row Functions	Aggregate Functions
Operate on a single row and return one result per row.	Operate on multiple rows and return a single result (e.g., SUM, AVG).
Examples UPPER(), LOWER(), SUBSTR()	*Examples* COUNT(), SUM(), AVG(), MAX(), MIN()

(c) The Cartesian Product in SQL refers to the result of joining two or more tables without any condition. This operation results in all possible combinations of rows from the participating tables.

For example, if Table A has 3 rows and Table B has 4 rows, the Cartesian Product will result in 12 rows (3 × 4).

(d) Functions for the specified operations:

(i) DAYNAME (Date)

(ii) SUBSTR(string, pos, n)

(iii) MONTHNAME(Date)

(iv) UPPER(string)

2. Write the output produced by the following SQL commands:

(a)
```
SELECT POW(2,3);
```
(b)
```
SELECT ROUND(123.2345, 2),
ROUND(342.9234,-1);
```
(c)
```
SELECT LENGTH("Informatics Practices");
```
(d)
```
SELECT YEAR("1979/11/26"),
MONTH("1979/11/26"),
DAY("1979/11/26"),
MONTHNAME("1979/11/26");
```
(e)
```
SELECT LEFT("INDIA",3), RIGHT("Computer
Science",4);
```
(f)
```
SELECT MID("Informatics",3,4),
SUBSTR("Practices",3);
```

Ans. (a) **Output** 8

(b) **Output** 123.23, 340

(c) **Output** 21

(d) **Output** 1979, 11, 26, November

(e) **Output** IND, ence

(f) **Output** form, actices

3. Consider the following table named "Product", showing details of products being sold in a grocery shop.

PCode	PName	UPrice	Manufacturer
P01	Washing Powder	120	Surf
P02	Tooth Paste	54	Colgate
P03	Soap	25	Lux
P04	Tooth Paste	65	Pepsodant
P05	Soap	38	Dove
P06	Shampoo	245	Dove

(a) Write SQL queries for the following:

(i) Create the table Product with appropriate data types and constraints.

(ii) Identify the primary key in Product.

(iii) List the Product Code, Product name and price in descending order of their product name. If PName is the same then display the data in ascending order of price.

(iv) Add a new column Discount to the table Product.

(v) Calculate the value of the discount in the table Product as 10 per cent of the UPrice for all those products where the UPrice is more than 100, otherwise the discount will be 0.

(vi) Increase the price by 12 per cent for all the products manufactured by Dove.

(vii) Display the total number of products manufactured by each manufacturer.

(b) Write the output(s) produced by executing the following queries on the basis of the information given above in the table Product:

(i) `SELECT PName, Average(UPrice) FROM Product GROUP BY Pname;`

(ii) `SELECT DISTINCT Manufacturer FROM Product;`

(iii) `SELECT COUNT(DISTINCT PName) FROM Notes Product;`

(iv) `SELECT PName, MAX(UPrice), MIN(UPrice) FROM Product GROUP BY PName;`

Ans. (a)

(i)
```
CREATE TABLE Product (
    PCode VARCHAR(10) PRIMARY KEY,
    PName VARCHAR(50),
    UPrice DECIMAL(10, 2),
    Manufacturer VARCHAR(50)
);
```

(ii) In the above CREATE TABLE statement, PCode is specified as the primary key.

(iii)
```
SELECT PCode, PName, UPrice
FROM Product
ORDER BY PName DESC, UPrice ASC;
```

(iv)
```
ALTER TABLE Product
ADD Discount DECIMAL(10, 2);
```

(v)
```
UPDATE Product
SET Discount = CASE WHEN UPrice >
        100 THEN UPrice * 0.10 ELSE 0 END;
```

(vi)
```
UPDATE Product
SET UPrice = UPrice * 1.12
WHERE Manufacturer = 'Dove';
```

(vii)
```
SELECT Manufacturer, COUNT(*)
AS TotalProducts
FROM Product
GROUP BY Manufacturer;
```

(b) (i) It shows error as there is no function average(). If the function is correct then the output will be

Output

PName	Average(UPrice)
Washing Powder	120.0
Tooth Paste	59.5
Soap	31.5
Shampoo	245.0

(ii) This query retrieves unique manufacturer names from the "Product" table.

Output

Manufacturer
Surf
Colgate
Lux
Pepsodant
Dove

(iii) There seems to be a typo or error in this query (Notes Product is not valid syntax). Assuming it's supposed to count distinct product names (PName):

Output

COUNT(DISTINCT PName)
4

(Counting distinct product names: Washing Powder, Tooth Paste, Soap, Shampoo)

(iv) This query retrieves the maximum and minimum unit prices (UPrice) for each product name (PName).

Output

PName	MAX(UPrice)	MIN(UPrice)
Washing Powder	120	120
Tooth Paste	65	54
Soap	38	25
Shampoo	245	245

Note For products where there's only one entry, MAX(UPrice) and MIN(UPrice) will be the same.

4. Using the CARSHOWROOM database given in the chapter, write the SQL queries for the following:

CarId	CarName	Price	Model	YearManu -facture	Fuel type
D001	Car1	582613.00	LXI	2017	Petrol
D002	Car1	673112.00	VXI	2018	Petrol
B001	Car2	567031.00	Si gmal.2	2019	Petrol
B002	Car2	647858.00	Del tal.2	2018	Petrol
E001	Car3	355205.00	5 STR STD	2017	CNG
E002	Car3	654914.00	CARE	2018	CNG
S001	Car4	514000.00	LXI	2017	Petrol
S002	Car4	614000.00	VXI	2018	Petrol

(a) Add a new column Discount in the INVENTORY table.

(b) Set appropriate discount values for all cars keeping in mind the following:

(i) No discount is available on the LXI model.

(ii) VXI model gives a 10% discount.

(iii) A 12% discount is given on cars other than LXI model and VXI model.

(c) Display the name of the costliest car with fuel type "Petrol".

(d) Calculate the average discount and total discount available on Car4.

(e) List the total number of cars having no discount.

Ans. (a)
```
ALTER TABLE INVENTORY
ADD COLUMN Discount DECIMAL(10, 2);
```
(b) (i)
```
UPDATE INVENTORY SET DISCOUNT = 0
WHERE MODEL = "LXI";
```
(ii)
```
UPDATE INVENTORY
SET Discount = Price * 0.10
WHERE Model = 'VXI';
```
(iii)
```
UPDATE INVENTORY
SET Discount = Price * 0.12
WHERE Model NOT IN ('LXI', 'VXI');
```
(c)
```
SELECT CarName, MAX(Price) AS MaxPrice
FROM INVENTORY
WHERE FuelType = 'Petrol';
```
(d)
```
SELECT AVG(Discount) AS AverageDiscount,
SUM(Discount) AS TotalDiscount
FROM INVENTORY
WHERE CarName = 'Car4';
```
(e)
```
SELECT COUNT(*) AS NoDiscountCars
FROM INVENTORY
WHERE Discount = 0;
```

5. Consider the following tables Student and Stream in the Streams_of_Students database. The primary key of the Stream table is StCode (stream code) which is the foreign key in the Student table. The primary key of the Student table is AdmNo (admission number).

AdmNo	Name	StCode
211	Jay	NULL
241	Aditya	S03
290	Diksha	S01
333	Jasqueen	S02
356	Vedika	S01
380	Ashpreet	S03

StCode	Stream
S01	Science
S02	Commerce
S03	Humanities

Write SQL queries for the following:

(a) Create the database Streams_Of_Students.

(b) Create the table Student by choosing appropriate data types based on the data given in the table.

(c) Identify the Primary keys from tables Student and Stream. Also, identify the foreign key from the table Stream.

(d) Jay has now changed his stream to Humanities. Write an appropriate SQL query to reflect this change.

(e) Display the names of students whose names end with the character 'a'. Also, arrange the students in alphabetical order.

(f) Display the names of students enrolled in Science and Humanities stream, ordered by student name in alphabetical order, then by admission number in ascending order (for duplicating names).

(g) List the number of students in each stream having more than 1 student.

(h) Display the names of students enrolled in different streams, where students are arranged in descending order of admission number.

(i) Show the Cartesian product on the Student and Stream table. Also mention the degree and cardinality produced after applying the Cartesian product.

(j) Add a new column 'TeacherIncharge" in the Stream table. Insert appropriate data in each row.

(k) List the names of teachers and students.

(l) If Cartesian product is again applied on Student and Stream tables, what will be the degree and cardinality of this modified table?

Ans. (a) `CREATE DATABASE Streams_Of_Students;`

(b)
```
CREATE TABLE Student (
    AdmNo INT PRIMARY KEY,
    Name VARCHAR(50),
    StCode CHAR(3),
        FOREIGN KEY (StCode) REFERENCES
Stream(StCode)
);
```

(c) **Primary key in Student table** AdmNo

Primary key in Stream table StCode

Foreign key in Student table referencing Stream table StCode

(d)
```
UPDATE Student
SET StCode = 'S03'
WHERE Name = 'Jay';
```

(e)
```
SELECT Name
FROM Student
WHERE Name LIKE '%a'
ORDER BY Name ASC;
```

(f)
```
SELECT S.Name
FROM Student S
JOIN Stream St ON S.StCode = St.StCode
WHERE St.Stream IN ('Science', 'Humanities')
ORDER BY S.Name ASC, S.AdmNo ASC;
```

(g)
```
SELECT St.Stream, COUNT(*) AS
Num_Students
FROM Student S
JOIN Stream St ON S.StCode = St.StCode
GROUP BY St.Stream
HAVING COUNT(*) > 1;
```

(h)
```
SELECT S.Name, St.Stream
FROM Student S
JOIN Stream St ON S.StCode = St.StCode
ORDER BY S.AdmNo DESC;
```

(i) To perform a Cartesian product (or cross join) on the Student and Stream tables, we'll combine every row from the Student table with every row from the Stream table, since there is no explicit join condition specified.

Cartesian Product (Student × Stream):

AdmNo	Name	StCode	Stream
211	Jay	NULL	S01
211	Jay	NULL	S02
211	Jay	NULL	S03
241	Aditya	S03	S01
241	Aditya	S03	S02
241	Aditya	S03	S03
290	Diksha	S01	S01
290	Diksha	S01	S02
290	Diksha	S01	S03
333	Jasqueen	S02	S01
333	Jasqueen	S02	S02
333	Jasqueen	S02	S03
356	Vedika	S01	S01
356	Vedika	S01	S02
356	Vedika	S01	S03
380	Ashpreet	S03	S01
380	Ashpreet	S03	S02
380	Ashpreet	S03	S03

Degree The Cartesian product of two tables results in a new table with a degree equal to the sum of the degrees of the original tables. In this case, the original tables have 2 and 1 columns respectively, so the resulting table has a degree of 5 (3 + 2).

Cardinality The cardinality (or size) of the Cartesian product is the product of the number of rows in each table. The Student table has 6 rows and the Stream table has 3 rows, so the Cartesian product will have 6 * 3 = 18 rows.

(j)
```
mysql > ALTER TABLE Stream
ADD COLUMN TeacherIncharge varchar(30);
mysql > UPDATE stream
SET TeacherIncharge = 'Ananyan Kant'
WHERE stream = 'Science';
mysql > UPDATE stream
SET TeacherIncharge = 'Joseph Turner'
WHERE stream = 'Commerce';
mysql > UPDATE stream
SET TeacherIncharge = 'Subham Gill'
WHERE stream = 'Humanities';
```

STCode	Stream	TeacherIncharge
S01	Science	Ananya Kant
S02	Commerce	Joseph Turner
S03	Humanities	Shubham Gill

(k)
```
SELECT Name, TeacherIncharge
FROM  Student s JOIN Stream st ON
                s.StCode = st.StCode;
```

(l) **Degree of the modified table** 6 (as one column is added in the stream table)

Cardinality of the modified table 18 (will remain the same)

EXAM PATTERN QUESTIONS

Objective Type Questions

Multiple Choice Questions

1. Which type of SQL function work with a single row at a time?
(a) Multiple-row functions
(b) Single-row functions
(c) Both (a) and (b)
(d) None of the above

2. Which of the following is the correct syntax of LCASE( ) function?
(a) LCASE (row_ name)
(b) LCE (column_name)
(c) LCASE (str/column_name)
(d) None of the above

3. The correct output of
```
SELECT TRIM (LEADING "&" FROM "&&& India &&&&"); is
```
(a) India &&& (b) India &&&&
(c) && India (d) &&& India

4. The string function that returns the index of the first occurrence of substring is ________.
(a) INSERT() (b) INSTR()
(c) INSTRING() (d) INFSTR()

5. What will be the output of the following query? CBSE 2024
```
SELECT SUBSTR ("G20 2023 INDIA", 5,4);
```
(a) G20 2 (b) 2023
(c) INDI (d) 023

6. Which MySQL string function is used to extract a substring from a given string based on a specified starting position and length ? CBSE 2024
(a) SUBSTRING_INDEX ()
(b) LENGTH ()
(c) MID ()
(d) TRIM ()

7. To remove the leading and trailing space from data values in a column of MySQL table, we use CBSE 2023
(a) LEFT () (b) RIGHT ()
(c) TRIM () (d) LTRIM ()

8. If the substring is not present in a string, the INSTR () returns CBSE 2023
(a) -1 (b) 1
(c) NULL (d) 0

9. Write the output of the following SQL command left ("Jammu Region",5);
(a) Region (b) Jammu
(c) Jammu Region (d) None of these

10. The return type of POWER( ) function is
(a) String (b) Date
(c) Numeric (d) None of these

11. The correct syntax of MOD ( ) function is
(a) MOD (Divisor, Dividend)
(b) MOD (Dividend)
(c) MOD (Divisor)
(d) MOD (Dividend, Divisor)

12. Which SQL function calculates a^b ? CBSE 2025
(a) MOD () (b) POWER ()
(c) RAISE () (d) ROUND ()

13. In which function, null values are excluded from the result returned?
(a) SUM (b) MAX
(c) MIN (d) All of these

14. Write the output of the following SQL command:
select round(458.45, -1);
(a) 450 (b) 460
(c) 458 (d) 500

15. What will be the output of the following query? CBSE 2024
```
SELECT POW (2, MOD (17,3));
```
(a) 8 (b) 1
(c) 0 (d) 4

16. Which of the following is the correct output of the following SQL command? CBSE 2023
```
SELECT ROUND (7876. 4568,2);
```
(a) 7876.46 (b) 7876.45
(c) 7900 (d) 7900.4568

17. **Which of the following is not a valid aggregate function in MySQL?** **CBSE 2023**

(a) COUNT () (b) SUM ()
(c) MAX () (d) LEN ()

18. **If column "Fees" contains the data set (5000,8000,7500,5000,8000), what will be the output after the execution of the given query?** **CBSE SQP 2022-23**

```
SELECT SUM (DISTINCT Fees) FROM student;
```

(a) 20500 (b) 10000 (c) 20000 (d) 33500

19. **Which one of the following is used to find the largest value from the given data in MySQL?** **CBSE SQP 2022-23**

(a) MAX( ) (b) MAXIMUM( )
(c) BIG( ) (d) LARGE( )

20. **In SQL, which function is used to display current date and time?** **CBSE SQP 2022-2023**

(a) Date () (b) Time ()
(c) Current () (d) Now ()

21. **What will be the output of the following SQL command?** **CBSE 2025**

```
SELECT MONTHNAME ('2024-08-02');
```

(a) 08 (b) 02
(c) February (d) August

22. **Which aggregate function returns the count of all rows in a specified table?**

(a) SUM (b) DISTINCT
(c) COUNT (d) None of these

23. **What values does the count(*) function ignore?**

(a) Repetitive values (b) Null values
(c) Characters (d) Integers

24. **Fill in the Blank** **CBSE SQP 2024-25**

The COUNT(*) function provides the total number of ______ within a relation (table) in a relational database.

(a) Columns (b) Unique values
(c)Not-null values (d)Rows

25. **Which SQL statement do we use to find out the total number of records present in the table ORDERS?** **CBSE SQP 2022-23**

(a) `SELECT * FROM ORDERS;`
(b) `SELECT COUNT (*) FROM ORDERS;`
(c) `SELECT FIND (*) FROM ORDERS;`
(d) `SELECT SUM () FROM ORDERS;`

26. **Which type of values will not be considered by SQL while executing the following statement?** **CBSE SQP 2022-23**

```
SELECT COUNT(column name) FROM inventory;
```

(a) Numeric value (b) text value
(c) Null value (d) Date value

27. **Aggregate functions are also known as** **CBSE 2023**

(a) scalar functions (b) single row functions
(c) multiple row functions (d) hybrid functions

28. **Which of the following is not an aggregate function in MySQL?** **CBSE 2024**

(a) AVG () (b) MAX ()
(c) LCASE () (d) MIN ()

29. **Which one of the following is not an aggregate function?** **CBSE SQP 2022-23**

(a) ROUND() (b) SUM()
(c) COUNT() (d) AVG()

30. **Which of the following is not an aggregate function in SQL?** **CBSE 2025**

(a) COUNT(*) (b) MIN ()
(c) LEFT () (d) AVG()

31. **Which of the following keyword sorts the records in ascending order by default?**

(a) GROUP BY (b) HAVING
(c) ORDER BY (d) None of these

32. **Ravisha has stored the records of all students of her class in a MySQL table. Suggest a suitable SQL clause that she should use to display the names of students in alphabetical order.** **CBSE 2023**

(a) SORT BY (b) ALIGN BY
(c) GROUP BY (d) ORDER BY

33. **To specify condition with a GROUP BY clause, ______clause is used.**

(a) USE (b) Where
(c) HAVING (d) LIKE

34. **What is the meaning of "HAVING" clause in MySQL?**

(a) To filter out the row values
(b) To filter out the column values
(c) To filter out the row and column values
(d) None of the above

35. **Match the following SQL functions/clauses with their descriptions:** **CBSE SQP 2024-25**

SQL Function		Description
P. MAX()	1.	Find the position of a substring in a string.
Q. SUBSTRING()	2.	Returns the maximum value in a column.
R. INSTR()	3.	Sorts the data based on a column.
S. ORDER BY	4.	Extracts a portion of a string.

(a) P-2, Q-4, R-3, S-1 (b) P-2, Q-4, R-1, S-3
(c) P-4, Q-3, R-2, S-1 (d) P-4, Q-2, R-1, S-3

36. **With respect to SQL, match the function given in column-II with categories given in column-I:** CBSE 2025

	Column I		Column II
(i)	Math function	(a)	COUNT()
(ii)	Aggregate function	(b)	ROUND()
(iii)	Date function	(c)	RIGHT()
(iv)	Text function	(d)	YEAR()

(a) (i) → (c), (ii) → (d), (iii) → (a), (iv) → (b)
(b) (i) → (b), (ii) → (a), (iii) → (d), (iv) → (c)
(c) (i) → (d), (ii) → (b), (iii) → (a), (iv) → (c)
(d) (i) → (b), (ii) → (c), (iii) → (d), (iv) → (a)

Fill in the Blanks

37. The .... functions of SQL are used to extract, change, format and alter character strings.

38. The SUBSTR( ) function returns the specified number of characters from a particular .... of a given string.

39. RTRIM function removes the .... from the characters of a string passed as an argument.

41. MID( ) function returns a .... of the specified length starting from the specified position.

41. The MOD( ) function returns the remainder of a number .... by another number.

42. .... function returns the square root of a given number.

43. The SQL function .... computes the number of rows in a table.

44. The SQL function .... obtains the smallest value in a selected column.

45. SQL stores date in .... format.

46. .... returns the name of the week day from a date specified as an argument.

47. The return type of DAYOFMONTH function is ....

48. The argument type of DAYOFYEAR function is ....

49. Aggregate functions are also known as ....

50. Columns can be sorted in descending sequence by using the .... keyword.

State Whether True or False

51. pos is an integer indicating the length of the substring.

52. SQRT ( ) returns the square root of a given number.

53. In TRUNCATE (M, N), M is the number to be truncated.

54. The MOD() function in SQL returns the quotient of division operation between two numbers. CBSE 2025

55. In SQL, the HAVING clause is used to apply filter on groups formed by the GROUP BY clause. CBSE SQP 2024-25

Assertion and Reason Based Questions

Assertion (A) and Reason (R) based questions. Mark the correct choice as

(a) Both (A) and (R) are true and (R) is the correct explanation for (A).
(b) Both (A) and (R) are true and (R) is not the correct explanation for (A).
(c) (A) is true and (R) is false.
(d) (A) is false but (R) is true.

56. **Assertion (A)** CHAR() return the character value of the given integer value according to the ASCII table.

Reason (R) CHAR() ignores the NULL value and by default returns a binary string.

57. **Assertion (A)** MID() returns a substring of the specified length starting from the specified position.

Reason (R) SELECT MID ('Environment', 4, 3); return the ron.

58. **Assertion (A)** SELECT RIGHT ('Program',4); Output will be '-ram';

Reason (R) It is used to return a specified number of characters from the right of the string. The number of characters returned is determined by the second argument.

59. **Assertion (A)** SELECT INSTR('Python Program', 'thon')' will produce the output 2.

Reason (R) INSTR() function takes two arguments as str (string) and sub_str (sub string) and returns the position of the first occurrence of a specified sub_str from a given str.

60. **Assertion (A)** The ROUND () function in SQL can be used to round off a number to a specified number of decimal places. CBSE 2025

Reason (R) The ROUND () function is a string function that accepts character values as input and returns numerical values as output.

61. **Assertion (A)** Aggregate functions are also known as group functions, they return a result in multiple rows based on table.

Reason (R) Aggregate functions return a single value, calculated from values in a column.

62. **Assertion (A)** Multiple row function work with data of multiple rows at a time and return a single output value.

Reason (R) SUM(), AVG(), MAX(), MIN(), COUNT() etc. are examples of aggregate functions.

Answers

1. (b) Single-row functions
2. (c) LCASE (str/column_name)
3. (b) India &&&&
4. (b) INSTR()
5. (b) 2023
6. (c) MID ()
7. (c) TRIM ()
8. (d) 0
9. (b) Jammu
10. (c) Numeric
11. (d) MOD (Dividend, Divisor)
12. (b) POWER ()
13. (d) All of these
14. (b) 460
15. (d) 4
16. (a) 7876.46
17. (d) LEN ()
18. (a) 20500
19. (a) MAX( )
20. (d) Now ()
21. (d) August
22. (c) COUNT
23. (b) Null values
24. (d)Rows
25. (b) `SELECT COUNT (*) FROM ORDERS;`
26. (c) Null value
27. (c) multiple row functions
28. (c) LCASE ()
29. (a) ROUND()
30. (c) LEFT ()
31. (c) ORDER BY
32. (d) ORDER BY
33. (c) HAVING
34. (a) To filter out the row values
35. (b) P-2, Q-4, R-1, S-3
36. (b) (i) → (b), (ii) → (a), (iii) → (d), (iv) → (c)
37. text
38. position
39. trailing space
40. substring
41. dividing
42. SQRT
43. COUNT
44. MIN
45. date/time
46. DAYNAME( )
47. integer
48. date
49. group functions
50. DESC
51. False
52. True
53. True
54. False
55. True
56. (c) (A) is true and (R) is false.
57. (a) Both (A) and (R) are true and (R) is the correct explanation for (A).
58. (d) (A) is false but (R) is true.
59. (d) (A) is false but (R) is true.
60. (c) (A) is true and (R) is false.
61. (d) (A) is false but (R) is true.
62. (a) Both (A) and (R) are true and (R) is the correct explanation for (A).

Subjective Type Questions

Very Short Answer Type Questions

1. How many types of single-row functions are there in MySQL?

Ans. The single-row functions have been categorised into three types such as:

(i) String/Text functions
(ii) Mathematical functions
(iii) Date/Time functions

2. How will you remove leading and trailing blank spaces from a character string?

Ans. By using TRIM() function

3. Write a command to display the first three characters of a string 'Computer'.

Ans. `mysql>SELECT SUBSTR('Computer',1,3);`

4. How to display the name 'RAHUL' and 'DEEPAK' into lowercase?

Ans. To convert a uppercase string into lowercase use LOWER() function

```
mysql>SELECT LOWER('RAHUL');
mysql>SELECT LOWER('DEEPAK');
```

5. Name any two text functions.

Ans. Two text functions are:

(i) UPPER( )
(ii) TRIM( )

6. Which function returns character string by converting each character to lower case.

Ans. LOWER( ) function

7. Mention the output of the following SQL query.

`mysql>SELECT MID(Class, 2,3);`

Ans. las

8. Write the output of the following query:

`mysql>SELECT SUBSTR(STUDENT,3,3);`

Ans. UDE

9. Consider the string: "Database Management System". Write suitable SQL queries for the following: CBSE SQP 2024-2025

(i) To extract and display "Manage" from the string.

(ii) Display the position of the first occurrence of "base" in the given string.

Ans. (i) `SELECT SUBSTRING('Database Management System', 10, 6);`
(ii) `SELECT INSTR('Database Management System', 'base');`

10. Consider the string, "Informatics Practices". Write suitable SQL queries for the following: CBSE 2025

(i) To convert the entire string to uppercase.

(ii) To display the total number of characters in the given string.

Ans. (i) Convert the entire string to uppercase:
```
SELECT UPPER('Informatics Practices');
```
(ii) Display the total number of characters in the string:
```
SELECT LENGTH('Informatics Practices');
```

11. Write the output of the statement given below.
```
mysql>SELECT ROUND(200.50, 1)
```
Ans. 200.5

12. `mysql>SELECT ROUND(6.5675,2);`
Write the output of the above SQL query.

Ans. 6.57

13. Which function is used to find the round off value of the specified floating point number?

Ans. ROUND()

14. Differentiate between COUNT ( ) and COUNT (DISTINCT) functions.

Ans. COUNT ( ) function returns the total number of records of a specified column whereas COUNT (DISTINCT) function returns the number of distinct rows in a specified table.

15. Write the output of the following SQL query.
```
SELECT POW(INSTR ('My_Database', '-',2);
```
Ans. 9

16. Which function is used to get the current date?

Ans. CURDATE() function is used to get the current date.

17. Which command is used to display the system date?

Ans. SELECT SYSDATE();

18. Name any three date functions.

Ans. MONTH(), YEAR(), DAY()

19. Write an example of MONTH( ) function.

Ans. `mysql>SELECT MONTH('2014-04-12');`
Output 4

20. Mention the output of the following SQL query.
```
mysql>SELECT DAYOFMONTH ('2013-01-29');
```
Ans. 29

21. Find out the output of the following command.
```
mysql>SELECT DATE('1991-04-02 01:45:55');
```
Ans. 1991-04-02

22. Name the function that is used to count the number of characters in a character expression.

Ans. LENGTH( ) function is used to return the number of characters in a character expression.

23. How will you display the length of the string 'CAPITAL OF INDIA IS DELHI'?

Ans. By using the following command
```
mysql>SELECT LENGTH ('CAPITAL OF INDIA IS DELHI');
```

24. Write the output of the following SQL query.
```
mysql>SELECT TRUNCATE(5.3456,1);
```
Ans. 5.3

25. How are NULL values treated by aggregate functions?

Ans. Aggregate functions do not consider NULL value. NULL is simply ignored by all the aggregate functions.

26. What is meant by NULL value in MySQL?

Ans. There are three different meanings of NULL value in MySQL :
(i) Field is not applicable.
(ii) Value is not available.
(iii) Value is available but not known at that time.

27. Why is it not allowed to give string and date type arguments for SUM( ) and AVG( ) functions?

Ans. String and date are not real numbers that we calculate. So, SUM( ) and AVG( ) functions are not valid for them.

28. Write a query to display the highest salary of the employee.

Ans. `mysql > SELECT MAX (Salary) FROM EMPLOYEE;`

29. Can a GROUP BY clause be used for more than one columns? Give example.

Ans. Yes;
```
SELECT Cust_Id, CustName, Grade, City FROM
CUSTOMER GROUP BY City, Grade;
```

30. Rashmi, a database administrator needs to display house wise total number of records of 'Red' and 'Yellow' house. She is encountering an error while executing the following query: CBSE SQP 2022-2023
```
SELECT HOUSE, COUNT (*) FROM STUDENT GROUP
BY HOUSE
WHERE HOUSE='RED' OR HOUSE= 'YELLOW';
```
Help her in identifying the reason of the error and write the correct query by suggesting the possible correction (s).

Ans. The problem with the given SQL query is that WHERE clause should not be used with Group By clause. To correct the error, HAVING clause should be used instead of WHERE. Corrected Query:

```
SELECT HOUSE, COUNT(*) FROM STUDENT GROUP
BY HOUSE HAVING HOUSE= 'RED' OR
HOUSE='YELLOW';
```

31. What is the purpose of Order By clause in SQL? Explain with the help of suitable example. **CBSE SQP 2022-2023**

Ans. The ORDER BY command is used to sort the result set in ascending or descending order.

The following SQL statement displays all the customer's names in alphabetical order:

```
SELECT Cname FROM Customers ORDER BY Cname;
```

32. Keshav has written the following query to find out the sum of bonus earned by the employees of WEST zone **CBSE 2023**

```
SELECT zone, TOTAL (bonus) FROM
Employee HAVING zone = 'WEST';
```

But he got an error. Identify the errors and rewrite the query by underlining the correction(s) done.

Ans. Correct query is

```
SELECT zone, SUM(bonus) FROM Employee
GROUP BY zone HAVING zone = "WEST";
```

33. Aryan, a database administrator, has grouped records of a table with the help of GROUP BY clause. **CBSE SQP 2021-22 Term II**

He needs to further filter groups of records generated through GROUP BY clause.

Suggest suitable clause for it and properly, explain its usage with the help of an example.

Ans. He needs to use the HAVING clause. Just as the WHERE clause filters individual records on a condition, the HAVING clause can be used to filter groups on basis of a condition.

Example

```
SELECT Dept, COUNT(*) FROM Emp GROUP BY
Dept;
```

Groups the records on Emp table by Dept and displays count of employees in each department.

```
SELECT Dept, COUNT(*) FROM Emp GROUP BY
Dept HAVING COUNT(*)>5;
```

Groups the records on Emp table by Dept and displays count of employees in each department, but only those departments are shown whose number of employees are >5.

Short Answer Type I Questions

34. Which function is used to display the position of occurrence of a string 'OUR' in string 'COURSE'? Explain.

Ans. The INSTR function searches for given second string into the first string and returns the position.

Syntax `INSTR(str1, str2)`

Example `mysql>SELECT INSTR('COURSE','OUR');`

The output will be 2 because the position of string 'OUR' is at 2 in the given string 'COURSE'.

35. Write the output of the following queries:

(i) `mysql>SELECT LENGTH('NAME');`

(ii) `mysql>SELECT MID('INFORMATION',3,2);`

Ans. (i) 4

(ii) FO

36. Consider the following table structure.

STUDENT (RollNo, Name, Class, Stream, Percentage)

Give the answer of the following questions on the basis of the above table structure

(i) Write a query to display the concatenated form of name and class.

(ii) Write a query to display the name of each student in uppercase letters with their ROLLNo, whose percentage is greater than 70.

Ans. (i) `mysql> SELECT CONCAT (Name, Class) FROM STUDENT;`

(ii) `mysql>SELECT UCASE (Name), RollNo FROM STUDENT WHERE Percentage>70;`

37. A character expression name contains 'try yourself'. Write a command to pick the following set of characters from it.

(i) First 3 characters

(ii) From 3rd to 7th character

Ans. (i) mysql>SELECT LEFT ('try yourself', 3);

(ii) mysql>SELECT SUBSTR ('try yourself', 3, 7);

38. (a) Consider the given table and write the following queries in MySQL: **CBSE 2024**

Table: Sports

Sid	SName	Fees	DateofPlay	CoachId
1	Karate	1200	2024-08-24	S1
2	Football	1800	2024-09-13	S2
3	Cricket	1500	2024-06-14	S3
4	Lawn Tennis	2500	2024-09-25	S4
5	Badminton	1800	2024-10-20	S5

(i) To display Sid and name of those sports which are to be played in the month of September.

(ii) To display all Sports names in lower case.

(iii) To display last two characters of all sports names whose fees is less than 1500.

Or

(b) **Predict the output of the following queries based on the table Sports given above:**

(i) `SELECT UCASE (TRIM(SName)) FROM Sports WHERE Sid = 5;`

(ii) `SELECT LEFT (SName, 3) FROM Sports WHERE DateofPlay > "2024-09-13";`

(iii) `SELECT SUBSTR (CoachId ,1) FROM Sports WHERE SName = "Cricket" or Fees >=2000;`

Ans. (i) `SELECT Sid, SName FROM Sports WHERE month (DateofPlay)=09;`

(ii) `SELECT LCASE(SName) FROM Sports;`

(iii) `SELECT RIGHT(SName,2) FROM Sports WHERE Fees < 1500;`

Or

(i) BADMINTON

(ii) LEFT(Sname,3)
Law
Bad

(iii) SUBSTR(CoachId,1)
S3
S4

39. While dealing with string data type in MySQL, its observed that sometimes unnecessary space character comes in between which hampers the successful executing of a string manipulation module. Name the suitable MySQL function(s) to remove leading, trailing and both type of space characters from a string. Also, give MySQL queries to depict the same. **CBSE SQP 2021-22 Term II**

Ans. (i) To remove leading spaces – LTRIM()

e.g. `SELECT LTRIM("##Spaces");`

Output

```
+-------------------+
| LTRIM ("   Spaces") |
+-------------------+
| Spaces            |
+-------------------+
```

(ii) To remove trailing spaces — RTRIM()

e.g. `SELECT RTRIM("Spaces##");`

Output

```
+-------------------+
| RTRIM ("Spaces   ") |
+-------------------+
| Spaces            |
+-------------------+
```

(iii) To remove spaces in both sides— TRIM()

e.g. `SELECT TRIM("###Spaces###");`

Output

```
+----------------------+
| TRIM ("   Spaces    ") |
+----------------------+
| Spaces               |
+----------------------+
```

40. Ms. Saumya is working on a MySQL table named 'Hotel' having following structure: **CBSE SQP 2021-22 Term II**

Field	Type	Null	Key	Default	Extra
user_id	varchar(20)	Yes		NULL	
name	varchar(20)	Yes		NULL	
city	varchar(20)	Yes		NULL	
mobile_no	varchar(11)	Yes		NULL	

She need to perform following task on the table:

(i) To fetch last 2 characters from the user_id column.

(ii) To display the values of name column in lower case.

(iii) To display 3 characters from 3rd place from the column city.

Suggest suitable SQL function for the same. Also write the query to achieve the desired task.

Ans. (i) `SELECT RIGHT(user_id,2) FROM hotel;`

(ii) `SELECT LOWER(name) FROM hotel;`

(iii) `SELECT MID(city,3,3) FROM hotel;`

41. Predict the output of the following queries: **CBSE SQP 2021-22 Term II**

(i) `SELECT INSTR('exams@cbse.nic.in','.');`

(ii) `SELECT SUBSTR('exams@cbse.nic.in',7,4);`

(iii) `SELECT LEFT('exams@cbse.nic.in',5);`

Ans. Output

(i) 11

(ii) cbse

(iii) exams

42. Which type of MySQL function accepts only numeric values? Give the name of some functions of that type.

Ans. Mathematical functions accept only numeric values and return the value of same type. These functions are used to perform mathematical operations on the database data.

Some mathematical functions are given below
POW()/POWER()
ROUND()
TRUNCATE()

43. Predict the output of the following queries:

(i) `mysql>SELECT POWER(3,2);`

(ii) `mysql>SELECT DATE('2009-1-21 02:01:04');`

Ans. (i) 9 (ii) 2009-1-21

44. Write the output of the following queries:

(i) `mysql>SELECT POW(6,3);`

(ii) `mysql>SELECT YEAR('2014-02-04');`

Ans. (i) 216 (ii) 2014

45. **A numeric data field NUM contains 34786.684. Write a command to round off NUM to.**

(i) **Whole number**

(ii) **Upto 1 decimal place.**

Ans. (i) mysql>SELECT ROUND (34786.684);

(ii) mysql>SELECT ROUND (34786.684, 1);

46. **What will be the output of the following?**

(i) `SELECT POWER (5, 3);`

(ii) `SELECT ROUND (2.67, 1);`

(iii) `SELECT RIGHT ('CALCUTTA', 5);`

(iv) `SELECT DAYOFMONTH ('2014-02-25');`

Ans. (i) 125 (ii) 2.7 (iii) CUTTA (iv) 25

47. **Explain the given below functions**

(i) **TRUNCATE()** (ii) **ROUND()**

Ans. (i) **TRUNCATE()** This function returns a number with some digits truncated. TRUNCATE() function just truncates the digits without rounding off them.

Syntax `TRUNCATE(n, m)`

(a) It returns value of argument n truncated to argument m decimal places.

(b) If argument m is given as 0 places, m can be negative to truncate (*i.e.,* make zero) m digits left of the decimal point.

(ii) **ROUND()** This function returns a number rounded off as per given specifications.

Syntax `ROUND(n,[m])`

It returns value of argument n rounded to m places right of the decimal point.

48. **Help Reshma in predicting the output of the following queries.** **CBSE SQP 2021-22 Term II**

(i) `SELECT ROUND(8.72,3);`

(ii) `SELECT ROUND(9.8);`

Ans. (i)

```
+-----------------+
| ROUND (8.72, 3) |
+-----------------+
| 8.720           |
+-----------------+
```

ROUND() function rounds a number to certain decimal places. Here, number of decimal places is 3 and the number is 8.72 . So, the output will be 8.720

(ii)

```
+-------------+
| ROUND (9.8) |
+-------------+
| 0           |
+-------------+
```

ROUND() function rounds a number to certain decimal places. Here, number of decimal places is 0 . So, as per rounding rules the integer part increases by 1 to give 10.

49. **Reena is working with functions of MySQL. Explain her following** **CBSE SQP 2021-22 Term II**

(i) **What is the purpose of NOW( ) function?**

(ii) **How many parameters does it accept?**

(iii) **What is the general format of its return type?**

Ans. (i) The NOW( )function returns the system date and time.

(ii) 0 parameters

(iii) "YYYY-MM-DD HH: MM : SS".

50. **In how many ways, we can find the current date using MySQL?**

Ans. The ways are

```
SELECT CURDATE();
SELECT CURRENT_DATE();
SELECT CURRENT_DATE;
```

51. **Which type of output does the following functions return?**

(i) **DATE()** (ii) **YEAR()**

(iii) **DAYNAME()** (iv) **NOW()**

Ans. (i) Date (ii) Number

(iii) String (iv) DateTime

52. **Write the output of following MySQL queries:**

(i) `Select ROUND(6.5675,2);`

(ii) `Select DAYOFMONTH(curdate());`

(iii) `Select MID ("PRE_BOARDCLASS12", 4,6);`

Ans. (i) 6.75

(ii) Day no of curdate(), Ex. If curdate is 05/02/2021 then output is 5.

(iii) _BOARD

53. **What is the use of COUNT function?**

Ans. COUNT() function returns the total number of values or rows of the specified field or column. COUNT (*) is a special function, as it returns the count of all rows in a specified table. It includes all the null and duplicate values.

54. **Which type of output does the following functions return?**

(i) **LENGTH()** (ii) **RTRIM()**

(iii) **POW()** (iv) **SUBSTR()**

Ans. (i) Number (ii) String

(iii) Number (iv) String

55. **What will be the output of the following queries on the basis of EMPLOYEE table?**

Table : EMPLOYEE

Emp_Id	Name	Salary
E01	Siya	54000
E02	Joy	NULL
E03	Allen	32000
E04	Neev	42000

(i) `SELECT AVG (Salary) FROM EMPLOYEE;`

(ii) `SELECT COUNT (Salary) FROM EMPLOYEE;`

(iii) `SELECT MIN (Salary) FROM EMPLOYEE;`

Ans. The output of the above queries

(i)

AVG(Salary)
42666.66

(ii)

COUNT(Salary)
3

(iii)

MIN(Salary)
32000

56. Give Employee table as follows:

Emp_Id	Name	Commission
101	Rahul Verma	NULL
102	Divya Arora	8900
103	Faizal Zaidi	NULL

What values will be following statements return?

(i) `SELECT COUNT (*) FROM Employee;`

(ii) `SELECT COUNT (Commission) FROM Employee;`

Ans. (i) 3 (ii) 1

57. Write the output (i-iii) for the following SQL commands. CBSE 2023

Table : FASHION

ID	Product	Price	Qty
F01	Kajal	970	10
F02	Foundation	2100	15
F03	Night Cream	1700	20
F04	Day Cream	1400	10
F05	Shampoo	1200	25
F06	Lipstick	850	32

(i) `SELECT COUNT(Product) FROM FASHION;`

(ii) `SELECT SUM (Price * Qty) FROM FASHION WHERE Product = "Night Cream:'`

(iii) `SELECT LEFT(Product,4) FROM FASHION WHERE Price >1500;`

Or

Find the output of the following SQL queries.

(i) `SELECT SUBSTR ("CLIMATE CHANGE", 4,4);`

(ii) `SELECT UCASE (RIGHT ("POPULATION",3);`

(iii) `SELECT LENGTH ("HAPPY") + 3;`

Ans. (i)

COUNT (Product)
6

(ii)

SUM (Price*Qty)
34000

(iii)

LEFT (Product,4)
Foun
Nigh

Or

(i) MATE

(ii) ION

(iii) 8

58. Write outputs for SQL queries (i) to (iii) which are based on the given table PURCHASE: CBSE SQP 2022-23

CNO	CNAME	CITY	QUANTITY	DOP
C01	GURPREET	NEW DELHI	150	2022-06-11
C02	MALIKA	HYDERABAD	10	2022-02-19
C03	NADAR	DALHOUSIE	100	2021-12-04
C04	SAHIB	CHANDIGARH	50	2021-10-10
C05	MEHAK	CHANDIGARH	15	2021-10-20

(i) `SELECT LENGTH(CNAME) FROM PURCHASE WHERE QUANTITY>100;`

(ii) `SELECT CNAME FROM PURCHASE WHERE MONTH(DOP)=3;`

(iii) `SELECT MOD (QUANTITY, DAY(DOP)) FROM PURCHASE WHERE CITY= 'CHANDIGARH';`

Ans. (i) 8

(ii) No Output

(iii) 0
15

Or

Discuss the significance of Group by clause in detail with the help of suitable example.

Ans. GROUP BY clause is used in a SELECT statement in combination with aggregate functions to group the result based on distinct values in a column.

59. Give the syntax of the ORDER BY clause.

Ans.
```
SELECT column_name(s)
FROM table_name
ORDER BY column_name(s) ASC/DESC;
```

60. What is the purpose of ORDER BY clause in MySQL? How is it different from GROUP BY clause?

Ans. ORDER BY clause is used to sort a particular field in either ascending order and descending order.

GROUP BY clause is used to group the rows that have the same value.

61. **Gopi Krishna is using a table EMPLOYEE. It has the following columns:**

Code, Name, Salary, Deptcode

He wants to display maximum salary departmentwise.

He wrote the following command:

```
SELECT Deptcode, MAX (Salary) FROM EMPLOYEE;
```

But he did not get desired result.

Rewrite the above query with necessary change to help him get the desired output.

Ans.
```
SELECT Deptcode, MAX (Salary)
FROM EMPLOYEE GROUP BY Deptcode;
```

62. **Mohan is using a table Employee. It has the following columns;**

```
Code, Name, Salary, Deptcode
SELECT Deptcode, MAX(Salary) FROM
Employee;
```

He wants to display maximum salary department wise. But he did not get the desired result. Rewrite the above query with necessary changes to help him get the desired result.

Ans.
```
SELECT Deptcode, MAX (Salary)
FROM Employee
GROUP BY Deptcode;
```

63. **Answer the following questions based on the table Salesman given below:** **CBSE 2024**

Table: Salesman

Salesman_Id	Name	City	Commission
5001	Neil Bhatt	Delhi	0.15
5002	Rohan Malik	Mumbai	0.13
5005	Ravi Mohan	Delhi	0.11
5006	Mehak Rai	Delhi	0.14
5007	Paul Lal	Bangalore	0.13
5003	Raman Sen	Kolkata	0.12

(i) How many tuples does the given table have?

(ii) Suggest the primary key for the given table.

(iii) Write the MySQL query to display all the records in descending order of commission.

Ans. (i) Number of tuples :6

(ii) Primary key – Salesman_id

(iii) Select * from Salesman order by commission Desc;

64. **Consider the table Patient given below and write SQL commands.** **CBSE 2023**

Table : Patient

Patientid	Name	City	Phone	DateofAdm	Department
1000001	Ritvik Garg	Delhi	68476213	2021-12-10	Surgery
1000002	Rahil Arora	Mumbai	36546321	2022-01-08	Medicine
1000003	Mehak Bhatt	Delhi	68421879	2022-02-02	Cardiology
1000004	Soumik Rao	Delhi	26543266	2022-01-11	Medicine
1000005	Suresh Sood	Bangalore	65432442	2021-03-09	Surgery

(i) Display the details of all patients who were admitted in January.

(ii) Count the total number of patients from Delhi.

(iii) Display the last 2 digits of the Patientid.

Ans. (i)
```
SELECT * FROM Patient WHERE
MONTH(DateofAdm)=1;
```
(ii)
```
SELECT COUNT (*) FROM Patient GROUP BY
CITY HAVING CITY = "Delhi";
```
(iii)
```
SELECT RIGHT (PatientId, 2) FROM Patient
WHERE Department = "Surgery";
```

65. **Shreya, a database administrator has designed a database for a clothing shop. Help her by writing answers of the following questions based on the given table:** **CBSE SQP 2022-23**

Table: Cloth

CCODE	CNAME	SIZE	COLOR	PRICE	DOP
C001	JEANS	XL	BLUE	990	2022-01-21
C002	T SHIRT	M	RED	599	2021-12-12
C003	TROUSER	M	GREY	399	2021-11-10
C004	SAREE	FREE	GREEN	1299	2019-11-12
C005	KURTI	L	WHITE	399	2021-12-07

(i) Write a query to display cloth names in lower case.

(ii) Write a query to display the lowest price of the cloths.

(iii) Write a query to count total number of cloths purchased of medium size.

***Or* (Option for part iii only)**

Write a query to count year wise total number of cloths purchased.

Ans. (i)
```
SELECT LOWER(CNAME) FROM CLOTH;
```
(ii)
```
SELECT MIN(PRICE) FROM CLOTH;
```

(iii)
```
SELECT COUNT(*) FROM CLOTH GROUP BY SIZE
HAVING SIZE='M';
```
Or
```
SELECT YEAR(DOP),COUNT(*) FROM CLOTH
GROUP BY YEAR(DOP);
```

66. **(A) Consider the following tables:** **CBSE SQP 2024-25**

Table 1

EMPLOYEE which stores Employee ID (EMP_ID), Employee Name (EMP_NAME), Employee City (EMP_CITY)

Table 2

PAYROLL which stores Employee ID (EMP_ID), Department (DEPARTMENT), Designation (DESIGNATION), and Salary (SALARY) for various employees.

Note *Attribute names are written within brackets.*

Table: EMPLOYEE

EMP_ID	EMP_NAME	EMP_CITY
1	ABHINAV	AGRA
2	KABIR	FARIDABAD
3	ESHA	NOIDA
4	PAUL	SEOUL
5	VICTORIA	LONDON

Table: PAYROLL

EMP_ID	DEPARTMENT	DESIGNATION	SALARY
1	SALES	MANAGER	75000
2	SALES	ASSOCIATE	50000
3	ENGINEERING	MANAGER	95000
4	ENGINEERING	ENGINEER	70000
5	MARKETING	MANAGER	65000

Write appropriate SQL queries for the following:

I. **Display department-wise average Salary.**

II. **List all designations in the decreasing order of Salary.**

III. **Display employee name along with their corresponding departments.**

Or

(B) Consider the following tables:

Table 1

ATHLETE, which stores AthleteID, Name, Country. The table displays basic information of the athletes

Table 2

MEDALS, which stores AthleteID, Sport, and Medals. The table displays the number of medals won by each athlete in their respective sports.

Table: ATHLETE

AthleteID	Name	COUNTRY
101	Arjun	INDIA
102	Priya	INDIA
103	Asif	UAE
104	Rozy	USA
105	David	DENMARK

Table: MEDALS

AthleteID	Sport	Medals
101	Swimming	8
102	Track	3
103	Gymnastics	5
104	Swimming	2
105	Track	6

Write appropriate SQL queries for the following:

I. **Display the sports-wise total number of medals won.**

II. **Display the names of all the Indian athletes in uppercase.**

III. **Display the athlete name along with their corresponding sports.**

Ans. (A)

I.
```
SELECT DEPARTMENT, AVG(SALARY) AS
AVG_SALARY FROM PAYROLL GROUP BY
DEPARTMENT;
```
II.
```
SELECT DESIGNATION FROM PAYROLL ORDER BY
SALARY DESC;
```
III.
```
SELECT EMPLOYEE.EMP_NAME,
PAYROLL.DEPARTMENT FROM EMPLOYEE JOIN
PAYROLL ON EMPLOYEE.EMP_ID =
PAYROLL.EMP_ID;
```
Or

(B)

I.
```
SELECT Sport, SUM(Medals) AS
Total_Medals FROM MEDALS GROUP BY Sport;
```
II.
```
SELECT UPPER(Name) FROM ATHLETE WHERE
Country = 'INDIA';
```
III.
```
SELECT A.Name, M.Sport  FROM ATHLETE A
JOIN MEDALS M ON A.AthleteID =
M.AthleteID;
```

67. (i) **Write the SQL statement to create a table, Customer with the following specifications:**

Table: Customer

Column Name	Data Type	Key
CID	Int	Primary Key
FName	Varchar(20)	
LName	Varchar(20)	
Age	Int	

(ii) **Write the SQL query to display all records in descending order of LName from the Table Customer.** **CBSE 2025**

Ans. (i) SQL statement to create the Customer table:

```
CREATE TABLE Customer (
    CID INT PRIMARY KEY,
    FName VARCHAR(20),
    LName VARCHAR(20),
    Age INT
);
```

(ii) SQL query to display all records in descending order of LName:

```
SELECT * FROM Customer ORDER BY LName DESC;
```

68. (a) **Given the following table** **CBSE 2025**

Table : STUDENTS

S_ID	NAME	AGE	CITY
1	Rahul	20	Delhi
2	Priya	22	Mumbai
3	David	21	Delhi
4	Neha	23	Bengaluru
5	Khurshid	22	Delhi

Table GRADES

S_ID	SUBJECT	GRADE
1	Math	A
2	English	B
3	Math	C
4	English	A
5	Math	B

Write SQL queries for the following:

(i) **To display the number of students from each city.**

(ii) **To find the average age of all students.**

(iii) **To list the names of students and their grades.**

Or

(b) **Consider the following table**

Table 1 : PRODUCTS

This table stores the basic details of the products available in a shop.

PID	PName	Category
201	Laptop	Electronics
202	Chair	Furniture
203	Desk	Furniture
204	Smartphone	NULL
205	Tablet	Electronics

Table 2 : SALES

This table records the number of units sold for each product.

SaleID	PID	UnitsSold
301	201	50
302	202	100
303	203	60
304	204	80
305	205	70

Write SQL queries for the following:

(i) **To delete those records from table SALES whose UnitsSold is less than 80.**

(ii) **To display names of all products whose category is not known.**

(iii) **To display the product names along with their corresponding units sold.**

Ans. (a) (i) To display the number of students from each city:

```
SELECT CITY, COUNT(*) AS Num_Students
FROM STUDENTS
GROUP BY CITY;
```

(ii) To find the average age of all students:

```
SELECT AVG(AGE) AS Average_Age
FROM STUDENTS;
```

(iii) To list the names of students and their grades:

```
SELECT STUDENTS.NAME, GRADES.GRADE
FROM STUDENTS
JOIN GRADES ON STUDENTS.S_ID = GRADES.SID;
```

Or

(b) (i) To delete those records from table SALES whose UnitsSold is less than 80:

```
DELETE FROM SALES
WHERE UnitsSold < 80;
```

(ii) To display names of all products whose category is not known:

```
SELECT PName
FROM PRODUCTS
WHERE Category IS NULL;
```

(iii) To display the product names along with their corresponding units sold:

```
SELECT PRODUCTS.PName, SALES.UnitsSold
FROM PRODUCTS
JOIN SALES ON PRODUCTS.PID = SALES.PID;
```

69. Write any two differences between UPDATE and ALTER TABLE commands of MySQL. CBSE 2024

Ans. Difference between UPDATE and ALTER TABLE :

UPDATE	ALTER TABLE
It is a DML command.	It is a DDL command.
Makes changes to data of a table.	Makes changes to structure of the table.
WHERE clause can be used with UPDATE command.	WHERE clause cannot be used with ALTER command.

Short Answer Type II Questions

70. Which SQL function is used to remove leading and trailing spaces from a character expression X, where X = 'INFORMATION ###PRACTICE####' (# denotes a blank space) and also give the output of X.

Ans. TRIM function is used to remove all leading and trailing spaces from the given character expression.

Syntax

```
TRIM ([{BOTH/ LEADING/ TRAILING} [remstr]
  FROM] str)
```

Example

```
mysql>SELECT TRIM
('INFORMATION###PRACTICE####');
```

Output

```
INFORMATION###PRACTICE
```

Spaces between 'INFORMATION' and 'PRACTICE' cannot be removed.

71. Differentiate between SUBSTR() and INSTR().

Ans.

SUBSTR()	INSTR()
It is used to extract a set of character from a string by specifying the character starting position and end position and length of characters to be fetched.	It is used to find the positon of any particular character in a word which returns numeric value.
`SELECT SUBSTR('Hello', 2,3);` **Output** ell	`SELECT INSTR('Hello','e')` **Output** 2

72. What is the difference between the functions DAYNAME( ) and DAYOFWEEK( )?

Ans. Differences between the DAYNAME( ) and DAYOFWEEK() functions are given below

DAYNAME( )	DAYOFWEEK( )
It returns the name of the weekday for date.	It returns the weekday index for date (1 = Sunday, 2 = Monday and so on).
Syntax `DAYNAME (date);`	**Syntax** `DAYOFWEEK (date);`
Query To display name of the weekday for date 21st Dec 2011.	**Query** To display the day of week for date 21st Dec 2011.
`mysql>SELECT DAYNAME ('2011-12-21');`	`mysql>SELECT DAYOFWEEK ('2011-12-21');`
Output Wednesday	**Output** 4

73. Mention the type of the functions given below with their purpose.
(i) CHAR( ) (ii) TRUNCATE( )
(iii) DAYOFMONTH( ) (iv) LEFT( )

Ans. (i) CHAR( ) It is a string function and returns the character for each integer passed.

(ii) TRUNCATE( ) It is a mathematical function and returns a number truncated upto specified number of digits.

(iii) DAYOFMONTH( ) It is a Date/Time function and returns the day of month for the specified date.

(iv) LEFT( ) It is a string function and returns the leftmost number of characters as specified.

74. (A) Rahul, who works as a database designer, has developed a database for a bookshop. This database includes a table BOOK whose column (attribute) names are mentioned below:
BCODE Shows the unique code for each book.
TITLE Indicates the book's title.
AUTHOR Specifies the author's name.
PRICE Lists the cost of the book.

CBSE SQP 2024-25

Table: BOOK

BCODE	TITLE	AUTHOR	PRICE
B001	MIDNIGHT'S CHILDREN	SALMAN RUSHDIE	500
B002	THE GOD OF SMALL THINGS	ARUNDHA TI ROY	450
B003	A SUITABLE BOY	VIKRAM SETH	600
B004	THE WHITE TIGER	ARAVIND ADIGA	399
B005	TRAIN TO PAKISTAN	KHUSHWA NT SINGH	350

I. Write SQL query to display book titles in lowercase.
II. Write SQL query to display the highest price among the books.
III. Write SQL query to display the number of characters in each book title.
IV. Write SQL query to display the Book Code and Price sorted by Price in descending order.

Or (B) Dr. Kavita has created a database for a hospital's pharmacy. The database includes a table named MEDICINE whose column (attribute) names are mentioned below:

MID Shows the unique code for each medicine.
MED_NAME Specifies the medicine name
SUPP_CITY Specifies the city where the supplier is located.
STOCK Indicates the quantity of medicine available.
DEL_DATE Specifies the date when the medicine was delivered.

Table: MEDICINE

MID	MED_NAME	SUPP_CITY	STOCK	DEL_DATE
M01	PARACETAMOL	MUMBAI	200	2023-06-15
M02	AMOXICILLIN	KOLKATA	50	2023-03-21
M03	COUGH SYRUP	BENGALURU	120	2023-02-10
M04	INSULIN	CHENNAI	135	2023-01-25
M05	IBUPROFEN	AHMEDABAD	30	2023-04-05

Write the output of the following SQL Queries.

I. `Select LENGTH(MED_NAME) from MEDICINE where STOCK > 100;`
II. `Select MED_NAME from MEDICINE where month(DEL_DATE) = 4;`
III. `Select MED_NAME from MEDICINE where STOCK between 120 and 200;`
IV. `Select max(DEL_DATE) from MEDICINE;`

Ans. (A) I. `SELECT LOWER(TITLE) AS title_lowercase FROM BOOK;`
II. `SELECT MAX(PRICE) AS highest_price FROM BOOK;`
III. `SELECT TITLE, LENGTH(TITLE) AS title_length FROM BOOK;`
IV. `SELECT BCODE, PRICE FROM BOOK ORDER BY PRICE DESC;`

Or (B) I.

LENGTH(MED_NAME)
11
11
7

II.

MED_NAME
IBUPROFEN

III.

MED_NAME
PARACETAMOL
COUGH SYRUP
INSULIN

IV.

max(DEL_DATE)
2023-06-15

75. Rupam created a MySQL table to store the details of Nobel prize winners. Help her to write the following MySQL queries: **CBSE 2024**

TABLE : NOBEL

Winner_Id	YEAR	SUBJECT	WINNER	COUNTRY	CATEGORY
1001	1970	Physics	Hannes Alfven	Sweden	Scientist
1002	1970	Physiology	Bernard Katz	NULL	Scientist
1003	1970	Literature	Aleksandr Solzhenitsyn	Russia	Linguist
1004	1971	Chemistry	Gerhard Herzberg	Germany	Scientist
1005	1978	Peace	Menachem Begin	Israel	Prime Minister
1006	1987	Economics	Robert Solow	USA	Economist
1007	1994	Literature	Kenzaburo Oe	Japan	Linguist

(i) Display the names of Nobel Prize winner in 'Literature' for the year 1970.
(ii) Display the subject and category of winners whose country is not known.
(iii) Display the details of all Nobel Prize winners who were Scientists.
(iv) Count total number of winners whose subject is Literature.

Ans. (i) `Select WINNER from NOBEL where SUBJECT="Literature" and YEAR=1970;`

(ii) `Select SUBJECT, CATEGORY from NOBEL where COUNTRY IS NULL;`

(iii) `Select * from NOBEL where CATEGORY="Scientist";`

(iv) `Select count(*) from NOBEL where SUBJECT="Literature";`

76. Consider the following table Schooldata **CBSE 2023**

Table : Schooldata

Admno	Name	Grade	Club	Marks	Gender
20150001	Sargam Singh	12	STEM	86	Male
20140212	Alok Kumar	10	SPACE	75	Male
20090234	Mohit Gaur	11	SPACE	84	Male
20130216	Romil Malik	10	READER	91	Male
20190227	Tanvi Batra	11	STEM	70	Female
20120200	Nomita Ranjan	12	STEM	64	Female

Write SQL queries for the following
(i) Display the average Marks secured by each Gender.
(ii) Display the minimum Marks secured by the students of Grade 10.
(iii) Display the total number of students in each Club where number of students are more than 1.

***Or* (Option for Part (iii) Only)**

Display the maximum and minimum marks secured by each gender.

Ans. (i) `SELECT Gender, AVG (Marks) FROM Schooldata GROUP BY Gender ;`

(ii) `SELECT MIN(Marks) FROM Schooldata WHERE GRADE=10;`

(iii) `SELECT Club, COUNT(*) FROM Schooldata GROUP BY Club HAVING COUNT(*)>1;`

Or

`SELECT Gender, MAX(Marks), MIN(Marks) FROM Schooldata GROUP BY Gender;`

77. **Satyam, a database analyst has created the following table:** CBSE SQP 2021-22 Term II

Table: Student

RegNo	SName	Stream	Optional	Marks
S1001	Akshat	Science	CS	99
S1002	Harshit	Commerce	IP	95
S1003	Devika	Humanities	IP	100
S1004	Manreen	Commerce	IP	98
S1005	Gaurav	Humanities	IP	82
S1006	Saurav	Science	CS	NULL
S1007	Bhaskar	Science	CS	95
S1007	Bhaskar	Science	CS	96

He has written following queries:

(a) `select sum(MARKS) from student where OPTIONAL= 'IP' and STREAM= 'Commerce';`

(b) `select max(MARKS)+min(MARKS) from student where OPTIONAL= 'CS';`

(c) `select avg(MARKS) from student where OPTIONAL= 'IP';`

(d) `select length(SNAME) from student where MARKS is NULL;`

Help him in predicting the output of the above given queries.

Or

Based on the above given table named 'Student', Satyam has executed following queries:

```
Select count(*) from student;
Select count(MARKS) from student;
```

Predict the output of the above given queries. Also give proper justifications of the output generated through each query.

Ans. **Output**

(a) 193 (b) 194 (c) 93.75 (d) 6

Or First query will produce the output 7.

Justification count (*) will count and display total number of rows (irrespective of any null value present in any of the column).

Second query will produce the output 6.

Justification count (col_name) will count and display total number of not null values in the specified column.

78. **Carefully observe the following table named 'stock':** CBSE SQP 2021-22 Term II

Table: stock

Pid	PName	Category	Qty	Price
1	Keyboard	IO	15	450
2	Mouse	IO	10	350
3	Wifi-router	NW	5	2600
4	Switch	NW	3	3000
5	Monitor	O	10	4500
6	Printer	O	4	17000

Write SQL queries for the following:

(a) **To display the records in decreasing order of price.**

(b) **To display category and category wise total quantities of products.**

(c) **To display the category and its average price.**

(d) **To display category and category wise highest price of the products.**

Ans. (a) `select * from stock order by Price desc;`

(b) `select Category, sum(Qty) from stock group by Category;`

(c) `select Category,avg(Price) from stock group by Category;`

(d) `select Category, max(Price) from stock group by Category;`

79. **What is the purpose of GROUP BY clause in MySQL? How is it different from ORDER BY clause?**

Ans. The GROUP BY clause can be used to combine all those records that have identical value in a particular field or a group of fields.

Whereas, ORDER BY clause is used to display the records either in ascending or descending order based on a particular field.

For ascending order, ASC is used and for descending order DESC is used. The default order is ascending order.

80. **How is HAVING clause similar to WHERE clause? How is HAVING clause different from WHERE clause? Explain with the help of examples of each.**

Ans. **Similarity** HAVING and WHERE both can be said to be as decision structures which are used in SQL to take an action to the database or more specifically on any table of database by matching a some sort of string or valued based on the values already present in tha database.

Difference A WHERE clause is used to filter records from a result. The filter occurs before any groupings are made. A HAVING clause is used to filter values from a group.

81. (a) **An educational institution is maintaining a database for storing the details of courses being offered. The database includes a table COURSE with the following attributes:** CBSE 2025

C_ID Stores the unique ID for each course.

C_NAME Stores the course's name.

INSTRUCTOR Stores the name of the course instructor.

DURATION Stores the duration of the course in hours.

Table: COURSE

C_ID	C_NAME	INSTRUCTOR	DURATION
C101	Data Structures	Dr. Alok	40
C102	Machine Learning	Prof. Sunita	60
C103	Web Development	Ms. Sakshi	45
C104	Database Management	Mr. Suresh	50
C105	Python Programming	Dr. Pawan	35

Write SQL queries for the following:

(i) To add a new record with following specifications:

C_ID C106

C_NAME Introduction to AI

INSTRUCTOR Ms. Preeti

DURATION 55

(ii) To display the longest duration among all courses.

(iii) To count total number of courses run by the institution.

(iv) To display the instructors' name in lower case.

Or **(b) Ashutosh, who is a manager, has created a database to manage employee records. The database includes a table named EMPLOYEE whose attribute names are mentioned below:**

EID Stores the unique ID for each employee.

EMP_NAME Stores the name of the employee.

DEPT Stores the department of the employee.

SALARY Stores the salary of the employee.

JOIN_DATE Stores the employee's joining date.

Table : EMPLOYEE

E_ID	EMP_NAME	DEPT	SALARY	JOIN_DATE
E01	ARJUN SINGH	SALES	75000	2019-11-01
E02	PRIYA JAIN	ENGINEERING	85000	2020-05-20
E03	RAVI SHARMA	MARKETING	60000	2018-08-14
E04	AYESHA	NULL	50000	2021-01-10
E05	RAHUL VERMA	FINANCE	40000	2017-06-25

(i) `Select SUBSTRING (EMP_NAME, 1 5) from EMPLOYEE where DEPT = 'ENGINEERING';`

(ii) `Select EMP_NAME from EMPLOYEE where month (JOIN_DATE) = 8;`

(iii) `Select EMP_NAME from EMPLOYEE where SALARY > 60000;`

(iv) `Select count (DEPT) from EMPLOYEE;`

Ans. (a) (i)
```
INSERT INTO COURSE (C_ID, C_NAME,
INSTRUCTOR, DURATION)
VALUES ('C106', 'Introduction to
AI', 'Ms. Preeti', 55);
```
(ii) `SELECT MAX(DURATION) FROM COURSE;`

(iii) `SELECT COUNT(*) FROM COURSE;`

(iv) `SELECT LOWER(INSTRUCTOR) FROM COURSE;`

Or

(b) (i) PRIYA

(Since PRIYA JAIN is in the ENGINEERING department, and SUBSTRING (EMP_NAME, 1, 5) extracts the first five characters.)

(ii) RAVI SHARMA

(Since RAVI SHARMA joined in August (08-14-2018).)

(iii) ARJUN SINGH

PRIYA JAIN

(Since ARJUN SINGH (?75,000) and PRIYA JAIN (?85,000) have salaries greater than ?60,000.)

(iv) 4

(There are 5 records, but one has NULL in the DEPT column, so only 4 are counted.)

Long Answer Type Questions

82. Write a query to extract a sub string from the string, "TAJMAHALAGRA1", which should be 5 characters long and start from 4th character of the given string. Also, give the syntax of the function that is being used in the query.

Ans. The MID function or SUBSTR function returns a substring starting from the specified position.

Syntax `MID(str, pos, len);`

or `SUBSTR (str, pos, len);`

str is a string from which a substring will be extracted.

pos is an integer indicating the position (within the str) from where extraction should start.

len is an integer indicating the length of the extracted string.

Query

```
mysql>SELECT MID ('TAJMAHALAGRA1', 4, 5);
```

Output

MAHAL

83. **Write down the syntax format of the following functions, with one example of each.**

(i) LCASE(str)
(ii) UCASE(str)
(iii) RIGHT(str)
(iv) POWER(m,n)
(v) RTRIM(str)

Ans. (i) Syntax LCASE (str)
Example `mysql>SELECT LCASE('MySQL');`
Output mysql

(ii) Syntax UCASE (str)
Example `mysql>SELECT UCASE('Mystring');`
Output MYSTRING

(iii) Syntax RIGHT (str,n)
Example `mysql>SELECT RIGHT('America',3);`
Output ica

(iv) Syntax POWER (m,n)
Example `mysql>SELECT POWER(2,2);`
Output 4

(v) Syntax RTRIM (str)
Example `mysql>SELECT RTRIM("##Arihant##");`
where # denotes space.
Output ##Arihant

84. **Write the resulting output of the following queries.**

(i) `mysql>SELECT LOWER ('INFORMATIONPRACTICE');`
(ii) `mysql>SELECT CONCAT('Great', 'India');`
(iii) `mysql>SELECT LENGTH('Delhi Public School');`
(iv) `mysql>SELECT SUBSTR('GREAT INDIA', 3, 6);`
(v) `mysql>SELECT ROUND(23.345, 2);`

Ans. (i) 'informationpractice' (ii) GreatIndia
(iii) 19 (iv) EAT IN
(v) 23.36

85. **Give the output of following commands.**

(i) `mysql>SELECT TRUNCATE (200.91,1);`
(ii) `mysql>SELECT LEFT ('Swati',4);`
(iii) `mysql>SELECT CHAR (83,72,85,67,72,73);`
(iv) `mysql>SELECT RTRIM('!!!!!Study is important !!!!!');` Where !!!!! denotes blank spaces
(v) `SELECT ROUND(3234.343, 1);`

Ans. (i) 200.9
(ii) Swat
(iii) SHUCHI
(iv) !!!!! Study is important
(v) 3234.3

86. **Write the output of following queries.**

(i) `mysql>SELECT POWER(9,3);`
(ii) `mysql>SELECT MID("SHUCHI GOYAL", 8,5);`
(iii) `mysql>SELECT RIGHT("Dushyant",5);`
(iv) `mysql>SELECT INSTR("SQL FUNCTIONS", "C");`
(v) `SELECT LEFT("Arihant",2);`

Ans. (i) 729 (ii) GOYAL
(iii) hyant (iv) 8 (v) Ar

87. **Consider the following table CLUB.**

Table : CLUB

COACH_ID	COACH NAME	AGE	SPORTS	Date_of_Joining	PAY
1	Rajesh	30	Karate	1999-08-25	1000
2	Anuj	35	Swimming	2000-01-05	750
3	Shuchi	25	Basketball	2005-01-04	1200
4	Reetika	28	Badminton	2002-08-25	1400
5	Virendra	32	Cricket	1996-05-17	1500

Give the answer of the following questions on the basis of the above table.

(i) **Write a query to display the substring of 4 characters of the name of each coach, starting from second character, with their age.**

(ii) **What will be the output of the following query?**
`mysql>SELECT CONCAT (COACHNAME, AGE) FROM CLUB WHERE AGE> 30;`

(iii) **Write a query to display the day for the Date_of_Joining column.**

(iv) **What will be the ouput of the following query?**
```
mysql>SELECT PAY *0.25 + 1000
  FROM CLUB
  WHERE COACHNAME LIKE 'R%';
```

(v) **Write a query to display 3 characters from left of coach name.**

Ans. (i) `mysql>SELECT SUBSTR (COACHNAME, 2,4), AGE FROM CLUB;`

(ii)

CONCAT (COACHNAME, AGE)
Anuj35
Virendra32

(iii) `mysql>SELECT DAY (Date_of_Joining);`

(iv)

PAY*0.25 + 1000
1250
1350

(v) `mysql>SELECT LEFT ('COACHNAME', 3);`

88. **Consider the table EXAM given below. Write the queries for (i) to (v).**

Table : EXAM

SNo	Name	Stipend	Subject	Average	Division
1	Karan	400	English	68	Ist
2	Aman	680	Mathematics	72	Ist
3	Javed	500	Accounts	67	Ist
4	Bishakh	200	Informatics	55	IInd
5	Sugandha	400	History	35	IIIrd
6	Suparna	550	Geography	45	IIIrd

(i) To list the names of those students, who have obtained division as Ist in ascending order of Name.

(ii) To count the number of students, who have either Accounts or Informatics as Subject.

(iii) To display maximum average.

(iv) To display a report listing Name, Subject and annual Stipend received assuming that the Stipend column has monthly stipend.

(v) Identify primary key from given attributes.

Ans. (i) `SELECT Name FROM EXAM WHERE Division = "Ist" ORDER BY Name;`

(ii) `SELECT COUNT (*) FROM EXAM WHERE Subject = "Accounts" OR Subject = "Informatics";`

(iii) `SELECT MAX (Average) As 'Highest Average' FROM EXAM;`

(iv) `SELECT Name, Subject, Stipend * 12 As 'Stipend' FROM Exam;`

(v) SNo

89. **Consider the table PERSONS given below. Write output for queries (i) to (v).**

Table : PERSONS

PID	SurName	FirstName	Gender	City	PinCode	Salary
1	Sharma	Geet	F	Udhamwara	182141	50000
2	Singh	Surinder	M	Kupwara Nagar	193222	75000
3	Jcob	Peter	M	Bhawani	185155	45000
4	Alvis	Thomas	M	Ahmed Nagar	380025	50000
5	Mohan	Gaurav	M	Nagar Coolangatta	390026	33000
6	Azmi	Simi	F	New Delhi	110021	40000
7	Kaur	Manpreet	F	Udhamwara	182141	42000

(i) `SELECT SurName FROM PERSONS WHERE Salary >= 50000;`

(ii) `SELECT SUM (Salary) FROM PERSONS WHERE Gender = 'F';`

(iii) `SELECT Gender, MIN (Salary) FROM PERSONS GROUP BY Gender;`

(iv) `SELECT Gender, COUNT (*) FROM PERSONS GROUP BY Gender;`

(v) `SELECT FirstName FROM PERSONS WHERE Salary > 50000;`

Ans.

(i)

SurName
Sharma
Singh
Alvis

(ii)

SUM(Salary)
132000

(iii)

Gender	MIN(Salary)
F	40000
M	33000

(iv)

Gender	COUNT(*)
F	3
M	4

(v)

FirstName
Surinder

90. Consider the table DOCTOR given below. Write commands in SQL for (i) to (ii) and output for (iii) to (v).

Table : DOCTOR

ID	DOCName	Department	DOJ	Gender	Salary
1	Amit Kumar	Orthopaedics	1993-02-12	M	35000
2	Anita Hans	Paediatrics	1998-10-16	F	30000
3	Sunita Maini	Gynaecology	1991-08-23	F	40000
4	Joe Thomas	Surgery	1994-10-20	M	55000
5	Gurpreet Kaur	Paediatrics	1999-11-24	F	52000
6	Anandini Burman	Oncology	1994-03-16	F	31000
7	Siddharth Dang	Surgery	1995-09-08	M	47000
8	Rama Mukherjee	Oncology	2000-06-27	F	54500

(i) Display the names and salaries of doctors in descending order of salaries.

(ii) Display names of each department alongwith total salary being given to doctors of that department.

(iii) `SELECT SUM (Salary) FROM DOCTOR WHERE Department = 'Surgery';`

(iv) `SELECT Department, COUNT (*) FROM DOCTOR GROUP BY Department;`

(v) `SELECT DOCName FROM DOCTOR WHERE Department LIKE "%gery%";`

Ans. (i) `SELECT DOCName, Salary FROM DOCTOR ORDER BY Salary DESC;`

(ii) `SELECT Department, SUM (Salary) FROM DOCTOR GROUP BY Department;`

(iii)

SUM(Salary)
102000

(iv)

Department	COUNT(*)
Orthopaedics	1
Paediatrics	2
Gynaecology	1
Surgery	2
Oncology	2

(v)

DOCName
Joe Thomas
Siddharth Dang

91. Write suitable SQL query for the following: **CBSE SQP 2024-25**

I. To display the average score from the test_results column (attribute) in the Exams table

II. To display the last three characters of the registration_number column (attribute) in the Vehicles table. (Note: The registration numbers are stored in the format DL-01-AV-1234)

III. To display the data from the column (attribute) username in the Users table, after eliminating any leading and trailing spaces.

IV. To display the maximum value in the salary column (attribute) of the Employees table.

V. To determine the count of rows in the Suppliers table.

Or Write suitable SQL query for the following:

I. Round the value of pi (3.14159) to two decimal places.

II. Calculate the remainder when 125 is divided by 8.

III. Display the number of characters in the word 'NewDelhi'.

IV. Display the first 5 characters from the word 'Informatics Practices'.

V. Display details from 'email' column (attribute), in the 'Students' table, after removing any leading and trailing spaces.

Ans. I. SELECT AVG(test_results) AS average_score FROM Exams;

II. SELECT RIGHT(registration_number, 3) AS last_three_characters FROM Vehicles;

III. SELECT TRIM(username) AS trimmed_username FROM Users;

IV. SELECT MAX(salary) AS max_salary

V. SELECT COUNT(*) AS row_count FROM Suppliers;

Or

I. `SELECT ROUND(3.14159, 2);`

II. `SELECT MOD(125,8);`

III. `SELECT LENGTH('NewDelhi');`

IV. `SELECT SUBSTRING('Informatics Practices', 1, 5);`

V. `SELECT TRIM(email) FROM Students;`

92. **Excellent Consultancy Pvt. Ltd. maintains two tables for all its employees.** **CBSE 2024**

Table : Employee

Employee_Id	First_Name	Last_Name	Salary	Joining_Date	Department
E101	Monika	Das	100000	2019-01-20	Finance
E102	Mehek	Verma	600000	2019-01-15	IT
E103	Manan	Pant	890000	2019-02-05	Banking
E104	Shivam	Agarwal	200000	2019-02-25	Insurance
E105	Alisha	Singh	220000	2019-02-28	Finance
E106	Poonam	Sharma	400000	2019-05-10	IT
E107	Anshuman	Mishra	123000	2019-06-20	Banking

Table : Reward

Employee_Id	Date_Reward	Amount
E101	2019-05-11	1000
E102	2019-02-15	5000
E103	2019-04-22	2000
E106	2019-06-20	8000

Write suitable SQL queries to perform the following task :

(i) Change the Department of Shivam to IT in the table Employee.

(ii) Remove the record of Alisha from the table Employee.

(iii) Add a new column Experience of integer type in the table Employee.

(iv) Display the first name, last name and amount of reward for all employees from the tables Employee and Reward.

(v) Display first name and salary of all the employees whose amount is less than 2000 from the tables Employee and Reward.

Or

Write suitable SQL queries for the following task:

(i) Display the year of joining of all the employees from the table Employee.

(ii) Display each department name and its corresponding average salary.

(iii) Display the first name and date of reward of those employees who joined on Monday from the tables Employee and Reward.

(iv) Display sum of salary of those employees whose reward amount is greater than 3000 from the tables Employee and Reward.

(v) Remove the table Reward.

Ans. (i) `Update Employee set Department = "IT" where First_name="Shivam";`

(ii) `Delete from Employee where First_Name ="Alisha";`

(iii) `Alter table Employee ADD Experience integer;`

(iv) `Select A.First_Name, A. Last_Name, B.Amount from Employee A , Reward B where A.Employee_ID= B. Employee_ID;`

(v) `Select A.First_Name , A. SALARY from Employee A , Reward B where A.Employee_ID= B. Employee_ID and B.AMOUNT<2000;`

Or (i) `Select year(Joining_Date) from Employee;`

(ii) `Select Department, avg(Salary) from Employee GROUP BY Department;`

(iii) `Select A.First_Name, B.Date_Reward from Employee A , Reward B where A.Employee_ID= B. Employee_ID and dayname (A.Joining_Date)="Monday";`

(iv) `Select sum(A.Salary) from Employee A , Reward B where A.Employee_ID= B. Employee_ID and B.Amount>3000;`

(v) `Drop table Reward;`

93. Consider a table PRODUCT with the following data. CBSE 2023

Table : PRODUCT

SNo	Itemname	Company	Stockdate	Price	Discount
1	Monitor	HP	2021-12-20	15499.739	15
2	Webcam	Logitech	2020-02-03	4890.90	5
3	Keyboard	Logitech	2022-08-19	1878.985	30
4	Mouse	HCL	2021-05-16	1200.00	7
5	Speakers	iBall	2021-10-19	NULL	25

Write SQL queries using SQL functions to perform the following operations.

(i) **Display the first 3 characters of all Itemnames.**

(ii) **Display the names of all items whose Stockday is "Monday".**

(iii) **Display the total price of all the products.**

(iv) **Display the maximum Price.**

(v) **Display the average Price of all the products by the company named 'Logitech'.**

Ans. (i) `SELECT LEFT (Itemname, 3) FROM PRODUCT;`

(ii) `SELECT Itemname FROM PRODUCT WHERE DAYNAME (Stockdate)= 'MONDAY';`

(iii) `SELECT SUM(Price) FROM PRODUCT;`

(iv) `SELECT MAX(Price) FROM PRODUCT;`

(v) `SELECT AVG(Price) FROM PRODUCT WHERE Company = "Logitech";`

94. Explain the following SQL functions using suitable examples. CBSE SQP 2022-23

(i) **UCASE()** (ii) **TRIM()** (iii) **MID()**
(iv) **DAYNAME()** (v) **POWER()**

Ans. (i) **UCASE()** It converts the string into upper case.

Example: `SELECT UCASE('welcome world');`

Output

WELCOME WORLD

(ii) **TRIM()** It removes the leading and trailing spaces from the given string.

Example `SELECT TRIM(' Welcome world ' );`

Output

Welcome world

(iii) **MID()** It extracts the specified number of characters from given string.

Example `SELECT MID(' Welcome world,4,,4);`

Output

Come

(iv) **DAYNAME()** It returns the weekday name for a given date

Example `SELECT DAYNAME('2022-07-22');`

Output

Friday

(v) **POWER()** It returns the value of a number raised to the power of another number.

Example `SELECT POW(6,2);`

Output

36

95. (a) Write SQL query for the following: CBSE 2025

(i) **To display sum total of all the values of the Score column, from STUDENTS table.**

(ii) **To display the first five characters of the Name column from STUDENTS table.**

(iii) **To display the values of Name column from the STUDENTS table, after removing the trailing spaces.**

(iv) **To retrieve the lowest score from the Score column of GRADES table.**

(v) **To increase the fee of all students by 100, in the STUDENTS table. (The name of the column is FEE)**

Or

(b) Write SQL queries for the following:

(i) **To calculate the square of 15.**

(ii) **To round the number 456.789 to the nearest integer.**

(iii) **To display the position of first occurrence of 'com' in the string 'mycommercial.com'.**

(iv) To display the name of the day for the date '2024-11-07'.

(v) To display the current date and time.

Ans. (a) (i) SELECT SUM(Score) FROM STUDENTS;

(ii) SELECT SUBSTRING (Name, 1, 5) FROM STUDENTS;

(iii) SELECT RTRIM(Name) FROM STUDENTS;

(iv) SELECT MIN(Score) FROM GRADES;

(v) UPDATE STUDENTS SET FEE = FEE + 100;

Or

(b) (i) SELECT POWER (15, 2);

(ii) SELECT ROUND (456.789, 0);

(iii) SELECT INSTR ('com', 'mycommercial.com');

(iv) SELECT DAYNAME ('2024-11-07');

(v) SELECT NOW ();

Case Study Based Questions

Case Study 1

A School in Delhi uses database management system to store student details. The school maintains a database 'school_record' under which there are two tables. **CBSE Question Bank**

Student Table This table maintains general details about every student enrolled in school.

StuLibrary Table This table stores details of issued books. BookID is the unique identification number issued to each book. Minimum issue duration of a book is one day.

Table : Student

Field	Type
StuID	numeric
StuName	varchar(20)
StuAddress	varchar(50)
StuFatherName	varchar(20)
StuContact	numeric
StuAadhar	numeric
StuClass	varchar(5)
StuSection	varchar(1)

Table : StuLibrary

Field	Type
BookID	numeric
StuID	numeric
Issued_date	date
Return_date	date

(i) Identify the SQL query which displays the data of StuLibrary table in ascending order of student ID.

I. `SELECT * FROM StuLibrary ORDER BY BookID;`

II. `SELECT * FROM StuLibrary ORDER BY StuID;`

III. `SELECT * FROM StuLibrary ORDER BY StuID ASC;`

IV. `SELECT * FROM StuLibrary ORDER BY StuID DESC;`

Choose the correct option.

(a) Both the queries (I) and (IV) will display the desired data.

(b) Both the queries (I) and (II) will display the desired data.

(c) Both the queries (III) and (IV) will display the desired data.

(d) Both the queries (II) and (III) will display the desired data.

(ii) The primary key for StuLibrary table is/are ....

(a) BookID (b) BookID,StuID (c) BookID,Issued_date (d) Issued_date

(iii) Which of the following SQL query will fetch ID of those issued books which have not been returned?

(a) `SELECT BookID FROM StuLibrary WHERE BookID IS NULL;`

(b) `SELECT BookID FROM StuLibrary WHERE StuID IS NULL;`

(c) `SELECT BookID FROM StuLibrary WHERE Issued_date IS NULL;`

(d) `SELECT BookID FROM StuLibrary WHERE Return_date IS NULL;`

(iv) The alternate key for Student table will be ....

(a) StuName (b) StuContact (c) StuAadhar (d) StuClass

Ans. (i) (*d*) Both queries II and III arrange the data in ascending order of StuID. The ASC clause is optional in ORDER BY.

(ii) (*a*) Each book will have an unique ID, so the BookID field can serve as primary key.

(iii) (*d*) The clause Return_date is NULL is used to find records whose Return_date is blank meaning, books not returned.

(iv) (*c*) Since aadhar number is unique for all citizens, hence it can serve as alternate key.

Case Study 2

Tejasvi Sethi, a car dealer has stored the details of all cars in her showroom in a table CARMARKET. The table CARMARKET has attributes CARCODE which is a primary key, CARNAME, COMPANY, COLOR, COST (in lakh) of the car and DOM which is the Date of Manufacture of the car. CBSE Question Bank

Table: CARMARKET

CARCODE	CARNAME	COMPANY	COLOR	COST	DOM
C01	BALENO	SUZUKI	BLUE	5.90	2019-11-07
C02	INDIGO	TATA	SILVER	12.90	2020-10-15
C03	GLC	MERCEDES	WHITE	62.38	2020-01-20
C04	A6	AUDI	RED	58.55	2018-12-29
C05	INNOVA	TOYOTA	BLACK	32.82	2017-11-10
C06	WAGON-R	SUZUKI	WHITE	12.11	2016-11-11
C07	BREZZA	SUZUKI	GOLDEN	9.80	2016-10-03

Choose the correct SQL query for (i) to (iv).

(i) Display the carname along with the charges rounded off to 1 digit after decimal place.

(a) `SELECT CARNAME,ROUND(COST) FROM CARMARKET;`

(b) `SELECT CARNAME,ROUND.COST(1) FROM CARMARKET;`

(c) `SELECT CARNAME,ROUND.COST() FROM CARMARKET;`

(d) `SELECT CARNAME, ROUND(COST,1) FROM CARMARKET;`

(ii) Display the carname, color and position of the character 'E' in the color of all the cars.

(a) `SELECT CARNAME,COLOR FROM CARMARKET WHERE COLOR LIKE "%E%";`

(b) `SELECT CARNAME,COLOR,INSTR(COLOR,'E') FROM CARMARKET;`

(c) `SELECT CARNAME,COLOR FROM CARMARKET WHERE COLOR = "%E%";`

(d) `SELECT CARNAME,COLOR,SUBSTR(COLOR,1,'E') FROM CARMARKET;`

(iii) Display the carname ,name of the company in lower case of all cars whose year (of dom) is 2020.

(a) `SELECT CARNAME,LCASE(COMPANY) FROM CARMARKET WHERE YEAR(DOM) = 2020;`

(b) `SELECT CARNAME,LCASE(COMPANY) FROM CARMARKET WHERE YEAROF(DOM) LIKE '2020%';`

(c) `SELECT CARNAME,LOWER(COMPANY) FROM CARMARKET WHERE DOM FROM '2020-01-01' TO '2020-12-31';`

(d) `SELECT CARNAME,LOWER(COMPANY) FROM CARMARKET WHERE YEARFROM(DOM) = 2020;`

(iv) Display the number of cars manufactured each year.

(a) `SELECT COUNT(*),YEAR(DOM) FROM CARMARKET WHERE YEAR(DOM) = DISTINCT;`

(b) `SELECT COUNT(*),YEAR(DOM) FROM CARMARKET GROUP BY YEAR(DOM);`

(c) `SELECT COUNT(CARMARKET),YEAR(DOM) FROM CARMARKET GROUP BY YEAR(DOM);`

(d) `SELECT COUNT(DISTINCT *),YEAR(DOM) FROM CARMARKET GROUP BY YEAR(DOM);`

Ans. (i) (*d*) The ROUND( ) function rounds a value to certain decimal places. Here the carname and the cost is to be displayed rounded to 1 decimal place.

(ii) (*b*) Here the carname, color and position of the character 'E' in the color of all the cars is to be displayed. The position of a string in another string can be obtained by the INSTR( ) function, which has been used in the query.

(iii) (*a*) Here the carname and name of the company is to be displayed in lower case of all cars whose year of manufacture is 2020. To convert a name to lowercase the LCASE( ) function can be used and to get the year from a date the YEAR( ) function can be used.

(iv) (*b*) Here the number of cars manufactured each year is to be shown. Hence, the records are grouped by YEAR(DOM) using GROUP BY and COUNT(*) gives the count of records.

Case Study 3

A Gift Gallery has different stores in India. Database Administrator Abhay wants to maintain database of their Salesmen in SQL to store the data. He has decided that

Name of the database GiftGallery

Name of the table Salesman

Attributes of the table Scode – Numeric, Sname – Character 25, Address - Character 25, Dofjoin - Date, Sales – Numeric and Area – Character 10

Consider the following records in 'Salesman' table and answer the given questions.

Table : Salesman

Scode	Sname	Address	Dofjoin	Sales	Area
100	Sushant	Delhi	2017/09/29	5000.90	East
101	Sushant	Gurgaon	2018/01/01	7000.75	East
102	Priya	Noida	2018/04/25	3450.45	West
103	Mohit	Delhi	2018/11/03	6000.50	North
104	Priyanshi	Delhi	2019/12/15	8000.62	North

(i) State the command that will give the output as

```
+-----------+
| Sname     |
+-----------+
| Sushant   |
| Priya     |
+-----------+
```

(a) `SELECT Sname FROM Salesman WHERE NOT Address ="Delhi";`

(b) `SELECT Sname FROM Salesman WHERE Address NOT IN("Delhi");`

(c) `SELECT Sname FROM Salesman WHERE Address !="Delhi";`

(d) All of the above

(ii) Which of the following commands will display the details of all sales record of North Area, regardless of case (whether North / NORTH / north).

(a) `SELECT * FROM Salesman WHERE Area LIKE UPPER 'North';`

(b) `SELECT * FROM Salesman WHERE Area = 'North' or 'NORTH' or north;`

(c) `SELECT * FROM Salesman WHERE upper(area)='NORTH';`

(d) `SELECT * FROM Salesman WHERE area= =upper("North");`

(iii) Help Priya to display sname and sales of east and west areas.

(a) `SELECT Sname, Sales FROM Salesman WHERE Area="East" AND Area="West";`

(b) `SELECT Sname, Sales FROM Salesman WHERE Area="East" OR Area="West";`

(c) `SELECT Sname, Sales FROM Salesman WHERE Area IN "East" AND "West";`

(d) `SELECT Sname, Sales FROM Salesman WHERE Area="East" , "West";`

Ans. (i) (*d*) Not Address ="Delhi", NOT IN("Delhi") !="Delhi" All the three mean is same thing. Hence, option (d) is correct.

(ii) (*c*) UPPER() function converts a string to uppercase, hence UPPER(area) ='NORTH' will convert the area to uppercase and then compare with "NORTH".

(iii) (*b*) To display the salesman name and sales of east and west areas an OR condition has to be used.

SELF ASSESSMENT TEST

Multiple Choice Questions

1. Which of the following performs a pre-defined task and returns some type of result?
   (a) Database (b) SQL function
   (c) Implementation (d) None of these
2. Which SQL function returns the character value of the given integer value according to the ASCII table?
   (a) CHAR( ) (b) CONCAT( )
   (c) LCASE( ) (d) LTRIM( )
3. Which aggregate function returns the count of a number of different values?
   (a) COUNT( ) (b) AVG( )
   (c) COUNT (DISTINCT) (d) None of these
4. Which of the following function returns the value of a number raised to the power of another number?
   (a) ROUND( ) (b) POWER( )
   (c) POW( ) (d) Both (b) and (c)

Fill in the Blanks

5. .... function returns the average value of a specified column.
6. .... work with data of multiple rows at a time and return a single output value.
7. The .... function is used to return a string after removing all prefix or suffix spaces from the given string.
8. The SIGN function is used for returning a value which indicates the .... of a number.
9. Aggregate functions do not consider ....

State whether True or False

10. RIGHT ( ) returns NULL if any argument is NULL.
11. In POW (M, N), N is an exponent of the exponentiation.

Assertion and Reason Based Questions

Assertion (A) and Reason (R) based questions. Mark the correct choice as

(a) Both (A) and (R) are true and (R) is the correct explanation for (A).
(b) Both (A) and (R) are true and (R) is not the correct explanation for (A).
(c) (A) is true and (R) is false.
(d) (A) is false but (R) is true.

12. **Assertion (A)** RTRIM() function takes a string argument and returns a new string with all the trailing space characters removed.
    Reason (R) TRIM() functions enables you to remove leading and trailing white space from string.
13. **Assertion (A)** COUNT(*) function returns a number of rows in a specified table.
    Reason (R) COUNT(*) function doesn't includes the number of duplicates and NULL values.

Very Short Answer Type Questions

14. Name some major string functions.
15. How to display the name RANI and DEEPA into lowercase?
16. What is the use of MIN( ) function?
17. Write down the name of the function used to remove leading spaces.

Short Answer Type Questions

18. Which function is used to display the position of occurrence of string 'OR' in string 'WORK'? Explain.
19. What is the output of the following query?
    ```
    mysql > SELECT LTRIM (RTRIM ('## ATHEN
    ##'));
    ```
20. Give an example of COUNT (DISTINCT) function.
21. Write the query according to the statements given below:
    (i) To display the first three letter of 'COMPUTER'.
    (ii) To display the day of the year for date 29th Sep 2012.
    (iii) How many characters are there in string 'WORLD ATLAS'?
22. Define Mathematical functions and its types.
23. Explain the HAVING clause with an example.

Long Answer Type Question

24. Answer the given below questions:
    (i) How to select unique records from a table?
    (ii) Name the operator is used in query for pattern matching.
    (iii) Write a query to remove leading spaces of string 'country'.

(iv) To display the month of the year for date '2009-06-18'.

(v) To display the name of day for date '2009-06-18'.

Case Study Based Question

25. Consider a database StudentScores that contains information about students from two tables: StudentDetails and Scores.

The StudentDetails table has the following columns:

- **StudentID (INT)** A unique identifier for each student.
- **StudentName (VARCHAR)** The name of the student.
- **DateOfBirth (DATE)** The date of birth of the student.

The Scores table has the following columns:

- **StudentID (INT)** The unique identifier for each student (foreign key from StudentDetails).
- **Subject (VARCHAR)** The subject name (e.g., Math, Science, English).
- **Marks (INT)** The marks obtained by the student in that subject.

Using this information, answer the following questions.

(i) What is the correct SQL query to find the month name of the student's date of birth for all students whose name contains "Raj"?

(a) `SELECT StudentName, MONTHNAME(DateOfBirth) FROM StudentDetails WHERE StudentName = 'Raj';`

(b) `SELECT StudentName, MONTHNAME(DateOfBirth) FROM StudentDetails WHERE StudentName LIKE '%Raj%';`

(c) `SELECT StudentName, MONTHNAME(DateOfBirth) FROM StudentDetails WHERE StudentName LIKE '_Raj_';`

(d) `SELECT StudentName, DAYNAME(DateOfBirth) FROM StudentDetails WHERE StudentName LIKE '%Raj%';`

(ii) Which query would calculate the rounded average of marks obtained by students in Math?

(a) `SELECT StudentName, ROUND(AVG(Marks)) AS AvgMarks FROM Scores WHERE Subject = 'Math';`

(b) `SELECT StudentName, AVG(Marks) AS AvgMarks FROM Scores WHERE Subject = 'Math';`

(c) `SELECT ROUND(AVG(Marks)) AS AvgMarks FROM Scores WHERE Subject = 'Math';`

(d) `SELECT AVG(ROUND(Marks)) AS AvgMarks FROM Scores WHERE Subject = 'Math';`

(iii) To retrieve students' names in uppercase who scored above 80 marks in Science, which of the following queries is correct?

(a) `SELECT UPPER(StudentName) FROM StudentDetails WHERE Marks > 80 AND Subject = 'Science';`

(b) `SELECT UPPER(StudentName) FROM Scores WHERE Marks > 80 AND Subject = 'Science';`

(c) `SELECT UCASE(StudentName) FROM StudentDetails JOIN Scores ON StudentDetails.StudentID = Scores.StudentID WHERE Marks > 80 AND Subject = 'Science';`

(d) `SELECT UPPER(StudentName) FROM StudentDetails JOIN Scores ON StudentDetails.StudentID = Scores.StudentID WHERE Marks > 80 AND Subject = 'Science';`

(iv) Which query would display the highest marks scored in each subject along with the subject name, ordered by subject name?

(a) `SELECT Subject, MAX(Marks) FROM Scores GROUP BY Subject ORDER BY Marks;`

(b) `SELECT Subject, MAX(Marks) FROM Scores GROUP BY Subject ORDER BY Subject;`

(c) `SELECT MAX(Marks), Subject FROM Scores GROUP BY Subject ORDER BY Marks;`

(d) `SELECT MAX(Marks), Subject FROM Scores GROUP BY Marks ORDER BY Subject;`

Answers

1. (b) 2. (a) 3. (c) 4. (d) 5. AVG
6. Aggregate functions 7. TRIM() 8. SIGN
9. NULL values 10. True 11. True 12. (b)
13. (c)
25. (i) → (b), (ii) → (c), (iii) → (d), (iv) → (b)

05

CHAPTER

Computer networks have revolutionized the use of computers. They are used in our everyday life from automated teller machine (ATM) to airline reservation system to electronic mail services.

YOUR STUDY GOALS

5.1 Components of Computer Network

5.2 Types of Networks

5.3 Network Devices

5.4 Network Topology

YOUR PRACTICE GOAL

- Objective Type Questions (33 Qs ; MCQs, True or False, Fill in the Blanks, Assertion and Reason)
- Subjective Type Questions (52 Qs ; VSA, SA, LA)
- Case Study Based Questions (Subjective Case Studies-3)

Computer Networks

A **computer network** is a collection of interconnected computers and other devices which are able to communicate with each other. Also defined as – collection of hardware components and computers interconnected by communication channels that allow sharing of resources and information.

The network size may vary from small to large depending on the number of computers it connects. A computer network can include different types of hosts (also called nodes) like server, desktop, laptop, cellular phones.

5.1 Components of Computer Network

Some major components of computer network are as follows:

Nodes

A node in a computer network is any device that can send, receive, or process data. This includes:

- **Computers** Desktops, laptops, workstations

- **Servers** Dedicated computers that provide services to other devices
- **Network Devices** Routers, switches, firewalls
- **Mobile Devices** Smartphones, tablets

Servers

A server is a computer that provides services to other computers (clients) on a network. These services can include:

- **File Sharing** Storing and distributing files
- **Printing** Managing print jobs
- **Email** Handling email messages
- **Web Services** Hosting websites and web applications
- **Database Management** Storing and managing data

Clients

A client is a computer that receives services from a server. Clients can be:

- **Individual Computers** Desktops, laptops, or mobile devices
- **Network Devices** Some network devices, like printers or switches, may act as clients for certain services.

Advantages / Uses of Computer Network

- **Resource Sharing** Computer network allows sharing of resources such as-
  - **Hardware Resources** Printer, Scanner, Photocopier, CD, DVD etc.
  - **Software Resources** ERPs, Open Source Software etc.
  - **Information Sharing** File sharing like documents, sheets, reports etc.
- **Increase Storage Capacity** Usually Server of Computer Network have large storage capacity. Total storage capacity of each node of computer network also increases storage capacity.
- **Cost Efficient** Computer Networks are cost effective as we can share one resources among many.
- **Collective User Interaction (Multi User Environment)** Computer Network allows many users to work together simultaneously on a project, a lot of time and effort is saved.
- **Improved Communication and information availability** WAN (Internet) enables instant access and sharing of information across diverse locations at any given time.

Disadvantages of Network

- If network are badly managed, services can become unusable and productivity fails.
- If software and files held centrally, it may be impossible to carry out any work if the central server fails.
- File security is more important especially if connected to WAN e.g., protection from viruses.
- To handle network of organisation you may need specialist staff to run the network.

Transmission Media

A transmission medium is a physical path between the transmitter and the receiver i.e. it is the channel through which data is sent from one place to another.

Types of Transmission Media

Guided Media	Unguided Media
• Fiber Optics	• Radio Waves
• Twisted	• Micro Waves
• Coaxial	• Infrared
	• Bluetooth

You may use the following QR code to learn transmission media in detail

5.2 Types of Network

Based on the geographical area covered and data transfer rate, computer networks are broadly categorised as:

1. PAN (Personal Area Network)

A Personal Area Network (PAN) is a small network typically used for connecting devices within a very limited range, such as within a room or an individual's workspace.

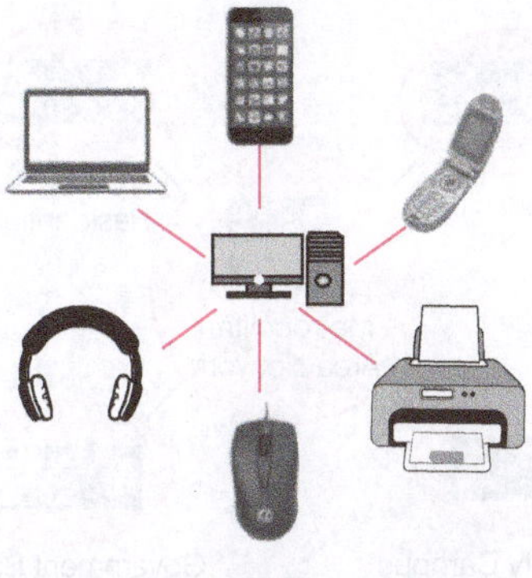

- **Range** Usually up to 10 meters (about 30 feet).
- **Application** Commonly used to connect personal devices like smartphones, tablets, laptops, and

printers. Bluetooth and infrared connections are typical examples of PAN technologies.

- **Example** Connecting your smartphone to a wireless headset via Bluetooth.

2. LAN (Local Area Network)

A Local Area Network (LAN) is a network that connects computers and devices within a specific area, such as a home, office, or school.

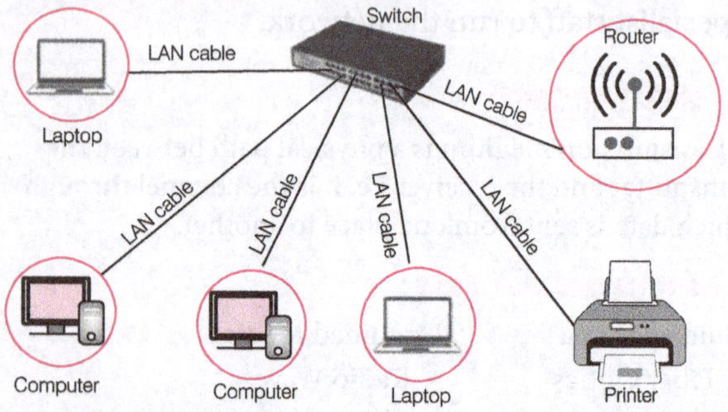

- **Range** Typically spans from a few meters to thousands of meters.
- **Application** Used to share resources like files, printers, and internet access within a building or campus. LANs can be wired (using Ethernet cables) or wireless (using Wi-Fi).
- **Example** The network in your school that connects all computers and printers in the computer lab.

3. MAN (Metropolitan Area Network)

A Metropolitan Area Network (MAN) covers a larger geographic area than a LAN but is smaller than a WAN. It connects computers within a metropolitan area, such as a large city, multiple cities or a large area with multiple buildings.

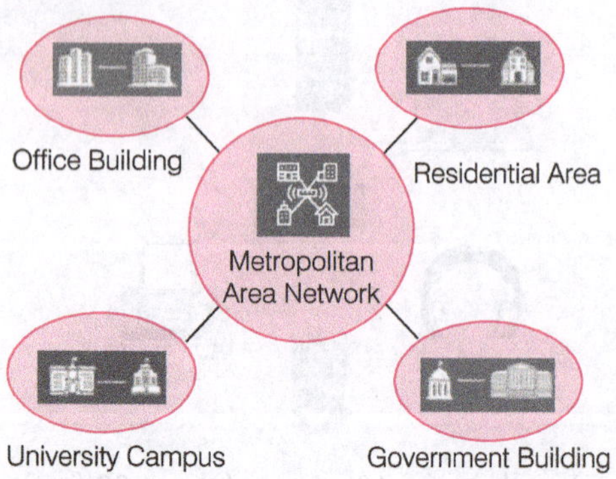

- **Range** Generally spans from a few kilometers to several tens of kilometers.
- **Application** Used to connect multiple LANs within a city or large campus. It supports high-speed data transfer and is often used by businesses, educational institutions, and government organizations.
- **Example** The network that connects several branch offices of a company within a city.

4. WAN (Wide Area Network)

A Wide Area Network (WAN) covers a vast geographic area, often spanning cities, countries, or even continents. It connects multiple LANs and MANs over large distances. A WAN could be formed by connecting a LAN to other LANs *via* wired or wireless media.

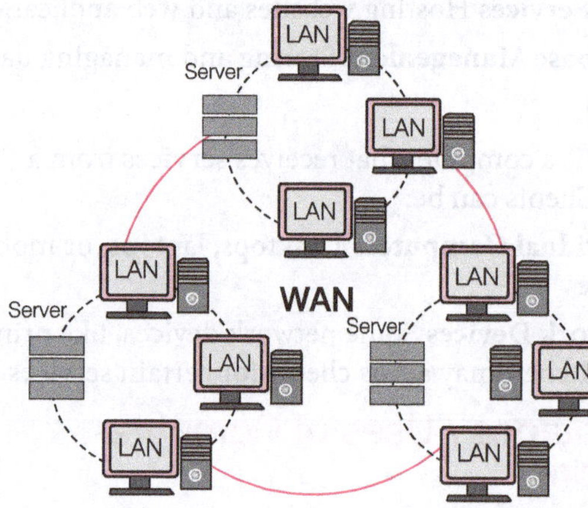

- **Range** Can span hundreds to thousands of kilometers.
- **Application** Used to connect networks across large distances and enables communication between remote locations. The Internet itself is the largest example of a WAN.
- **Example** The network connecting a company's headquarters with its branches located in different countries.

> **Mistake Alert!**
>
> Student might get confused about the distance covered by LAN, MAN and WAN. LAN provides connectivity in small areas like homes and offices. MAN covers an intermediate scale like a city. WAN spans over large distances connecting cities, and countries.

5.3 Network Devices

Some common network devices that are essential for communication between a computer and a network include:

Repeater

A repeater is a network device used to extend the range of a network signal. It receives the signal, amplifies it, and then retransmits it to cover greater distances. This helps in maintaining signal strength over long distances or through obstacles.

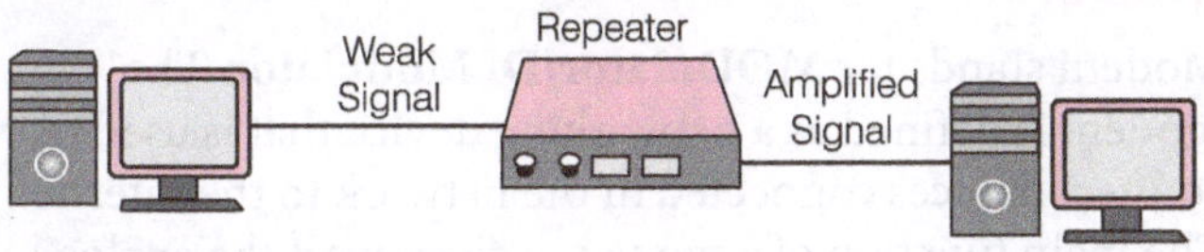

Application

- **Long-Distance Connections** Repeater is used in networks that span large distances, such as in wide-area networks (WANs).
- **Signal Boosting** It is used to boost signal strength in a network to ensure that data reaches its destination without degradation.

Hub

A hub is a basic network device that connects multiple computers or network devices through wires. It allows them to communicate with each other within the same network segment. Hubs are used to connect various devices, such as computers, printers, and servers, in a network. They act as a central point where all devices are connected.

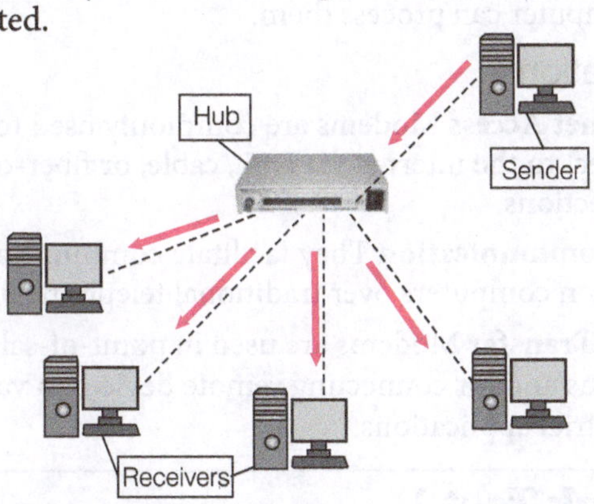

Hubs come in two main types:

- **Active Hub** Has built-in electronics to amplify the signal and manage data transmission.
- **Passive Hub** Simply acts as a connector without amplifying the signal or managing data.

Application

- **Simple Networks** Hubs are used in small or simple network setups where high-speed data transfer and security are not critical.
- **Low Cost** They are relatively inexpensive and easy to set up.

Router

A router is a network device that connects different networks together. It acts as a traffic manager, directing data packets between networks and ensuring they reach their correct destination.

> **TEACHER TIP**
> A router is a device like a switch that routes data packets based on their IP addresses.

Application

- **Interconnect Networks** Connects multiple networks, like home and internet networks.
- **Traffic Management** Directs data to the correct destination based on IP addresses.
- **Security** Can provide security features like firewalls to protect against unauthorized access.

Gateway

A gateway in a computer network is a device that connects two different networks, often with different protocols, and allows communication between them. It acts as a translator, converting data from one network protocol to another.

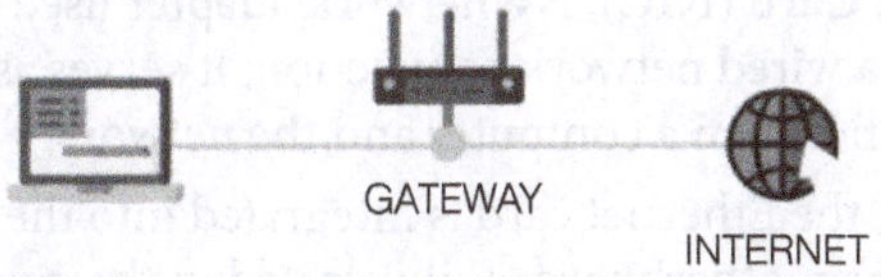

Application

- **Internet Gateways** A home router acts as a gateway, allowing devices in a local network (LAN) to communicate with external networks like the internet.
- **Cloud Networking** Gateways facilitate secure connections between local enterprise networks and cloud services.
- **VoIP** In Voice over IP, gateways convert voice data between telephone networks and IP-based networks.

Switch

A switch in computer networks is a device that connects multiple devices (like computers, printers, etc.) within a local area network (LAN) and facilitates communication between them.

It works by receiving data packets from a device, identifying the destination device's Media Access Control (MAC) address, and then forwarding the data to the appropriate device.

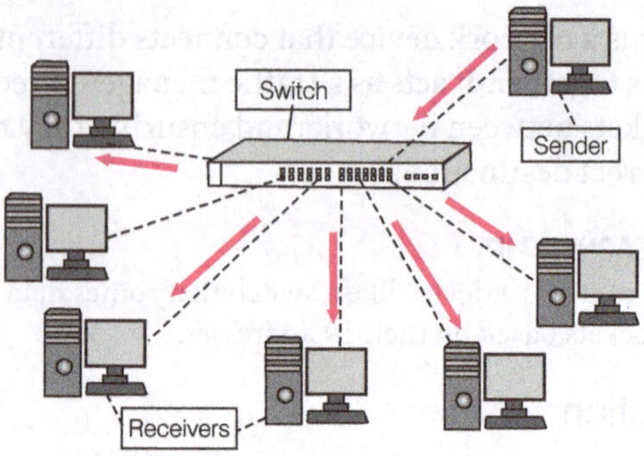

Application

- **LANs** Used to connect computers and devices in a local network for sharing resources like printers and internet access.
- **Network Segmentation** Helps segment networks into smaller parts, reducing traffic and improving performance.
- **VLANs** Switches can create Virtual LANs (VLANs) for better network management and security.

Ethernet Card

An Ethernet card, commonly referred to as a **Network Interface Card** (NIC), is a network adapter used to establish a wired network connection. It serves as the interface between a computer and the network.

Typically, the Ethernet card is integrated into the computer's motherboard, as illustrated in the given figure. The Ethernet cable connects the computer to the network *via* the NIC.

Ethernet cards can support data transfer speeds ranging from 10 Mbps to 1 Gbps (1000 Mbps). Each NIC has a unique MAC address, which helps to identify the computer on the network.

Application

- **Internet Access** Enables wired internet connection for computers, printers, and routers.
- **Local Area Network (LAN)** Used to connect devices within a LAN for sharing files, printers, and other resources.
- **Data Transfer** Essential for high-speed, reliable data transfer in office or home networks.

Modem

Modem stands for **MODulator/DEModulator**. The modem is defined as a networking device that is used to connect devices connected in the network to the internet. The main function of a modem is to convert the analog signals that come from telephone wire into a digital form. In digital form, these converted signals are stored in the form of 0s and 1s.

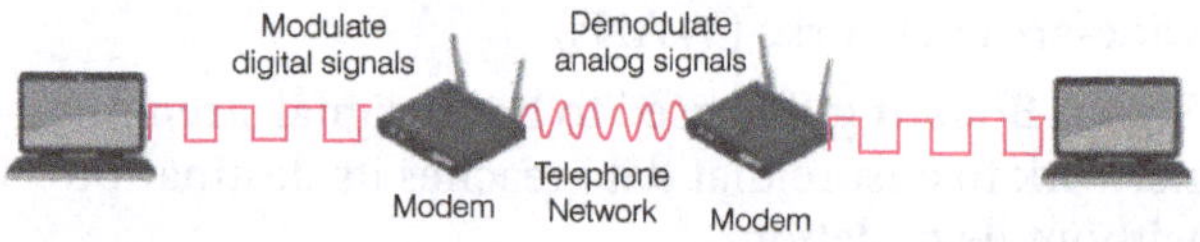

Functions

1. **Modulation** When sending data, the modem modulates digital signals (0s and 1s) into analog signals (waveforms) suitable for transmission over various media.
2. **Demodulation** Upon receiving data, it demodulates the analog signals back into digital form so that the computer can process them.

Application

- **Internet Access** Modems are commonly used to connect to the internet via DSL, cable, or fiber-optic connections.
- **Telecommunication** They facilitate communication between computers over traditional telephone lines.
- **Data Transfer** Modems are used in point-of-sale systems and for connecting remote devices in various industrial applications.

Quick Test 1

1. Mention any four networking goals. **CBSE SQP 2022-23**
2. What is the primary function of a gateway in computer network? Explain briefly. **CBSE 2024**
3. Name the device for the following: **NCERT**
   (a) It stands for Modulator Demodulator
   (b) It regenerates the signals.
4. What type of network connects devices within a small area like a room or office?
5. Which network device forwards data packets based on the MAC address?

5.4 Network Topology

Network topology refers to the arrangement of different elements like nodes, links, or devices in a computer network. It defines how these components are connected and interact with each other. Understanding various types of network topologies helps in designing efficient and robust networks.

Common types of topologies are

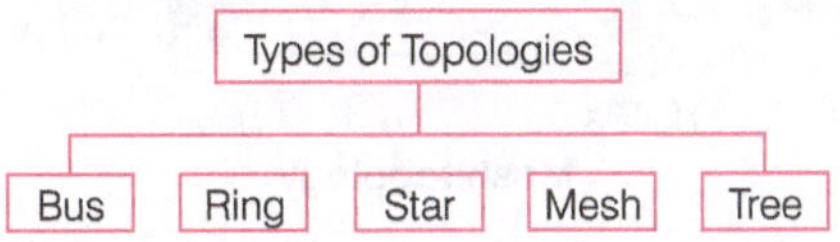

Bus Topology

Bus topology refers to a network arrangement where all devices are connected to a cable known as the "bus," which serves as the medium for data transmission. Each device directly connects to the bus cable, forming a structure. Consequently, any data transmitted by one device becomes accessible to all devices that are part of the network.

To ensure transmission without signal interference or disruption, the bus cable incorporates two endpoints called "terminators."

These terminators prevent signals from bouncing back within the system. To connect a computer to the backbone cable, a drop cable is used.

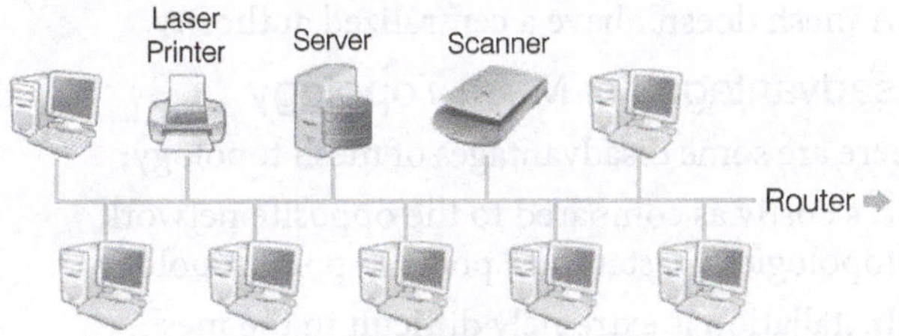

Bus topology

Note *The bus is mainly a passive type of network. This means that it does not amplify signals. It simply transmits them across devices.*

Advantages of Bus Topology

There are several advantages associated with using bus topology:

- It is known for being straightforward and hassle-free when it comes to installation and maintenance.
- Compared to many other topologies, bus topology requires less cable length and fewer devices. This ultimately leads to cost reduction and simplifies network management.
- The network allows for the addition or removal of devices without causing any disruption to any of the available devices in a network.
- It enables broadcast communication, where data from one device can be simultaneously sent to all devices.

Disadvantages of Bus Topology

Apart from the advantages that we just discussed, bus topology also has some disadvantages. These are:

- It has low performance and reliability. Here, the data transmission speed and quality depend on the length and condition of the bus cable.
- As we already know, all the devices that are part of this topology can access the transmitted data. Therefore, it has low security and privacy.
- It has a high collision probability; the reason behind it is multiple devices can try to send data at the same time, which in turn causes interference and data loss.
- Low fault tolerance, as any damage to the bus cable and the whole network will not work.

Star Topology

A star may be a topology for a Local Area Network (LAN) during which all nodes are individually connected to a central connection point, sort of a hub or a switch.

A star takes more cable than e.g. a bus, but the benefit is that if a cable fails, just one node is going to be brought down. Each device within the network is connected to a central device called a hub.

If one device wants to send data to another device, it's first to send the data/information to the hub then the hub transmits that data to the designated device. The number of links required to connect nodes in the star topology is N, where N is the number of nodes. The hub, switch, or concentrator manages and controls all functions of the network.

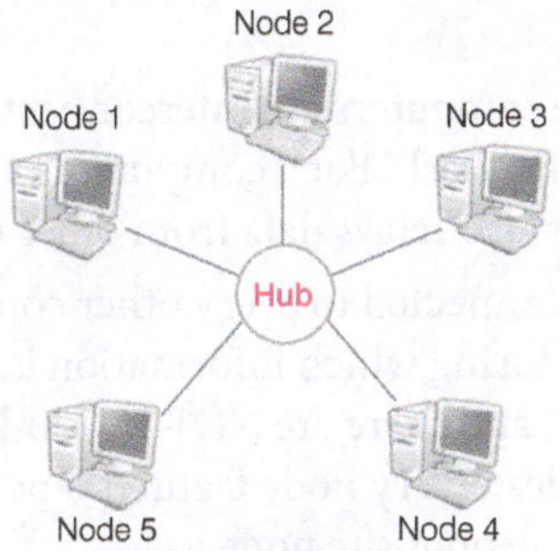

Star topology

Advantages of Star Topology

There are several advantages of using star topology:

- It is very reliable – if one cable or device fails then all the others will still work.
- It is high-performing as no data collisions can occur.
- It is less expensive because each device only needs one I/O port and wishes to be connected to the hub with one link.
- Easy fault detection because the links are often easily identified.
- No disruptions to the network when connecting or removing devices.
- Each device requires just one port i.e. to attach to the hub.
- If N devices are connected to each other in star, then the amount of cables required to attach them is N. So, it's easy to line up.

Disadvantages of Star Topology

There are some disadvantages of star topology:

- Requires more cable than a linear bus.
- If the connecting network device (network switch) fails, the nodes attached are disabled and can't participate in network communication.
- More expensive than linear bus topology due to the value of the connecting devices (network switches).
- If the hub goes down everything goes down, none of the devices can work without the hub.
- Hub requires more resources and regular maintenance because it's the central system of Star.
- Extra hardware is required (hubs or switches) which adds to the cost.
- Performance is predicated on the one concentrator i.e. hub.

Mesh Topology

In mesh, all the computers are interconnected to every other during a network. Each computer not only sends its own signals but also relays data from other computers.

The nodes are connected to every other completely via a dedicated link during which information is travel from nodes-to-nodes and there are N(N-1)/2 links in mesh if there are N nodes. Every node features a point-to-point connection to the opposite node.

The connections within the mesh are often wired or wireless.

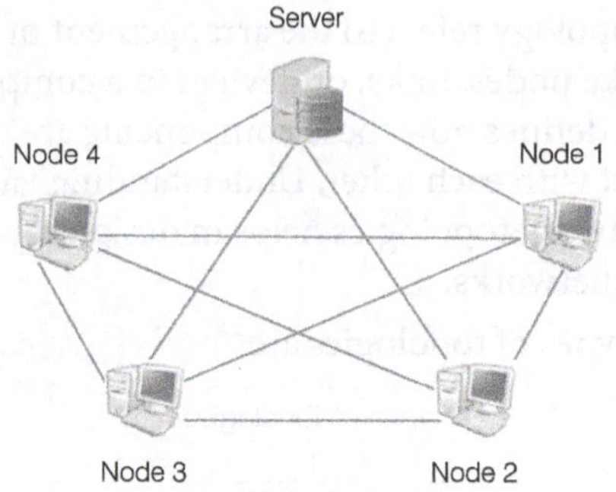

Mesh topology

Advantages of Mesh Topology

There are several advantages of using mesh topology:

- Failure during a single device won't break the network.
- There is no traffic problem as there is a dedicated point to point links for every computer.
- Fault identification is straightforward.
- This topology provides multiple paths to succeed in the destination and tons of redundancy.
- It provides high privacy and security.
- Data transmission is more consistent because failure doesn't disrupt its processes.
- Adding new devices won't disrupt data transmissions.
- This topology has robust features to beat any situation.
- A mesh doesn't have a centralized authority.

Disadvantages of Mesh Topology

There are some disadvantages of mesh topology:

- It's costly as compared to the opposite network topologies i.e. star, bus, point to point topology.
- Installation is extremely difficult in the mesh.
- Power requirement is higher as all the nodes will need to remain active all the time and share the load.
- Complex process.
- The cost to implement mesh is above other selections.
- There is a high risk of redundant connections.
- Each node requires a further utility cost to think about.
- Maintenance needs are challenging with a mesh

Tree Topology

Tree Topology is a topology which is having a tree structure in which all the computers are connected like the branches which are connected with the tree. In Computer Network, tree topology is called a combination of a Bus and Star network topology.

Tree network topology is considered to be the simplest topology in all the topologies which is having only one route between any two nodes on the network.

The pattern of connection resembles a tree in which all branches spring from one root hence (Tree Topology). Tree topology is one of the most popular among the four network topologies.

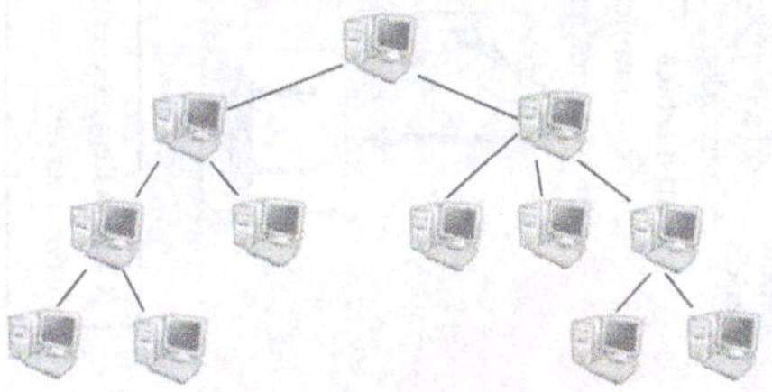

Tree topology

Advantages of Tree Topology

- This topology is the combination of bus and star topology.
- This topology provides a hierarchical as well as central data arrangement of the nodes.
- As the leaf nodes can add one or more nodes in the hierarchical chain, this topology provides high scalability.
- The other nodes in a network are not affected if one of their nodes gets damaged or does not work.
- Tree topology provides easy maintenance and easy fault identification can be done.
- Point-to-point wiring for individual segments.
- Tree Topology is highly secure and reliable.

Disadvantages of Tree Topology

- This network is very difficult to configure as compared to the other network topologies.
- The length of a segment is limited & the limit of the segment depends on the type of cabling used.
- Due to the presence of a large number of nodes, the network performance of tree topology becomes a bit slow.
- If the computer on the first level is erroneous, the next-level computer will also go under problems.
- Requires a large number of cables compared to star and ring topology.
- The Backbone appears as the failure point of the entire segment of the network.
- Treatment of the topology is pretty complex and the establishment cost increases as well.

Quick Test 2

1. Write any one advantage and one disadvantage of star topology. **CBSE 2024**
2. Identify the type of topology from the following: **NCERT**
   (a) Each node is connected with the help of a single cable.
   (b) Each node is connected with central switching through independent cables.
3. Give one advantage and disadvantage each of Bus and Star topology. **CBSE 2022**
4. In a tree topology, how are devices connected?
5. How does a mesh topology ensure network reliability?

Mind Map

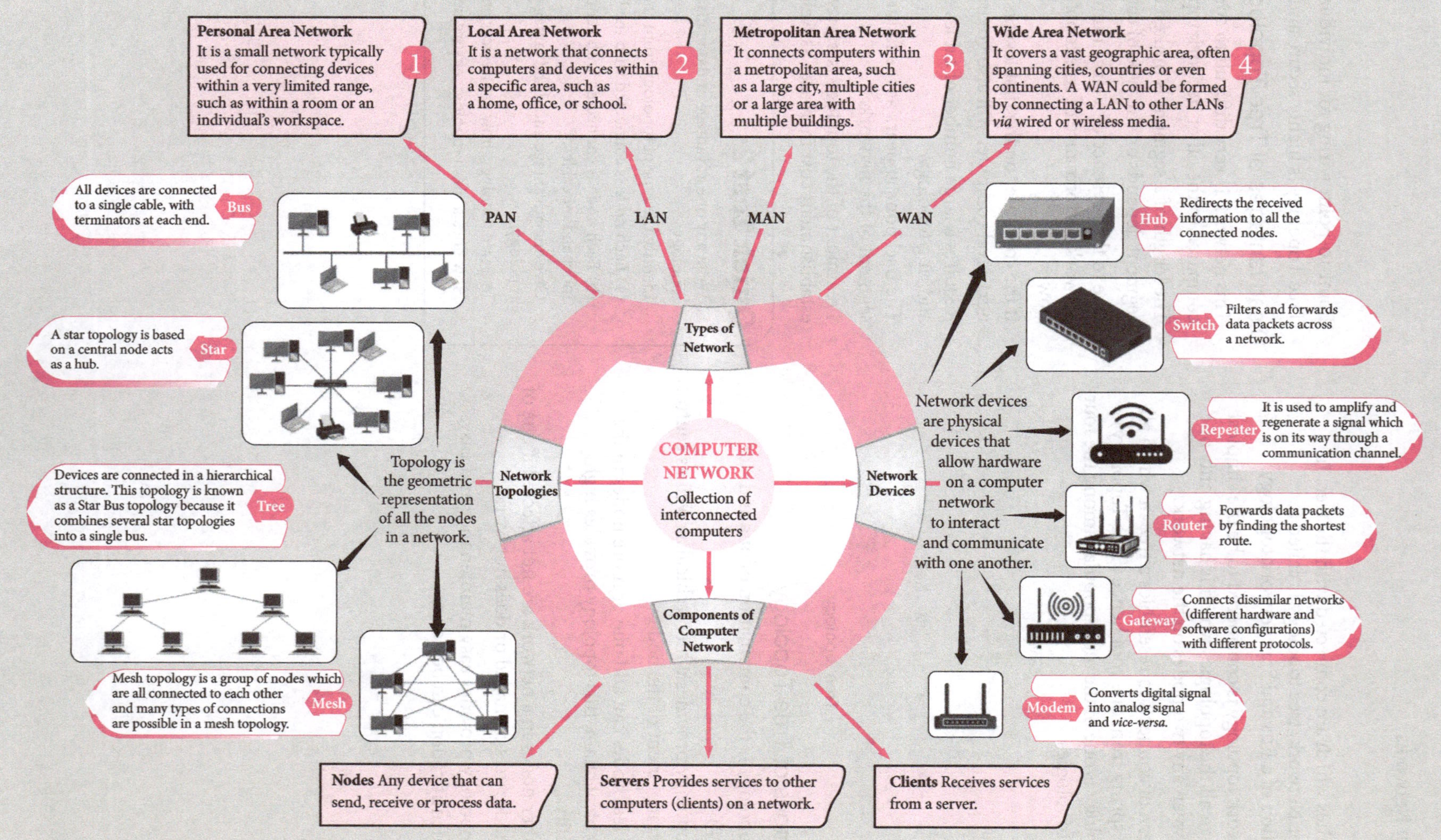

COMPUTER NETWORK
Collection of interconnected computers
Types of Network
PAN
LAN
MAN
WAN
Personal Area Network It is a small network typically used for connecting devices within a very limited range, such as within a room or an individual's workspace. 1
Local Area Network It is a network that connects computers and devices within a specific area, such as a home, office, or school. 2
Metropolitan Area Network It connects computers within a metropolitan area, such as a large city, multiple cities or a large area with multiple buildings. 3
Wide Area Network It covers a vast geographic area, often spanning cities, countries or even continents. A WAN could be formed by connecting a LAN to other LANs *via* wired or wireless media. 4
Network Topologies
Topology is the geometric representation of all the nodes in a network.
Bus All devices are connected to a single cable, with terminators at each end.
Star A star topology is based on a central node acts as a hub.
Tree Devices are connected in a hierarchical structure. This topology is known as a Star Bus topology because it combines several star topologies into a single bus.
Mesh Mesh topology is a group of nodes which are all connected to each other and many types of connections are possible in a mesh topology.
Network Devices
Network devices are physical devices that allow hardware on a computer network to interact and communicate with one another.
Hub Redirects the received information to all the connected nodes.
Switch Filters and forwards data packets across a network.
Repeater It is used to amplify and regenerate a signal which is on its way through a communication channel.
Router Forwards data packets by finding the shortest route.
Gateway Connects dissimilar networks (different hardware and software configurations) with different protocols.
Modem Converts digital signal into analog signal and *vice-versa*.
Components of Computer Network
Nodes Any device that can send, receive or process data.
Servers Provides services to other computers (clients) on a network.
Clients Receives services from a server.

NCERT Folder

1. Fill in the blanks:

(a) To transmit data for sharing on a network, it has to be divided into smaller chunks called ________.

(b) The set of rules that decide the functioning of a network is called ________.

(c) A LAN can be extended up to a distance of ______ km.

(d) The ________ connects a local area network to the internet.

(e) The ________ topology is of hierarchical nature.

Ans. (a) packets. (b) protocol.
(c) 1 (d) router
(e) tree

2. Define a network. What is the need of forming a network?

Ans. A network is a collection of interconnected devices that communicate with each other to share resources and information.

Networks are needed to enable data sharing, improve communication, and provide access to shared resources like printers and the internet.

3. Give any two examples of networks.

Ans. Examples of computer network are

- Social networking
- Mobile networking
- Network of computers
- Airlines, railway, banks, hospitals networks.

4. Differentiate between:

(a) MAN and WAN **(b) Router and Gateway**

(c) Bus and star topology

Ans. (a) MAN and WAN

MAN (Metropolitan Area Network)	WAN (Wide Area Network)
Covers a city or a large town.	Covers a large geographical area, often across countries.
Usually managed by a single organization or entity, like a city or a large campus.	Often spans multiple organizations, cities, or countries.
Typically has higher speeds within its coverage area.	Speeds can vary due to the longer distances involved.
Example Network connecting branches within a city.	**Example** The internet or a network connecting branches worldwide.

(b) Router and Gateway

Router	Gateway
Connects multiple networks and directs data packets between them.	Connects two different networks with varying protocols, acting as a translator.
Operates at the network layer of the OSI model.	Operates at multiple layers, often including the application layer.
Primarily used within similar types of networks (e.g., LAN to LAN).	Used to connect different network types (e.g., LAN to WAN).
Less complex, mainly focused on forwarding data packets based on IP addresses.	More complex, as it performs protocol conversions and other data processing.

(c) Bus and star topology

Bus Topology	Star Topology
Has a single central cable (backbone) that connects all devices.	Has a central hub or switch to which all devices are connected.
Data sent by a device travels through the entire cable.	Data sent by a device goes directly to the central hub, which then forwards it to the intended device.
If the central cable fails, the entire network goes down.	If a single cable connecting a device fails, only that device is affected; the rest of the network remains operational.
Slower data transmission as more devices are connected.	Faster data transmission as each device has a direct connection to the hub.
Difficult to troubleshoot.	Easier to troubleshoot.

EXAM PATTERN QUESTIONS

Objective Type Questions

Multiple Choice Questions

1. Which of the following is a collection of independent computers and other hardware interconnected by communication channels?

(a) Computer (b) Networking
(c) Sharing (d) None of these

2. Which of the following is an advantage of networking?

(a) Application sharing (b) File sharing
(c) User communication (d) All of the above

3. Network formed between computers which are spread across the continents is called

(a) LAN (b) WAN
(c) MAN (d) WLAN

4. Which type of network covers a small geographical area like a single office, building, or school campus? CBSE SQP 2024-25

(a) PAN (b) MAN (c) LAN (d) WAN

5. Riya wants to transfer pictures from her mobile phone to her laptop. She uses Bluetooth Technology to connect two devices. Which type of network will be formed in this case? CBSE SQP 2023-24, Competency Based Que.

(a) PAN (b) LAN (c) MAN (d) WAN

6. Television cable network is an example of: CBSE SQP 2022-23

(a) LAN (b) WAN
(c) MAN (d) Internet

7. Someone's internet is slow. They realize their computer's data isn't being changed into a signal that can travel over phone lines. They need a device to fix this. Which device changes computer data into a signal for phone lines and back again? Competency Based Que.

(a) Microwave (b) Satellite
(c) Modem (d) Gateway

8. Which of the following device may operate at different network speeds depending on the protocol standard they support?

(a) Router (b) Ethernet card
(c) RJ45 Connector (d) None of these

9. Identify the networking device responsible for routing data packets based on their destination addresses. CBSE SQP 2024-25

(a) Modem (b) Hub
(c) Repeater (d) Router

10. Fill in the Blank:

The modem at the sender's computer end acts as a ________. CBSE SQP 2023-24

(a) Model (b) Modulator
(c) Demodulator (d) Convertor

11. Geometric arrangement of devices on the network is called

(a) topology (b) protocols
(c) media (d) LAN

12. In which of the topology, network components are connected to the same cable?

(a) Star (b) Ring
(c) Bus (d) Mesh

13. A company needs a network where all computers are connected to each other. This is to make sure the network keeps working even if some connections break. Which network setup works best for this? Competency Based Que.

(a) Ring Setup
(b) Star Setup
(c) Bus Setup
(d) Mesh Setup

14. In which of the network topologies do all devices connect to a central point, such as a switch or hub? CBSE SQP 2024-25

(a) Star (b) Bus
(c) Tree (d) Mesh

15. In .... topology, the devices are arranged in the form of multiple branches in hierarchical manner. CBSE 2024

(a) Star (b) Tree
(c) Mesh (d) Bus

16. Which of the following topologies is very efficient and all nodes are connected to a central hub? CBSE 2023

(a) Star (b) Tree (c) Bus (d) Ring

Fill in the Blanks

17. ______ of computers helps the user to share data files.

18. Users can share ______ using networking.

19. ______ acts as a centralised connection to several computers with the central node or server.

20. The antenna transmits the radio signals to those equipment, which has ______.

21. Hub is associated with ______ network.

State whether True or False

22. Networking of computer helps the user to share data files.

23. RJ45 connector is commonly used in telephony applications and networking.

24. WAN refers to a small network communication.

25. Passive hub amplifies the signal as it moves from one device to another.

26. Star topology is an extension and variation of bus topology.

Assertion and Reason Based Questions

Assertion and Reason based questions. Mark the correct choice as

(a) Both A and R are true, and R is the correct explanation of A.

(b) Both A and R are true, but R is not the correct explanation of A.

(c) A is true, but R is false.

(d) A is false, but R is true.

27. Assertion (A) LAN (Local Area Network) is suitable for connecting devices across different cities.

Reason (R) LANs are typically designed for small areas such as homes, offices, or schools, usually spanning a few meters to a few hundred meters.

28. Assertion (A) A repeater amplifies or regenerates signals to ensure data transmission over longer distances without degradation.

Reason (R) A repeater works by receiving a weakened signal, amplifying it, and transmitting it further along the network.

29. Assertion (A) A hub improves network performance by sending data packets directly to the intended recipient device.

Reason (R) Hubs broadcast data packets to all connected devices, which may lead to traffic congestion in the network.

30. Assertion (A) A router assigns IP addresses to devices in a network.

Reason (R) A router uses DHCP (Dynamic Host Configuration Protocol) to automatically assign IP addresses to devices.

31. Assertion (A) A switch broadcasts data to all devices in a network, leading to potential traffic congestion.

Reason (R) A switch uses MAC addresses to forward data only to the intended device, unlike hubs that broadcast to all devices.

32. Assertion (A) Bus topology is cost-effective and simple to install.

Reason (R) It requires less cable length and fewer devices compared to other topologies.

33. Assertion (A) Mesh topology provides high privacy and security for data transmission.

Reason (R) Each computer in a mesh network is interconnected with every other computer.

Answers

1. (b) Networking
2. (d) All of the above
3. (b) WAN
4. (c) LAN
5. (a) PAN
6. (c) MAN
7. (c) Modem
8. (b) Ethernet card
9. (c) Repeater
10. (b) Modulator
11. (a) topology
12. (c) Bus
13. (d) Mesh Setup
14. (a) Star
15. (b) Tree
16. (a) Star
17. Networking
18. Files
19. Hub
20. Wi-Fi cards
21. star
22. True
23. True
24. False
25. False
26. False
27. (d) A is false, but R is true.
28. (a) Both A and R are true, and R is the correct explanation of A.
29. (d) A is false, but R is true.
30. (a) Both A and R are true, and R is the correct explanation of A.
31. (d) A is false, but R is true.
32. (a) Both A and R are true, and R is the correct explanation of A.
33. (a) Both A and R are true, but R is the correct explanation of A.

Subjective Questions

Very Short Answer Type Questions

1. Name the term defined by given below statement:
"A group of computers connected to each other by a link."

Ans. Computer network.

2. Which cable networks are used for LAN connections?

Ans. Twisted pair and fibre optic cables are used for LAN connections.

3. List down the types of computer networks.

Ans. Following are the three main types of computer networks, based upon the geographical area as follows

(i) Local Area Network (LAN)
(ii) Metropolitan Area Network (MAN)
(iii) Wide Area Network (WAN)

4. Which type of network (out of LAN, PAN and MAN) is formed, when you connect two mobiles using bluetooth to transfer a picture file?

Ans. When two mobiles are connected using bluetooth to transfer a picture file, a PAN (Personal Area Network) is created.

5. Arrange the following network in ascending order of their area: LAN, PAN, WAN, MAN

Ans. PAN < LAN < MAN < WAN

6. Name any two components required for networking.

Ans. Switch/hub and repeaters.

7. What is the purpose of switch in a network?

Ans. A switch is a networking device, which is used to connect different LAN segments of a network.

8. Why is a switch called an intelligent hub?

Ans. A switch is also known as intelligent hub because a hub forwards each incoming packet (data) to all the hub ports. Whereas, a switch forwards each incoming packet to the specified recipient.

9. What is the advantage of using switch over hub?

Ans. Switch provides a dedicated line at full bandwidth between two devices but hub doesn't provide a dedicated line. Hub share the bandwidth.

10. Beauty lines fashion incorporation is a fashion company with design unit and market unit 135 m away from each other. The company recently connected their LANs using Ethernet cable to share the stock related information. But after joining their LAN's they are not able to show the information due to loss of signal in between. Competency Based Que.

Which device out of the following should you suggest to be installed for a smooth communication?

(i) Modem (ii) Repeater (iii) UPS

Ans. (ii) They should use repeater. As repeater is a device used to amplify the signals.

11. What is the function of a gateway? CBSE 2022

Ans. The gateway is a node in a network, which serves as a proxy server and a firewall system, that prevents the unauthorised access.

12. What is a modem?

Ans. Modem stands for Modulator/Demodulator, which converts analog signal into digital signal and again digital signal into analog signal. It is used to connect the computers and transmit data using telephone lines.

13. A company wants to form a network on their five computers to a server within the company premises. Represent star and ring topologies diagrammatically for this network. Competency Based Que.

Ans.

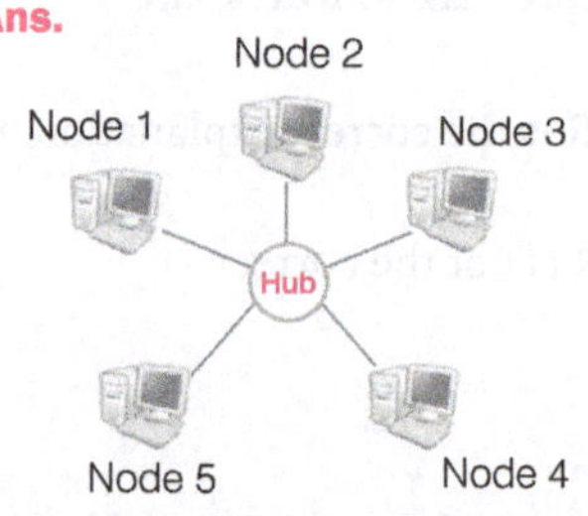

Star topology

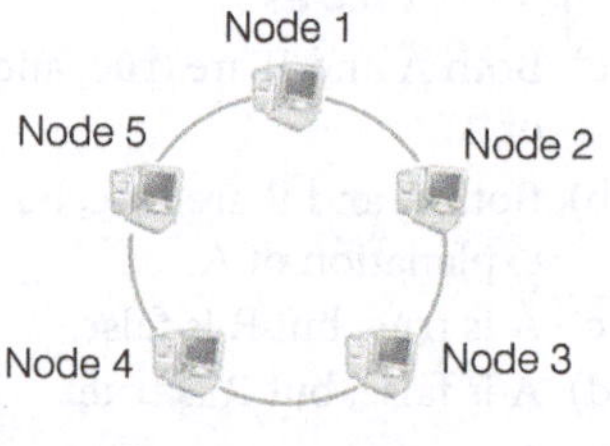

Ring topology

Short Answer Type I Questions

14. Write some benefits of networking.

Ans. Some benefits of networking are

(i) File sharing
(ii) Hardware sharing
(iii) Application sharing
(iv) User communication
(v) Access to remote database

15. How do computer networks reduce hardware costs of an organization? Explain with the help of example.

Ans. Computer networks reduce hardware costs in an organization by enabling resource sharing, which eliminates the need for each employee to have dedicated devices for every task.

For example, a network allows multiple computers to share a single printer, reducing the need for each employee to own a separate printer. Similarly, shared servers can store data centrally, reducing the need for personal storage devices for each employee. This sharing of resources significantly cuts down on the purchase and maintenance costs of hardware.

16. Write down any two points of differences between LAN, MAN and WAN.

Ans. Two major points of differences among LAN, MAN and WAN are as follows

Basics	LAN	MAN	WAN
Geographical Area	Generally within a building	Within a city	Across the continents
Distance	Upto 5 km	Upto 160 km	Unlimited

17. Write a short note on LAN and PAN.

Ans. **LAN** A Local Area Network is a computer network covering a small geographical area like a home, office or small group of building such as building in a school. Computer connected to a LAN can share information and peripheral equipments.

PAN It stands for Personal Area Network. It is a computer network used for communication among computer and different technological devices close to it. Technologies such as bluetooth and infrared communication form a wireless PAN around the device.

18. Explain a scenario where a company operating in multiple cities should use a combination of LAN, MAN, and WAN networks. Justify the use of each network type in this scenario. Competency Based Que.

Ans. In a company with offices in multiple cities, each office can use a Local Area Network (LAN) to connect computers, printers, and other devices within the building for fast data exchange.

For offices spread across the same city, a Metropolitan Area Network (MAN) can be used to connect these LANs, facilitating seamless communication and resource sharing within that city.

To connect offices in different cities or countries, a Wide Area Network (WAN) is required, as it spans large geographic distances, allowing the company's branches to communicate and share data globally. Each network type optimizes cost and efficiency based on the required range and data-sharing needs.

19. Which device is used to connect dissimilar networks?

Ans. A gateway is a device, which is used to connect dissimilar networks. The gateway establishes an intelligent connection between a local network and external network, which are completely different in structure. Gateway also serve as proxy server and a firewall system that prevents the unauthorised access.

20. Identify the following devices

(i) An intelligent device that connects several nodes to form a network and redirects the received information only to intended node(s).

(ii) A device that regenerates (amplifies) the received signal and re-transmits it to its destinations.

Ans. (i) Switch (ii) Repeater

21. Identify the following devices

(i) A device that is used to connect different types of networks. It performs the necessary translation so that the connected networks can communicate properly. Competency Based Que.

(ii) A device that converts data from digital bit stream into an analog signal and *vice-versa*.

Ans. (i) Router (ii) Modem

22. Mr. GopiNath Associate Manager of Unit Nations corporate recently discovered that the communication between his company's accounts office and HR office is extremely slow and signals drop quite frequently. These offices are 120 metre away from each other and connected by an Ethernet cable. Competency Based Que.

(i) Suggest him a device which can be installed in between the office for smooth communication.

(ii) What type of network is formed by having this kind of connectivity out of LAN, MAN and WAN?

Ans. (i) The device that can be installed between the office for smooth communication is repeater.

(ii) The type of network is Local Area Network (LAN).

23. Define hub and write its functions and types.

Ans. A hub connects several computers together and acts as a central node or server.

Function of a hub

- Interconnects number of computers or users.
- All the incoming data packets received by the hub are send to all hub ports and from their, the data is sent to all the computers, connected in a hub network.

Hub are of two types

(i) **Active hub** It acts as repeater. It amplifies the signal as these move from one device to another.

(ii) **Passive hub** It simply passes the signal from one connected device to another.

24. What are the functions of the following devices?

(i) Repeater

(ii) Switch

Ans. (i) **Repeater** It is a network device, that amplifies and restores signals for long distance transmission.

It interconnects identical network. Useful for long distance transmission, as they assure that there is no loss of data packets on the way.

(ii) **Switch** It is a device used to segment networks into different subnetworks, called subnets or LAN segments. This prevents traffic overloading. Switches are responsible for filtering, i.e. transforming data in a specific way and forwarding packets.

25. Define repeaters with its two types.

Ans. Repeaters are used to amplify the signals, when they are transported over a long distance.

Repeaters are of two types

(i) **Amplifier** It amplifies or boosts the incoming signals. So, it amplifies both the signal and any concurrent noise.

(ii) **Signal repeater** It only amplifies the signal and filters out the noise signals. So, we get only the clear signal at the receiver end.

26. Mention the advantages of switch over a hub?

Ans. Advantages of a switch over a hub:

- A switch directs data to specific devices, reducing collisions.
- It increases network efficiency and security by segmenting traffic.
- A switch operates at the data link layer, making it more intelligent and faster than a hub.

27. Explain how a router differs from a switch in a network. Additionally, in which types of networks (LAN, MAN, or WAN) are routers typically used, and why?

Ans. A router directs data packets between different networks, often over wide areas, and makes decisions based on IP addresses. Routers are crucial for connecting separate networks and are primarily used in WAN (Wide Area Network) and MAN (Metropolitan Area Network) setups to link multiple local networks or remote networks over large distances.

A switch, on the other hand, operates within a single network (typically a LAN) to connect multiple devices. Switches use MAC addresses to forward data within the local network, optimizing internal communication but not routing data across different networks.

28. Write one advantage of bus topology of network. Also, illustrate how four computers can be connected with each other using star topology of network?

Ans. Advantage of bus topology In bus topology, computers can be connected with each other using server (host) along with a single length of cable.

Four computers can be connected with each other using star topology in the following way:

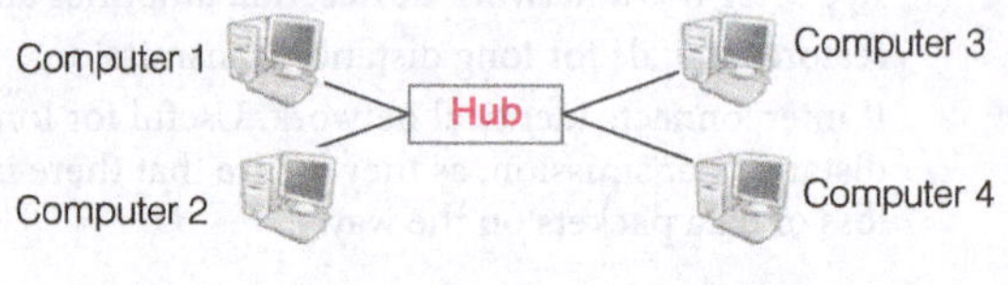

29. Define tree topology. Also, write down its two limitations.

Ans. A tree topology is an extension and variation of bus topology. Its basic structure is like an inverted tree, where the root acts as a server.

Limitations

- Long cables are required for this kind of topologies.
- There is the dependence on the root node.

30. How is it easier to diagnose fault in Star topology than in Bus topology?

Ans. Star topology is easier to diagnose fault than bus topology because in a star topology, each device is connected to a central hub or switch. If a device fails, it can be easily isolated, and the rest of the network continues to function. In bus topology, a fault in the central bus can affect the entire network, making diagnosis harder.

31. State reason why star topology requires more cable length than bus topology.

Ans. Star topology requires more cable length than bus topology because in star topology, each device is connected individually to the central hub or switch, requiring more cabling. In bus topology, all devices are connected to a single central cable, so less cabling is needed.

Short Answer Type II Questions

32. Write the difference between LAN and MAN.

Ans. Differences between LAN and MAN are as follows

LAN	MAN
LAN stands for Local Area Network.	MAN stands for Metropolitan Area Network.
LAN's ownership is private.	MAN's ownership can be private or public.
The speed of LAN is high.	The speed of MAN is average.
There is more fault tolerance in LAN.	There is less fault tolerance in MAN.
LAN's design and maintenance is easy.	MAN's design and maintenance is difficult than LAN.
LAN's cost is high but less than MAN.	MAN's cost is higher than LAN.

33. When the computer network uses telephone lines as communication channel then MODEM is used as a data communication device. Now, explain the working of MODEM.

Ans. MODEM performs the task of modulation at sender's site and DEModulation at the receiver's site. Basically, our computer generates data in the form of digital signals, which need to be forwarded to the receiver through telephone lines. Since, telephone lines can carry only analog signals. So, digital signals need to be converted to analog signals at sender's site, this is called modulation.

At receiver's site, again analog signals should be converted back to the original digital signals, then this is called demodulation.

34. **Name the different types of network topologies and brief their advantages?**

Ans. Refer to text on page no. 159-161 (Network topology).

35. **Write one advantage of star topology over bus topology and one advantage of bus topology over star topology.**

Ans. **Advantage of star topology over bus topology** The star topology is the most reliable as there is a direct connection of every nodes in the network with the central node, so any problem in any node will affect the particular node only. While in bus topology, if problem exists in common medium, it will affect the entire node.

Advantage of bus topology over star topology Extension of network is very easy in bus topology. We can connect new node along its length. While in star topology, it is difficult to expand, as the new node has to connect all the way to central node and there is not available port in central node.

Long Answer Type Questions

36. **Trine Tech Corporation (TTC) is a professional consultancy company. The company is planning to set up their new offices in India with its hub at Hyderabad. As a network adviser, you have to understand their requirement and suggest them the best available solutions. Their queries are mentioned as (i) to (v) below.**

Physical locations of the blocks of TTC

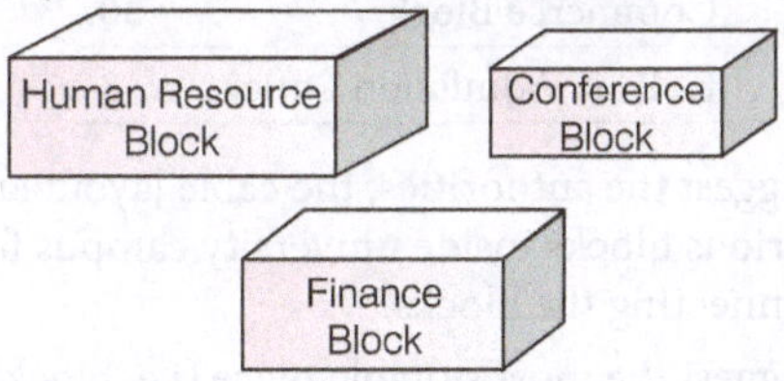

Block to block distance (in metre)

Block (From)	Block (To)	Distance
Human Resource	Conference	110
Human Resource	Finance	40
Conference	Finance	80

Expected number of computers to be in each block

Block	Computers
Human Resource	25
Finance	120
Conference	90

(i) Which will be the most appropriate block, where TTC should plan to install their server?

(ii) Draw a block to block cable layout to connect all the buildings in the most appropriate manner for efficient communication.

(iii) What will be the best possible connectivity out of the following, you will suggest to connect the new set up of offices in Bengalore with its London based office.
- Satellite Link
- Infrared
- Ethernet

(iv) Which of the following device will be suggested by you to connect each computer in each of the buildings?
- Switch
- Modem
- Gateway

(v) The company is planning to connect its admission office in Hyderabad which is more than 1000 km from company. Which type of network will be formed?

Ans. (i) TTC should install its server in finance block as it is having maximum number of computers.

(ii)

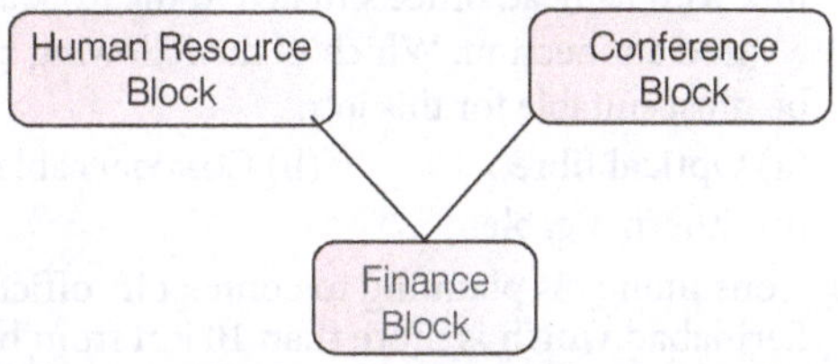

The above layout is based on minimum cable length required, which is 120 metres in the above case.

(iii) Satellite Link (iv) Switch (v) WAN

37. **Granuda consultants are setting up a secured network for their office campus at Faridabad for their day-to-day office and web based activities. They are planning to have connectivity among 3 buildings and the head office situated in Kolkata.**

Answer the questions (i) to (v) after going through the building positions in the campus and other details, which are given below.

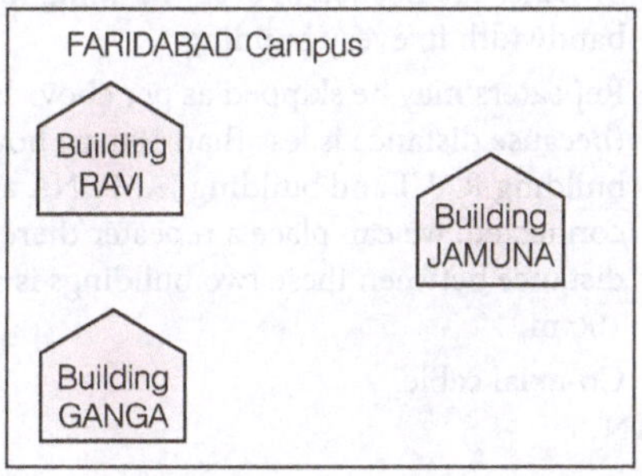

Distance between various buildings

Building RAVI to Building JAMUNA	120 m
Building RAVI to Building GANGA	50 m
Building GANGA to Building JAMUNA	65 m
Faridabad Campus to Head Office	1460 km

Competency Based Que.

Number of computers

Building RAVI	25
Building JAMUNA	150
Building GANGA	51
Head Office	10

(i) Suggest the most suitable place (i.e. block) to house the server of this organisation. Also, give a reason to justify your suggested location.

(ii) Suggest a cable layout of connections between the building inside the campus.

(iii) Suggest the placement of the following devices with justification:
(a) Switch (b) Repeater

(iv) The organisation is planning to provide a high speed link with its head office situated in the Kolkata using a wired connection. Which of the following cable will be most suitable for this job?
(a) Optical fibre (b) Co-axial cable
(c) Ethernet cable

(v) Consultancy is planning to connect its office in Faridabad which is more than 10 km from head office. Which type of network will be formed?

Ans. (i) The most suitable place to house the server is JAMUNA because it has maximum number of computers.

(ii)

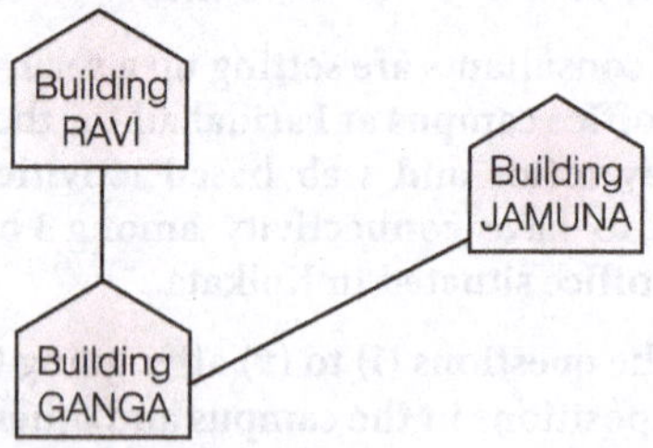

(iii) (a) Switches are needed in every building to share bandwidth in every building.

(b) Repeaters may be skipped as per above layout, (because distance is less than 100 m) however, if building RAVI and building JAMUNA are directly connected, we can place a repeater there as the distance between these two buildings is more than 100 m.

(iv) (b) Co-axial cable.

(v) MAN

38. Freshminds University of India is starting its first campus in Ana Nagar of South India with its centre admission office in Kolkata. The university has three major blocks comprising of Office block, Science block and Commerce block is in 5 km area campus.

As a network expert, you need to suggest the network plan as per (i) to (v) to the authorities keeping in mind the distance and other given parameters.

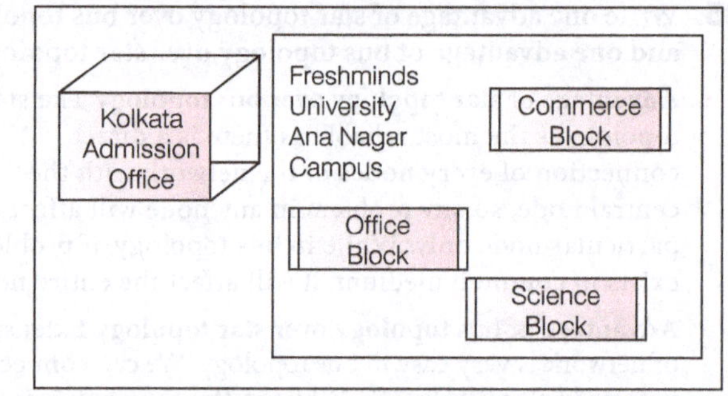

Expected wire distance between various locations

Office Block to Science Block	90 m
Office Block to Commerce Block	80 m
Science Block to Commerce Block	15 m
Kolkata Admission Office to Ana Nagar Campus	450 km

Expected number of computers to be installed at various locations in the university are as follows:

Office Block	10
Science Block	140
Commerce Block	30
Kolkata Admission Office	8

(i) Suggest the authorities, the cable layout amongst various blocks inside university campus for connecting the blocks.

(ii) Suggest the most suitable place (i.e. block) to house the server for this university with a suitable reason.

(iii) Suggest an efficient device from the following to be installed in each of the block to connect all the computers.
(a) Modem
(b) Switch
(c) Gateway

(iv) Suggest the most suitable (very high speed) service to provide data connectivity between admission office located in Kolkata and the campus located in Ana Nagar from the following options:
- Telephone line

- Fixedline dial-up connection
- Co-axial cable network
- GSM
- Leased line
- Satellite connection.

(v) University is planning to connect its campus in Kolkata which is more than 100 km. Which type of network will be formed? **Competency Based Que.**

Ans. (i)

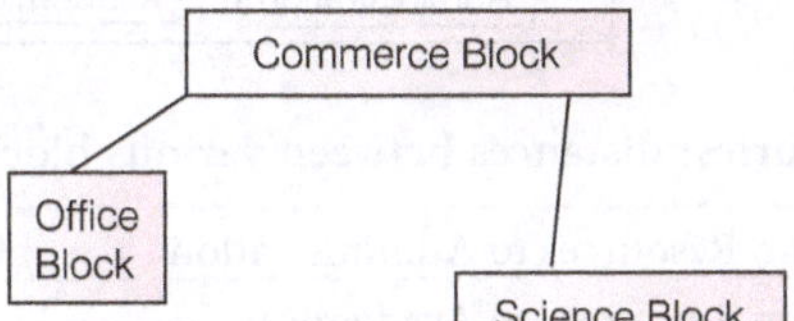

(ii) The most suitable place to house the server is Science Block as it has maximum number of computers. Thus, reducing the cabling cost and increases efficiency of network.

(iii) (b) Switch is the device to be installed in each of the blocks to connect all the computers.

(iv) Satellite connection.

(v) MAN

39. Quick Learn University is setting up its academic blocks at Prayag Nagar and planning to set up a network. The university has three academic blocks and one human resource centre as shown in the diagram below:

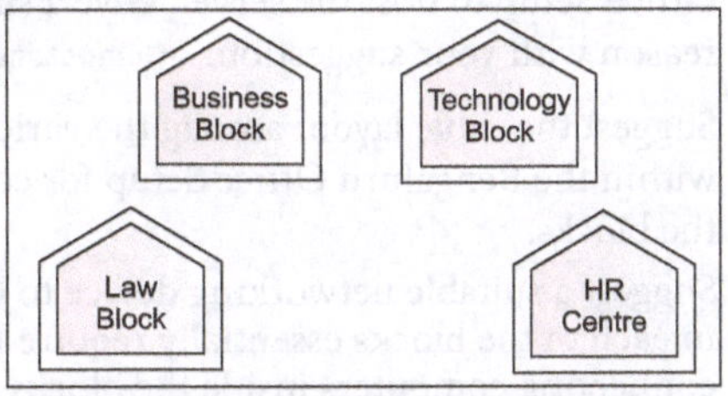

Centre to centre distance between various blocks/centre is as follows:

Law Block to Business Block	40 m
Law Block to Technology Block	80 m
Law Block to HR Centre	105 m
Business Block to Technology Block	30 m
Business Block to HR Centre	35 m
Technology Block to HR Centre	15 m

Number of computers in each of the blocks/centre are as follows:

Law Block	15
Technology Block	40
HR Centre	115
Business Block	25

(i) Suggest the most suitable place (i.e. block/centre) to install the server of this university with a suitable reason.

(ii) Suggest an ideal layout for connecting these block/centre for a wired connectivity.

(iii) Which device you will suggest to be placed/installed in each of these blocks/centre to efficiently connect all the computers with in these blocks/centre ?

(iv) The university is planning to connect its admission office in the closest big city, which is more than 250 km from university, which type of network (out of LAN, MAN or WAN) will be formed? Justify your answer. **Competency Based Que.**

(v) Expand the following:
- LAN
- WAN

Ans. (i) HR centre as it has maximum number of computers.

(ii)

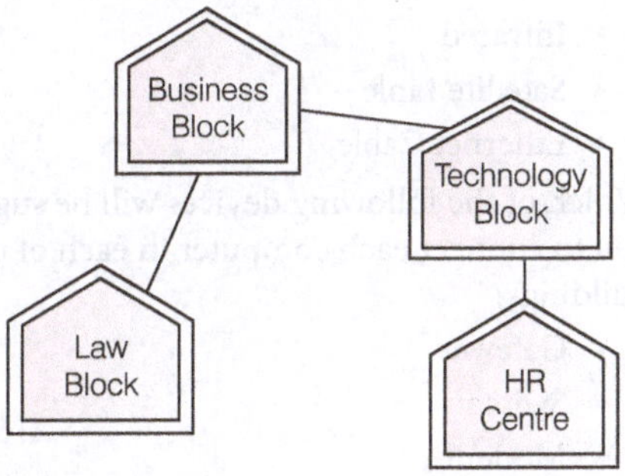

(iii) Switch.

(iv) WAN as it is another city.

(v) • Local Area Network
• Wide Area Network

40. Tech Up Corporation (TUC) is a professional consultancy company. The company is planning to set up their new offices in India with its hub at Hyderabad. As a network adviser, you have to understand their requirement and suggest to them the best available solutions. Their queries are mentioned as (i) to (v) below.

Physical locations of the blocks of TUC

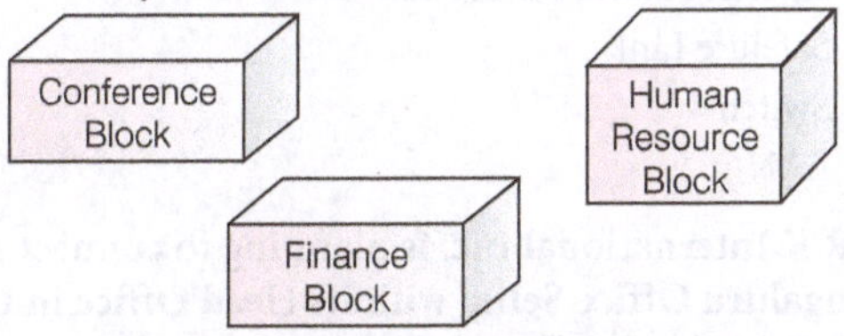

Block to block distances (in metre)

Block (From)	Block (To)	Distance
Human Resource	Conference	60
Human Resource	Finance	120
Conference	Finance	80

Expected number of computers to be installed in each block

Block	Computers
Human Resource	125
Finance	25
Conference	60

(i) What will the most appropriate block, where TUC should plan to install their server?

(ii) Draw a block to block cable layout to connect all the buildings in the most appropriate manner for efficient communication.

(iii) What will be the best possible connectivity out of the following, you will suggest to connect the new setup of offices in Bengalore with its London based office?

- Infrared
- Satellite Link
- Ethernet Cable

(iv) Which of the following devices will be suggested by you to connect each computer in each of the buildings?

- Gateway
- Switch
- Modem

(v) Company is planning to connect its block in its office which is less than 1 km. Which type of network will be formed? **Competency Based Que.**

Ans. (i) TUC should install its server in Human Resource Block as it has maximum number of computers.

(ii)

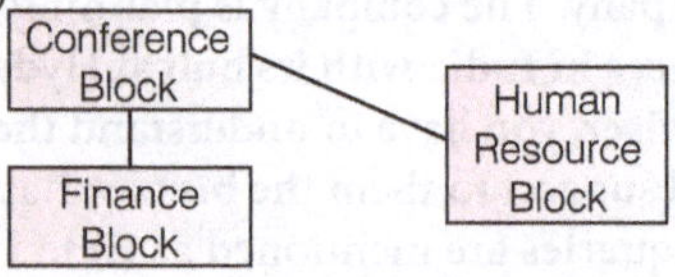

The above layout is based on the minimum length of cable required, i.e. 140 m.

(iii) Satellite Link

(iv) Switch

(v) LAN

41. **G.R.K International Inc. is planning to connect its Bengaluru Office Setup with its Head Office in Delhi. The Bengaluru Office G.R.K. International Inc. is spread across an area of approx. 1 square kilometres consisting of 3 blocks. Human Resources, Academics and Administration. You as a network expert have to suggest answers to the five queries (i) to (v) raised by them.**

Note **Keep the distances between blocks and number of computers in each block in mind, while providing them the solutions.**

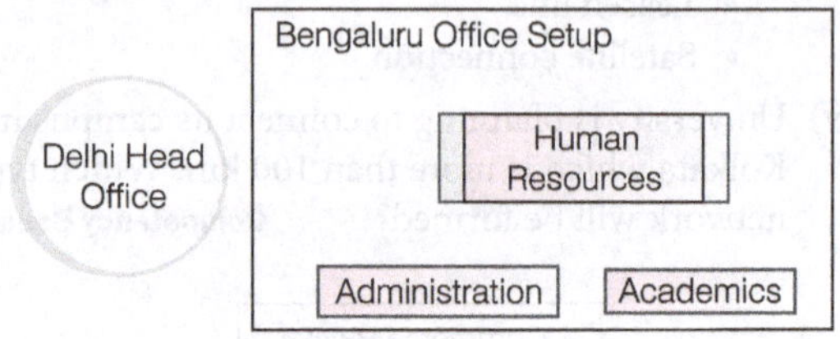

Shortest distances between various blocks

Human Resources to Administration	100m
Human Resources to Academics	65m
Academics to Administration	110m
Delhi Head Office to Bengaluru Office Setup	2350 km

Number of computers installed at various blocks

Block	Number of Computers
Human Resources	155
Administration	20
Academics	100
Delhi Head Office	20

(i) Suggest the most suitable block in the Bengaluru Office Setup to host the server. Give a suitable reason with your suggestion. **Competency Based Que.**

(ii) Suggest the cable layout among the various blocks within the Bengaluru Office Setup for connecting the blocks.

(iii) Suggest a suitable networking device to be installed in each of the blocks essentially required for connecting computers inside the blocks with fast and efficient connectivity.

(iv) Suggest the most suitable media to provide secure, fast and reliable data connectivity between Delhi Head Office and the Bengaluru Office Setup.

(v) Expand the following:

- WAN
- MAN

Ans. (i) Human Resources, because it has maximum number of computers.

(ii)

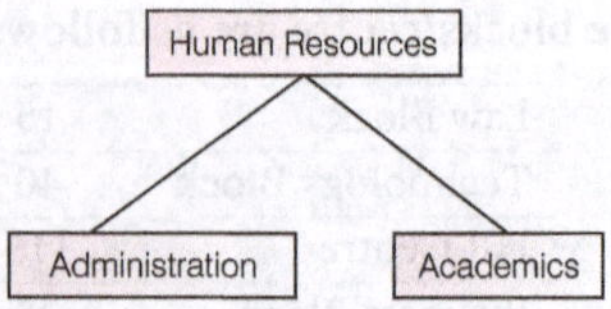

(iii) Hub/Switch.

(iv) Satellite.

(v) • Wide Area Network
• Metropolitan Area Network

42. Expertia Professional Global (EPG) in an online corporate training provider company for IT related courses. The company is setting up their new campus in Mumbai.

Physical locations of the buildings of EPG

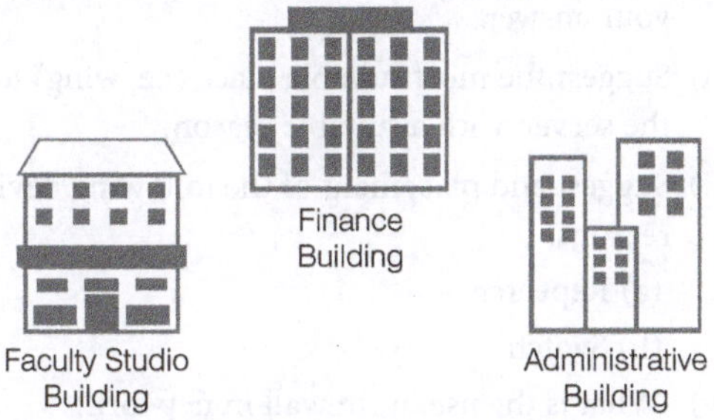

You as a network expert have to study the physical locations of various buildings and the number of computers to be installed. In the planning phase, provide the best possible answers for the queries (i) to (v) raised by them.

Building to building distance (in metre)

From	To	Distance
Administrative Building	Finance Building	60
Administrative Building	Faculty Studio Building	120
Finance Building	Faculty Studio Building	70

Expected computers to be installed in each building

Buildings	Computers
Administrative Building	20
Finance Building	40
Faculty Studio Building	120

(i) Suggest the most appropriate building, where EPG should plan to install the server.

(ii) Suggest the most appropriate building to building cable layout to connect all three buildings for efficient communication.

(iii) Which type of network out of the following is formed by connection the computers of these three buildings?
(a) LAN (b) MAN (c) WAN

(iv) Which wireless channel out of the following should be opted by EPG to connect to students of all over the world?
(a) Infrared (b) Microwave (c) Satellite

(v) Expand the following:
• MAN
• PAN

Ans. (i) EPG should install the server in the Faculty Studio Building as it has maximum number of computers.

(ii)

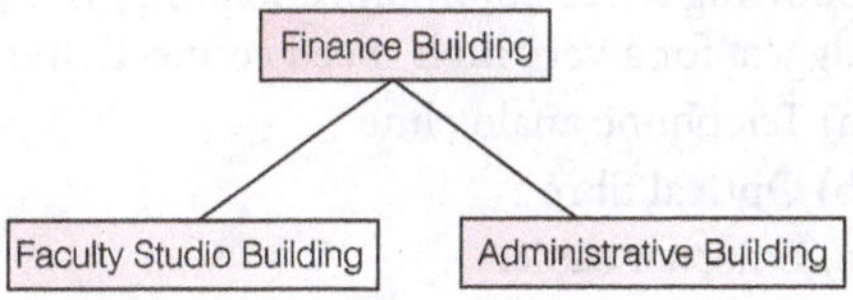

(iii) (a) LAN (Local Area Network).

(iv) (c) Satellite.

(v) • Metropolitan Area Network
• Personal Area Network

43. Learn Together is an educational NGO. It is setting up its new campus at Jabalpur for its web-based activities. The campus has four compounds as shown in the diagram below: **Competency Based Que.**

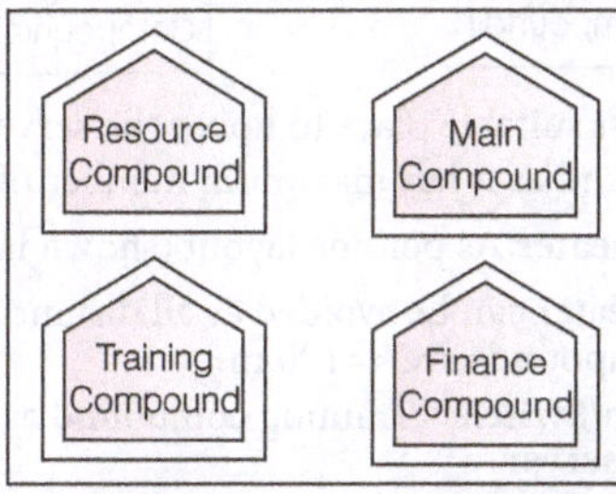

Centre to centre distance between various compounds as per architectural drawing (in m) is as follows

Main Compound to Resource Compound	110 m
Main Compound to Training Compound	115 m
Main Compound to Finance Compound	35 m
Resource Compound to Training Compound	25 m
Resource Compound to Finance Compound	135 m
Training Compound to Finance Compound	100 m

Expected number of computers in each compound are as follows

Main Compound	5
Resource Compound	15
Training Compound	150
Finance Compound	20

(i) Suggest a cable layout of connections between the compounds.

(ii) Suggest the most suitable place (i.e. compound) to house the server for this NGO. Also, provide a suitable reason for your suggestion.

(iii) Suggest the placement of the following devices with justification:
(a) Repeater
(b) Hub/Switch

(iv) The NGO is planning to connect its international office situated in Mumbai, which out of the following wired communication link, will you suggest for a very high speed connectivity?
(a) Telephone analog line
(b) Optical fibre
(c) Ethernet cable.

(v) Expand the following:
- LAN
- PAN

Ans. (i)

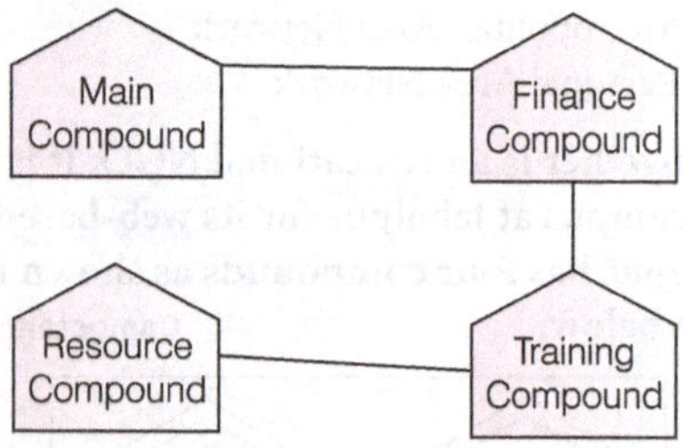

(ii) The most suitable place to house the server is Training Compound as it has maximum number of computers.

(iii) (a) **Repeater** As per one layout (shown in (i)), the repeater can be avoided as all distances between the compounds are <=100 m.
(b) **Hub/Switch** Training compound as it is hosting the server.

(iv) (b) Optical fibre.

(v) • Local Area Network
• Personal Area Network

44. Institute of Distance Learning is located in Pune and is planning to go in for networking of four wings for better interaction. The details are shown below: **Competency Based Que.**

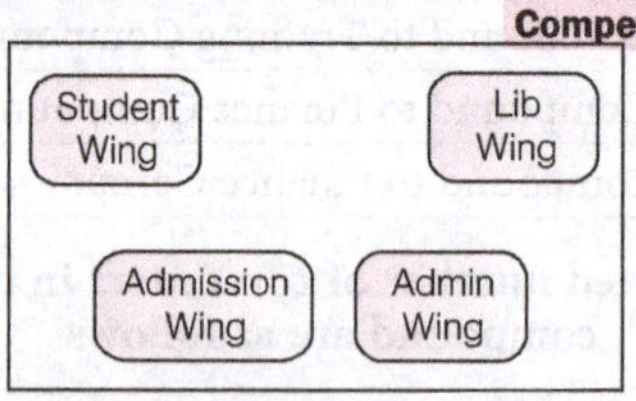

The distance between various wings

Student Wing to Admin Wing	150 m
Student Wing to Admission Wing	100 m
Student Wing of Lib Wing	325 m
Admission Wing to Admin Wing	100 m
Admission Wing to Lib Wing	125 m
Admin Wing to Lib Wing	90 m

Number of computers

Student Wing	225
Admission Wing	50
Admin Wing	10
Lib Wing	25

(i) Suggest the type of networking (LAN, MAN, WAN) for connecting Lib Wing to Admin Wing. Justify your answer.

(ii) Suggest the most suitable place (i.e. wing) to house the server, with a suitable reason.

(iii) Suggest and placement of the following devices with reasons.
(a) Repeater
(b) Switch

(iv) What is the use of firewall in network?

(v) Expand the term MODEM.

Ans. (i) Since, the distance between Lib Wing and Admin Wing is small. So type of networking is small, i.e. LAN.

(ii) Since, maximum number of computers are in Student Wing, so suitable place to house the server is Student Wing.

(iii) (a) Repeater should be installed between Student Wing and Admin Wing as distance is more than 60 m.
(b) Switch should be installed in each wing to connect several computers.

(iv) Firewall prevents unauthorised access in the network.

(v) Modulator Demodulator

45. Bias Methodologies is planning to expand their network in India, starting with three cities in India to build infrastructure for research and development of their chemical products. **Competency Based Que.**

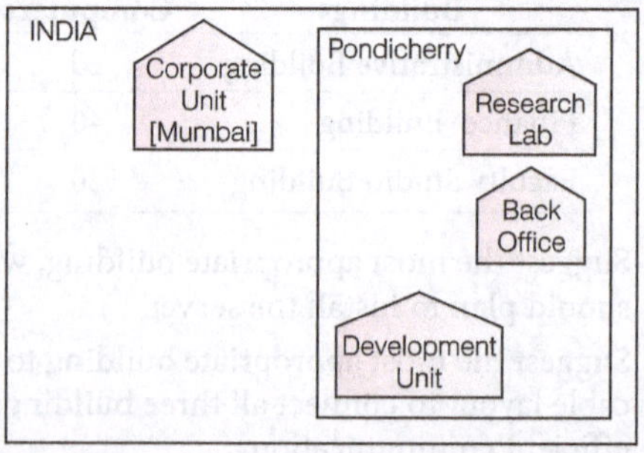

The company has planned to set up their main office in Pondicherry at three different locations and have named their offices as Back Office, Research Lab and Development Unit. The company has one more research office namely Corporate Unit in Mumbai. A rough layout of the same is as follows:

Approximate distance between these offices are as follows

From	To	Distance
Research Lab	Back Office	110 m
Research Lab	Development Unit	16 km
Research Lab	Corporate Unit	1800 km
Back Office	Development Unit	13 km

In continuation of the above, the company experts have planned to install the following number of computers in each of their offices

Research Lab	158
Back Office	79
Development Unit	90
Corporate Unit	51

(i) Suggest the type of network required (out of LAN, MAN, WAN) for connecting each of the following office units.
- Research Lab and Back Office
- Research Lab and Development Unit.

(ii) Which one of the following device, will you suggest for connecting all the computers with in each of their office units?
- Switch/Hub
- Modem
- Telephone.

(iii) Which of the following communication medium, will you suggest to be procured by the company for connecting their local office units in Pondicherry for very effective (high speed) communication?
- Telephone cable
- Optical fibre
- Ethernet cable.

(iv) Suggest a cable/wiring layout for connecting the company's local office units located in Pondicherry. Also, suggest an effective method/technology for connecting the company's office unit located in Mumbai.

(v) Which building is suitable to install the server with suitable reason?

Ans. (i) • LAN • MAN.

(ii) Switch/Hub.

(iii) Optical fibre.

(iv)

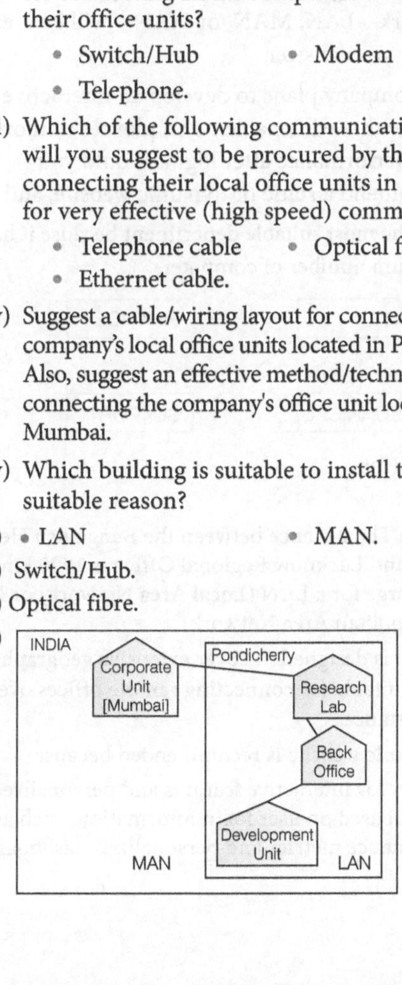

An effective method/technology for connecting the company's offices–unit located in Mumbai is dial-up or broadband.

(v) Research lab is suitable to install the server because it has maximum number of computers.

46. Gargi Education Service Ltd. is an educational organisation. It is planning to set up its India campus at Nepal with its head office at Mumbai. The Nepal campus has 4 main buildings– ADMIN, ENGINEERING, BUSINESS and MEDIA. **Competency Based Que.**

You as a network expert have to suggest the best network related solutions for their problems raised in (i) to (v), keeping in mind the distance between the buildings and other given parameters.

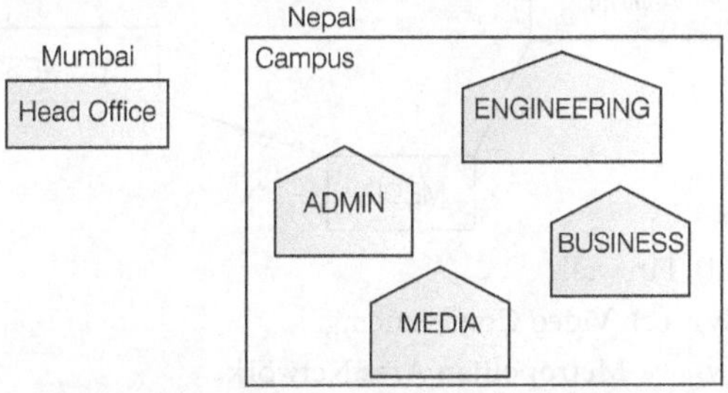

Shortest distance between various buildings

ADMIN To ENGINEERING	50 m
ADMIN To BUSINESS	80 m
ADMIN To MEDIA	45 m
ENGINEERING To BUSINESS	60 m
ENGINEERING To MEDIA	50 m
BUSINESS To MEDIA	45 m
Mumbai Head Office To Nepal Campus	2175 m

Number of computers installed at various buildings are as follows

ADMIN	110
ENGINEERING	75
BUSINESS	40
MEDIA	10
Mumbai Head Office	20

(i) Suggest the most appropriate location of the server inside the Nepal Campus (out of 4 buildings), to get the best connectivity for maximum number of computers. Justify your answer.

(ii) Suggest and draw the cable layout to efficiently connect various buildings within the Nepal Campus for connecting the computers.

(iii) Which hardware device will you suggest to be procured by the company to be installed to protect and control the Internet uses within the campus.

(iv) Which of the following will you suggest to establish the online face-to-face communication between the people in the ADMIN office of Nepal Campus and Mumbai Head Office?
(a) Cable TV (b) E-mail
(c) Video Conferencing (d) Text Chat

(v) Expand the following:
• MAN • PAN

Ans. (i) ADMIN is the most appropriate location of the Nepal Campus because it has maximum number of computers.

(ii)

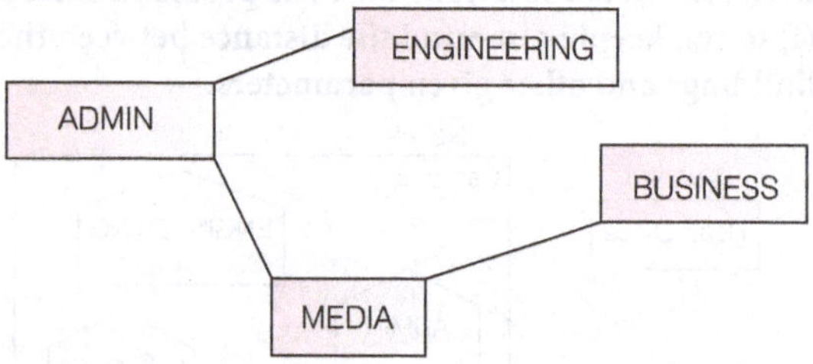

(iii) Firewall.
(iv) (c) Video Conferencing.
(v) • Metropolitan Area Network
• Personal Area Network

47. ABC Pvt. Ltd., a multinational technology company, is looking to establish its Indian Head Office in Bengaluru, and a regional office branch in Lucknow. The Bengaluru head office will be organized into four departments: HR, FINANCE, TECHNICAL, AND SUPPORT. As a network engineer, you have to propose solutions for various queries listed from (i) to (v).

CBSE SQP 2024-25
Competency Based Que.

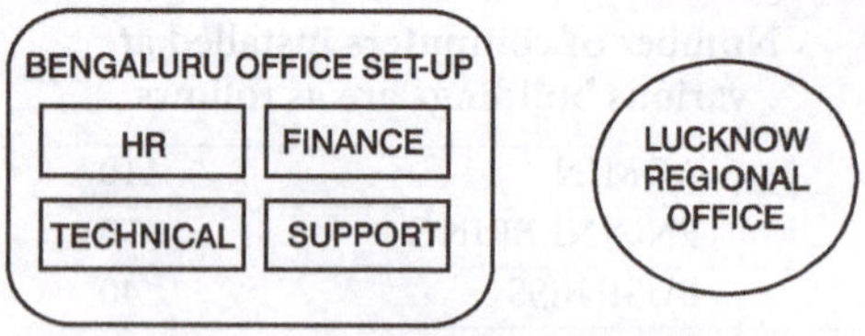

The shortest distances between the departments/offices are as follows:

HR to FINANCE	65 m
HR to TECHNICAL	80 m
HR to SUPPORT	70 m
FINANCE to TECHNICAL	60 m
FINANCE to SUPPORT	75 m
TECHNICAL to SUPPORT	50 m
BENGALURU OFFICE to LUCKNOW	1900 km

The number of computers in each department/office is as follows:

HR	175
FINANCE	35
TECHNICAL	50
SUPPORT	15
LUCKNOW OFFICE	40

(i) Suggest the most suitable department in the Bengaluru Office Setup, to install the server. Also, give a reason to justify your suggested location.

(ii) Draw a suitable cable layout of wired network connectivity between the departments in the Bengaluru Office.

(iii) Which networking device would you suggest the company to purchase to interconnect all the computers within a department in Bengaluru Office?

(iv) The company is considering establishing a network connection between its Bengaluru Head Office and Lucknow regional office. Which type of network—LAN, MAN, or WAN—will be created? Justify your answer.

(v) The company plans to develop an interactive website that will enable its employees to monitor their performance after login. Would you recommend a static or dynamic website, and why?

Ans. (i) HR is the most suitable department because it has maximum number of computers.

(ii)

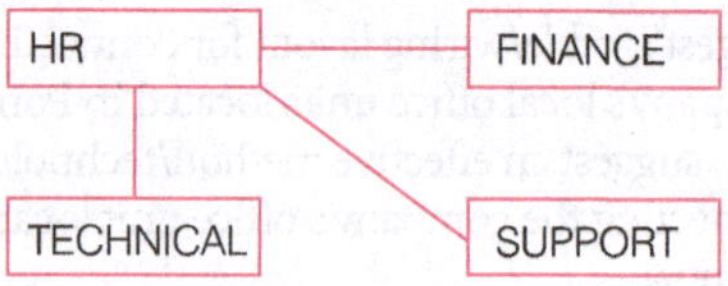

(iii) Switch/Hub
(iv) WAN

Reason The distance between the Bengaluru Head Office and Lucknow Regional Office is 1900 km, which is too large for a LAN (Local Area Network) or MAN (Metropolitan Area Network).

A WAN is designed to cover extensive geographic areas and is suitable for connecting remote offices over such long distances.

(v) A dynamic website is recommended because

It allows for interactive features and personalized content based on user login information, such as performance metrics and personalized dashboards.

It can display real-time data updates, which is crucial for monitoring employee performance and other metrics.

48. FULLMAN Tech, Bengaluru is a company that deals with software development. They have different divisions HR (H1), Sales (H2), Production (H3) and Marketing (H4). The layout of the Bengaluru branch is **CBSE 2024**

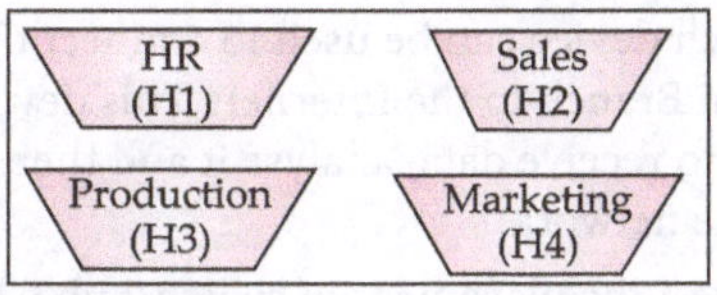

The management wants to connect all the divisions as well as all the computers of each division (H1, H2, H3 and H4). **Competency Based Que.**

Distance between the divisions are as follows:

H1 to H2	76 m
H1 to H3	185 m
H1 to H4	88 m
H2 to H3	140 m
H2 to H4	125 m
H3 to H4	160 m

Number of computers in each of the division:

Division	Number of Computers
H1	140
H2	340
H3	180
H4	260

Based on the above specifications, answer the following questions:

(i) Suggest the topology and draw the most efficient cable layout for connecting all the divisions of Bengaluru branch.

(ii) FULLMAN Tech is expanding its reach and therefore it establishes a new office in Delhi. Out of LAN, MAN, and WAN what kind of network will be created to connect Bengaluru office with Delhi Office?

(iii) Suggest the division for the placement of server in Bengaluru branch. Explain the reason for your selection.

(iv) Suggest the placement of the following devices in Bengaluru branch :

(a) Repeater (b) Switch/Hub

(v) The company's manager Ms. Ritu is worried as to how she can extend and modify the functionality of the web browser. Help her by giving names of any two tools.

Ans. (i) Star Topology

Layout

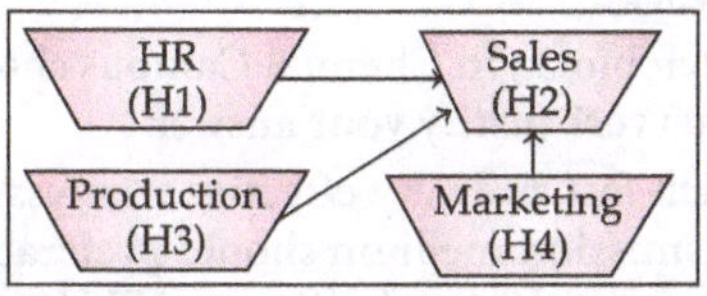

(ii) WAN

(iii) H2 , as it has the largest number of computers.

(iv) (a) Repeater

H2 to H3

H2 to H4

(b) Switch/Hub in all the buildings

(v) Browser apps, add-ons, plug-ins, and extensions

49. Meticulous EduServe is an educational organization. It is planning to setup its India campus at Chennai with its head office at Delhi. The Chennai campus has 4 main buildings – ADMIN, ENGINEERING, BUSINESS and MEDIA **CBSE SQP 2023-24** **Competency Based Que.**

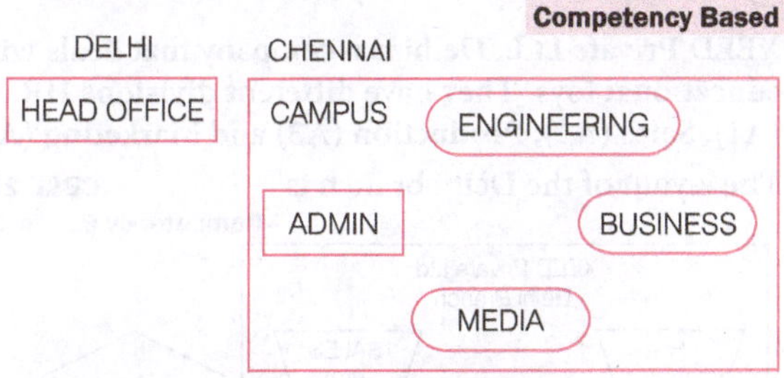

Block to Block distances (in Mtrs.)

From	To	Distance
ADMIN	ENGINEERING	55 m
ADMIN	BUSINESS	90 m
ADMIN	MEDIA	50 m
ENGINEERING	BUSINESS	55 m
ENGINEERING	MEDIA	50 m
BUSINESS	MEDIA	45 m
DELHI HEAD OFFICE	CHENNAI CAMPUS	2175 km

Number of computers in each of the blocks/Center is as follows:

ADMIN	110
ENGINEERING	75
BUSINESS	40
MEDIA	12
DELHI HEAD	20

(i) Suggest and draw the cable layout to efficiently connect various blocks of buildings within the CHENNAI campus for connecting the digital devices.

(ii) Which network device will be used to connect computers in each block to form a local area network?

(iii) Which block, in Chennai Campus should be made the server? Justify your answer.

(iv) Which fast and very effective wireless transmission medium should preferably be used to connect the head office at DELHI with the campus in CHENNAI?

(v) Is there a requirement of a repeater in the given cable layout?

Ans. (i) Bus topology

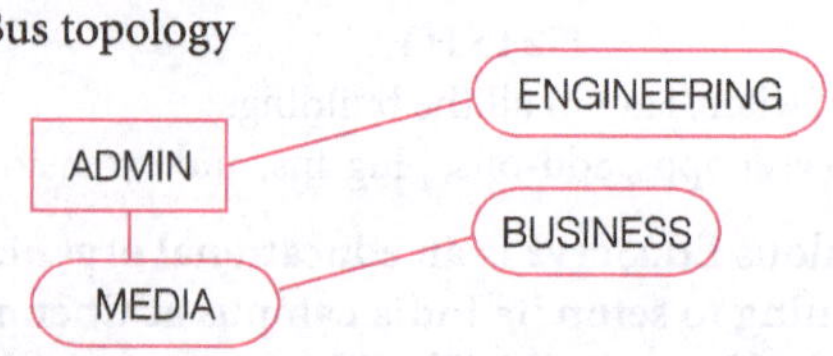

(ii) Switch

(iii) Admin block, as it has maximum number of computers.

(iv) Microwave (v) No

50. XEED Private Ltd., Delhi is a company that deals with educational toys. They have different divisions HR (A1), Sales (A2), Production (A3) and Marketing (A4).

The layout of the Delhi branch is **CBSE 2023** **Competency Based Que.**

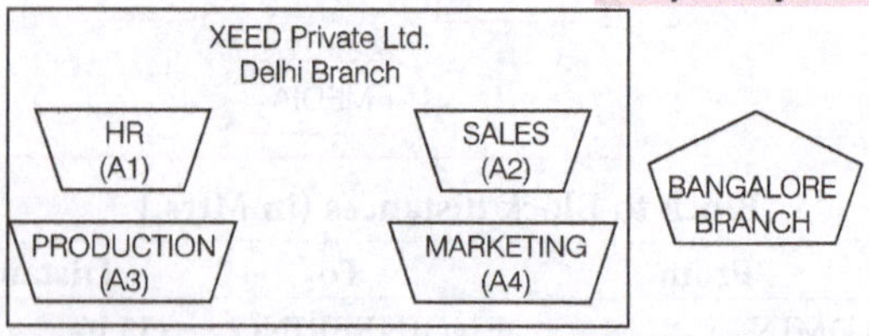

The company also has a branch in Bangalore. The management wants to connect all the divisions as well as all the computers of each division (A1, A2, A3, A4).

Distance between the wings are as follows

A3 to A1	25 m
A1 to A2	40 m
A2 to A4	25 m
A4 to A3	20 m
A3 to A2	30 m
A1 to A4	170 m
Delhi Head Office to Bangalore Office	2154 km

Number of computers in each of the wing

A1	50
A2	40
A3	110
A4	60

Based on the above specifications, answer the following questions.

(i) Suggest the topology and draw the most suitable cable layout for connecting all the divisions of Delhi branch.

(ii) Suggest the kind of network required (out of LAN, MAN, WAN) for connecting Production (A3) with the Bangalore branch.

(iii) Which device can be used to connect the network of Delhi Branch to the Internet? This device should be able to receive data, analyse it and then transmit it to the network.

(iv) Suggest the placement of switch/hub with justification.

(v) Many employees were finding it difficult to cope up with work pressure and hence were showing stress related symptoms. In order to improve the mental health of its employees, HR planned to conduct an online session with a mental health expert from Mumbai. Out of the options given below, suggest the protocol that will help to send the voice signals over Internet to conduct the session successfully.

(a) FTP (b) SMTP

(c) VoIP (d) POP

Ans. (i) Star Topology

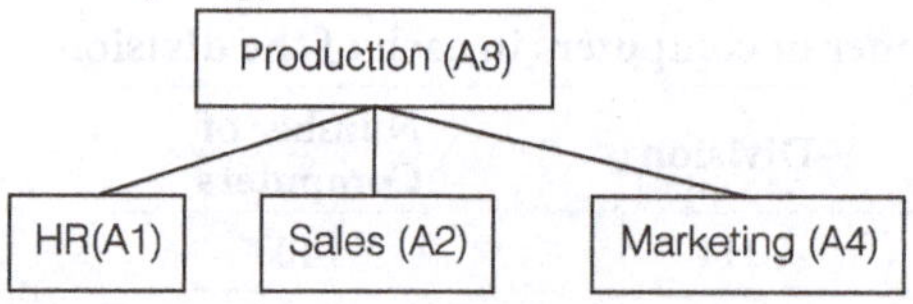

(ii) WAN (iii) Router

(iv) Switch should be placed in each block.

(v) (c) VoIP

51. Prime Computer services Ltd. is an international educational organization. It is planning to set up its India campus at Mumbai with its head office in Delhi. The Mumbai office campus has four main buildings-ADMIN, ACCOUNTS, EXAMINATION and RESULT. **CBSE SQP 2022-2023**

You as a network expert have to suggest the best network related solutions for their problems raised in (i) to (v), keeping in mind the distances between the buildings and other given parameters.

Competency Based Que.

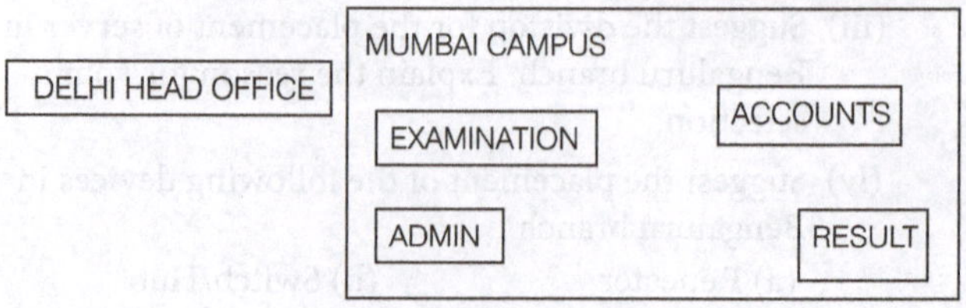

Shortest distances between various buildings

ADMIN to ACCOUNTS	55 m
ADMIN to EXAMINATION	90 m
ADMIN to RESULT	50 m
ACCOUNTS to EXAMINATION	55 m
ACCOUNTS to RESULT	50 m
EXAMINATION to RESULT	45 m
DELHI HEAD OFFICE to MUMBAI CAMPUS	2150 m

Number of computers installed at various buildings are as follows:

ADMIN	110
ACCOUNTS	75
EXAMINATION	40
RESULT	12
DELHI HEAD OFFICE	20

(i) Suggest the most appropriate location of the server inside the MUMBAI campus (out of the four buildings) to get the best connectivity for maximum number of computers. Justify your answer.

(ii) Suggest and draw cable layout to efficiently connect various buildings within the MUMBAI campus for a wired connectivity.

(iii) Which networking device will you suggest to be procured by the company to interconnect all the computers of various buildings of MUMBAI campus?

(iv) Company is planning to get its website designed which will allow students to see their results after registering themselves on its server. Out of the static or dynamic, which type of website will you suggest?

(v) Which of the following will you suggest to establish the online face to face communication between the people in the ADMIN office of Mumbai campus and Delhi head office?

(a) Cable TV (b) Email
(c) Video conferencing (d) Text chat

Ans. (i) Server should be installed in Admin department as it has maximum number of computers.

(ii)

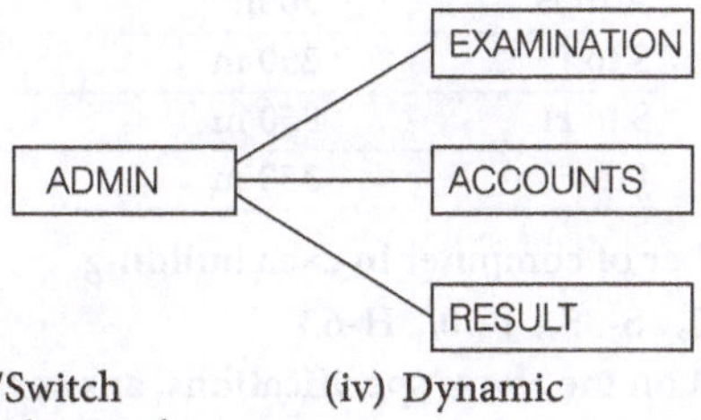

(iii) Hub/Switch (iv) Dynamic

(v) (c) Video conferencing

52. **XYZ Technologies, Hyderabad is a company that deals with data science and AI projects. They have different divisions ADMIN, SALES, PRODUCTION and SERVICE.** **CBSE 2025**

The layout of the Hyderabad branch is:

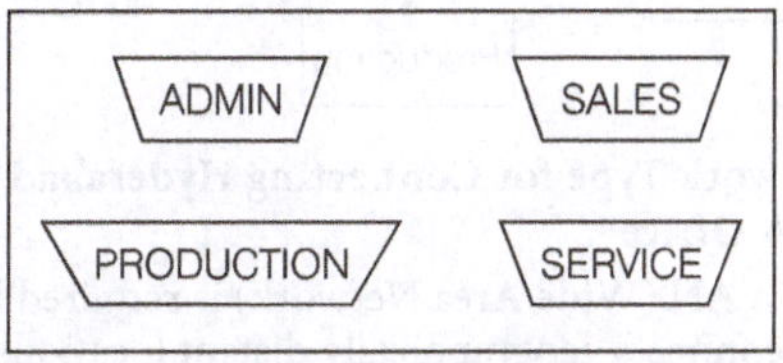

The management wants to connect all the divisions as well as the computers of each division (ADMIN, SALES, PRODUCTION and SERVICE).

Distance between the divisions are as follows:

ADMIN to SALES	69 m
ADMIN to PRODUCTION	84 m
ADMIN to SERVICE	60 m
SALES to PRODUCTION	110 m
SALES to SERVICE	135 m
PRODUCTION to SERVICE	90 m

Number of computers in each division

Division	Number of computers
ADMIN	40
SALES	75
PRODUCTION	120
SERVICE	20

Based on the above specifications, answer the following questions: **Competency Based Que.**

(i) Suggest the topology and draw the most suitable cable layout for connecting all the divisions in the Hyderabad office.

(ii) XYZ Technologies is having its head office in USA. Out of LAN, MAN and WAN, which kind of network will be created to connect Hyderabad office with USA Office? Justify your answer.

(iii) Suggest the division for the placement of server. Explain the reason for your selection.

(iv) Suggest the placement of Switch/Hub with justification.

(v) Where will a repeater be placed in the suggested network layout? Justify your answer.

Ans. (i) **Suggested Topology and Cable Layout**

Topology Star Topology is the most suitable because it ensures efficient communication and easy troubleshooting.

Cable Layout Use Fiber Optic Cables for high-speed connectivity between divisions due to long distances.

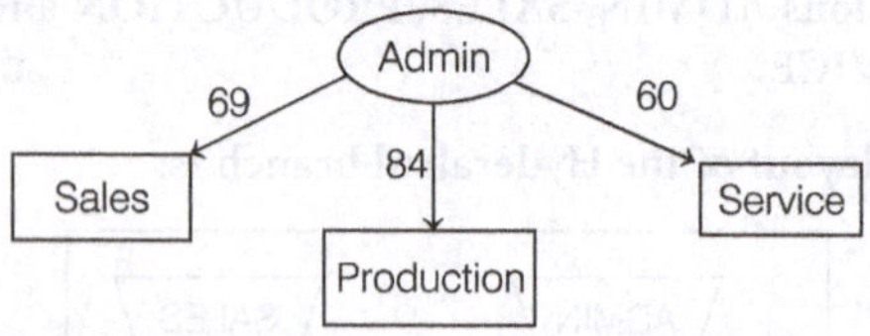

(ii) **Network Type for Connecting Hyderabad Office to USA Office**

- WAN (Wide Area Network) is required because it connects geographically distant locations (Hyderabad, India to the USA).
- **Justification** WAN is suitable for connecting global offices using internet, leased lines, or VPNs.

(iii) **Placement of Server**

The server should be placed in the PRODUCTION division because:

1. PRODUCTION has the highest number of computers (120), requiring fast access to data.
2. Placing the server centrally ensures equal distribution of network load.

(iv) **Placement of Switch/Hub**

Switches should be placed in each division to connect the computers within the division efficiently.

Justification

1. Switches provide better bandwidth and security compared to hubs.
2. Each division can communicate efficiently while being connected to the central network.

(v) **Placement of Repeater**

A repeater should be placed between SALES and SERVICE (135m distance) to boost the signal strength.

Justification Since Ethernet cables support up to 100 meters without signal degradation, placing a repeater between SALES and SERVICE ensures uninterrupted data transmission.

Case Study Based Questions

Case Study 1

ABC Pvt Ltd. is setting up the network in Bengaluru. There are four departments named as Market, Finance, Legal and Sales.

Distance between various buildings is as follows:

Market to Finance	80 m
Market to Legal	180 m
Market to Sales	100 m
Legal to Sales	150 m
Legal to Finance	100 m
Finance to Sales	50 m

Number of computers in the building:

Market	20
Legal	10
Finance	08
Sales	42

Based on the above specifications, answer the following questions.

(i) Suggest the best possible topology to be used.

(ii) Suggest the most suitable building to place the server.

(iii) Suggest the placement of hub/switch in the network.

(iv) The organisation is planning to link its sale counter situated in various part of the same city. Which type of network will be formed?

(v) Which communication media will you suggest to be procured by the company for connecting their offices for very effective and fast communication?

Ans. (i) Star topology.

(ii) Sales is the most suitable building to place the server because it has maximum number of computers.

(iii) Each building should have hub/switch and modem in case internal connection is required.

(iv) MAN (Metropolitan Area Network) can be carried out in a city network.

(v) For connecting offices for very effective and fast communication is optical fiber.

Case Study 2

Delhi Public School in Meerut is starting up the network between its different wings.

There are four building named as S, J, A and H. The distance between various buildings is as follows:

A to S	200 m
A to J	150 m
A to H	50 m
S to J	250 m
S to H	350 m
J to H	350 m

Number of computer in each building

A-200, S-35, J-50, H-63

Based on the above specifications, answer the following questions.

(i) Suggest the best possible topology to be used.
(ii) Suggest the most suitable building to place the server.
(iii) Suggest the placement of Hub/switch.
(iv) The organisation also has enquiry office in another City about 50-60 km away in hilly region. Suggest the suitable transmission media to inter-connect school and enquiry office.
(v) The organisation also has Head office in another Country (Japan). Suggest the suitable transmission media to inter-connect school and enquiry office.

Ans. (i) Star topology
(ii) Server can be placed in the A building as it has the maximum number of computers.
(iii) Hub/Switch is required in all blocks.
(iv) Radio waves can be used in hilly region as they can travel through obstacles.
(v) Satellite links are used to provide communications over very large distances (global coverage).

Case Study 3

"Anutulya Creations"-A start-up fashion house has set up its main centre at Kanpur, Uttar Pradesh for its dress designing, production and dress supplying activities. It has 4 blocks of buildings.

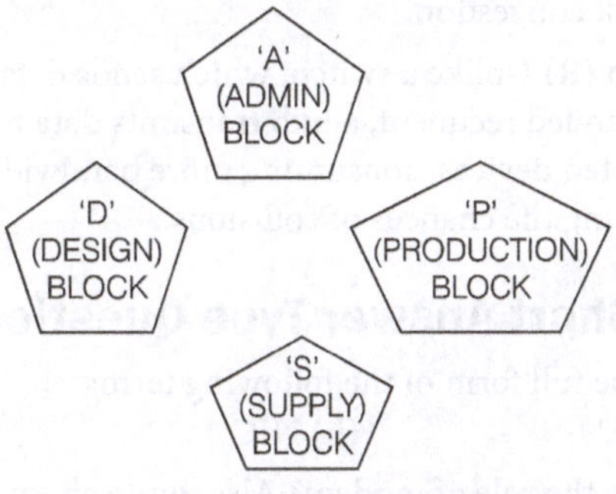

Distance between the various blocks

A to D	—	50 m
A to P	—	60m
A to S	—	110 m
D to S	—	60 m
P to S	—	50 m
P to D	—	150 m

Numbers of computers in each block

Block A	—	20
Block D	—	80
Block P	—	15
Block S	—	8

Based on the above specifications, answer the following questions.

(i) Out of LAN, WAN and MAN, what type of network will be formed if we interconnect different computers of the campus? Justify.
(ii) Suggest the topology, which should be used to efficiently connect various blocks of buildings within Kanpur centre for fast communication.
Also, draw the cable layout for the same.
(iii) Suggest the placement of the following device with justification.
(a) Repeater (b) Hub/Switch
(iv) Now-a-days, video-conferencing software is being used frequently by the company to discuss the product details with the clients. Name any one video conferencing software.
Also, mention the protocol which is used internally in video conferencing software.

CBSE SQP 2021-22 Term II

Ans. (i) A LAN network is formed. LAN or Local Area Network is a network of systems spread in a small area ranging from about 500m to 1km approx. Here the distances between the offices is maximum 150 m.
(ii) Star topology should be used.

Cable layout

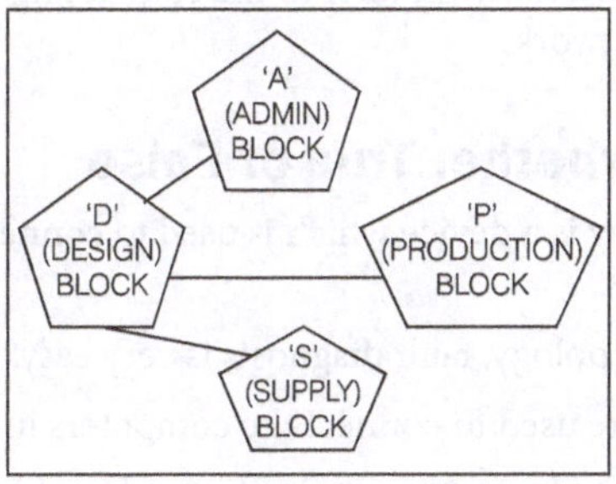

(iii) (a) **Repeater** A to S and P to D.
Since, the distances between the blocks are 110m and 150m respectively a repeater will be required to amplify the signals.
(b) **Switch/Hub** should be placed in each building to connect various computer together.
(iv) **Video conferencing softwares** Zoom, Google Meet
Protocol VoIP (Voice over Internet Protocol)

SELF ASSESSMENT TEST

Multiple Choice Questions

1 It is used to amplify the feeble signals when they are transported over a long distance.
(a) Switch (b) Repeater (c) Gateway (d) Hub

2 Which network device is primarily responsible for forwarding data packets between different networks and ensuring they reach their destination using IP addresses?
(a) Hub (b) Switch (c) Router (d) Repeater

3 Computer connected with LAN
(a) work fast (b) go online
(c) can E-mail
(d) can share information or peripheral devices

4 In which topology all the nodes are directly connected to the central node?
(a) Star (b) Bus (c) Ring (d) Tree

Fill in the Blanks

5 A .... in a computer network is any device that can send, receive or process data.

6 In .... topology, the nodes are interlinked in the form of tree.

7 .... of a network refer to the connecting media used in the network.

State whether True or False

8 A gateway is a device which is used to connect dissimilar networks.

9 In star topology, fault diagnosis is very easy.

10 Cables are used to connect the computers in WAN.

11 The name bluetooth is derived from Harald Bluetooth, a king in Denmark.

Assertion and Reason Based Questions

Assertion and Reason based questions. Mark the correct choice as

(a) Both A and R are true, and R is the correct explanation of A.
(b) Both A and R are true, but R is not the correct explanation of A.
(c) A is true, but R is false.
(d) A is false, but R is true.

12 **Assertion (A)** Wide Area Network (WAN) is typically used to connect geographically dispersed locations over long distances.

Reason (R) WANs are designed to span large geographical areas, such as cities, countries, or even continents, using public or leased communication lines.

13 **Assertion (A)** Router is responsible for forwarding data packets between different networks.

Reason (R) Routers operate at the network layer and use IP addresses to route packets to their destination across interconnected networks.

14 **Assertion (A)** Mesh topology offers high fault tolerance due to the multiple paths between devices.

Reason (R) In Mesh topology, every device is connected to every other device, allowing data to reach its destination through alternate paths if one connection fails.

15 **Assertion (A)** Hub is a network device that broadcasts data to all devices connected to it, leading to potential network congestion.

Reason (R) Unlike a switch, which sends data only to the intended recipient, a hub transmits data to all connected devices, consuming more bandwidth and increasing the chances of collisions.

Very Short Answer Type Questions

16 Give the full form of the following terms
(i) LAN (ii) NIC

17 What is the role of modem? Also, write about its functions.

Short Answer Type Questions

18 Mention one advantage of networking.

19 Give an advantage of using star topology over bus topology.

20 Compare the mesh topology and star topology.

21 What do you understand by mesh topology? Write two advantages and disadvantages of mesh topology.

Long Answer Type Questions

22 Explain the key differences between a Router and a Gateway in terms of their roles in a network.

Additionally, discuss how the function of these devices can vary in different types of networks like LAN, MAN, and WAN.

23 The Cyber Mind Organisation has set up its new branch at Mizoram for its office and web-based activities. It has four wings of buildings as shown in the diagram.

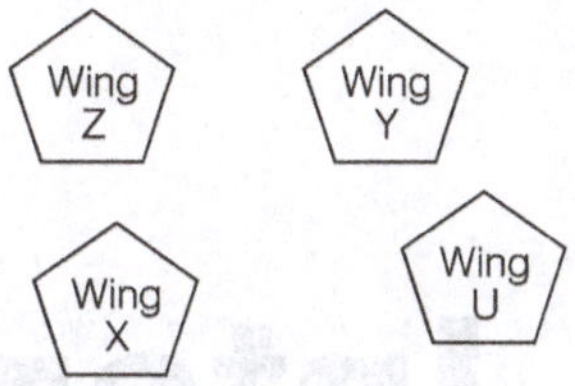

Centre to centre distances between various blocks

Wing X to Wing Z	40 m
Wing Z to Wing Y	60 m
Wing Y to Wing X	135 m
Wing Y to Wing U	70 m
Wing X to Wing U	165 m
Wing Z to Wing U	80 m

Number of computers

Wing X	50
Wing Z	130
Wing Y	40
Wing U	15

(i) Suggest a most suitable cable layout of connection between the wings and topology.

(ii) Suggest the most suitable place (i.e. Wing) to house the server of this organisation with a suitable reason, with justification.

(iii) Suggest the placement of the following device with justification :
(a) Repeater
(b) Hub/Switch

(iv) The organisation is planning to link its head office situated in Delhi with the office at Mizoram. Suggest an economic way to connect it; the company is ready to compromise on the speed of connectivity. Justify your answer.

Case Study Based Questions

24 ABC Pvt Ltd is a company with multiple offices across different cities. In each office, employees need to access company data and communicate with each other seamlessly. The head office is in a metropolitan city, with smaller branches spread across various regions. Due to the size and geographical spread of the network, the company needs a reliable setup. They use different network types, devices, and topologies for efficient communication. The head office connects multiple branches using a dedicated wide area network, while individual offices use smaller, more localized networks. The IT team is tasked with setting up network topologies and selecting the right network devices to optimize data transfer.

Based on the case study above, answer the following questions:

(i) Which network type is most likely used to connect the head office with branches in different cities?
(a) PAN (b) LAN
(c) MAN (d) WAN

(ii) The network type used within each office, connecting computers and devices in a limited geographical area, is likely:
(a) PAN (b) LAN
(c) MAN (d) WAN

(iii) To connect multiple devices within each office and ensure efficient data transfer without any data collision, which device should the IT team choose?
(a) Hub (b) Switch
(c) Modem (d) Repeater

(iv) If the IT team wants to connect two different network types within the company, such as LAN in the office and a WAN for external communication, which device would be most suitable?
(a) Router (b) Switch
(c) Hub (d) Repeater

(v) To ensure that if one cable fails, other devices on the network can continue to communicate, which network topology would be best for the head office?
(a) Star (b) Bus
(c) Mesh (d) Tree

Answers

1. (b) 2. (c) 3. (d) 4. (a) 5. Node
6. Tree 7. Topology 8. True 9. True
10. False 11. True 12. (a) 13. (a) 14. (a)
15. (a)
24. (i) → (d), (ii) → (b), (iii) → (b), (iv) → (a), (v) → (c)

06

CHAPTER

The internet allows any computer to communicate with any other computer that is also connected to the internet.

▼ YOUR STUDY GOALS

▼ YOUR PRACTICE GOAL

- Objective Type Questions (40 Qs ; MCQs, True or False, Fill in the Blanks, Assertion and Reason)
- Subjective Type Questions (42 Qs ; VSA, SA, LA)
- Case Based Questions (Objective Case Studies-5)

Internet

The internet is composed of a large number of smaller interconnected networks. These networks may link tens, hundreds, or thousands of computers. The Internet is the global network of computing devices including desktop, laptop, servers, tablets, mobile phones, other handheld devices as well as peripheral devices such as printers, scanners, etc. Today, smart electronic appliances like TV, AC, refrigerator, fan, light, etc., can also communicate through the Internet.

6.1 History of Internet

US defense department had sponsored a project ARPANET acronym for (Advanced Research Project Agency NETwork) in the year 1969.

It was a first and a small project run through internet technology. NSFnet was created by the National Science Foundation which was more capable than ARPANET. The linking of these two and some other networks was named INTERNET.

Working of Internet

- Computers on the Internet are connected to each other through small networks.
- These networks are connected through the gateways to the Internet Backbone.
- They communicate using TCP/IP.
- TCP breaks message into smaller packets and resembles these smaller packets into original message.
- IP handles the address part of each packet.

Advantages of Internet

- Greater access to information reduces research time.
- Allows you to easily communicate with other people.
- Global reach enables one to connect everyone on the Internet.
- Publishing documents on the Internet saves paper.
- A valuable resource for companies to advertise and conduct business.

Disadvantages of Internet

- Cyber frauds may take place involving credit/debit card numbers and details.
- Unsuitable and undesirable material is available that sometimes can be used by notorious people such as terrorists.
- It is a major source of computer viruses.
- Messages sent across the Internet can be easily intercepted and are open to abuse by others.
- It is difficult to check the accuracy of information available on the Internet.

Uses of the Internet

The Internet may be used to exchange information with people all over the world, communicate across great distances, and locate information or answers fast on almost any subject.

Here are some examples of specific uses for the Internet

- Using social media and content sharing.
- Instant messaging, video conferencing, Internet Relay Chat (IRC), Internet telephony, and email are all examples of electronic communication. These all are used through the Internet.
- Access to online degree programs, courses, and workshops for education and self-improvement.
- Searching for jobs- to advertise available positions, submit job applications, and hire candidates identified on social networking sites like LinkedIn, both employers and applicants use the Internet.

Applications of Internet

There are various applications of the internet, such as www, Email, Chat, VoIP

WWW or World Wide Web

The World Wide Web (WWW), often called the Web, is a system of interconnected webpages and information that you can access using the Internet. It was created to help people share and find information easily, using links that connect different pages together. The Web allows us to browse websites, watch videos, shop online, and connect with others around the world through our computers and phones.

It is a project created, by **Tim Berner Lee** in 1989, for researchers to work together effectively at CERN. It is an organization, named the World Wide Web Consortium (W3C), which was developed for further development of the web. **This organization is directed by Tim Berner's Lee, aka the father of the web.**

By october of 1990, Tim had written the three fundamental technologies that remain the foundation of today's web

1. **HTML** (HyperText Markup Language) is a standard language used for designing and structuring web pages. It enables web content to be displayed consistently across different devices and platforms globally.

   HTML uses tags to define how content is presented in a web browser. The basic structure of every webpage is built using HTML, making it the foundation for web design.

2. **HTTP** (HyperText Transfer Protocol) is a set of rules used for retrieving and transferring web pages and other resources across the web.

   Its more secure and encrypted version is HTTPS (HyperText Transfer Protocol Secure), which ensures secure communication over the internet by encrypting data.

3. **URI** (Uniform Resource Identifier) is a unique identifier used to locate a resource on the web. It can identify a resource (whether hardware or software) by its location, its name, or both.

   A URL (Uniform Resource Locator) is a specific type of URI that not only identifies the resource but also provides the method (protocol) and location for accessing it. It's a unique identifier that identifies the location of a resource on the Internet.

   URLs are often referred to as web addresses or website addresses because web pages are the most common resource that end users use URLs to find. Other resources include CSS documents, videos, and images. Every file stored on a server has a unique URL, which tells a web browser how and where to retrieve that resource.

We actively use web addresses by typing them into the web browser's address bar. End users also interact with web addresses when they click a hyperlink on web pages, bookmark lists, or emails.

Components of a URL There are several parts of a URL; some are present in all web addresses and others are optional.

However, each part has a specific purpose to help you access anything online. Consider the following URL structure:

https://www.example.com:8080/products/page1.html?search=keyword#section1

In this web address:

- **Protocol** https://
- **Subdomain** www
- **Domain** example.com
- **Port** 8080
- **Path** /products/page1.html
- **Query parameters** ?search=keyword
- **Fragment identifier** #section1

Note *These days it is not mandatory to mention protocol and subdomain while entering a URL. The browser automatically prefixes it.*

TEACHER TIP

The Domain Name System (DNS) is like the internet's phone book. It helps you find websites by translating easy-to -remember names (like www.example.com) into the numerical IP addresses (like 192.0.2.1) that computers use to locate each other on the internet. Without DNS, you would have to remember long strings of numbers to visit your favorite websites.

Types of URL There are two types of URL:

1. **Absolute URL** An absolute URL provides the complete path to a resource, including the protocol, domain, and the file or resource location.

   Example
   https://www.example.com/images/logo.png

2. **Relative URL** A relative URL provides a path relative to the current page or directory. It does not include the domain or protocol.

   Example /images/logo.png

The **World Wide Web** (WWW) is based on client/server software design. A client/server software design requires two types of software to work in communication environment

(i) **Client Software** It is a type of software, which is used by a client (or user) to request some information from web server. e.g. Web browsers

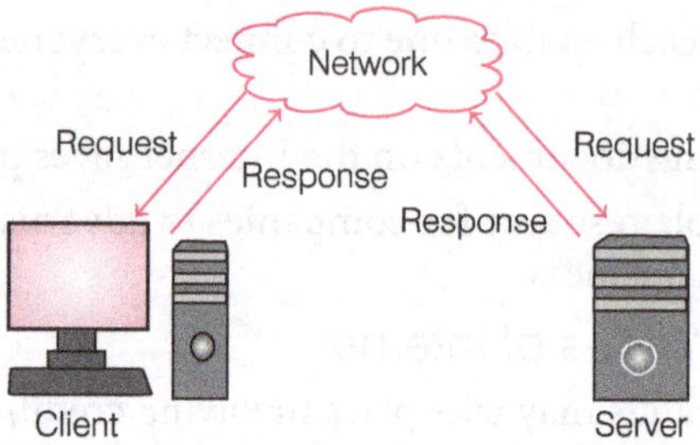

(ii) **Server Software** It is a type of software, which is used by the server to answer the requests and provide the required information. e.g. Microsoft, Oracle, etc.

It is possible to use your local computer as a server but usually you want to have a fixed server, which runs 24 × 7 hours. So, more advanced and large systems are used as a server instead of local computers.

Difference Between Internet and WWW

- Some students use the words "internet" and "World Wide Web" interchangeably. They believe they are the same, although this is not the case. The difference between the Internet and WWW (World Wide Web) is essential to understand.
- WWW or web is one of the key services offered by the internet. The World Wide Web, or simply "web," is the term for the collection of web pages that you view on your computer or other device using the internet.
- On the other hand, the internet is the network of interconnected computers on which the web runs and the conduit through which emails and data pass. The internet has made many things feasible for humans, such as playing online games, electronic mail, internet calling, chatting, file sharing, etc.

6.2 Web Server

Web server is a program which processes the network requests of the users and serves them with files that create web pages. This exchange takes place using Hypertext Transfer Protocol (HTTP).

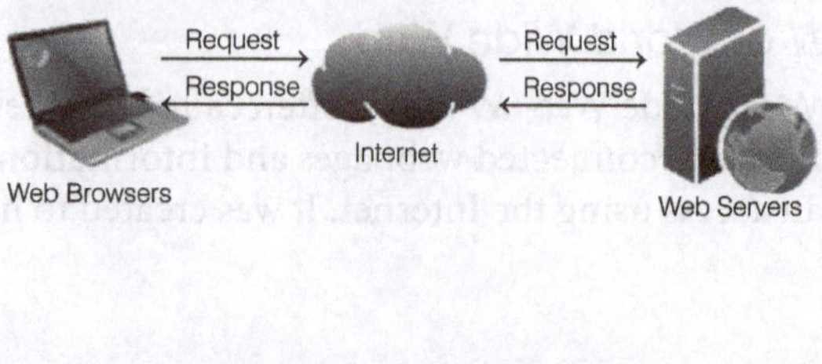

Basically, web servers are computers used to store HTTP files which makes a website and when a client requests a certain website, it delivers the requested website to the client.

For example, you want to open Facebook on your laptop and enter the URL in the search bar of google. Now, the laptop will send an HTTP request to view the Facebook webpage to another computer known as the webserver. This computer (webserver) contains all the files (usually in HTTP format) which make up the website like text, images, gif files, etc.

After processing the request, the webserver will send the requested website-related files to your computer and then you can reach the website.

Note *A 404 error, also known as a "404 Not Found" and "The requested URL was not found" error, occurs when a web server can't find a requested resource, such as a webpage or file.*

A web server provides several key services, including:

1. **Hosting Websites** Serves HTML, CSS, JavaScript, and multimedia content to users' web browsers.
2. **File Storage and Management** Allows users to upload, download, and manage files, including images, videos, and documents.
3. **Processing Dynamic Content** Supports the execution of server-side scripts (e.g., PHP, Python, ASP.NET) to generate dynamic web pages.
4. **HTTP Request Handling** Manages incoming HTTP or HTTPS requests and sends appropriate responses (e.g., web pages, API data).
5. **Security Services** Provides SSL/TLS encryption for secure data transmission, and implements security measures like firewalls, authentication, and access controls.
6. **Logging and Monitoring** Tracks server activity, including user access, errors, and performance metrics for analysis.
7. **Load Balancing** Distributes incoming traffic across multiple servers to ensure optimal performance and availability.
8. **Database Connectivity** Facilitates communication between web applications and databases to retrieve and store data.

There are many web servers available in the market both free and paid. Some of them are: Apache HTTP server, Microsoft Internet Information Services (IIS) etc.

Hosting a Website

Web hosting is a service that allows a website or web page to be accessible via the Internet, making it part of the World Wide Web.

To host a website, you need to upload the site's files (HTML, CSS, JavaScript, images, databases, etc.) from your local computer onto a server that is connected to the Internet. This can be done either using your own server or by renting server resources like CPU, RAM, and storage from a cloud service provider. The web hosting service typically requires a payment to access resources such as RAM, disk space, and bandwidth. These resources can be scaled based on the website's needs, depending on the traffic and loads on the site.

Every web server, whether it's local or cloud-based, is assigned a unique numeric address called an IP address. However, since it's difficult for users to remember numeric IP addresses, this address is mapped to a domain name, a more user-friendly textual identifier.

The domain name is entered into a browser's URL bar to access the website, and it must be registered with an authorized agency.

To host a website, follow these key steps:

1. **Select a Web Hosting Service** Choose a reliable web hosting provider. The provider will offer web server space and essential services like database support, bandwidth, backups, firewall, and email services. The selection depends on the features and services you want to offer on your website.
2. **Register a Domain Name** Pick a suitable domain name for your website, and register it through a domain name registrar. The domain name is essentially the website's address on the internet (e.g., www.example.com).
3. **Configure Web Space** After purchasing web hosting, create login credentials with the required access rights for managing your hosting account. Note down the IP address of the server where your site will be hosted.
4. **Upload Your Website** Develop your website and upload it to the web server using tools like FTP (File Transfer Protocol) or file management provided by the host. You can use CMS (Content Management System) platforms like WordPress if you're not building the site from scratch.

5. **Link Domain to Web Hosting** Connect your domain name to your hosting provider by updating DNS settings. This ensures that when someone types your domain name, they are directed to your hosted website.
6. **Test and Launch** Once everything is set up, test your website to ensure it works correctly. After testing, your site is live for users worldwide!

Quick Test 1

1. Rushil thought www and internet are synonyms i.e., they meant same and can be used interchangeably. But the teacher said that they are not same. Help him to understand the meaning of both the terms with the help of a suitable example of each. **CBSE 2022**
2. What is Internet and how does it differ for World Wide Web(WWW)? **CBSE SQP 2024-2025**
3. Expand URL. Identify the protocol and domain in the following URL: **CBSE 2024**
   https: // epathshala. nic. in/ topics. php? len = en
4. What protocol is used by web servers to communicate with clients?

6.3 Web Browser

The web browser is an application software to explore WWW (World Wide Web). It provides an interface between the server and the client and it requests to the server for web documents and services.

It works as a compiler to render HTML which is used to design a webpage. Whenever we search for anything on the internet, the browser loads a web page written in HTML, including text, links, images, and other items such as style sheets and JavaScript functions.

Browsers are of two types

(i) **Text-Based Web Browsers** are the web browsers that support text only, i.e. these browsers do not support graphics. e.g. Linux.

(ii) **Graphical-Based Web Browsers** provide a Graphical User Interface (GUI) where the user can jump from one web page to another by clicking on the hyperlink on a web page. e.g. Chrome, Internet Explorer, Mozilla Firefox, etc.

Web Browser Toolbar

A major part of the user interface for a browser is the toolbar. This appears at the top of the browser window, above the viewing pane and it can perform a number of critical functions.

Major functions of browser toolbar are as follows

(i) **Back** Open previously opened page.

(ii) **Forward** It allows you to move forward through your history, to where you were before you used the Back button.

(iii) **Address Bar** This is a text box that displays the URL of the current page.

(iv) **Stop** This will be found either just inside the address bar or just next to it. It only appears when the page is currently in the process of loading. If you click it, the page will stop loading.

(v) **Refresh** The Refresh or Reload button looks like a circular arrow. This button repeats the request that led to the current page, which usually cause the same page to load into the browser again.

(vi) **Bookmark** This allows you to bookmark the URL, saving it to your browser.

Commonly used Web Browsers

There are many web browsers in use today. The most common of these are Google Chrome, Safari, Edge, Firefox, Samsung Internet, Opera etc.

TEACHER TIP

Mosaic was the first web browser developed by the National Centre for Supercomputing Application (NCSA). The initial web browsers like Mosaic used to support HTML documents containing plain text (static website) only, but nowadays with the advancement of technology, modern web browsers allow us to view interactive and dynamic websites.

Browser Settings

Every web browser has specific settings that determine how it functions. These settings may relate to privacy, search engine preferences, download options, auto signatures, autofill and autocomplete features, themes, and more.

Customizing these settings allows users to tailor the browser to their needs.

Mozilla Firefox

It is an open source web browser which is available free of cost and can be easily downloaded from the internet. To change the browser setting in firefox click the **Open** menu (☰) in the upper-right corner, and click on **Settings** in the menu.

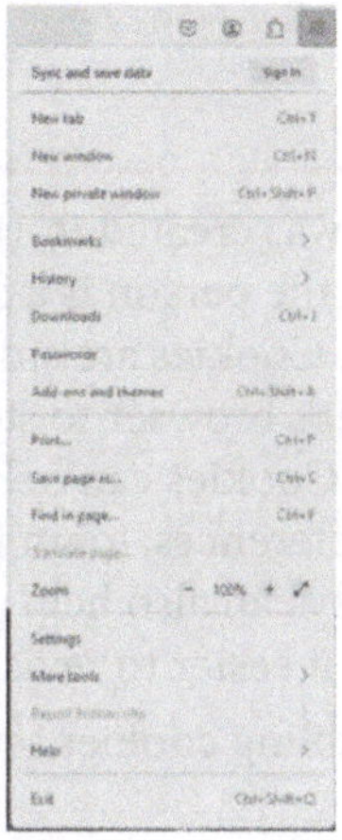

Key Panels in Firefox Settings

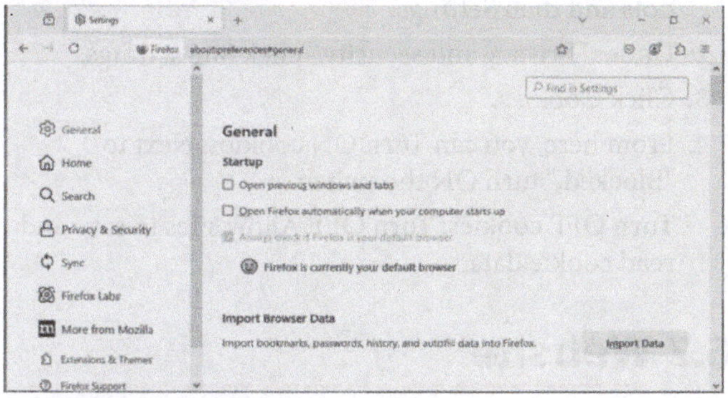

- **General Panel** Here, you can manage:
  - Default browser settings
  - Language preferences and text appearance
  - File download settings
  - Updates for the browser
  - Network settings
- **Appearance Panel** This allows you to adjust the theme of your browser and customize the layout.
- **Search Engine Panel** You can select or modify the default search engine that firefox uses for searches.
- **Privacy and Security Panel** This section is crucial for protecting your data.

  It includes:
  - Enhanced tracking protection
  - Managing saved passwords and autofill settings
  - Browsing history management
  - Cookies and site data preferences
  - Permissions for pop-ups and site notifications
- **Sync Panel** This panel enables you to set up and manage your Google account, which allows you to sync your bookmarks, history, and settings across devices.

Similarly, you can open the settings pages in other web browsers and choose the settings for your web browsers.

6.4 Add-ons

Most web browsers allow you to install extensions, also called "add-ons." Extensions are small applications that add features and functionality to your browser and enhance or modify how web pages are displayed.

How Add-ons are Installed

1. Open Mozilla Firefox.
2. At the top of the page, click Extensions.

3. In the Find add-ons search field, type a phrase or extension you want to find. You can also browse recommended extensions using the category buttons.

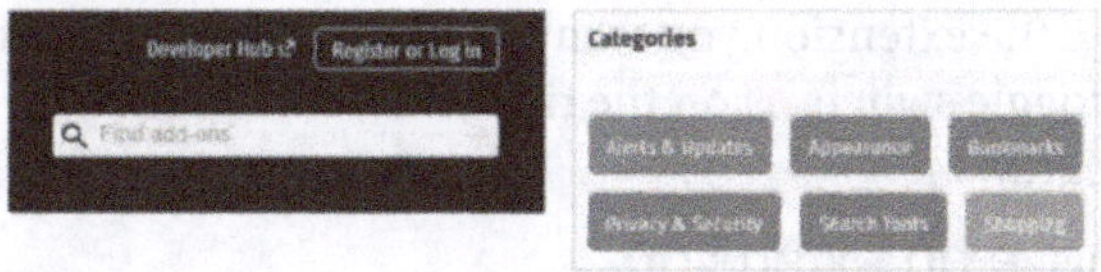

4. When you find an extension you want to install, click the Add to Firefox button.
5. In the upper-right corner of the screen, click the Add button.

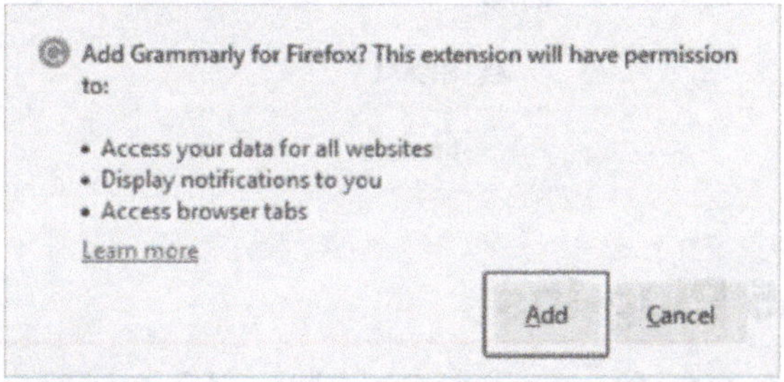

6. When the installation is complete, a notification is displayed.

How to Remove Add-ons

1. Open Mozilla Firefox.
2. In the upper-right corner of the window, click the Open menu icon.

3. In the drop-down menu, select Add-ons and themes.
4. On the left side of the Add-ons Manager tab, click Extensions.

5. In the center of the screen, the extensions are listed under Manage Your Extensions.

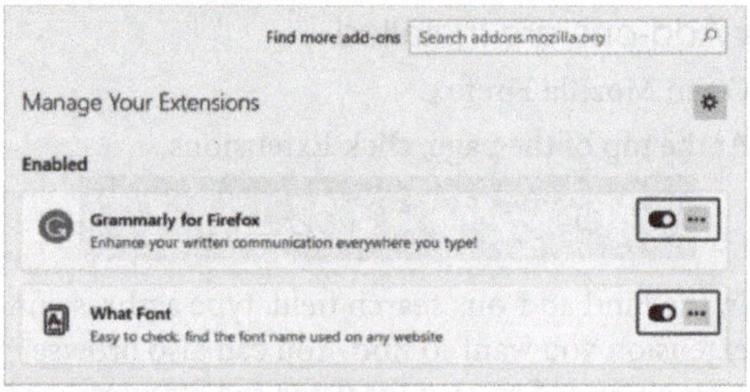

Disable an extension

Locate the extension you want to disable. Then, click the blue toggle switch on the right side, changing it to gray.

Remove an extension

Locate the extension you want to remove. On the right side, click the menu icon and select Remove from the drop-down menu.

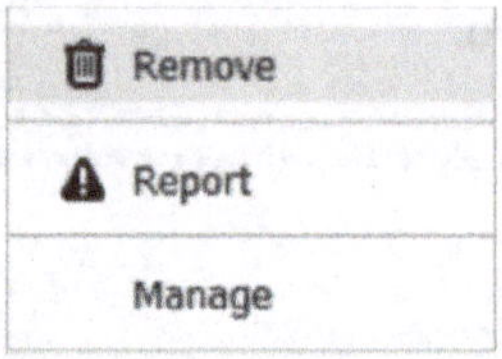

6.5 Plug-ins

They are software components that add features to an existing computer program. A plug-in functions a little bit differently from add-ons , allowing websites to embed and render content through the use of software such as Adobe, Java, QuickTime, or Microsoft Silverlight. These plug-ins allow you to do things in your browser such as view PDF files or watch videos on sites such as Netflix.

Similarly you can install and remove plug-ins in your web browser like add-ons.

6.6 Cookies

First cookie software was created in 1994 at Netscape, for determining whether the person is a first time visitor or a re-visitor of their site. Cookies are small text files that websites send to a user's browser to store information about the user's visit. Cookies can help websites remember a user's preferences, login information, and browsing history. They can also help personalize a user's experience and make it easier to revisit a website.

For enabling and disabling cookies settings ,you can do the following

1. Open Chrome and at the top right, click on triple dots and then Settings.
2. Under "Privacy and security," click Site settings.
3. Click Cookies.
4. From here, you can Turn ON cookies: Next to "Blocked," turn ON the switch.

   Turn OFF cookies: Turn OFF Allow sites to save and read cookie data.

6.7 Website

A website is a collection of interconnected web pages written in HTML (HyperText Markup Language). To be accessible to users globally, a website must be hosted on a web server, which is a computer connected to the internet. Key characteristics of a website include:

- **Hyperlinks and Hypertext** Web pages are linked together, allowing users to navigate seamlessly.
- **Common Design and Interface** Websites typically share a consistent look and feel across all pages.
- **Additional Content** Websites may include images, videos, and other digital assets that enhance the user experience.

Components of a Website

1. **Web Host** The server that hosts the website.
2. **Address (URL)** The URL is the address users enter into their web browsers to access a website. The web server delivers the requested website based on this address.

3. **Homepage** This is the first page that visitors see when they access a website.
4. **Design** The design encompasses the overall aesthetic of the website, achieved through elements like navigation menus, graphics, and layout.
5. **Content** All the web pages on the website.
6. **Navigation Structure** This defines how the pages are organized and linked. A well-structured navigation menu helps users to easily find the information on the site.

6.8 Web Page

A webpage is a digital document linked to the World Wide Web that can be viewed by anyone with internet access and a web browser. It can include various types of information, such as text, images, graphics, animations, videos, sounds, and more.

Webpages are primarily written in HTML (HyperText Markup Language), allowing them to be displayed on the internet. Users can access a webpage by entering its URL (Uniform Resource Locator) in the address bar of a web browser.

Types of Web Page

A web page can be of two types:

- **Static Web Page** A web page which displays same kind of information whenever a user visits, is known as a static web page. A static web page written *via* HTML code and generally has .htm or .html as extension.
- **Dynamic Web Page** An interactive web page is a dynamic web page. A dynamic web page uses scripting languages to display changing content on the web page. Such a page generally has .php, .asp or .jsp as extension.

6.9 Electronic Mail

Email, or electronic mail, refers to the transmission of messages or data between computers over the internet. To send an email, you need an active internet connection, an email service provider, a personal email address, and the recipient's email address.

Email Address

An email address identifies a user's electronic mailbox and consists of two main parts– the **local part** and the **domain.** The local part typically contains the username of the user, while the domain indicates the email service provider being used.

The local part can include letters, numbers, or periods, whereas the domain varies based on the specific service provider.

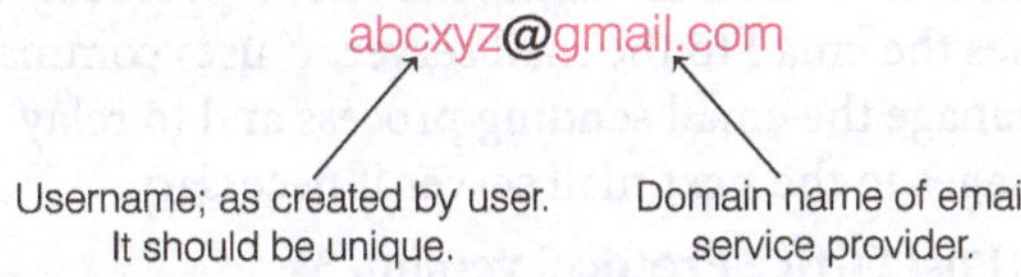

Note *The topmost popular email providers are: G-mail, Yahoo Mail, Microsoft (Outlook) GMX Mail etc.*

The common email facilities available for users:

1. **Composing Emails** Creating new emails and attaching files. This process is often referred to as composing.
2. **Sending and Receiving Emails** Users can send emails to multiple recipients at once.
3. **Carbon Copy (CC) and Blind Carbon Copy (BCC)** Sending copies of emails to other addresses without disclosing all recipients.
4. **Forwarding Emails** Sharing received emails with other users.
5. **Spam Filtering** Identifying and managing unwanted spam emails.

Note ***Spam*** *mail is defined as irrelevant or inappropriate message sent on the Internet to a large number of people whereas* ***Junk mail*** *is unwanted or unsolicited advertising or promotional material received through mail or email. These two terms typically are used interchangeably.*

6. **Organizing Emails** Sorting emails into folders and subfolders for better management.
7. **Contact Management** Creating and managing email addresses of known contacts.
8. **Email Signatures** Setting up automatic signatures or footers that appear at the end of each email.
9. **Printing and Saving Emails** Options to print emails or save them as files.
10. **Email Search** Finding emails by searching through addresses or subject lines.

Electronic Mail Protocol

E-mail protocols are set of rules that help the client to properly transmit the information to or from the mail server. Here, we will discuss various protocols such as:

SMTP (Simple Mail Transfer Protocol)

- SMTP is primarily used for sending emails from a client to a server or between servers. It ensures that emails are transmitted to the appropriate destination.
- When a user sends an email, the SMTP protocol pushes the email to the mail server. It uses commands to manage the email sending process and to relay messages to the next mail server if necessary.

POP3 (Post Office Protocol version 3)

- POP3 is used by email clients to retrieve emails from a mail server. It downloads emails to the client and usually deletes them from the server after retrieval.
- When a user checks their email, POP3 allows the email client to connect to the mail server, download new messages, and remove them from the server (unless configured otherwise).

IMAP (Internet Message Access Protocol)

- IMAP is another protocol for retrieving emails, but unlike POP3, it allows users to manage their emails directly on the server.
- IMAP synchronizes the email client with the server, allowing users to view, organize, and manage their emails without downloading them. This means that messages remain on the server, enabling access from multiple devices.

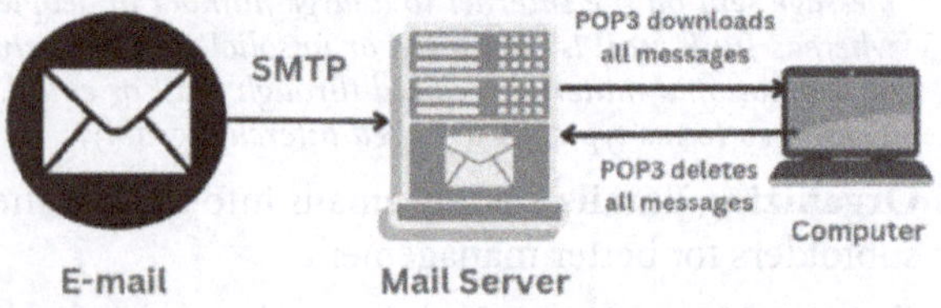

6.10 Chat

Chatting is a form of communication facilitated by the internet, allowing live transmission of text messages between sender and receiver. It can be point-to-point (one sender to one receiver) or broadcast (one sender to many).

Modern chatting includes text, voice, video, and web conferencing. With numerous applications and websites available, online chatting has made conversations accessible, enabling people from around the world to connect easily. If you want to chat ,you need to log ON to a server that provides chat facility.There are many sites that provide chat facility. These sites mostly provide you chat facility *via* **chat rooms.**

A chat room is an online platform that enables users to communicate with each other in real time. Chat rooms are typically hosted on a server with an internet connection, enabling members from around the world to hold conversations about various topics. Examples of chat room software are: Slack, Skype, Google Meet and Google Chat.

Following are the most common type of chatting:

- **Instant Messaging (IM)** The most widespread form of chatting, IM involves real-time, text-based communication between two or more users. Popular platforms like WhatsApp, Messenger, and Slack use this method.
- **Internet Relay Chat (IRC)** An older form of text-based chat that is not owned by any company. Users participate *via* channels or private messages using client programs. It's used for group discussions or one-on-one conversations.
- **ICQ (I Seek You)** A messaging program similar to IM but allows users to join chat rooms and communicate with multiple people simultaneously. ICQ supports file and link sharing.
- **Voice Chatting** A type of chatting where users communicate through audio over the internet. It's essentially an internet-based phone call, allowing free and unlimited voice communication with a good internet connection.
- **Video Chatting** This involves face-to-face communication using a webcam and is conducted over the internet. It requires a high-speed connection and a quality camera, making it more demanding than text or voice chats.

6.11 VoIP

VoIP (Voice over Internet Protocol) is a technology that allows people to make voice calls using an internet connection instead of a traditional analog phone line. It converts voice signals into digital data that can be transmitted over the internet.

Common VoIP services include Skype, Zoom, WhatsApp, and Google Meet etc.

Advantages of VoIP

- Reduces communication costs, especially for long-distance calls
- Allows calls from anywhere with internet access
- Provides free advanced features like video calls and conference calling
- Easy to scale for businesses
- Integrates with other communication tools
- Enables multi-device calling

Disadvantages of VoIP

- Requires reliable, fast internet connection
- Doesn't work during power outages
- Potential call quality issues due to network problems
- Security vulnerabilities
- Limited emergency service access
- May require hardware and software investments
- Requires learning new systems

Quick Test 2

1. Name any two popular web browsers. **CBSE SQP 2021-2022**
2. Give examples of any two plug-ins. **CBSE 2022**
3. Explain the terms Web page and Home Page. **CBSE SQP 2022-2023**
4. Expand the following terms: **CBSE SQP 2023-2024**
   POP3, URL
5. What is a web server? How is it different from web browser? **CBSE 2023**
6. I : **CBSE SQP 2021-2022 Term II**
   - am a small text file
   - created on a user's computer
   - contain small pieces of data — like a username, password and user's browsing history as well as preferences may help to improve user's web browsing experience.

   Who am I?
7. What are cookies? How can we disable cookies? **CBSE 2022**

NCERT Folder

1. Fill in the blanks:

(a) ________ is a standard naming convention used for accessing resources over the Internet.

(b) ________ is a collection of related web pages.

(c) A ________ is a computer that provides services to other programs or computers.

Ans. (a) URL

(b) Website

(c) server

2. Expand the following:

(a) ARPANET

(b) ISP

(c) URL

Ans. (a) ARPANET – Advanced Research Projects Agency Network

(b) ISP – Internet Service Provider

(c) URL – Uniform Resource Locator

3. Differentiate between:

(a) Website and web page

(b) Static and Dynamic web pages

Ans. (a) Differentiate between website and web page

Website	Web page
A collection of webpages about a particular organization is called website.	A single HTML document is called webpage.
A website does not have any extension.	A web page has an extension.

(b) Differentiate between static and dynamic web pages

Static Web page	Dynamic Web page
A static web page is one whose content always remains same for all users.	A dynamic web page is one whose content is different for different users.
They are less complex and thus take less time to load than dynamic web pages.	They are more complex and thus take more time to load than static web pages.

4. Give any three applications on the Internet.

Ans. Three applications on the Internet include web browsing (like Chrome or Firefox), email services (like Gmail or

Outlook), and social networking (like Facebook or Twitter).

5. Name any two mail service providers.

Ans. Two mail service providers are Gmail and Outlook.

6. Explain VoIP.

Ans. Refer to text on page no. 192 (VoIP).

7. What is DNS?

Ans. DNS (Domain Name System) is a system that translates domain names (like www.example.com) into IP addresses, allowing browsers to locate and load websites.

8. Sahil, a Class X student, has just started understanding the basics of Internet and web technologies. He is a bit confused in between the terms "World Wide Web" and "Internet". Help him in understanding both the terms with the help of suitable examples of each.

Ans. The Internet is the global network of interconnected computers, while the World Wide Web (WWW) is a collection of websites and web pages accessed via the Internet.

Example Internet is like the roads connecting cities (computers), while WWW is like the shops and buildings (websites) along those roads.

9. Murugan wants to send a report on his trip to the North East to his mentor. The report contains images and videos. How can he accomplish his task through the Internet?

Ans. Murugan can send his report through email or file-sharing services like Google Drive or Dropbox. These services allow uploading files, including images and videos, and sharing them over the Internet with his mentor.

10. Mampi is planning to open a company that deals with rural handicrafts. She wants to advertise about handicrafts on a social platform. Which Internet service she should use and why?

Ans. Mampi should use social media platforms like Facebook, Instagram, or Pinterest.

These platforms have large user bases and tools for targeted advertising, ideal for reaching potential customers interested in rural handicrafts.

11. Ruhani wants to edit some privacy settings of her browser. How can she accomplish her task?

Ans. Ruhani can accomplish this by accessing her browser's settings menu. There, she can adjust privacy settings like clearing browsing history, cookies, and managing site permissions to control how websites track her online activity.

12. Shubham wants to play a video in his browser but he is not able to do so. A message on the screen instructs him to install the Adobe Flash Player plugin. Help him to add it in his browser.

Ans. Shubham can install Adobe Flash Player by visiting Adobe's official website and downloading the plugin compatible with his browser.

Once downloaded, he can follow the installation instructions to add it to his browser.

13. When Joe typed a URL in the address bar of his browser, Error 404 was displayed? Why did this happen? What can be done to avoid it?

Ans. Error 404 means the webpage Joe tried to access couldn't be found on the server. This happens if the URL is incorrect or the page has been moved or deleted.

To avoid it, Joe should ensure the URL is correct and the webpage exists, or use search engines to find the correct webpage.

Mind Map

Hosting a Website It is a service that allows a website or web page to be accessible *via* the Internet, making it part of the World Wide Web.

Web Server

Web server is a program which processes the network requests of the users and serves them with files that create web pages. This exchange takes place using HyperText Transfer Protocol (HTTP).

History of Internet

- US defense department had sponsored a project **ARPANET** in the year 1969. It was a first and a small project run through internet technology.
- **NSFnet** was created by the National Science Foundation which was more capable than ARPANET.
- The linking of these two and some other networks was named **INTERNET**.

Web Browser

It is an application software to explore WWW (World Wide Web).
It provides an interface between the server and the client and it requests to the server for web documents and services.

Types of Web Browsers

Text-Based Web Browsers Support text only, i.e. these browsers do not support graphics. e.g. Linux.

Graphical-Based Web Browsers Provide a Graphical User Interface (GUI) where the user can jump from one web page to another by clicking on the hyperlink on a web page. e.g. Chrome, Internet Explorer, Mozilla Firefox, etc.

Browser Settings

Add-ons Most web browsers allow you to install extensions, also called "add-ons." Extensions are small applications that add features and functionality to your browser and enhance or modify how web pages are displayed.

Plug-ins A plug-in functions a little bit differently from add-ons , allowing websites to embed and render content through the use of software such as Adobe, Java, QuickTime, or Microsoft Silverlight.

Cookies Cookies are small text files that websites send to a user's browser to store information about the user's visit.

INTERNET

The internet is a global network of computers that are connected and can communicate with each other.

Website

A website is a collection of interconnected web pages written in HTML (HyperText Markup Language).

Web Page A webpage is a digital document linked to the World Wide Web that can be viewed by anyone with internet access and a web browser.

Types of Web Page

A **static web page** written via HTML code and generally has .htm or .html as extension.

A **dynamic web page** uses scripting languages to display changing content on the web page. Such a page generally has .php, .asp or .jsp as extension.

APPLICATIONS OF INTERNET

WWW or World Wide Web The WWW, often called the Web, is a system of interconnected webpages and information that you can access using the Internet.

Electronic Mail or Email It refers to the transmission of messages or data between computers over the internet.

Chat Chatting is a form of communication facilitated by the internet, allowing live transmission of text messages between sender and receiver. It can be point-to-point or broadcast.

VoIP (Voice over Internet Protocol) It converts voice signals into digital data that can be transmitted over the internet.

- **HTML** (HyperText Markup Language) is a standard language used for designing and structuring web pages.
- **HTTP** (HyperText Transfer Protocol) is a set of rules used for retrieving and transferring web pages and other resources across the web.
- **URI** (Uniform Resource Identifier) is a unique identifier used to locate a resource on the web. A **URL** (Uniform Resource Locator) is a specific type of URI that not only identifies the resource but also provides the method (protocol) and location for accessing it.

- **Email Address** An email address identifies a user's electronic mailbox and consists of two main parts– the local part and the domain. The local part typically contains the username of the user, while the domain indicates the email service provider being used.
- **Electronic Mail Protocol** E-mail protocols are set of rules that help the client to properly transmit the information to or from the mail server. e.g. SMTP (Simple Mail Transfer Protocol), POP3 (Post Office Protocol version 3) and IMAP (Internet Message Access Protocol)

EXAM PATTERN QUESTIONS

Objective Type Questions

Multiple Choice Questions

1. There are numerous websites, which provide search facility for searching the contents on

(a) Internet (b) Website (c) Web page (d) LAN

2. The first network is

(a) ARPANET (b) Internet
(c) NSFnet (d) NET

3. Which part of TCP/IP is responsible for dividing a file or message into very small parts, at the source computer?

(a) TCP (b) IP
(c) Both (a) and (b) (d) None of these

4. In Internet Protocol (IP), data is organised in the form of

(a) bundles (b) packets
(c) switches (d) parts

5. In URL, http://www.arihant.com/index.htm, which component identifies the path of a web page?

(a) http (b) www.arihant.com
(c) /index.htm (d) All of these

6. Every web page on the Internet has a unique address. This address is known as **CBSE 2025**

(a) Domain Name
(b) Protocol
(c) Uniform Resource Locater
(d) Network Topology

7. Which of the following web server was specially developed for the UNIX platform?

(a) Microsoft IIS
(b) Netscape enterprise web server
(c) Apache web server
(d) None of the above

8. Which of the following is not a web browser? **CBSE 2023**

(a) Opera (b) Google Chrome
(c) Linux (d) Mozilla Firefox

9. Which amongst the following is not an example of a browser? **CBSE SQP 2022-23**

(a) Chrome (b) Firefox
(c) Avast (d) Edge

10. A browser is

(a) the program to connect to internet
(b) the program to create websites
(c) the program used to view sites on web
(d) All of the above

11. Which of the following is a text based web browser?

(a) Opera (b) Lynx
(c) Safari (d) All of these

12. Which of the following is based on first web browser software mosaic?

(a) Opera
(b) Netscape navigator
(c) Internet Explorer
(d) Google chrome

13. _______ are similar to regular apps or programs, but only run when the browser runs.

(a) Add-ons (b) Plug-ins
(c) Both (a) and (b) (d) None of these

14. Temporary data files stored by websites in our computer can be used to track our online activities and also to personalize browsing experience. **CBSE 2025**

These files are known as:

(a) Plug-ins (b) Add-ons
(c) Cookies (d) Bookmarks

15. Home page helps viewers to find out what they can find on the particular site. Home page is the

(a) first page of a website (b) index page
(c) about page (d) None of these

16. Which of the following website is not used for job search?

(a) monster.com (b) recruitment.com
(c) naukri.com (d) myspace

17. By default, web pages are saved in the _______ folder.

(a) Download (b) Document
(c) Picture (d) Music

18. The WWW is made up of the set of interconnected _______ that are linked together over the internet.

(a) Electronic documents (b) Web pages
(c) Files (d) All of these

19. Which of the following is the online textual or multimedia conversation?

(a) VoIP (b) Chatting
(c) HTML (d) None of these

20. Which of the following protocol allows delivery of voice communication over IP network?

(a) VoIP (b) FTP
(c) TCP/IP (d) PPP

21. Which protocol is used while communicating through video calls on the Internet? **CBSE 2025**

(a) Video Over Internet Protocol
(b) Voice Over Internet Protocol
(c) Internet Protocol
(d) Video Audio Over Internet Protocol

Fill in the blanks

22. The address of location of the document on WWW is called ______.

23. The primary function of a ______ is to deliver web pages on the request of client using the HTTP.

24. A ______ is a software application for retrieving, presenting and traversing information resources on the WWW.

25. Web pages that are connected together with hyperlinks is called a ______.

26. A web page which displays same kind of information whenever a user visits, is known as ______.

27. ______ is a method of exchanging digital messages from sender to one or more recipients.

State Whether True or False

28. TCP/IP can be called as backbone of Internet.

29. HTML uses Internet address in a special format called a URL.

30. Safari web browser is a product of Microsoft Corporation USA.

31. A website displays related information on a specific topic.

32. Static web page is an interactive web page.

Assertion and Reason Based Questions

Assertion (A) and Reason (R) Type questions. Choose the correct option as:

(a) Both Assertion (A) and Reason (R) are true, and Reason (R) is the correct explanation of Assertion (A)
(b) Both Assertion (A) and Reason (R) are true, but Reason (R) is not the correct explanation of Assertion (A)
(c) Assertion (A) is True, but Reason (R) is False
(d) Assertion (A) is False, but Reason (R) is True

33. Assertion (A) The Internet and the World Wide Web (WWW) are the same.

Reason (R) The WWW is a service contained inside the infrastructure of the Internet, using protocols like HTTP.

34. Assertion (A) The first working model of the Internet was ARPANET, developed in the 1960s.

Reason (R) ARPANET used packet switching to allow multiple computers to work on a single network.

35. Assertion (A) The Internet allows users to send emails, photos, and videos instantly across the globe.

Reason (R) The Internet is a global network of billions of computers and electronic devices that enables communication and access to information

36. Assertion (A) Add-ons are lightweight extensions that enhance specific browser functionalities.

Reason (R) Add-ons are standalone programs that support multiple applications apart from the browser.

37. Assertion (A) Internet cookies are text files that contain small pieces of data, like a username, password and user's preferences while surfing the internet. **CBSE SQP 2022-23**

Reason (R) To make browsing the Internet faster & easier, its required to store certain information on the server's computer.

38. Assertion (A) Cookies improve user experience on websites by storing session data and user preferences.

Reason (R) Cookies increase the privacy of users by preventing websites from tracking their activities.

39. Assertion (A) A static web page does not change for each person visiting the web page. **CBSE 2023**

Reason (R) When a web server receives a request for a dynamic web page, it locates and updates the page and sends it to the browser of the client.

40. Assertion (A) VoIP calls are more cost-effective for long-distance communication compared to traditional phone calls.

Reason (R) VoIP uses an internet connection to transmit voice data, reducing costs compared to analog phone lines.

Answers

1. (a) Internet
2. (a) ARPANET
3. (a) TCP
4. (b) packets
5. (c) /index.htm
6. (c) Uniform Resource Locator
7. (c) Apache web server
8. (c) Linux
9. (c) Avast
10. (d) All of the above
11. (b) Lynx
12. (b) Netscape Navigation
13. (a) Add-ons
14. (c) Cookies
15. (a) first page of a website
16. (d) myspace
17. (b) Document
18. (b) Web pages
19. (b) Chatting
20. (a) VoIP
21. (b) Voice Over Internet Protocol (VoIP)
22. URL
23. Webserver
24. Web browser
25. Website
26. static web page
27. E-mail
28. True
29. False
30. False
31. True
32. False
33. (d)Assertion (A) is False, but Reason (R) is True
34. (a) Both Assertion (A) and Reason (R) are true, and Reason (R) is the correct explanation of Assertion (A)
35. (a) Both Assertion (A) and Reason (R) are true, and Reason (R) is the correct explanation of Assertion (A)
36. (c)Assertion (A) is True, but Reason (R) is False
37. (c) Assertion (A) is True, but Reason (R) is False
38. (c)Assertion (A) is True, but Reason (R) is False
39. (b) Both Assertion (A) and Reason (R) are true, but Reason (R) is not the correct explanation of Assertion (A)
40. (a) Both Assertion (A) and Reason (R) are true, and Reason (R) is the correct explanation of Assertion (A)

Subjective Type Questions

Very Short Answer Type Questions

1. Why is Internet so popular?

Ans. Due to its extensible use and sharing of data, Internet becomes so popular.

2. Write two advantages of using Internet.

Ans. (i) It is used for communication, entertainment, searching information and for providing many types of services.
(ii) It provides the facility of E-mail.

3. What can a user do with WWW?

Ans. Using WWW, a user can download files, listen to music, view video files and jump to other documents or websites by using hypertext links.

4. Can we use URL to access a web page? How?

Ans. Yes, as a location on a Web server, which is called a website and each website has a unique address known as URL. So, URL can be used to access a web page.

5. Define the structure of URL with example.

Ans.

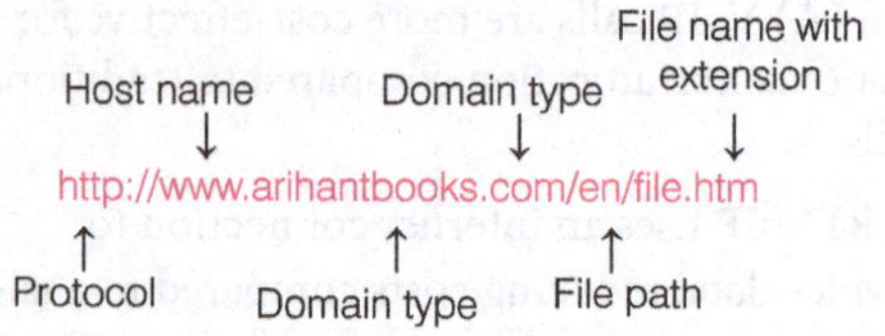

6. Give one difference between XML and HTML. CBSE SQP 2023-24

Ans. XML (eXtensible Markup Language) is used for storing and transporting data, while HTML (HyperText Markup Language) is used for creating web pages and displaying content in browsers.

7. Write the relationship between a website and a web server.

Ans. Web server is a computer with an Internet connection on which a website is hosted.

8. Navya has just created a website for her company and now need to host it. Briefly discuss the role of a web server in hosting a website. CBSE SQP 2021-22 Term II, Competency Based Que.

Ans. A web server stores the website's files and delivers them to users' browsers over the internet. It processes requests from users and sends the appropriate web pages, handling communication between the user and the website.

9. What is the role of a web browser in Internet surfing?

Ans. A web browser is a software program that allows a user to locate and display web pages that acts as Internet surfing.

10. Distinguish between website and web browser.

Ans. Website is a place on the net servers to keep web pages while the web browser is a software application for retrieving, presenting and traversing information resources on the WWW.

11. How will you change the browser setting in google chrome?

Ans. In the upper right corner, click on Google Chrome triple dots (⋮) icons and then click on the Settings option in the menu. In the Settings window, we can change the settings.

12. What is the use of add-on on web browser?

Ans. Add-ons extend a browser's functionality by adding new features, such as ad-blocking, security tools, or customization options for a better browsing experience.

13. What is the role of plug-ins?

Ans. Plug-ins is a piece of software that acts as an add-on to a web browser and gives the browser additional functionality.

14. What is the role of plug-ins?

Ans. Plug-ins is a piece of software that acts as an add-on to a web browser and gives the browser additional functionality.

15. Explain the concept of browser cookies and mention one advantages of using them? CBSE SQP 2024-25

Ans. Browser cookies are small data files stored on a user's device by websites to remember information. One advantage is that they enable personalized experiences, like keeping users logged in.

16. What do you understand by the term cookies? Give any two benefits of cookies. CBSE 2023

Ans. Cookies are small text files stored on a user's computer by websites to track and store information about the user's preferences and activity.

Two benefits Remembering login credentials, saving time for users.

Personalizing user experience by retaining preferences like language settings.

It processes requests from users and sends the appropriate web pages, handling communication between the user and the website.

17. Priyanka, a beginner in IT field has just started learning web technologies. Help her in understanding the difference between website and web pages with the help of a suitable general example of each. CBSE SQP 2021-22 Term II, Competency Based Que.

Ans. Difference between a website and web pages:

(i) A website is a collection of related web pages under one domain, like an entire book containing many pages (e.g., an online book store).

(ii) A web page is a single document that can be viewed in a web browser, like a page of a book (e.g., a homepage).

18. Mr. Lal owns a factory which manufactures automobile spare parts. Suggest him the advantages of having a web page for his factory. Competency Based Que.

Ans. The web page provides the information to the clients about his factory of spare parts. Moreover, he can receive the order on the Internet from the clients using the web page.

19. Aman, a freelance web site developer, has been assigned a task to design few web pages for a book shop. Help Aman in deciding out of static web page and dynamic web page, what kind of web pages should be designed by clearly differentiating between static and dynamic web pages on at least two points. Competency Based Que.

Ans. Aman should design dynamic web pages for the book shop. Here's why:

1. **Content Update** Dynamic web pages can be easily updated with real-time information like book availability, prices, and promotions, while static pages require manual updates.
2. **User Interaction** Dynamic pages allow users to interact with the website, such as searching for books or adding items to a cart, while static pages cannot handle.

20. Write any one advantage of using E-mail.

Ans. E-mails are easy to use. You can organise your daily correspondence, send and receive electronic messages and save them on computers.

21. Rashmi has to send e-email to Raees. She also wants to send the same e-email to Anjali but does not want Raees to know about it. Which option out of Cc and Bcc should Rashmi use to enter the Email address of Anjali. Competency Based Que.

Ans. Bcc (Blind Carbon Copy)

22. What is the difference between e-mail and chat?

Ans. E-mail is an asynchronous communication method where messages are sent and received with a delay, while chat is real-time, allowing instant communication between users.

23. What do you mean by IRC?

Ans. IRC (Internet Relay Chat) is an application layer protocol that facilitates communication in the form of text. The chat process works on a client/server networking model.

24. What is VoIP?

Ans. VoIP (Voice over Internet Protocol) is simply the transmission of voice traffic over IP based networks. VoIP has been around in one form or another, since 1973 when it began as an experiment by US.

Short Answer Type I Questions

25. How do Internet help us?

Ans. Internet can be useful for us in following ways:

(i) Allows organisations to advertise their products.

(ii) Provides information.

(iii) Easily communicate with other people.

(iv) Save paper as we can publish documents on the Internet.

26. Write three disadvantages of using Internet.

Ans. The three disadvantages of using Internet are as follows:

(i) Cyber frauds
(ii) Information misuse
(iii) Computer virus circulation

27. Explain any two attributes of WWW.

Ans. Two attributes of WWW are as follows:

(i) **User-friendly** The WWW resource works smoothly with most web browsers, such as Internet Explorer, Firefox etc.

(ii) **Multimedia document** WWW allows users to create and display web pages that contains various graphics, audio, video, animation and text.

28. Riya has typed the following text in the address bar http://www.cbse.international.com/help.htm
Explain to her the main concept of URL and domain name with reference to the example given above. **Competency Based Que.**

Ans. URL (Uniform Resource Locator) is the complete address of a document on the web, whereas a domain name specifies the location of document's web server. A domain name is a component of the URL used to access websites.

Given example (http://www.cbse.international.com/help.htm) is a URL.

In this URL, www.cbse.international.com is the domain name.

29. Explain the difference between an absolute URL and a relative URL, providing examples.

Ans. An absolute URL provides the complete path to a resource, including the protocol, domain, and specific file location (e.g., https://www.example.com/images/logo.png).

A relative URL offers a path relative to the current page or directory and does not include the domain (e.g., /images/logo.png), making it useful for linking within the same site.

30. Distinguish between server and web server.

Ans. Differences between server and web server are as follows:

Server	Web Server
These servers arrange the run environment for enterprises applications.	These servers arrange the run environment for web application.
These servers utilize more resources.	These servers utilize less resources.
In this server, multithreading is supported.	In this server, multi-threading is not supported.

31. Give any two points of difference between Static web page and Dynamic web page. **CBSE 2025**

Ans.

Static webpage	Dynamic webpage
Static webpages are generally simple HTML written pages in which all the data is static in nature and it does not get changed until someone changes it manually.	Dynamic webpages are the pages written in some more complex language such as ASP.NET in which the data is rendered after some interpretation. It can produce distinctive content for different calls.
Static webpages are generally written in simpler languages such as HTML, JavaScript, CSS, etc.	Dynamic webpages are written in more complex languages such as CGI, AJAX, ASP, ASP.NET, etc.

32. How is an E-mail different from a chat?

Ans. In order to chat, you need have an account on the same service as the person you are chatting with. On the other hand, in case of E-mail, it is not necessary, i.e. you can have an account from any provider and you can establish your own.

33. What do you mean by instant messaging?

Ans. Refer to text on page no. 192 (instant messaging).

Short Answer Type II Questions

34. Discuss the advantages and disadvantages of the Internet regarding communication and social interaction.

Ans. The internet has many advantages and disadvantages for communication and social interaction, including:

Advantages

- **Communication** The internet has made communication faster and more efficient, and has made it easier to connect with others.
- **Global connections** The internet allows for virtual communication and global connections.
- **E-commerce** The internet has made e-commerce possible.
- **Online education** The internet has made online education possible.
- **Information** The internet provides an abundance of information.

Disadvantages

- **Fake news** The internet has led to the proliferation of fake news and disinformation.
- **Personal information** The internet can lead to loss of personal information.
- **Internet addiction** The internet can lead to internet addiction and time wastage.
- **Mental health** The internet can lead to physical and mental health issues.
- **Social isolation** Extensive internet use, particularly of social media, can be correlated with loneliness and social isolation.

- **Intimate relationships** Internet use can degrade intimate relationships, particularly due to viewing online pornography.

35. Discuss the functioning of a web server with its explanation.

Ans. A web server is a program that runs on a computer connected to the Internet. It is simply a computer with an Internet connection that runs software designed to send out HTML, DHTML, XML or Java based pages and other file formats such as multimedia files.

A web server provides four major functions:

(i) Surfing web pages.
(ii) Running gateway programs and returning output.
(iii) Controlling access to the server.
(iv) Monitoring and logging server access statistics.

36. Differentiate between Static and Dynamic website.

Ans. Difference between static and dynamic websites

Static website	Dynamic website
Content of web pages cannot be change at runtime.	Content of web pages can be changed.
No interaction with database possible.	Interaction with database is possible
It is faster to load as compared to dynamic website.	It is slower than static website.
HTML, CSS, Javascript is used for developing the website.	Server side languages such as PHP, Node.js are used.
Same content is delivered everytime the page is loaded.	Content may change everytime the page is loaded

Long Answer Type Questions

37. Why is Internet called Network of Networks?

Ans. Internet is called Network of Networks because it is global network of computers that are linked together by cables and telephone lines making communication possible among them. It can be defined as a global network over a million of smaller heterogeneous computer networks. The network which consists of thousands of network spanning the entire globe is known as Internet.

The Internet is a worldwide collection of networked computers, which are able to exchange information with each other very quickly.

In Internet, most computers are not connected directly, they are connected to smaller networks, which in turn are connected through gateways to the Internet backbone. A gateway is a device that connects dissimilar networks. A backbone is central interconnecting structure that connects one or more networks.

38. Explain cookies and also write steps for enabling or disabling cookies setting.

Ans. **Refer to text on page no 190 (Cookies).**

39. Explain the following:

- **POP3**
- **SMTP**
- **IMAP**

Ans. Refer to text on page no. 192 (Electronic mail protocol).

40. Explain the following terms:

(i) WWW (ii) Web browser
(iii) Web page (iv) Web hosting (v) Chat

Ans. (i) Refer to text on page no. 185.
(ii) Refer to text on page no. 188.
(iii) Refer to text on page no. 191.
(iv) Refer to text on page no. 187.
(v) Refer to text on page no. 192.

41. What do you understand by chatting?

Ans. Refer to text on page no. 192 (Chat).

42. Define Voice over Internet Protocol (VoIP). Also, explain its advantages.

Ans. Refer to text on page no. 192-193. (VoIP)

Case Study Based Questions

Case Study 1

Samarth is the hardware engineer of "Happy School". He has been given the task of installing a network in the school lab which has around 40 computers.

(i) Suggest the most suitable type of network topology he should use in order to maximise speed and make each computer indepenent of network breakdowns.

(a) Bus topology (b) Star topology
(c) Ring topology (d) Mesh topology

(ii) In order to allow data transfer from server to only the intended computers which network device is required in the lab to connect the computers?

(a) Switch (b) Hub
(c) Router (d) Gateway

(iii) After setting up the lab and Internet in the lab, Samarth is now required to enable videos and animations to be played on the web browser for students of multimedia class.

Which browser tool /service can be used for the same?

(a) Plug-ins (b) Add-ons
(c) Control Panel (d) Download Settings

(iv) During an international exchange program the students need to connect to a classroom in Russia using Skype. Samarth helps the students to connect. Which type of network service is being used ?

(a) Instant messaging (b) Email messaging
(c) VoIP (d) WWW

(v) Samarth has asked students of class 7 to identify different parts of URL. Help the students to choose the correct option for label 1 and 2.

(a) 1-Domain Name 2-Protocol (b) 1-Protocol 2-Domain Name
(c) 1-Domain name 2-sub-domain (d) 1-Protocol 2-sub-domain

CBSE Question Bank

Ans. (i) (*b*) Star topology is the best and allows central fault diagnosis and easy detection of faults . Hence, it should be used.

(ii) (*a*) Switch is a device that connects multiple computers in a network and also allows simultaneous communicaton between multiple nodes of the network.

(iii) (*b*) Add-ons are additionally installable components to a browser that adds to its capability to support additional features.

(iv) (*c*) VoIP or Voice over Internet Protocol is service that allows real time sharing of audio, video and data.

(v) (*b*) Here https is the protocol name and www.cbse.gov.in is the domain under which the pages of the web site are available.

Case Study 2

Refer to the following diagram and answer the questions given below.

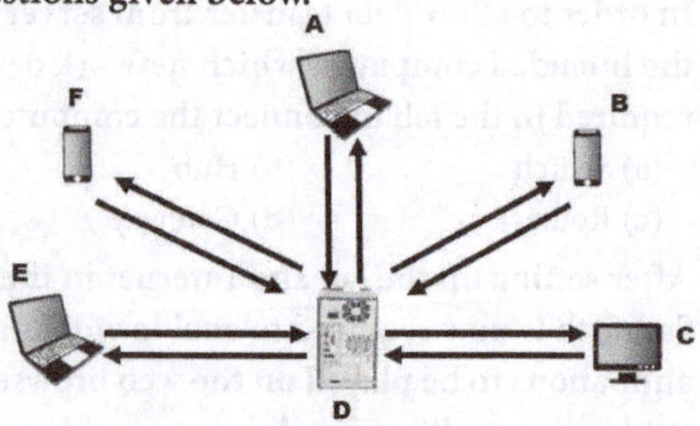

(i) Which of the following device acts as a server?

(a) A (b) B
(c) C (d) D

(ii) The arrow from device D to pointing to A represents?

(a) HTTP request
(b) HTTP response
(c) Both (a) and (b)
(d) All of the above

(iii) Which of the following device(s) can have IP addresses?

(a) A (b) D
(c) F (d) All of these

(iv) Identify the network topology of the above network.

(a) Ring
(b) Star
(c) Bus
(d) None of the above

(v) …… is a protocol (set of rules) used when transmitting files (data) over the world wide web.

(a) FTP (b) HTTP
(c) SMP (d) None of these

CBSE Question Bank

Ans. (i) (*d*) As seen from the diagram D is the central computer in the network to which all other systems are connected. Hence, it is acting as the server.

(ii) (*b*) As D is the server here, hence an arrow from D to A represents a response for a request from the client A.

(iii) (*d*) Any device that is connected to a network must have a network provided address called the IP address. Hence all the devices will have an IP address.

(iv) (*b*) As we know in star topology all nodes are connected to the central server by independent cables. The configuration here is star topology.

(v) (*b*) The HTTP protocol is used for transmitting web files containing text , images and other dynamic content.

Case Study 3

The school offers Wi-Fi to the students of Class XII. For communication, the network security-staff of the school is having a registered URL "schoolwifi.edu". On 17th September 2017, emails were received by all the students regarding expiry of their passwords. Instructions were also given renew their password within 24 hours by clicking on particular URL provided.

On the bases of the given information, answer the questions given below: **CBSE Question Bank**

(i) Specify which type of cybercrime is it.
(a) Spamming (b) Phishing
(c) Identity Theft (d) Hacking

(ii) URL stands for ________ .
(a) Universal Resource Loader
(b) Uniform Resource Locator
(c) United Research Loader
(d) Uniform Resource Loader

(iii) Unsolicited commercial email is known as:
(a) Malware
(b) Virus
(c) Spam
(d) Spyware

(iv) WiFi stands for ______ .
(a) Wireless Internet Frequent Interface
(b) Wireless Functioning
(c) Wireless Fidelity
(d) Wire Free Internet

(v) Ideally, what characters should be used in a password to make it strong?
(a) Letters and numbers only
(b) Mixed Case (Upper and Lower)
(c) Special characters
(d) All of these

Ans. (i) (b) The fraudulent act of stealing others personal information by an authenticated looking E-mail, message or call is called phishing. Prompting to click on a link is an attempt to steal information.

(ii) (b) URL stands for Uniform Resource Locator.

(iii) (c) Bulk unwanted or unsolicited mails from unknown sources filling the mailbox is called spamming.

(iv) (c) Wi-Fi stands for Wireless Fidelity.

(v) (d) Passwords should such that they cannot be easily guessed or cracked. Hence, it should have a mix of letter, digits and special characters and combination of upper and lowercase alphabets.

Case Study 4

Vidya Devi, a retired school principal, was inspired by her granddaughter who uses technology for her day to day activities. Being a learner and teacher all her life, she wanted to open an E-mail account and interact with her friends and family.

Her granddaughter created an E-mail account for her and gradually she started sending mails to her friends and family. This was a big achievement for her. Her granddaughter explained how E-mails are sent, how to create an E-mail address, what protocols are used. Some of these details were too technical for her, but she never gave up. There are few doubts/misconceptions in her mind, help her to find the solutions of her doubts by the given questions. CBSE Question Bank

(i) Unsolicited E-mail advertising is known as ______.
(a) newsgroup (b) junk ads
(c) spam (d) None of these

(ii) Which of the following is the correct format of E-mail address?
(a) name@website@info
(b) name@website.info
(c) www.nameofwebsite.com
(d) name.website.com

(iii) Mail access starts with client when user needs to download E-mail from the ________ .
(a) mail box (b) mail server
(c) IP server (d) Internet

(iv) To use E-mail service, one needs to register with ________ .
(a) Internet Service Provider
(b) E-mail Service Provider
(c) a company
(d) No need to register

(v) Bcc stands for to send the copy of mail.
(a) Black carbon copy (b) Blue carbon copy
(c) Blind carbon copy (d) Block chain copy

Ans. (i) (c) Bulk unwanted or unsolicited mails from unknown sources filling the mail box is called spamming.

(ii) (b) Email ids have a format that starts with the user name followed by "@" and the web site name/domain name where the user name has a space or mail box.

(iii) (a) User Emails are stored in the user's mail box, hence whenever the user wants to access the mails, they have to be obtained from the mail box.

(iv) (a) To use the internet services, a user needs to register with an Internet service provider.

(v) (c) Bcc stands for blind carbon copy. Bcc is a way of sending copies of an E-mail to other people.

Case Study 5

Ramanpreet has to work on his science project which deals with electromagnetic waves. A lot of research work is required by him for the same. He uses Google Chrome to search for the relevant matter. CBSE Question Bank

(i) Google chrome is an example of a
(a) website
(b) web browser
(c) web page
(d) None of the above

(ii) He finally locates some useful information and clicks on the link provided to access the website. The link is actually known as _____.

(a) domain name
(b) web page
(c) URL
(d) IP address

(iii) As Ramanpreet works on his project, he collects and curates information. Whenever he clicks on the link the same piece of information is shown and the content is not clickable. Ramanpreet is accessing a/an ________ website.

(a) dynamic
(b) textual
(c) outdated
(d) static

(iv) A web cookie is a small piece of data that is ______

(a) sent from a website and stored in user's web browser while a user is browsing a website
(b) sent from user and stored in the server while a user is browsing a website
(c) sent from root server to all servers
(d) sent from the root server to other root servers

(v) HTML stands for ________

(a) HyperText Markup Link
(b) HyperText Markup Language
(c) Hybrid Text Markup Language
(d) HyperText Manipulation Language

Ans. (i) (b) Google chrome is one of the popular web browsers that can be used for browsing, searching web sites and web pages.

(ii) (c) A URL or Uniform resource locator is a link to a remote web resource.

(iii) (d) A static website contains information that can be seen and used, but they do not have any dynamic behavior to give additional information/features or to take to an additional resource.

(iv) (a) A cookie is a small text file that is usually created by a web site to store personal user information to give convenient and personalized browsing experiences.

(v) (b) HTML stands for HyperText Markup Language, A language used to create web pages.

SELF ASSESSMENT TEST

Multiple Choice Questions

1 The vast network of computers that connects millions of people all over the world is called

(a) LAN (b) Web
(c) Hypertext (d) Internet

2 Which of the following is a wide area network of Internet that supports different web protocols?

(a) WWW (b) Protocol
(c) Web server (d) URL

3 Which web page uses scripting languages to display changing content on the web page?

(a) Static web page
(b) Hybrid web page
(c) Dynamic web page
(d) None of the above

4 Browsers are helpful to view

(a) home pages
(b) web pages
(c) index pages
(d) personal pages

5 In Google Chrome, where can you customize privacy settings, change the default search engine, and manage download options?

(a) Appearance Panel
(b) Address Bar
(c) Settings Menu
(d) Toolbar

Fill in the Blanks

6 Basic purpose of URL is to locate .... on the internet.

7 .... is the web address for a website or a web page.

8 A/An .... is a program or a computer that connects to and requests information from a server.

State whether True or False

9 The first part of the URL is called a protocol identifier.

10 A static web page generally has .htm or .html as extension.

11 The purpose of HTTP is to set up communication rules between servers.

Assertion and Reason Based Questions

Assertion (A) and Reason (R) Type questions. Choose the correct option as:

(a) Both Assertion (A) and Reason (R) are true, and Reason (R) is the correct explanation of Assertion (A)
(b) Both Assertion (A) and Reason (R) are true, but Reason (R) is not the correct explanation of Assertion (A)
(c) Assertion (A) is True, but Reason (R) is False
(d) Assertion (A) is False, but Reason (R) is True

12 **Assertion (A)** The Internet enables users to communicate instantly with each other across the world.

Reason (R) The Internet is a global network of interconnected computers and electronic devices that facilitates access to information, communication, and various online services.

13 **Assertion (A)** The World Wide Web (WWW) is the same as the Internet.

Reason (R) The WWW is a system of interconnected webpages that allows users to access and share information using the Internet.

14 **Assertion (A)** Graphical-based web browsers provide a Graphical User Interface (GUI), allowing users to interact with web pages through clickable elements like hyperlinks.

Reason (R) Graphical-based web browsers only support text-based content and cannot display images or videos.

15 **Assertion (A)** The Address Bar in a web browser displays the URL of the current page.

Reason (R) The Address Bar only appears when loading a new page and disappears once the page has fully loaded.

Very Short Answer Type Questions

16. Write any one disadvantage of Internet.
17. Write the element of URL syntax.
18. Describe the advantage of home page.
19. What do you mean by graphical based web browser?

Short Answer Type Questions

20. How will you change the browser setting in opera?
21. Explain the advantages of E-mail.

22. Write the process to install the add-ons.
23. Differentiate between the static and dynamic web page.

Long Answer Type Questions

24. Explain the working of Internet.
25. Describe the browser setting in different web browsers.
26. Explain the components of E-mail messages.

Case Study Based Question

27. Ravi is a high school student who is learning about the Internet and its various applications. He frequently uses the web to research information for his projects, communicates with friends and family through email and chat, and recently started exploring Voice over Internet Protocol (VoIP) applications to make voice calls over the internet. Ravi is also curious about the structure of websites and web pages and has learned about static and dynamic web pages. His teacher explained to him how web servers host websites, making them accessible over the Internet.

Ravi has learned that URLs (Uniform Resource Locators) are essential for accessing web pages and that browsers are software applications that enable users to view and navigate websites. He experimented with different browsers and explored settings, add-ons, and plug-ins to improve his browsing experience. Ravi is now familiar with cookies and understands how they help in storing information about his browsing sessions.

Based on this information, answer the following questions:

(i) Which of the following best describes a URL?
(a) It is a protocol used to transfer data over the Internet.
(b) It is the address used to locate a resource on the web.
(c) It is a software application for viewing web pages.
(d) It is a service that enables voice communication over the internet.

(ii) What is the primary difference between a static and a dynamic web page?
(a) Static pages allow for real-time data changes, while dynamic pages do not.
(b) Static pages are fixed and do not change, while dynamic pages can update content based on user interaction.
(c) Static pages are hosted on local servers, while dynamic pages are hosted on remote servers.
(d) Static pages require a database connection, while dynamic pages do not.

(iii) Which application would Ravi use if he wants to make voice calls over the Internet?
(a) Web browser
(b) Chat application
(c) VoIP
(d) Email client

(iv) Which of the following statements is true about cookies?
(a) Cookies store data to help websites remember information about users' browsing sessions.
(b) Cookies are software applications that enable browsing.
(c) Cookies allow users to view and edit web pages directly.
(d) Cookies are security protocols used to protect user data.

(v) Which feature of a web browser allows Ravi to install additional functionality, such as ad blockers or language translators?
(a) Browser settings (b) URL bar
(c) Add-ons and plug-ins (d) Cookies

Answers

1. (d) 2. (a) 3. (c) 4. (b) 5. (c)
6. Resources 7. URL 8. Client 9. True
10. True 11. True 12. (a) 13. (c) 14. (c)
15. (c)
27. (i) → (b), (ii) → (b), (iii) → (c), (iv) → (a), (v) → (c)

07

CHAPTER

Societal Impacts

Today, IT is an integral part of almost every individual. With such importance of IT in our everyday life, it brings us some advantages and disadvantages along with.

▼ YOUR STUDY GOALS

7.1 Digital Footprint
7.2 Digital Society and Netizens
7.3 Data Protection
7.4 Software Licensing
7.5 Software Piracy
7.6 Cyber Crime
7.7 Indian Information Technology Act (IT Act)
7.8 E-Waste: Hazards and Management
7.9 Impact on Health Due to Digital Device Usage

▼ YOUR PRACTICE GOAL

- Objective Type Questions (71 Qs ; MCQs, True or False, Fill in the Blanks, Assertion and Reason)
- Subjective Type Questions (47 Qs ; VSA, SA, LA)
- Case Study Based Questions (Objective Case Study-1, Subjective Case Study-1)

Societal impact is the effect that research or actions have on people, communities and the environment. It can include changes to culture the economy, education, health and the environment and quality of life.

7.1 Digital Footprint

A digital footprint refers to the trail of data you leave behind when you use the internet. This includes all the information that is collected about you from various online activities, such as:

- **Social Media Posts** Everything you share, like, or comment on platforms like Facebook, Twitter, or Instagram.
- **Browsing History** The websites you visit, the searches you perform, and the content you view online.
- **Online Transactions** Purchases made through e-commerce sites, including payment information and delivery addresses.

- **Emails and Messages** Correspondence sent via email or messaging apps.
- **Location Data** Information collected through your devices, which can reveal where you go and how often you visit certain places.

Types of Digital Footprint

Digital footprints can be categorized into two main types:

1. Active Digital Footprint

This consists of the data that you intentionally share online. Whenever you post a status update, share a photo, or comment on a blog, you are creating an active digital footprint.

Examples

- Social media posts
- Blog entries
- Comments on forums or articles

2. Passive Digital Footprint

This refers to the data collected about you without your direct input. It is generated by your online activities and interactions, often tracked by websites and apps.

Examples

- Cookies that track your browsing habits
- Metadata from photos (like GPS coordinates)
- Analytics data collected by websites to monitor user behavior

Importance of Understanding Digital Footprints

Understanding your digital footprint is crucial for several reasons:

- **Privacy Concerns** Being aware of what information is available online can help you manage your privacy.
- **Reputation Management** Your digital footprint can impact how others perceive you, including potential employers or educational institutions.
- **Online Safety** Recognizing the types of data collected can help you make informed choices about sharing information online.

7.2 Digital Society and Netizens

The **digital society** represents the growing trend of utilizing digital technologies across all aspects of human activity.

However, being online also necessitates awareness of how to conduct ourselves, relate to others, and uphold ethics, morals, and values.

A **digital citizen**, commonly referred to as a **netizen**, is anyone who engages with digital technology and the Internet.

Being a responsible netizen involves practicing safe, ethical, and legal use of digital technology. A good netizen should follow net etiquette, communication etiquette, and social media etiquette to ensure a positive online experience for themselves and others.

Net Etiquettes

Net etiquette refers to the proper manners and behavior we should exhibit while engaging with others on the Internet. Here are some key points to keep in mind:

1. **Be Respectful** Treat everyone online with the same respect you would show in person. Avoid using offensive language, making derogatory remarks, or engaging in cyberbullying.
2. **Practice Ethical Behavior** Always ensure that your actions online are ethical. This includes respecting copyright laws, giving credit for others' work, and avoiding plagiarism. If you use someone else's ideas, make sure to cite them appropriately.
3. **Think Before You Post** Before sharing any content, think about its impact. Consider how your words and actions may affect others. Once something is posted online, it can be difficult to remove or change.
4. **Be Responsible** Take responsibility for your online behavior. If you make a mistake or hurt someone, apologize sincerely. Being accountable for your actions helps build trust and fosters a positive online environment.
5. **Maintain Privacy** Be cautious about sharing personal information. Protect your privacy and the privacy of others by not sharing sensitive details online.
6. **Be Mindful of Tone** Communication online lacks the non-verbal cues present in face-to-face conversations. Use clear language and avoid sarcasm or humor that might be misinterpreted.
7. **Engage Positively** Contribute to discussions in a constructive manner. Offer support and encouragement to others rather than criticism.

Communication Etiquettes in Digital Communication

Digital communication encompasses various platforms such as email, texting, instant messaging, cell phone conversations, audio/video conferencing, and social networking sites. While these tools facilitate connection and knowledge sharing, adhering to communication etiquettes is essential for effective interaction. The key etiquettes to follow:

(A) Be Precise

- **Respect Time** Avoid cluttering communication with unnecessary emails or comments. Respond promptly only to relevant messages and understand that not everyone can provide instant replies due to varying priorities.
- **Respect Data Limits** Be mindful of file sizes when sharing attachments. Opt for compressed files or use cloud storage solutions like Google Drive, Microsoft OneDrive, or Dropbox to share larger files, ensuring efficient use of data and bandwidth.

(B) Be Polite

- **Maintain Courtesy** Regardless of the communication format—synchronous (real-time) or asynchronous (delayed responses)—always engage politely and constructively. Avoid aggressive or abusive language, even in disagreements, to foster a respectful environment.

(C) Be Credible

- **Cultivate Trust** Comments, replies, and posts can significantly influence your credibility over time. Be cautious with your contributions; they shape how others perceive you. In discussion forums, users often review previous comments to gauge reliability. Aim to build a reputation for credible and thoughtful input.

Social Media Etiquettes

In today's digital age, social media has become an integral part of our lives. Platforms like Facebook, Instagram, Twitter, and YouTube offer us the power to connect with people across the globe, share our thoughts, and express ourselves creatively. However, with great power comes great responsibility. It's crucial to navigate these platforms with care and consideration.

Some essential social media etiquettes to keep in mind are:

1. Protect Your Privacy

- **Strong Passwords** Create complex passwords that are difficult to guess and change them regularly.
- **Selective Friend Requests** Be cautious about accepting friend requests from strangers.
- **Privacy Settings** Understand and utilize the privacy settings on each platform to control who can see your posts and information.
- **Beware of Phishing Scams** Be aware of suspicious messages or links that may ask for personal information.

2. Be Mindful of Your Online Presence

- **Think Before You Post** Once something is online, it's difficult to remove completely. Consider the potential consequences of your posts.
- **Respectful Communication** Engage in respectful and constructive conversations, avoiding cyberbullying and hate speech.
- **Fact-Checking** Before sharing information, verify its authenticity from credible sources.
- **Digital Footprint** Be aware of your digital footprint and how it can impact your future opportunities.

3. Ethical Usage

- **Copyright and Intellectual Property** Respect copyright laws and avoid sharing copyrighted material without permission.
- **Privacy of Others** Don't share personal information about others without their consent.
- **Online Etiquette** Follow basic netiquette, such as using proper grammar and punctuation.

Email Etiquettes

Email Etiquettes refer to the proper and professional way of communicating through email. Some key points are:

- **Use a Clear Subject Line** The subject should reflect the content of the email briefly and clearly.
- **Greet Appropriately** Begin with a formal greeting like "Dear [Name]" or "Hello" depending on the recipient.
- **Be Concise** Keep your email brief and to the point, avoiding unnecessary details.
- **Use Proper Grammar and Spelling** Always proofread for errors and use proper language.
- **Avoid All Caps** Writing in all caps can be perceived as shouting.

- **Professional Tone** Maintain a respectful and polite tone, even in disagreements.
- **End Politely** Close with appropriate sign-offs like "Regards," or "Best wishes," followed by your name.
- **Use BCC and CC Thoughtfully** Avoid spamming unnecessary recipients; only include people who need to be informed.

7.3 Data Protection

Data protection refers to the practices, safeguards, and binding rules put in place to protect our personal information and ensure that it remain in control. In short, we should be able to decide whether or not we want to share some information, who has access to it, for how long, for what reason, and be able to modify some of this information, and more.

Consequences of Unprotected Data/Data breaches

- Suffer from security breach/attack
- Physical data loss
- Hit with a virus
- Targeted by hackers
- Suffer from DDoS(Distributed denial of service)
- Lose of money
- Intellectual property at risk
- Damage downtime

How we can protect our personal data online?

- Through Encrypt our Data
- Keep Passwords Private
- Don't Overshare on Social Networking Sites
- Use Security Software
- Avoid Phishing Emails
- Be Wise About Wi-Fi
- Be Alert to Impersonators
- Safely Dispose of Personal Information

Intellectual Property Right (IPR)

Intellectual Property (IP) is a property created by a person or group of persons using their own intellect for ultimate use in commerce and which is already not available in the public domain.

Examples of IP Property which are, an invention relating to a product or any process, a new design, a literary or artistic work and a trademark (a word, a symbol and / or a logo, etc.).

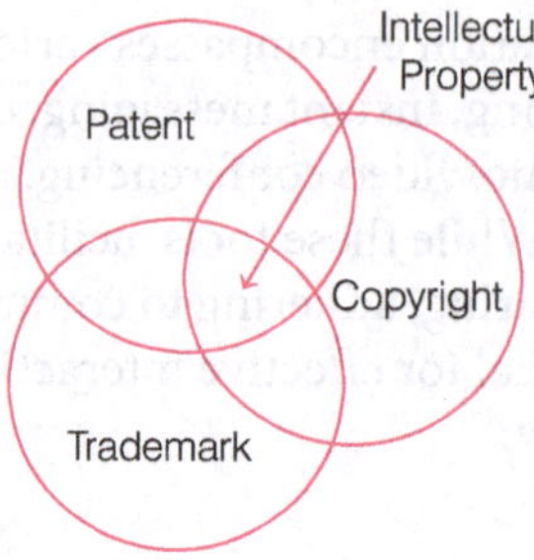

Intellectual Property Right legally protected through

- **Copyrights** It protects the ideas, examples would be written works, music, art, etc.
- **Trademarks** It is something that protects the symbols, colors, phrases, sounds, design etc.
- **Patents** It is used for protecting new inventions, ideas, or processes. Patent holders need to pay periodic government renewal fees. An approved patent is for a limited time period. Know more about Patents Act in India.

Violation of IPR

Violation of Intellectual Property Rights (IPR) refers to the unauthorized use or infringement of the exclusive rights granted to creators and inventors. This includes various forms of violations:

1. **Plagiarism** is the act of using someone else's work, ideas, or expressions without proper acknowledgement, presenting them as one's own. It undermines the original creator's contribution and can lead to academic and professional consequences.
2. **Copyright infringement** occurs when someone uses a protected work—such as music, literature, or software—without permission from the copyright holder. This can include unauthorized reproduction, distribution, or display of the work, violating the creator's exclusive rights.

TEACHER TIP
Plagiarism means using other's work and not giving adequate citation for use.
Copyright infringement means using another person's work, without permission or without paying for it, if it is being sold.

3. **Trademark infringement** involves the unauthorized use of a registered trademark or a confusingly

similar mark, which can mislead consumers about the source of goods or services. This can damage the brand's reputation and dilute its value, leading to legal disputes.

Quick Test 1

1. Give an example of passive digital footprint.
2. What is the fullform of IPR?
3. Where is patent used?
4. What do you mean by net etiquettes?

7.4 Software Licensing

A software license is a document that provides legally binding guidelines to the person who holds it for the use and distribution of software.

It typically provide end users with the right to make one or more copies of the software without violating copyrights.

It also defines the responsibilities of the parties entering into the license agreement and may impose restrictions on how the software can be used.

Software licensing terms and conditions usually include fair use of the software, the limitations of liability, warranties and disclaimers and protections.

Benefits of Using Licensed Software

- Using Unlicensed Software Against the Law
- The Right Software License Can Save our Money
- We can Receive Around-The-Clock License Support

Software copyright is used by software developers/software companies/proprietary software companies to prevent the unauthorized copying of their softwares.

Free and open source licenses also rely on copyright law to enforce their terms.

Reason for copyright of software

Software development is an asset Protect our rights:

- It protects software structures
- It protects software code,sequencing and organization
- It enhances protection against license agreements

Types of Public Licenses

Public licenses are legal tools that allow creators to specify how others can use their work. Understanding these licenses is essential, especially in the digital age, where sharing and collaboration are common.

Here, we'll focus on two major types of public licenses: Creative Commons (CC) and GNU General Public License (GPL).

1. Creative Commons (CC)

Creative Commons licenses are used for a wide range of creative works, including websites, music, films, and literature. These licenses enable creators to easily share their work with others while still retaining certain rights.

Features

- **Free Distribution** Works licensed under CC can be shared freely. This means anyone can download, use, and share the work without asking for permission.
- **Flexibility** Creators can choose how they want their work to be used. They can allow others to modify it, use it commercially, or restrict certain uses.
- **Encouraging Collaboration** By allowing sharing and modification, CC promotes collaboration and creativity in the community.

2. GNU General Public License (GPL)

The GNU General Public License is primarily used for software licensing. It was created to ensure that software remains free for users.

The GPL aims to give users the freedom to run, study, share, and modify software, promoting an open-source approach.

Features

- **User Freedom** Users can not only use the software but also modify its source code. This means they can improve it or tailor it to their needs.
- **Sharing Modifications** If someone modifies a GPL-licensed program and wants to share it, they must also distribute their modifications under the same GPL license. This ensures that future users also have the same freedoms.
- **Commercial Use** Users or companies can charge a fee for distributing GPL-licensed software. They can also provide it for free. This flexibility allows for both community sharing and commercial opportunities.

Distinction Between GPL and Other Licenses

- GPL vs. Freeware Licenses (e.g., Skype, Adobe Acrobat Reader)

- Freeware licenses allow personal use and copying but prohibit commercial distribution.
- GPL vs. Proprietary Licenses
- Proprietary licenses restrict copying and distribution under copyright law.

3. Free and Open Source Software (FOSS)

FOSS is available freely and allows access to its source code for modification, correction, and improvement. FOSS has a large community of users and developers contributing to its development.

Examples

- Linux kernel-based operating systems (e.g., Ubuntu, Fedora).
- Popular tools such as Libre Office (office package) and Mozilla Firefox (browser).

7.5 Software Piracy

Software piracy refers to the unauthorized use, distribution, or reproduction of software. This includes making copies without the permission of the copyright owner. Purchasing a software license does not automatically grant the right to make additional copies. Permission from the copyright owner is required. Software piracy constitutes copyright infringement, whether it is done for resale, free distribution, or personal use.

Consequences of Software Piracy

- **Performance Degradation** Pirated software often lacks updates, leading to security vulnerabilities and decreased performance of computer systems.
- **Economic Impact** It harms the software industry, resulting in significant financial losses and negatively affecting the economy of a country.

Creative Commons

Creative Commons (CC) is a non-profit organization that promotes the sharing of creative and academic works globally. It provides a platform for individuals to access, share, and utilize various works without infringing copyright or intellectual property rights, as proper attribution to the creators is ensured.

Features

- **Free Licenses**: CC offers copyright licenses at no cost, allowing creators to grant permissions for the use and distribution of their works in a standardized manner.
- **Rights to Share and Use** Authors can allow others to share, use, and adapt their creations, facilitating collaboration and innovation.
- **Wide Applicability** The CC licenses cover all forms of creative works, including art, music, literature, films, images, educational resources, and software.
- **CC Search** The platform includes a search feature to help users easily locate CC-licensed materials.
- **Customizable Terms** Creators have the freedom to specify the conditions under which their work can be used.

The owner of a work can combine these conditions to create six different types of CC licenses, as listed in Table:

License Name	License icon	Description
Attribution	CC BY	This license lets others distribute, remix, tweak, and build upon your work, even commercially, as long as they credit you for the original creation.
Attribution-ShareAlike	CC BY SA	This license lets others remix, tweak, and build upon your work even for commercial purposes, as long as they credit you and license their new creations under the identical terms.
Attribution-NoDerivs	CC BY ND	This license lets others reuse the work for any purpose, including commercially; however, it cannot be shared with others in adapted form, and credit must be provided to you.
Attribution-NonCommercial	CC BY NC	This license lets others remix, tweak, and build upon your work non-commercially, and although their new works must also acknowledge you and be non-commercial.
Attribution-NonCommercial-ShareAlike	CC BY NC SA	This license lets others remix, tweak, and build upon your work non-commercially, as long as they credit you and license their new creations under the identical terms.
Attribution-NonCommercial-NoDerivs	CC BY NC ND	This license is the most restrictive of our six main licenses, only allowing others to download your works and share them with others as long as they credit you, but they can't change them in any way or use them commercially.

Quick Test 2

1. why is data protection important?
2. what does ipr stand for?
3. give one example of violating intellectual property rights.
4. What is a software license?
5. What is the main benefit of using licensed software?
6. What is the GNU General Public License (GPL)?
7. What does Creative Commons (CC) license enable?
8. What is software piracy?

7.6 Cyber Crime

Cyber crime refers to criminal activities conducted in a digital environment. In these crimes, a computer may be the target, or it may be used as a tool to commit the offense.

Cyber crimes can affect individuals, groups, organizations, or even nations, often causing physical harm, financial loss, or mental distress.

Cyber criminals may attack computers or networks to disable or damage data and services. They often spread viruses and malware to steal confidential information for blackmail or extortion.

A computer virus consists of malicious code that replicates itself, potentially destroying data or corrupting systems. Malware is designed to gain unauthorized access to computer systems.

Types of Cyber Crime

1. Hacking

Hacking is the act of gaining unauthorized access to a computer, computer network, or any digital system. Hackers typically possess technical expertise in hardware and software, often exploiting bugs or vulnerabilities to break into systems.

Types of Hackers

1. **Ethical Hacking (White Hat Hackers)**

- Ethical hacking refers to hacking performed with positive intent, aimed at improving security.
- Ethical hackers, known as white hat hackers, are specialists in identifying vulnerabilities or loopholes in systems during testing.
- Their goal is to help improve software security by discovering weaknesses and reporting them to the system or website owner.
- Ethical hackers prepare organizations against potential cyberattacks by ensuring system robustness.

2. Non-Ethical Hacking (Black Hat Hackers or Crackers)

- Non-ethical hackers engage in unauthorized access with the intent to steal sensitive data, damage systems, or exploit them for malicious purposes.
- These hackers are called black hat hackers or crackers.
- Their focus is on security breaches, identity theft, financial gain, sabotage, or leaking sensitive information.
- They use their skills illegally to harm systems, businesses, or individuals, often causing financial or reputational damage.

2. Phishing and Fraud Emails

Phishing is an unlawful activity where fake websites or emails that appear to be original or authentic are used to fraudulently collect sensitive personal details.

These details often include usernames, passwords, banking, and credit card information. Common Methods of Phishing:

1. Email Spoofing

- In this method, a fake or forged email address is used to deceive the user into believing the email is from a legitimate source (e.g., bank, educational institution).
- These emails often contain logos and designs resembling real organizations, making them harder to detect.
- By closely inspecting the URL, you may find that it is fake, even though it closely mimics an official address.

2. Phone Calls and Text Messages:

- In addition to emails, phishing attempts can be made through fraudulent phone calls or text messages.
- These attempts may ask for personal information under the guise of a trusted authority.

Key Tips to Avoid Phishing

- Always check the URL or sender's email address carefully.
- Be wary of any unsolicited request for sensitive information.
- Never click on suspicious links or provide personal details through unsecured platforms.

3. Identity Theft

Identity theft occurs when personal information is stolen from computers or computer networks and used unlawfully to commit fraud.

The stolen data often includes a user's identifiable personal details, such as:

- Demographic information
- Email ID
- Banking credentials
- Passport number
- PAN (Permanent Account Number)
- Aadhaar number

Hackers misuse this stolen data, often for monetary gain, making this a type of phishing attack. There are various ways in which criminals can exploit an individual's stolen identity. Below are a few examples:

1. **Financial Identity Theft** The stolen identity is used for financial gain, such as making unauthorized purchases or accessing bank accounts.
2. **Criminal Identity Theft** Criminals use the victim's identity to avoid detection of their true identity, often in situations involving law enforcement.
3. **Medical Identity Theft** Criminals seek medical treatment or obtain prescription drugs using the victim's identity, causing potential health risks to the victim.
4. **Cyberbullying** Cyberbullying is the act of harassing, threatening, or humiliating someone using digital platforms like social media, messaging apps, or online forums.

   It often involves spreading harmful messages or images and can have serious emotional and psychological effects on the victim.
5. **Cyberstalking** Cyberstalking refers to the use of the internet to monitor, harass, or intimidate someone repeatedly and persistently. It may involve tracking online activities, sending threatening messages, or hacking into personal accounts to frighten or control the victim.
6. **Spamming** Spamming is the practice of sending unsolicited, irrelevant, or repetitive messages, often in bulk, to a large number of people, usually via email or messaging platforms. Spams are typically used for advertising or phishing purposes and can clog communication channels.
7. **Ransomware** Ransomware is a type of cybercrime where attackers gain unauthorized access to a computer and prevent users from accessing their data, often by encrypting it.

   The attacker then demands a ransom, usually in cryptocurrency, to restore access. In some cases, the attacker threatens to release sensitive or personal information unless the ransom is paid.

   Ransomware can infect systems in various ways:

   - Visiting malicious or unsecure websites
   - Downloading software from untrustworthy sources
   - Opening infected email attachments in spam mails
   - Clicking on malicious ads (malvertising)

Safeguarding Against Cyber Crime

Cyber crime poses significant challenges, but these can be effectively addressed through vigilance and legal assistance.

The essential safety measures to minimize the risk of cyber crime are:

- **Regularly Backup Important Data** Ensure you keep copies of critical information to prevent loss from cyber attacks.
- **Utilize Updated Antivirus Software** Protect your devices by using reputable antivirus software and keeping it regularly updated.
- **Avoid Pirated Software** Download software only from trusted sources and secure (HTTPS) websites to mitigate risks.
- **Keep System Software Updated** Regularly update your operating system, internet browser, and application software to fix vulnerabilities.
- **Steer Clear of Untrusted Websites** Avoid visiting or downloading content from websites that are not verified or seem suspicious.
- **Heed Browser Warnings** Pay attention to alerts about doubtful websites lacking valid security certificates and avoid them.
- **Use Strong Passwords** Create complex passwords for online accounts, change them periodically, and avoid reusing passwords across different sites.
- **Be Cautious on Shared Computers** When using someone else's device, refrain from allowing the

browser to save passwords or autofill sensitive information; use private browsing modes instead.

- **Decline Cookies on Unknown Sites** Be cautious about agreeing to cookie usage on unfamiliar websites.
- **Shop Securely Online** Conduct transactions such as shopping or ticketing only on well-known and secure websites.
- **Secure Your Home Network** Protect your home wireless network with a strong password and change it regularly to prevent unauthorized access.

7.7 Indian Information Technology Act (IT Act)

With the growth of the Internet, many cases of cyber crimes, frauds, cyber attacks, and cyber bullying have been reported. The nature of these fraudulent activities and crimes is contineously changing. To address such issues, many countries have implemented legal measures to protect sensitive personal data and safeguard the rights of Internet users.

In India, the Information Technology Act, 2000 (commonly referred to as the IT Act), which was amended in 2008, provides guidelines for the processing, storage, and transmission of sensitive information. This act is essential for enabling people to perform transactions over the Internet, such as credit card payments, without fear of misuse.

Features of the IT Act

1. **Legal Framework** The act establishes a legal framework for electronic governance by recognizing electronic records and digital signatures.
2. **Cyber Crime Identification** It outlines various cyber crimes and specifies penalties for these offenses.
3. **Reporting Cyber Crimes** In many Indian states, cyber cells have been established in police stations where individuals can report cyber crimes.
4. **Cyber Appellate Tribunal** This tribunal has been set up to resolve disputes arising from cyber crimes, such as:
    - Tampering with computer source documents
    - Hacking into computer systems
    - Using someone else's password
    - Publishing sensitive personal data without consent

Quick Test 3

1. What is the difference between ethical hacking and non-ethical hacking?
2. How does ransomware infect a system?
3. What role does the Indian Information Technology Act (IT Act), 2000 play in cyber crime?
4. What is the key purpose of phishing attacks?

7.8 E-Waste: Hazards and Management

E-waste, or electronic waste, encompasses discarded electrical and electronic devices that are no longer in use. Common examples include:

- Computers and laptops
- Mobile phones
- Televisions
- Tablets
- Music systems
- Speakers
- Printers
- Scanners

As the lifespan of these gadgets nears its end, they become e-waste, contributing to one of the fastest-growing environmental hazards worldwide. The increased use of electronic equipment has led to a significant rise in discarded products, and the lack of awareness and proper skills for managing e-waste exacerbates the problem.

The Growing Concern of E-Waste

Waste Electrical and Electronic Equipment (WEEE) has become a major global concern. E-waste constitutes over 5% of municipal solid waste, making proper disposal and management critical to minimizing environmental and societal damage.

Environmental Impact of E-Waste

E-waste significantly impacts the environment in various ways:

1. **Pollution Sources**
    - **Air Pollution** When e-waste is improperly disposed of, it emits harmful gases and fumes into the atmosphere. Dust particles laden with heavy metals contribute to air quality degradation.

- **Water Pollution** Improper disposal can lead to the leaching of harmful chemicals into the ground. When these contaminants reach groundwater, they render it unsafe for human consumption, animal life, and agriculture.
- **Soil Pollution** The chemicals from e-waste can seep into the soil, causing severe contamination that affects plant growth and soil health.

2. **Toxic Materials** Many electronic products contain toxic substances like lead, mercury, and cadmium. When these materials enter the environment through careless disposal, they pose serious health risks to humans and wildlife.
3. **Landfill Issues** Discarded e-waste often ends up in landfills, where it takes years to decompose. The accumulation of electronic devices in landfills contributes to environmental degradation and resource wastage.

Impact of E-Waste on Humans

E-waste, or electronic waste, poses significant risks to human health due to the presence of toxic metals and chemicals in electronic devices. When improperly disposed of, these materials can leach into the environment, leading to serious health consequences. Here are some of the key impacts:

1. **Lead Poisoning**
   - Lead is commonly found in devices such as monitors and batteries.
   - It can enter the human body through contaminated food, water, air, or soil.
   - Lead poisoning can severely affect the kidneys, brain, and central nervous system, with children being particularly at risk, potentially leading to developmental issues and learning disabilities.
2. **Beryllium Exposure**
   - When e-waste is incinerated, components like electronic circuit boards release beryllium.
   - This substance can lead to skin diseases, allergic reactions, and a heightened risk of lung cancer.
   - The burning of insulated wires to recover copper can also lead to neurological disorders due to harmful byproducts.
3. **Mercury Toxicity**
   - Mercury is another hazardous element found in various electronic devices.
   - Exposure can result in serious respiratory disorders, neurological damage, and impairment of cognitive functions, leading to long-term health issues.
4. **Cadmium Poisoning**
   - Cadmium is commonly present in semiconductors and resistors.
   - It poses risks to the kidneys, liver, and bones, and chronic exposure can lead to severe health conditions, including bone fragility and kidney dysfunction.
5. **Plastic Pollution**
   - Most electronic devices contain plastics that can release toxic chemicals when they degrade or burn.
   - The combustion of these plastics can produce dioxins and furans, which are highly toxic and carcinogenic.
   - These chemicals can accumulate in the food chain and affect human health, leading to reproductive issues and various cancers.

Management of E-Waste

E-waste management involves the efficient disposal of electronic waste (e-waste) to minimize its harmful effects on humans and the environment.

While it is impossible to completely eliminate e-waste, several steps can be taken to mitigate its impact. The most effective strategies for e-waste management are Reduce, Reuse, and Recycle.

1. **Reduce**
   - To limit e-waste generation, consumers should buy electronic and electrical devices based on their actual needs. Avoid impulse purchases or acquiring unnecessary gadgets.
   - Use devices to their full capacity and avoid premature disposal.
   - Proper maintenance can extend the lifespan of electronic devices, reducing the frequency of replacements.
2. **Reuse**
   - Devices that are still operational should be reused, either by donating them to those in need or selling them.

- This process involves repairing and selling older electronic goods at lower prices, allowing them to serve a new purpose.

3. **Recycle**
   - Recycling involves converting electronic devices that cannot be repaired or reused into materials that can be repurposed.
   - Many companies and non-governmental organizations (NGOs) facilitate recycling by offering door-to-door pickup services for e-waste, making it easier for households and offices to dispose of their unwanted electronics responsibly.

E-Waste Management in India

E-waste management is a critical environmental issue in India, governed by a combination of legal frameworks and guidelines designed to mitigate pollution caused by electronic waste.

The Environmental Protection Act, 1986, serves as the cornerstone of this effort, introducing the "Polluter Pays Principle."

This principle holds that any entity causing pollution is liable for the costs associated with restoring the environment.

Key Provisions and Guidelines

1. **Responsibility of Manufacturers** According to the Central Pollution Control Board (CPCB), manufacturers of electronic equipment bear the responsibility for the safe disposal of their products once they become e-waste.

   This legal accountability encourages manufacturers to design products that are easier to recycle and dispose of safely.
2. **CPCB Guidelines** The CPCB has established a formal set of guidelines for the handling and disposal of e-waste.

   These guidelines detail the necessary steps for proper recycling and disposal to minimize environmental impact.
3. **Department of Information Technology (DIT)** The DIT, under the Ministry of Communication and Information Technology, has issued a comprehensive technical guide titled "Environmental Management for the Information Technology Industry in India." This guide outlines best practices for recycling and reusing e-waste within the IT sector, promoting environmentally responsible behavior.
4. **Awareness and Recycling Programs** To raise awareness among consumers regarding e-waste recycling, many prominent smartphone and computer manufacturers have initiated various recycling programs.

   These programs aim to educate consumers on how to dispose of their electronic devices responsibly and highlight the importance of recycling.

7.9 Impact on Health Due to Digital Device Usage

As digital technologies have become integral to various fields, our time spent in front of screens—whether on mobile phones, laptops, desktops, televisions, gaming consoles, or music devices—has significantly increased.

This shift has brought about several health concerns, both physical and mental, primarily due to improper posture and excessive screen time.

Physical Health Concerns

1. **Ergonomics and Posture** Ergonomics is the science of designing and arranging workspaces, including furniture and equipment, to ensure safety and comfort for users.

   Proper ergonomics can reduce bodily strain, fatigue, and the risk of injuries caused by prolonged device use.

   Maintaining an ergonomic setup involves adjusting the viewing distance and angle of screens, which can alleviate eye strain, backaches, and neck pain.
2. **Eye Strain** Extended screen time can lead to symptoms such as dry, watery, or itchy eyes, commonly referred to as digital eye strain. To combat this, it's recommended to periodically focus on distant objects and take breaks for outdoor activities.
3. **Musculoskeletal Issues** Poorly arranged workspaces can result in bad posture, leading to chronic conditions such as backaches, neck and shoulder pain. Additionally, overuse of keyboards (both

physical and virtual) not aligned ergonomically can cause painful conditions in the wrists and fingers.

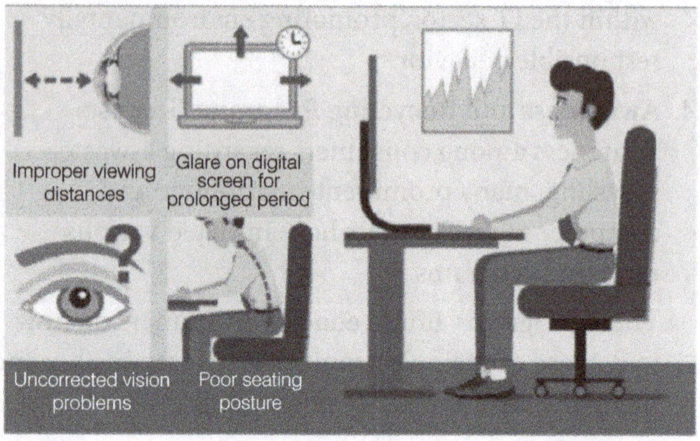

Mental and Psychological Health Concerns

1. **Addiction and Dependence** Excessive time spent online can lead to addictive behaviors, negatively impacting mental health and overall well-being.
2. **Stress and Fatigue** Continuous interaction with digital devices can contribute to stress and physical fatigue. The combination of mental strain from prolonged focus and physical discomfort can exacerbate feelings of exhaustion.
3. **Obesity** A sedentary lifestyle associated with excessive screen time can lead to weight gain and obesity, further affecting physical and mental health.

Quick Test 4

1. What is e-waste?
2. Name two toxic substances commonly found in e-waste.
3. How does e-waste contribute to air pollution?
4. What principle holds manufacturers responsible for the disposal of their electronic products in India?
5. Mention one guideline provided by the CPCB for e-waste management.

NCERT Folder

1. After practicals, Atharv left the computer laboratory but forgot to sign off from his email account. Later, his classmate Revaan started using the same computer. He is now logged in as Atharv. He sends inflammatory email messages to few of his classmates using Atharv's email account. Revaan's activity is an example of which of the following cyber crime? Justify your answer.

(a) Hacking (b) Identity theft

(c) Cyber bullying (d) Plagiarism

Ans. (b) Revaan's actions constitute identity theft because he is impersonating Atharv by sending emails from his account without permission, effectively using Atharv's identity for malicious purposes.

2. Rishika found a crumpled paper under her desk. She picked it up and opened it. It contained some text which was struck off thrice. But she could still figure out easily that the struck off text was the email ID and password of Garvit, her classmate. What is ethically correct for Rishika to do?

(a) Inform Garvit so that he may change his password.

(b) Give the password of Garvit's email ID to all other classmates.

(c) Use Garvit's password to access his account.

Ans. (a) Ethically, Rishika should inform Garvit about the discovered information so he can take necessary actions to protect his account, rather than sharing the password or using it for unauthorized access.

3. Suhana is down with fever. So, she decided not to go to school tomorrow. Next day, in the evening she called up her classmate, Shaurya and enquired about the computer class. She also requested him to explain the concept. Shaurya said, "Mam taught us how to use tuples in python". Further, he generously said, "Give me some time, I will email you the material which will help you to understand tuples in python". Shaurya quickly downloaded a 2-minute clip from the Internet explaining the concept of tuples in python. Using video editor, he added the text "Prepared by Shaurya" in the downloaded video clip. Then, he emailed the modified video clip to Suhana. This act of Shaurya is an example of —

(a) Fair use (b) Hacking

(c) Copyright infringement (d) Cyber crime

Ans. (c) Shaurya's action of downloading a video, modifying it by adding his own text, and sharing it without permission from the original creator is an example of copyright infringement. This violates the intellectual property rights of the original creator of the video.

4. After a fight with your friend, you did the following activities. Which of these activities is not an example of cyber bullying?

(a) **You sent an email to your friend with a message saying that "I am sorry".**

(b) **You sent a threatening message to your friend saying "Do not try to call or talk to me".**

(c) **You created an embarrassing picture of your friend and uploaded on your account on a social networking site.**

Ans. (a) This action is an attempt to apologize and mend the relationship, which is not an example of cyberbullying. Cyberbullying involves using digital platforms to harm, threaten, or embarrass someone, which applies to the other two options (b and c).

5. Sourabh has to prepare a project on "Digital India Initiatives". He decides to get information from the Internet. He downloads three web pages (webpage 1, webpage 2, webpage 3) containing information on Digital India Initiatives. Which of the following steps taken by Sourabh is an example of plagiarism or copyright infringement? Give justification in support of your answer.

(a) **He read a paragraph on " Digital India Initiatives" from webpage 1 and rephrased it in his own words. He finally pasted the rephrased paragraph in his project.**

(b) **He downloaded three images of " Digital India Initiatives" from webpage 2. He made a collage for his project using these images.**

(c) **He downloaded "Digital India Initiative" icon from web page 3 and pasted it on the front page of his project report.**

Ans. (b) Downloading and using images without permission or proper attribution violates copyright laws.

(c) Using logos or icons without authorization is a form of copyright infringement, as these are often protected by intellectual property laws.

However, (a) is not plagiarism because Sourabh rephrased the content in his own words, which is allowed as long as proper attribution is given.

6. Match the following:

	Column A		Column B
A.	Plagiarism	(i)	Fakers, by offering special rewards or money prize asked for personal information, such as bank account information.
B.	Hacking	(ii)	Copy and paste information from the Internet into your report and then organise it.
C.	Credit card fraud	(iii)	The trail that is created when a person uses the Internet.
D.	Digital Foot Print	(iv)	Breaking into computers to read private emails and other files.

Ans. A → (ii), B → (iv), C → (i), D → (iii)

7. You got the below shown SMS from your bank querying a recent transaction. Answer the following —

(a) **Will you SMS your pin number to the given contact number?**

(b) **Will you call the bank helpline number to recheck the validity of the SMS received?**

Ans. (a) No (b) Yes

8. Preeti celebrated her birthday with her family. She was excited to share the moments with her friend Himanshu. She uploaded selected images of her birthday party on a social networking site so that Himanshu can see them. After few days, Preeti had a fight with Himanshu. Next morning, she deleted her birthday photographs from that social networking site, so that Himanshu cannot access them. Later in the evening, to her surprise, she saw that one of the images which she had already deleted from the social networking site was available with their common friend Gayatri. She hurriedly enquired Gayatri "Where did you get this picture from?". Gayatri replied "Himanshu forwarded this image few minutes back". Help Preeti to get answers for the following questions. Give justification for your answers so that Preeti can understand it clearly.

(a) **How could Himanshu access an image which I had already deleted?**

(b) **Can anybody else also access these deleted images?**

(c) **Had these images not been deleted from my digital footprint?**

Ans. (a) Even though you deleted the image from your profile, it may still exist on the platform's servers or in other users' accounts. Himanshu received the photo before you deleted it, so he still has access to it.

(b) Yes, if the deleted images were shared with other friends before deletion, they can still access them. Deleting an image from your profile does not remove it from those who received or saved it.

(c) Correct, deleting an image from your account does not eliminate it from your digital footprint. Copies may still exist online, including on other users' devices or cloud storage.

9. The school offers wireless facility (wifi) to the Computer Science students of Class XI. For communication, the network security staff of the school have a registered URL schoolwifi.edu. On 17 September 2017, the following email was mass distributed to all the Computer Science students of Class XI. The email claimed that the password of the students was about to expire. Instructions were given to go to URL to renew their password within 24 hours.

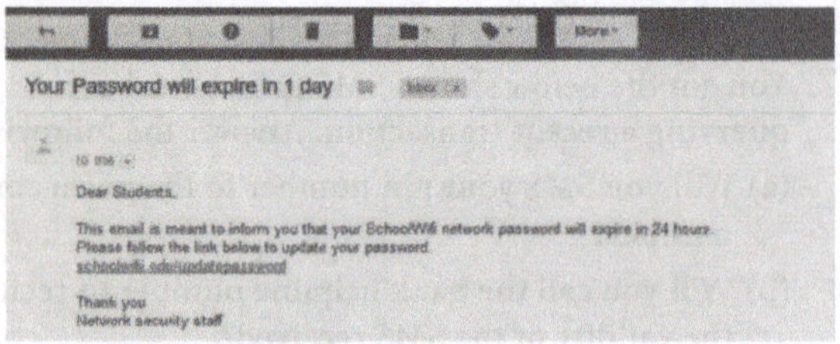

(a) Do you find any discrepancy in this email?

(b) What will happen if the student will click on the given URL?

(c) Is the email an example of cyber crime? If yes, then specify which type of cyber crime is it. Justify your answer.

Ans. (a) Yes

(b) If the student clicks on the URL, they may be directed to a fraudulent website designed to capture their personal information or credentials.

(c) Yes, the email is an example of cybercrime, specifically phishing, as it seeks to deceive individuals into providing sensitive information by impersonating a legitimate source.

10. You are planning to go for a vacation. You surfed the Internet to get answers for the following queries —

(a) Weather conditions

(b) Availability of air tickets and fares

(c) Places to visit

(d) Best hotel deals

Which of your above mentioned actions might have created a digital footprint?

Ans. Surfing the Internet for weather conditions, checking air ticket availability and fares, and researching places to visit and hotel deals all contribute to your digital footprint. These actions leave behind data that can be tracked and analyzed by websites and online services.

11. How would you recognise if one of your friends is being cyber bullied?

(a) Cite the online activities which would help you detect that your friend is being cyber bullied?

(b) What provisions are in IT Act 2000, (amended in 2008) to combact such situations.

Ans. (a) Signs of cyberbullying include sudden changes in online behavior, withdrawal from social media, or excessive secrecy about online activities. Look for negative comments, harassment in messages, or derogatory posts about your friend.

(b) The IT Act 2000, amended in 2008, includes provisions against cyberbullying, such as Section 66A (sending offensive messages) and Section 67 (publishing or transmitting obscene material), allowing for legal action against offenders.

12. Write the differences between the following —

(a) Copyrights and Patents

(b) Plagiarism and Copyright infringement

(c) Non-ethical hacking and Ethical hacking

(d) Active and Passive footprints

(e) Free software and Free and open source software

Ans. (a) Copyrights protect original works of authorship, while patents protect inventions and processes for a limited time.

(b) Plagiarism is using someone else's work without credit, whereas copyright infringement is the unauthorized use of copyrighted material.

(c) Non-ethical hacking involves unauthorized access for malicious purposes, while ethical hacking is conducted to improve security with permission.

(d) Active footprints involve direct interaction with the target system, whereas passive footprints gather information without direct interaction.

(e) Free software allows users to run, modify, and share it freely, while free and open source software also provides access to the source code for modification and distribution.

13. If you plan to use a short text from an article on the web, what steps must you take in order to credit the sources used?

Ans. Always provide proper attribution by including the author's name and the publication date, and link back to the original source if possible.

14. When you search online for pictures, how will you find pictures that are available in the free public domain. How can those pictures be used in your project without copyright violations?

Ans. Use search filters for "public domain" or "Creative Commons" licenses to find free images, and ensure to follow the usage guidelines specified for each image.

15. Describe why it is important to secure your wireless router at home. Search the Internet to find the rules to create a reasonably secure password. Create an imaginary password for your home router. Will you share your password for home router with following people. Justify your answer.

(a) Parents **(b) Friends**

(c) Neighbours **(d) Home tutors**

Ans. Securing your wireless router is essential to protect your home network from unauthorized access, data theft, and potential cyber threats. A secure password should include a mix of upper and lowercase letters, numbers, and special characters, ideally at least 12 characters long.

Imaginary Password: W1r3l3ss!S3cur3$2024

Sharing Justification:

(a) **Parents** Yes, they need access for online activities.

(b) **Friends** Maybe, if they visit often and require internet access.

(c) **Neighbours** No, to prevent unauthorized access to your network.

(d) **Home tutors** Yes, if they require internet access for tutoring.

16. List down the steps you need to take in order to ensure

(a) your computer is in good working condition for a longer time.

(b) smart and safe Internet surfing.

Ans. (a) Regularly update software, perform antivirus scans, clean hardware components, and ensure proper ventilation.

(b) Use strong, unique passwords, avoid clicking on suspicious links, and utilize privacy settings on social media and browsers.

17. What is data privacy? Websites that you visit collect what type of information about you?

Ans. Data Privacy refers to the protection of personal information that individuals share online. It involves controlling how personal data is collected, used, and shared by organizations.

Websites typically collect the following types of information about you:

1. **Personal Information** Name, email address, phone number, etc.
2. **Browsing History** Pages visited, time spent, and interactions on the site.
3. **Device Information** IP address, device type, operating system, and browser type.
4. **Location Data** Geolocation based on IP address or GPS.
5. **Cookies and Tracking Data** Information stored on your device to track your activity across sessions and sites.

18. In the computer science class, Sunil and Jagdish were assigned the following task by their teacher.

(a) Sunil was asked to find information about "India, a Nuclear power". He was asked to use Google Chrome browser and prepare his report using Google Docs.

(b) Jagdish was asked to find information about "Digital India". He was asked to use Mozilla Firefox browser and prepare his report using Libre Office Writer.

What is the difference between technologies used by Sunil and Jagdish?

Ans. Sunil used Google Chrome and Google Docs, which are proprietary software, while Jagdish used Mozilla Firefox and LibreOffice Writer, which are open-source software.

19. Cite examples depicting that you were a victim of following cyber crime. Also, cite provisions in IT Act to deal with such a cyber crime.

(a) Identity theft **(b) Credit card account theft**

Ans. (a) Someone used my personal information to create a fake social media profile. IT Act Section 66C deals with punishment for identity theft.

(b) My credit card details were stolen and used for unauthorized transactions. IT Act Section 66C and Section 43 address credit card fraud and unauthorized access.

20. Neerja is a student of Class XI. She has opted for Computer Science. Neerja prepared the project assigned to her. She mailed it to her teacher. The snapshot of that email is shown below.

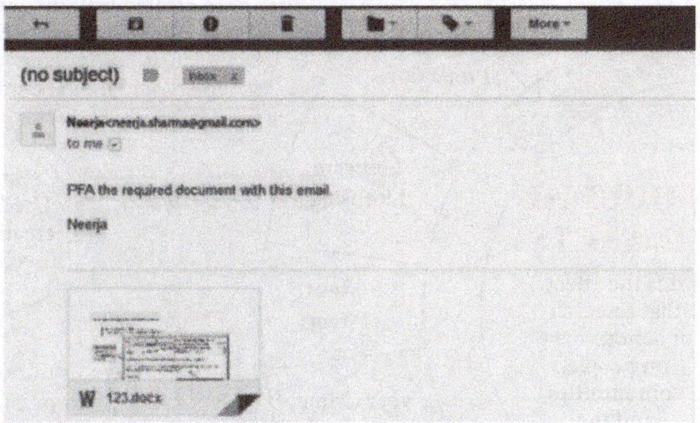

Find out which of the following email etiquettes are missing in it. Justify your answer.

(a) Subject of the mail **(b) Formal greeting**

(c) Self-explanatory terms **(d) Identity of the sender**

(e) Regards

Ans. The following email etiquettes are missing in the provided screenshot:

1. **Subject of the Email** This is essentially the title of the email. A well-crafted subject line encourages readers to open your message.
2. **Formal Greeting** The screenshot lacks a formal greeting, as it does not include words like "Hi," "Hello," "Dear," or "Respected."
3. **Self-Explanatory Terms** The email screenshot does not include clear, self-explanatory terms, making it difficult to understand the email's content at a glance.
4. **Identity of the Sender** The screenshot only displays the sender's name, which does not fully establish their identity.
5. **Closing Regards** Including a closing line such as "Regards" shows respect towards the recipient, which is absent in the screenshot.

Mind Map

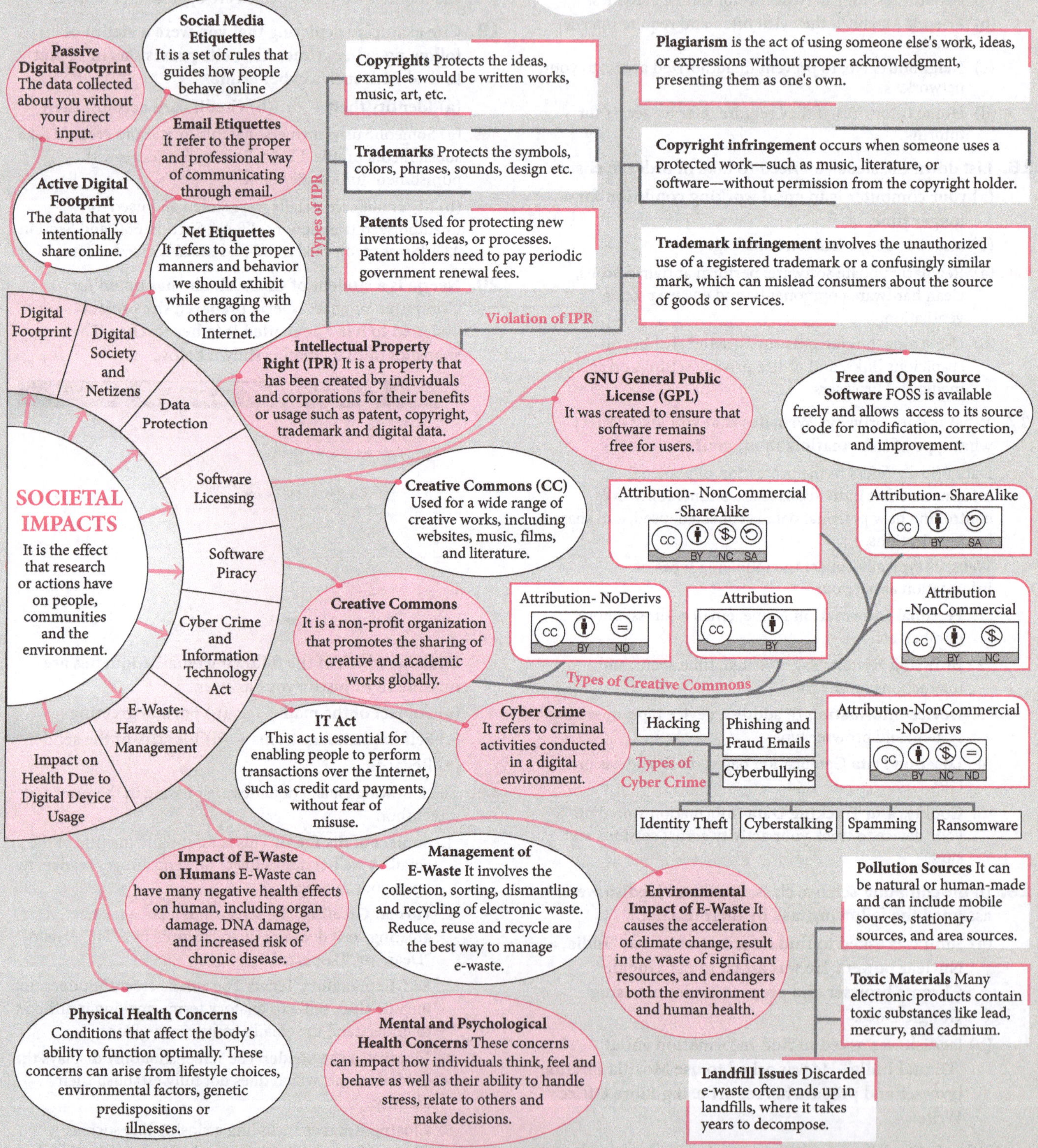

SOCIETAL IMPACTS
It is the effect that research or actions have on people, communities and the environment.
Digital Footprint
Digital Society and Netizens
Data Protection
Software Licensing
Software Piracy
Cyber Crime and Information Technology Act
E-Waste: Hazards and Management
Impact on Health Due to Digital Device Usage
Passive Digital Footprint The data collected about you without your direct input.
Active Digital Footprint The data that you intentionally share online.
Social Media Etiquettes It is a set of rules that guides how people behave online
Email Etiquettes It refer to the proper and professional way of communicating through email.
Net Etiquettes It refers to the proper manners and behavior we should exhibit while engaging with others on the Internet.
Intellectual Property Right (IPR) It is a property that has been created by individuals and corporations for their benefits or usage such as patent, copyright, trademark and digital data.
Types of IPR
Copyrights Protects the ideas, examples would be written works, music, art, etc.
Trademarks Protects the symbols, colors, phrases, sounds, design etc.
Patents Used for protecting new inventions, ideas, or processes. Patent holders need to pay periodic government renewal fees.
Violation of IPR
Plagiarism is the act of using someone else's work, ideas, or expressions without proper acknowledgment, presenting them as one's own.
Copyright infringement occurs when someone uses a protected work—such as music, literature, or software—without permission from the copyright holder.
Trademark infringement involves the unauthorized use of a registered trademark or a confusingly similar mark, which can mislead consumers about the source of goods or services.
GNU General Public License (GPL) It was created to ensure that software remains free for users.
Free and Open Source Software FOSS is available freely and allows access to its source code for modification, correction, and improvement.
Creative Commons (CC) Used for a wide range of creative works, including websites, music, films, and literature.
Creative Commons It is a non-profit organization that promotes the sharing of creative and academic works globally.
Types of Creative Commons
Attribution- NonCommercial -ShareAlike
CC BY NC SA
Attribution- ShareAlike
CC BY SA
Attribution- NoDerivs
CC BY ND
Attribution
CC BY
Attribution -NonCommercial
CC BY NC
Attribution-NonCommercial -NoDerivs
CC BY NC ND
IT Act This act is essential for enabling people to perform transactions over the Internet, such as credit card payments, without fear of misuse.
Cyber Crime It refers to criminal activities conducted in a digital environment.
Types of Cyber Crime
Hacking
Phishing and Fraud Emails
Cyberbullying
Identity Theft
Cyberstalking
Spamming
Ransomware
Impact of E-Waste on Humans E-Waste can have many negative health effects on human, including organ damage. DNA damage, and increased risk of chronic disease.
Management of E-Waste It involves the collection, sorting, dismantling and recycling of electronic waste. Reduce, reuse and recycle are the best way to manage e-waste.
Environmental Impact of E-Waste It causes the acceleration of climate change, result in the waste of significant resources, and endangers both the environment and human health.
Pollution Sources It can be natural or human-made and can include mobile sources, stationary sources, and area sources.
Toxic Materials Many electronic products contain toxic substances like lead, mercury, and cadmium.
Landfill Issues Discarded e-waste often ends up in landfills, where it takes years to decompose.
Physical Health Concerns Conditions that affect the body's ability to function optimally. These concerns can arise from lifestyle choices, environmental factors, genetic predispositions or illnesses.
Mental and Psychological Health Concerns These concerns can impact how individuals think, feel and behave as well as their ability to handle stress, relate to others and make decisions.

EXAM PATTERN QUESTIONS

Objective Type Questions

Multiple Choice Questions

1. In which of the following, users share their activities intentionally like social media activities, online chatting?

(a) Passive data trace (b) Active digital footprint
(c) Both (a) and (b) (d) None of these

2. Rama was unable to understand how the recruiters were able to know about her digital activity when she has not shared anything with them. The recruiters might have checked .... of Rama. Competency Based Que.

(a) Carbon Footprint (b) Water Footprint
(c) Online print (d) Digital Footprint

3. The digital footprint that we leave online unintentionally is called CBSE 2023

(a) active digital footprint (b) passive digital footprint
(c) true digital footprint (d) false digital footprint

4. ___________ is the trail of data we leave behind when we visit any website (or use any online application or portal) to fill-in data or perform any transaction. CBSE SQP 2022-23

(a) Offline phishing (b) Offline footprint
(c) Digital footprint (d) Digital phishing

5. The trail that is automatically created, when a person uses the Internet on any digital devices like laptops, smart phones, tablets etc is called CBSE 2021-22 Term I

(a) cyberbullying (b) phishing
(c) digital footprint (d) digital activity

6. We should exhibit proper manners and etiquettes while being online. Choose the right netiquette(s). CBSE SQP 2021-22 Term I

(a) Avoid cyber bullying
(b) Respect otherís privacy
(c) No copyright violation
(d) All of the above

7. What is plagiarism? CBSE SQP 2024-25

(a) Using copyrighted material without giving proper acknowledgement to the source
(b) Downloading illegal software.
(c) Spreading misinformation online.
(d) Hacking into computer systems.

8. Ridhima purchased a license for a copy of a software and made additional copies without the permission of the copyright owner. This act of hers is known as .... Competency Based Que.

(a) Trademark Infringement (b) Identity Theft
(c) Copyright Infringement (d) Patent

9. What can an individual do to enhance the privacy of data stored digitally? CBSE 2024

(a) Share sensitive information on social media platforms.
(b) Use your date of birth as your password.
(c) Regularly update software installed on your device.
(d) Download and install software from unknown sources.

10. .... is the gaining of unauthorized access to data in a computer system. CBSE 2024

(a) Phishing (b) Plagiarism
(c) Hacking (d) Copyright violation

11. .... help in data protection through copyrights, patents and trademarks. CBSE 2024

(a) Data Privacy Right
(b) Right to Innovation
(c) Intellectual Property Rights (IPR)
(d) Right to Data Protection

12. Copyright, Patent and Trademark comes under: CBSE SQP 2023-24

(a) Intellectual Property Right
(b) Individual Property Right
(c) Industrial Property Right
(d) International Property Right

13. Ramandeep is a young woman with great aspirations and has a good team of like-minded people. She along with her team members started a company to sell handicrafts online and also designed a logo for their company. What type of intellectual property does this logo represent? Competency Based Que.

(a) Patents (b) Copyright
(c) Design (d) Trademark

14. Legal term to describe the rights of a creator of original creative or artistic work is: CBSE SQP 2022-23

(a) Copyright (b) Copyleft
(c) GPL (d) FOSS

15. **The rights of the owner of information to decide, how much information is to be shared/exchanged /distributed, are collectively known as ______.** CBSE 2021-22 Term I

(a) Intelligent Portable Rights
(b) Intellectual Property Rights
(c) Interactive Property Rights
(d) Instance Portability Rights

16. **Raheem created a unique computer software and wants to protect his creation from being copied or used without his permission. He is considering to apply for legal protection. Which type of intellectual property protection should Raheem apply for, to safeguard his software?** CBSE 2025

(a) Copyright (b) Plagiarism
(c) Trademark (d) Lease

17. **Which of the following is an example of copy left license?**

(a) GPL (b) BSD
(c) MIT (d) All of these

18. **The software that is free for anyone, and its source code is available for access, modification, correction, and improvement is called ....** CBSE 2024

(a) Proprietary software (b) Commercial software
(c) FOSS (d) Copyrighted software

19. **________ is not a FOSS tool.** CBSE SQP 2023-24

(a) Libre Office
(b) Mozilla Firefox
(c) Google Chrome
(d) Python

20. **Linux, MySQL and Mozilla Firefox software come under ________ category.** CBSE SQP 2021-22 Term I

(a) proprietary (b) FOSS
(c) freeware (d) shareware

21. **________ is a non-profit organization that aims to build a publicly accessible global platform where a range of creative and academic work is shared freely.** CBSE SQP 2023-24

(a) Creative Cost (b) Critical Commons
(c) Creative Commons (d) Creative Common

22. **There is only 1 day left for Ravisha to submit her Science project. Therefore, she performed the following activities to complete her task. Which of the following activities can be considered as plagiarism?** CBSE 2021-22 Term I, Competency Based Que.

(a) Downloaded the images that were marked as CC and pasted in her project file.
(b) Copied the content from some website and pasted in her file.
(c) Copied the content from the website and gave references about the same in the project.
(d) Downloaded and installed the open source software for typing the synopsis.

23. **Which of the following is one of the strongest crime committed in the virtual world?**

(a) Cyber stalking (b) Cyber bullying
(c) Cyber trolls (d) None of these

24. **Which of the following term used to describe any fraudulent business or scheme that takes money or other goods from an unsuspecting person?**

(a) Spreading rumours online (b) Illegal downloads
(c) Scams (d) Cyber stalking

25. **Identify the type of cybercrime that involves sending fraudulent emails to deceive individuals into revealing sensitive information.** CBSE SQP 2024-25

(a) Hacking (b) Phishing
(c) Cyberbullying (d) Cyberstalking

26. **By restricting the server and encrypting the data, a software company's server is unethically accessed in order to obtain sensitive information. The attacker blackmails the company to pay money for getting access to the data, and threatens to publish sensitive information unless price is paid. This kind of attack is known as:** CBSE SQP 2023-24, Competency Based Que.

(a) Phishing (b) Identity Theft
(c) Plagiarism (d) Ransomware

27. **Which of the following is a type of cybercrime where objectionable and demeaning comments are posted on social media platform about a person, such that he/she is mentally harassed?** CBSE 2023

(a) Phishing (b) Hacking
(c) Cyber bullying (d) Identity theft

28. **Which of the following is not a type of cyber crime?** CBSE SQP 2022-23

(a) Data theft
(b) Installing antivirus for protection
(c) Forgery
(d) Cyber bullying

29. **Abdul deleted all his chats from all his social media accounts and he thinks that all his traces are deleted completely. Is he right in thinking so?** CBSE 2021-22 Term I, Competency Based Que.

(a) Yes (b) No
(c) May be (d) Not sure

30. **............ is a cybercrime in which a target or targets are contacted by E-mail, telephone or text message by someone posing as a legitimate institution to lure**

individuals into providing sensitive data such as personally identifiable information, banking and credit card details and passwords. **CBSE SQP 2021-22 Term I**

(a) Plagiarism (b) Phishing
(c) Cyber stalking (d) Hacking

31. **Rohit forgot his laptop in his car and when he came back, he found his laptop was missing. This act is** **Competency Based Que.**

(a) cybercrime (b) phishing
(c) theft (d) plagiarism

32. **Priya received an email that appeared to be from her bank, asking her to update her account information by clicking on a link. She clicked the link to enter her details, but immediately after, some amount was debited from her account. What type of cybercrime did Priya fall victim to?** **CBSE 2025**

(a) Cyber stalking (b) Phishing
(c) Fishing (d) Cyber bullying

33. **Which section was introduced in IT Act amendment 2008?**

(a) 66 (b) 66A (c) 66B (d) 66C

34. **Primary law in India for matters related to e-commerce and cyber crime is** **CBSE 2023**

(a) IT Act 1995 (b) IT Act 2000
(c) IT Act 1998 (d) IT Act 2010

35. **______ may also be defined as discarded computers, office electronic equipment, mobile phones, television sets etc.**

(a) Electronic devices (b) E-waste
(c) Electronic worm (d) None of these

36. **e-waste refers to:** **CBSE SQP 2024-25**

(a) Software that has become obsolete
(b) Data that has been deleted from a storage device
(c) Viruses that infect computers
(d) Electronic devices that are no longer in use

37. **When e-waste such as electronic circuit boards are burnt for disposal, the elements contained in them create a harmful chemical called _______ which causes skin diseases, allergies and an increased risk of lung cancer.** **CBSE SQP 2023-24**

(a) Hydrogen (b) Beryllium
(c) Chlorine (d) Oxygen

38. **E-waste is responsible for the degradation of our environment if not properly treated or disposed of. Some of the feasible methods of E-waste management are reduce, _____ and recycle.** **CBSE 2023**

(a) reuse (b) recheck
(c) resubmit (d) regular

39. **What is an example of e-waste?** **CBSE SQP 2022-23**

(a) A ripened mango (b) Unused old shoes
(c) Unused old computers (d) Empty cola cans

40. **Feasible method(s) to manage e-Waste.** **CBSE SQP 2021-22 Term I**

(a) Reducing (b) Reusing
(c) Recycling (d) All of these

41. **E-waste is becoming one of the fastest growing environmental hazards in the world today. If it is not properly treated or disposed of it can cause serious health hazards, therefore the _____ has issued a formal set of guidelines for proper handling and disposal of e-Waste.** **CBSE 2021-22 Term I**

(a) Central Pollution Control Board (CPCB)
(b) Department of Information Technology (DIT)
(c) Waste Electrical and Electronic Equipment (WEEE)
(d) Information Communication Technology (ICT)

42. **With the outset of Covid-19, schools started online classes but due to continuous online classes, student's health issues also started. Health practitioner advised the parents to follow a few health tips. Which of the following health tip should not be suggested?** **Competency Based Que.**

(a) The sitting posture should be correct.
(b) Breaks should be taken in between the online classes.
(c) To protect the eyes the gadgets should be placed above eye level.
(d) Wash the eyes regularly.

43. **Excessive screen time and poor posture can lead to:** **CBSE 2025**

(a) Faster Internet Speeds
(b) Eye strain and other health issues
(c) Better vision and bone density
(d) Improved physical health

Fill in the Blanks

44. A __________ is a unique data trace of a user's activities, actions, communications or transition in digital media.

45. The word netiquette is a combination of ________ and ________.

46. _________ is the process of safeguarding important information from corruption, compromise or loss.

47. Directly copying text, word is called __________.

48. Plagiarism occurs due to lack of __________.

49. _______ gives full control to the patentee to decide whether or how the invention can be used by others.

50. _________ arise when piracy occurs between companies.

51. The hallmark of __________ grants the use of one or more copies of software.

52. __________ refers to the unauthorised duplication of computer software.

53. __________ refers to attempts to gain information from undisclosed areas.

54. Any crime committed using computers and internet is termed as __________.

55. __________ is a form of cybercrime that takes place online when a criminal used technology to harass or threaten a person or an organisation.

56. __________ comprises of the electronic products that are no longer useful to us.

57. The E-waste management involves proper __________ and __________ of the disposed material.

State whether True and False

58. Netiquette is short for Network Etiquette.

59. If someone comes out with a new idea/original idea, then it is that person's intellectual property.

60. Selling of software illegally for temporary use as on rent basis is called soft lifting.

61. Criminals who perform those illegal activities are often referred to as crackers.

62. E-waste is mostly made up of metal and plastic components.

Assertion and Reason Based Questions

Assertion (A) and Reason (R) based questions. Mark the correct choice as

(a) Both (A) and (R) are true and (R) is the correct explanation for (A).

(b) Both (A) and (R) are true and (R) is not the correct explanation for (A).

(c) (A) is true and (R) is false.

(d) (A) is false but (R) is true.

63. **Assertion (A)** Digital communication etiquette only applies to formal communication channels such as emails and official meetings.

Reason (R) Digital communication encompasses various platforms including social networking sites, texting, and instant messaging.

64. **Assertion (A)** Software licenses provide users with the right to make copies of the software without violating copyrights.

Reason (R) Software licensing terms usually include fair use of the software, limitations of liability, warranties, and protections.

65. **Assertion (A)** Creative Commons licenses allow creators to retain all rights to their works while permitting others to use them.

Reason (R) CC licenses enable free distribution, allowing anyone to download and share the work without permission.

66. **Assertion (A)** Ethical hackers are individuals who use their skills to harm systems and exploit vulnerabilities.

Reason (R) Ethical hackers aim to improve system security by identifying weaknesses.

67. **Assertion (A)** Ransomware attacks often involve the encryption of user data and demand a ransom for its release.

Reason (R) Ransomware can infect systems through downloading software from untrustworthy sources.

68. **Assertion (A)** Cyber Bullying can have serious, emotional and psychological effects on victims.

Reason (R) Online Bullying is not a crime while offline bullying is a crime. **CBSE 2024**

69. **Assertion (A)** E-waste management is critical to minimizing environmental and societal damage.

Reason (R) E-waste constitutes over 5% of municipal solid waste, leading to pollution and health risks.

70. **Assertion (A)** Lead poisoning from e-waste affects only adults and does not pose risks to children.

Reason (R) Children are particularly vulnerable to lead poisoning, which can lead to developmental issues and learning disabilities.

71. **Assertion (A)** The Environmental Protection Act, 1986, does not address e-waste management in India.

Reason (R) The Act introduces the "Polluter Pays Principle," making manufacturers responsible for e-waste disposal.

Answers

1. (b) Active digital footprint
2. (d) Digital Footprint
3. (b) passive digital footprint
4. (c) Digital footprint
5. (c) digital footprint
6. (d) All of the above
7. (a)Using copyrighted material without giving proper acknowledgement to the source
8. (c) Copyright Infringement
9. (c) Regularly update software installed on your device.
10. (c) Hacking
11. (c) Intellectual Property Rights (IPR)
12. (a) Intellectual Property Right
13. (d) Trademark
14. (a) Copyright
15. (b) Intellectual Property Rights
16. (a) Copyright
17. (a) GPL
18. (c) FOSS
19. (c) Google Chrome
20. (b) FOSS
21. (c) Creative Commons
22. (a) Downloaded the images that were marked as CC and pasted in her project file.
23. (b) Cyber bullying
24. (c) Scams
25. (b) Phishing
26. (d) Ransomware
27. (c) Cyber bullying
28. (b) Installing antivirus for protection
29. (b) No
30. (b) Phishing
31. (c) theft
32. (b) Phising
33. (b) 66A
34. (b) IT Act 2000
35. (b) E-waste
36. (d)Electronic devices that are no longer in use
37. (b) Beryllium
38. (a) reuse
39. (c) Unused old computers
40. (d) All of these
41. (a) Central Pollution Control Board (CPCB)
42. (c) To protect the eyes the gadgets should be placed above eye level.
43. (b) Eye Stain and other health issue
44. Digital footprint
45. net and etiquette
46. Data protection
47. Plagiarism
48. Knowledge
49. Patent
50. Digital property rights
51. proprietary software license
52. Software piracy
53. Hacking
54. cyber crime
55. Cyber stalking
56. E-waste
57. recycling, recovery
58. True
59. True
60. False
61. True
62. True
63. (d) (A) is false but (R) is true.
64. (a) Both (A) and (R) are true and (R) is the correct explanation for (A).
65. (d) (A) is false and (R) is true.
66. (d) (A) is false and (R) is true.
67. (a) Both (A) and (R) are true and (R) is the correct explanation for (A).
68. (c) (A) is true and (R) is false.
69. (a) Both (A) and (R) are true, and (R) is the correct explanation for (A).
70. (d) (A) is false and (R) is true.
71. (d) (A) is false, but (R) is true.

Subjective Type Questions

Very Short Answer Type Questions

1. Now-a-days all of us frequently use social media to connect with our friends. Give any two netiquettes that we should follow while communicating on social media. **Competency Based Que.**

Ans. (i) Respect other's privacy by not sharing personal information, photos or videos that another person may not want published online.

(ii) Avoid replying to negative comments with more negative comments.

2. Mention any four net etiquettes. **CBSE SQP 2022-2023**

Ans. The four net etiquettes are:

(i) No copyright violation

(ii) Share the expertise with others on the internet

(iii) Avoid cyber bullying

(iv) Respect other's privacy and diversity

3. What is the importance of data protection?

Ans. The importance of data protection increases as the amount of data created and stored continues to grow at unprecedented rates.

4. Explain the controls of intellectual property rights.

Ans. (i) Avoid joint ownership
(ii) Get exact match domains
(iii) Safeguard with strong access control

5. Define the content management system of digital property right.

Ans. Content management system is the back end of our website, check who has access to this section of our website, and make sure that they don't have unrestricted access to the site.

6. Name three types of law that can help to restrict software piracy.

Ans. The following are the three types of law that can help to restrict software piracy
(i) Copyright
(ii) Patent
(iii) Trademark

7. What are intellectual property rights (IPR), and why are they important in the digital world?

Ans. **Intellectual Property Rights (IPR)** These are legal rights that protect the creations of the human intellect. The nature of these works can be artistic, literary or technical etc.

Importance in the digital world These rights help prevent the unauthorized use or reproduction of digital content and ensure that creators are fairly compensated and incentivized for their original work.

8. Explain plagiarism with an example. **CBSE 2023**

Ans. Plagiarism is an act of copying another person's idea, words or work and pretend that they are our own.
The intentions behind plagiarism could be malicious or it could be done accidently.
e.g. A technical writer copies chunks of wording from documentation that she finds online for several products similar to the one she is writing about.

9. Give the examples of permissive license.

Ans. Examples of permissive license are MIT license, BSD license, Apache license etc.

10. A small tech startup, is considering using open source software to develop their new project management tool. They are evaluating the benefits and potential challenges of adopting open source solutions. **CBSE 2025**

(i) Identify one key benefit of using open source software for the development of project management tool.

(ii) Give any two examples of open source softwares.

Ans. (i) **Key benefit of using open-source software for developing a project management tool**

Cost-effectiveness Open-source software is typically free to use, reducing the overall development costs.

(ii) **Two examples of open-source software**

1. **Linux** An open-source operating system widely used for servers and desktops.
2. **LibreOffice** A free and open-source office suite that includes word processing, spreadsheets, and presentation applications.

11. Write any one point to prevent the hacking.

Ans. Create complex password to prevent the hacking.

12. What is the use of cyber bullying?

Ans. Cyber bullying is the use of technology like the Internet, E-mail, cell phones, social media or picture to harass, threaten or target a person.

13. Which measure is used to avoid online scam?

Ans. Do not click on any link in a mail that tells you to change any of you passwords or security code.

14. What are the factors in rise of cybercrimes?

Ans.
- Spread of computers
- Increasing use to broadband
- Increasing financial motivation for computer crime.

15. What is provided by IT Act?

Ans. An IT Act provides legal recognition for transactions carried out by means of electronic data interchange and other means of electronic communication.

16. List any four benefits of e-waste management. **CBSE SQP 2022-23**

Ans. The e-waste management:
(i) Saves the environment and natural resources
(ii) Allows for recovery of precious metals
(iii) Protects public health and water quality
(iv) Saves landfill space

17. Give any two impacts on the environment that are caused when e-waste is carelessly thrown or dumped in landfills or dumping grounds. **CBSE 2025**

Ans. **Environmental Impacts of Improper E-Waste Disposal:**

1. **Soil Contamination** Toxic substances like mercury, lead, and cadmium from e-waste can leach into the soil, degrading its quality and harming plant life.
2. **Water Pollution** Hazardous chemicals from e-waste can seep into groundwater or nearby water bodies, posing risks to aquatic ecosystems and contaminating drinking water sources.

18. Sumit got good marks in all the subjects. His father gifted him a laptop. He would like to make Sumit aware of health hazards associated with inappropriate and excessive use of laptop. Help his father to list the points which he should discuss with Sumit. **Competency Based Que.**

Ans. Sumit's father should discuss risks like eye strain, posture problems, and repetitive strain injuries (RSI) due to prolonged laptop use. He should also advise taking regular breaks and maintaining ergonomic habits to prevent health issues.

19. Mention two health concerns associated with excessive use of Digital Devices.

Ans. Two health concerns associated with excessive use of digital devices are:

(i) Eye strain or Computer Vision Syndrome (CVS) due to prolonged screen time.

(ii) Musculoskeletal problems like neck and back pain from poor posture.

Short Answer Type I Questions

20. What is meant by digital footprint?

Ans. On the internet, a digital footprint is the word used to describe the trail, traces or footprints that people leave online. This is information transmitted online, such as forum registration, e-mails and attachments, uploading videos or digital images.

21. Differentiate between the active digital footprint and passive digital footprints. CBSE SQP 2023-24

Ans. **Active Digital Footprint** This is the data that users intentionally share online. It includes information posted on social media, comments on blogs, and any content created by the user, such as photos or videos. Users have control over this type of footprint.

Passive Digital Footprint This refers to the data collected about users without their direct input. It includes information like browsing history, location data, and cookies that track online behavior. Users usually have less control over this type of footprint.

22. What are the major factors that about the reasons behind plagiarism?

Ans. Following are the major factors about the reasons behind plagiarism.

(i) Being lazy
(ii) Lack of enforcement
(iii) Fear of failure
(iv) Not having enough knowledge
(v) Lack of management skills

23. Intellectual property right means that the person who produces the information is the only one who can use that information. Now, explain the need of protecting intellectual property right. Competency Based Que.

Ans. The intellectual property rights must be protected because of protecting them

(i) encourages individuals and business to create new software and new software applications, as well as improving existing applications.

(ii) ensures new ideas and technologies are widely distributed.

(iii) promotes investment in the national economy.

24. What do you understand by plagiarism? Why is it a punishable offence? Mention any two ways to avoid plagiarism. CBSE SQP 2022-23

Ans. Plagiarism is the act of using or stealing someone else's intellectual work, ideas etc. and passing it as your own work. In other words, plagiarism is a failure in giving credit to its source.

Plagiarism is a fraud and violation of Intellectual Property Rights. Since IPR holds a legal entity status, violating its owners right is a legally punishable offence.

Any two ways to avoid plagiarism:

1. Be original
2. Cite/acknowledge the source

25. Using copyright, software piracy can be stopped. How?

Ans. The copyright in the work of authorship immediately becomes the property of the author, who created the work. Only the author or those deriving their rights through the author, can rightfully claim copyright.

26. What is digital property rights? Write the names of some digital property rights.

Ans. Digital property includes data, internet accounts and other rights in the digital world, including contractual rights and intellectual property rights.

Data are the files and information stored and used by computers. Digital property right dispute arise when some form of counterfeiting or piracy occurs between companies.

27. Explain the use of creative common license.

Ans. Creative common (CC) is an internationally active non-profit organisation that provides free licenses for creators to use when making their source code available to the public. These licenses help the creator to give permission for others to use the source code in advance under certain conditions.

28. What do you mean by cyber stalking?

Ans. Cyber stalking is a crime in which the attacker harasses a victim using electronic communication, such as e-mail or Instant Messaging (IM), or messages posted to a website or a discussion group. Cyber stalking messages differ from ordinary spam in that a cyber stalker targets a specific victim with often threatening messages.

29. Manohar received an email from a company, named Makemoney Pvt. Ltd., claiming that Manohar has won ₹ 20 lakhs in a survey done online. In order to claim the prize money, he was required to answer few security questions such as his Name, Account number, PAN card details, Phone number and OTP for

verification purposes. For this, he had to click on the link provided in the email. Competency Based Que.

Answer the following questions

(i) Should Manohar give the required details to the company?

(ii) What is the activity depicted above?

(iii) What should he do with this email ?

Ans. (i) No

(ii) Fraud/Scam

(iii) He should never click on the given link.

30. What do you understand by the term hacking? Write any two measures that one should take to avoid being the victim of hacking. CBSE 2023

Ans. Hacking means stealing of required information byseeking and exploiting weakness of a computer or a computer network.

To prevent hacking, following points are to be used

(i) Create complex passwords.

(ii) Logout of accounts when you are done with them.

31. Ravi is a student studying in grade 12. He frequently uses the internet for various activities such as social networking, online shopping, and to research for school projects. Recently, he noticed that he receives targeted advertisements based on his browsing history and is concerned about his digital footprint. Additionally, Ravi has encountered instances of cyberbullying and is unsure how to handle them. Help Ravi by answering the following questions: CBSE 2025

(i) What are digital footprints, and how are they created?

(ii) Write any two net etiquettes that Ravi should follow to ensure respectful and responsible online behavior.

(iii) How can Ravi protect himself from cyberbullying? Mention any one protective measure.

Ans. (i) **Digital footprints** refer to the traces of online activities a user leaves behind, such as browsing history, social media interactions, and online purchases. They are created when users visit websites, use apps, or engage in online communication.

(ii) **Two net etiquettes Ravi should follow:**

1. **Be respectful** – Avoid posting hurtful or offensive comments.
2. **Think before sharing** – Verify information before posting and avoid sharing personal details publicly.

(iii) **One protective measure against cyberbullying:**

Block and report the bully on the platform and inform a trusted adult or authority.

32. Police officials arrested four members of an interstate gang for allegedly duping many people from different states on the pretext of providing them with holiday packages after creating fake websites of Tours and Travels. The cyber criminals sent fraudulent emails containing links to fraudulent websites created by them. The victim in his complaint told police that he was offered a holiday package to Dubai for a total of 10 times in the next 10 years and was charged ₹ 1.45 lakh through his credit card. CBSE 2024, Competency Based Que.

Answer the following questions pertaining to the given news byte:

(i) Identify the type of cybercrime mentioned in above case.

(ii) Which Act deals with such crimes in India?

(iii) Suggest any one precaution that can be taken to avoid falling prey to such criminals.

Ans. (i) Phishing

(ii) IT Act 2000

(iii) Check the authenticity of the websites by their address

Check for the https:// and padlock.

Do not respond to unknown mail ids.

Do not ever click on links.

33. Nadar has recently shifted to a new city and school. She does not know many people in her new city and school. But all of a sudden, someone is posting negative, demeaning comments on her social networking profile etc. She is also getting repeated mails from unknown people. Every time she goes online, she finds someone chasing her online. CBSE SQP 2022-23, Competency Based Que.

(i) What is this happening to Nadar?

(ii) What immediate action should she take to handle it?

(iii) Is there any law in India to handle such issues? Discuss briefly.

Ans. (i) Nadar has become a victim of cyber bullying and cyber stalking.

(ii) She must immediately bring it into the notice of her parents and school authorities. And she must report this cyber crime to local police with the help of her parents.

(iii) Yes. The Information Technology Act, 2000 (also known as ITA-2000, or the IT Act) is the primary law in India dealing with cybercrime and electronic commerce.

34. Explain the features of IT Act 2000.

Ans. (1) It helps to promote E-commerce

(2) It includes high penalty for cyber crime

(3) It provides filing online forms

(4) It enhances the corporate business

35. Explain the scope of IT Act.

Ans. (i) IT Act 2000 is not applicable on the attestation for making will of any body.

(ii) Attestation for giving power of attorney of property is not possible via electronic record.

(iii) A contract of sale of any immovable property.

(iv) IT Act 2000 is not applicable on the attestation for creating trust via electronic way. Physical attestation is must.

36. What are the advantages of E-waste recycling?

Ans. The key advantages of E-waste recycling are:

(i) Conserves natural resources

(ii) Protects environment

(iii) Create Jobs

(iv) Saves landfill space

(v) Save money

37. Ayesha's family is replacing their old computer with a new one. They decide to throw the old computer in a nearby empty field/plot. **CBSE SQP 2024-25, Competency Based Que.**

I. Explain any one potential environmental hazard associated with improper e-waste disposal.

II. Suggest one responsible way to Ayesha's family for proper disposal of their old computer.

III. Describe the importance of recycling in e-waste management.

Ans. I. **Environmental hazard** Improper disposal of e-waste can release toxic chemicals like lead and mercury into the soil and water, harming plants, animals, and human health.

II. **Responsible disposal** Ayesha's family can take the old computer to a certified e-waste recycling center to ensure safe and eco-friendly disposal.

III. **Importance of recycling** Recycling helps recover valuable materials from e-waste, reduces the need for new resources, and minimizes the environmental impact of waste in landfills.

38. ABC Electronics, a popular electronics retail chain, has been a prominent player in the market for years. However, recent concerns over environmental degradation and e-waste have prompted the company to rethink its strategies and practices. As the newly appointed sustainability manager, you've been asked to answer the following questions:

(i) Considering the environmental concerns associated with e-waste, outline any one negative impact of the electronic products on the environment.

(ii) Gopal is a college student who recently bought his new smartphone from ABC electronics. He's excited about the new features and improved performance of his new device. However, he's now left with his old smartphone, which is still functional but considered outdated. Suggest him any one action that he can take for his old smartphone.

(iii) Provide any one recommendation on how ABC Electronics can responsibly manage its e-waste while minimizing harm to the environment. **CBSE 2024, Competency Based Que.**

Ans. (i) When electronics are improperly disposed and end up in landfills, toxic chemicals are released, impacting the earth's air, soil, water and ultimately, human health.

(ii) He can remove his old data to a proper media and sell it to a proper vendor who can either repair it or extract the useful components from the old smartphone and make it usable.

(iii) They can contact a proper e-Waste recycler, who can collect the e-wastes from ABC Electronics and reuse , recycle the electronic wastes of the company.

39. Mention any three health hazards associated with inappropriate and excessive use of gadgets. **CBSE SQP 2023-24**

Ans. Health Hazards of Excessive Gadget Use

1. **Eye Strain** Prolonged screen time can lead to digital eye strain, causing discomfort and visual problems.
2. **Sleep Disturbances** Excessive use of gadgets, especially before bedtime, can disrupt sleep patterns and lead to insomnia.
3. **Physical Health Issues** Extended use can result in posture-related problems, such as back pain and repetitive strain injuries.

Short Answer Type II Questions

40. List the guidelines to avoid plagiarism.

Ans. Follow the below given guidelines to avoid plagiarism:

(i) To avoid plagiarism, instead of copying the language of the book as it is, try to put it is your own language/words.

(ii) One should have a clear understanding of plagiarism and its consequences, so that no one perform it unintentionally.

(iii) If copying someone elseís work in our task, word for word, then do not forget enclosing it is quotes and also mention its source.

(iv) Another way is to credit the author has write which was useful for your task and not taking credit for its yourself.

41. Richa, recently started using her social media account. Within a few days, she befriends many people she knows and some that she does not know. After some time, she starts getting negative comments on her posts. She also finds that her pictures are being shared online without her permission. **CBSE SQP 2023-24, Competency Based Que.**

Based on the given information, answer the questions given below.

(i) Identify the type of cybercrime she is a victim of.

(ii) Under which act, she can lodge a complaint to the relevant authorities?

(iii) Suggest her any two pre cautionary measures which she should take in future while being online to avoid any such situations.

Ans. (i) **Type of Cybercrime** Richa is a victim of cyberbullying (due to negative comments) and unauthorized sharing of personal images (invasion of privacy).

(ii) **Relevant Act for Complaint** She can lodge a complaint under the Information Technology Act, 2000 (specifically sections related to cyberbullying and privacy violations).

(iii) **Precautionary Measures**

1. **Adjust Privacy Settings** Richa should set her social media accounts to private, limiting access to her posts and pictures only to approved friends.
2. **Be Selective with Friend Requests** She should only accept friend requests from people she knows personally to reduce the risk of negative interactions.

42. What are the disadvantages of E-waste recycling?

Ans. Some disadvantages of E-waste recycling are:

1. **Environmental Pollution** Improper recycling processes can release harmful chemicals into the environment, contaminating soil and water.
2. **Health Risks** Workers in e-waste recycling facilities may be exposed to toxic substances, leading to serious health issues.
3. **Resource Intensity** The recycling process can be energy-intensive and may not always be economically viable, consuming more resources than it recycles.
4. **Data Security** Improper handling of electronic devices can lead to data breaches if sensitive information is not adequately destroyed.
5. **Inefficient Practices** Many recycling facilities may lack proper technology and expertise, resulting in inefficient recycling methods and loss of valuable materials.
6. **Limited Infrastructure** In some regions, there may be insufficient recycling infrastructure, leading to improper disposal instead of recycling.

Long Answer Type Questions

43. Explain the rules for good netiquette.

Ans. Below are the rules to follow for good netiquette

(i) Avoid posting offensive comments online.

(ii) Never spam other by sending large amounts of unsolicited e-mail.

(iii) Do not troll people in web forums or website comments by repeatedly annoying them.

(iv) Do not use offensive language.

(v) Do not trust other when you are new.

(vi) Avoid replying to negative comments with more negative comments.

(vii) Stick the topic when posting in online forums or when commenting on photos or videos such as Youtube or facebook comments.

44. Explain the software license with its types.

Ans. A software license is a license agreement that given an individual, company or an organisation permission to use a software program. It typically provides end users with the right to one or more copies of the software without violating copyrights. Software licenses typically are the either proprietary or free and open source.

(i) **Proprietary software license** The hallmark of proprietary software license it that the software publisher grants the use of one or more copies of software under the End user License Agreement (EULA) but ownership of those copies remains with the software publisher. This feature of proprietary software licenses means that certain rights regarding the software are reserved by the software publisher.

In other words, without acceptance of the license, the end user may not use the software at all. One example of such a proprietary software license is the license for microsoft windows.

(ii) **Free and open source software license** It refers to the software that users can softely run, adopt and redistribute without legal restraint. Open source software refers to freedom to use, share and/or modify the source code and allow copies to other users. Open source softwares are further classified into permissive license and copyleft license.

45. Differentiate between copyright and licensing

Ans. Differentiation between copyright and licensing:

Copyright	Licensing
Legal protection granting creators exclusive rights to their original works.	Permission granted by the copyright holder to use the work under specified conditions.
Automatically owned by the creator upon creation.	Ownership remains with the copyright holder; licensee only gets usage rights.

Copyright	Licensing
Lasts for the life of the creator plus 70 years (in many jurisdictions).	Duration varies; can be temporary or long-term based on agreement.
Copyright can be transferred or sold.	Licensing can be exclusive or non-exclusive, allowing multiple licenses or just one.
Infringement can lead to legal action against unauthorized use.	License violation can also lead to legal consequences, but depends on license terms.
Includes literary, artistic, musical works, etc.	Includes various types like open-source, proprietary, public domain licenses.

46. Define the most common types of cyber crime.

Ans. Refer to text on page 213-214 (Types of cyber crime).

47. What is E-waste management? Explain E-waste management in India.

Ans. Refer to text on page no. 216-217 (Management of E-waste, E-waste management in India).

Case Study Based Questions

Case Study 1

Smridh has recently changed his school, so he is not aware of the people, but someone is posting negative , demeaning comments on his social media profile. He is also getting repeated mails from unknown people. Everytime he goes online, he finds someone chasing him online. CBSE Question Bank

(i) **Smridh is a victim of ___________.**
(a) eavesdropping (b) stolen identity
(c) phishing (d) cyber stalking

(ii) **The action that Smridh should take :**
(a) He should only share with his friends
(b) He should not share with anyone as it can cause serious problem
(c) He should immediately report to the police
(d) He should bring to the notice of his parents and school authorities

(iii) **___________. is a set of moral principles that governs the behaviour of a group or an individual and regulates the use of computers.**
(a) Copyright (b) Computer ethics
(c) Property rights (d) Privacy law

(iv) **Smridh needs to protect his personal information or data from unintentional and intentional attacks and disclosure which is termed as ___________...**
(a) digital right (b) copyright
(c) privacy (d) intellectual property

(v) **The act of fraudulently acquiring someone's personal and private information, such as online account names, login information and passwords is called as __________**
(a) phishing (b) fraud
(c) scam (d) plagiarism

Ans. (i) (d) Cyber stalking is the use of the Internet or other electronic means to stalk or harass an individual, group or organization. Smridh is also getting such anonymous mails and negative comments.

(ii) (d) The incidents should be reported to the parents, school authorities and the cyber crime cell since this would keep him safe from future troubles. If ignored these can put him into a deeper web of cyber problems.

(iii) (b) Computer ethics refer to all the ethical , behavioral characteristics that computer users and professionals should have and perform accordingly.

(iv) (c) The protection of one's personal confidential information from web criminals is privacy.

(v) (a) Phishing is the fraudulent act of obtaining confidential information of people by an authentic looking E-mail , phone call or message.

Case Study 2

Sumit has to prepare a project on "Swachh Bharat Shreshth Bharat". He decides to get information from the Internet. He downloads three web pages (webpage1, webpage 2, webpage 3) containing information on the given topic.

1. **He read a paragraph on from webpage 1 and rephrased it in his own words. He finally pasted the rephrased paragraph in his project.**
2. **He downloaded three images of from webpage 2. He made a collage for his project using these images.**
3. **He also downloaded an icon from web page 3 and pasted it on the front page of his project report.**

(i) **Step1 is an example of........**
(a) Plagiarism (b) Paraphrasing
(c) Copyright infringement
(d) Intellectual Property right

(ii) Step 2 an act of ....

(a) plagiarism

(b) copyright infringement

(c) Intellectual Property Right

(d) Digital Footprints

(iii) Step 3 an act of ....

(a) Plagiarism

(b) Paraphrasing

(c) copyright infringement

(d) Intellectual Property right

(iv) A website is a collection of ....

(a) Web Servers (b) Web pages

(c) Browsers (d) Hyperlinks

(v) The process of getting web pages, images and files from a web server to local computer is called

(a) FTP

(b) Uploading

(c) Downloading

(d) Remote

Ans. (i) (b) Step 1 is an example of paraphrasing .

(ii) (a) Step 2 an act of plagiarism.

(iii) (c) Step 3 an act of copyright infringement.

(iv) (b) A website is a collection of web pages.

(v) (c) The process of getting web pages, images and files from a web server to local computer is called downloading.

SELF ASSESSMENT TEST

Multiple Choice Questions

1 Which form of cyber crime refers to offensive comments posted online targeting people?
(a) Cyber bullying (b) Cyber stalking
(c) Cyber trolls (d) Both (a) and (b)

2 Reason(s) behind plagiarism is/are
(a) fear of failure (b) being lazy
(c) competition (d) All of these

3 Which of the following is not the form of software piracy?
(a) Softlifting (b) Renting
(c) Hard disk loading (d) Site hosting

4 Which of the following is an example of computer virus?
(a) Bomber (b) Whale
(c) Eliza (d) All of these

5 Which type of virus infects the directory of your computer by changing the path that indicates the location of a file?
(a) File system virus (b) Macro virus
(c) Boot sector virus (d) All of these

6 Which type of firewall provides protection to a local network?
(a) Software firewall (b) Hardware firewall
(c) Both (a) and (b) (d) None of these

Fill in the Blanks

7 IT Act 2000 includes high penalty for ……… .

8 The word ……… has emerged from a latin word plagiarius which means kidnapping.

9 ……… is a term that encapsulates the legal issues related to the use of Internet.

10 Spam is usually defined as ……… .

11 ……… is a combination of alphabets and symbols.

State whether True or False

12 Copyrights are automatically granted to creators and authors.

13 Avoid posting inframmatory or offensive comments online.

14 CC stands for Create Common.

15 Never reply to E-mails from any unknown or unreliable source.

16 Those who execute such threats are known as attackers.

17 Strong passwords are like names, birth dates, phone numbers, etc.

18 Each pair of files is divided into three parts the public key, private key and protected key.

Assertion and Reason Based Questions

Assertion (A) and Reason (R) based questions. Mark the correct choice as

(a) Both (A) and (R) are true and (R) is the correct explanation for (A).
(b) Both (A) and (R) are true and (R) is not the correct explanation for (A).
(c) (A) is true and (R) is false.
(d) (A) is false but (R) is true.

19 **Assertion (A)** Using licensed software helps protect the software developer's rights and prevents unauthorized use of the software.

Reason (R) Licensed software provides legally binding guidelines for usage and distribution, including restrictions on making additional copies without permission.

20 **Assertion (A)** Improper disposal of e-waste can cause air, water, and soil pollution.

Reason (R) E-waste contains toxic substances like lead, mercury, and cadmium, which can leach into the environment and harm ecosystems.

Very Short Answer Type Questions

21 What is meant by Apache license?

22 Give the examples of cyber stalking.

23 Write the form of BSD license.

Short Answer Type Questions

24 Explain the violation of IPR.

25 Explain any one example of copyleft license.

26 How will you avoid the spam?

27 What are the policies of cyber crime?

28 How will you avoid the spam?

29 What is the use of password cracking?

Long Answer Type Questions

30 What do you mean by information technology? Explain its importance in various fields.

31 Define the following:
(i) Adware
(ii) Phishing
(iii) Password cracking
(iv) Sweeper
(v) Denial of service

Case Study Based Question

32 Ravi, a college student, has been using the internet extensively for his academic and social activities. He often shares personal photos and thoughts on social media platforms like Facebook and Instagram. Recently, he came across a website offering free software downloads and was intrigued by the idea of using it for his studies. However, he later found out that some of the software was pirated, and he unknowingly violated copyright laws by using it. Furthermore, Ravi has received unsolicited emails asking for personal information, which could potentially be a phishing attack. At the same time, he has noticed an increasing amount of e-waste accumulating due to the frequent upgrading of his electronic devices. Ravi is also concerned about the impact of prolonged use of his phone and laptop on his health.

Based on the case study, answer the following questions:

(i) What is Ravi's digital footprint?
(a) The traces of his physical activities
(b) The online record of his activities and interactions
(c) The number of followers on his social media
(d) His profile pictures on the internet

(ii) Which of the following is considered a violation of intellectual property rights (IPR) in Ravi's case?
(a) Sharing personal photos on social media
(b) Downloading and using pirated software
(c) Sending emails to friends
(d) Upgrading his phone

(iii) Ravi received unsolicited emails asking for personal details. What is this an example of?
(a) Cyberbullying
(b) Phishing
(c) Hacking
(d) Data protection violation

(iv) What is the primary concern related to e-waste in Ravi's case?
(a) It harms the environment if not disposed of properly
(b) It can be used to create new devices
(c) It increases the value of electronics
(d) It has no impact on health

(v) How can Ravi reduce the health risks associated with prolonged use of his phone and laptop?
(a) Avoid using his devices completely
(b) Use devices only in the evening
(c) Take regular breaks and maintain proper posture
(d) Increase screen brightness for better visibility

Answers

1. (a)	2. (d)	3. (b)	4. (d)	5. (a)
6. (b)	7. Cyber crime		8. Plagiarism	
9. Cyberlaw		10. Unsolicited bulk mail		
11. Password		12. True	13. True	14. False
15. True	16. True	17. False	18. False	19. (a)
20. (a)				

32. (i) → (b); (ii) → (a); (iii) → (b); (iv) → (a); (v) → (c)

PRACTICAL WORK

1. DATA HANDLING

AIM 1. **Create a panda's series from a dictionary of values and a ndarray.**

Procedure **From a Dictionary**

```
import pandas as pd
data = {'A': 10, 'B': 20, 'C': 30}
series = pd.Series(data)        # Create a Series from the dictionary
print(series)
```

```
Output                                   Clear
A    10
B    20
C    30
dtype: int64

=== Code Execution Successful ===
```

From a NumPy Array

```
import pandas as pd
import numpy as np
data = np.array([1, 2, 3, 4, 5])        # Create a NumPy array
series = pd.Series(data)                # Create a Series from the NumPy array
print(series)
```

```
Output                                   Clear
0    1
1    2
2    3
3    4
4    5
dtype: int64

=== Code Execution Successful ===
```

AIM 2. **Given a Series, print all the elements that are above the 75th percentile.**

Procedure

```
import pandas as pd
data = {'A': 10, 'B': 20, 'C': 30, 'D': 40, 'E': 50}
series = pd.Series(data)
percentile_75 = series.quantile(0.75)        # Calculate the 75th percentile
for index, value in series.items():
            # Filter and print elements above the 75th percentile
    if value > percentile_75:
        print(f"{index}: {value}")
```

```
Output                                   Clear
E: 50

=== Code Execution Successful ===
```

AIM 3. **Create a DataFrame quarterly sales where each row contains the item category, item name, and expenditure. Group the rows by the category and print the total expenditure per category.**

Procedure

```
import pandas as pd
   # Create a sample DataFrame with quarterly sales data
data = {
    'Item Category': ['Electronics', 'Electronics', 'Appliance', 'Furniture', 'Furniture'],
    'Item Name': ['TV', 'Laptop', 'Refrigerator', 'Sofa', 'Chair'],
    'Expenditure (Q1)': [1000, 1500, 2000, 3000, 1000],
    'Expenditure (Q2)': [1200, 1800, 2500, 3500, 1500],
    'Expenditure (Q3)': [1100, 1600, 2200, 3200, 1200],
    'Expenditure (Q4)': [1300, 1700, 2300, 3800, 1300]
}
df = pd.DataFrame(data)
   # Group DataFrame by 'Item Category' and calculate total expenditure per category
total_expenditure = df.groupby('Item Category')[['Expenditure (Q1)', 'Expenditure (Q2)',
'Expenditure (Q3)', 'Expenditure (Q4)']].sum()
   # Print the DataFrame with total expenditure per category
print(total_expenditure)
```

Output

```
               Expenditure (Q1)  Expenditure (Q2)  Expenditure (Q3)  \
Item Category
Appliance                  2000              2500              2200
Electronics                2500              3000              2700
Furniture                  4000              5000              4400

               Expenditure (Q4)
Item Category
Appliance                  2300
Electronics                3000
Furniture                  5100
```

AIM 4. **Create a DataFrame for examination result and display row labels, column labels data types of each column and the dimensions.**

Procedure

```
import pandas as pd
   # Create a DataFrame with sample data
data = {'Student': ['Alice', 'Bob', 'Charlie', 'David'],
        'Maths': [85, 92, 78, 95],
        'Science': [90, 88, 85, 92],
        'English': [88, 90, 82, 93]}
df = pd.DataFrame(data)
   # Display row and column labels
print("Row Labels:", df.index)
print("Column Labels:", df.columns)
   # Display data types of each column
print("Data Types:", df.dtypes)
   # Display dimensions of the DataFrame
print("Dimensions:", df.shape)
   # Print the DataFrame
print(df)
```

```
Output                                                              Clear
Row Labels: RangeIndex(start=0, stop=4, step=1)
Column Labels: Index(['Student', 'Maths', 'Science', 'English'], dtype='object')
Data Types: Student    object
Maths       int64
Science     int64
English     int64
dtype: object
Dimensions: (4, 4)
   Student  Maths  Science  English
0    Alice     85       90       88
1      Bob     92       88       90
2  Charlie     78       85       82
3    David     95       92       93

=== Code Execution Successful ===
```

AIM 5. Filter out rows based on different criteria such as duplicate rows.

Procedure

```
import pandas as pd
import numpy as np
   # Create a sample DataFrame with some duplicate and problematic rows
data = {
    'name': ['Anurag', 'Bobby', 'Arnav', 'Deepak', 'Abhishek', 'Ram', 'Varun', 'Govind'],
    'age': [25, 30, 35, 25, 25, 40, 30, 45],
    'city': ['New York', 'London', 'Paris', 'Tokyo', 'New York', 'Berlin', 'London', 'Sydney'],
    'salary': [50000, 60000, 75000, np.nan, 50000, 80000, 60000, 90000]
}
df = pd.DataFrame(data)
   # 1. Remove completely duplicate rows (all columns)
df_no_duplicates = df.drop_duplicates()
   # 2. Remove duplicate rows based on specific columns
df_unique_names = df.drop_duplicates(subset=['name'])
   # 3. Keep the first occurrence of duplicate rows
df_first_occurrence = df.drop_duplicates(keep='first')
   # 4. Keep the last occurrence of duplicate rows
df_last_occurrence = df.drop_duplicates(keep='last')
   # 5. Filter out rows with missing values
df_no_missing = df.dropna()
   # 6. Filter rows based on a condition (e.g., age > 30)
df_older = df[df['age'] > 30]
   # 7. Filter rows based on multiple conditions
df_filtered = df[(df['age'] > 30) & (df['salary'] > 70000)]
   # 8. Filter using .query() method
df_query_filtered = df.query('age > 30 and salary > 70000')
   # 9. Complex filtering with isin()
cities_to_keep = ['New York', 'London']
df_selected_cities = df[df['city'].isin(cities_to_keep)]
   # 10. Filtering out rows based on regex
df_name_filter = df[df['name'].str.contains('^[A-C]')]
   # Print out the results
print("Original DataFrame:")
print(df)
```

```
print("\n1. No Duplicates (all columns):")
print(df_no_duplicates)
print("\n2. Unique Names:")
print(df_unique_names)
print("\n5. No Missing Values:")
print(df_no_missing)
print("\n6. Age > 30:")
print(df_older)
print("\n7. Age > 30 and Salary > 70000:")
print(df_filtered)
print("\n9. Selected Cities:")
print(df_selected_cities)
print("\n10. Names starting with A-C:")
print(df_name_filter)
```

Output

```
Original DataFrame:
       name  age      city   salary
0    Anurag   25  New York  50000.0
1     Bobby   30    London  60000.0
2     Arnav   35     Paris  75000.0
3    Deepak   25     Tokyo      NaN
4  Abhishek   25  New York  50000.0
5       Ram   40    Berlin  80000.0
6     Varun   30    London  60000.0
7    Govind   45    Sydney  90000.0

1. No Duplicates (all columns):
       name  age      city   salary
0    Anurag   25  New York  50000.0
1     Bobby   30    London  60000.0
2     Arnav   35     Paris  75000.0
3    Deepak   25     Tokyo      NaN
4  Abhishek   25  New York  50000.0
5       Ram   40    Berlin  80000.0
6     Varun   30    London  60000.0
7    Govind   45    Sydney  90000.0

2. Unique Names:
       name  age      city   salary
0    Anurag   25  New York  50000.0
1     Bobby   30    London  60000.0
2     Arnav   35     Paris  75000.0
3    Deepak   25     Tokyo      NaN
4  Abhishek   25  New York  50000.0
5       Ram   40    Berlin  80000.0
6     Varun   30    London  60000.0
7    Govind   45    Sydney  90000.0

5. No Missing Values:
       name  age      city   salary
0    Anurag   25  New York  50000.0
1     Bobby   30    London  60000.0
2     Arnav   35     Paris  75000.0
4  Abhishek   25  New York  50000.0
5       Ram   40    Berlin  80000.0
6     Varun   30    London  60000.0
7    Govind   45    Sydney  90000.0
```

```
6. Age > 30:
     name  age    city   salary
2   Arnav   35   Paris  75000.0
5     Ram   40  Berlin  80000.0
7  Govind   45  Sydney  90000.0

7. Age > 30 and Salary > 70000:
     name  age    city   salary
2   Arnav   35   Paris  75000.0
5     Ram   40  Berlin  80000.0
7  Govind   45  Sydney  90000.0

9. Selected Cities:
       name  age      city   salary
0    Anurag   25  New York  50000.0
1     Bobby   30    London  60000.0
4  Abhishek   25  New York  50000.0
6     Varun   30    London  60000.0
```

AIM 6. Importing and exporting data between pandas and CSV file.

Procedure 1. **Importing Data (Reading) from a CSV File** To read data from a CSV file into a pandas DataFrame, you can use the pd.read_csv() function. This function reads the contents of the CSV file and loads it into a DataFrame.

Syntax

```
import pandas as pd
# Read a CSV file into a DataFrame
df = pd.read_csv('file_name.csv')
```

Example

```
import pandas as pd
# Read CSV file into DataFrame
df = pd.read_csv('data.csv')
# Display the first 5 rows of the DataFrame
print(df.head())
```

Output

```
     Name  Age       City
0    Amit   25  New Delhi
1   Bobby   26     Mumbai
2  Deepak   23    Chennai
3  Anurag   22        Goa
4  Lalita   25     Jaipur
```

Note By default, read_csv() assumes the first row of the CSV file contains column headers. You can modify its behavior using parameters like header, index_col, and dtype if needed.

2. **Exporting Data (Writing) to a CSV File** To export data from a pandas DataFrame to a CSV file, you can use the to_csv() method.

Syntax

```
# Write a DataFrame to a CSV file
df.to_csv('file_name.csv', index=False)
```

The index=False argument prevents pandas from writing row numbers (index) into the CSV file. If you want to include the index, you can omit this argument or set it to True.

Example

```
import pandas as pd
# Assume we have a DataFrame df
df = pd.DataFrame({
    'Name': ['Amit', 'Bobby', 'Deepak', 'Anurag', 'Lalita', 'Arnav', 'Govind'],
    'Age': [25, 26, 23, 22, 25, 21, 22],
    'City': ['New Delhi', 'Mumbai', 'Chennai', 'Goa', 'Jaipur', 'Pune', 'Meerut']
})
# Export DataFrame to CSV
df.to_csv('output.csv', index=False)
```

2. VISUALIZATION

AIM 1. **Given the school result data, analyses the performance of the students on different parameters, e.g subject wise or class wise.**

Student ID	Name	Class	Math	Science	English	History	Geography
101	Arnav	10A	85	92	78	88	90
102	Bobby	10A	75	80	65	72	78
103	Ram	10A	90	95	85	92	94
104	Deepak	10B	82	88	75	80	84
105	Lalita	10B	78	82	70	75	78
106	Anurag	10B	95	98	90	92	96
107	Govind	11A	88	92	85	88	90
108	Vaibhav	11A	72	78	65	70	74
109	Abhishek	11A	92	96	88	90	94
110	Varun	11B	80	84	75	80	82

Procedure

```
import pandas as pd
import matplotlib.pyplot as plt
   # Table data in DataFrame format
data = {
    'Student ID': [101, 102, 103, 104, 105, 106, 107, 108, 109, 110],
    'Name': ['Arnav', 'Bobby', 'Ram', 'Deepak', 'Lalita', 'Anurag', 'Govind', 'Vaibhav',
                                                                  'Abhishek', 'Varun'],
    'Class': ['10A', '10A', '10A', '10B', '10B', '10B', '11A', '11A', '11A', '11B'],
    'Math': [85, 75, 90, 82, 78, 95, 88, 72, 92, 80],
    'Science': [92, 80, 95, 88, 82, 98, 92, 78, 96, 84],
    'English': [78, 65, 85, 75, 70, 90, 85, 65, 88, 75],
    'History': [88, 72, 92, 80, 75, 92, 88, 70, 90, 80],
    'Geography': [90, 78, 94, 84, 78, 96, 90, 74, 94, 82]
}
df = pd.DataFrame(data)
   # Subject-wise analysis: Calculates the avg. score for each subject.
   # Selecting only numeric columns explicitly.
subject_wise_avg = df[['Math', 'Science', 'English', 'History', 'Geography']].mean()
print("Subject-wise Average Scores:")
print(subject_wise_avg)
   # Class-wise analysis: Calculates the avg. score for each class.
class_wise_avg = df.groupby('Class')[['Math', 'Science', 'English', 'History',
                                                                  'Geography']].mean()
print("\nClass-wise Average Scores:")
print(class_wise_avg)
   # Visualizations using matplotlib
   # 1. Bar plot for subject-wise average scores.
plt.figure(figsize=(10, 6))
plt.bar(subject_wise_avg.index, subject_wise_avg.values, color='skyblue')
```

```
plt.title('Subject-wise Average Scores', fontsize=16)
plt.xlabel('Subject', fontsize=12)
plt.ylabel('Average Score', fontsize=12)
plt.xticks(rotation=45)
plt.grid(axis='y', linestyle='--', alpha=0.7)
plt.tight_layout()    # Adjust layout for better fit
plt.show()
  # 2. Bar plot for class-wise average scores.
class_wise_avg.plot(kind='bar', figsize=(10, 6))
plt.title('Class-wise Average Scores', fontsize=16)
plt.xlabel('Class', fontsize=12)
plt.ylabel('Average Score', fontsize=12)
plt.xticks(rotation=0)
plt.grid(axis='y', linestyle='--', alpha=0.7)
plt.tight_layout()    # Adjust layout for better fit
plt.show()
```

Output

```
Subject-wise Average Scores:
Math         83.7
Science      88.5
English      77.6
History      82.7
Geography    86.0
dtype: float64

Class-wise Average Scores:
            Math    Science    English    History  Geography
Class
10A    83.333333  89.000000  76.000000  84.000000  87.333333
10B    85.000000  89.333333  78.333333  82.333333  86.000000
11A    84.000000  88.666667  79.333333  82.666667  86.000000
11B    80.000000  84.000000  75.000000  80.000000  82.000000
```

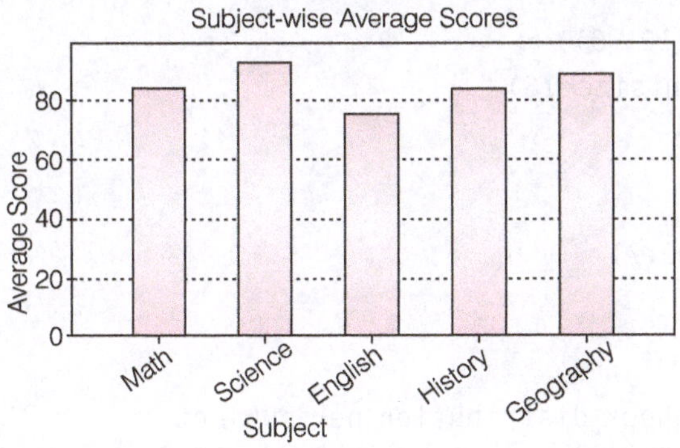

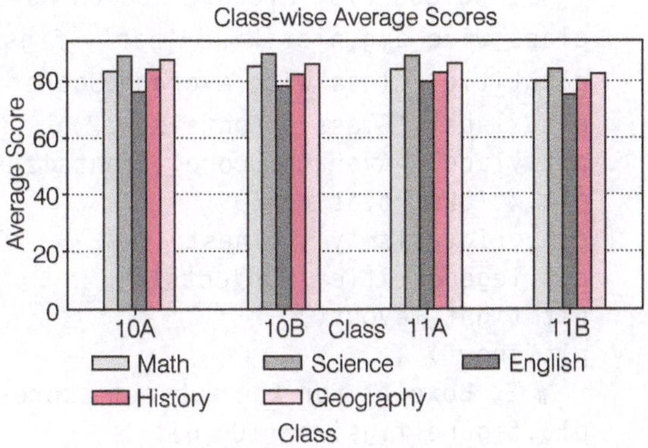

AIM 2. For the Data frames created above, analyze, and plot appropriate charts with title and legend.

Procedure

```
import pandas as pd
import matplotlib.pyplot as plt
  # Table data in DataFrame format
data = {
   'Student ID': [101, 102, 103, 104, 105, 106, 107, 108, 109, 110],
   'Name': ['Arnav', 'Bobby', 'Ram', 'Deepak', 'Lalita', 'Anurag', 'Govind', 'Vaibhav',
                                                              'Abhishek', 'Varun'],
   'Class': ['10A', '10A', '10A', '10B', '10B', '10B', '11A', '11A', '11A', '11B'],
   'Math': [85, 75, 90, 82, 78, 95, 88, 72, 92, 80],
```

```
    'Science': [92, 80, 95, 88, 82, 98, 92, 78, 96, 84],
    'English': [78, 65, 85, 75, 70, 90, 85, 65, 88, 75],
    'History': [88, 72, 92, 80, 75, 92, 88, 70, 90, 80],
    'Geography': [90, 78, 94, 84, 78, 96, 90, 74, 94, 82]
}
df = pd.DataFrame(data)
   # Subject-wise analysis: Average scores for each subject
subject_wise_avg = df[['Math', 'Science', 'English', 'History', 'Geography']].mean()
print("Subject-wise Average Scores:")
print(subject_wise_avg)
   # Class-wise analysis: Average scores for each class
class_wise_avg = df.groupby('Class')[['Math', 'Science', 'English', 'History',
                                                            'Geography']].mean()
print("\nClass-wise Average Scores:")
print(class_wise_avg)
   # Visualizations using matplotlib
   # 1. Subject-wise average scores bar chart
plt.figure(figsize=(10, 6))
plt.bar(subject_wise_avg.index, subject_wise_avg.values, color='skyblue',
                                                           label='Avg. Score')
plt.title('Subject-wise Average Scores', fontsize=16)
plt.xlabel('Subject', fontsize=12)
plt.ylabel('Average Score', fontsize=12)
plt.xticks(rotation=45)
plt.grid(axis='y', linestyle='--', alpha=0.7)
plt.legend()
plt.tight_layout()
plt.show()
   # 2. Class-wise average scores bar chart
class_wise_avg.plot(kind='bar', figsize=(10, 6))
plt.title('Class-wise Average Scores', fontsize=16)
plt.xlabel('Class', fontsize=12)
plt.ylabel('Average Score', fontsize=12)
plt.xticks(rotation=0)
plt.grid(axis='y', linestyle='--', alpha=0.7)
plt.legend(title='Subjects')
plt.tight_layout()
plt.show()
   # 3. Boxplot for the subject scores to check distribution per subject
plt.figure(figsize=(10, 6))
df[['Math', 'Science', 'English', 'History', 'Geography']].boxplot()
plt.title('Boxplot of Subject Scores', fontsize=16)
plt.ylabel('Scores', fontsize=12)
plt.grid(True)
plt.tight_layout()
plt.show()
   # 4. Line plot for individual student performance across subjects
plt.figure(figsize=(12, 6))
for i, row in df.iterrows():
    plt.plot(df.columns[3:], row[3:], marker='o', label=row['Name'])
```

```
plt.title('Individual Student Performance Across Subjects', fontsize=16)
plt.xlabel('Subjects', fontsize=12)
plt.ylabel('Scores', fontsize=12)
plt.xticks(rotation=45)
plt.legend(loc='center left', bbox_to_anchor=(1, 0.5), title='Students')
plt.grid(True)
plt.tight_layout()
plt.show()
```

Output

```
Subject-wise Average Scores:
Math         83.7
Science      88.5
English      77.6
History      82.7
Geography    86.0
dtype: float64

Class-wise Average Scores:
            Math    Science    English    History  Geography
Class
10A    83.333333  89.000000  76.000000  84.000000  87.333333
10B    85.000000  89.333333  78.333333  82.333333  86.000000
11A    84.000000  88.666667  79.333333  82.666667  86.000000
11B    80.000000  84.000000  75.000000  80.000000  82.000000
```

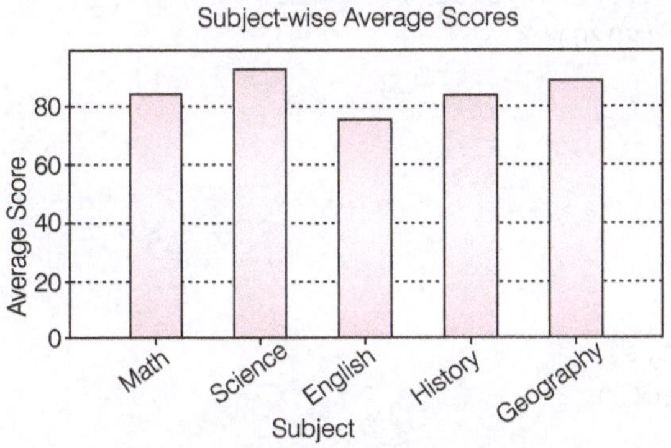

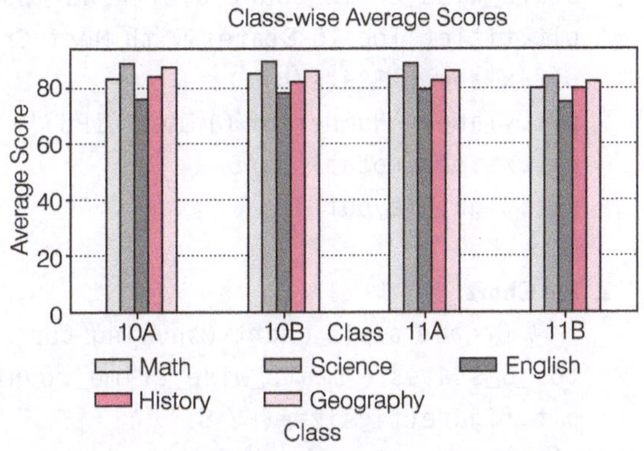

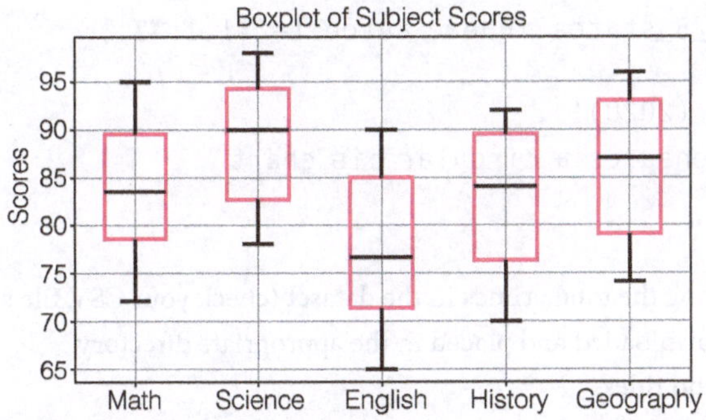

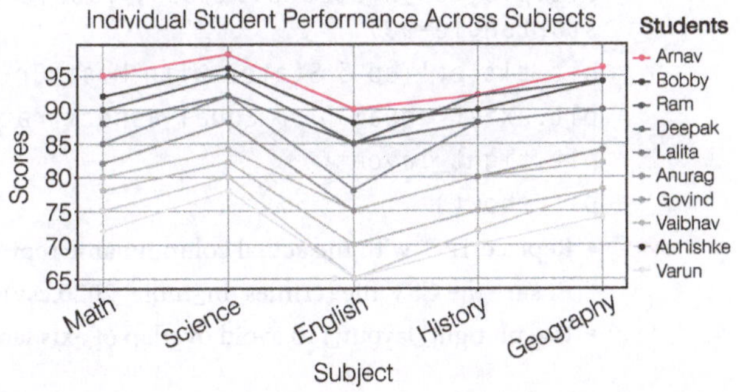

AIM 3. Take data of your interest from an open source (e.g. data.gov.in), aggregate and summarize it. Then plot it using different plotting functions of the Matplotlib library.

Procedure

Step 1 Import libraries and download data (assuming we have downloaded the CSV file)

```
import pandas as pd
import matplotlib.pyplot as plt
  # Load the CSV file (replace the path with the actual path of the file)
```

```
    # Example: crimes_in_india_2020.csv should be downloaded and available in the working
                                                                                 directory
data = pd.read_csv('crimes_in_india_2020.csv')
    # Display the first few rows of the dataset to understand its structure
print(data.head())
```

Step 2 Data Aggregation and Summarization

Let's explore crimes by state:

```
    # Group data by 'State/UT' and calculate the total number of crimes for each state
state_wise_crime_count = data.groupby('State/UT')['IPC'].sum()
    # Sort the states by the total number of crimes in descending order
state_wise_crime_count = state_wise_crime_count.sort_values(ascending=False)
    # Print the top 10 states with the most crimes
print("Top 10 States/UTs with the Most Crimes (2020):")
print(state_wise_crime_count.head(10))
```

Step 3 Data Visualization using Matplotlib

1. **Bar Chart**

```
# Create a bar chart
plt.figure(figsize=(12, 8))
state_wise_crime_count.plot(kind='bar', color='skyblue')
plt.title('Top 10 States with Most Crimes (2020)')
plt.xlabel('State/UT')
plt.ylabel('Number of Crimes (IPC)')
plt.xticks(rotation=45)
plt.tight_layout()
plt.show()
```

2. **Pie Chart**

```
    # Create a pie chart (showing top 5 states)
top_5_states = state_wise_crime_count.head(5)
plt.figure(figsize=(8, 8))
plt.pie(top_5_states.values, labels=top_5_states.index, autopct='%1.1f%%',
startangle=90)
plt.title('Top 5 States with Most Crimes (2020)')
plt.axis('equal')  # Equal aspect ratio ensures a circular pie chart
plt.tight_layout()
plt.show()
```

Note
- Replace 'IPC' with the actual column name representing the total crimes in the dataset (check your CSV file structure).
- Ensure the CSV file (crimes_in_india_2020.csv) is downloaded and placed in the appropriate directory.
- Use plt.tight_layout() to avoid overlap of axis labels and titles.

3. DATA MANAGEMENT

AIM 1. Create a student table with the student id, name, and marks as attributes where the student id is the primary key.

Procedure

```
CREATE TABLE students
(   student_id INT PRIMARY KEY,
    name VARCHAR(50),
    marks INT
);
INSERT INTO students (student_id, name, marks)
VALUES (1, 'Anurag', 99), (2, 'Aniket', 92), (3, 'Vijay', 78), (4, 'Abhishek', 98),
       (5, 'Lalita', 95);
SELECT * FROM students
```

Output

Students

student_id	name	marks
1	Anurag	99
2	Aniket	92
3	Vijay	78
4	Abhishek	98
5	Lalita	95

AIM 2. Insert the details of a new student in the above table.

Procedure

```
INSERT INTO students (student_id, name, marks)
VALUES (6, 'Rohan', 75);
```

Output

Students

student_id	name	marks
1	Anurag	99
2	Aniket	92
3	Vijay	78
4	Abhishek	98
5	Lalita	95
6	Rohan	75

AIM 3. Delete the details of a student in the above table.

Procedure

```
DELETE FROM students WHERE student_id = 3;
```

Output

Students

student_id	name	marks
1	Anurag	99
2	Aniket	92
4	Abhishek	98
5	Lalita	95
6	Rohan	75

AIM 4. **Use the select command to get the details of the students with marks more than 80.**

Procedure
```
SELECT * FROM students
WHERE marks > 80;
```

Output

student_id	name	marks
1	Anurag	99
2	Aniket	92
4	Abhishek	98
5	Lalita	95

AIM 5. **Find the min, max, sum, and average of the marks in a student marks table.**

Procedure
```
SELECT MIN(marks) AS min_marks,
       MAX(marks) AS max_marks,
       SUM(marks) AS total_marks,
       AVG(marks) AS avg_marks
FROM students;
```

Output

min_marks	max_marks	total_marks	avg_marks
75	99	459	91.8

AIM 6. **Find the total number of customers from each country in the table (customer ID, customer Name, country) using group by.**

Procedure
```
SELECT country, COUNT(*) AS total_customers
FROM customers
GROUP BY country;
```

AIM 7. **Write a SQL query to order the (student ID, marks) table in descending order of the marks.**

Procedure
```
SELECT student_id, marks
FROM students
ORDER BY marks DESC;
```

Output

student_id	marks
1	99
4	98
5	95
2	92
6	75

CBSE

EXAMINATION PAPER 2025

INFORMATICS PRACTICES

Time : 3 Hours

Max. Marks : 70

General Instructions

1. Please check this question paper contains 37 questions.
2. All questions are compulsory. However, internal choices have been provided in some questions. Attempt only one of the choices in such questions.
3. The paper is divided into 5 Sections- A, B, C, D and E.
4. Section A consists of 21 questions (1 to 21). Each question carries 1 Mark.
5. Section B consists of 7 questions (22 to 28). Each question carries 2 Marks.
6. Section C consists of 4 questions (29 to 32). Each question carries 3 Marks.
7. Section D consists of 2 case study type questions (33 to 34). Each question carries 4 Marks.
8. Section E consists of 3 questions (35 to 37). Each question carries 5 Marks.
9. All programming questions are to be answered using Python Language only.
10. In case of MCQ, text of the correct answer should also be written.

SECTION A

1. State whether the following statement is True or False:
In Python ,we cannot create an empty DataFrame.

2. What will be the output of the following SQL command?

```
SELECT MONTHNAME ('2024-08-02');
```

(a) 08 (b) 02 (c) February (d) August

3. Temporary data files stored by websites in our computer can be used to track our online activities and also to personalize browsing experience.
These files are known as:

(a) Plug-ins (b) Add-ons
(c) Cookies (d) Bookmarks

4. Which of the following is not an aggregate function in SQL?

(a) COUNT(*) (b) MIN ()
(c) LEFT () (d) AVG()

5. Raheem created a unique computer software and wants to protect his creation from being copied or used without his permission. He is considering to apply for legal protection. Which type of intellectual property protection should Raheem apply for, to safeguard his software?

(a) Copyright (b) Plagiarism
(c) Trademark (d) Lease

6. What is the default index type for a Pandas Series if not explicitly specified?

(a) String (b) List
(c) Numeric (d) Boolean

7. In Python which function of matplotlib library is used to save a plot?

(a) save () (b) saveplot()
(c) export() (d) savefig()

8. State whether the following statement is True or False:
The MOD() function in SQL returns the quotient of division operation between two numbers.

9. Which of the following data structure is used for storing one-dimensional labelled data in Python Pandas?

(a) Integer (b) Dictionary
(c) Series (d) DataFrame

10. Priya received an email that appeared to be from her bank, asking her to update her account information by clicking on a link. She clicked the link to enter her details, but immediately after, some amount was debited from her account. What type of cybercrime did Priya fall victim to?

(a) Cyber stalking (b) Phishing
(c) Fishing (d) Cyber bullying

11. Which SQL function calculates a^b?

(a) MOD () (b) POWER ()
(c) RAISE () (d) ROUND ()

12. Which protocol is used while communicating through video calls on the Internet?

(a) Video Over Internet Protocol
(b) Voice Over Internet Protocol
(c) Internet Protocol
(d) Video Audio Over Internet Protocol

13. Which of the following Python statements will be used to select a specific element having index as points, from a Pandas Series named ser?

(a) ser.element (points) (b) ser.select (points)
(c) ser [points] (d) ser.show [points]

14. Excessive screen time and poor posture can lead to:

(a) Faster Internet Speeds
(b) Eye strain and other health issues
(c) Better vision and bone density
(d) Improved physical health

15. Which of the following libraries defines an ndarray in Python?

(a) pandas (b) numpy (c) matplotlib (d) scipy

16. With respect to SQL, match the function given in Column II with categories given in Column I:

	Column I		Column II
(i)	Math function	(a)	COUNT()
(ii)	Aggregate function	(b)	ROUND()
(iii)	Date function	(c)	RIGHT()
(iv)	Text function	(d)	YEAR()

Options

(a) (i) → (c), (ii) → (d), (iii) → (a), (iv) → (b)
(b) (i) → (b), (ii) → (a), (iii) → (d), (iv) → (c)
(c) (i) → (d), (ii) → (b), (iii) → (a), (iv) → (c)
(d) (i) → (b), (ii) → (c), (iii) → (d), (iv) → (a)

17. Which of the following Python statements is used to change a column label in a DataFrame, df?

(a) df =df.rename ({old_name: new_name}, axis='columns')
(b) df =df.rename (old_name, new_name), axis='columns'
(c) df = df.change_name (old_name, new_name, axis='bar')
(d) df =df.update({old_name: new_name}, axis='bar')

18. In Python Pandas, DataFrame.____[ ] is used for label indexing with DataFrames.

(a) label (b) index
(c) labindex (d) loc

19. Every web page on the Internet has a unique address. This address is known as

(a) Domain Name
(b) Protocol
(c) Uniform Resource Locater
(d) Network Topology

Directions (Q.Nos.20 and 21) *are Assertion (A) and Reason (R) type questions. Choose the correct option as:*

(a) Both Assertion (A) and Reason (R) are True and Reason (R) is the correct explanation for Assertion (A).
(b) Both Assertion (A) and Reason (R) are True and Reason (R) is not the correct explanation for Assertion (A).
(c) Assertion (A) is True and Reason (R) is False.
(d) Assertion (A) is False, but Reason (R) is True.

20. Assertion (A) The drop() method in Pandas can be used to delete rows and columns from a DataFrame.

Reason (R) The axis parameter in the drop() method specifies whether to delete rows (axis=0) or columns (axis=1).

21. Assertion (A) The ROUND () function in SQL can be used to round off a number to a specified number of decimal places.

Reason (R) The ROUND () function is a string function that accepts character values as input and returns numerical values as output.

SECTION B

22. (a) Mention any two main points of difference between Series and DataFrame of Python Pandas.

Or (b) Explain how we can access elements of a series using slicing. Give an example to support your answer.

23. A small tech startup, is considering using open source software to develop their new project management tool. They are evaluating the benefits and potential challenges of adopting open source solutions.

(i) Identify one key benefit of using open source software for the development of project management tool.

(ii) Give any two examples of open source software.

24. Consider the string, "Informatics Practices". Write suitable SQL queries for the following:

(i) To convert the entire string to uppercase.
(ii) To display the total number of characters in the given string.

25. (a) Give any two points of difference between Static web page and Dynamic web page.

Or

(b) Describe the role of a router in a network.

26. **What is a Database Management System(DBMS)? Mention any two examples of DBMS.**

27. **Give any two impacts on the environment that are caused when e-waste is carelessly thrown or dumped in landfills or dumping grounds.**

28. (a) Rohit is trying to create a Pandas Series from scalar values. His code has some mistakes. Rewrite the correct code and underline the corrections made.

```
import pandas
data = [50, 15,40]
series = pd.series (data, Index=['x', 'y', 'z'])
Print (series)
```

Or (b) Complete the given Python code to generate the following output:

```
     COLOUR    NAME    QTY
0    Red       Apple   10
1    Blue      Berry   15
2    Green     Guava   20
```

```
import ______as pd
data=[{'COLOUR': 'Red', 'NAME': 'Apple',
'QTY':10},{'COLOUR': 'Blue', 'NAME':
'Berry','QTY':15},{ ______,'NAME': 'Guava', 'QTY':20}]
df=pd.DataFrame(___)
print(__)
```

SECTION C

29. **Ravi is a student studying in grade 12. He frequently uses the internet for various activities such as social networking, online shopping, and to research for school projects. Recently, he noticed that he receives targeted advertisements based on his browsing history and is concerned about his digital footprint. Additionally, Ravi has encountered instances of cyberbullying and is unsure how to handle them. Help Ravi by answering the following questions:**

(i) What are digital footprints, and how are they created?

(ii) Write any two net etiquettes that Ravi should follow to ensure respectful and responsible online behavior.

(iii) How can Ravi protect himself from cyberbullying? Mention any one protective measure.

30. (a) Write a Python program to create the following DataFrame using a Dictionary of Series:

	City	State
0	Mumbai	Maharashtra
1	Dehradun	Uttarakhand
2	Bengaluru	Karnataka
3	Hyderabad	Telangana

(b) Write a Python program to create a Pandas Series as shown below from an ndarray containing the numbers 10, 20, 30, 40, 50 with corresponding indices 'A', 'B', 'C', 'D', 'E'.

```
A    10
B    20
C    30
D    40
E    50
```

31. (i) Write the SQL statement to create a table, Customer with the following specifications:

Table : Customer

Column Name	Data Type	Key
CID	Int	Primary key
FName	Varchar (20)	
LName	Varchar (20)	
Age	Int	

(ii) Write the SQL query to display all records in descending order of LName from the Table Customer.

32. (a) Given the following table:

Table : STUDENTS

S_ID	NAME	AGE	CITY
1	Rahul	20	Delhi
2	Priya	22	Mumbai
3	David	21	Delhi
4	Neha	23	Bengaluru
5	Khurshid	22	Delhi

Table : GRADES

S_ID	SUBJECT	GRADE
1	Math	A
2	English	B
3	Math	C
4	English	A
5	Math	B

Write SQL queries for the following:

(i) To display the number of students from each city.

(ii) To find the average age of all students.

(iii) To list the names of students and their grades.

Table 1 : PRODUCTS

This table stores the basic details of the products available in a shop.

PID	PName	Category
201	Laptop	Electronics
202	Chair	Furniture
203	Desk	Furniture
204	Smartphone	NULL
205	Tablet	Electronics

Table 2 : SALES

This table records the number of units sold for each product.

SaleID	PID	UnitsSold
301	201	50
302	202	100
303	203	60
304	204	80
305	205	70

Write SQL queries for the following:

(i) To delete those records from table SALES whose UnitsSold is less than 80.

(ii) To display names of all products whose category is not known.

(iii) To display the product names along with their corresponding units sold.

SECTION D

33. Gurkirat has to fill in the blanks in the given Python program that generates a line plot as shown below. The given line plot represents the temperature (in degree Celcius) over five days as given in the table:

Days	Temperature
Day 1	30
Day 2	32
Day 3	31
Day 4	29
Day 5	28

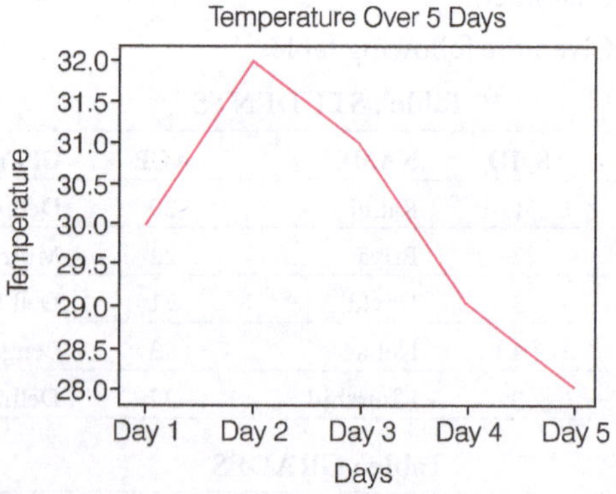


```
import_____ as plt # Statement-1
days = ['Day 1', 'Day 2', 'Day 3', 'Day 4', 'Day 5']
temp = [30, 32, 31, 29, 28]
plt. ____ (days, temp) # Statement-2
plt.xlabel ('____') # Statement-3
plt.ylabel ('Temperature')
plt.title ('____') # Statement-4
plt.show()
```

Write the missing statements according to the given specifications:

(i) Write the suitable code to import the required module in the blank space in the line marked as Statement-1.

(ii) Fill in the blank in Statement-2 with a suitable Python function name to create a line plot.

(ii) Refer to the graph shown and fill in the blank in Statement-3 to display the appropriate label for x-axis.

(iv) Refer to the graph shown and fill in the blank in Statement-4 to display the suitable chart title.

34. (a) An educational institution is maintaining a database for storing the details of courses being offered. The database includes a table COURSE with the following attributes:

C_ID Stores the unique ID for each course.

C_NAME Stores the course's name.

INSTRUCTOR Stores the name of the course instructor.

DURATION Stores the duration of the course in hours.

Table: COURSE

C_ID	C_NAME	INSTRUCTOR	DURATION
C101	Data Structures	Dr. Alok	40
C102	Machine Learning	Prof. Sunita	60
C103	Web Development	Ms. Sakshi	45
C104	Database Management	Mr. Suresh	50
C105	Python Programming	Dr. Pawan	35

Write SQL queries for the following:

(i) To add a new record with following specifications:

C_ID C106

C_NAME Introduction to AI

INSTRUCTOR Ms. Preeti

DURATION 55

(ii) To display the longest duration among all courses.

(iii) To count total number of courses run by the institution.

(iv) To display the instructors' name in lower case.

Or

(b) Ashutosh, who is a manager, has created a database to manage employee records. The database includes a table named EMPLOYEE whose attribute names are mentioned below:

EID Stores the unique ID for each employee.

EMP_NAME Stores the name of the employee.

DEPT Stores the department of the employee.

SALARY Stores the salary of the employee.

JOIN_DATE Stores the employee's joining date.

Table : EMPLOYEE

EID	EMP_NAME	DEPT	SALARY	JOIN_DATE
E01	ARJUN SINGH	SALES	75000	2019-11-01
E02	PRIYA JAIN	ENGINEERING	85000	2020-05-20
E03	RAVI SHARMA	MARKETING	60000	2018-08-14
E04	AYESHA	NULL	50000	2021-01-10
E05	RAHUL VERMA	FINANCE	40000	2017-06-25

Write the output of the following SQL Queries:

(i) `Select SUBSTRING (EMP_NAME, 1, 5) from EMPLOYEE where DEPT = 'ENGINEERING';`

(ii) `Select EMP_NAME from EMPLOYEE where month (JOIN_DATE) = 8;`

(iii) `Select EMP_NAME from EMPLOYEE where SALARY > 60000;`

(iv) `Select count (DEPT) from EMPLOYEE;`

SECTION E

35. **XYZ Technologies, Hyderabad is a company that deals with data science and AI projects. They have different divisions ADMIN, SALES, PRODUCTION and SERVICE.**

The layout of the Hyderabad branch is:

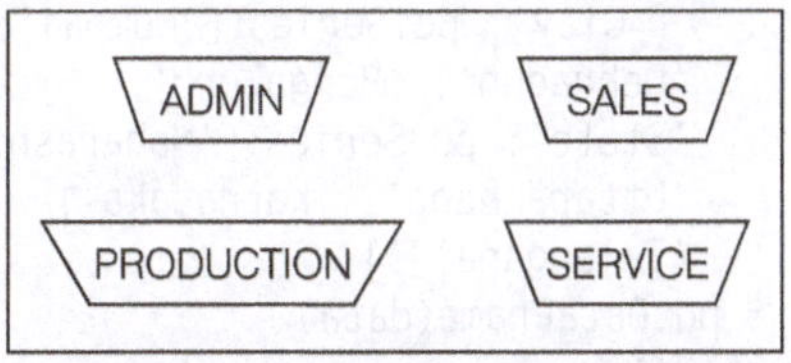

The management wants to connect all the divisions as well as the computers of each division (ADMIN, SALES, PRODUCTION and SERVICE).

Distance between the divisions are as follows:

ADMIN to SALES	69 m
ADMIN to PRODUCTION	84 m
ADMIN to SERVICE	60 m
SALES to PRODUCTION	110 m
SALES to SERVICE	135 m
PRODUCTION to SERVICE	90 m

Number of computers in each division:

Division	Number of Computers
ADMIN	40
SALES	75
PRODUCTION	120
SERVICE	20

Based on the above specifications, answer the following questions:

(i) Suggest the topology and draw the most suitable cable layout for connecting all the divisions in the Hyderabad office.

(ii) XYZ Technologies is having its head office in USA. Out of LAN, MAN and WAN, which kind of network will be created to connect Hyderabad office with USA Office? Justify your answer.

(iii) Suggest the division for the placement of server. Explain the reason for your selection.

(iv) Suggest the placement of Switch/Hub with justification.

(v) Where will a repeater be placed in the suggested network layout? Justify your answer.

36. **Consider the DataFrame Doctor shown below:**

	DID	Name	Department	Fee
0	101	Dr. Joe	ENT	1500
1	102	Dr. Salma	UROLOGY	1600
2	103	Dr. Jeet	ORTHO	1550
3	104	Dr. Neha	ENT	1200
4	105	Dr. Vikram	ORTHO	1700

Write suitable Python statements for the following

(i) To print the last three rows of the DataFrame Doctor.

(ii) To display the names of all doctors.

(iii) To add a new column 'Discount' with value of 200 for all doctors.

(iv) To display rows with index 2 and 3.

(v) To delete the column 'Department'.

37. (a) Write SQL query for the following:

(i) To display sum total of all the values of the Score column, from STUDENTS table.

(ii) To display the first five characters of the Name column from STUDENTS table.

(iii) To display the values of Name column from the STUDENTS table, after removing the trailing spaces.

(iv) To retrieve the lowest score from the Score column of GRADES table.

(v) To increase the fee of all students by 100, in the STUDENTS table. (The name of the column is FEE)

Or (b) Write SQL queries for the following:

(i) To calculate the square of 15.

(ii) To round the number 456.789 to the nearest integer.

(iii) To display the position of first occurrence of 'com' in the string 'mycommercial.com'.

(iv) To display the name of the day for the date '2024-11-07'.

(v) To display the current date and time.

Answers

1. False	**2.** (d)	**3.** (b)	**4.** (c)	**5.** (a)	
6. (c)	**7.** (d)	**8.** False	**9.** (c)	**10.** (d)	
11. (b)	**12.** (b)	**13.** (b)	**14.** (c)	**15.** (b)	
16. (b)	**17.** (a)	**18.** (d)	**19.** (c)	**20.** (a)	**21.** (c)

22. (a) Two main differences between Series and DataFrame in Python Pandas:

1. **Dimensionality**

Series A one-dimensional labeled array capable of holding any data type (integers, strings, floating point numbers, Python objects, etc.).

DataFrame A two-dimensional labeled data structure with columns, akin to a table in a database or a spreadsheet.

2. **Structure**

Series Consists of an index and a single data column.

DataFrame Comprises multiple columns, each of which can be a different data type, along with both row and column indices.?

Or (b) Refer to text on page no. 6-7 (Accessing Elements from Series (Indexing and Slicing)).

23. Refer to Ques. 10 on page 228 (Very Short Answer Type).

24. Refer to Ques. 10 on page 131 (Very Short Answer Type).

25. Refer to Ques. 31 on page 200 (Short Answer Type I).

26. Refer to Ques. 3 on page 104 (Very Short Answer Type).

27. Refer to Ques. 17 on page 228 (Very Short Answer Type).

28. (a)
```
import pandas as pd
    # Corrected from 'pandas' to 'pd'
data = 50
    # Changed from list to scalar value
series = pd.Series(data, index=['x', 'y', 'z'])
    # Corrected 'series' to 'Series' and
                          'Index' to 'index'
print(series)
```

Or (b)
```
import pandas as pd
data = [{'COLOUR': 'Red', 'NAME': 'Apple',
    'QTY': 10},{'COLOUR': 'Blue', 'NAME':
    'Berry', 'QTY': 15},{'COLOUR': 'Green',
    'NAME': 'Guava', 'QTY': 20}]
df = pd.DataFrame(data)
print(df)
```

29. Refer to Ques. 31 on page 230 (Short Answer Type I).

30. (a)
```
import pandas as pd
data = {'City': pd.Series(['Mumbai',
    'Dehradun', 'Bengaluru', 'Hyderabad']),
    'State': pd.Series(['Maharashtra',
    'Uttarakhand', 'Karnataka',
    'Telangana'])}
df = pd.DataFrame(data)
print(df)
```

Or (b)
```
import pandas as pd
data = [10, 20, 30, 40, 50]
indices = ['A', 'B', 'C', 'D', 'E']
series = pd.Series(data, index=indices)
print(series)
```

31. Refer to Ques. 39 on page 107 (Short Answer Type I).

32. Refer to Ques. 68 on page 138 (Short Answer Type I).

33. Refer to Ques. 31 on page 76 (Short Answer Type II).

34. Refer to Ques. 81 on page 142 (Short Answer Type II).

35. Refer to Ques. 52 on page 179 (Long Answer Type).

36. (i) `print(Doctor.tail(3))`

(ii) `print(Doctor['Name'])`

(iii)
```
Doctor['Discount'] = 200
print(Doctor)
```

(iv) `print(Doctor.loc[2:3])`

(v)
```
Doctor.drop(columns=['Department'],
inplace=True)
print(Doctor)
```

37. Refer to Ques. 95 on page 148 (Long Answer Type).

SAMPLE QUESTION PAPER 1

A Highly Simulated Sample Question Paper for CBSE Class XII Examination

INFORMATICS PRACTICES

Time : 3 Hours **Max. Marks : 70**

General Instructions

1. Please check this question paper contains 37 questions.
2. All questions are compulsory. However, internal choices have been provided in some questions. Attempt only one of the choices in such questions.
3. The paper is divided into 5 Sections- A, B, C, D and E.
4. Section A consists of 21 questions (1 to 21). Each question carries 1 Mark.
5. Section B consists of 7 questions (22 to 28). Each question carries 2 Marks.
6. Section C consists of 4 questions (29 to 32). Each question carries 3 Marks.
7. Section D consists of 2 case study type questions (33 to 34). Each question carries 4 Marks.
8. Section E consists of 3 questions (35 to 37). Each question carries 5 Marks.
9. All programming questions are to be answered using Python Language only.
10. In case of MCQ, text of the correct answer should also be written.

SECTION A

[21 × 1 = 21]

1. **State whether the following statement is True and False:**

A pandas Series cannot have string values as indices.

2. **The MySQL function returns the specified number of characters from a particular position of a given string.**

(a) MID () (b) SUBSTRING ()
(c) SUBSTR () (d) All of these

3. **Which type of network is formed, when you connect two mobiles using bluetooth to transfer a picture file?**

(a) LAN (b) MAN (c) PAN (d) WAN

4. **Consider a table DOCTOR(ID, DocName, Department, DOJ,Gender, Salary) . Which of the following query will display the names and salaries of doctors in descending order of salaries.**

(a) `SELECT DocName, Salary FROM DOCTOR ORDER BY Salary DESC;`
(b) `SELECT DocName, Salary FROM DOCTOR WHERE ORDER BY Salary ASC;`
(c) `SELECT DocName, Salary FROM DOCTOR ORDER BY Salary ASC;`
(d) `SELECT DocName, Salary FROM DOCTOR WHERE ORDER BY Salary DESC;`

5. **............ is a cyber crime in which a target or targets are contacted by E-mail, telephone or text message by someone posing as a legitimate institution to lure individuals into providing sensitive data such as personally identifiable information, banking and credit card details and passwords.**

(a) Plagiarism (b) Phishing (c) Cyber stalking (d) Hacking

6. **What is a correct syntax to return the values of first row of a Pandas DataFrame? Assuming the name of the DataFrame is dfRent.**

(a) `dfRent[0]` (b) `dfRent.loc[1]`
(c) `dfRent.loc[0]` (d) `dfRent.iloc[0]`

7. **Out of the following, which function cannot be used for customization of charts in Python?**

(a) xlabel() (b) color() (c) title() (d) xticks()

8. **State whether the following statement is True and False:**

The SQL DISTINCT keyword is used to return only duplicate rows from a query result.

9. **Which of the following statements will read a csv file "Emp.csv" from "c:\\Data" folder.**

(a) pd.readcsv('C:\\Data\\Emp.csv')
(b) pd.read ('C:\\Data\\Emp.csv')
(c) pd.read_csv('C:\\Emp.csv')
(d) pd.read_csv('C:\\Data\\Emp.csv')

10. **Which of the following is/are the benefit(s) of e-Waste management?**

(a) Saving the environment (b) Creating jobs
(c) Recovery of precious metals (d) All of these

11. Fill in the Blank:

The ________ keyword is used to retrieve only distinct (unique) values from a column in a SELECT statement.

(a) UNIQUE (b) DISTINCT (c) PRIMARY (d) GROUP

12. Which network topology requires a central controller or hub?

(a) Ring (b) Bus (c) Star (d) Mesh

13. Which of the following will not display the last 5 elements from the series S1?

(a) S1.tail() (b) S1.tail(5)
(c) S1.Tail() (d) None of these

14. .... is a set of moral principles that governs the behaviour of a group or an individual and regulates the use of computers.

(a) Copyright (b) Computer ethics
(c) Property rights (d) Privacy law

15. The term e-Waste can also be called as

(a) WEEE (b) WEST
(c) WET (d) None of these

16. Match the following SQL functions/clauses with their descriptions:

SQL Function	Description
P. COUNT()	1. Returns the average value in a column.
Q. AVG()	2. Counts the number of rows in a result set.
R. CONCAT()	3. Joins two strings together.
S. DISTINCT	4. Removes duplicate rows from the result set.

(a) P-2, Q-1, R-3, S-4 (b) P-1, Q-2, R-4, S-3
(c) P-3, Q-4, R-2, S-1 (d) P-4, Q-1, R-3, S-2

17. Fill in the Blank

The method used to remove missing data from a Pandas DataFrame is ________.

(a) dropna() (b) fillna()
(c) isnull() (d) notnull()

18. Which of the following is an incorrect example of savefig( ) function?

(a) plt.savefig("bar1.pdf") (b) plt.savefig("bar1.png")
(c) plt.savefig("bar1.eps") (d) plt.savefig("bar1.ppt")

19. What is the term for the data communication system within a building or campus?

(a) MAN (b) LAN
(c) PAN (d) WAN

Directions (Q. Nos. 20 and 21) *are Assertion (A) and Reason (R) Type questions. Choose the correct option as*

(a) Both Assertion (A) and Reason (R) are true, and Reason (R) is the correct explanation of Assertion (A)
(b) Both Assertion (A) and Reason (R) are true, but Reason (R) is not the correct explanation of Assertion (A)
(c) Assertion (A) is True, but Reason (R) is False
(d) Assertion (A) is False, but Reason (R) is True

20. **Assertion (A)** Some time we want to combine the two DataFrame using the merge() function.

Reason (R) Merging operation can be performed only with common values of column not with specific column.

21. **Assertion (A)** The `SELECT` statement is used to retrieve data from a database.

Reason (R) `SELECT` is a Data Control Language (DCL) command in SQL.

SECTION B

[7 × 2 = 14]

22. (A) What is a DataFrame in Pandas? Give a suitable example to support your answer.

Or (B) What do you understand by slicing in a Pandas Series? Give two examples of slicing in a Series.

23. What is phishing and how can it be avoided?

24. Predict the output of following queries

(i) `SELECT MOD(16,7);`

(ii) `SELECT CONCAT ('Honesty', 'is', 'the', 'best', 'policy');`

25. (A) Write down any two points of differences among LAN, MAN and WAN.

Or (B) Define home page. Give two advantages of home page.

26. State differences between date functions NOW( ) and DAY( ) of MySQL.

27. Give any two measures to avoid online scams.

28. (A) The Python code written below has syntactical errors. Rewrite the correct code and underline the corrections made.

```
import Pandas as pd
data = {'A': 1, 'B': 2, 'C': 3}
my_series = Pd.Series(data)
print(my_series)
```

Or (B) Complete the given Python code to given two DataFrames 'df1' and 'df2', merge them on the 'ID' column to get a single DataFrame 'merged_df'.

```
import ______ as pd
df1 = pd.DataFrame({'ID': [1, 2, 3], 'Name':
                    ['Riya', 'Preeti', 'Neeta']})
df2 = pd.DataFrame({'ID': [1, 2, 4], 'Age':
                    [25, 30, 22]})
merged_df = pd.merge(df1, df2, on=______)
print(merged_df)
```

SECTION C

[4 × 3 = 12]

29. **Nadar has recently shifted to a new city and school. She does not know many people in her new city and school. But all of a sudden, someone is posting negative, demeaning comments on her social networking profile, etc.**

She is also getting repeated mails from unknown people. Every time she goes online, she finds someone chasing her online.

(i) What is this happening to Nadar?

(ii) What immediate action should she take to handle it?

(iii) Is there any law in India to handle such issues? Discuss briefly.

30. **Write a small Python code to create a DataFrame with headings (a and b) from the list given below**

[[10, 20], [30, 40], [50, 60], [70, 80]]

Or **Consider two objects A and B. A is a list whereas B is a Series. Both have values 20, 35, 75, 110.**

What will be the output of the following two statements considering that the above objects have been created already?

(i) `print (A*3)`

(ii) `print (B*3)`

Justify your answer.

31. **I. Write an SQL statement to create a table named CUSTOMER, with the following specifications:**

Column Name	Data Type	Key
CustomerID	Numeric	Primary Key
CustomerName	Varchar(30)	
Age	Numeric	
JoiningDate	Date	

II. Write an SQL Query to insert the following data into the CUSTOMER table:

1025, John Doe, 28, 2023-08-15

32. **(A) Consider the table DOCTOR given below.**

Table : DOCTOR

ID	DOCName	Department	DOJ	Gender	Salary
1	Amit Kumar	Orthopaedics	1993-02-12	M	35000
2	Anita Hans	Paediatrics	1998-10-16	F	30000
3	Sunita Maini	Gynaecology	1991-08-23	F	40000
4	Joe Thomas	Surgery	1994-10-20	M	55000
5	Gurpreet Kaur	Paediatrics	1999-11-24	F	52000
6	Anandini Burman	Oncology	1994-03-16	F	31000
7	Siddharth Dang	Surgery	1995-09-08	M	47000
8	Rama Mukherjee	Oncology	2000-06-27	F	54500

Table : Docdetails

DocID	Visitdays	Fees
1	MWF	1200
2	WFS	1000
3	WFS	600
4	MWF	700
5	TWS	800
6	TWS	1200
7	MWF	1600
8	TWS	1900

Write SQL queries for the following:

(i) Display the names and salaries of doctors in descending order of salaries.

(ii) Display names of each department along with total salary being given to doctors of that department.

(iii) Display the number of doctors in each department.

Or (B) Consider the following tables:

Table 1: EMPLOYEE

EmployeeID	Name	Department
201	Alice	HR
202	Bob	IT
203	Charlie	Finance
204	Diana	IT
205	Eve	HR

Table 2: PROJECTS

EmployeeID	Project	Hours
201	Recruitment	30
202	Development	40
203	Audit	25
204	Development	20
205	Hiring	35

Write appropriate SQL queries for the following:

(i) Display the total number of hours worked on each project.

(ii) Display the names of all employees who have worked on more than 30 hours.

(iii) Display the employee names along with their corresponding projects.

SECTION D

[2 × 4 = 8]

33. During a practical exam, a student, Ravi, has to fill in the blanks in a Python program that generates a line chart. This line chart represents the monthly sales of a store over four months.

Month	Sales (in $)
January	1500
February	2000
March	1800
April	2200

Help Ravi to complete the code.

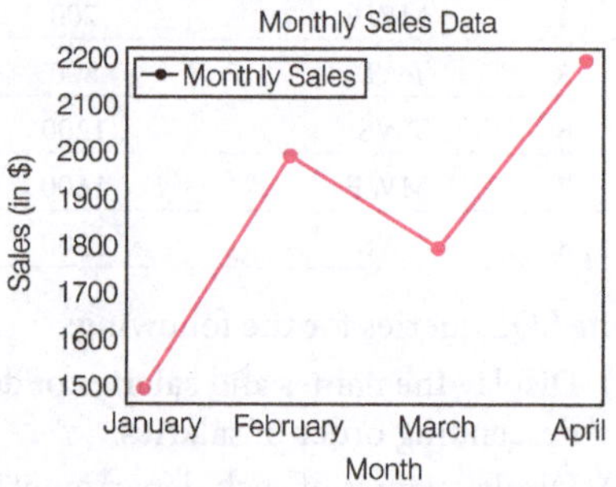


```
import ____ as plt                          #Statement-1
months = ['January', 'February', 'March', 'April']
sales = [1500, 2000, 1800, 2200]
plt.plot(months, _____, marker='o', label='Monthly
Sales')                                     #Statement-2
plt.xlabel('Month')
plt._____('Sales (in $)')                   #Statement-3
plt.legend()
plt.title('_____')                          #Statement-4
plt.show()
```

I. Write the suitable code for the import statement in the blank space in the line marked as Statement-1.

II. Refer to the graph shown above and fill in the blank in Statement-2 with suitable Python code.

III. Fill in the blank in Statement-3 with the name of the function to set the label on the y-axis.

IV. Refer to the graph shown above and fill the blank in Statement-4 with a suitable chart title.

34. (A) Predict the output of the following queries

Table : Doctor

DoctorID	Dname	Dept	Charges	VisitDays
D01	R. Sharma	ENT	1000	Mon
D02	D. Basak	ENT	1500	Wed
D03	M. Agarwal	PAED	6000	Sat
D04	E. Joseph	Ortho	1200	Sun
D05	M. Fernandes	Ortho	4000	Thu

(i) `Select Dname from Doctor where VisitDays IN ("Mon","Wed");`

(ii) `Select Dept,Count(*) from Doctor Group by Dept;`

(iii) `Select right(Dname,3) from Doctor where Charges >4000;`

Or

(B) Tejasvi Sethi, a car dealer has stored the details of all cars in her showroom in a table CARMARKET. The table CARMARKET has attributes CARCODE which is a primary key, CARNAME, COMPANY, COLOR, COST (in lakh) of the car and DOM which is the Date of Manufacture of the car.

Table: CARMARKET

CARCODE	CARNAME	COMPANY	COLOR	COST	DOM
C01	BALENO	SUZUKI	BLUE	5.90	2019-11-07
C02	INDIGO	TATA	SILVER	12.90	2020-10-15
C03	GLC	MERCEDES	WHITE	62.38	2020-01-20
C04	A6	AUDI	RED	58.55	2018-12-29
C05	INNOVA	TOYOTA	BLACK	32.82	2017-11-10
C06	WAGON-R	SUZUKI	WHITE	12.11	2016-11-11
C07	BREZZA	SUZUKI	GOLDEN	9.80	2016-10-03

Help her by writing answers of the following questions based on the given table.

(i) Display the carname along with the charges rounded off to 1 digit after decimal place.

(ii) Display the carname ,name of the company in lower case of all cars whose year (of dom) is 2020.

(iii) Display the number of cars manufactured each year.

(iv) Display the carname, color and position of the character 'E' in the color of all the cars.

SECTION E

3 × 5 = 15

35. **Ideal IT Service Ltd is a software development organisation. It is planning to set up its Indian campus at Delhi with its head office at Mumbai. The Delhi campus has 4 main buildings PLANNING, ANALYSIS, DESIGN and IMPLEMENTATION.**

You as a network expert have to suggest the best network related solution for their problem raised in (i) to (v), keeping in the mind the distance between the building and other given parameter.

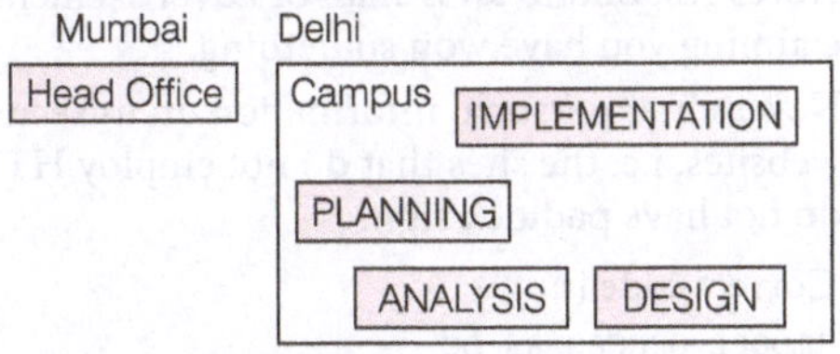

Shortest distance between various buildings:

PLANNING to IMPLEMENTATION	65
PLANNING to DESIGN	100
PLANNING to ANALYSIS	60
IMPLEMENTATION to DESIGN	65
IMPLEMENTATION to ANALYSIS	60
ANALYSIS to DESIGN	55
Mumbai Head Office to Delhi Campus.	1725 km.

Number of computers installed at various buildings are as follows

PLANNING	130
IMPLEMENTATION	85
DESIGN	50
ANALYSIS	22
Mumbai Head Office	30

(i) Suggest the most appropriate location of the server inside the Delhi campus (out of the 4 buildings), to get best connectivity for maximum number of computers, justify your answer.

(ii) Suggest and draw the cable layout to efficiently connect various buildings within the Delhi campus for connecting the computers.

(iii) Which hardware device will you suggest to be procured by the company to be installed to protect and control the Internet uses within the campus?

(iv) Which of the following communication media, will you suggest to be installed for connecting their Delhi campus for very effective (High speed) communication?

(a) Telephone line (b) Optical fibre
(c) Ethernet cable.

(v) What is the use of firewall in building network?

36. **Consider the given DataFrame'Stock':**

	Name	Price
0	Item1	150
1	Item2	180
2	Item3	225
3	Item4	500

(i) Add a column called Special_Price with the following data: [135, 150, 200, 440].

(ii) Add a new book named 'The Secret' having price 800.

(iii) Remove the column Special_Price.

(iv) Update the price of 'Item2' to 190.

(v) Filter the DataFrame to show only items with a price greater than 200.

37. **(A) Write suitable SQL query for the following:**

(i) To display the minimum value from the price column (attribute) in the Products table.

(ii) To display the first five characters of the phone_number column (attribute) in the Contacts table. (Note: The phone numbers are stored in the format +91-989-436-7090)

(iii) To display the data from the column (attribute) email in the Customers table, after eliminating any leading and trailing spaces.

(iv) To display the average value in the age column (attribute) of the Members table.

(v) To determine the count of distinct values in the category column (attribute) of the Items table.

Or

(B) Write SQL queries:

(i) To display the name of the month for the current date.

(ii) To display the leftmost 5 characters from the string "INFORMATICS PRACTICES".

(iii) To display the position of the first occurrence of "iya" in the string "Kendriya Vidyalaya".

(iv) To display the column NAME in uppercase from table STUDENT.

(v) To compute the remainder of 120 and 7 using SQL function.

Answers

1. False 2. (d) 3. (c) 4. (a) 5. (b)
6. (d) 7. (b) 8. False 9. (d) 10. (d)
11. (b) 12. (c) 13. (c) 14. (b) 15. (a)
16. (a) 17. (a) 18. (d) 19. (b) 20. (c) 21. (c)

22. (A) A DataFrame is a two-dimensional, size-mutable, and heterogeneous data structure in pandas, similar to a table or spreadsheet, where data is aligned in rows and columns.

Example:

```
import pandas as pd
data = {
  'Name': ['Alice', 'Bob', 'Charlie'],
  'Age': [25, 30, 35]
}
df = pd.DataFrame(data)
print(df)
```

Or

(B) Slicing in a Series involves selecting a subset of data based on labels or integer indices.

Examples:

```
import pandas as pd
s = pd.Series([10, 20, 30, 40, 50])
```

Example 1: Slicing by index

```
print(s[1:4])
```

Output: 1 20, 2 30, 3 40

Example 2: Slicing by labels

```
print(s.loc[1:3])
```

Output: 1 20, 2 30, 3 40

23. Phishing is a fraudulent attempt to obtain sensitive information via deceptive emails or websites. It can be avoided by verifying the source and not clicking on suspicious links.

24. (i) 2
(ii) Honestyisthebestpolicy

25. (A) Two major points of differences among LAN, MAN and WAN are as follows

Basics	LAN	MAN	WAN
Geographical Area	Generally within a building	Within a city	Across the continents
Distance	Upto 5 km	Upto 160 km	Unlimited

Or

(B) A home page is the first page of a website.
Two advantages of home page are as follows
(i) It helps viewers to find out what they can find on that site.
(ii) Publicity of an individual or a community.

26.

NOW( )	DAY( )
This function returns the current date and time in the format 'YYYY-MM-DD HH:MM:SS' or YYYYMMDDHHMMSS format.	This function returns the day of the month (from 1 to 31) from a date specified as an argument.
Syntax `SELECT NOW();`	**Syntax** `SELECT DAY('2021-09-31');`

27. (i) Never respond to an E-mail or advertisement claiming you have won something.
(ii) Never enter personal information on unsecure websites, i.e. the sites that do not employ HTTPs and do not have padlock sign.

28. (A) Correct code is:

```
import pandas as pd
data = {'A': 1, 'B': 2, 'C': 3}
my_series = pd.Series(data)
print(my_series)
```

Or (B) Correct code is:

```
import pandas as pd
df1 = pd.DataFrame({'ID': [1, 2, 3], 'Name':
                    ['Riya', 'Preeti', 'Neeta']})
df2 = pd.DataFrame({'ID': [1, 2, 4], 'Age':
                    [25, 30, 22]})
merged_df = pd.merge(df1, df2, on='ID')
print(merged_df)
```

29. (i) Nadar has become a victim of cyber bullying.
(ii) She must immediately bring it into the notice of her parents and school authorities. And she must report this cyber crime to local police with the help of her parents.
(iii) Yes, Information Technology Act, 2000 (also known as ITA-2000, or the IT Act) is the primary law in India dealing with cybercrime and electronic commerce.

30.

```
import pandas as pd
df1=pd.DataFrame ([[10, 20], [30, 40]],
    columns = ['a', 'b'])
df2=pd.DataFrame ([[50, 60], [70, 80]],
    columns = ['a', 'b'])
df = df1.append (df2)
```

Or

(i) Will give the output as
[20, 35, 75, 110, 20, 35, 75, 110, 20, 35, 75, 110]

(ii) Will give the output as

```
0    60
1    105
2    225
3    330
```

Justification

In the first statement, A represents a list so when a list is multiplied by a number, it is replicated that many number of times.

In the second statement, B represents a Series. When a Series is multiplied by a number then each element of the Series is multiplied by that number.

31. I.
```
CREATE TABLE CUSTOMER (
    CustomerID NUMERIC PRIMARY KEY,
    CustomerName VARCHAR(30),
    Age NUMERIC,
    JoiningDate DATE
    );
```
II.
```
INSERT INTO CUSTOMER (CustomerID,
CustomerName, Age, JoiningDate)
VALUES (1025, 'John Doe', 28, '2023-08-15');
```

32. (A)

(i)
```
SELECT DOCName, Salary FROM DOCTOR
ORDER BY Salary DESC;
```
(ii)
```
SELECT Department, SUM (Salary) FROM
DOCTOR GROUP BY Department;
```
(iii)
```
SELECT Department, COUNT(*) FROM
DOCTOR GROUP BY Department;
```

Or (B)

(i)
```
SELECT Project, SUM(Hours) AS Total_Hours
FROM PROJECTS GROUP BY Project;
```
(ii)
```
SELECT e.Name FROM EMPLOYEE e JOIN PROJECTS
p ON e.EmployeeID = p.EmployeeID WHERE
p.Hours > 30;
```
(iii)
```
SELECT e.Name, p.Project FROM EMPLOYEE e
JOIN PROJECTS p ON e.EmployeeID =
p.EmployeeID;
```

33. I. matplotlib.pyplot   II. sales

III. ylabel   IV. Monthly Sales Data

34. (A)

(i) Dname

R. Sharma

D. Basak

(ii)

Dept	Count(*)
ENT	2
PAED	1
Ortho	2

(iii) right(Dname,3)

wal

Or (B)

(i)
```
SELECT CARNAME, ROUND(COST,1) FROM
CARMARKET;
```
(ii)
```
SELECT CARNAME, LOWER(COMPANY) FROM
CARMARKET WHERE YEAR(DOM) = 2020;
```
(iii)
```
SELECT COUNT(*),YEAR(DOM) FROM
CARMARKET GROUP BY YEAR(DOM);
```
(iv)
```
SELECT CARNAME, COLOR,INSTR(COLOR,'E')
FROM CARMARKET;
```

35. (i) The PLANNING will be the most appropriate location for the server because it has the maximum number of computers.

(ii)

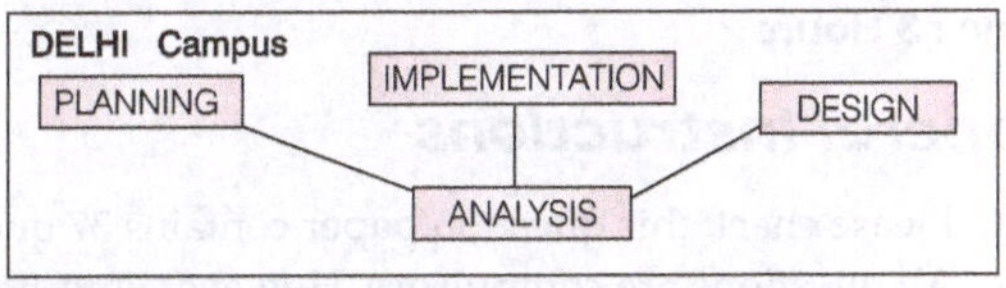

(iii) Firewall, because it is used to filter the data comes from other network to protect the Internet uses within the campus.

(iv) (b) Optical fibre because it is used for very high speed wired communication.

(v) Firewall is a type of software or hardware device that helps to protect your computer from being attacked over the Internet.

36. (i)
```
df['Special_Price'] = [135, 150, 200, 440]
print(df)
```
(ii)
```
new_row = {'Name': 'The Secret', 'Price': 800,
'Special_Price': None}
df = df.append(new_row, ignore_index=True)
print(df)
```
(iii)
```
df = df.drop(columns=['Special_Price'])
print(df)
```
(iv)
```
df.loc[df['Name'] == 'Item2', 'Price'] = 190
print(df)
```
(v)
```
filtered_df = df[df['Price'] > 200]
print(filtered_df)
```

37. (A) (i)
```
SELECT MIN(price) FROM Products;
```
(ii)
```
SELECT LEFT(phone_number, 5) FROM
Contacts;
```
(iii)
```
SELECT TRIM(email) FROM Customers;
```
(iv)
```
SELECT AVG(age) FROM Members;
```
(v)
```
SELECT COUNT(DISTINCT category) FROM
Items;
```

Or

(B) (i)
```
SELECT MONTHNAME (CURDATE());
```
(ii)
```
SELECT SUBSTR('INFORMATICS PRACTICES', 1,
5) AS Leftmost_5_Chars;
```
(iii)
```
SELECT INSTR('Kendriya Vidyalaya', 'iya')
AS Position;
```
(iv)
```
SELECT UPPER(NAME) AS Uppercase_Name FROM
STUDENT;
```
(v)
```
SELECT MOD(120, 7) AS Remainder;
```

SAMPLE QUESTION PAPER 2

A Highly Simulated Sample Question Paper for CBSE Class XII Examination

INFORMATICS PRACTICES

Time : 3 Hours **Max. Marks : 70**

General Instructions

1. Please check this question paper contains 37 questions.
2. All questions are compulsory. However, internal choices have been provided in some questions. Attempt only one of the choices in such questions.
3. The paper is divided into 5 Sections- A, B, C, D and E.
4. Section A consists of 21 questions (1 to 21). Each question carries 1 Mark.
5. Section B consists of 7 questions (22 to 28). Each question carries 2 Marks.
6. Section C consists of 4 questions (29 to 32). Each question carries 3 Marks.
7. Section D consists of 2 case study type questions (33 to 34). Each question carries 4 Marks.
8. Section E consists of 3 questions (35 to 37). Each question carries 5 Marks.
9. All programming questions are to be answered using Python Language only.
10. In case of MCQ, text of the correct answer should also be written.

SECTION A

21 × 1 = 21

1. State whether the following statement is True or False:

A Pandas Series must have a unique index for each element.

2. The function which returns the name of the week day from a date specified as an argument.

(a) DAY() (b) DAYNAME()
(c) MONTHNAME() (d) DAY_NAME()

3. Which device connects different networks and routes data between them?

(a) Switch (b) Hub (c) Router (d) Bridge

4. Which SQL command will display the structure of a table?

(a) Describe (b) Show
(c) Structure (d) None of the above

5. Which of the following is not an e-Waste?

(a) Books (b) Laptop
(c) Monitor (d) Motherboard

6. Given the code:

```
datastud=[['Shreya',20,30],['Rakhi',23,50],
                                        ['Priya',45,90]]
dfs=pd.DataFrame(datastud)
```

The statement to add the column names 'Name','Eng','IP' to the DataFrame will be

(a) `dfs.fields= ['Name','Eng','IP']`
(b) `dfs.rows= ['Name','Eng','IP']`
(c) `dfs.columns=['Name','Eng','IP']`
(d) None of these

7. Which argument keyword can be used to emphasize each point with a specified marker in plotting?

(a) marker_points (b) marker
(c) ring (d) types

8. State whether the following statement is True or False:

The ORDER BY clause in SQL sorts the results in ascending order by default.

9. Which of the following functions is used to import a dataframe from csv file ?

(a) read_csv() (b) import_csv()
(c) to_csv() (d) export_csv()

10. e-Waste is becoming one of the fastest growing environmental hazards in the world today. If it is not properly treated or disposed of it can cause serious health hazards, therefore the ______ has issued a formal set of guidelines for proper handling and disposal of e-Waste.

(a) Central Pollution Control Board (CPCB)
(b) Department of Information Technology (DIT)
(c) Waste Electrical and Electronic Equipment (WEEE)
(d) Information Communication Technology (ICT)

11. **Fill in the Blank**

The _______ clause is used to group rows that have the same values into summary rows.

(a) HAVING (b) GROUP BY
(c) ORDER BY (d) SELECT

12. **Which protocol is used for secure communication over a computer network?**

(a) HTTP (b) FTP (c) SSH (d) SNMP

13. **Which of the following can be used to specify the data while creating a DataFrame?**

(a) Series (b) List of Dictionaries
(c) Structured ndarray (d) All of these

14. **Which of the following can be called as cyber-crime?**

(a) Stealing someone's computer
(b) Harassing someone over Internet
(c) Downloading copyright free movies over Internet
(d) Sending emails to known people

15. **To display last five rows of a series object "M", you may write**

(a) M.Head() (b) M.Tail(5)
(c) M.Head(5) (d) M.tail()

16. **Match the following SQL functions/clauses with their descriptions:**

SQL Function	Description
P. NOW()	1. Returns the system date and time.
Q. GETDATE()	2. Returns the current date.
R. DATE()	3. Extracts the date part from a datetime.
S. CURDATE()	4. Returns the current date and time.

(a) P-4, Q-1, R-3, S-2 (b) P-2, Q-3, R-1, S-4
(c) P-1, Q-4, R-3, S-2 (d) P-4, Q-3, R-2, S-1

17. **Fill in the Blank**

While creating a DataFrame Sunil wanted to specify the datatype, ______ property will help him to do so.

(a) datatype (b) type
(c) dtype (d) dt

18. **Which is/are the parameter(s) that can be used in grid() function to specify the line properties?**

(a) color
(b) linestyle
(c) linewidth
(d) All of these

19. **Network formed between computers which are spread across the continents is called**

(a) LAN (b) WAN
(c) MAN (d) WLAN

Directions (Q. Nos. 20 and 21) *are Assertion (A) and Reason (R) Type questions. Choose the correct option as*

(a) Both Assertion (A) and Reason (R) are true, and Reason (R) is the correct explanation of Assertion (A)
(b) Both Assertion (A) and Reason (R) are true, but Reason (R) is not the correct explanation of Assertion (A)
(c) Assertion (A) is True, but Reason (R) is False
(d) Assertion (A) is False, but Reason (R) is True

20. **Assertion (A)** DataFrame.count() function will display the sum of the values from the data frame.

Reason (R) axis=0 ,argument is to used to find sum column-wise.

21. **Assertion (A)** The SQL command `ALTER TABLE` is used to modify the structure of an existing table.

Reason (R)`ALTER TABLE` can be used to add or delete columns from an existing table.

SECTION B

7 × 2 = 14

22. **(A) Write Python code to do the following based on the given dataframe DF:**

Rollno	Name	Age	Marks
11	Aruna	18	68
12	Mohini	14	47
13	Kiya	13	78
14	Lakshami	16	87
15	Ravisha	14	60

(a) display students having marks more than 50.
(b) display name and marks column only.

Or

(B) Write a program to create a series object using a dictionary that stores the number of boys in each from IX to XII your school.

Note: Assume four class names are Ninth, Tenth, Eleventh and Twelfth having 10, 20, 12, 16 boys respectively and pandas library has been imported as pd.

23. **What is the need for secure passwords?**

24. **Write SQL queries for the following :**

(i) Add a constraint in table EMP1 that declares column Designation NOT NULL.
(ii) DROP table EMP1.

25. **(A) What is the web browser? Name any four web browsers.**

Or **(B) Discuss the structure of an E-mail message in brief.**

26. **Differentiate Primary key and Foreign key.**

27. **Write about preventive measures about health concerns due to overuse of Digital technology.**

28. (A) Consider the following DataFrame, Class :

	Enroll	Name	Score	Percentage
A1	1	Rahul	76	78
A2	2	Kiyaan	82	76
A3	3	Karan	78	89
A4	4	Prashant	92	88

Write commands to :

(i) Add a new column 'Grade' to the DataFrame.

(ii) Add a new row with values (5, Kirti, 69, 72).

Or

(B) Series object S1 stores the amount of product

A 4000
B 5200
C 6500
D 3800
E 4600

Write a program to display which product made more than 6000.

SECTION C

4×3=12

29. Simran often shares personal information and photos on various social networking sites. She is unaware of the potential risks associated with this behavior.

(i) What is a digital footprint, and how does it relate to Simran's online activity?

(ii) What are some potential risks of sharing too much personal information online?

(iii) How can Simran protect her digital footprint?

30. (A) Write the code to create the following DataFrame

	Name	Marks	Subject
a	Abhi	75	Maths
b	Chirag	82	Science
c	Tushar	69	English
d	Mahi	70	Science
e	Vanshika	92	Computer

Or

(B) Write a program to create a series object using a dictionary that stores the number of students in each house of class 12B of your school.

Note Assume four house names are Beas, Chenab, Ravi and Satluj having 18, 2, 20, 18 students respectively and pandas library has been imported as pd.

31. I. Write an SQL statement to create a table named DOCTORS, with the following specifications:

DoctorID: INTEGER, Primary Key, Auto Increment

FirstName: VARCHAR(50), cannot be NULL
LastName: VARCHAR(50), cannot be NULL

Specialization: VARCHAR(100), cannot be NULL
DateOfJoining: DATE, cannot be NULL
Salary: DECIMAL(10, 2)

II. Write SQL Query to insert the following data in the DOCTORS Table:

1, Anil, Sharma, Cardiologist, 2015-05-20, 120000.50

32. (A) Consider the following tables CABHUB and CUSTOMER.

CABHUB

Vcode	Vehicle Name	Make	Colour	Capacity	Charges
100	Innova	Toyota	WHITE	7	15
102	SX4	Suzuki	BLUE	4	14
104	C Class	Mercedes	RED	4	35
105	A-Star	Suzuki	WHITE	3	14
108	Indigo	Tata	SILVER	3	12

CUSTOMER

Ccode	Cname	Vcode
1	Hemant Sahu	101
2	Raj Lal	108
3	Feroza Shah	105
4	Ketan Dhal	104

Write SQL commands for the following statements:

(i) To display the names of all the white coloured vehicles.

(ii) To display name of vehicle name and capacity of vehicles in ascending order of their sitting capacity.

(iii) To display the customer name and the corresponding name of the vehicle hired by them.

Or

(B) Consider the following tables EMPLOYEE and DEPARTMENT.

EMPLOYEE

TCode	TName	DepCde	Salary	Age	JoinDate
15	Sameer Sharma	123	75000	39	01-Apr-2007
21	Ragvinder K	101	86000	29	11-Nov-2005
34	Rama Gupta	119	52500	43	03-Mar-2010
46	CR Menon	103	67000	38	12-Jul-2004
77	Mohan Kumar	103	63000	55	25-Nov-2000
81	Rajesh Kumar	119	74500	48	11-Dec-2008
89	Sanjeev P	101	92600	54	12-Jan-2009
93	Pragya Jain	123	32000	29	05-Aug-2006

DEPARTMENT

DepCde	DepName	DepHead
101	ACCOUNTS	Rajiv Kumar
103	HR	P K Singh
119	IT	Yogesh Kumar
123	RESEARCH	Ajay Dutta

Write SQL commands for the following statements:

(i) To display all DepName along with the DepCde in descending order of DepCde.

(ii) To display the average age of Employees in DepCde as 103.

(iii) To display the name of DepHead of the Employee named "Sanjeev P"

SECTION D

2 × 4 = 8

33. During a practical exam, a student Mehek has to fill in the blanks in a Python program that generates a bar chart. This bar chart represents the Sales of cars in one month.

CarName	Sale %
Maruti Suzuki XUV	60
Thar	30
Hyundai Verna	50
Toyota	55

Help her to complete the code

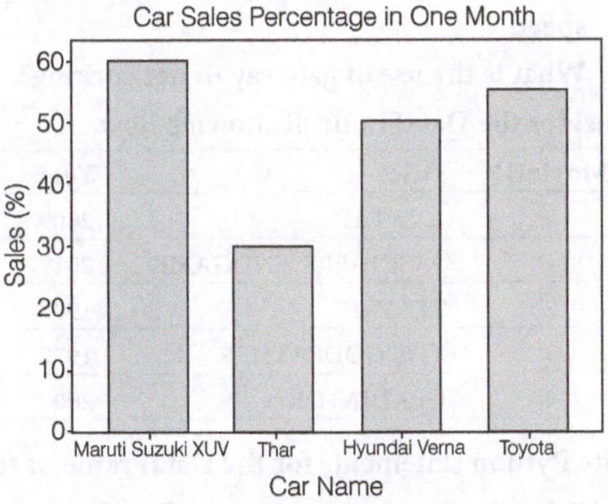


```
import ________ as plt                        #Statement -1
car_names = ['Maruti Suzuki XUV', 'Thar',
             'Hyundai Verna', 'Toyota']
sales = [60, 30, 50, 55]
plt.bar(car_names, ________, color=['blue',
       'green', 'red', 'purple'])  #Statement -2
plt.________('Car Sales Percentage in One
                          Month')    #Statement-3
plt.xlabel('Car Name')
plt.________('Sales (%)')             #Statement -4
plt.show()
```

I. Write the suitable code for the import statement in the blank space in the line marked as Statement-1.

II. Refer to the graph shown above and fill in the blank in Statement-2 with suitable Python code.

III. Refer the graph shown above and fill the blank in Statement-3 with suitable Chart Title.

IV. Fill in the blank in Statement-4 with the name of the function to set the label on the y-axis.

34. (A) Consider the following table Graduate and write SQL commands for (i) to (iv).

Table : Graduate

SNo	Name	Stipend	Subject	Average	Div
1	Karan	400	Physics	68	1
2	Divakar	450	Computers	68	1
3	Divya	300	Chemistry	62	2
4	Arun	350	Physics	63	1
5	Sabina	500	Mathematics	70	1
6	John	400	Chemistry	55	2
7	Robert	250	Physics	64	1
8	Rubina	450	Mathematics	68	1
9	Vikas	500	Computers	62	1
10	Mohan	300	Mathematics	57	2

(i) List the Names of those students who obtained Div 1.

(ii) Display a report, listing Name , Stipend , Subject and amount of stipend received in a year assuming that the Stipend is paid every month.

(iii) Display first three characters of student Name where/whose SNo is 7.

(iv) Display the student Names having 2nd division.

Or

(B) Mr. Manav, a database administrator in "Global Educational and Training Institute" has created following table named "Training" for the upcoming training schedule:

Table : Training

Training_Id	Name	Email_Id	Topic	City	Fee
ND01	Mr. Rajan	raj@gmail. com	Cyber Security	New Delhi	10000
GU01	Ms. Urvashi	urv@yahoo.com	ICT in Education	Gurugram	15000
FD01	Ms. Neena	neenarediff.com	Cyber Security	Faridabad	12000
ND02	Mr. Vinay	NULL	ICT in Education	New Delhi	13000
GU02	Mr. Naveen	nav@gmail.com	Cyber Security	Gurugram	NULL

Predict the output of the following queries:

(i) `SELECT SUBSTR(City,2,4) FROM Training WHERE Topic != 'Cyber Security';`

(ii) `SELECT NAME FROM Training WHERE INSTR (Email_Id, '@')=0;`

(iii) `SELECT Topic , COUNT(*) FROM Training GROUP BY Topic;`

(iv) `SELECT MAX (Fee) AS Max_Fee FROM Training;`

SECTION E

3×5=15

35. Knowledge supplement organisation has set up its new centre at Bangalore for its office and web based activities. It has 4 blocks of buildings as shown in the diagram below.

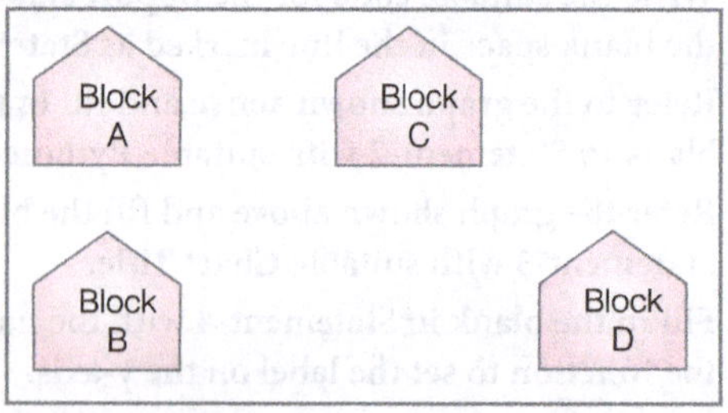

Centre to centre distances between various blocks

Block A to Block B	50 m
Block B to Block C	150 m
Block C to Block D	25 m
Block A to Block D	170 m
Block B to Block D	125 m
Block A to Block C	90 m

Number of Computers

Block A	25
Block B	50
Block C	125
Block D	10

(i) Suggest a cable layout of connections between the blocks.

(ii) Suggest the most suitable place (i.e. block) to house the server of this organisation with a suitable reason.

(iii) Suggest the placement of the following devices with justification.

(a) Repeater

(b) Hub/Switch

(iv) The organisation is planning to link its front office situated in the city in a hilly region, where cable connection is not feasible, suggest an economic way to connect it with reasonably high speed.

(v) What is the use of gateway in networking?

36. Consider the DataFrame df shown below.

MovieID	Title	Year	Rating
0	AVATAR	2009	7.8
1	AVENGERS: ENDGAME	2019	8.4
2	TITANIC	1997	7.9
3	THE GODFATHER	1972	9.2
4	GLADIATOR	2000	8.5

Write Python statements for the DataFrame df to:

(i) Print the first four rows of the DataFrame df.

(ii) Display the movie titles of all the movies.

(iii) Remove the column Rating.

(iv) Display the data of the Title column from indexes 0 to 2 (both included).

(v) Rename the column name Year to Release Year.

37. **(A) Consider the table furniture:**

item_id	item_name	price	quantity	manufacturer
1	Chair	150	30	ABC Furnishings
2	Table	300	20	XYZ Interiors
3	Sofa	500	15	ABC Furnishings
4	Desk	200	25	DEF Designs

Write suitable SQL queries for the following:

(i) To display the average price of all items from the furniture table.

(ii) To display the first three characters of the item_name column from the furniture table.

(iii) To display the data from the manufacturer column in the furniture table, after eliminating any leading and trailing spaces.

(iv) To display the maximum value in the price column of the furniture table.

(v) To determine the count of rows in the furniture table.

Or

(B) Heena has created a table ' student' with the attributes id varchar(20), name varchar(50), city varchar(50), contactno varchar(11) She wants to write the queries for the following. Help her write the queries for the same.

(i) To extract the first four characters from the name

(ii) To display the names in the lower case

(iii) To display the characters from 4th position of column city

(iv) Display the remainder of 100 divided by 9.

(v) Remove all the expected leading and trailing spaces from a column Name of the table 'Student'.

Answers

1. False	**2.** (b)	**3.** (c)	**4.** (a)	**5.** (a)	**6.** (c)	**7.** (b)
8. True	**9.** (a)	**10.** (a)	**11.** (b)	**12.** (c)	**13.** (d)	**14.** (b)
15. (d)	**16.** (b)	**17.** (c)	**18.** (d)	**19.** (b)	**20.** (d)	**21.** (a)

SAMPLE QUESTION PAPER 3

A Highly Simulated Sample Question Paper for CBSE Class XII Examination

INFORMATICS PRACTICES

Time : 3 Hours **Max. Marks : 70**

General Instructions

1. Please check this question paper contains 37 questions.
2. All questions are compulsory. However, internal choices have been provided in some questions. Attempt only one of the choices in such questions.
3. The paper is divided into 5 Sections- A, B, C, D and E.
4. Section A consists of 21 questions (1 to 21). Each question carries 1 Mark.
5. Section B consists of 7 questions (22 to 28). Each question carries 2 Marks.
6. Section C consists of 4 questions (29 to 32). Each question carries 3 Marks.
7. Section D consists of 2 case study type questions (33 to 34). Each question carries 4 Marks.
8. Section E consists of 3 questions (35 to 37). Each question carries 5 Marks.
9. All programming questions are to be answered using Python Language only.
10. In case of MCQ, text of the correct answer should also be written.

SECTION A

21 × 1 = 21

1. State whether the following statement is True or False:

A Pandas Series does not support vectorized operations.

2. Which of the following is not an aggregate function?

(a) AVG() (b) ADD()
(c) MAX() (d) COUNT()

3. In which format, a simple date value in MySQL exists?

(a) MM-YYYY-DD
(b) YYYY-MM-DD
(c) DD-MM-YYYY
(d) None of the above

4. We can use the aggregate functions in select list or the .... clause of a select statement. But they cannot be used in a .... clause.

(a) WHERE, HAVING
(b) GROUP BY, HAVING
(c) HAVING, WHERE
(d) GROUP BY, WHERE

5. Rohit forgot his laptop in his car and when he came back, he found his laptop was missing. This act is

(a) cybercrime
(b) phishing
(c) theft
(d) plagiarism

6. A DataFrame is created by a dictionary carrying 3 keys and 4 values against each of the keys. ________ columns will be there in the DataFrame.

(a) 2 (b) 1 (c) 3 (d) 4

7. How to activate a style (for example, you want to activate 'fivethirtyeight' style) in Matplotlib?

(a) plt.style.use('fivethirtyeight')
(b) plt.style.apply('fivethirtyeight')
(c) plt.style('fivethirtyeight')
(d) plt.style.activate('fivethirtyeight')

8. State whether the following statement is True or False:

In SQL, the HAVING clause is used to apply filters on groups formed by the GROUP BY clause.

9. Which of the following functions is used to import a dataframe from csv file ?

(a) read_csv() (b) import_csv()
(c) to_csv() (d) export_csv()

10. The rights of the owner of information to decide, how much information is to be shared/exchanged /distributed, are collectively known as ....

(a) Intelligent Portable Rights
(b) Intellectual Property Rights
(c) Interactive Property Rights
(d) Instance Portability Rights

11. Fill in the Blank

The SQL keyword __________ is used to arrange the result set of a query in ascending or descending order.

(a) FILTER (b) ORDER BY
(c) SORT (d) GROUP BY

12. Which protocol is primarily used to transfer web pages over the internet?

(a) FTP (b) HTTP
(c) SMTP (d) SSH

13. What is the correct way to get the first 5 rows of a DataFrame df?

(a) df.head(5) (b) df.top(5)
(c) df.rows(5) (d) df.show(5)

14. A/An .... is a unique data trace of a user's activities, actions, communications or transactions in digital media.

(a) digital handprint (b) digital footprint
(c) offline footprint (d) offline handprint

15. The pop() method can be used for

(a) Series (b) DataFrame
(c) Both (a) and (b) (d) None of these

16. Match the following SQL aggregate functions with their operations:

SQL Function	Operation
P. SUM()	1. Finds the largest value.
Q. AVG()	2. Calculates the sum of values.
R. COUNT()	3. Computes the average value.
S. MAX()	4. Counts the number of rows.

(a) P-2, Q-3, R-4, S-1 (b) P-1, Q-4, R-3, S-2
(c) P-3, Q-2, R-1, S-4 (d) P-4, Q-1, R-2, S-3

17. Fill in the Blank:

__________ method in Pandas can be used to change the index of rows and columns of a Series or Dataframe.

(a) rename()
(b) reindex()
(c) reframe()
(d) None of the above

18. Using Python Matplotlib __________ can be used to display information as a series of data points.

(a) line chart
(b) bar graph
(c) histogram
(d) None of the above

19. A network having span of a city is called:

(a) LAN (b) WAN
(c) MAN (d) Internet

Directions (Q. Nos. 20 and 21) *are Assertion (A) and Reason (R) Type questions. Choose the correct option as*

(a) Both Assertion (A) and Reason (R) are true, and Reason (R) is the correct explanation of Assertion (A)
(b) Both Assertion (A) and Reason (R) are true, but Reason (R) is not the correct explanation of Assertion (A)
(c) Assertion (A) is True, but Reason (R) is False
(d) Assertion (A) is False, but Reason (R) is True

20. Assertion (A) Pandas.head() is used to display first 5 records of any Series or DataFrame.

Reason (R) It displays the last 3 rows.

21. Assertion (A) In SQL, the ALTER TABLE statement can be used to delete a table from the database.

Reason (R) The ALTER TABLE statement is used to modify the structure of a table, not delete it.

SECTION B

7 × 2 = 14

22. (A) Write a program to create a series from a given Tuple data data=(100,"Aavya Verma",96.3,"A").

Or

(B) Carefully observe the following code:

```
import pandas as pd
Year1 = {'L1':5000,'L2':8000,'L3':12000,
                              'L4': 18000}
Year2 = {'X' :13000,'Y':14000,'Z':12000}
totSales = {1: Year1,2: Year2}
df= pd.DataFrame (totSales)
print(df)
```

Answer the following:

(i) List the index of the DataFrame df

(ii) List the column names of DataFrame df.

23. Define the following terms

(a) Digital Footprints
(b) Phishing

24. Write a query to display name, job, salary and hiredate of employees who are hired between may 20, 1990 and December 31,1991. Order the query in ascending order of hiredate. (table emp).

25. (A) Write the short note on the following

(i) Web server (ii) Mesh topology

Or **(B) List two disadvantages of internet.**

26. What is the use of Having clause? How is it different from the where clause?

27. Why are netiquettes important?

28. (A) The Python code written below has syntactical errors. Rewrite the correct code and underline the corrections made.

```
import pandas as pd
data = {'A': [1, 2, 3], 'B': [4, 5, 6]}
df = Pd.dataFrame(data)
result = df[df 'A' > 1 'B']
```

Or (B) Complete the given Python code: to display the last 3 rows of the DataFrame df using Pandas.

```
import _______ as pd
data = {'Name': ['John', 'Jane', 'Mike',
        'Emily'],'Age': [25, 30, 22, 28]}
df = pd.DataFrame(_______)
print(df._____(_____))
```

SECTION C

4×3=12

29. Ravi has been receiving threatening messages from an anonymous user on social media. These messages have started affecting his mental health and daily life. The user also posts harmful comments about Ravi, spreading false information.

(i) What is happening to Ravi?

(ii) What steps should Ravi take to address the cyberbullying?

(iii) What legal recourse does Ravi have under Indian law?

30. (A) Write the code in Python to create the following DataFrame.

	Name	Subject	Marks
1	Abhi	Mathematics	46
2	Vanshika	Science	76
3	Riya	Science	70
4	Chirag	Mathematics	82
5	Tushar	Commerce	72
6	Khushal	Physical	80
7	Mahi	Art	78

Or (B) Write a Python program to create a Pandas Series as GI_tag as shown below using a dictionary. Note that the left column indicates that indices and the right column displays the data.

Kashmir Saffron	Agriculture	Jammu & Kashmir
Manipuri Black Rice	Food Stuff	Manipur
Kandangi Saree	Handicraft	Tamil Nadu
Kalpi Handmade Paper	Handicraft	Uttar Pradesh

31. I. Write an SQL statement to create a table named EMPLOYEES, with the following specifications:

- EmployeeID (integer, primary key, auto-increment)
- FirstName (varchar, up to 50 characters)
- LastName (varchar, up to 50 characters)
- DateOfBirth (date)
- Salary (decimal with 2 decimal places)

II. Write an SQL query to insert the following data into the EMPLOYEES table:

1, Ronit, Rawat, 1985-09-25, 55000.00

32. (A) Given a table Drinks, write SQL queries to get the following:

Table : Drinks

DrinkID	Drinkname	Type	Cost
D01	PepsiCola	SoftDrinks	45
D02	CocaCola	SoftDrinks	40
D03	MineralWater	Gen	25
D04	SodaWater	Booster	30
D05	Mangodrink	Children	50

(i) Display the last 4 characters of the drinknames in uppercase.

(ii) Display each drinkname and the cost increased to double using a function.

(iii) Display the type and cost of the drinks whose drinkname has the word "cola" in it, using a mySQL function.

Or (B) Write SQL commands for (i) to (iii) on the basis of table Student

Table : Student

S.no	Name	Stream	Fees	Age	Sex
1.	Arun Kumar	Computer	750.00	17	M
2.	DivyaJaneja	Computer	750.00	18	F
3.	KesharMehra	Biology	500.00	16	M
4.	Harish Singh	Eng. Dr	350.00	18	M
5.	Prachi	Economics	300.00	19	F
6.	Nisha Arora	Computer	750.00	15	F
7.	Dinesh Kumar	Economics	300.00	16	M
8.	SarikaVaswani	Biology	500.00	15	F

(i) List the name of all students, who have taken stream as Computer.

(ii) To count the number of female students.

(iii) To display the number of students stream wise.